T0229151

PROBABILISTIC REASONING
IN INTELLIGENT SYSTEMS:
Networks of Plausible Inference

REVISED SECOND PRINTING

THE MORGAN KAUFMANN SERIES
IN REPRESENTATION AND REASONING

Series editor, Ronald J. Brachman
(AT&T Bell Laboratories)

BOOKS

James Allen, James Hendler, and Austin Tate, editors
Readings in Planning (1990)

James F. Allen, Henry A. Kautz, Richard N. Pelavin, and Josh D. Tenenberg
Reasoning About Plans (1991)

Ronald J. Brachman and Hector Levesque, editors
Readings in Knowledge Representation (1985)

Ernest Davis
Representations of Commonsense Knowledge (1990)

Thomas L. Dean and Michael P. Wellman
Planning and Control (1991)

Matthew L. Ginsberg, editor
Readings in Nonmonotonic Reasoning (1987)

Judea Pearl
Probabilistic Reasoning in Intelligent Systems: Networks of Plausible Inference (1988)

Glenn Shafer and Judea Pearl, editors
Readings in Uncertain Reasoning (1990)

John Sowa, editor
Principles of Semantic Networks: Explorations in the Representation of Knowledge (1991)

Daniel S. Weld and John de Kleer, editors
Readings in Qualitative Reasoning about Physical Systems (1990)

David E. Wilkins
Practical Planning: Extending the Classical AI Planning Paradigm (1988)

PROCEEDINGS

Principles of Knowledge Representation and Reasoning:
Proceedings of the First International Conference (KR 89)
edited by Ronald J. Brachman, Hector J. Levesque, and Raymond Reiter

Proceedings of the Second International Conference (KR 91)
edited by James Allen, Richard Fikes, and Eric Sandewall

The Frame Problem in Artificial Intelligence: Proceedings of the 1987 Conference
edited by Frank M. Brown (1987)

Reasoning about Actions and Plans: Proceedings of the 1986 Workshop
edited by Michael P. Georgeff and Amy L. Lansky (1987)

Theoretical Aspects of Reasoning about Knowledge:
Proceedings of the First Conference (TARK 1986)
edited by Joseph P. Halpern

Proceedings of the Second Conference (TARK 1988)
edited by Moshe Y. Vardi

Proceedings of the Third Conference (TARK 1990)
edited by Rohit Parikh

PROBABILISTIC REASONING IN INTELLIGENT SYSTEMS:

Networks of Plausible Inference

REVISED SECOND PRINTING

Judea Pearl

Department of Computer Science
University of California
Los Angeles

MORGAN KAUFMANN PUBLISHERS, INC.
An Imprint of Elsevier
San Francisco, California

Editor and President	Michael B. Morgan
Production Manager	Shirley Jowell
Text Design	Rick Van Genderen
Cover Design	Rick Van Genderen
Composition	Technically Speaking Publications
Copy Editor	Daniel Pearl
Proofreader	Linda Medoff

Grateful acknowledgement is made to the following for permission to reprint previously published material.

North-Holland, Amsterdam: Excerpts from Pearl, J., Fusion, Propogation, and Structuring in Belief Networks, *Artificial Intelligence* 29 (1986) 241-288; Pearl, J., Evidential Reasoning Using Stochastic Simulation of Causal Models, *Artificial Intelligence* 33 (1087) 173-215; Pearl, J., On Evidential Reasoning in a Heirarchy of Hypotheses, *Artificial Intelligence* 28 (1986) 9-15; and Pearl, J., Distributed Revision of Composite Beliefs, *Artificial Intelligence* 29 (1986) 241-288; Pearl, J., Embracing Causality in Default Reasoning, 35 *Artificial Intelligence* (1988) 259-271. Reprinted here with the permission of the publisher.

Pearl, J., Bayesian Decision Methods, *Encyclopedia of Artificial Intelligence* , Editor-in-Chief Stuart C. Shapiro, Vol. 1, pp 48-45 (1987). With permission of the publisher John Wiley & Sons.

Morgan Kaufmann Publishers, Inc.
An Imprint of Elsevier
Editorial Office:
340 Pine Street, Sixth Floor
San Francisco, CA 94104

Permissions may be sought directly from Elsevier's Science and Technology Rights Department in Oxford, UK. Phone: (44) 1865 843830, Fax: (44) 1865 853333, e-mail: permissions@elsevier.co.uk. You may also complete your request on-line via the Elsevier homepage: http://www.elsevier.com by selecting "Customer Support" and then "Obtaining Permissions".

Library of Congress Cataloging-in-Publication Data

Pearl, Judea.
    Networks of belief.
    Bibliography: p.
    Includes index.
    1. Probabilities. 2. Inference (Logic) I. Title.

ISBN-13: 978-1-55860-479-7   ISBN-10: 1-55860-479-0
Transferred to Digital Printing 2009

In memory of my brother Beni

Preface

This book is the culmination of an investigation into the applicability of proba-bilistic methods to tasks requiring automated reasoning under uncertainty. The result is a computation-mided interpretation of probability theory, an interpretation that exposes the qualitative nature of this ceturies-old formalism, its solid epistemological foundation, its compatibility with human intuition and, most importantly, its amenibility to network representations and to parallel and distri-buted computation. From this vantage point I have attempted to provide a coherent account of probability as a language for reasoning with partial beliefs and bind it, in a unifying perspective, with other artificial intelligence (AI) approaches to uncertainty, such as the Dempster-Shafer formalism, truth maintenance systems, and nonmonotonic logic.

Probabilistic Reasoning has been written with a variety of readers in mind. It should be of interest to scholars and researchers in AI, decision theory, statistics, logic, philosophy, cognitive psychology, and the management sciences. Specifically, AI researchers can take an earnest look at probability theory, now that it is phrased in their language, and probabilists should be challenged by the new issues that emerge from the AI experiment. In addition, practitioners in the areas of knowledge-based systems, operations research, engineering, and statistics will find a variety of theoretical and computational tools that should be of immediate practical use. Application areas include diagnosis, forecasting, image understand-ing, multi-sensor fusion, decision support systems, plan recognition, planning and control, speech recognition – in short, almost any task requiring that conclusions be drawn from uncertain clues and incomplete information.

The book is also intended as a textbook for graduate-level courses in AI, opera-tions research, and applied probability. In teaching this material at various levels of sophistication, I have found that the conceptual tools students acquire by treat-ing the world probabilistically grow in value, even (perhaps especially) when the students go on to pursue other formalisms.

To my own surprise, most of these chapters turned out to be fairly self-contained, demanding only a basic understanding of the results established in pre-vious chapters.

Chapter 1 identifies the basic AI paradigms of dealing with uncertainty and highlights the unique qualitative features that make probability theory a loyal guardian of plausible reasoning. Chapter 2 introduces the basic principles of

Bayesian inference and discusses some epistemological issues that emerge from this formalism. Those who have had no previous exposure to probability theory (some computer science students fall into this category) might wish to consult an introductory textbook and should follow closely the examples in Chapter 2 and work the exercises at the end of that chapter. In general, an elementary course in probability theory or decision analysis should be sufficient for mastering most of the book.

The casual reader seeking a painless glimpse at the basic issues of uncertainty should read the less technical sections in each chapter. These are indicated by a single asterisk (*) in the Contents. Chapters 1, 9, and 10 will prove especially useful for those seeking a comprehensive look at how the various formalisms are related, and how they measure up to each other under the acid test of human intuition.

The more technically oriented reader will want to follow the sections marked with a double asterisk (**), glancing occasionally at the definitions and results of other sections. This path leads the reader from traditional Bayesian inference and its graphical representations, into network propagation techniques (Chapters 4 and 5) and decision analysis (Chapter 6), and then into belief functions (Chapter 9) and default reasoning (Chapter 10). Knowledge engineers and developers of expert systems, for example, are advised to go straight to Section 3.3, then read Chapters 4, 5, 6, 7, and 9.

The most advanced sections, dealing with topics closer to current research frontiers, are marked with a triple asterisk (***). These include the theory of graphoids (Chapter 3), learning methods (Chapter 8), and probabilistic semantics for default reasoning (Section 10.2).

The reader should not view these markings as strict delineators. Just as an advanced ski run has flat stretches and a beginner's run has a mogul or two, there will be occasional pointers to human-style reasoning in the midst of technical discussions, and references to computational issues in the midst of philosophical discussions. Some reviewers advised me to avoid this hybrid style of writing, but I felt that retreating toward a more traditional organization would deny the reader the sense of excitement that led me to these explorations. By confessing the speculative nature of my own curiosity I hope to encourage further research in these areas.

I owe a great debt to many people who assisted me with this work. First, I would like to thank the members of the Cognitive Systems Laboratory at UCLA, whose work and ideas formed the basis of many of these sections: Avi Dechter, Rina Dechter, Hector Geffner, Dan Geiger, Moises Goldszmidt, Jin Kim, Itay Meiri, Javier Pinto, Prasadram Ramachandra, George Rebane, Igor Roizen, Rony Ross, and Thomas Verma. Rina and Hector, in particular, are responsible for wresting me from the security blanket of probability theory into the cold darkness of constraint networks, belief functions, and nonmonotonic logic.

My academic and professional colleagues have been generous with their time and ideas. I have been most influenced by the ideas of Stephen Lauritzen, Glenn Shafer, and David Spiegelhalter, and my collaborations with Azaria Paz and Norman Dalkey have been very rewarding. Helpful comments on selected sections were offered by Ernest Adams, Moshe Ben-Bassat, Alan Bundy, Norman Dalkey, Johan de Kleer, Arthur Dempster, Richard Duda, David Heckerman, David Etherington, Max Henrion, Robert Goldman, Richard Jeffrey, Henry Kyburg, Vladimir Lifschitz, John Lowrance, David McAllester, John Pollock, Gregory Provan, Lenhart Schubert, Ross Shachter, Glenn Shafer and Michael Wellman.

The National Science Foundation deserves acknowledgment for sponsoring the research that led to these results, with special thanks to Y.T. Chien, Joe Dekens, and the late Ken Curtis, who encouraged my research when I was still a junior faculty member seeking an attentive ear. Other sponsors include Lashon Booker of the Navy Research Laboratory, Abraham Waksman of the Air-Force Office of Scientific Research, and Richard Weis of Aerojet Electro Systems.

The manuscript was most diligently typed, processed, illustrated and proofed by Gina George and Jackie Trang, assisted by Nina Roop and Lillian Casey. I thank the publisher for accommodating my idiosyncracies, and special thanks to a very special copy editor, Danny Pearl, whose uncompromising stance made these pages readable.

Finally, I owe a great debt to the rest of my family: to Tammy for reminding me why it all matters, to Michelle for making me feel useful and even drawing some of the figures, and especially to my wife Ruth for sheltering me from the travails of the real world and surrounding me with so much love, support, and hope.

J.P.
Los Angeles, California
June 1988

Preface to the Fourth Printing

The upsurge in research in and applications of Bayesian networks has necessitated a large number of refinements within the original pagination of the first printing. Summaries of and references to new developments were added to the bibliographical sections at the end of each chapter and are also reflected in the revised set of exercises. One major development that could not be included is the transition from the probabilistic to the causal interpretation of Bayesian networks, which led to a calculus of interventions (*Biometrica* 82(4):669–710, December 1995) and counterfactuals (*UAI*-94, July 1994, 46-54). I hope to introduce these exciting developments in the near future.

J.P.
Los Angeles, California
February 1997

Contents

Chapter **1**
UNCERTAINTY IN AI SYSTEMS: AN OVERVIEW   1

1.1   INTRODUCTION*   1
      1.1.1   Why Bother with Uncertainty?   1
      1.1.2   Why Is It a Problem?   2
      1.1.3   Approaches to Uncertainty   2
      1.1.4   Extensional vs. Intensional Approaches   3

1.2   EXTENSIONAL SYSTEMS: MERITS, DEFICIENCIES,
      AND REMEDIES*   4
      1.2.1   Computational Merits   4
      1.2.2   Semantic Deficiencies   6
      1.2.3   Attempted Remedies and their Limitations   9

1.3   INTENSIONAL SYSTEMS AND NETWORK
      REPRESENTATIONS*   12
      1.3.1   Why Networks?   12
      1.3.2   Graphoids and the Formalization of Relevance and
              Causality   13

1.4   THE CASE FOR PROBABILITIES*   14
      1.4.1   Why Should Beliefs Combine Like Frequencies?   15
      1.4.2   The Primitive Relationships of Probability
              Language   16
      1.4.3   Probability as a Faithful Guardian of Common
              Sense   19

___

* Basic Issues
** Technical and Substantive Discussions
*** Advanced Research
For a detailed explanation of these levels, see Preface.

1.5	QUALITATIVE REASONING WITH PROBABILITIES*	23
	1.5.1 Softened Logic vs. Hardened Probabilities	24
	1.5.2 Probabilities and the Logic of "Almost True"	25
1.6	BIBLIOGRAPHICAL AND HISTORICAL REMARKS	26

Chapter 2
BAYESIAN INFERENCE   29

2.1	BASIC CONCEPTS	29
	2.1.1 Probabilistic Formulation and Bayesian Inversion*	29
	2.1.2 Combining Predictive and Diagnostic Supports*	34
	2.1.3 Pooling of Evidence*	36
	2.1.4 Recursive Bayesian Updating*	37
	2.1.5 Multi-Valued Hypotheses**	39
2.2	HIERARCHICAL MODELING	42
	2.2.1 Uncertain Evidence (Cascaded Inference)*	42
	2.2.2 Virtual (Intangible) Evidence*	44
	2.2.3 Predicting Future Events**	47
	2.2.4 Multiple Causes and "Explaining Away"*	49
	2.2.5 Belief Networks and the Role of Causality*	50
2.3	EPISTEMOLOGICAL ISSUES OF BELIEF UPDATING	52
	2.3.1 Patterns of Plausible Inference: Polya vs. Bayes?*	52
	2.3.2 The Three Prisoners Paradox: When the Bare Facts Won't Do*	58
	2.3.3 Jeffrey's Rule and the Problem of Autonomous Inference Agents*	62
2.4	BIBLIOGRAPHICAL AND HISTORICAL REMARKS	70
EXERCISES		73

Chapter 3
MARKOV AND BAYESIAN NETWORKS: Two Graphical
Representations of Probabilistic Knowledge   77

3.1	FROM NUMERICAL TO GRAPHICAL REPRESENTATIONS	78
	3.1.1 Introduction*	78

3.1.2   An Axiomatic Basis for Probabilistic
        Dependencies**   82
3.1.3   On Representing Dependencies by Undirected
        Graphs*   90
3.1.4   Axiomatic Characterization of Graph-Isomorph
        Dependencies***   93

3.2   MARKOV NETWORKS   96
      3.2.1   Definitions and Formal Properties***   96
      3.2.2   Illustrations**   100
      3.2.3   Markov Network as a Knowledge Base***   104
      3.2.4   Decomposable Models**   108

3.3   BAYESIAN NETWORKS   116
      3.3.1   Dependence Semantics for Bayesian Networks** 117
      3.3.2   Bayesian Network as a Knowledge Base**   122
      3.3.3   How Expressive Are Bayesian Networks?***   126

3.4   BIBLIOGRAPHICAL AND HISTORICAL REMARKS   131

EXERCISES   134
APPENDIX 3-A Proof of Theorem 3   139
APPENDIX 3-B Proof of Theorem 4   141

Chapter 4
BELIEF UPDATING BY NETWORK PROPAGATION   143

4.1   AUTONOMOUS PROPAGATION AS A
      COMPUTATIONAL PARADIGM   144
      4.1.1   Constraint Propagation and Rule-based
              Computation*   145
      4.1.2   Why Probabilistic Reasoning Seems to Resist
              Propagation*   148

4.2   BELIEF PROPAGATION IN CAUSAL TREES   150
      4.2.1   Notation**   150
      4.2.2   Propagation in Chains**   153
      4.2.3   Propagation in Trees**   162

4.3   BELIEF PROPAGATION IN CAUSAL POLYTREES
       (SINGLY CONNECTED NETWORKS)   175
       4.3.1   Propagation Rules**   177
       4.3.2   Canonical Models of Multicausal Interactions**   184

4.4   COPING WITH LOOPS   195
       4.4.1   Clustering Methods*   197
       4.4.2   The Method of Conditioning (Reasoning by
                Assumptions)*   204
       4.4.3   Stochastic Simulation**   210

4.5   WHAT ELSE CAN BAYESIAN NETWORKS
       ·COMPUTE?   223
       4.5.1   Answering Queries*   223
       4.5.2   Introducing Constraints*   225
       4.5.3   Answering Conjunctive Queries**   226

4.6   BIBLIOGRAPHICAL AND HISTORICAL REMARKS   232

EXERCISES   234
APPENDIX 4-A Auxilliary Derivations for Section 4.5.3   236

Chapter 5
DISTRIBUTED REVISION OF COMPOSITE BELIEFS   239

5.1   INTRODUCTION   239

5.2   ILLUSTRATING THE PROPAGATION SCHEME   241
       5.2.1   Belief Updating (A Review)*   242
       5.2.2   Belief Revision*   245

5.3   BELIEF REVISION IN SINGLY CONNECTED
       NETWORKS   250
       5.3.1   Deriving the Propagation Rules***   251
       5.3.2   Summary of Propagation Rules*   255
       5.3.3   Reaching Equilibrium and Assembling a
                Composite Solution**   257
       5.3.4   Comparison to Belief Updating*   259
       5.3.5   Coping with Loops*   260

5.4   DIAGNOSIS OF SYSTEMS WITH MULTIPLE
       FAULTS   263
       5.4.1   An Example: Electronic Circuit**   263
       5.4.2   Initialization**   265
       5.4.3   Fault Interpretation**   267
       5.4.4   Finding the Second-Best Interpretation**   271

5.5   APPLICATION TO MEDICAL DIAGNOSIS   272
       5.5.1   The Causal Model*   273
       5.5.2   Message Propagation**   275
       5.5.3   Choosing the Best Interpretation*   278
       5.5.4   Generating Explanations*   279
       5.5.5   Reversibility vs. Perseverance*   280

5.6   THE NATURE OF EXPLANATIONS   281
       5.6.1   Accepting vs. Assessing Beliefs*   281
       5.6.2   Is a Most-Probable Explanation Adequate?*   283
       5.6.3   Circumscribing Explanations*   285

5.7   CONCLUSIONS   286

5.8   BIBLIOGRAPHICAL AND HISTORICAL REMARKS   287

EXERCISES   288

Chapter **6**
DECISION AND CONTROL   289

6.1   FROM BELIEFS TO ACTIONS: INTRODUCTION TO
       DECISION ANALYSIS   289
       6.1.1   Rational Decisions and Quality Guarantees*   289
       6.1.2   Consequences, Payoffs, and Lotteries*   290
       6.1.3   Calibrating the Value of a Lottery*   292
       6.1.4   The Axioms of Utility Theory**   294
       6.1.5   Utility Functions*   297

6.2   DECISION TREES AND INFLUENCE DIAGRAMS   299
       6.2.1   Decision Trees*   299
       6.2.2   Planning with Decision Trees*   300
       6.2.3   Influence Diagrams*   306

6.3   THE VALUE OF INFORMATION   313
        6.3.1   Information Sources and Their Values**   313
        6.3.2   Myopic Assessments of Information Sources**   314

6.4   RELEVANCE-BASED CONTROL   318
        6.4.1   Focusing Attention**   318
        6.4.2   Utility-Free Assessment of Information
                 Sources***   319
        6.4.3   Controlling Attention*   324
        6.4.4   Summary*   326

6.5   BIBLIOGRAPHICAL AND HISTORICAL REMARKS   327

EXERCISES   328

Chapter 7
**TAXONOMIC HIERARCHIES, CONTINUOUS VARIABLES,
AND UNCERTAIN PROBABILITIES**   333

7.1   EVIDENTIAL REASONING IN TAXONOMIC
        HIERARCHIES   333
        7.1.1   Taxonomic vs. Causal Hierarchies*   333
        7.1.2   Evidence Propagation in Taxonomic Hierarchies*   337
        7.1.3   Probabilistic Justification**   340
        7.1.4   Psychological and Computational Characteristics*   342

7.2   MANAGING CONTINUOUS VARIABLES   344
        7.2.1   Plausible Reasoning about Uncertain Quantities*   344
        7.2.2   Propagating Estimates and Ranges**   346
        7.2.3   Qualitative Patterns of Reasoning**   351
        7.2.4   Discussion*   355

7.3   REPRESENTING UNCERTAINTY ABOUT
        PROBABILITIES   357
        7.3.1   The Semantics of Probabilities of Probabilities*   358
        7.3.2   De Finetti's Paradigm of Uncertain Contingencies*   359
        7.3.3   A Formal Definition of Network-Induced
                 Confidence Measures**   363

        7.3.4   The Effect of Evidence on Confidence: An
                Example**   366
        7.3.5   Conclusions*   372

7.4   BIBLIOGRAPHICAL AND HISTORICAL REMARKS   372

EXERCISES   374
APPENDIX 7-A Derivation of Propagation Rules For Continuous
                Variables   375

Chapter 8
LEARNING STRUCTURE FROM DATA   381

8.1   CAUSALITY, MODULARITY, AND TREE
        STRUCTURES*   383

8.2   STRUCTURING THE OBSERVABLES   387
        8.2.1   Chow's Method of Constructing Trees**   387
        8.2.2   Structuring Causal Polytrees**   390
        8.2.3   Conclusions: Causation or Covariation?*   396

8.3   LEARNING HIDDEN CAUSES   398
        8.3.1   Problem Definition and Nomenclature***   398
        8.3.2   Star-Decomposable Triplets***   401
        8.3.3   A Tree-Reconstruction Procedure***   402
        8.3.4   Extensions to Normal Variables***   405
        8.3.5   Conclusions and Open Questions*   407

8.4   BIBLIOGRAPHICAL AND HISTORICAL REMARKS   408

EXERCISES   409
APPENDIX 8-A Proof of Theorems 1 and 2   411
APPENDIX 8-B Conditions for Star-Decomposability (*After
                Lazarfeld [1966]*)   412

Chapter 9
**NON-BAYESIAN FORMALISMS FOR MANAGING
UNCERTAINTY**   415

9.1   THE DEMPSTER-SHAFER THEORY   416
        9.1.1   Basic Concepts*   416

9.1.2   Comparing Bayesian and Dempster-Shafer
Formalisms*   421
9.1.3   Dempster's Rule of Combination**   428
9.1.4   More on the Nature of Probability Intervals*   438
9.1.5   Applications to Rule-based Systems**   440
9.1.6   Bayes vs. Dempster-Shafer: A Semantic Clash*   447

9.2   TRUTH MAINTENANCE SYSTEMS   450
9.2.1   Naming the Assumptions*   451
9.2.2   Uncertainty Management in an ATMS**   454
9.2.3   Incidence Calculus*   456

9.3   PROBABILISTIC LOGIC**   457

9.4   BIBLIOGRAPHICAL AND HISTORICAL REMARKS   462

EXERCISES   465

Chapter 10
LOGIC AND PROBABILITY: THE STRANGE
CONNECTION   467

10.1   INTRODUCTION TO NONMONOTONIC
REASONING*   467
10.1.1   Reiter's Default Logic*   468
10.1.2   Problems with Default Logics*   470
10.1.3   Empirical vs. Procedural Semantics in Default
Reasoning*   473

10.2   PROBABILISTIC SEMANTICS FOR DEFAULT
REASONING   481
10.2.1   ε-semantics***   482
10.2.2   Axiomatic Characterization and a System of
Defeasible Inference***   485
10.2.3   Relevance-based Conventions***   491
10.2.4   Do People Use the Logic of Extreme
Probabilities?*   493

10.3   EMBRACING CAUSALITY IN DEFAULT
        REASONING   497
        10.3.1   How Old Beliefs Were Established Determines
                 Which New Beliefs Are Evoked*   497
        10.3.2   More on the Distinction Between Causal and
                 Evidential Support*   499
        10.3.3   The C-E System: A Coarse Logical Abstraction of
                 Causal Directionality*   501
        10.3.4   Implicit Suppressors and the Need for Finer
                 Abstractions*   507

10.4   A PROBABILISTIC TREATMENT OF THE YALE
        SHOOTING PROBLEM   509
        10.4.1   The Problem and its Solution*   509
        10.4.2   Concluding Dialogue*   513

10.5   BIBLIOGRAPHICAL AND HISTORICAL REMARKS   516

EXERCISES   518

Bibliography   521

Author Index   539

Subject Index   545

Chapter **1**

UNCERTAINTY IN AI SYSTEMS: AN OVERVIEW

I consider the word probability as meaning
the state of mind with respect to an assertion,
a coming event, or any other matter on which
absolute knowledge does not exist.
— August De Morgan, 1838

1.1 INTRODUCTION

1.1.1 Why Bother with Uncertainty?

Reasoning about any realistic domain always requires that some simplifications be made. The very act of preparing knowledge to support reasoning requires that we leave many facts unknown, unsaid, or crudely summarized. For example, if we choose to encode knowledge and behavior in rules such as "Birds fly" or "Smoke suggests fire," the rules will have many exceptions which we cannot afford to enumerate, and the conditions under which the rules apply (e.g., seeing a bird or smelling smoke) are usually ambiguously defined or difficult to satisfy precisely in real life. Reasoning with exceptions is like navigating a minefield: Most steps are safe, but some can be devastating. If we know their location, we can avoid or defuse each mine, but suppose we start our journey with a map the size of a postcard, with no room to mark down the exact location of every mine or the way they are wired together. An alternative to the extremes of ignoring or enumerating exceptions is to *summarize* them, i.e., provide some warning signs to indicate which areas of the minefield are more dangerous than others. Summarization is essential if we wish to find a reasonable compromise between safety and speed of movement. This book studies a language in which summaries of exceptions in the minefield of judgment and belief can be represented and processed.

1.1.2 Why Is It a Problem?

One way to summarize exceptions is to assign to each proposition a numerical measure of uncertainty and then combine these measures according to uniform syntactic principles, the way truth values are combined in logic. This approach has been adopted by first-generation expert systems, but it often yields unpredictable and counterintuitive results, examples of which will soon be presented. As a matter of fact, it is remarkable that this combination strategy went as far as it did, since uncertainty measures stand for something totally different than truth values. Whereas truth values in logic characterize the formulas under discussion, uncertainty measures characterize *invisible* facts, i.e., exceptions not covered in the formulas. Accordingly, while the syntax of the formula is a perfect guide for combining the visibles, it is nearly useless when it comes to combining the invisibles. For example, the machinery of Boolean algebra gives us no clue as to how the exceptions to $A \rightarrow C$ interact with those of $B \rightarrow C$ to yield the exceptions to $(A \wedge B) \rightarrow C$. These exceptions may interact in intricate and clandestine ways, robbing us of the modularity and monotonicity that make classical logic computationally attractive.

Although formulas interact in intricate ways, in logic too, the interactions are visible. This enables us to calculate the impact of each new fact *in stages*, by a process of derivation that resembles the propagation of a wave: We compute the impact of the new fact on a set of syntactically related sentences S_1, store the results, then propagate the impact from S_1 to another set of sentences S_2, and so on, without having to return to S_1. Unfortunately, this computational scheme, so basic to logical deduction, cannot be justified under uncertainty unless one makes some restrictive assumptions of *independence*.

Another feature we lose in going from logic to uncertainty is *incrementality*. When we have several items of evidence, we would like to account for the impact of each of them individually: Compute the effect of the first item, then absorb the added impact of the next item, and so on. This, too, can be done only after making restrictive assumptions of independence. Thus, it appears that uncertainty forces us to compute the impact of the entire set of past observations to the entire set of sentences in one global step—this, of course, is an impossible task.

1.1.3 Approaches to Uncertainty

AI researchers tackling these problems can be classified into three formal schools, which I will call *logicist*, *neo-calculist*, and *neo-probabilist*. The logicist school attempts to deal with uncertainty using nonnumerical techniques, primarily nonmonotonic logic. The neo-calculist school uses numerical representations of uncertainty but regards probability calculus as inadequate for the task and thus invents entirely new calculi, such as the Dempster-Shafer calculus, fuzzy logic, and certainty factors. The neo-probabilists remain within the traditional framework of probability theory, while attempting to buttress the theory with computational facilities needed to perform AI tasks. There is also a school of researchers taking an informal, heuristic approach [Cohen 1985; Clancey 1985; Chandrasekaran and Mittal 1983], in which uncertainties are not given explicit notation but are instead embedded in domain-specific procedures and data structures.

This taxonomy is rather superficial, capturing the syntactic rather than the semantic variations among the various approaches. A more fundamental taxonomy can be drawn along the dimensions of *extensional* vs. *intensional* approaches.† The extensional approach, also known as *production* systems, *rule-based* systems, and *procedure-based* systems, treats uncertainty as a generalized truth value attached to formulas and (following the tradition of classical logic) computes the uncertainty of any formula as a function of the uncertainties of its subformulas. In the intensional approach, also known as *declarative* or *model-based*, uncertainty is attached to "states of affairs" or subsets of "possible worlds." Extensional systems are computationally convenient but semantically sloppy, while intensional systems are semantically clear but computationally clumsy. The trade-off between semantic clarity and computational efficiency has been the main issue of concern in past research and has transcended notational boundaries. For example, it is possible to use probabilities either extensionally (as in PROSPECTOR [Duda, Hart, and Nilsson 1976]) or intensionally (as in MUNIN [Andreassen et al. 1987]). Similarly, one can use the Dempster-Shafer notation either extensionally [Ginsberg 1984] or intensionally [Lowrance, Garvey, and Strat 1986].

1.1.4 Extensional vs. Intensional Approaches

Extensional systems, a typical representative of which is the certainty-factors calculus used in MYCIN [Shortliffe 1976], treat uncertainty as a generalized truth value; that is, the certainty of a formula is defined to be a unique function of the certainties of its subformulas. Thus, the connectives in the formula serve to select the appropriate weight-combining function. For example, the certainty of the conjunction $A \wedge B$ is given by some function (e.g., the minimum or the product) of

---

† These terms are due to Perez and Jirousek (1985); the terms *syntactic* vs. *semantic* are also adequate.

the certainty measures assigned to A and B individually. By contrast, in intensional systems, a typical representative of which is probability theory, certainty measures are assigned to sets of worlds, and the connectives combine sets of worlds by set-theory operations. For example, the probability $P(A \wedge B)$ is given by the weight assigned to the intersection of two sets of worlds—those in which A is true and those in which B is true—but $P(A \wedge B)$ cannot be determined from the individual probabilities $P(A)$ and $P(B)$.

Rules, too, have different roles in these two systems. The rules in extensional systems provide licenses for certain symbolic activities. For example, a rule $A \xrightarrow{m} B$ may mean "If you see A, then you are given the license to update the certainty of B by a certain amount which is a function of the rule strength m." The rules are interpreted as a summary of past performance of the problem solver, describing the way an agent normally reacts to problem situations or to items of evidence. In intensional systems, the rules denote elastic constraints about the world. For example, in the Dempster-Shafer formalism (see Chapter 9) the rule $A \xrightarrow{m} B$ does not describe how an agent reacts to the finding of A, but asserts that the set of worlds in which A and $\neg B$ hold simultaneously has low likelihood and hence should be excluded with probability m. In the Bayesian formalism the rule $A \xrightarrow{m} B$ is interpreted as a conditional probability expression $P(B \mid A) = m$, stating that among all worlds satisfying A, those that also satisfy B constitute a fraction of size m. Although there exists a vast difference between these two interpretations (as will be shown in Chapters 9 and 10), they both represent summaries of factual or empirical information, rather than summaries of past decisions. We will survey intensional formalisms in Section 1.3, but first, we will briefly discuss their extensional rivals.

1.2 EXTENSIONAL SYSTEMS: MERITS, DEFICIENCIES, AND REMEDIES

1.2.1 Computational Merits

A good way to show the computational merits of extensional systems is to examine the way rules are handled in the certainty-factors formalism [Shortliffe 1976] and contrast it with probability theory's treatment of rules. Figure 1.1 depicts the combination functions that apply to serial and parallel rules, from which one can form a *rule network*. The result is a modular procedure for determining the certainty of a conclusion, given the credibility of each rule and the certainty of the premises (i.e., the roots of the network). To complete the calculus we also need to define combining functions for conjunction and negation. Setting mathematical details aside, the point to notice is that the same combination function applies uniformly to any two rules in the system, regardless of what other rules might be in the neighborhood.

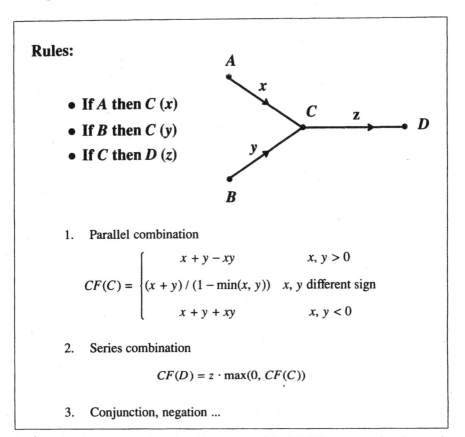

Rules:

- **If A then C (x)**
- **If B then C (y)**
- **If C then D (z)**

1. Parallel combination

$$CF(C) = \begin{cases} x + y - xy & x, y > 0 \\ (x + y) / (1 - \min(x, y)) & x, y \text{ different sign} \\ x + y + xy & x, y < 0 \end{cases}$$

2. Series combination

$$CF(D) = z \cdot \max(0, CF(C))$$

3. Conjunction, negation ...

Figure 1.1. *Certainty combination functions used in MYCIN. x, y, and z denote the credibilities of the rules.*

Computationally speaking, this uniformity mirrors the modularity of inference rules in classical logic. For example, the logical rule "If A then B" has the following procedural interpretation: "If you see A anywhere in the knowledge base, then regardless of what other things the knowledge base contains and regardless of how A was derived, you are given the license to assert B and add it to the database." This combination of *locality* ("regardless of other things") and *detachment* ("regardless of how it was derived") constitutes the principle of *modularity*. The numerical parameters that decorate the combination functions in Figure 1.1 do not alter this basic principle. The procedural license provided by the rule $A \xrightarrow{x} B$ reads as follows: "If you see the certainty of A undergoing a change δ_A, then regardless of what other things the knowledge base contains and regardless of how δ_A was triggered, you are given an unqualified license to modify the current certainty of B by some amount δ_B, which may depend on x, on δ_A, and on the current certainty of B."†

To appreciate the power of this interpretation, let us compare it with that given by an intensional formalism such as probability theory. Interpreting rules as conditional probability statements, $P(B \mid A) = p$, does not give us license to do anything. Even if we are fortunate enough to find A true in the database, we still cannot assert a thing about B or $P(B)$, because the meaning of the statement is "If A is true and A is the *only* thing that you know, then you can attach to B a probability p." As soon as other facts K appear in the database, the license to assert $P(B) = p$ is automatically revoked, and we need to look up $P(B \mid A, K)$ instead. The probability statement leaves us totally impotent, unable to initiate any computation, unless we can verify that everything else in the knowledge base is irrelevant. This is why verification of irrelevancy is so crucial in intensional systems.

In truth, such verifications are crucial in extensional systems too, but the computational convenience of these systems and their striking resemblance to logical derivation tempt people to neglect the importance of verifying irrelevancy. We shall now describe the semantic penalties imposed when relevance considerations are ignored.

1.2.2 Semantic Deficiencies

The price tag attached to extensional systems is that they often yield updating that is incoherent, i.e., subject to surprises and counterintuitive conclusions. These problems surface in several ways, most notably

1. improper handling of bidirectional inferences,

2. difficulties in retracting conclusions, and

3. improper treatment of correlated sources of evidence.

We shall describe these problems in order.

THE ROLE OF BIDIRECTIONAL INFERENCES

The ability to use both predictive and diagnostic information is an important component of plausible reasoning, and improper handling of such information leads to rather strange results. A common pattern of normal discourse is that of

---

† The observation that the rules refer to changes rather than absolute values was made by Horvitz and Heckerman [1986].

abductive reasoning—if A implies B, then finding that B is true makes A more credible (Polya [1954] called this an *induction* pattern [see Section 2.3.1]). This pattern involves reasoning both ways, from A to B and from B to A. Moreover, it appears that people do not require two separate rules for performing these inferences; the first rule (e.g., "Fire implies smoke") provides the license to invoke the second (e.g., "Smoke makes fire more credible"). Extensional systems, on the other hand, require that the second rule be stated explicitly and, even worse, that the first rule be removed. Otherwise, a cycle would be created where any slight evidence in favor of A would be amplified via B and fed back to A, quickly turning into a stronger confirmation (of A and B), with no apparent factual justification. The prevailing practice in such systems (e.g., MYCIN) is to cut off cycles of that sort, permitting only diagnostic reasoning and no predictive inferences.

Removal of its predictive component prevents the system from exhibiting another important pattern of plausible reasoning, one that we call *explaining away*: If A implies B, C implies B, and B is true, then finding that C is true makes A *less* credible. In other words, finding a second explanation for an item of data makes the first explanation less credible. Such interaction among multiple causes appears in many applications (see Sections 2.2.4, 2.3.1, 4.3.2, and 10.2). For example, finding that the smoke could have been produced by a bad muffler makes fire less credible. Finding that my light bulb emits red light makes it less credible that the red-hued object in my hand is truly red.

To exhibit this sort of reasoning, a system must use bidirected inferences: from evidence to hypothesis (or explanation) and from hypothesis to evidence. While it is sometimes possible to use brute force (e.g., enumerating all exceptions) to restore "explaining away" without the danger of circular reasoning, we shall see that any system that succeeds in doing this must sacrifice the principles of modularity, i.e., locality and detachment. More precisely, every system that updates beliefs modularly at the natural rule level and that treats all rules equally is bound to defy prevailing patterns of plausible reasoning.

THE LIMITS OF MODULARITY

The principle of locality is fully realized in the inference rules of classical logic. The rule "If P then Q" means that if P is found true, we can assert Q with no further analysis, even if the database contains some other knowledge K. In plausible reasoning, however, the luxury of ignoring the rest of the database cannot be maintained. For example, suppose we have a rule R_1 = "If the ground is wet, then assume it rained (with certainty c_1)." Validating the truth of "The ground is wet" does not permit us to increase the certainty of "It rained" because the knowledge base might contain strange items such as K = "The sprinkler was on last night." These strange items, called *defeaters* or *suppressors* (Section 10.3), are sometimes easy to discover (as with K' = "The neighbor's grass is dry," which directly opposes "It rained"), but sometimes they hide cleverly behind syntactical innocence. The neutral fact K = "Sprinkler was on" neither supports nor opposes the possibility of rain, yet K manages to undercut the rule R_1. This undercutting cannot be implemented in an extensional system; once R_1 is invoked, the increase in the certainty of "It rained" will never be retracted, because no rule would normally connect "Sprinkler was on" to "It rained." Imposing such a connection by proclaiming "Sprinkler was on" as an explicit exception to R_1 defeats the spirit of modularity by forcing the rule-writer to pack together items of information that are only remotely related to each other, and it burdens the rules with an unmanageably large number of exceptions.

Violation of detachment can also be demonstrated in this example. In deductive logic, if K implies P and P implies Q, then finding K true permits us to deduce Q by simple chaining; a derived proposition (P) can trigger a rule $(P \rightarrow Q)$ with the same vigor as a directly observed proposition can. Chaining does not apply in plausible reasoning. The system may contain two innocent-looking rules—"If the ground is wet then it rained" and "If the sprinkler was on then the ground is wet"—but if you find that the sprinkler was on, you obviously do not wish to conclude that it rained. On the contrary, finding that the sprinkler was on only takes away support from "It rained."

As another example, consider the relationships shown in Figure 1.2. Normally an alarm sound alerts us to the possibility of a burglary. If somebody calls you at the office and tells you that your alarm went off, you will surely rush home in a hurry, even though there could be other causes for the alarm sound. If you hear a radio announcement that there was an earthquake nearby, and if the last false alarm you recall was triggered by an earthquake, then your certainty of a burglary will diminish. Again, this requires going both ways, from effect to cause (*Radio* $\rightarrow$ *Earthquake*), and from cause to effect (*Earthquake* $\rightarrow$ *Alarm*), and then from effect to cause again (*Alarm* $\rightarrow$ *Burglary*). Notice what pattern of reasoning results from such a chain, though: We have a rule, "If A (*Alarm*) then B (*Burglary*)"; you listen to the radio, A becomes more credible, and the conclusion B becomes less credible. Overall, we have "If $A \rightarrow B$ and A becomes more credible, then B becomes less credible." This behavior is clearly contrary to everything we expect from local belief updating.

In conclusion, we see that the difficulties plaguing classical logic do not stem from its nonnumeric, binary character. Equally troublesome difficulties emerge when truth and certainty are measured on a grey scale, whether by point values, by interval bounds, or by linguistic quantifiers such as "likely" and "credible." There seems to be a basic struggle between procedural modularity and semantic coherence, independent of the notation used.

CORRELATED EVIDENCE

Extensional systems, greedily exploiting the licenses provided by locality and detachment, respond only to the magnitudes of the weights and not to their origins.

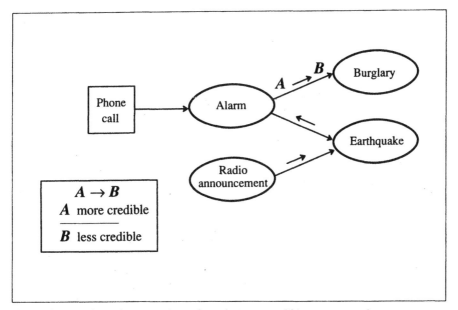

Figure 1.2. *Making the antecedent of a rule more credible can cause the consequent to become less credible.*

As a result they will produce the same conclusions whether the weights originate from identical or independent sources of information. An example from Henrion [1986b] about the Chernobyl disaster helps demonstrate the problems encountered by such a local strategy. Figure 1.3 shows how multiple, independent sources of evidence would normally increase the credibility of a hypothesis (e.g., *Thousands dead*), but the discovery that these sources have a common origin should reduce the credibility. Extensional systems are too local to recognize the common origin of the information, and they would update the credibility of the hypothesis as if it were supported by three independent sources.

1.2.3 Attempted Remedies and their Limitations

The developers of extensional systems have proposed and implemented powerful techniques to remedy some of the semantic deficiencies we have discussed. The remedies, most of which focus on the issue of correlated evidence, take two approaches:

1. *Bounds propagation*: Since most correlations are unknown, certainty measures are combined under two extreme assumptions—that the components have a high positive correlation, and that they have a high

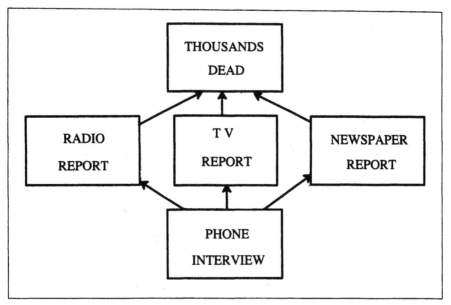

Figure 1.3. *The Chernobyl disaster example (after Henrion) shows why rules cannot combine locally.*

negative correlation. This yields upper and lower bounds on the combined certainty, which are entered as inputs to subsequent computations, producing new bounds on the certainty of the conclusions. This approach has been implemented in INFERNO [Quinlan 1983] and represents a local approximation to Nilsson's probabilistic logic [Nilsson 1986] (see Section 9.3).

2. *User-specified combination functions*: A system named RUM [Bonissone, Gans, and Decker 1987] permits the rule-writer to specify the combination function that should apply to the rule's components. For example, if a, b, and c stand for the weights assigned to propositions A, B, and C in the rule

$$A \wedge B \to C \ ,$$

the user can specify which of the following three combination functions should be used:

$$T_1(a, b) = \max(0, a + b - 1),$$

$$T_2(a, b) = ab,$$

or

$$T_3(a, b) = \min(a, b).$$

These functions (called *T norms*) represent the probabilistic combinations obtained under three extreme cases of correlation between *A* and *B*: highly negative, zero, and highly positive.

Cohen, Shafer, and Shenoy [1987] have proposed a more refined scheme, where for any pair of values $P(A)$ and $P(B)$, the user is permitted to specify the value of the resulting probability, $P(C)$.

The difficulties with these correlation-handling techniques are several. First, the bounds produced by systems such as INFERNO are too wide. For example, if we are given $P(A) = p$ and $P(B \mid A) = q$, then the bounds we obtain for $P(B)$ are

$$pq \leq P(B) \leq 1 - p(1 - q),$$

which for small p approach the unit interval $[0, 1]$. Second, to handle the intricate dependencies that may occur among rules it is not enough to capture pair-wise correlations; higher-order dependencies are often necessary [Bundy 1985]. Finally, even if one succeeds in specifying higher-order dependencies, a much more fundamental limitation exists: Dependencies are dynamic relationships, created and destroyed as new evidence is obtained. For example, dependency between the propositions "It rained last night" and "The sprinkler was on" is created once we find out that the ground is wet. The dependence between a child's shoe size and reading ability is destroyed once we find out the child's age. Thus, correlations and combination functions specified at the knowledge-building phase may quickly become obsolete once the program is put into use.

Heckerman [1986a, 1986b] delineated precisely the range of applicability of extensional systems. He proved that any system that updates certainty weights in a modular and consistent fashion can be given a probabilistic interpretation in which the certainty update of a proposition *A* is some function of the likelihood ratio

$$\lambda = \frac{P(Evidence \mid A)}{P(Evidence \mid \neg A)}.$$

In MYCIN, for example, the certainty factor *CF* can be interpreted as

$$CF = \frac{\lambda - 1}{\lambda + 1}.$$

Once we have a probabilistic interpretation, it is easy to determine the set of structures within which the update procedure will be semantically valid. It turns out that a system of such rules will produce coherent updates if and only if the rules form a directed tree, i.e., no two rules may stem from the same premise. This limitation explains why strange results were obtained in the burglary example of Figure 1.2. There, the alarm event points to two possible explanations, *Burglary* and *Earthquake*, which amounts to two evidential rules stemming from the premise, *Alarm*.

Hájek [1985] and Hájek and Valdes [1987] have developed an algebraic theory that characterizes an even wider range of the extensional systems and combining functions, including those based on Dempster-Shafer intervals. The unifying properties common to all such systems is that they form an ordered Abelian group. Again, the knowledge base must form a tree so that no evidence is counted twice via alternative paths of reasoning.

1.3 INTENSIONAL SYSTEMS AND NETWORK REPRESENTATIONS

We have seen that handling uncertainties is a rather tricky enterprise. It requires a fine balance between our desire to use the computational permissiveness of extensional systems and our ability to refrain from committing semantic sins. It is like crossing a minefield on a wild horse. You can choose a horse with good instincts, attach certainty weights to it and hope it will keep you out of trouble, but the danger is real, and highly skilled knowledge engineers are needed to prevent the fast ride from becoming a disaster. The other extreme is to work your way by foot with a semantically safe intensional system, such as probability theory, but then you can hardly move, since every step seems to require that you examine the entire field afresh. We shall now examine means for making this movement brisker.

In intensional systems, the syntax consists of declarative statements about states of affairs and hence mirrors world knowledge rather nicely. For example, conditional probability statements such as "Most birds fly" are both empirically testable and conceptually meaningful. Additionally, intensional systems have no problem handling bidirected inferences and correlated evidence; these emerge as built-in features of one globally coherent model (see Chapters 2 and 4). However, since the syntax does not point to any useful procedures, we need to construct special mechanisms that convert the declarative input into routines that answer queries. Such a mechanism is offered by techniques based on *belief networks,* which will be a central topic of discussion in this book.

1.3.1 Why Networks?

Our goal is to make intensional systems operational by making relevance relationships explicit, thus curing the impotence of declarative statements such as $P(B \mid A) = p$. As mentioned earlier, the reason one cannot act on the basis of such declarations is that one must first make sure that other items in the knowledge base are irrelevant to B and hence can be ignored. The trick, therefore, is to encode knowledge in such a way that the ignorable is recognizable, or better yet, that the unignorable is quickly identified and is readily accessible. Belief networks encode relevancies as neighboring nodes in a graph, thus ensuring that by consulting the neighborhood one gains a license to act; what you don't see locally doesn't matter. In effect, what network representations offer is a dynamically updated list of all currently valid licenses to ignore, and licenses to ignore constitute permissions to act.

Network representations are not foreign to AI systems. Most reasoning systems encode relevancies using intricate systems of pointers, i.e., networks of indices that group facts into structures, such as frames, scripts, causal chains, and inheritance hierarchies. These structures, though shunned by pure logicians, have proved to be indispensable in practice, because they place the information required to perform an inference task close to the propositions involved in the task. Indeed, many patterns of human reasoning can be explained only by people's tendency to follow the pathways laid out by such networks.

The special feature of the networks discussed in this book is that they have clear semantics. In other words, they are not auxiliary devices contrived to make reasoning more efficient but are an integral part of the semantics of the knowledge base, and most of their features can even be derived from the knowledge base.

Belief networks play a central role in two uncertainty formalisms: probability theory, where they are called *Bayesian networks, causal nets,* or *influence diagrams,* and the Dempster-Shafer theory (see Chapter 9), where they are referred to as *galleries* [Lowrance, Garvey, and Strat 1986], *qualitative Markov networks* [Shafer, Shenoy, and Mellouli 1988], or *constraint networks* [Montanari 1974]. Probabilistic networks will be given a formal treatment in Chapter 3 and will serve as a unifying theme throughout this book. In the next subsection we briefly discuss the theory of graphoids, which provides formal semantics for graphical representations in terms of information relevance.

1.3.2 Graphoids and the Formalization of Relevance and Causality

A central requirement for managing intensional systems is to articulate the conditions under which one item of information is considered relevant to another, given what we already know, and to encode knowledge in structures that display these conditions vividly as the knowledge undergoes changes. Different formalisms give rise to different definitions of relevance. For example, in probability theory, relevance is identified with dependence; in database theory, with induced constraints—two variables are said to be relevant to each other if we can restrict the range of values permitted for one by constraining the other.

The essence of relevance can be identified with a structure common to all of these formalisms. It consists of four axioms which convey the simple idea that when we learn an irrelevant fact, the relevance relationships of all other propositions remain unaltered; any information that was irrelevant remains irrelevant, and that which was relevant remains relevant. Structures that conform to these axioms are called *graphoids* [Pearl and Paz 1985] and will be treated more fully in Chapter 3. Interestingly, both undirected graphs and directed acyclic graphs conform to the graphoids axioms (hence the name) if we associate the sentence "Variable X is irrelevant to variable Y once we know Z" with the graphical condition "Every path from X to Y is intercepted by the set of nodes corresponding to Z." (A special definition of intercept is required for directed graphs [see Section 3.3.1]).

With this perspective in mind, graphs, networks, and diagrams can be viewed as inference engines devised for efficiently representing and manipulating relevance relationships. The topology of the network is assembled from a list of local relevance statements (e.g., direct dependencies). This input list implies (using the graphoid axioms) a host of additional statements, and the graph ensures that a substantial portion of the latter can be verified by simple graphical procedures such as path tracing and path blocking. Such procedures enable one to determine, at any state of knowledge Z, what information is relevant to the task at hand and what can be ignored. Permission to ignore, as we saw in Section 1.1, is the fuel that gives intensional systems the power to act.

The theory of graphoids shows that a belief network can constitute a sound and complete inference mechanism relative to probabilistic dependencies, i.e., it identifies, in polynomial time, every conditional independence relationship that logically follows from those used in the construction of the network (see Section 3.3). Similar results hold for other types of relevance relationships, e.g., partial correlations and constraint-based dependencies. The essential requirement for soundness and completeness is that the network be constructed *causally,* i.e., that we identify the most relevant predecessors of each variable recursively, in some total order, say temporal. (Once the network is constructed, the original order can be forgotten; only the partial order displayed in the network matters.)

It is this soundness and completeness that gives causality such a central role in this book, and perhaps in knowledge organization in general. However, the precise relationship between causality as a representation of irrelevancies and causality as a commitment to a particular inference strategy (e.g., chronological ignorance [Shoham 1986]) has yet to be fully investigated.

1.4 THE CASE FOR PROBABILITIES

The aim of artificial intelligence is to provide a computational model of intelligent behavior, most importantly, commonsense reasoning. The aim of probability theory is to provide a coherent account of how belief should change in light of partial or uncertain information. Since commonsense reasoning always applies to incomplete information, one might naturally expect the two disciplines to share language, goals, and techniques. However, ever since McCarthy and Hayes [1969] proclaimed probabilities to be "epistemologically inadequate," AI researchers have shunned probability adamantly. Their attitude has been expressed through commonly heard statements like "The use of probability requires a massive amount of data," "The use of probability requires the enumeration of all possibilities," and "People are bad probability estimators." "We do not have those numbers," it is often claimed, and even if we do, "We find their use inconvenient."

Aside from the obvious corrections to these claims, this book will try to communicate the idea that "probability is not really about numbers; it is about the structure of reasoning," as Glenn Shafer recently wrote.† We will emphasize, for example, that when a physician asserts, "The chances that a patient with disease D will develop symptom S is p," the thrust of the assertion is not the precise magnitude of p so much as the specific reason for the physician's belief, the context or assumptions under which the belief should be firmly held, and the sources of information that would cause this belief to change. We will also stress that probability theory is unique in its ability to process context-sensitive beliefs, and what makes the processing computationally feasible is that the information needed for specifying context dependencies can be represented by graphs and manipulated by local propagation.

1.4.1 Why Should Beliefs Combine Like Frequencies?

On the surface, there is really no compelling reason that beliefs, being mental dispositions about unrepeatable and often unobservable events, should combine by the laws of proportions that govern repeatable trials such as the outcomes of gambling devices. The primary appeal of probability theory is its ability to express useful *qualitative* relationships among beliefs and to process these relationships in a way that yields intuitively plausible conclusions, at least in cases where intuitive judgments are compelling. A summary of such qualitative relationships will be given in the next subsection. What we wish to stress here is that the fortunate match between human intuition and the laws of proportions is not a coincidence. It came about because beliefs are formed not in a vacuum but rather as a distillation of sensory experiences. For reasons of storage economy and generality we forget the actual experiences and retain their mental impressions in the forms of averages, weights, or (more vividly) abstract qualitative relationships that help us determine future actions. The organization of knowledge and beliefs must strike a delicate balance between the computational resources these relationships consume and the frequency of their use. With these considerations in mind, it is

---

† Personal communication.

hard to envision how a calculus of beliefs can evolve that is substantially different from the calculus of proportions and frequencies, namely probability.

1.4.2 The Primitive Relationships of Probability Language

Although probabilities are expressed in numbers, the merit of probability calculus rests in providing a means for articulating and manipulating qualitative relationships that are found useful in normal discourse. The following four relationships are viewed as the basic primitives of the language:

1. Likelihood ("Tim is *more likely* to fly than to walk").

2. Conditioning ("*If* Tim is sick, he can't fly").

3. Relevance ("Whether Tim flies *depends on whether* he is sick").

4. Causation ("Being sick *caused* Tim's inability to fly").

LIKELIHOOD

The qualitative relationship of the form "A is more likely than B" has traditionally been perceived as the prime purpose of using probabilities. The practical importance of determining whether one event is more likely than another is best represented by the fact that probability calculus was pioneered and developed by such ardent gamblers as Cardano (1501-1576) and De Moivre (1667-1754). However, the importance of likelihood relationships goes beyond gambling situations or even management decisions. Decisions depending on relative likelihood of events are important in every reasoning task because likelihood translates immediately to *processing time*—the time it takes to verify the truth of a proposition, to consider the consequence of a rule, or to acquire more information. A reasoning system unguided by likelihood considerations (my ex-lawyer is a perfect example of one) would waste precious resources in chasing the unlikely while neglecting the likely.

Philosophers and decision theorists have labored to obtain an axiomatic basis for probability theory based solely on this primitive relationship of "more likely," namely, to identify conditions under which an ordering of events has a numerical representation P that satisfies the properties of probability functions [Krantz et al. 1971; Fine 1973; Fishburn 1986]. More recently, the task of devising a nonnumeric logic for manipulating sentences that contain the qualifier likely has received considerable attention [Halpern and Rabin 1987; Fagin and Halpern 1988] and has turned out to be a tougher challenge than expected.

CONDITIONING

Probability theory adopts the autoepistemic phrase "...given that what I know is C" as a primitive of the language. Syntactically, this is denoted by placing C behind the conditioning bar in a statement such as $P(A \mid C) = p$. This statement combines the notions of knowledge and belief by attributing to A a degree of belief p, given the knowledge C. C is also called the *context* of the belief in A, and the notation $P(A \mid C)$ is called *Bayes conditionalization*. Thomas Bayes (1702–1761) made his main contribution to the science of probability by associating the English phrase "...given that I know C" with the now-famous ratio formula

$$P(A \mid C) = \frac{P(A, C)}{P(C)} \tag{1.1}$$

[Bayes 1763], which has become a definition of conditional probabilities (see Eq. (2.8)).

It is by virtue of Bayes conditionalization that probability theory facilitates nonmonotonic reasoning, i.e., reasoning involving retraction of previous conclusions (see Section 1.5). For example, it is perfectly acceptable to assert simultaneously $P(Fly(a) \mid Bird(a)) = HIGH$ and $P(Fly(a) \mid Bird(a), Sick(a)) = LOW$. In other words, if all we know about individual a is that a is a bird, we jump to the conclusion that a most likely flies. However, upon learning that a is also sick, we retract our old conclusion and assert that a most likely cannot fly.

To facilitate such retraction it is necessary both that the original belief be stated with less than absolute certainty and that the context upon which we condition beliefs be consulted constantly to see whether belief revision is warranted. The dynamic of belief revision under changing contexts is not totally arbitrary but must obey some basic laws of plausibility which, fortunately, are embedded in the syntactical rules of probability calculus. A typical example of such a plausibility law is the rule of the *hypothetical middle*:

> If two diametrically opposed assumptions impart two different degrees of belief onto a proposition Q, then the unconditional degree of belief merited by Q should be somewhere between the two.

For example, our belief that Tim flies given that Tim is a bird must be between our belief that Tim flies given that he is a sick bird and our belief that Tim flies given that he is a healthy bird. Such a qualitative, commonsense restriction is built into the syntax of probability calculus via the equality

$$P(B \mid C) = \alpha P(B \mid C, A) + (1 - \alpha) P(B \mid C, \neg A), \tag{1.2}$$

where $\alpha = P(A \mid C)$ is some number between 0 and 1. Other typical patterns of plausible reasoning are those of abduction and "explaining away," mentioned in Section 1.2.2 and further elaborated in Section 2.3.1.

RELEVANCE

Relevance is a relationship indicating a potential change of belief due to a specified change in knowledge (see Section 1.3.2). Two propositions A and B are said to be relevant to each other in context C if adding B to C would change the likelihood of A. Clearly, relevance can be defined in terms of likelihood and conditioning, but it is a notion more basic than likelihood. For example, a person might be hesitant to assess the likelihood of two events but feel confident about judging whether or not the events are relevant to each other. People provide such judgments swiftly and consistently because—we speculate—relevance relationships are stored explicitly as pointers in one's knowledge base.

Relevance is also a primitive of the language of probability because the language permits us to specify relevance relationships directly and qualitatively before making any numerical assessment. Later on, when numerical assessments of likelihood are required, they can be added in a consistent fashion, without disturbing the original relevance structure (see Chapter 3).

CAUSATION

Causation is a ubiquitous notion in man's conception of his environment, yet it has traditionally been considered a psychological construct, outside the province of probability or even the physical sciences [Russell 1913]. In Section 3.3 we present a new account of causation, according to which it can be given a nontemporal probabilistic interpretation based solely on the notion of relevance. The temporal component of causation [Suppes 1970; Shoham 1988] is viewed merely as a convenient indexing standard chosen to facilitate communication and predictions.

Causation is listed as one of the four basic primitives of the language of probability because it is an indispensable tool for structuring and specifying probabilistic knowledge (see Sections 3.3 and 10.4) and because the semantics of causal relationships are preserved by the syntax of probabilistic manipulations; no auxiliary devices are needed to force conclusions to conform with people's conception of causation. The following is a brief summary of our notion of causation, to be further developed in Sections 3.3, 8.2, and 10.3.

Causation is a language with which one can talk efficiently about certain structures of relevance relationships, with the objective of separating the relevant from the superfluous. For example, to say that a wet pavement was a direct cause of my slipping and breaking a leg is a concise way of identifying which events should no longer be considered relevant to my accident, once the wetness of the pavement is confirmed. The facts that it rained that day, that the rain was welcomed by farmers, and that my friend also slipped and broke his leg should no longer be considered relevant to the accident once we establish the truth of *Wet pavement* and identify it as the direct cause of the accident.

The asymmetry conveyed by causal directionality is viewed as a notational device for encoding still more intricate patterns of relevance relationships, such as *nontransitive* and *induced* dependencies. For example, by designating *Rain* and *Sprinkler* as potential causes of the wet pavement we permit the two causes to be independent of each other and still both be relevant to *Wet pavement* (hence forming a nontransitive relationship). Moreover, by this designation we also identify the consequences *Wet pavement* and *Accident* as potential sources of new dependencies between the two causes; once a consequence is observed, its causes can no longer remain independent, because confirming one cause lowers the likelihood of the other. This connection between nontransitive and induced dependencies is, again, a built-in feature of the syntax of probability theory—the syntax ensures that nontransitive dependencies always induce the appropriate dependencies between causes (see Exercise 3.10).

To summarize, causal directionality conveys the following pattern of dependency: Two events do not become relevant to each other merely by virtue of predicting a common consequence, but they do become relevant when the consequence is actually observed. The opposite is true for two consequences of a common cause; typically the two become independent upon learning the cause. (Chapter 8 deals with using this asymmetry to identify causal directionality in nontemporal empirical data.)

1.4.3 Probability as a Faithful Guardian of Common Sense

In the preceding subsections we presented qualitative patterns of commonsense reasoning that are naturally embedded within the syntax of probability calculus. Among these intuitive patterns are nonmonotonicity (context sensitivity), abduction, "explaining away," causation, and hypothetical middle. It is possible to assemble some of these desirable patterns of inference and pose them as axioms that render probability calculus "inevitable," i.e., to show that any calculus respecting these desired patterns behaves as if it were driven by a probability engine. This route was a favorite preoccupation of many philosophers, most notably Ramsey [1931], de Finetti [1937], Cox [1946], Good [1950], and Savage [1954]. Cox assembled seven semi-qualitative arguments for the conditional relation $(A \mid B)$ (to read, "The plausibility of A conditioned on the evidence B") and showed that they lead to Bayes' ratio formula (Eq. (1.1)) and thus to probability calculus. This axiomatic approach placed probability on firm qualitative ground, but it has also been the subject of lively debates and refutations (e.g., Savage [1962], Lindley [1982], and Shafer [1986a]). When posed as a stand-alone axiomatic system, any chosen subset of reasoning patterns is vulnerable to criticism because we can always imagine a situation where one of the axioms ceases to be necessary, thus discrediting the entire system. The interested reader is referred to the classical literature on the foundations of probability [Fine 1973; Krantz et al. 1971].

The approach taken in this book is somewhat different. We take for granted that probability calculus is unique in the way it handles context-dependent information and that no competing calculus exists that closely covers so many qualitative aspects of plausible reasoning. So the calculus is worthy of exploitation, emulation, or at the very least, serious exploration. We therefore take probability calculus as an initial model of human reasoning from which more refined models may originate, if needed. By exploring the limits of using probability calculus in machine implementations of plausible inference, we hope to identify conditions under which extensions, refinements, and simplifications are warranted.

Obviously, there are applications where strict adherence to the dictates of probability theory would be computationally infeasible, and there compromises will have to be made. Still, we find it more comfortable to compromise an ideal theory that is well understood than to search for a new surrogate theory, with only gut feeling for guidance.

The merits of a theory-based approach are threefold:

1. The theory can be consulted to ensure that compromises are made only when necessary and that their damage is kept to a minimum.

2. When system performance does not match expectations, knowing which compromises were made helps identify the adjustments needed.

3. Compromised theories facilitate scientific communication; one need specify only the compromises made, treating the rest of the theory as common knowledge.

HOW BAD ARE THOSE NUMBERS?

People are notoriously bad numerical estimators. They find it hard to assess absolute probabilities as well as distances, weights, and times. A person would much rather assert qualitatively that one object is heavier than another than assess the absolute weight of a given object. Still, the lack of an accurate scale does not preclude the use of the laws of physics when it comes to deciding which bag is lighter, the one containing 2000 dimes or the one containing 1000 quarters. It is quite conceivable that a person has never before seen bags containing thousands of coins, yet the limited experience gathered from handling small quantities of coins, teaching us that two dimes are lighter than one quarter, can be amplified by the laws of physics and extended to situations never seen before. We might assign a single dime a rough weight estimate of 10 grams, consult our experience and assign a quarter an estimate of 30 grams, then multiply the two estimates by the respective numbers of coins and compare the results. The absolute estimates in this example can be completely off, but as long as their ratio reflects genuine experience, the conclusions will still be useful. (Deriving these conclusions symbolically, using axioms to describe how weights combine, often requires much more work.) In other words, if we strongly believe in the rules by which exact quantities combine, we can use the same combination rules on the rough estimates at hand.

This heuristic strategy gives reasonably good results for several reasons. First, by using reliable combination rules, we make the utmost use of the available knowledge and keep the damage due to imprecision from extending beyond well-defined boundaries. Second, when we commit ourselves to a particular set of numbers, no matter how erroneous, the consistency of the model prevents us from reaching inconsistent conclusions. For example, we will never reach a conclusion that the 2000-dime bag is lighter than the 1000-quarter bag and a simultaneous conclusion that 3000 dimes are heavier than 1500 quarters. Finally, and most importantly for dealing with uncertainty in AI systems, adhering to a coherent model of reality helps us debug our inferences when they do not match expectations. In our coin example, if it turns out, contrary to calculations, that the 2000 dimes are not lighter than the 1000 quarters, we know immediately that we have either wrongly estimated the relative weights of a dime and a quarter or miscounted the coins in the bags; we need not tamper with the rules of inference or with their calculus of combination. In general, we know precisely how the model should be refined or improved.

ON THE USEFULNESS OF NUMBERS

If people prefer to reason qualitatively, why should machines reason with numbers? Probabilities are summaries of knowledge that is left behind when information is transferred to a higher level of abstraction. The summaries can be encoded logically or numerically; logic enjoys the advantages of parsimony and simplicity, while numbers are more informative and sometimes are necessary.

The minefield metaphor used in Section 1.1 will help illustrate the usefulness of numerical summarization. Imagine that before we start our journey across the minefield, we are given access to a complete record of the field, specifying in full detail the exact location of each mine as recorded six months earlier by the team that laid these mines. However, since we cannot carry with us the entire record, we must somehow summarize that information on a miniature map, the size of a postcard. There are many ways we might summarize the data on the postcard, but one of the most effective methods is to color the map to reflect the density of mines in any given area: the darker the color, the higher the density. Viewing dark colors as high numbers, this is the essence of numerical summarization of uncertainty. Why is this scheme effective?

Imagine that you start your journey by pursuing what appears to be a rather safe path to your destination. After two days you reach a roadblock; the path chosen is not usable and an alternative path must be found. Here is where the color code begins to show its usefulness. While traversing the original path you passed many side roads branching out from the one you chose. At the time, these junctions were abandoned because your path appeared more promising, but now that your first choice turned into a disappointment, you must look back at those branching points and decide which one to pursue next. Had you summarized your decisions using a bi-valued predicate, say "possible" or "not possible," you would now be at a loss. Among those marked "possible," you would not know which one is actually the least dangerous and the quickest, especially in light of the new roadblocks you have discovered. The colored map provides exactly this information.

To make the analogy closer to mental reasoning tasks, let us further imagine that we can communicate with headquarters and ask them to wire us a more detailed map of any region under consideration. The question is which map we should request. In the absence of priority ranking among the viable alternatives, precious time will be wasted transmitting and examining maps that, in view of the new road conditions discovered, will again lead to dead ends. The function of colored maps, and of numeric labels in general, is to prioritize the flow of information and focus on items more likely to yield beneficial results.

The translation to reasoning tasks is obvious. Raw experiential data is not amenable to reasoning activities such as prediction and planning; these require that data be abstracted into a representation with a coarser grain. Probabilities are summaries of details lost in this abstraction, similar in role to the colors on our maps. The importance of maintaining such summaries in AI systems can be appreciated in the context of planning systems, where a major obstacle has been the impracticability of enumerating all preconditions that might trigger, inhibit, or enable a given event. (This problem is known as the *qualification* problem [McCarthy 1980], a refinement of the infamous *frame* problem [McCarthy and Hayes 1969; Brown 1987]). Probabilistic formalisms enable us to *summarize* the presumed existence of exceptional conditions without explicating the details of their interactions unless the need arises. Probability does not offer a complete solution to the frame problem because it does not provide rules for recomputing the summaries when unanticipated refinements are warranted. It does, however, provide a way to express summaries of unexplicated information, procedures for manipulating these summaries, and criteria for deciding when additional chunks of knowledge warrant explication.

To show what is still needed, let us examine how an ideal system might reason about the burglar alarm situation of Figure 1.2. Upon receiving the phone call from your neighbor, only the burglary hypothesis is triggered; your decision whether to drive home or stay at work is made solely on the basis of the parameter $P(False\ alarm)$, which summarizes all other (unexplicated) causes for an alarm sound. After a moment's reflection, the possibility of an April Fools' Day joke may enter your mind, in which case a two-stage inference chain is assembled, governed by two probabilistic parameters, $P(False\ alarm)$ and $P(Prank\ call)$. Later, when the possibility of an earthquake enters consideration, the parameter

P(*False alarm*) undergoes a partial explication; a fragment of knowledge is brought over from the remote frame of earthquake experiences and is appended to the link *Burglary* → *Alarm* as an alternative cause or explanation. The catchall hypothesis *All other causes* shrinks (to exclude earthquakes), and its parameters are readjusted. The radio announcement strengthens your suspicion in the earthquake hypothesis and permits you to properly readjust your decisions without elaborating the mechanics of the pressure transducer used in the alarm system. The remote possibility of having forgotten to push the reset button will be invoked only if it is absolutely needed for explaining some observed or derived phenomenon, e.g., finding your home burglarized and your alarm system silent.

Systems using probabilistic formalisms have so far drawn inferences from static knowledge bases, where the set of variables, their relationships, and all probabilistic parameters are provided by external agents, at predetermined levels of granularity. This is far from the reasoning pattern just portrayed by our burglary example, where relationships are explicated, refined, and quantified mechanically when the need arises. Clearly, what is lacking is the ability to transfer information back and forth between knowledge strata at different levels of abstraction, the ability to identify how information in one strata bears on information in another, and a means of properly adjusting the parameters of each item transferred.† Research toward the development of such facilities should bring together logic's aptitude for handling the visible and probability's ability to summarize the invisible.

1.5 QUALITATIVE REASONING WITH PROBABILITIES

In the preceding section we described some of the merits of using numerical representations in reasoning tasks. There are applications, however, where categorical abstractions may suffice and knowledge can be summarized by hard logical facts, merely distinguishing the possible from the impossible. For example, when the number of possibilities is small, instead of calculating which option is preferred we might settle for an indication of which option is still a candidate for exploration. In such cases we enter the province of logical analysis, and the problem becomes one of representing exceptions and reflecting nonmonotonic reasoning. The connection between probability theory and nonmonotonic logic will be expounded more fully in Chapter 10. Here we merely outline how probability theory, even stripped of all its numbers, can be useful as a paradigm facilitating purely qualitative reasoning.

---

†   Variable precision logic [Michalski and Winston 1986] is an attempt to formulate this dynamics.

1.5.1 *Softened Logic vs. Hardened Probabilities*

The ills of classical logic have often been attributed to its rigid, binary character. Indeed, when one tries to explain why logic would not predict the obvious fact that penguin are birds but do not fly, the first thing that one tends to blame is logic's rigid stance toward exceptions to the rule "Birds fly." It is therefore natural to assume that once we soften the constraints of Boolean logic and allow truth values to be measured on a grey scale, these problems will disappear. There have been several such attempts. Rich [1983] proposed a likelihood-based interpretation of default rules, managed by certainty-factors calculus. Ginsberg [1984] and Baldwin [1987] have pursued similar aspirations using the Dempster-Shafer notion of belief functions (see Chapter 9). While these attempts can produce valuable results (revealing, for instance, how sensitive a conclusion is to the uncertainty of its premises), the fundamental problem of monotonicity remains unresolved. For example, regardless of the certainty calculus used, these analyses always yield an increase in the belief that penguins can fly if one adds the superfluous information that penguins are birds and birds normally fly. Identical problems surface in the use of incidence calculus and softened versions of truth-maintenance systems [Falkenhainer 1986; D'Ambrosio 1987].

Evidently, it is not enough to add a soft probabilistic veneer to a system that is built on hard monotonic logic. The problem with monotonic logic lies not in the hardness of its truth values, but rather in its inability to process context-dependent information. Logic does not have a device equivalent to the conditional probability statement "$P(B|A)$ is high," whose main function is to define the context A under which the proposition B can be believed and to make sure that the only context changes permitted are those that do not change the belief in B (e.g., going from $A = Birds$ to $A' = Feathered\ birds$).

Lacking an appropriate logical device for conditionalization, the natural tendency is to interpret the English sentence "If A then B" as a softened version of the material implication constraint $A \supset B$. A useful consequence of such softening is the freedom from outright contradictions. For example, while the classical interpretation of the three rules "Penguins do not fly," "Penguins are birds," and "Birds fly" yields a blatant contradiction, attaching uncertainties to these rules renders them manageable. They are still managed in the wrong way, however, because the material-implication interpretation of if–then rules is so fundamentally wrong that its maladies cannot be rectified simply by allowing exceptions in the form of shaded truth values. The source of the problem lies in the property of transitivity, $(a \rightarrow b, b \rightarrow c) \Longrightarrow a \rightarrow c$, which is inherent to the material-implication interpretation. On some occasions rule transitivity must be totally suppressed, not merely weakened, or else strange results will surface. One such occasion occurs in property inheritance, where subclass specificity should override superclass properties. Another occurs in causal reasoning, where predictions should not trigger explanations (e.g., "Sprinkler was on" predicts "Ground is wet,"

"Ground is wet" suggests "It rained," yet "Sprinkler was on" should not suggest "It rained"). In such cases, softening the rules weakens the flow of inference through the rule chain but does not bring it to a dead halt, as it should.

Apparently what is needed is a new interpretation of if–then statements, one that does not destroy the context sensitivity of probabilistic conditionalization. McCarthy [1986] remarks that *circumscription*† indeed provides such an interpretation. In his words:

> Since circumscription doesn't provide numerical probabilities, its probabilistic interpretation involves probabilities that are either infinitesimal, within an infinitesimal of one, or intermediate—without any discrimination among the intermediate values. The circumscriptions give conditional probabilities. Thus we may treat the probability that a bird can't fly as an infinitesimal. However, if the rare event occurs that the bird is a penguin, then the conditional probability that it can fly is infinitesimal, but we may hear of some rare condition that would allow it to fly after all.

Rather than contriving new logics and hoping that they match the capabilities of probability theory, we can start with probability theory, and if we can't get the numbers or we find their use inconvenient, we can extract the infinitesimal approximation as an idealized abstraction of the theory, while preserving its context-dependent properties. In this way, a nonmonotonic logic should crystallize that is guaranteed to capture the context-dependent features of natural defaults.

1.5.2 Probabilities and the Logic of "Almost True"

This program was in fact initiated over twenty years ago by the philosopher Ernest Adams, who developed a logic of conditionals based on probabilistic semantics [Adams 1966]. The sentence "If A then B" is interpreted to mean that the conditional probability of B given A is very close to 1 but is short of actually being 1. An adaptation of Adams's logic to default schemata of the form $Bird(x) \rightarrow Fly(x)$, where x is a variable, is described in Section 10.2. The resulting logic is nonmonotonic relative to learning new facts, in accordance with McCarthy's desiderata. For example, learning that Tweety is a bird will yield the conclusion that Tweety can fly. Subsequently learning that Tweety is also a penguin will yield the opposite conclusion: Tweety can't fly. Further, learning that Tweety is black and white will not alter this belief, because black and white is a typical color combination for penguins. However, and this is where Adams's logic falls short of expectations, learning that Tweety is clever would force us to

---

† Circumscription is a system developed by McCarthy for nonmonotonic reasoning. With circumscription, the conclusions are sanctioned relative to the minimal models of the theory.

retract all previously held beliefs about Tweety's flying and answer, "I don't know." The logic is so conservative that it never jumps to conclusions that some new rule schemata might invalidate (just in case clever penguins *can* fly). In other words, the logic does not capture the usual convention that unless we are told otherwise, properties are presumed to be irrelevant to each other.

Attempts to enrich Adams's logic with relevance-based features are reported in Geffner and Pearl [1987b] and briefly described in Section 10.2.5. The idea is to follow a default strategy similar to that of belief networks (Section 3.1): Dependencies exist only if they are mentioned explicitly or if they follow logically from other explicit dependencies. However, whereas the stratified method of constructing belief networks ensures that all relevant dependencies were already encoded in the network, this can no longer be assumed in the case of partially specified models of isolated default rules. A new logic is needed to capture the conventions by which we proclaim properties to be irrelevant to each other.

There is another dimension along which probabilistic analysis can assist current research into nonmonotonic logics—the logics provide no criterion for testing whether a database comprising default rules is internally consistent. The prevailing attitude is that once we tolerate exceptions we might as well tolerate anything [Brachman 1985]. There is a sharp qualitative difference, however, between exceptions and outright contradictions. For example, the statement "Red penguins can fly" can be accepted as a description of a world in which redness defines an abnormal type of penguin, but the statements "Typically, birds fly" and "Typically, birds do not fly" stand in outright contradiction to each other, and because there is no world in which the two statements can hold simultaneously, they will inevitably lead to strange, inconsistent conclusions. While such obvious contradictions can easily be removed from the database [Touretzky 1986], more subtle ones might escape detection, e.g., "Birds fly," "Birds are feathered animals," "Feathered animals are birds," and "Feathered animals do not fly." Adams's logic provides a criterion for detecting such inconsistencies, in the form of three axioms that should never be violated. These axioms, and their implied graphical test for consistency, will be discussed in Sections 10.1 and 10.2.

1.6 BIBLIOGRAPHICAL AND HISTORICAL REMARKS

Broad surveys of uncertainty formalisms proposed for AI can be found in Prade [1983], Thompson [1985], Stephanou and Sage [1987], and the works collected in Kanal and Lemmer [1986] and Smets et al. [1988]. The February 1987 issue of *Statistical Science*, devoted to the calculus of uncertainty in artificial intelligence and expert systems, includes a lively debate between advocates of the Bayesian methods and advocates of the Dempster-Shafer approach. The February 1988 issue of *Computational Intelligence* offers a similar debate between advocates of the probabilistic and logicist schools in AI.

Systems—primarily expert systems—that provide practical solutions to various problems of reasoning with uncertainty include MYCIN [Shortliffe 1976], INTERNIST [Miller, Poole, and Myers 1982; Pople 1982], PROSPECTOR [Duda, Hart, and Nilsson 1976], MEDAS [Ben-Bassat et al. 1980], INFERNO [Quinlan 1983], RUM [Bonissone, Gans, and Decker 1987], MUM [Cohen et al. 1987], MDX [Chandrasekaran and Mittal 1983], and MUNIN [Andreassen et al. 1987]. Of these, only MEDAS and MUNIN would be classified as intensional systems; the rest are extensional (i.e., rule-based) systems. An in-depth study of rule-based systems, including the uncertainty management technique used in MYCIN, can be found in Buchanan and Shortliffe [1984] and the survey articles by Davis, Buchanan, and Shortliffe [1977] and Buchanan and Duda [1983]. Critical discussions of the use of probabilistic reasoning in medical decisions are given in Szolovits and Pauker [1978] and Pauker and Kassirer [1987].

Cox's [1946] argument for the use of probability theory has also been expounded by Reichenbach [1949] and restated in Horvitz, Heckerman, and Langlotz [1986] and Cheeseman [1988] for an AI audience. Heckerman [1986b] has generalized Cox's argument to measures of confirmation, i.e., the impact evidence has on the belief in a hypothesis. A stronger argument, based entirely on qualitative axioms, has been developed by Aleliunas [1988], who included the hypothetical-middle pattern (Section 1.4.2) as one of his axioms.

Arguments based on pragmatic considerations go back to Ramsey [1931] and de Finetti [1937]. These are often called "Dutch book" arguments, because they show that a gambler deviating from the rules of probability calculus will, in the long run, lose against an opponent who adheres to those rules. Lindley [1982] introduced a pragmatic argument based on the notion of a scoring rule, i.e., a payoff function that depends both on one's degree of belief in an event and on whether the event actually occurred (see Exercise 6.9). He showed that under rather general conditions, an agent can maximize his expected payoffs only by adopting the axioms of probability theory. Rebuttals to this argument are given in the discussion following Lindley's article.

Our treatment of MYCIN's certainty calculus (Figure 1.1) follows that of Heckerman [1986a]. A coherent treatment of bidirectional inferences in trees was given in Pearl [1982] and will be described in Section 4.2. The distinction between rebutting and undercutting defeaters (Section 1.2.2) was first made in Pollock [1974], and the example of an object observed in red light is his. A probabilistic model for such defeaters was proposed by Kim and Pearl [1983] and implemented in CONVINCE [Kim 1983; Kim and Pearl 1987] (see Section 4.3). A logic-based model was proposed in Pearl [1988b] and will be described in Section 10.3.

Bibliographical references for graphoids and nonmonotonic logic are in Chapters 3 and 10, respectively.

References to recent literature on various approaches to uncertainty in AI can be found in the following volumes:

Kanal L.N.; and Rosenfeld A. (series eds.). 1986-1991. Uncertainty in Artificial Intelligence 1-6 [1] Elsevier Science Publishers B.V. (North-Holland).

Shafer, G., and Pearl, J. (Eds.). 1990. *Readings in Uncertain Reasoning*, Morgan Kaufmann, Palo Alto, CA.

Neapolitan , R.E. 1990. *Probabilistic Reasoning in Expert Systems: Theory and Algorithms*, Wiley, New York.

Shachter, R., (ed.), Special Issue on Influence Diagrams, *Networks: an International Journal*, Vol. 20, No. 5, August 1990.

Oliver, R.M., and Smith, J.Q. (Eds.). 1990. *Influence Diagrams, Belief Nets and Decision Analysis*, Sussex, England: John Wiley & Sons, Ltd.

The following articles describe general uncertainty-management systems:

Andersen, S. K., et al. 1989. "HUGIN — A Shell for Building Bayesian Belief Universes for Expert Systems," *Proceedings, IJCAI-89*, 1080-1085.

Poole, D. "Representing Diagnostic Knowledge for Probabilistic Horn Abduction," *Proceedings IJCAI-91*, Sydney, Australia, August, 1991, 1129-1137.

Srinivas, S. and Breese, J., 1989. *IDEAL: Influence Diagram Evaluation and Analysis in Lispu*, Rockwell International Science Center, Palo Alto, CA.

Systems designed for specific applications include:

Heckerman, D.E., Horvitz, E.J., and Nathwany, B.N. 1990. "Toward normative expert systems: The Pathfinder project." Technical Report KSL-90-08, Medical Computer Science Group, Section on Medical Informatics, Stanford University, Stanford, CA. (diagnosis of pathological findings)

Peng, Y., and Reggia, J.A. 1990. *Abductive Inference Models for Diagnostic Problem-Solving*, Springer-Verlag, New York. (medical diagnosis)

Levitt, T.S., Agosta, J.M., and Binford, T.O. 1990. "Model-Based Influence Diagrams for Machine Vision," *UAI* 5, 371-388.

Charniak, E., and Goldman, R. 1991. "A Probabilistic Model of Plan Recognition, " *Proceedings, AAAI-91*, Anaheim, CA, 160-165. (story understanding)

Agogino, A.M., Srinivas, S. and Schneider, K. 1988. "Multiple sensor expert system for diagnostic reasoning, monitoring and control of mechanical systems, *Mechanical Systems and Signal Processing*, 2(2), 165-85.

Abramson, B. 1991. "ARCO1: An application of belief networks to the oil market," *Proceedings of the 1991 Conference on Uncertainty in AI*, Los Angeles, CA., Morgan Kaufmann, 1-8. (economic forcasting)

---

[1]   In subsequent references, these volumes will be denoted *UAI*-1 through *UAI*-6.

Chapter *2*

BAYESIAN INFERENCE

---

*The purpose I mean is, to show what reason
we have for believing that there are in the
constitution of things fixed laws according to
which events happen...*
— *Richard Price, 1763*

(Introduction to Bayes' essay)

2.1 BASIC CONCEPTS

2.1.1 Probabilistic Formulation and Bayesian Inversion

Bayesian methods provide a formalism for reasoning about partial beliefs under
conditions of uncertainty. In this formalism, propositions are given numerical
parameters signifying the degree of belief accorded them under some body of
knowledge, and the parameters are combined and manipulated according to the
rules of probability theory. For example, if A stands for the statement "Ted
Kennedy will seek the nomination for president in 1992," then $P(A \mid K)$ stands for a
person's subjective belief in A given a body of knowledge K, which might include
that person's assumptions about American politics, specific proclamations made by
Kennedy, and an assessment of Kennedy's past and personality. In defining belief

expressions, we often simply write $P(A)$ or $P(\neg A)$, leaving out the symbol K. This abbreviation is justified when K remains constant, since the main purpose of the quantifier P is to *summarize* K without explicating it. However, when the background information undergoes changes, we need to identify specifically the assumptions that account for our beliefs and articulate explicitly K or some of its elements.

In the Bayesian formalism, belief measures obey the three basic axioms of probability theory:

$$0 \leq P(A) \leq 1 \tag{2.1}$$

$$P(Sure\ proposition) = 1 \tag{2.2}$$

$$P(A\ or\ B) = P(A) + P(B) \ \ \text{if } A \text{ and } B \text{ are mutually exclusive.} \tag{2.3}$$

The third axiom states that the belief assigned to any set of events is the sum of the beliefs assigned to its nonintersecting components. Hence, since any event A can be written as the union of the joint events (A and B) and (A and $\neg B$), their associated probabilities are given by

$$P(A) = P(A, B) + P(A, \neg B), \tag{2.4}$$

where $P(A, B)$ is short for $P(A\ and\ B)$. More generally, if B_i, $i = 1, 2,...,n$, is a set of exhaustive and mutually exclusive propositions (called a *partition* or a *variable*), then $P(A)$ can be computed from $P(A, B_i)$, $i = 1, 2,...,n$, using the sum

$$P(A) = \sum_i P(A, B_i). \tag{2.5}$$

For example, the probability of A = "The outcomes of two dice are equal" can be computed by summing over the joint events (A and B_i) $i = 1, 2,...,6$, where B_i stands for the proposition "The outcome of the first die is i," yielding

$$P(A) = \sum_i P(A, B_i) = 6 \times \frac{1}{36} = \frac{1}{6}. \tag{2.6}$$

A direct consequence of Eqs. (2.2) and (2.4) is that a proposition and its negation must be assigned a total belief of unity,

$$P(A) + P(\neg A) = 1, \tag{2.7}$$

because one of the two statements is certain to be true.

The basic expressions in the Bayesian formalism are statements about *conditional probabilities*—e.g., $P(A\,|\,B)$—which specify the belief in A under the assumption that B is known with absolute certainty. If $P(A\,|\,B) = P(A)$, we say that A and B are *independent*. If $P(A \mid B,C) = P(A \mid C)$, we say that A and B are *conditionally independent* given C.

Contrary to the traditional practice of defining conditional probabilities in terms of joint events,

$$P(A \mid B) = \frac{P(A, B)}{P(B)}, \qquad (2.8)$$

Bayesian philosophers see the conditional relationship as more basic than that of joint events, i.e., more compatible with the organization of human knowledge. In this view, B serves as a pointer to a context or frame of knowledge, and $A \mid B$ stands for an event A in the context specified by B (e.g., a symptom A in the context of a disease B). Consequently, empirical knowledge invariably will be encoded in conditional probability statements, while belief in joint events, if it is ever needed, will be computed from those statements via the product

$$P(A, B) = P(A \mid B) P(B), \qquad (2.9)$$

which is equivalent to Eq. (2.8). For example, it was somewhat unnatural to assess

$$P(A, B_i) = \frac{1}{36}$$

directly in Eq. (2.6). The mental process underlying such assessment presumes that the two outcomes are independent, so to make this assumption explicit the probability of the joint event (*Equality*, B_i) should be assessed from the conditional event (*Equality* $\mid B_i$) via the product

$$P(Equality \mid B_i)P(B_i) = P(Outcome\ of\ second\ die\ is\ i \mid B_i)P(B_i) = \frac{1}{6} \times \frac{1}{6} = \frac{1}{36}.$$

As in Eq. (2.5), the probability of any event A can be computed by conditioning it on any set of exhaustive and mutually exclusive events B_i, $i = 1, 2, ...,n$:

$$P(A) = \sum_i P(A \mid B_i) P(B_i). \qquad (2.10)$$

This decomposition provides the basis for hypothetical or "assumption-based" reasoning in the Bayesian formalism. It states that the belief in any event A is a weighted sum over the beliefs in all the distinct ways that A might be realized. For example, if we wish to calculate the probability that the outcome X of the first die will be greater than the outcome Y of the second, we can condition the event $A: X > Y$ on all possible values of X and obtain

$$P(A) = \sum_{i=1}^{6} P(Y < X \mid X = i) P(X = i)$$

$$= \sum_{i=1}^{6} P(Y < i) \frac{1}{6} = \sum_{i=1}^{6} \sum_{j=1}^{i-1} P(Y = j) \frac{1}{6}$$

$$= \frac{1}{6} \sum_{i=2}^{6} \frac{i-1}{6} = \frac{5}{12}.$$

It is worth reemphasizing that formulas like Eq. (2.10) are always understood to apply in some larger context K, which defines the assumptions taken as common knowledge (e.g., the fairness of dice rolling). Eq. (2.10) is really a shorthand notation for the statement

$$P(A \mid K) = \sum_{i} P(A \mid B_i, K) P(B_i \mid K). \tag{2.11}$$

Another useful generalization of the product rule (Eq. (2.9)) is the so-called *chain rule* formula. It states that if we have a set of n events, $E_1, E_2, ..., E_n$, then the probability of the joint event $(E_1, E_2, ... , E_n)$ can be written as a product of n conditional probabilities:

$$P(E_1, E_2, ..., E_n) = P(E_n \mid E_{n-1}, ..., E_2, E_1) ... P(E_2 \mid E_1) P(E_1). \tag{2.12}$$

This product can be derived by repeated application of Eq. (2.9), in any convenient order.

The heart of Bayesian techniques lies in the celebrated inversion formula,

$$P(H \mid e) = \frac{P(e \mid H) P(H)}{P(e)}, \tag{2.13}$$

which states that the belief we accord a hypothesis H upon obtaining evidence e can be computed by multiplying our previous belief $P(H)$ by the likelihood $P(e \mid H)$ that e will materialize if H is true. $P(H \mid e)$ is sometimes called the posterior probability (or simply *posterior*), and $P(H)$ is called the prior probability (or *prior*). The denominator $P(e)$ of Eq. (2.13) hardly enters into consideration because it is merely a normalizing constant $P(e) = P(e \mid H) P(H) + P(e \mid \neg H) P(\neg H)$, which can be computed by requiring that $P(H \mid e)$ and $P(\neg H \mid e)$ sum to unity.

Whereas a formal mathematician might dismiss Eq. (2.13) as a tautology stemming from the definition of conditional probabilities,

$$P(A \mid B) = \frac{P(A, B)}{P(B)} \quad \text{and} \quad P(B \mid A) = \frac{P(A, B)}{P(A)}, \qquad (2.14)$$

the Bayesian subjectivist regards Eq. (2.13) as a normative rule for updating beliefs in response to evidence. In other words, while the mathematician views conditional probabilities as mathematical constructs, as in Eq. (2.14), the Bayes adherent views them as primitives of the language and as faithful translations of the English expression "..., given that I know A." Accordingly, Eq. (2.14) is not a definition but an empirically verifiable relationship between English expressions. It asserts, among other things, that the belief a person attributes to B after discovering A is never lower than that attributed to $A \wedge B$ before discovering A. Also, the ratio between these two beliefs will increase proportionally with the degree of surprise $[P(A)]^{-1}$ one associates with the discovery of A.

The importance of Eq. (2.13) is that it expresses a quantity $P(H \mid e)$—which people often find hard to assess—in terms of quantities that often can be drawn directly from our experiential knowledge. For example, if a person at the next gambling table declares the outcome "Twelve," and we wish to know whether he was rolling a pair of dice or spinning a roulette wheel, our models of the gambling devices readily yield the quantities $P(Twelve \mid Dice)$ and $P(Twelve \mid Roulette)$— 1/36 for the former and 1/38 for the latter. Similarly, we can judge the prior probabilities $P(Dice)$ and $P(Roulette)$ by estimating the number of roulette wheels and dice tables at the casino. Issuing a direct judgment of $P(Dice \mid Twelve)$ would have been much more difficult; only a specialist in such judgments, trained at the very same casino, could do it reliably.

To complete this brief introduction, we need to discuss the notion of *probabilistic models*. A probabilistic model is an encoding of probabilistic information that permits us to compute the probability of every well-formed sentence S in accordance with the axioms of Eqs. (2.1) through (2.3). Starting with a set of atomic propositions A, B, C,..., the set of well-formed sentences consists of all Boolean formulas involving these propositions, e.g., $S = (A \vee B) \wedge \neg C$. The traditional method of specifying probabilistic models employs a joint distribution function, namely, a function that assigns nonnegative weights to every *elementary event* (an elementary event being a conjunction in which every atomic proposition or its negation appears once), such that the sum of the weights adds up to 1. For example, if we have three atomic propositions, A, B, and C, a joint distribution function should assign nonnegative weights to all eight combinations: $(A \wedge B \wedge C)$, $(A \wedge B \wedge \neg C)$, ..., $(\neg A \wedge \neg B \wedge \neg C)$, such that the eight weights sum to 1.

It is sometimes convenient to view the conjunctive formulas corresponding to elementary events as points, and to regard other formulas as sets made up of these points. Since every Boolean formula can be expressed as a disjunction of elementary events, and since the elementary events are mutually exclusive, we can always compute $P(S)$ using the additive axiom (Eq. (2.3)). Conditional probabilities can be computed the same way, using Eq. (2.14). Thus, any joint probability function represents a complete probabilistic model.

Joint distribution functions are mathematical constructs of primarily theoretical use. They allow us to determine quickly whether we have sufficient information to specify a complete probabilistic model, whether the information we have is consistent, and at what point additional information is needed. The criterion is simply to check whether the information available is sufficient for uniquely determining the probability of every elementary event in the domain, and whether the probabilities add up to 1.

In practice, however, joint distribution functions are rarely specified explicitly. In the analysis of continuous random variables, the distribution functions are given by algebraic expressions such as those describing normal or exponential distributions, while for discrete variables, indirect representation methods have been developed, where the overall distribution is inferred from local relationships among small groups of variables. Network approaches, the most promising of these representations, provide the basis of discussion throughout this book. Their use will be illustrated in the following few sections, then given a more formal treatment in Chapter 3.

2.1.2 *Combining Predictive and Diagnostic Supports*

The essence of Bayes' Rule (Eq. (2.13)) is conveniently portrayed using the *odds* and *likelihood ratio* parameters. Dividing Eq. (2.13) by the complementary form for $P(\neg H \mid e)$, we obtain

$$\frac{P(H \mid e)}{P(\neg H \mid e)} = \frac{P(e \mid H)}{P(e \mid \neg H)} \frac{P(H)}{P(\neg H)} . \qquad (2.15)$$

Defining the *prior odds* on H as

$$O(H) = \frac{P(H)}{P(\neg H)} = \frac{P(H)}{1 - P(H)} \qquad (2.16)$$

and the *likelihood ratio* as

$$L(e \mid H) = \frac{P(e \mid H)}{P(e \mid \neg H)}, \qquad (2.17)$$

the *posterior odds*

$$O(H \mid e) = \frac{P(H \mid e)}{P(\neg H \mid e)} \qquad (2.18)$$

are given by the product

$$O(H \mid e) = L(e \mid H) \, O(H). \qquad (2.19)$$

Thus, Bayes' Rule dictates that the overall strength of belief in a hypothesis H, based on both our previous knowledge K and the observed evidence e, should be the product of two factors: the prior odds $O(H)$ and the likelihood ratio $L(e \mid H)$. The first factor measures the *predictive* or *prospective* support accorded to H by the background knowledge alone, while the second represents the *diagnostic* or *retrospective* support given to H by the evidence actually observed.

Strictly speaking, the likelihood ratio $L(e \mid H)$ might depend on the content of the tacit knowledge base K. However, the power of Bayesian techniques comes primarily from the fact that in causal reasoning the relationship $P(e \mid H)$ is fairly local, namely, given that H is true, the probability of e can be estimated naturally and is not dependent on many other propositions in the knowledge base. For example, once we establish that a patient suffers from a given disease H, it is natural to estimate the probability that he will develop a certain symptom e. The organization of medical knowledge rests on the paradigm that a symptom is a stable characteristic of the disease and should therefore be fairly independent of other factors, such as epidemic conditions, previous diseases, and faulty diagnostic equipment. For this reason the conditional probabilities $P(e \mid H)$, as opposed to $P(H \mid e)$, are the atomic relationships in Bayesian analysis. The former possess modularity features similar to logical production rules. They convey a degree of confidence in rules such as "If H then e," a confidence that persists regardless of what other rules or facts reside in the knowledge base.

EXAMPLE 1: Imagine being awakened one night by the shrill sound of your burglar alarm. What is your degree of belief that a burglary attempt has taken place? For illustrative purposes we make the following judgments: (a) There is a 95% chance that an attempted burglary will trigger the alarm system—$P(Alarm \mid Burglary) = 0.95$; (b) based on previous false alarms, there is a slight (1 percent) chance that the alarm will be triggered by a mechanism other than an attempted burglary—$P(Alarm \mid No\ burglary) = 0.01$; (c) previous crime patterns indicate that there is a one in ten thousand chance that a given house will be burglarized on a given night—$P(Burglary) = 10^{-4}$.

Putting these assumptions together using Eq. (2.19), we obtain

$$O(Burglary \mid Alarm) = L(Alarm \mid Burglary) \, O(Burglary)$$

$$= \frac{0.95}{0.01} \frac{10^{-4}}{1-10^{-4}} = 0.0095.$$

So, from

$$P(A) = \frac{O(A)}{1 + O(A)},\tag{2.20}$$

we have

$$P(Burglary \mid Alarm) = \frac{0.0095}{1+0.0095} = 0.00941.$$

Thus, the retrospective support imparted to the burglary hypothesis by the alarm evidence has increased its degree of belief almost a hundredfold, from one in ten thousand to 94.1 in ten thousand. The fact that the belief in burglary is still below 1% should not be surprising, given that the system produces a false alarm almost once every three months. Notice that it was not necessary to estimate the absolute values of the probabilities $P(Alarm \mid Burglary)$ and $P(Alarm \mid No\ burglary)$. Only their ratio enters the calculation, so a direct estimate of this ratio could have been used instead.

2.1.3 Pooling of Evidence

Assume that the alarm system consists of a collection of N burglary detection devices, each one sensitive to a different physical mechanism (air turbulence, temperature variation, pressure, radar waves, etc.) and each one producing a distinct sound.

Let H stand for the event that a burglary took place and let e^k stand for the evidence obtained from the k-th detector, with e_1^k representing an activated detector and e_0^k representing a silent detector. The reliability (and sensitivity) of each detector is characterized by the probabilities $P(e_1^k \mid H)$ and $P(e_1^k \mid \neg H)$, or more succinctly by their ratio:

$$L(e_1^k \mid H) = \frac{P(e_1^k \mid H)}{P(e_1^k \mid \neg H)}.\tag{2.21}$$

If some detectors are triggered while others remain silent, we have conflicting evidence on our hands, and the combined belief in the hypothesis H is computed by Eq. (2.19):

$$O(H \mid e^1, e^2, ..., e^N) = L(e^1, e^2, ..., e^N \mid H)\ O(H).\tag{2.22}$$

Eq. (2.22) could require an enormous data base, because we need to specify the probabilities of activation for every subset of detectors, conditioned on H and on $\neg H$. Fortunately, reasonable assumptions of conditional independence can reduce this storage requirement drastically. Assuming that the state of each detector depends only on whether a burglary took place and is thereafter independent of the state of other detectors, we can write

$$P(e^1, e^2, ..., e^N \mid H) = \prod_{k=1}^{N} P(e^k \mid H) \qquad (2.23)$$

and

$$P(e^1, e^2, ..., e^N \mid \neg H) = \prod_{k=1}^{N} P(e^k \mid \neg H), \qquad (2.24)$$

which lead to

$$O(H \mid e^1, e^2, ..., e^N) = O(H) \prod_{k=1}^{N} L(e^k \mid H). \qquad (2.25)$$

Thus, the individual characteristics of each detector are sufficient for determining the combined impact of any group of detectors.

2.1.4 Recursive Bayesian Updating

One of the attractive features of Bayes' updating rule is its amenability to recursive and incremental computation schemes. Let H denote a hypothesis, $e_n = e^1, e^2, ..., e^n$ denote a sequence of data observed in the past, and e denote a new fact. A brute-force way to calculate the belief in H, $P(H \mid e_n, e)$ would be to append the new datum e to the past data e_n and perform a global computation of the impact on H of the entire data set $e_{n+1} = \{e_n, e\}$. Such a computation would be uneconomical for several reasons. First, the entire stream of past data must be available at all times. Also, as time goes on and the set e_n increases, the computation of $P(H \mid e_n, e)$ becomes more and more complex. Under certain conditions, this computation can be significantly curtailed by incremental updating; once we have computed $P(H \mid e_n)$, we can discard the past data and compute the impact of the new datum by the formula

$$P(H \mid e_n, e) = P(H \mid e_n) \frac{P(e \mid e_n, H)}{P(e \mid e_n)}. \qquad (2.26)$$

Thus, comparing Eq. (2.26) and Eq. (2.13), we see that the old belief $P(H \mid e_n)$ assumes the role of the prior probability in the computation of new impact; it completely summarizes the past experience and for updating need only be multiplied by the likelihood function $P(e \mid e_n, H)$, which measures the probability of the new datum e, given the hypothesis and the past observations.

This recursive formulation still would be cumbersome but for the fact that the likelihood function is often independent of the past data and involves only e and H. For example, the likelihood that a patient will develop a certain symptom, given that he definitely suffers from a disease H, is normally independent of what symptoms the patient had in the past. This conditional independence condition, which gave rise to the product expression in Eqs. (2.23) through (2.25), allows us to write

$$P(e \mid e_n, H) = P(e \mid H) \quad \text{and} \quad P(e \mid e_n, \neg H) = P(e \mid \neg H), \qquad (2.27)$$

and after dividing Eq. (2.26) by the complementary equation for $\neg H$, we obtain

$$O(H \mid e_{n+1}) = O(H \mid e_n)\, L(e \mid H), \qquad (2.28)$$

which also is obtainable from the product form of Eq. (2.25).

Eq. (2.28) describes a simple recursive procedure for updating the posterior odds—upon the arrival of each new datum e, we multiply the current posterior odds $O(H \mid e_n)$ by the likelihood ratio of e. This procedure sheds new light on the relationship between the prior odds $O(H)$ and the posterior odds $O(H \mid e_n)$; the latter can be viewed as the prior odds relative to the next observation, while the former are nothing but posterior odds that have evolved from previous observations not included in e_n.

If we take the logarithm of Eq. (2.28), the incremental nature of the updating process becomes more apparent. Writing

$$\log O(H \mid e_n, e) = \log O(H \mid e_n) + \log L(e \mid H), \qquad (2.29)$$

we can view the log of the likelihood ratio as a weight, carried by the evidence e, which additively sways the belief in H one way or the other. Evidence supporting the hypothesis carries positive weight, and evidence that opposes it carries negative weight.

The simplicity and appeal of the log-likelihood calculation has led to a wide variety of applications, especially in intelligence-gathering tasks. For each new report, an intelligence analyst can estimate the likelihood ratio L. Using a log-log paper, the contribution of the report can easily be incorporated into the already accumulated overall belief in H. This method also facilitates retracting or revising beliefs in case a datum is found to be in error. If the erroneous datum is e, and the correct one is e', then to rectify the error one need only compute the difference

$$\Delta = \log L(e' \mid H) - \log L(e \mid H)$$

and add Δ to the accumulated log-odds of Eq. (2.29).

The ability to update beliefs recursively depends heavily on the conditional independence relation formulated in Eqs. (2.23) and (2.24) and will exist only when knowledge of H (or $\neg H$) renders past observations totally irrelevant with regard to future observations. It will not be applicable, for example, if the hypothesis H influences the observations only indirectly, via several causal links. For instance, suppose that in our burglar alarm example we cannot hear the alarm sound directly but must rely on the testimony of other people. Because the burglary hypothesis has an indirect influence on the witnesses, the testimony of one witness (regarding the alarm) affects our expectation of the next witness's testimony even when we are absolutely sure that a burglary has occurred. The two testimonies will, however, become independent once we know the actual state of the alarm system. For that reason, decision analysts (e.g., Kelly and Barclay [1973], Schum and Martin [1982]) have gone to great lengths to retain incremental updating in the context of "cascaded" inferencing. The issue will be discussed further in Section 2.2 and will be given full treatment, using network propagation techniques, in Chapter 4.

2.1.5 Multi-Valued Hypotheses

The assumption of conditional independence in Eqs. (2.23) and (2.24) is justified if both the failure of a detector to react to an attempted burglary and the factors that can cause it to be activated prematurely depend solely on mechanisms intrinsic to the individual detection systems, such as low sensitivity and internal noise. But if false alarms can be caused by external circumstances affecting a select group of sensors, such as a power failure or an earthquake, then the two hypotheses $H = $ *Burglary* and $\neg H = $ *No burglary* may be too broad to allow sensor independence, and additional refinement of the hypothesis space may be necessary. This condition usually occurs when a proposition or its negation encompasses several possible states, each associated with a distinct set of evidence. For example, the hypothesis *Burglary* encompasses either *Break-in through the door* or *Break-in through a window,* and since each mode of entry has a distinct effect on the sensors, the modes ought to be spelled out separately. Similarly, the state *No burglary* allows the possibilities *Ordinary peaceful night, Night with earthquake,* and *Attempted entry by the neighbor's dog,* each influencing the sensors in a unique way. Eq. (2.24) might hold for each of these conditions, but not for their aggregate, *No burglary.* For this reason, it is often necessary to refine the hypothesis space beyond binary propositions and group the hypothesis into multi-valued *variables,* where each variable reflects a set of exhaustive and mutually exclusive hypotheses.

EXAMPLE 2: We assign the variable $H = \{H_1, H_2, H_3, H_4\}$ to the following set of conditions:

$H_1 = $ *No burglary, animal entry.*
$H_2 = $ *Attempted burglary, window break-in.*
$H_3 = $ *Attempted burglary, door break-in.*
$H_4 = $ *No burglary, no entry.*

Each evidence variable E^k can also be multi-valued (e.g., $e_1^k = $ *No sound* , $e_2^k = $ *Low sound*, $e_3^k = $ *High sound*), in which case the causal link between H and E^k is quantified by an $m \times n$ matrix M^k, where m and n are the number of values that H and E^k, respectively, might take, and the (i, j)-th entry of M^k stands for

$$M_{ij}^k = P(e_j^k | H_i). \tag{2.30}$$

For example, the matrix below could represent the sensitivity of the k-th detector to the four conditions in H:

	e_1^k (no sound)	e_2^k (low sound)	e_3^k (high sound)
H_1	0.5	0.4	0.1
H_2	0.06	0.5	0.44
H_3	0.5	0.1	0.4
H_4	1	0	0 .

Given a set of evidence readings $e^1, e^2, ..., e^k, ..., e^N$, the overall belief in the i-th hypothesis H_i is (by Eq. (2.13))

$$P(H_i | e^1, ..., e^N) = \alpha P(e^1, ..., e^N | H_i) P(H_i), \tag{2.31}$$

where $\alpha = [P(e^1, ..., e^N)]^{-1}$ is a normalizing constant to be computed by requiring that Eq. (2.31) sum to unity (over i). Assuming conditional independence with respect to each H_i, we obtain

$$P(H_i | e^1, ..., e^N) = \alpha P(H_i)[\prod_{k=1}^{N} P(e^k | H_i)]. \tag{2.32}$$

Thus, the matrices $P(e^k | H_i)$ now play the role of the likelihood ratios in Eq. (2.25). If for each detector reading e^k we define the *likelihood vector*

$$\lambda^k = (\lambda_1^k, \lambda_2^k, ..., \lambda_m^k), \tag{2.33}$$

$$\lambda_i^k = P(e^k | H_i), \tag{2.34}$$

then Eq. (2.32) is computed by a simple vector-product process. First the individual likelihood vectors are multiplied together, term by term, to form an overall likelihood vector $\Lambda = \lambda^1, ..., \lambda^N$, namely,

$$\Lambda_i = \prod_{k=1}^{N} P(e^k | H_i). \tag{2.35}$$

Then we obtain the overall belief vector $P(H_i | e^1, ..., e^N)$ by the product

$$P(H_i | e^1, ..., e^N) = \alpha P(H_i)\Lambda_i, \tag{2.36}$$

which is reminiscent of Eq. (2.25).

Note that only the relative magnitudes of the conditional probabilities in Eq. (2.34) need be estimated; their absolute magnitudes do not affect the final result because α can be determined later, via the requirement $\sum_i P(H_i | e^1, ..., e^N) = 1$.

EXAMPLE 3: Let us assume that our alarm system contains two detectors having identical characteristics, given by the matrix of Example 2. Furthermore, let us represent the prior probabilities for the hypotheses in Example 2 with the vector $P(H_i) = (0.099, 0.009, 0.001, 0.891)$ and assume that detector 1 was heard to issue a high sound while detector 2 remained silent. From Eq. (2.34) we have

$$\lambda^1 = (0.1, 0.44, 0.4, 0), \quad \lambda^2 = (0.5, 0.06, 0.5, 1),$$

$$\Lambda = \lambda^1 \lambda^2 = (0.05, 0.0264, 0.2, 0),$$

$$P(H_i | e^1, e^2) = \alpha (4.95, 0.238, 0.20, 0)10^{-3} = (0.919, 0.0439, 0.0375, 0),$$

from which we conclude that the chance of an attempted burglary (H_2 or H_3) is $0.0439 + 0.0375 = 8.14\%$.

Of course, the updating of belief need not be delayed until all the evidence is collected but can be carried out incrementally. For example, if we first observe $e^1 = High\ sound$, our belief in H calculates to

$$P(H_i | e^1) = \alpha (0.0099, 0.00396, 0.0004, 0) = (0.694, 0.277, 0.028, 0).$$

This probability now serves as a prior belief with respect to the next datum, and after we observe $e^2 = No\ sound$, it updates to

$$P(H_i | e^1, e^2) = \alpha' \lambda_i^2 \cdot P(H_i | e^1) = \alpha'(0.347, 0.0166, 0.014, 0)$$

$$= (0.919, 0.0439, 0.0375, 0),$$

as before. Thus, the quiescent state of detector 2 lowers the probability of an attempted burglary from 30.5% to 8.14%.

2.2 HIERARCHICAL MODELING

2.2.1 Uncertain Evidence (Cascaded Inference)

One often hears the claim that Bayesian techniques cannot handle uncertain evidence because the basic building block in these techniques is the relationship $P(A \mid B)$, which requires that the conditioning event B be known with certainty. To see the difficulties that led to this myth, let us modify slightly the alarm scenario.

EXAMPLE 4: Mr. Holmes receives a telephone call from his neighbor Dr. Watson, who states that he hears the sound of a burglar alarm from the direction of Mr. Holmes's house. While preparing to rush home, Mr. Holmes recalls that Dr. Watson is known to be a tasteless practical joker, and he decides to first call another neighbor, Mrs. Gibbon, who, despite occasional drinking problems, is far more reliable.

Since the evidence variable $S = Sound$ is now uncertain, we cannot use it as evidence in Eq. (2.19) but instead must apply Eq. (2.19) to the actual evidence at hand, $W = Dr.\ Watson's\ testimony$, and write

$$O(H \mid W) = L(W \mid H)O(H). \qquad (2.37)$$

Unfortunately, the task of estimating $L(W \mid H)$ will be more difficult than estimating $L(S \mid H)$, because it requires mentally tracing a two-step process, as shown in Figure 2.1. Even if we obtain $L(W \mid H)$, we will not be able to combine it with other possible testimonies, say Mrs. Gibbon's (G), through a simple process of multiplication as in Eq. (2.35), because those testimonies will no longer be conditionally independent with respect to H. What Mrs. Gibbon is about to say depends only on whether an alarm sound can be heard in the neighborhood, not on whether a burglary actually took place. Thus, we cannot assume $P(G \mid Burglary, W) = P(G \mid Burglary)$; the joint event of a burglary and Dr. Watson's testimony constitutes stronger evidence for the occurrence of the alarm sound than does the burglary alone.

Given the level of detail used in our story, it is more reasonable to assume that the testimony (W and G) and the hypothesis (H) are mutually independent once we know whether the alarm sound was actually triggered. In other words, each neighbor's testimony depends directly on the alarm sound (S) and is influenced only indirectly by the possible occurrence of a burglary (H) or by the other testimony (see Figure 2.1).

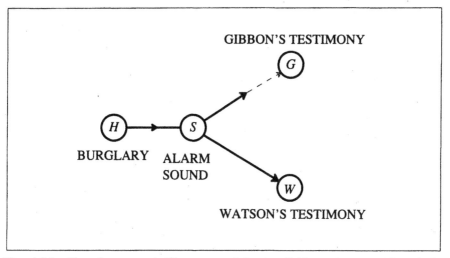

Figure 2.1. *The alarm sound (S), supported by unreliable testimonies (W and G), represents an uncertain evidence for a burglary (H).*

These considerations can easily be incorporated into the Bayesian formalism. Using Eq. (2.11), we simply condition and sum Eq. (2.31) over all possible states of the intermediate variable S and obtain

$$P(H_i \mid G, W) = \alpha P(G, W \mid H_i) P(H_i)$$
$$= \alpha P(H_i) \sum_j P(G, W \mid H_i, S_j) P(S_j \mid H_i), \qquad (2.38)$$

where S_j, $j=1$, 2 stands for the two possible states of the alarm system, namely, $S_1 = $ *Sound ON* and $S_2 = $ *Sound OFF*. Moreover, the conditional independence of G, W, and H_i with respect to the mediating variable S allows us to state

$$P(G, W \mid H_i, S_j) = P(G \mid S_j) P(W \mid S_j), \qquad (2.39)$$

and Eq. (2.38) becomes

$$P(H_i \mid G, W) = \alpha P(H_i) \sum_j P(G \mid S_j) P(W \mid S_j) P(S_j \mid H_i). \qquad (2.40)$$

The final computation can be interpreted as a three-stage process. First, the local likelihood vectors $P(G \mid S_j)$ and $P(W \mid S_j)$ are multiplied to obtain a combined likelihood vector

$$\Lambda_j(S) = P(e \mid S_j) = P(G \mid S_j) \, P(W \mid S_j), \qquad (2.41)$$

where e stands for the total evidence collected (G and W). Second, the vector $\Lambda_j(S)$ is multiplied by the link matrix $M_{ij} = P(S_j \mid H_i)$ to form the likelihood vector of the top hypothesis $\Lambda_i(H) = P(e \mid H_i)$. Finally, using the product rule of Eq. (2.24), we multiply $\Lambda_i(H)$ by the prior probability $P(H_i)$ to compute the overall belief in H_i.

This process demonstrates the psychological and computational roles of the mediating variable S. The conditional independence associated with S makes it a convenient anchoring point from which reasoning "by assumptions" can proceed effectively, because it decomposes the reasoning task into a set of independent subtasks. It permits us to use local chunks of information taken from diverse domains (e.g., $P(H_i)$, $P(G \mid S_j)$, $P(W \mid S_j)$, $P(S_j \mid H_i)$) and fit them together to form a global inference $P(H \mid e)$ in stages, using simple, local vector operations. It is this role which prompts us to posit that conditional independence is not a grace of nature for which we must wait passively, but rather a psychological necessity which we satisfy actively by organizing our knowledge in a specific way. An important tool in such organization is the identification of intermediate variables that induce conditional independence among observables; if such variables are not in our vocabulary, we create them. In medical diagnosis, for instance, when some symptoms directly influence each other, the medical profession invents a name for that interaction (e.g., "syndrome," "complication," "pathological state") and treats it as a new auxiliary variable that induces conditional independence; dependency between any two interacting symptoms is fully attributed to the dependencies of each on the auxiliary variable. It may be to reap the computational advantages associated with such independence that we organize most of our knowledge in causal hierarchies (see Chapter 8).

2.2.2 Virtual (Intangible) Evidence

Let us imagine a new development in the story of Mr. Holmes.

EXAMPLE 5: When Mr. Holmes calls Mrs. Gibbon, he soon realizes that she is somewhat tipsy. Instead of answering his question directly, she goes on and on about her latest back operation and about how terribly noisy and crime-ridden the neighborhood has become. When he finally hangs up, all Mr. Holmes can glean from the conversation is that there is probably an 80% chance that Mrs. Gibbon did hear an alarm sound from her window.

The Holmes-Gibbon conversation is the kind of evidence that is hard to fit into any formalism. If we try to estimate the probability $P(e \mid Alarm\ sound)$ we will get ridiculous numbers because it entails anticipating, describing, and assigning probabilities to all the possible paths Mrs. Gibbon's conversation might have taken under the circumstances. Alternatively, if we try to directly estimate $P(Alarm\ sound \mid e)$, we must be careful to clearly specify what other information was consulted in producing the estimate.

These difficulties arise whenever the task of gathering evidence is delegated to autonomous interpreters who, for various reasons, cannot explicate their interpretive process in full detail but nevertheless often produce informative conclusions that summarize the evidence observed. In our case, Mr. Holmes provides us with a direct mental judgment, based on Mrs. Gibbon's testimony, that the hypothesis *Alarm sound* should be accorded a confidence measure of 80%. The interpretation process remains hidden, however, and we cannot tell how much of the previously obtained evidence was considered in the process. Thus, it is impossible to integrate this probabilistic judgment with previously established beliefs unless we make additional assumptions.

The prevailing convention in the Bayesian formalism is to assume that probabilistic summaries of virtual evidence are produced independently of previous information; they are interpreted as local binary relations between the evidence and the hypothesis upon which it bears, independent of other information in the system. For this reason, we cannot interpret Mr. Holmes's summary as literally stating $P(S \mid G) = 0.80$. $P(S \mid G)$ should be sensitive to variations in crime rate information—$P(H)$—or equipment characteristics—$P(S \mid H)$. The impact of Gibbon's testimony should be impervious to such variations. Therefore, the measure $P(S \mid G)$ cannot represent the impact the phone conversation has on the truth of *Alarm sound*.

The likelihood ratio, on the other hand, meets this locality criterion, and for that reason probabilistic summaries of virtual evidence are interpreted as conveying likelihood information.† For example, Mr. Holmes's summary of attributing 80% credibility to the *Alarm sound* event can be interpreted as

$$P(G \mid Alarm\ sound) : P(G \mid No\ alarm\ sound) = 4{:}1. \qquad \textbf{(2.42)}$$

More generally, if the variable upon which the tacit evidence e impinges most directly has several possible states, $S_1, S_2, ..., S_i, ...$, we instruct the interpreter to estimate the relative magnitudes of the terms $P(e \mid S_i)$, perhaps by eliciting estimates of the ratios $P(e \mid S_i) : P(e \mid S_1)$. Since the absolute magnitudes do not

---

† It is interesting to note that an identical assumption has been tacitly incorporated into the calculus of certainty factors [Shortliffe 1976] if one interprets CF to stand for $(\lambda - 1) / (\lambda + 1)$ [Heckerman 1986b].

affect the calculations, we can update the beliefs as though this likelihood vector originated from an ordinary, logically definable event e.

For example, assuming that Mr. Watson's phone call already contributed a likelihood ratio of 9:1 in favor of the hypothesis *Alarm sound*, the combined weight of Watson's and Gibbon's testimonies would yield a likelihood vector $\Lambda_i(S) = P(W, G|S_i) = (36, 1)$. Now we can integrate this vector into the computation of Eq. (2.38). Using the numbers given in Example 1, we get

$$\Lambda_i(H) = \sum_j \Lambda_j(S)P(S_j|H_i) = \begin{pmatrix} 0.95 & 0.05 \\ 0.01 & 0.99 \end{pmatrix} \begin{pmatrix} 36 \\ 1 \end{pmatrix} = \begin{pmatrix} 34.25 \\ 1.35 \end{pmatrix},$$

$$P(H_i|G, W) = \alpha \, \Lambda_i(H) \, P(H_i) = \alpha \, (34.25, 1.35) \, (10^{-4}, 1 - 10^{-4})$$
$$= (0.00253, 0.99747). \tag{2.43}$$

It is important to verify that Mr. Holmes's 80% summarization is indeed based only on Mrs. Gibbon's testimony and not on prejudicial beliefs borrowed from the previous evidence (e.g., Watson's testimony or crime rate information); otherwise we are in danger of counting the same information twice. The likelihood ratio is in fact the only reasonable interpretation of Mr. Holmes's summarization that reflects a local binary relationship between the hypothesis and the evidence, unaffected by previous information [Heckerman 1986b].

An effective way of eliciting pure likelihood ratio estimates is to present the interpreter with a direct query: "How much more likely are we to obtain such an evidence under H, compared with the denial of H?" Alternatively, we can ask the interpreter to imagine that the evidence arrives in some standard state of belief, then request an estimate of how much the degree of belief in the hypothesis would be modified because of the evidence. In our example, if Mr. Holmes had a "neutral" belief in S before conversing with Mrs. Gibbon—$P(Alarm) = P(No\ alarm) = 1/2$—then the after-conversation estimate $P(Alarm|G) = 80\%$ would indeed correspond to a likelihood ratio of 4:1 in favor of *Alarm*. Bayesian practitioners claim that people are capable of retracing the origins of their beliefs and of entertaining hypothetical questions such as "What if you didn't receive Watson's call?" or "What is the increase in belief due to Gibbon's testimony alone?" This explains why interpretations of virtual evidence often are cast in terms of absolute probabilities, rather than probability changes or probability ratios. Evidently, the interpreter begins with some standard level of belief in the hypothesis (not necessary 50%), mentally assimilates the impact of the observed evidence, and then reports the updated posterior probability that emerges. However, it is not the final value but the ratio between the initial value and the final value that characterizes the impact of the evidence on the hypothesis, as this ratio is the only quantity that remains impervious to changes in the initial standard chosen. This issue will be discussed further in Section 2.3.3.

2.2.3 Predicting Future Events

One of the attractive features of causal models in the Bayesian formulation is the ease they lend to the prediction of future events such as the denouement of a social episode, the outcome of a given test, and the prognosis of a given disease. The need to facilitate such predictive tasks may in fact be the very reason that human beings have adopted causal schema for encoding experiential knowledge.

EXAMPLE 6: Immediately after his conversation with Mrs. Gibbon, as Mr. Holmes is preparing to leave his office, he recalls that his daughter is scheduled to arrive home at any minute. If greeted by an alarm sound, she probably ($P = 0.70$) would phone him for instructions. Now he wonders whether he should wait a few more minutes in case she calls.

To estimate the likelihood of our new target event, D = *Daughter will call*, we have to add a new causal link to the graph of Figure 2.1. Assuming that hearing an alarm sound is the only event that would induce Mr. Holmes's daughter to call, the new link, shown in Figure 2.2, should emanate from the variable S and be quantified by the following $P(D \mid S)$ matrix:

		D	
		will call	will not call
S	on	0.7	0.3
	off	0.0	1.0

Accordingly, to compute $P(D \mid All\ evidence)$ we write

$$P(D \mid e) = \sum_j P(D \mid S_j, e)\, P(S_j \mid e) = \sum_j P(D \mid S_j)\, P(S_j \mid e), \qquad (2.44)$$

which means that the lengthy episodes with Mr. Watson and Mrs. Gibbon impart their influence on D only via the belief $P(S_j \mid e)$ that they induce on S.

It is instructive to see how $P(S_j \mid e)$ can be obtained from the previous calculation of $P(H_i \mid e)$. A natural temptation would be to use the updated belief

$P(H_i | e)$ as a new prior probability and, through rote, to write the conditioning equation

$$P(S_j | e) = \sum_i P(S_j | H_i)\, P(H_i | e). \tag{2.45}$$

This equation, however, is valid only in a very special set of circumstances. It would be wrong in our example because the changes in the belief of H actually originated from corresponding changes in S; reflecting these back to S would amount to counting the same evidence twice. The correct conditioning equation should be

$$P(S_j | e) = \sum_i P(S_j | H_i, e)\, P(H_i | e) \tag{2.46}$$

instead of Eq. (2.45). Since $P(S_j | H_i)$ may be different than $P(S_j | H_i, e)$, it follows that the evidence obtained affects not only the belief in H and S but also the strength of the causal link between H and S. At first glance, this realization makes Bayesian methods appear to be useless in handling a large number of facts; having to recalculate all the link matrices each time a new piece of evidence arrives would be an insurmountable computational burden.

Fortunately, there is a simple way of updating beliefs that circumvents this difficulty and uses only the original link matrices (see Chapter 4 for elaboration). The calculation of $P(S_j | e)$, for instance, can be performed as follows: Treating S as an intermediate hypothesis, Eq. (2.13) dictates

$$P(S_j | e) = \alpha P(e | S_j)\, P(S_j) \tag{2.47}$$

The term $P(e | S_j)$ is the likelihood vector $\Lambda_j(S)$, which earlier was calculated as (36, 1), while the prior $P(S_j)$ is given by the matrix multiplication

$$P(S_j) = \sum_i P(S_j | H_i)\, P(H_i) = (10^{-4},\ 1-10^{-4}) \begin{bmatrix} 0.95 & 0.05 \\ 0.01 & 0.99 \end{bmatrix} = (0.0101,\ 0.9899).$$

Together, we have

$$P(S_j | e) = \alpha\,(36,\ 1)\,(0.0101,\ 0.9899) = (0.2686,\ 0.7314),$$

which gives the event S_1 = *Alarm sound on* a credibility of 26.86% and gives the predicted event D = *Daughter will call* the probability

$$P(D | e) = \sum_i P(D | S_i)\, P(S_i | e) = (0.2686,\ 0.7314) \begin{bmatrix} 0.7 \\ 0 \end{bmatrix} = 0.188. \tag{2.48}$$

2.2.4 Multiple Causes and "Explaining Away"

Consider the following situation:

EXAMPLE 7: As he is debating whether or not to rush home, Mr. Holmes remembers reading in the instruction manual of his alarm system that the device is sensitive to earthquakes and can be accidentally ($P = 0.20$) triggered by one. He realizes that if an earthquake had occurred, it surely ($P = 0.40$) would be on the news. So he turns on his radio and waits for either an announcement over the air or a call from his daughter.

Mr. Holmes perceives two episodes as potential causes for the alarm sound—an attempted burglary and an earthquake. Though burglaries can be safely assumed to be independent of earthquakes, a positive radio announcement reduces the likelihood of a burglary, since it "explains away" the alarm sound. It does this even though the two causal events are perceived as individual variables (see Figure 2.2); general knowledge about earthquakes rarely intersects knowledge about burglaries.

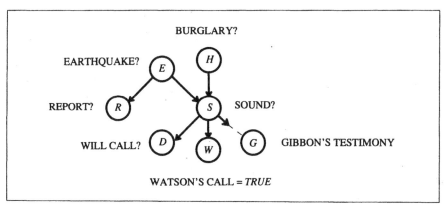

Figure 2.2. *A network depicting predicted events (D), explanatory variables (E and H) and evidence variables (W, G and R).*

This interaction among multiple causes is a prevailing pattern of human reasoning. (See Section 1.2.2.) When a physician discovers evidence in favor of one disease, it reduces the perceived likelihood of other diseases, although the patient may well be suffering from two or more disorders simultaneously. A suspect who provides an alternative explanation for being present at the scene of the crime appears less likely to be guilty, even though the explanation furnished does not preclude his having committed the crime.

To model this "sideways" interaction a matrix M should be assessed, giving the distribution of the consequence variable as a function of every possible combination of the causal variables. In our example, we should specify $M = P(S \mid E, H)$ where E stands for the variable $E = \{Earthquake, No\ earthquake\}$ and H stands for the hypothesis variable $H = \{Burglary, No\ Burglary\}$. Although this matrix is identical in form to the one described in Eq. (2.30), where several causal variables from example 2 were combined into one compound variable $\{H_1, H_2, H_3, H_4\}$, treating E and H as two separate entities has an advantage: it allows us to relate each of the variables to a separate set of evidence without consulting the other. For example, we can quantify the relation between E and $R = Radio\ announcement$ by the probabilities $P(R \mid E)$ without having to consider the irrelevant event of burglary, as would be required by compounding the pair (E, H) into one variable. Moreover, upon confirmation of R, we can update the beliefs of E and H in two separate steps, mediated by the updating of S. This more closely resembles the local process used by people in tracing lines of evidence. (An updating scheme for networks with multiple-parent nodes is described in Section 4.3.)

If the number of causal factors k is large, estimating M may be troublesome because in principle it requires a table of size 2^{k+1}. In practice, however, people conceptualize causal relationships by creating hierarchies of small clusters of variables, and the interactions among the factors in each cluster are normally categorized into prestored, prototypical structures, each requiring about k parameters. Common examples of such prototypical structures are noisy OR-gates (i.e., any one of the factors is likely to trigger the effect), noisy AND-gates, and various enabling mechanisms (i.e., factors identified as having no influence of their own except that they enable other influences to become effective). In Example 7, it is reasonable to assume that the influences of burglaries and earthquakes on alarm systems is of the noisy OR-type; accordingly, only two parameters are needed, one describing the sensitivity of the alarm to earthquakes (in the absence of burglaries), the other describing its sensitivity to burglaries (in the absence of earthquakes). These prototypical structures will be treated formally in Section 4.3.2.

2.2.5 Belief Networks and the Role of Causality

In the preceding discussion we twice resorted to the use of diagrams. Figures 2.1 and 2.2 were not, however, presented merely for mnemonic or illustrative purposes. We will see that they convey important conceptual information, far more meaningful than the numerical estimates of the probabilities involved. The formal properties of such diagrams, called *Bayesian belief networks*, will be discussed in Section 3.3; here, we briefly outline their salient features.

Formally, Bayesian networks are directed acyclic graphs in which each node represents a random variable, or uncertain quantity, which can take on two or more possible values. The arcs signify the existence of direct causal influences between the linked variables, and the strengths of these influences are quantified by conditional probabilities. Informally, the structure of a Bayesian network can be determined by a simple procedure: We assign a vertex to each variable in the domain and draw arrows toward each vertex X_i from a select set Π_{X_i} of vertices perceived to be direct causes of X_i. The strengths of these direct influences are then quantified by assigning to each variable X_i a link matrix $P(x_i \mid \Pi_{X_i})$, which represents judgmental estimates of the conditional probabilities of the event $X_i = x_i$, given any value combination Π_{X_i} of the parent set Π_{X_i}. The conjunction of these local estimates specifies a complete and consistent global model (i.e., a joint distribution function) on the basis of which all probabilistic queries can be answered. The overall joint distribution function over the variables $X_1, ..., X_n$, is given by the product

$$P(x_1, x_2, ..., x_n) = \prod_{i=1}^{n} P(x_i \mid \Pi_{X_i}). \qquad (2.49)$$

So, for example, the joint distribution corresponding to the network of Figure 2.2 is given by

$$P(h, e, r, s, d, w, g) = P(h)\, P(e)\, P(r \mid e)\, P(s \mid e, h)\, P(d \mid s) \qquad (2.50)$$
$$P(w \mid s)\, P(g \mid s),$$

where lowercase symbols stand for the particular values (*TRUE* or *FALSE*) of the corresponding variables.

The advantage of network representation is that it allows people to express directly the fundamental qualitative relationship of "direct dependency." The network then displays a consistent set of additional direct and indirect dependencies and preserves it as a stable part of the model, independent of the numerical estimates. For example, Figure 2.2 demonstrates that the radio report (R) does not change the prospects of Holmes's daughter phoning (D), once we verify the actual state of the alarm system (S). This fact is conveyed by the network topology—showing S blocking the path between R and D—even though it was not considered explicitly during the construction of the network. It can be inferred visually from the linkages used to put the network together, and it will remain part of the model regardless of the numerical estimates of the link matrices.

The directionality of the arrows is essential for displaying *nontransitive* dependencies, i.e., S depends on both E and H, yet E and H are marginally independent (they become dependent only if S or any of its descendants are known). If the arcs were stripped of their arrows, some of these relationships would be misrepresented. It is this computational role of identifying what information is or is not relevant in any given situation that we attribute to the mental construct of causation. Causality modularizes our knowledge as it is cast from experience. By displaying the irrelevancies in the domain, causal schemata minimize the number of relationships that need to be considered while a model is constructed, and in effect legitimizes many future local inferences. The prevailing practice in rule-based expert systems of encoding knowledge by evidential rules (i.e., if effect then cause) is deficient in this respect. It usually fails to account for induced dependencies between causes (e.g., an earthquake explaining away the alarm sound), and if one ventures to encode these by direct rules, the number of rules becomes unmanageable [Shachter and Heckerman 1987].

In Chapter 3, we will present a formal characterization of dependencies expressible in both causal and non-causal networks. In Chapters 4 and 5 we will show that belief networks can also be used as inference engines, where the network topology provides both the storage locations and the timing information to sequence the computational steps involved in answering probabilistic queries. Examples of such queries are "What are the chances of a burglary, given that the radio announced an earthquake and my daughter did not call?" and "What is the most likely explanation of Watson's phone call?" Answers to such queries will be assembled by local, parallel message-passing processes, with minimal external supervision. The essential role of causality will be explored further in Chapters 8 and 10. Before advancing to these topics, we will use the next few sections to further elaborate on the philosophy of Bayesian inference and the role of networks in shaping human judgment.

2.3 EPISTEMOLOGICAL ISSUES OF BELIEF UPDATING

2.3.1 Patterns of Plausible Inference: Polya vs. Bayes?

In our previous discussion we suggested that once we encode knowledge in probabilistic terms and adhere to the rules of probability calculus, we are guaranteed never to produce paradoxical or counterintuitive conclusions. This raises an interesting question about how people produce intuitively acceptable conclusions using mechanisms that seem to involve only qualitative, nonnumerical relationships. If such mechanisms work for people, can we simulate them on digital machines and thus facilitate commonsense reasoning? This is indeed the ultimate objective of many works in AI, most notably nonmonotonic logics. The goal is to capture the patterns of plausible reasoning in nonnumerical terms, as principles governing English sentences that contain linguistic hedges such as "typically," "likely," and "surely." In this subsection we discuss some of the difficulties associated with using the logical approach instead of the probabilistic approach. A more detailed discussion will be given in Chapter 10.

POLYA'S PATTERNS OF PLAUSIBLE INFERENCE

George Polya (1887–1985) was one of the first mathematicians to attempt a formal characterization of qualitative human reasoning. In his 1954 book *Mathematics and Plausible Reasoning*, Polya argued that the process of discovery, even in as formal a field as mathematics, is guided by nondeductive inference mechanisms, entailing a lot of guesswork. "Patterns of plausible inference" was his term for the principles governing this guesswork.

Among the conspicuous patterns listed by Polya, we find the following four:

1. *Inductive patterns:* "The verification of a consequence renders a conjecture more credible."

    For example, the conjecture "It rained last night" becomes more credible when we verify the consequence "The ground is wet."

2. *Successive verification of several consequences:* "The verification of a new consequence counts more or less if the new consequence differs more or less from the former, verified consequences."

    For example, if in trying to substantiate the conjecture "All ravens are black," we observe n Australian ravens, all of them black, our subsequent confidence in the conjecture will be increased substantially if the $(n + 1)$-th raven is a black Brazilian raven rather than another black Australian raven.

3. *Verification of improbable consequences:* "The verification of a consequence counts more or less according as the consequence is more or less improbable in itself."

    For example, the conjecture "It rained last night" obtains more support from "The roof is leaking" than from the more common observation "The grass is wet."

4. *Inference from analogy:* "A conjecture becomes more credible when an analogous conjecture turns out to be true."

    For example, the conjecture "Of all objects displacing the same volume, the sphere has the smallest surface" becomes more credible when we prove the related theorem "Of all curves enclosing the same area, the circle has the shortest perimeter."

Polya also identified three main sub-patterns of inductive reasoning:

1. *Examining a consequence:* same as (1) above.

2. *Examining a possible ground:* "Our confidence in a conjecture can only diminish when a possible ground for the conjecture is exploded."

3. *Examining a conflicting conjecture:* "Our confidence in a conjecture can only increase when an incompatible rival conjecture is exploded."

These patterns can be further refined depending on whether propositions are verified categorically or just become more credible (Polya called this *shaded verification*).

Polya summarized the patterns and subpatterns by the following table:

		(1) Demonstrative	(2) Shaded Demonstrative	(3) Shaded Inductive	(4) Inductive
1.	Examining a consequnce	$A \rightarrow B$ B false	$A \rightarrow B$ B less cr.	$A \rightarrow B$ B more cr.	$A \rightarrow B$ B true
		A false	A less cr.	As. more cr.	A more cr.
2.	Examining a possible ground	$A \leftarrow B$ B true	$A \leftarrow B$ B more cr.	$A \leftarrow B$ B less cr.	$A \leftarrow B$ B false
		A true	A more cr.	As. less cr.	A less cr.
3.	Examining a conflicting conjecture	$A|B$ B true	$A|B$ B more cr.	$A|B$ B less cr.	$A|B$ B false
		A false	A less cr.	As. more cr.	A more cr.

In this table, $A \rightarrow B$ means that A implies B, *cr.* is short for "credible," *s.* is short for "somewhat," and $A \mid B$ means that A is incompatible with B, i.e., A and B cannot both be true at the same time.

The patterns for "Examining a possible ground" are logically equivalent to those for "Examining a consequence." For example, entry (2,2) follows from (1,2) because $A \rightarrow B$ is logically equivalent to $(\neg B) \rightarrow (\neg A)$ and "B more cr." is equivalent to "$\neg B$ less cr." It still makes sense to restate row 2 separately since people do not readily perceive logical identities as psychological necessities; redundant inference rules are useful for dealing with logically equivalent but syntactically different situations.

WHY POLYA PREFERRED PROBABILITIES OVER LOGIC

When stated individually, each pattern in Polya's table appears plausible and is supported by many examples. However, after extracting many such conspicuous primitive patterns, Polya stopped short of proposing them as syllogistic axioms (or inference rules) for a new logic, capable of manipulating concepts such as "credible," "more credible," and "somewhat credible." Instead, Polya shelved this promising prospect and retreated to the safety of probability calculus—from which, supposedly, all the qualitative patterns of plausible inference should follow naturally and automatically, leaving no need to express them in symbolic terms.

The reason for Polya's sharp retreat is explained in Chapter 15 of his book and is based on the realization that primitive patterns of plausible reasoning, as reasonable as they appear and as syntactically similar as they are to logical syllogisms, are of basically different character than those syllogisms. Polya identified four basic differences between the two modes of reasoning, the most important being a feature he called *self-sufficiency* (today we use the term *monotonicity*)—new information, as long as it does not conflict with the premises, will never change the conclusions reached by demonstrative inferences.

> Nothing is needed beyond the premises to validate the conclusion and nothing can invalidate it if the premises remain solid.

By contrast, credibility levels established by plausible inferences are not "durable," as they may change with new information and are sensitive to the entire content of one's knowledge base. In Polya's words:

> In opposition to demonstrative inference, plausible inference leaves indeterminate a highly relevant point: the "strength" or the "weight" of the conclusion. This weight may depend not only on clarified grounds such as those expressed in the premises, but also on unclarified unexpressed grounds somewhere in the background of the person who draws the conclusion.

This is indeed the violation of modularity discussed in Chapter 1. Polya claimed, however, that in each inferential step the direction of change depends only on the premises considered at that step. For example, in the inductive pattern above, the credibility of the hypothesis can only increase with the discovery of its consequence, regardless of what background information we possess. This, we shall soon demonstrate, is not entirely correct (see also Figure 1.2). The gap between demonstrative and plausible inferences is, in fact, wider than that identified by Polya, i.e., not only the strength of the conclusions but also their "direction" depends on "unclarified unexpressed grounds somewhere in the background...."

Notwithstanding this oversight, Polya apparently chose the calculus of probability as a surrogate for logic because he believed that if things are set up properly, probability calculus will preserve all the qualitative patterns of plausible reasoning and, as a bonus, will provide the correct strengths of the conclusions. Polya, in fact, showed that all the patterns of his table follow from probability theory. For example, here is Polya's probabilistic proof of the inductive pattern

$$(A \rightarrow B) \ \& \ B \Longrightarrow A \ more \ credible: \qquad (2.51)$$

Assume that in knowledge state S_1, A and B accrue the credibility measures $P(A)$ and $P(B)$, respectively, and that in state S_2, B is known to be true, i.e., $P_2(B) = 1$. One can defend the validity of Eq. (2.51) by showing that the inequality $P(A \mid B) > P(A)$ holds in all cases. Indeed, using Bayes' Rule (Eq. (2.13)) and the fact that $A \rightarrow B$ implies $P(B \mid A) = 1$, we obtain

$$P(A \mid B) = \frac{P(B \mid A)P(A)}{P(B)} = \frac{P(A)}{P(B)}, \qquad (2.52)$$

and, since $P(B) \leq 1$, we have

$$P(A \mid B) \geq P(A), \tag{2.53}$$

with equality holding iff either $P(A) = 0$ or $P(B) = 1$. Thus, it appears as though probability calculus lends unqualified confirmation to the inductive pattern (Eq. (2.51)).

Unfortunately, the above proof has a major flaw. The inequality in Eq. (2.53) is valid only in the rare and uninteresting case when B is the only new piece of information by which S_2 differs from S_1. To be used as a syllogistic rule of inference, the inductive pattern of Eq. (2.51) must be universally applicable to any two knowledge states S_1 and S_2. Yet, if S_2 differs from S_1 by two facts, say B and C, Eq. (2.51) no longer holds. An extreme case is when C directly opposes A. For example, consider the following three events:

$A = $ "It rained last night."
$B = $ "My grass is wet."
$C = $ "My neighbor's grass is dry."

Any reasonable probabilistic model would yield

$$P(A \mid B) > P(A) \qquad \text{but} \qquad P(A \mid B, C) < P(A).$$

Although the left-hand side of Eq. (2.51) is satisfied in this example, the right-hand side of Eq. (2.51) contradicts our expectations whenever S_2 entails both B and C.

This might be construed as an artificial and harmless example, because the knowledge base should also contain the rule $C \rightarrow \neg A$, which eventually will establish the falsity of A after Eq. (2.51) temporarily raises its credibility. A more convincing criticism would be to demonstrate the failure of Eq. (2.51) when C has no relation whatsoever to A. For example:

$A = $ "It rained last night."
$B = $ "My grass is wet."
$C = $ "The sprinkler was on last night."

Here, the falsity of Eq. (2.51) could produce paradoxical and irreversible consequences. Perhaps it was this realization that prevented Polya from proposing his patterns as inference rules for a logic of plausible reasoning.

IF BAYES NEVER ERRS, WHY DID POLYA?

It is instructive, at this point, to reiterate the fundamental difference between the role of premises in logic and that of conditioning events in probability calculus (see Chapter 1). In logic, the truth of a premise B is all that is required for deducing the conclusion A. In probability calculus, the expression $P(A \mid B)$ specifically identifies B as the *only* information available—aside from the tacit knowledge base K, which we assume to be constant. This distinction is also reflected in significant computational differences between the two formalisms. The statement

$$P(A \mid B) = p$$

denotes totally different operational semantics than the production rule

$$\text{If } B \text{ then } A \quad \text{(with certainty } p\text{).} \tag{2.54}$$

The latter constitutes a carte blanche to execute a certain transformation on the database *whenever* it entails the truth of B, regardless of what other information it contains. The former permits us to draw certain conclusions (about the probability of A) *only when* the database entails B and no other information that can affect A once we know B.

This difference may explain why the designers of first-generation expert systems preferred the rule-based approach over straightforward Bayes' conditioning. The latter seems to require that we inspect the entire database at each step of the computation to see if it contains any new information that is relevant to A and not fully accounted for in B. In subsequent chapters, we shall see that networks provide an effective scheme for indexing this information so that local inspections are sufficient. On the other hand, systems based on rules such as Eq. (2.54) invariably run into the same paradoxical difficulties that plagued Polya's patterns. For example, such systems would draw the same conclusion from Eq. (2.54) whether B was established by $C' = $ "My shoes are muddy" or by $C = $ "The sprinkler was on last night." This is a clear violation of common sense. Section 10.3 provides a remedy to this problem, within the framework of rule-based systems.

It is also interesting to inquire why Polya's patterns are considered plausible if they are not supported by probability theory and they lead to paradoxical conclusions. The answer lies in the type of assumptions we all make when asked to judge the plausibility of an argument. Apparently, the inductive pattern (Eq. (2.51)) appears plausible to most people, because we tacitly assume that the truth of B is the *only* relevant change known to have taken place in the world. In other words, unless otherwise stated, all belief values, especially of events that precede B, are presumed to persist unaltered. Since changes in the belief of other propositions (e.g., "The sprinkler was on") are not mentioned in Eq. (2.51), we presume that in the transition from S_1 to S_2 the truth of B ("The grass is wet") was established by direct observation or reliable testimony and not as a consequence of other, unmentioned changes.

So far, we have discussed the difficulties associated with the nonmodularity of plausible inferences, i.e., the impropriety of drawing conclusions from certain truths in the database without checking other truths that may reside there. The following discussion will focus on an even tougher problem, *query sensitivity*, which stems not from neglecting facts that were learned but from neglecting to specify which facts could have been learned. In other words, plausible reasoning, unlike logical deduction, is sensitive not only to the information at hand but also to the query process by which the information was obtained.

2.3.2 The Three Prisoners Paradox: When the Bare Facts Won't Do

Three prisoners, A, B, and C, have been tried for murder, and their verdicts will be read and their sentences executed tomorrow morning. They know only that one of them will be declared guilty and will be hanged to die while the other two will be set free; the identity of the condemned prisoner is revealed to the very reliable prison guard, but not to the prisoners themselves.

In the middle of the night, Prisoner A calls the guard over and makes the following request: "Please give this letter to one of my friends—to one who is to be released. You and I know that at least one of them will be freed." The guard takes the letter and promises to do as told. An hour later Prisoner A calls the guard again and asks, "Can you tell me which of my friends you gave the letter to? It should give me no clue regarding my own status because, regardless of my fate, each of my friends had an equal chance of receiving my letter." The guard answers, "I gave the letter to Prisoner B; he will be released tomorrow." Prisoner A returns to his bed and thinks, "Before I talked to the guard, my chances of being executed were one in three. Now that he has told me that B will be released, only C and I remain, and my chances of dying have gone from 33.3% to 50%. What did I do wrong? I made certain not to ask for any information relevant to my own fate...."

SEARCHING FOR THE BARE FACTS

So far, we have the classical Three Prisoners story as described in many books of mathematical puzzles (e.g., Gardner [1961]). Students are asked to test which of the two values, 1/3 or 1/2, reflects prisoner A's updated chances of perishing at dawn.† Let us attempt to resolve the issue using formal probability theory.

---

† A survey conducted in the author's class in 1984 showed 23 students in favor of 1/2 and 3 students in favor of 1/3. (The proportion was reversed in 1987, when class notes became available.)

Let I_B stand for the proposition "Prisoner B will be declared innocent," and let G_A stand for the proposition "Prisoner A will be declared guilty." Our task is to compute the probability of G_A given all the information obtained from the guard, i.e., to compute $P(G_A | I_B)$. Since $G_A \supset I_B$, we have $P(I_B | G_A) = 1$, and we can write

$$P(G_A | I_B) = \frac{P(I_B | G_A) P(G_A)}{P(I_B)} = \frac{P(G_A)}{P(I_B)} = \frac{1/3}{2/3} = 1/2. \qquad (2.55)$$

Thus, when facts are wrongly formulated, even the tools of probability calculus are insufficient safeguards against drawing counterintuitive or false conclusions. (Readers who are not convinced that the answer 50% is false are invited to eavesdrop on Prisoner A's further reflections: "... Worse yet, by sheer symmetry, my chances of dying would also have risen to 50% if the guard had named C instead of B—so my chances must have been 50% to begin with. I must be hallucinating. ....")

The fallacy in the preceding formulation arose from omitting the full context in which the answer was obtained by Prisoner A. By *context* we mean the entire range of answers one could possibly obtain (as in Eq. (2.30)), not just the answer actually obtained. In our example, it is important to know not only that the guard said, "B will be released," but also that the only other possible reply was "C will be released." Had the guard's answer, "B will be released," been a reply to the query "Will B die tomorrow?" the preceding analysis would have been correct.

A useful way of ensuring that we have considered the full context is to condition our analysis on events actually observed, not on their implications. In our example, the information in

$$I_B = \text{"}B \text{ will be declared innocent."}$$

was inferred from a more direct observation,

$$I'_B = \text{"Guard said that } B \text{ will be declared innocent."}$$

If we compute $P(G_A | I'_B)$ instead of $P(G_A | I_B)$, we get the correct answer:

$$P(G_A | I'_B) = \frac{P(I'_B | G_A) P(G_A)}{P(I'_B)} = \frac{1/2 \cdot 1/3}{1/2} = 1/3. \qquad (2.56)$$

The calculations in Eq. (2.56) differ from those in Eq. (2.55) in two ways. First, G_A subsumed I_B but does not subsume I'_B, because it is possible for A to be the condemned man and hear the guard report, "C will be released." Second, $P(I'_B)$ is 1/2, whereas $P(I_B)$ was 2/3. These differences exist because I'_B implies I_B but not vice versa; even if B is to be released, the guard can truthfully report, "C will be released"—if A is slated to die.

The lesson of the Three Prisoners paradox is that we cannot assess the impact of new information by considering only propositions implied by the information; we must also consider what information *could have* been reported.

THE THOUSAND PRISONER PROBLEM

Here is an extreme example, in which knowledge of the query context is even more important. Imagine you are one of one thousand prisoners awaiting sentencing with the knowledge that only one of you has been condemned. By sheer luck, you find a computer printout (with a court seal on it) listing 998 prisoners; each name is marked "innocent," and yours is not among them. Should your chances of dying increase from 1/1000 to 1/2? Most people would say yes, and rightly so.

Imagine, however, that while poring anxiously over the list you discover the query that produced it: "Print the names of any 998 innocent right-handed prisoners." If you are the only left-handed person around, would you not breathe a sigh of relief? Again, most people would.

Though the discovery of the query adds no logical conclusions to our knowledge base, it alters drastically the relative likelihood of events that remain unsettled. In other words, the range of possibilities is the same before and after you discover the query: Either you or the other unlisted prisoner will die. Yet the query renders the death of the other prisoner much more likely, because while you can blame your exclusion from the list on being left-handed, the other prisoner has no explanation except being found guilty. If the list contained 999 names marked "innocent," knowledge of the query would have no impact on your beliefs, because the only possible conclusion would be that you had been found guilty.

Again we see the computational virtues and epistemological weaknesses of crisp logic: It allows us to dispose of the query once we learn its ramifications but prevents the ramifications learned from altering the likelihood of uncertain events. Indeed, if we wish to determine merely which events are possible we need not retain the queries; the bare information will suffice. But if we are concerned also with the relative likelihood of these possible events, then the query process is necessary. If the process is unknown, then several likely processes can be conjectured and their average computed (see next subsection).

But first, let us return to the jail cell. Mathematically, the discovery of the query should restore your confidence of innocence to its original value of 99.9%, but psychologically you are more frightened than you were before you found the list. In your intuition, the realization that you are one of the only two potentially guilty individuals evidently carries more weight than Bayesian arithmetic does. Still, intuition is a multifaceted resource, and pondering further, you should muster intuitive support for the Bayesian conclusion as well: Finding the query after seeing the list should have the same effect as seeing the list after the query. In the second case, once you know the query, the list is useless to you, because it can contain neither your name nor the name of the guilty prisoner. Consequently, your chances of being found guilty should revert to 1/1000.

WHAT IF WE DON'T KNOW THE QUERY?

In the Three Prisoners story, we assumed that if both B and C were pardoned, the guard would give the letter to one or the other with equal ($\frac{1}{2}$) probability. What if we do not know the process by which the letter recipient is chosen, when A is condemned? The conditional probability $P(I'_B|G_A)$ can vary from 0 (the guard avoids B), to 1 (the guard avoids C). Likewise, the marginal probability $P(I'_B)$ can vary from $\frac{1}{3}$ to $\frac{2}{3}$. Treating $q = P(I'_B|G_A)$ as a variable, Eq. (2.56) can be written as follows:

$$P(G_A|I'_B) = \frac{P(I'_B|G_A)\,P(G_A)}{P(I'_B|G_A)\,P(G_A) + P(I'_B|G_B)\,P(G_B) + P(I'_B|G_C)\,P(G_C)}$$
$$= \frac{q\,^1/_3}{q\,^1/_3 + 0 + 1 \cdot {}^1/_3} = \frac{q}{1+q}. \tag{2.57}$$

Thus, as q varies from 0 to 1, $P(G_A|I'_B)$ varies from 0 to $\frac{1}{2}$.

Philosophers disagree on how to treat ignorance of this sort. Some favor the use of probability intervals, where the upper and lower probabilities represent the boundaries of our convictions, while others prefer an interpolation rule that selects a single probability model having some desirable properties. The Dempster-Shafer (D-S) formalism (see Chapter 9) is an example of the interval-based approach, while maximum-entropy techniques [Tribus 1969, Jaynes 1979] represent the single model approach.

Bayesian technique lies somewhere in between. For example, in the absence of information about the selection process used by the guard, several plausible models of the process are articulated, and their likelihoods are assessed. In our example, we may treat the critical parameter q as a random variable ranging from 0 to 1 and assess a probability distribution $f(q)$ on q, reflecting the likelihood that the guard will exhibit a bias q in favor of selecting B. This method yields a unique distribution on the variables previously considered, via

$$P(G_A|I'_B) = \int_0^1 \frac{q}{1+q}\, f(q|I'_B)\,dq = \frac{\displaystyle\int_0^1 q\,f(q)\,dq}{1 + \displaystyle\int_0^1 q\,f(q)\,dq}, \tag{2.58}$$

but the method simultaneously maintains a distinction between conclusions based on definite models and conclusions based on uncertain models. For example, the knowledge that the choice between B and C is made at random is modeled by $q = \frac{1}{2}$, while total lack of knowledge about the process is represented by $f(q) = 1$, $0 \le q \le 1$. Though both models yield the same point values of $\frac{1}{3}$ for

$P(G_A | I'_B)$, they differ substantially in the way they allow new facts to be assimilated. Suppose Prisoner A recalls that the guard had a fistfight with C yesterday. This fact can easily be incorporated if q is a random variable (by updating $f(q)$), but not if q is a fixed value. The problem of representing uncertainty about probabilities will be discussed further in Section 7.3.

2.3.3 Jeffrey's Rule and the Problem of Autonomous Inference Agents

The Three Prisoners puzzle shows that before we can determine the implications of a new fact in our knowledge base, we must know the process by which the fact was learned—in particular, what other facts could have been gathered in that process. Such detailed knowledge is not always available; we often must respond to new information without having the slightest idea how it was collected. These situations occur when the gathering of information is delegated to autonomous agents, each using private procedures which for various reasons cannot be explicated in full detail.

OBSERVATION BY CANDLE LIGHT

Richard Jeffrey was the first to recognize the importance of this problem, and he devised a rule for handling it [Jeffrey 1965]. The autonomous agents used in Jeffrey's original example are our sensory organs, as described in the following passage:

> The agent inspects a piece of cloth by candlelight and gets the impression that it is green, although he concedes that it might be blue or, even (but very improbably), violet. If G, B and V are the propositions that the cloth is green, blue and violet, respectively, then the outcome of the observation might be that, whereas originally his degrees of belief in G, B and V were 0.30, 0.30 and 0.40, his degrees of belief in those same propositions after the observation are 0.70, 0.25 and 0.05. If there were a proposition E in his preference ranking [i.e., knowledge base] which described the precise quality of his visual experience in looking at the cloth, one would say that what the agent learned from the observation was that E is true. If his original subjective probability assignment was *prob*, his new assignment should then be $prob_E$, and we would have
>
> $$prob\ G = .30 \quad prob\ B = .30 \quad prob\ V = .40$$
>
> representing his opinions about the color of the cloth before the observation, but would have
>
> $$prob(G\ |E) = .70 \quad prob(B\ |E) = .25 \quad prob(V\ |E) = .05$$
>
> representing his opinions about the color of the cloth after the observation.... When the agent looks at the piece of cloth by candlelight there is a particular complex

pattern of physical stimulation of his retina, on the basis of which his beliefs about the possible colors of the cloth change in the indicated ways. However, the pattern of stimulation need not be describable in the language he speaks; and even if it is, there is every reason to suppose that the agent is quite unaware of what that pattern is, and is quite incapable of uttering or identifying a correct description of it. Thus, a complete description of the pattern of stimulation includes a record of the firing times of all the rods and cones in the outer layer of retinal neurons during the period of the observation. Even if the agent is an expert physiologist, he will be unable to produce or recognize a correct record of this sort on the basis of his experience during the observation.

With this story in mind, Jeffrey wonders how the new information should be used to influence other propositions that depend on the color of the cloth:

Then the problem is this: Given that a passage of experience has led the agent to change his degrees of belief in certain propositions $B_1, B_2, ..., B_n$ from their original values,

$$prob\, B_1, prob\, B_2, ..., prob\, B_n$$

to new values,

$$PROB\, B_1, PROB\, B_2, ..., PROB\, B_n,$$

how should these changes be propagated over the rest of the structure of his beliefs? If the original probability measure was *prob*, and the new one is *PROB*, and if A is a proposition in the agent's preference ranking [i.e., knowledge base] but is not one of the n propositions whose probabilities were directly affected by the passage of experience, how shall *PROB A* be determined?

Jeffrey's solution is based on the critical assumption that the propositions B selected to summarize the experience possess a special property: "...while the observation changed the agent's degree of belief in B and in certain other propositions, it did not change the *conditional degree of belief* in any propositions on the evidence B or on the evidence $\neg B$" (italics added). Thus, if $B_1, B_2, ..., B_n$ are exhaustive and mutually exclusive propositions (like *Green*, *Blue*, and *Violet* in the candlelight example), Jeffrey maintains that, for every proposition A not "directly affected by the passage of experience," we should write

$$PROB\, (A \mid B_i) = prob\, (A \mid B_i) \quad i = 1, 2, ..., n. \tag{2.59}$$

This, together with the additivity of *PROB*, leads directly to

$$PROB(A) = \sum_i prob\, (A \mid B_i)\, PROB(B_i), \tag{2.60}$$

a formula now known as *Jeffrey's Rule* of updating, or the rule of *probability kinematics*.

The convenience of the rule is enticing in a way that is reminiscent of the logical rules of deduction; we need not know anything about how $prob(B_i)$ was updated to $PROB(B_i)$—only the net result matters. We simply take $PROB(B_i)$ as a new set of priors and apply the textbook formula of Eq. (2.10). Unfortunately, the rule is applicable only in situations where the criterion of Eq. (2.59) holds, and this condition, as we shall soon see, is not easy to test.

Traditional probabilistic analysis gives us a way to decide when Eqs. (2.59) and (2.60) are applicable, based on Bayes' conditioning. If we denote by e the evidence actually observed and equate $PROB(A)$ with $prob(A \mid e)$, we get the *Bayes conditionalization formula,*

$$prob(A \mid e) = \sum_i prob(A \mid B_i, e) \, prob(B_i \mid e), \qquad \textbf{(2.61)}$$

which coincides with Eq. (2.60) only when A and e are conditionally independent given B_i, i.e., only when

$$prob(A \mid B_i, e) = prob(A \mid B_i). \qquad \textbf{(2.62)}$$

However, philosophers might argue that it sometimes makes no sense to equate $PROB(A)$ with $prob(A \mid e)$ or even to talk about $prob(A \mid e)$, e being an elusive, non-propositional experience. Indeed, the textbook definition of conditional probability, $P(A \mid e) = P(A, e) / P(e)$, suggests that before $P(A \mid e)$ can be computed one must have the joint probability $P(A, e)$, so e must already be integrated in one's knowledge base as a proposition that might later be an object of attention. This condition clearly is not met in the candlelight story; the sensory experience responsible for the color judgment cannot have been anticipated in anyone's knowledge base. In such cases, so the argument goes, Bayes conditionalization is not applicable and should give way to the more general Jeffrey's Rule. Likewise, the conditional independence criterion of Eq. (2.62) is a quality ascertainable only by Bayes conditionalization and therefore is clearly inadequate for delineating the class of propositions A to which Jeffrey's Rule applies.

While no alternate criterion for testing Eq. (2.59) is formulated in Jeffrey's book, some hint is provided by the requirement that A "is not one of the n propositions whose probabilities were directly affected by the passage of experience." Jeffrey apparently believed that the question of whether a proposition A is affected directly or indirectly can be decided on qualitative grounds, prior to defining joint distributions. In this sense, he pioneered the idea that dependence relationships are the fundamental building blocks of probabilistic knowledge, more basic than numerical distributions (a position that will be developed further in Chapter 3).

In a subsequent publication [Jeffrey 1968], Jeffrey replaced the notion of directness with that of a *basis,* where a basis B for an observation is defined as the set of propositions $B_1, B_2,..., B_n$ that satisfy Eq. (2.59) for every A not in B. This way, the validity of Eq. (2.60) is automatically guaranteed to hold for every A not in B, but from a practical viewpoint the problem of determining the basis associated with a given observation remains unresolved.

To demonstrate the type of information required for determining the applicability of Jeffrey's Rule, let us return to the candlelight example and assign two alternative meanings to proposition A.

Case 1 e — B — A: Assume that the proposition A stands for the statement "The cloth will be sold the next day," and we know the chances of selling the cloth depend solely on its color:

$$P(A \mid Green) = 0.40, \quad P(A \mid Blue) = 0.40, \quad \text{and}$$

$$P(A \mid Violet) = 0.80. \tag{2.63}$$

Eq. (2.60), then, allows us to calculate the updated belief in the salability of the cloth, based only on the color inspection (see Figure 2.3). Prior to the test, our belief in selling the cloth measured

$$prob(A) = (0.4)(0.3) + (0.4)(0.3) + (0.8)(0.4) = 0.56 \,,$$

and once the test results become known, our belief should change to

$$PROB(A) = (0.4)(0.7) + (0.4)(0.25) + (0.8)(0.05) = 0.42 \,.$$

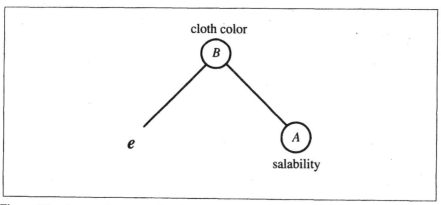

Figure 2.3. *A network representing the conditional independence of A and e, given B.*

Bayes conditionalization would yield the same result, because the salability of the cloth depending only on its color is interpreted as A and e being conditionally independent, and therefore

$$P(A \mid Color, e) = P(A \mid Color), \tag{2.64}$$

which legitimizes Jeffrey's assumption that

$$PROB(A \mid B_i) = prob(A \mid B_i),$$

as long as we identify $PROB(A \mid B_i)$ with $P(A \mid B_i, e)$. In other words, modern Bayesians take the liberty of writing equations such as Eq. (2.64) even though $P(A \mid Color, e)$ is available nowhere and cannot be computed numerically. The equation does convey the qualitative information expressed in the story—that color is the only factor relevant to salability—and it thus draws legitimacy not from numerical probability values but from a more reliable knowledge source: people's qualitative reasoning about dependencies.

Note that Jeffrey's Rule is equivalent to the Bayesian treatment of virtual evidence (Section 2.2.2), using the likelihood vector

$$\Lambda_i(B) \triangleq P(e \mid B_i) = \alpha \, \frac{PROB(B_i)}{prob(B_i)} = \alpha \left(\frac{0.70}{0.30}, \frac{0.25}{0.30}, \frac{0.05}{0.40} \right)$$

$$= \alpha \, (2.330, \, 0.833, \, 0.125). \tag{2.65}$$

Indeed, in Section 2.2.2 we saw that the likelihood vector requires no absolute probability assessments and therefore avoids the difficulties associated with non-propositional evidence (e.g., the visual stimulus in the candlelight story). We also argued that the assumption of conditional independence means that the likelihood vector is the only stable component in the relation between the evidence and the impacted variable B, making it more reliable to assess than the final product $PROB(B_i)$. Thus, an alternate way of viewing the impact of sensory experience on one's knowledge is to replace the former by a likelihood vector impinging on the basis B. (A similar idea was advanced by Field [1978].)

To demonstrate the volatility of the assumption in Eq. (2.59), let us choose an example where it is obviously violated.

Case 2 A — e — B: Imagine that the main interest of our candlelight observer lies not in the color of the cloth but rather in the chemical composition of the candle wax. The agent inspects the color of the cloth, adjusts his belief from $prob(B_i)$ to $PROB(B_i)$, and then wonders how to update $prob(A)$, where A is the proposition that the wax is a notoriously cheap brand known to produce flames deficient in violet content.

Are we justified in using Jeffrey's Rule? Since the color of the cloth (B_i) is of no relevance to A prior to the observation, we have $prob(A \mid B_i) = prob\ A$. If we blindly apply Eq. (2.60), we obtain a paradoxical result,

$$PROB\ (A) = \sum_i prob(A)\ PROB\ (B_i) = prob\ (A), \tag{2.66}$$

which states that no matter how violet or greenish the cloth looks under the candlelight, the observer's belief regarding the makeup of the wax ought to remain unaltered.

Is there any information in the story that should warn us against applying Jeffrey's Rule here? Modern Bayesians claim that even though we lack the knowledge required for precise description of the measurement process, our qualitative understanding of the process is sufficient to alert us to the falsity of $P(A \mid B_i, e) = P(A \mid B_i)$ and thus protect us from drawing a false conclusion like Eq. (2.66). Colloquially, we say that in Case 1, the color of the cloth "stood between" the evidence and A (the salability of the cloth), while in Case 2 it was the evidence that mediated between the colors and A (the brand of wax), as shown in Figure 2.4.

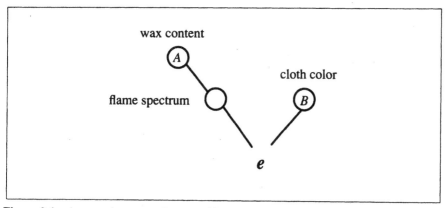

Figure 2.4. *A network representing an evidence (e) mediating between A and B.*

One might argue that Jeffrey's original account also prevents us from applying his rule to Case 2 because A presumably should qualify as "one of the n propositions whose probabilities were directly affected by the passage of experience." But the criterion by which this passage of experience can be termed "direct" is rather hard to define. In other words, it is hard to see how the visual experience bears directly on the nature of the wax (A) when it is the flame that mediates between the two (see Figure 2.4). If anything, B seems more directly affected by e than A is; the agent's judgment about the color was reported first, and color bears a closer semantic relation to visual experience than wax chemistry does.

If the road map outlining one's passage of experience is so crucial for understanding the structure of stories (i.e., which propositions should be affected by the evidence and how), it is unfortunate that the philosophical literature on probability kinematics does not provide a more complete analysis of this crucial source of information. Evidently, some believed that this road map is so deeply entrenched in human intuition that no further explication is required.

Neo-Bayesian philosophers go one step beyond Jeffrey. They say any assertions one wishes to make about "passage of experience" ought to be explicated formally, using the familiar syntax of probability calculus. For example, one's intuition that A is not directly affected by the passage of experience ought to be written in the format of Eq. (2.62), treating e as a genuine propositional entity. On the surface, this requirement seems vacuous. If one interprets Eq. (2.62) merely as a notation for expressing intuitions about the "passage of experience," then Bayes conditionalization—$P(A \mid e)$—ceases to be a statement about the numeric magnitudes of $P(A)$ and $P(A \mid e)$ and becomes no more informative than the verbal, intuitive sentences it purports to replace. However, there is a profound significance to the use of the $P(* \mid *)$ syntax instead of some other notation.

First, it embodies the claim that passages of experience have traffic laws of their own and that these laws are similar, if not identical, to those governing Bayes conditionalization. For example, one traffic law states that it is inconsistent for an agent to assert, "B stands between e and a pair of propositions $\{A_1, A_2\}$" without also asserting, "B and A_1 together stand between e and A_2." This consistency requirement holds both in Bayes conditionalization and in the road map metaphor. Thus, even if one insists that statements such as Eq. (2.62) represent qualitative facts about the passage of experience, not conditional probabilities, by agreeing to manipulate these sentences by the rules of Bayes conditionalization one is guaranteed never to violate any of the traffic laws that govern the roadmaps of experience. The question of whether graphical representation of dependencies can yield similar guarantees is treated in Chapter 3.

Second, the use of the $P(* \mid *)$ syntax to define criteria such as Eq. (2.62) suggests procedures a person should use to test mentally the validity of the criterion in any given situation. Eq. (2.62) instructs a person to imagine first that the cloth has a definite color, say $B_i = Green$, then test whether any visual experience e could significantly sway the belief in A one way or the other. In Case 1 the answer is clearly no, because the salability was proclaimed to be a function only of the cloth color. In Case 2, however, this mental exercise would evoke some vivid scenarios that could sway our belief. For example, a green cloth that appears totally violet under the candlelight would induce a different opinion about the candle's wax than a green cloth that appears totally yellow under candlelight. Thus, Bayes conditionalization has syntactic and psychological merits beyond the numerical definition

$$P(A \mid B) = \frac{P(A, B)}{P(B)}$$

that appears in most textbooks on probability theory.

Case 2 carries two messages. First, we demonstrated again that even when we cannot describe precisely the observed evidence e, the qualitative elements of the story are sufficient for judging whether the situation meets Jeffrey's criterion, or the conditional independence requirement $P(A \mid B_i, e) = P(A \mid B_i)$. Second, we demonstrated that Jeffrey's Rule is invalid not only when A is directly affected by the passage of experience; it is enough that A branches off someplace on the path from e to B, as in Figure 2.4. A more striking example is provided by the diamond structure of Figure 2.5. Here, B is clearly more directly affected by e than A is, as B stands between e and A, yet Eq. (2.62) will be violated.

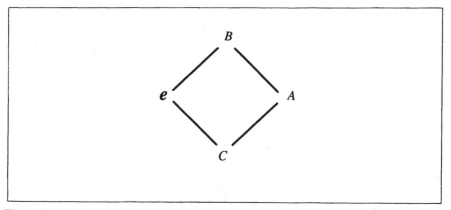

Figure 2.5. *A is not affected directly by the passage of experience, yet the observation e changes the conditional degree of belief in A given B.*

So far, we have used the diagrams in Figures 2.3 through 2.5 primarily as mnemonic devices to distinguish among the cases discussed and to make an occasional association with Jeffrey's "passage of experience" notion. However, the preceding discussion also demonstrates a rather useful pattern produced by graphical representations (Figures 2.3 through 2.5): Jeffrey's Rule is applicable if and only if B separates A from e. This may be what Jeffrey meant by requiring that A not be "one of the n propositions whose probabilities were directly affected by the passage of experience." The notion of *separation* and its relation to information independence will be given formal treatment in Chapter 3.

SUMMARY

Jeffrey's Rule of belief updating was devised to replace Bayes conditioning in cases where the evidence cannot be articulated propositionally. Our analysis shows that to determine whether the rule is valid in any specific case, one must have topological knowledge about one's belief structure, namely, which beliefs are directly related and which are only indirectly related. If such knowledge is available, it can be faithfully represented by the syntax of conditional independence sentences, and traditional Bayes' methods can be used to update beliefs. Thus, the question arises whether it is *ever* necessary to avoid conditionalization in formal belief updating.

Since simple criteria based on graphical considerations lead to conclusions that match our intuition, perhaps human intuition itself can be represented by networks of relations, and perhaps intuitive judgments are really mental tracings of those networks. These suggestions motivate the discussion of dependency graphs in Chapter 3.

2.4 BIBLIOGRAPHICAL AND HISTORICAL REMARKS

The Italian mathematician Gerolamo Cardano (1501-1576) is believed to be the first to have formulated the notion of probability in gambling in terms of the number of distinguishable ways that events may occur. This development marks a radical (if somewhat tardy) change in cultural attitudes toward uncertainty. Although fascination with the unpredictability of gambling devices goes back to the time of the Pharaohs [David 1962], these devices were not perceived as possessing inherent elements of uncertainty; instead, they were seen as means of communicating with a source of knowledge (e.g., deity) that was basically deterministic [Hacking 1975].

Cardano's "objective" view of probability developed into a rather sophisticated mathematical theory of combinatorics, in the hands of Fermat (1601-1665), Pascal (1623-1662), Huygens (1629-1695), James Bernoulli (1654-1705), DeMoivre (1667- 1754), and LaPlace (1749-1827), until in 1837 Denis Poisson gave it a new twist by defining probability as a limit of a long-run relative frequency. Emile Borel (1871-1956) and A. N. Kolmogorov are credited with developing the modern axiomatic foundations of mathematical probability, of which Eqs. (2.1) through (2.3) are a simplified version [Kolmogorov 1950]. Kolmogorov's axiomatization of probability is responsible for the unfortunate tradition of treating Eq. (2.8) as a definition of conditional probability, rather than a theorem that follows from more primitive axioms about conditioning.

In parallel to these mathematical developments, an alternative view of probability came into being with Bernoulli's suggestion that probability is a "degree of confidence" that an individual attaches to an uncertain event. This concept, aided by Bayes' Rule [Bayes 1763], blossomed in the writings of LaPlace and De Morgan and later in the works of Keynes [1921] and Jeffreys [1939]. However, the established communities of statisticians and mathematical probabilists viewed this "subjectivist" intrusion with suspicion. It was not until the 1950s, with the development of statistical decision theory (see Section 6.5), that

Bayesian methods gained their current momentum. The two defining attributes of the Bayesian school are (1) willingness to accept subjective opinions as an expedient substitute for raw data and (2) adherence to Bayes conditionalization as the primary mechanism for updating beliefs in light of new information. The articles in Kyburg and Smokler [1980] deal with the philosophical underpinning of the Bayesian revival.

A critical analysis of Bayes conditionalization can be found in Shafer [1982, 1985, 1986b]: According to Shafer, it was DeMoivre who first formulated the idea that the occurrence of one event can change the probability of another and who proved the multiplication rule of Eq. (2.9) using the method of expectation. Bayes gave a version of DeMoivre's proof for his rule (Eq. (2.13)), while interpreting it as providing the subjective probabilities of past events. Exercise 2.2 gives a modern version of the example used in Bayes' original essay [Bayes 1763]. Alternatives to Bayes conditioning—including Jeffrey's rule and Dempster's rule (see Chapter 9)—have been discussed by Diaconis and Zabell [1986]. Jeffrey's rule constitutes the minimum entropy extension of *prob* (·), and Lemmer and Barth [1982] first proposed it for belief updating in expert systems. The formal identity between Jeffrey's rule and virtual conditionalization (as in Eq. (2.65)) renders the two semantically equivalent, i.e., beliefs updated by Jeffrey's rule cannot be distinguished from those updated by Bayes' conditionalization on some virtual evidence. Another alternative to Bayes' conditionalization, called *imaging*, was introduced by Lewis [1976] and was used to represent counterfactual conditionals.

The Three Prisoners story is one of many well-known puzzles that illustrate the need for specifying the query process in tasks involving inference from observations (see Exercise 2.6). Shafer [1985] calls this query process a *protocol* and views it as a disadvantage of Bayes conditioning, since we must assign probabilities for all possible ways information may be obtained. Our discussion in Section 2.3.2 attempts to convince the reader that formalisms that ignore the query process altogether (see Chapter 9 for examples) are bound to be insensitive to an important component of human reasoning. In the Thousand Prisoners story, for example, such systems will not attach any significance to discovering the query after seeing the list; beliefs will remain the same, based solely on the one-in-two model (see Exercise 9.5b).

Our treatment of virtual evidence (Section 2.2.2), using the vector of likelihood-ratios, sidesteps the requirement of specifying a full protocol in advance (see Exercise 2.7). This option expands the repertoire of Bayes analysis by permitting us to assimilate evidence by means other than straight conditioning, and it simultaneously facilitates the manipulation of belief updates within the traditional syntax of probability calculus.

There are, of course, items of information that cannot and should not be handled as evidential data, but must be treated as constraints on—or specificational adjustments to—the probabilistic model we currently possess. Conditional sentences are typical examples of such information. For example, the sentence "If Joe goes to the party Mary will not go" must be treated as a meta-level constraint in the form of conditional probability and not as evidence to be conditioned upon (see Exercises 10.1 and 10.2). On the other hand, the sentence "Joe and Mary will not both go to the party," though logically equivalent to the previous sentence, is a form of information that can be treated as evidence for conditionalization.   The difference is that conditionalization changes the probability of Joe's going to the party while constraint-based updating leaves this probability intact. The purpose of the English word *if* is to convey a distinction between these two modes of assimilating information and to instruct the listener to refrain from straight conditioning.

The papers in Harper et al. [1981] provide a cross section of the philosophical literature dealing with conditionals. Section 10.2 illustrates how conditional information can be absorbed in the form of specification constraints, following the work of Adams [1975].

The treatment of Jeffrey's rule (Section 2.3) is further expanded in Pearl [1990][1].

Recent works on foundational issues of probability have focused on higher-order probabilities[2][3] (see also Section 7.3) and on the development of logics for reasoning about probabilities.[4][5][6]

[1]   Pearl, J. Jeffrey's Rule, Passage of Experience, and *Neo*-Bayesianism. H.E. Kyburg, Jr. et al., (eds.), *Knowledge Representation and Defeasible Reasoning*, 1990, Kluwer Academic Publishers, 245-264.

[2]   Haddawy, P., and Frisch, A.M. Modal logics of higher-order probability. In Shachter et al., (eds.), *Uncertainty in AI* 4, North Holland, 1990, 133-148.

[3]   Fagin, R., and Halpern, J. Y., Reasoning about Knowledge and Probability: Preliminary Report, in *Proceedings, 2nd Conference on Theoretical Aspects of Reasoning about Knowledge*, Morgan-Kaufmann, 1988, 277-293.

[4]   Fagin, R., Halpern, J.Y., and Megiddo, N., A logic for reasoning about probabilities, *Information and Computation*, 87 (1/2), 1990, 78-128.

[5]   Bacchus, F., *Representing and reasoning with probabilistic knowledge*, Cambridge, MA: The MIT Press, 1990.

[6]   Kyburg, H., Evidential Probability, *Proceedings IJCAI-91*, Sydney, Australia, 1991, 1196-1203.

Exercises

2.1.   There are three urns labeled one, two, and three. These urns contain, respectively, three white and three black balls, four white and two black balls and one white and two black balls. An experiment consists of selecting an urn at random, then drawing a ball from it.

    a.   Find the probability of selecting urn 2 and drawing a black ball.

    b.   Find the probability of drawing a black ball.

    c.   Find the conditional probability that urn 2 was selected, given that a black ball was drawn.

It may be helpful to label the possible outcomes $(1, B)$, $(1, W)$, $(2, B)$, $(2, W)$, $(3, B)$, $(3, W)$.

2.2.   A billiard table has unit length, measured from left to right. A ball is rolled on this table, and when it stops, a partition is placed at its stopping position, a distance x from the left end of the table. A second ball is now rolled between the left end of the table and the partition, and its stopping position, y, is measured.

    a.   Answer qualitatively: How does knowledge of y affect our belief about x? Is x more likely to be near y, far from y, or near the midpoint between y and 1?

    b.   Justify your answer for (**a**) by quantitative analysis. Assume each stopping position is uniformly distributed over its feasible range.

2.3.   Let the hypothesis variable $H = \{H_1, H_2, H_3, H_4\}$ stand for the following set of exhaustive and mutually exclusive conditions

    H_1 = *No burglary, animal entry.*
    H_2 = *Attempted burglary, window break-in.*
    H_3 = *Attempted burglary, door break-in.*
    H_4 = *No burglary, no entry.*

with prior probabilities $P(H_i) = (0.099, 0.009, 0.001, 0.891)$. Let the alarm system contain two detectors, E^1 and E^2, with the following sensitivity matrices:

	e_1^1	e_2^1	e_3^1
H_1	0.5	0.4	0.1
H_2	0.06	0.5	0.44
H_3	0.5	0.1	0.4
H_4	1.0	0	0

	e_1^2	e_2^2	e_3^2
H_1	0.8	0.1	0.1
H_2	0.8	0.1	0.1
H_3	0.1	0.1	0.8
H_4	0.9	0.05	0.05.

a. What is the probability of burglary if detector E^1 is *OFF* ($E^1 = e_1^1$) and E^2 is *HIGH* ($E^2 = e_3^2$)?

b. Repeat problem (a) under the following conditions:

- A reliable witness claims to have heard detector E^1, but she cannot tell whether it was *High sound* (e_3^1) or *Low sound* (e_2^1).

- A second reliable witness claims detector E^2 was definitely not in *High sound* state but there is a slight (5%) chance that it issued a *Low sound* (e_2^2).

c. You are considering adding to your alarm system a new detector E^3, with the following sensitivity matrix:

	OFF	*ON*
H_1	0.1	0.9
H_2	0.9	0.1
H_3	0.9	0.1
H_4	1	0

What is the probability that E^3 will be activated under the conditions described in problem (b)?

d. You are considering installing a monitor E^4 at your office, connected directly to detector E^1. The relation between E^1 and E^4 is characterized by the matrix

	$E^4 = OFF$	$E^4 = ON$
$E^1 = OFF$	0.9	0.1
$E^1 = LOW$	0.2	0.8
$E^1 = HIGH$	0.1	0.9 .

What is the probability that E^4 will turn on under the conditions of problem (**b**).

2.4. **a.** Verify which entries in Table 1 (page 54) are unconditionally supported by probability theory and which must be qualified with additional assumptions about context.

b. Which of the entries are violated in the Three Prisoners story.

2.5. How would Jeffrey's rule handle the Three Prisoners problem?

2.6. I have three cups and one ball. I put the ball under one of the cups and mix up the cups. You must pick the cup with the ball under it. You choose one without inspecting its content. Then I remove one of the other cups and show you that it does not have a ball under it. Now I give you the chance to change your choice of cups. Should you do it? How is this puzzle related to the Three Prisoners story?

2.7. **a.** Formulate Case 2 of the candlelight story using a Bayesian approach, and determine what additional information is required for computing $P(A \mid e)$. (Recall: e is non-propositional, so the absolute value of $P(e \mid \cdot)$ is meaningless).

b. Assume reasonable values for the missing information and compute $P(A \mid e)$.

Chapter *3*

MARKOV AND BAYESIAN NETWORKS:

Two Graphical Representations of Probabilistic Knowledge

Probability is not really about numbers;
it is about the structure of reasoning.
— G. Shafer

In this chapter, we shall seek effective graphic representations of the dependencies embedded in probabilistic models. First, we will uncover a set of axioms for the probabilistic relation "X is independent of Y, given Z" and offer the set as a formal definition for the notion of informational dependency. Given an initial set of independence relationships, the axioms permit us to infer new independencies by nonnumeric, logical manipulations. Using this axiomatic basis, we will identify structural properties of probabilistic models that can be captured by graphical representations and compare two such representations, *Markov networks* and *Bayesian networks*. A Markov network is an undirected graph whose links represent symmetrical probabilistic dependencies, while a Bayesian network is a directed acyclic graph whose arrows represent causal influences or class-property relationships. After establishing formal semantics for both network types, we shall explore their power and limitations as knowledge representation schemes in inference systems.

77

3.1 *FROM NUMERICAL TO GRAPHICAL REPRESENTATIONS*

3.1.1 *Introduction*

Scholarly textbooks on probability theory have created the impression that to construct an adequate representation of probabilistic knowledge, we must literally define a *joint distribution function* $P(x_1,...,x_n)$ on all propositions and their combinations, this function serving as the primary basis for all inferred judgments. While useful for maintaining consistency and proving mathematical theorems, this view of probability theory is totally inadequate for representing human reasoning.

Consider, for example, the problem of encoding an arbitrary joint distribution, $P(x_1,...,x_n)$, for n propositional variables. To store $P(x_1,...,x_n)$ explicitly would require a table with 2^n entries, an unthinkably large number by any standard. Even if we found some economical way of storing $P(x_1,...,x_n)$ —or rules for generating it—there would remain the problem of computing from it the probabilities of propositions people consider interesting. For example, computing the marginal probability $P(x_i)$ would require summing $P(x_1,...,x_n)$ over all 2^{n-1} combinations of the remaining $n-1$ variables. Similarly, computing the conditional probability $P(x_i \mid x_j)$ via its textbook definition

$$P(x_i \mid x_j) = \frac{P(x_i, x_j)}{P(x_j)}$$

would entail dividing two marginal probabilities, each a result of summation over an exponentially large number of variable combinations. Human performance shows the opposite pattern of complexity: probabilistic judgments on a small number of propositions (especially two-component conditional statements such as the likelihood that a patient suffering from a given disease will develop a certain type of complication) are issued swiftly and reliably, while judging the likelihood of a conjunction of propositions entails much difficulty and hesitancy. This suggests that the elementary building blocks of human knowledge are not entries of a joint-distribution table. Rather, they are low-order marginal and conditional probabilities defined over small clusters of propositions.

Another problem with purely numerical representations of probabilistic information is their lack of *psychological meaningfulness*. The numerical representation can produce coherent probability measures for all propositional sentences, but it often leads to computations that a human reasoner would not use. As a result, the process leading from the premises to the conclusions cannot be followed, tested, or justified by the users, or even the designers, of the reasoning system. Even simple tasks such as computing the impact of a piece of evidence $E = e$ on a hypothesis $H = h$ via

$$P(h \mid e) = \frac{P(h, e)}{P(e)} = \frac{\displaystyle\sum_{x_i \,:\, X_i \neq H, E} P(x_1, ..., x_n)}{\displaystyle\sum_{x_i \,:\, X_i \neq E} P(x_1, ..., x_n)}$$

require a horrendous number of meaningless arithmetic operations, unsupported by familiar mental processes.

THE QUALITATIVE NOTION OF DEPENDENCE

The most striking inadequacy of traditional theories of probability lies in the way these theories address the notion of independence. The traditional definition of independence uses equality of numerical quantities, as in $P(x, y) = P(x) \cdot P(y)$, suggesting that one must test whether the joint distribution of X and Y is equal to the product of their marginals in order to determine whether X and Y are independent. By contrast, people can easily and confidently detect dependencies, even though they may not be able to provide precise numerical estimates of probabilities.

A person who is reluctant to estimate the probability of being burglarized the next day or of having a nuclear war within five years can nevertheless state with ease whether the two events are dependent, namely, whether knowing the truth of one proposition will alter the belief in the other. Likewise, people tend to judge the three-place relationship of conditional dependency (i.e., X influences Y, given Z) with clarity, conviction, and consistency. For example, knowing the time of the last pickup from a bus stop is undeniably relevant for assessing how long we must wait for the next bus. However, once we learn the whereabouts of the next bus, the previous knowledge no longer provides useful information. These commonsense judgments are issued qualitatively, without reference to numerical probabilities, and could not possibly rely on arithmetic manipulation of precise probabilities.

Evidently, the notions of relevance and dependence are far more basic to human reasoning than the numerical values attached to probability judgments. In a commonsense reasoning system, therefore, the language used for representing probabilistic information should allow assertions about dependency relationships to be expressed qualitatively, directly, and explicitly. The verification of dependencies should not require lengthy numerical manipulations but should be accomplished swiftly with a few primitive operations on the salient features of the representation scheme. Once asserted, these dependency relationships should remain a part of the representation scheme, impervious to variations in numerical inputs. For example, one should be able to assert categorically that a nuclear disaster is independent of a home burglary; the system should retain and reaffirm this independence despite changes in the estimated likelihoods of these and other events in the system.

Making effective use of information about dependencies is essential in reasoning. If we have acquired a body of knowledge K and now wish to assess the truth of proposition A, it is important to know whether it is worthwhile to consult another proposition B, which is not in K. In other words, before we examine B, we need to know if its truth value can generate new information that is relevant to A and is not available from K. Without this knowledge, an inference engine might spend precious time on derivations bearing no relevance to the task at hand. Relevance information, if available, can confine the engine's attention to derivations that truly are needed for the target conclusion. But how can we encode relevance information in a symbolic system?

Explicit encoding is clearly impractical; the number of (A, B, K) combinations needed is astronomical, because relevance and dependency are relationships that vary depending on the information available at any given time. Acquisition of new facts may destroy existing dependencies as well as create new ones. For example, learning a child's age destroys the dependency between height and reading ability, and learning that a patient suffers from a given symptom creates new dependencies among the diseases that could account for the symptom. The first kind of change will be called *normal* as it fits the normal picture that learning reduces dependencies, and the second will be called *induced* as it permits learned facts to induce new dependencies. What logic would facilitate these two modes of reasoning?

In probability theory, the notion of informational relevance is given quantitative underpinning through the device of *conditional independence,* which successfully captures our intuition about how dependencies should change in response to new facts. A proposition A is said to be independent of B, given the information K, if

$$P(A \mid B, K) = P(A \mid K),$$

namely, if once K is given, the probability of A will not be affected by the discovery of B. This formulation can represent both normal and induced dependencies: A and B could be marginally dependent (i.e., dependent when K is unknown) and become conditionally independent given K; conversely, A and B could be marginally independent and become dependent given K. Thus, in principle, probability theory could provide the machinery for identifying the propositions that are relevant to each other under a given state of knowledge.

But we have already argued that it is unreasonable to expect people or machines seeking relevance information to resort to numerical equality tests. Human behavior suggests that relevance information is inferred qualitatively from the organizational structure of human memory, not calculated from numerical values assigned to its components. Accordingly, it would be interesting to explore how assertions about relevance can be inferred qualitatively, and whether assertions equivalent to those made about probabilistic dependencies can be derived *logically* without reference to numerical quantities. This task will be discussed in Section 3.1.2, which establishes an axiomatic basis for probabilistic dependencies and examines whether the set of axioms matches our intuitive notion of informational relevancy.

WHY GRAPHS?

.A logic of dependency might be useful for verifying whether a set of dependencies asserted by an agent is consistent and whether a new dependency follows from the initial set. We could not guarantee, however, that the verification would be tractable or that any sequence of inferences would match mental steps taken by humans. To facilitate psychological meaningfulness, we must make sure most derivations in the logic correspond to simple local operations on structures depicting commonsense associations. We call such structures *dependency graphs.*

The nodes in these graphs represent propositional variables, and the arcs represent local dependencies among conceptually related propositions. Graph representations meet our earlier requirements of explicitness, saliency, and stability. The links in the graph permit us to express directly and qualitatively the dependence relationships, and the graph topology displays these relationships explicitly and preserves them, under any assignment of numerical parameters.

It is not surprising, therefore, that graphs are the most common metaphor for conceptual dependencies. Models of human memory are often portrayed in terms of associational graphs (e.g., semantic networks [Woods 1975], constraint networks [Montanari 1974], inference networks [Duda, Hart, and Nilsson 1976], conceptual dependencies [Schank 1972], and conceptual structures [Sowa 1984]). Graph concepts are so entrenched in our language (e.g., "threads of thoughts," "lines of reasoning," "connected ideas," "far-fetched arguments") that one wonders if people can reason any other way except by tracing links and arrows and paths in some mental representation of concepts and relations. The next question to ask is what aspects of informational relevance and probabilistic dependence can be represented graphically. In other words, what types of dependencies and independencies are deducible from the topological properties of a graph? This question will be addressed in Sections 3.2 (undirected graphs) and 3.3 (directed graphs).

Despite the prevailing use of graphs as metaphors for communicating and reasoning about dependencies, the task of capturing informational dependencies by graphs is not at all trivial. We have no problem configuring a graph which represents phenomena with explicit notions of neighborhood or adjacency (e.g., families, electronic circuits, communication networks). However, in modeling conceptual relations, such as causation, association, and relevance, it is often hard to distinguish direct neighbors from indirect neighbors; constructing a graph for the relation therefore becomes more delicate. The notion of conditional independence in probability theory is a perfect example. For a given probability distribution P and any three variables X, Y, Z, it is straightforward to verify whether knowing Z renders X independent of Y, but P does not dictate which variables should be regarded as direct neighbors. Thus, many different topologies might be used to display P's dependencies. We shall also see that some useful properties of dependencies and relevancies cannot be represented graphically. The challenge is to devise graphical schemes that minimize these deficiencies; Markov and Bayesian networks are two such schemes.

CHAPTER OVERVIEW

This chapter is organized as follows: Section 3.1.2 uncovers a set of axioms for the probabilistic relation "X is independent of Y, given Z" and offers the set as a formal definition for the notion of informational dependency. Sections 3.1.3 and 3.1.4 examine those properties of dependencies that can be captured by graphical representations. Sections 3.2 and 3.3 compare two such representations, *Markov networks* and *Bayesian networks*. For both network types, we shall establish (1) a formal description of the dependencies portrayed by the networks, (2) an axiomatic description of the class of dependencies that can be captured by the network, (3) methods of constructing the network from either hard data or subjective judgments, and (4) a summary of properties relevant to the network's use as a knowledge representation scheme.

3.1.2 An Axiomatic Basis for Probabilistic Dependencies

NOTATION AND DEFINITIONS

We will consider a finite set U of discrete random variables (also called partitions or attributes), where each variable $X \in U$ may take on values from a finite domain D_X. We will use capital letters for variable names (e.g., X, Y, Z) and lowercase letters (e.g., x, y, z) for specific values taken by variables. Sets of variables will be denoted by boldfaced capital letters (e.g., X, Y, Z), and assignments of values to the variables in these sets (also called *configurations*), will be denoted by boldfaced lowercase letters (e.g., x, y, z). For example, if Z stands for the set of variables $\{X, Y\}$, then z represents the configuration $\{x, y\}$: $x \in D_X$, $y \in D_Y$. When the distinction between variables and sets of variables requires special emphasis, Greek letters α, β, γ,... will be used to represent individual variables.

We shall repeatedly use the short notation $P(x)$ for the probabilities $P(X = x)$, $x \in D_X$, and we will write $P(z)$ for the set of variables $Z = \{X, Y\}$, meaning

$$P(Z = z) = P(X = x, Y = y) \qquad x \in D_X, y \in D_Y.$$

(In the rare event that we run out of symbols, variable names will be used as arguments of probability statements, e.g., $P(X, Y)$, which is equivalent to $P(x, y)$.)

DEFINITION: *Let $U = \{\alpha, \beta, \ldots\}$ be a finite set of variables with discrete values. Let $P(\cdot)$ be a joint probability function over the variables in U, and let $X, Y,$ and Z stand for any three subsets of variables in U. X and Y are said to be **conditionally independent given Z** if*

$$P(x \mid y, z) = P(x \mid z) \quad whenever \quad P(y, z) > 0. \tag{3.1}$$

Eq. (3.1) is a terse way of saying the following: for any configuration x of the variables in the set X and for any configurations y and z of the variables in Y and Z satisfying $P(Y = y, Z = z) > 0$, we have

$$P(X = x \mid Y = y, Z = z) = P(X = x \mid Z = z). \tag{3.2}$$

We will use the notation $I(X,Z,Y)_P$ or simply $I(X,Z,Y)$ to denote the conditional independence of X and Y given Z; thus,

$$I(X, Z, Y)_P \text{ iff } P(x \mid y, z) = P(x \mid z) \tag{3.3}$$

for all values $x, y,$ and z such that $P(y, z) > 0$. Unconditional independence (also called *marginal independence*) will be denoted by $I(X, \varnothing, Y)$, i.e.,

$$I(X, \varnothing, Y) \text{ iff } P(x \mid y) = P(x) \text{ whenever } P(y) > 0. \tag{3.4}$$

Note that $I(X, Z, Y)$ implies the conditional independence of all pairs of variables $\alpha \in X$ and $\beta \in Y$, but the converse is not necessarily true.

The following is a partial list of (equivalent) properties satisfied by the conditional independence relation $I(X, Z, Y)$ [Lauritzen 1982]:

$$I(X, Z, Y) \Longleftrightarrow P(x, y \mid z) = P(x \mid z) P(y \mid z), \tag{3.5a}$$

$$I(X, Z, Y) \Longleftrightarrow \exists f, g : P(x, y, z) = f(x, z) g(y, z), \tag{3.5b}$$

$$I(X, Z, Y) \Longleftrightarrow P(x, y, z) = P(x \mid z) P(y, z). \tag{3.5c}$$

The proof of these properties can be derived by elementary means from Eq. (3.3) and the basic axioms of probability theory. The properties are based on the numeric representation of P and therefore would be inadequate as an axiomatic system.

AXIOMATIC CHARACTERIZATION

We now ask what logical conditions, void of any reference to numerical forms, should constrain the relationship $I(X, Z, Y)$ if in some probability model P it stands for the statement "X is independent of Y, given that we know Z."

THEOREM 1: *Let X, Y, and Z be three disjoint subsets of variables from **U**. If $I(X, Z, Y)$ stands for the relation "X is independent of Y, given Z" in some probabilistic model P, then I must satisfy the following four independent conditions:*

- *Symmetry:*
$$I(X, Z, Y) \Longleftrightarrow I(Y, Z, X) \tag{3.6a}$$

- *Decomposition:*
$$I(X, Z, Y \cup W) \Longrightarrow I(X, Z, Y) \ \& \ I(X, Z, W) \tag{3.6b}$$

- *Weak Union:*
$$I(X, Z, Y \cup W) \Longrightarrow I(X, Z \cup W, Y) \tag{3.6c}$$

- *Contraction:*
$$I(X, Z, Y) \ \& \ I(X, Z \cup Y, W) \Longrightarrow I(X, Z, Y \cup W). \tag{3.6d}$$

If P is strictly positive, then a fifth condition holds:

- *Intersection:*
$$I(X, Z \cup W, Y) \ \& \ I(X, Z \cup Y, W) \Longrightarrow I(X, Z, Y \cup W). \tag{3.6e}$$

REMARKS:

1. The symbol $\cup$ in $Y \cup W$ represents a union of variable sets and should not be confused with logical disjunction. More specifically, it stands for the *conjunction* of events asserted by instantiating the set union $Y \cup W$. For example, $I(X, \varnothing, Y \cup W)$ stands for

    $$P(X = x, Y = y, W = w) = P(X = x) \, P(Y = y, W = w) \ \forall \, x, y, w.$$

    A simpler notation, $I(X, \varnothing, YW)$, will occasionally be used.

2. The requirement that the arguments of $I(\cdot)$ be disjoint was made for the sake of future clarity. Theorem 1 can be extended to include overlapping subsets as well, using an additional axiom,

    $$I(X, Z, Z). \tag{3.6f}$$

From Eqs. (3.6*a*) through (3.6*d*) and Eq. (3.6*f*) one can prove the theorem

$$I(X, Z, Y) \Longleftrightarrow I(X - Z, Z, Y - Z),$$

stating that the parts of X and Y that do not overlap Z are sufficient to determine whether $I(X, Z, Y)$ holds. Thus, once $I(\cdot)$ is defined on the set of disjoint triplets (X, Y, Z) it is also defined on the set of all triplets. Note that both $I(X, Z, Z)$ and $I(X, Z, \varnothing)$ follow from Eq. (3.3).

3. The proof of Theorem 1 can be derived from Eq. (3.3) and from the basic axioms of probability theory [Dawid 1979]. That Eqs. (3.6*a*) through (3.6*e*) are logically independent can be demonstrated by letting U contain four elements and showing that it is always possible to contrive a subset I of triplets (from the subsets of U) that violates one property and satisfies the other four.

INTUITIVE INTERPRETATION OF THE AXIOMS

Eqs. (3.6*a*) through (3.6*e*) can be interpreted as follows: The *symmetry* axiom states that in any state of knowledge Z, if Y tells us nothing new about X, then X tells us nothing new about Y. The *decomposition* axiom asserts that if two combined items of information are judged irrelevant to X, then each separate item is irrelevant as well. The *weak union* axiom states that learning irrelevant information W cannot help the irrelevant information Y become relevant to X. The *contraction* axiom states that if we judge W irrelevant to X after learning some irrelevant information Y, then W must have been irrelevant before we learned Y. Together, the weak union and contraction properties mean that irrelevant information should not alter the relevance of other propositions in the system; what was relevant remains relevant, and what was irrelevant remains irrelevant. The *intersection* axiom states that unless Y affects X when W is held constant or W affects X when Y is held constant, neither W nor Y nor their combination can affect X.

GRAPHICAL INTERPRETATIONS

The operational significance of these axioms and their role as inference rules can best be explained with a graph metaphor. Let $I(X, Z, Y)$ stand for the phrase "Z separates X from Y," i.e., "The removal of a set Z of nodes from the graph (together with their associated edges) would render the nodes in X disconnected from those in Y." The validity of Eqs. (3.6*a*) through (3.6*e*) is clearly depicted by the chain $X - Z - Y - W$ and by the schematics of Figure 3.1.

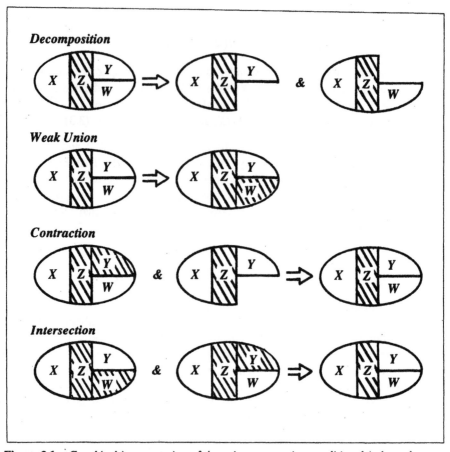

Figure 3.1. *Graphical interpretation of the axioms governing conditional independence.*

Symmetry simply states that if Z separates X from Y, it also separates Y from X. Decomposition asserts that if Z separates X from the compound set $S = Y \cup W$, it also separates X from every subset of S. Weak union provides conditions under which a separating set Z can be augmented by additional elements W and still separate X from Y. The condition is that the added subset W should come from the section of space that was initially separated from X by Z. Contraction provides conditions for reducing the size of the separating set; it permits the deletion of a subset Y from the separator $Z \cup Y$ if the remaining part, Z, separates the deleted part, Y, from X. Intersection states that if within some set of variables $S = X \cup Y \cup Z \cup W$, X can be separated from the rest of S by two different subsets, S_1 and S_2 (i.e., $S_1 = Z \cup Y$ and $S_2 = Z \cup W$), then the intersection of S_1 and S_2 is sufficient to separate X from the rest of S.

THE INTERSECTION AXIOM AND STRICTLY POSITIVE DISTRIBUTIONS

The intersection axiom is the only one that requires $P(x) > 0$ for all x, and it will not hold if the variables in U are constrained by logical dependencies. For instance, if Y stands for the proposition "The water temperature is above freezing" and W stands for "The water temperature is above 32°F," then knowing the truth of either proposition clearly renders the other superfluous. Contrary to the intersection axiom, however, Y and W might still be relevant to a third proposition X ("We will enjoy swimming in that water," for example). The intersection axiom will hold if we regard these logical constraints as having some small probability ε of being violated.

The assumption $P \geq \varepsilon > 0$ means every event or combination of events, no matter how outrageous, has some chance of being true. When examining empirical facts, making this assumption is not as strange as it seems. For example, it is possible for the water temperature to be above freezing but below 32°F (if it is very salty, for instance). Once we accept such a possibility we must reject the statement that knowing either of these facts renders the other superfluous relative to any X. If X represents our concern about swimming in the water, then the temperature becomes the relevant fact, and whether it is frozen is irrelevant. On the other hand, if our interest is ice fishing, the frozenness, not the temperature, is relevant. This is exactly what Eq. (3.6e) claims: if two properties exert influence on X, then (at a sufficiently high level of detail) it is impossible that each of the two properties will render the other irrelevant. Such symmetrical exclusion is possible only with analytical or definitional properties (e.g., Y = "The water temperature is above 32°F," W = "The water temperature is not equal to or lower than 32°F") and not with properties defined by independent empirical tests.

GRAPHS VS. GRAPHOIDS

Decomposition and weak union are strikingly similar to vertex separation in graphs, but are much weaker. In graphs, two sets of vertices are said to be separated if there exists no path between an element of one set and an element of the other. The decomposition property (Eq. (3.6b)), on the other hand, reflects only one-way implication; a variable X may be independent of each individual variable in set Y and still be dependent on the entire set. For example, let Y be the outcomes of a set of fair coins, and let X be a variable that gets the value 1 whenever an even number of coins turn up "heads" and gets 0 otherwise. X is independent of every element and every proper subset of Y, yet X is completely determined by the entire set Y. Weak union is also weaker than vertex separation. If Z is a cutset of vertices that separates X from Y in some graph, then enlarging Z keeps X and Y separated. Weak union, on the other hand, severely restricts the conditions under which a separating set Z can be enlarged with elements W; it states that W should be chosen from a set that, like Y, is already separated from X by Z.

Any three-place relation $I(\cdot)$ that satisfies Eqs. (3.6a) through (3.6d) is called a *semi-graphoid.* If it also obeys Eq. (3.6e), it is called a *graphoid* [Pearl and Paz 1985]. Eqs. (3.6a) through (3.6d) are satisfied by many dependency models. Besides vertex separation in undirected graphs, they also hold in directed graphs (see Section 3.3), and they govern information dependencies based on partial correlations [Pearl and Paz 1985], embedded multi-valued dependencies (EMVDs) in relational databases [Fagin 1977], and qualitative constraints [Shafer, Shenoy, and Mellouli 1988]. Because of this generality, the semi-graphoid axioms have been proposed as the basis of information dependencies.

Qualitative formulations of dependencies are accompanied by extra properties, whereas the probabilistic formulation seems to be completely characterized by these four axioms and therefore is more general. This observation can be expressed more formally.

COMPLETENESS CONJECTURE [Pearl and Paz 1985]: *The set of axioms in Eqs. (3.6a) through (3.6d) is **complete** when I is interpreted as a conditional independence relation. In other words, for every three-place relation I satisfying Eqs. (3.6a) through (3.6d), there exists a probability model P such that*

$$P(x|y, z) = P(x|z) \quad iff \quad I(X, Z, Y).$$

If the intersection axiom (Eq. (3.6e)) also is satisfied, then there exists a positive P satisfying the above relation.

While no proof has yet been found for this conjecture, all known properties of conditional independence (those valid for all P) have been shown to be derivable from Eqs. (3.6a) through (3.6d). A thorough treatment of the completeness problem, as well as completeness results for special types of probabilistic dependencies, are given by Geiger and Pearl [1988a].

WHY AXIOMATIC CHARACTERIZATION?

Axiomatizing the notion of probabilistic dependence is useful for three reasons. First, it allows us to conjecture and derive interesting and powerful theorems that may or may not be obvious from the numerical representation of probabilities. For example, the chaining rule [Lauritzen 1982],

$$I(X, Y, Z) \ \& \ I(X \cup Y, Z, W) \implies I(X, Y, W),$$

follows directly from Eqs. (3.6a) through (3.6d) and is important for recursively constructing directed graph representations (see Section 3.3). Another interesting theorem is the mixing rule [Dawid 1979],

$$I(X, Z, Y \cup W) \ \& \ I(Y, Z, W) \implies I(X \cup W, Z, Y),$$

which also follows from Eqs. (3.6a) through (3.6d). The mixing rule, with symmetry and decomposition, constitutes a complete axiomatization of marginal independencies, i.e., independence statements where the knowledge set Z is fixed [Geiger and Pearl 1988a]. The rule states that for each of the variables X, Y, W to be independent of the other two, it is enough that just one of them be independent of the other two and that the remaining pair be mutually independent. Generalizing recursively to n variables, the rule states that for n variables to be mutually independent, it is enough that one of them be independent of the other $n - 1$, and that the remaining $n - 1$ be mutually independent.

Second, the axioms can be viewed as qualitative inference rules used to derive new independencies from some initial set. For example, an expert might provide us with an initial set Σ of qualitative independence judgments in the form of triplets (X, Z, Y), and we may wish to test whether a new triplet $\sigma = (X', Z', Y')$ follows from Σ. This task, called the *membership problem* [Beeri 1980] may in principle be undecidable, because to test whether σ follows from Σ we must test whether σ holds in every distribution that satisfies Σ, and the number of distributions is infinite. If, however, we can derive σ by repeated application of sound axioms, we can guarantee that σ follows from Σ without searching the vast space of probability distributions. If, in addition, the set of axioms is complete, we are also guaranteed that every σ that follows from Σ eventually will be derived from Σ by repeated application of the axioms. In other words, the decidability of the membership problem hinges upon finding a complete set of axioms for conditional independence. Closely related to the membership problem is the task of verifying whether a mixed set Σ' of dependencies and independencies is *consistent*, namely, whether no subset of Σ' implies the negation of another. Thus, with a sound and efficient inference mechanism we can test and maintain consistency in a database of dependency information.

Finally, an axiomatic system provides a parsimonious and convenient code for comparing the features of several formalisms of dependency (e.g., probabilistic vs. qualitative) as well as the expressive power of various representations of such formalisms. In Sections 3.2 and 3.3, for example, we will use the axioms to compare the expressive powers of directed and undirected graphs, and to reveal what types of dependencies cannot be captured by graphical representations.

SUMMARY

The probabilistic relation of conditional independence possesses a set of qualitative properties that are consistent with our intuitive notion of "X is irrelevant to Y, once we learn Z." These properties, which are also satisfied by vertex separation in graphs, are captured by the axioms in Eq. (3.6). The defining axioms convey the idea that when we learn an irrelevant fact, the relevance relationships among other propositions remain unaltered; any information that was relevant remains relevant, and irrelevant information remains irrelevant. The axioms established can be used as inference rules for deriving new independencies and for defining the common features among various formalisms of dependence.

3.1.3 On Representing Dependencies by Undirected Graphs

WHAT'S IN A MISSING LINK?

Suppose we have a collection $U = \{\alpha, \beta, ...\}$ of interacting elements, and we decide to represent their interactions by an undirected graph G, in which the nodes correspond to individual elements of U. Naturally, we would like to display independence between two elements as a lack of connection between their corresponding nodes in G; conversely, dependent elements should correspond to connected nodes in G. This requirement alone, however, does not take full advantage of the expressive power of graphical representation. It treats all connected components of G as equivalent and does not attribute any special significance to the structure of each connected component.

Clearly, if graph topology is to convey meaning beyond connectedness, a semantic distinction must be drawn between *direct* connection and *indirect* connection. This means that the absence of a direct link between two elements α and β should reflect an interaction that is *conditional*, i.e., it may become stronger, weaker, or zero, depending on the state of other elements in the system, especially those that lie on the paths connecting α and β and thus *mediate* between them.

As an example, consider a group of two males $\{M_1, M_2\}$ and two females $\{F_1, F_2\}$ who occasionally engage in pairwise heterosexual activities. The lack of direct contact between the two males and between the two females can be represented by the diamond-shaped graph of Figure 3.2, which can also be used to represent conditional dependencies between various propositions. For example, if by m_i (or f_i) we denote the proposition that male M_i (or female F_i) will carry a certain disease within a year, then the topology of the network in Figure 3.2 asserts that f_1 and f_2 are independent given m_1 and m_2, namely, once we know for sure whether M_1 and M_2 will carry the disease, knowing the truth of f_1 ought not change our belief in f_2.†

---

† This assumes, of course, that we are dealing with a known disease whose spreading mechanism is well understood. Otherwise, while we are still learning the disease characteristic, knowledge of f_1 may help decide the more basic question of whether the disease is contagious at all, and this information will and should have an effect on f_2.

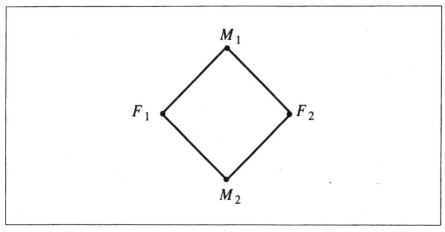

Figure 3.2. *An undirected graph representing interactions among four individuals.*

This conditional independence reflects a model whereby the disease spreads only by direct contact. Note that the links in this network are undirected, namely, either partner might be the originator of the disease. This does not exclude asymmetric interactions (e.g., the disease may be more easily transferable from males to females than the other way around). Such information, if available, will be contained in the numerical parameters that eventually will characterize the links in the network—they will be described in Section 3.2.3.

In summary, the semantics of the graph topology are defined by the meaning of the missing links, which tells us what other elements mediate the interactions between nonadjacent elements. This process of mediation will now be compared to the probabilistic relation of conditional independence $I(X, Z, Y)$, Eq. (3.1), which formalizes the intuitive statement "Knowing Y tells me nothing new about X if I already know Z."

DEPENDENCY MODELS AND DEPENDENCY MAPS

Let $U = \{\alpha, \beta,...\}$ be a finite set of elements (e.g., propositions or variables), and let X, Y, and Z stand for three disjoint subsets of elements in U. Let M be a *dependency model*, that is to say, a rule that assigns truth values to the three-place predicate $I(X, Z, Y)_M$, or in other words determines a subset I of triplets (X, Z, Y) for which the assertion "X is independent of Y given Z" is true. Any probability distribution P is a dependency model, because for any triplet (X, Z, Y) we can test the validity of $I(X, Z, Y)$ using Eq. (3.1). Our task is to characterize the set of dependency models capturable by graphs, including models that provide no explicit notion of adjacency. In other words, we are given the means to test whether a given subset Z of elements *intervenes* in a relation between the elements of X and those of Y, but it is up to us to decide how to connect the elements in a graph that encodes these interventions.

An undirected graph $G = (V, E)$ is characterized by a set V of nodes (or vertices) and a set E of edges that connect certain pairs of nodes in V. By a *graphical representation* of a dependency model M, we mean a direct correspondence between the elements in U (of M) and the set of vertices in V (of G), such that the topology of G reflects some properties of M. When this correspondence is established, we will make no distinction between U and V but will write $G = (U, E)$.

Ideally, if a subset Z of nodes in a graph G intercepts all paths between the nodes of X and those of Y (written $< X \mid Z \mid Y >_G$), then this interception should correspond to conditional independence between X and Y given Z, namely,

$$< X \mid Z \mid Y >_G \implies I(X, Z, Y)_M,$$

and conversely,

$$I(X, Z, Y)_M \implies < X \mid Z \mid Y >_G.$$

This correspondence would provide a clear graphical representation for the notion that X does not affect Y directly, that the variables in Z mediate between them. Unfortunately, we are about to see that these two requirements are too strong; there often is no way of using vertex separation in a graph to display *all* dependencies and independencies embodied in a dependency model, even if the model portrays simple, everyday experiences.

DEFINITION: *An undirected graph G is a **dependency map** (or D-map) of M if there is a one-to-one correspondence between the elements of U and the nodes V of G, such that for all disjoint subsets X, Y, Z of elements we have*

$$I(X, Z, Y)_M \implies < X \mid Z \mid Y >_G. \tag{3.7}$$

*Similarly, G is an **independency map** (or I-map) of M if*

$$I(X, Z, Y)_M \impliedby < X \mid Z \mid Y >_G. \tag{3.8}$$

*G is said to be a **perfect map** of M if it is both a D-map and an I-map.*

A D-map guarantees that vertices found to be connected are indeed dependent in M (from the contrapositive form of Eq. (3.7)); it may, however, display a pair of dependent variables as a pair of separated vertices. An I-map, conversely, guarantees that vertices found to be separated correspond to independent variables but does not guarantee that all those shown to be connected are in fact dependent. Empty graphs are trivial D-maps, while complete graphs are trivial I-maps.

It is clear that many reasonable models of dependency have no perfect maps. An example is a model in which $I(X, Z, Y)$ exhibits *induced dependencies*, i.e., totally unrelated propositions become relevant to each other when we learn new facts. Such a model, implying both $I(X, Z_1, Y)_M$ and $\neg I(X, Z_1 \cup Z_2, Y)_M$, cannot have a graph representation that is both an *I*-map and a *D*-map, because graph separation always satisfies

$$< X \mid Z_1 \mid Y >_G \implies < X \mid Z_1 \cup Z_2 \mid Y >_G$$

for any two subsets Z_1 and Z_2 of vertices. Thus, being a *D*-map requires G to display Z_1 as a cutset separating X and Y, while G's being an *I*-map prevents $Z_1 \cup Z_2$ from separating X and Y. No graph can satisfy both requirements simultaneously.

This weakness in the expressive power of undirected graphs severely limits their ability to represent informational dependencies. Consider an experiment with two coins and a bell that rings whenever the outcomes of the two coins are the same. If we ignore the bell, the coin outcomes, X and Y, are mutually independent, i.e., $I(X, \emptyset, Y)$, but if we notice the bell (Z), then learning the outcome of one coin should change our opinion about the other coin, i.e., $\neg I(X, Z, Y)$. How can we graphically represent the simple dependencies between the coins and the bell, or between any two causes leading to a common consequence? If we take the naive approach and assign links to (Z, X) and (Z, Y), leaving X and Y unlinked, we get the graph $X—Z—Y$. This graph is not an *I*-map because it (wrongly) asserts that X and Y are independent given Z. If we add a link between X and Y we get the trivial *I*-map of a complete graph, which no longer reflects the obvious fact that the two coins are genuinely independent (the bell being a passive device that does not affect their interaction). In Section 3.3, we will show that such dependencies can be represented completely with the richer language of directed graphs. For now, let us further examine the representational capabilities of undirected graphs.

Our inability to provide graphical representations for some models of dependency (e.g., induced dependency) raises the need to delineate the class of models that *do* lend themselves to graphical representation. This we do in the following section by establishing an axiomatic characterization of the family of relations that are isomorphic to vertex separation in graphs.

3.1.4 Axiomatic Characterization of Graph-Isomorph Dependencies

DEFINITION: *A dependency model M is said to be a* **graph-isomorph** *if there exists an undirected graph* $G = (U, E)$ *that is a perfect map of M, i.e., for every three disjoint subsets* $X, Y,$ *and* Z *of* U, *we have*

$$I(X, Z, Y)_M \iff < X \mid Z \mid Y >_G. \tag{3.9}$$

THEOREM 2 [Pearl and Paz 1985]: *A necessary and sufficient condition for a dependency model M to be a graph-isomorph is that $I(X, Z, Y)_M$ satisfies the following five independent axioms (the subscript M is dropped for clarity):*

- *Symmetry:*
$$I(X, Z, Y) \Longleftrightarrow I(Y, Z, X) \tag{3.10a}$$

- *Decomposition:*
$$I(X, Z, Y \cup W) \Longrightarrow I(X, Z, Y) \& I(X, Z, W) \tag{3.10b}$$

- *Intersection:*
$$I(X, Z \cup W, Y) \& I(X, Z \cup Y, W) \Longrightarrow I(X, Z, Y \cup W) \tag{3.10c}$$

- *Strong union:*
$$I(X, Z, Y) \Longrightarrow I(X, Z \cup W, Y) \tag{3.10d}$$

- *Transitivity:*
$$I(X, Z, Y) \Longrightarrow I(X, Z, \gamma) \text{ or } I(\gamma, Z, Y). \tag{3.10e}$$

REMARKS:

1. γ is a singleton element of U, and all three arguments of $I(\cdot)$ must represent disjoint subsets.

2. The axioms are clearly satisfied for vertex separation in graphs. Eq. (3.10e) is the contrapositive form of connectedness transitivity, stating that if X is connected to some vertex γ and γ is connected to Y, then X must also be connected to Y. Eq. (3.10d) states that if Z is a vertex cutset separating X from Y, then removing additional vertices W from the graph leaves X and Y still separated. Eq. (3.10c) states that if X is separated from W with Y removed and X is separated from Y with W removed, then X must be separated from both Y and W.

3. Eqs. (3.10c) and (3.10d) imply the converse of Eq. (3.10b), meaning I is completely defined by the set of triplets (α, Z, β) in which α and β are individual elements of U:

$$I(X, Z, Y) \Longleftrightarrow (\forall \alpha \in X) (\forall \beta \in Y) I(\alpha, Z, \beta).$$

Equivalently, we can express the axioms in Eq. (3.10) in terms of such triplets. Note that the union axiom, Eq. (3.10d), is unconditional and therefore stronger than Eq. (3.6c), which is required for probabilistic dependencies. Eq. (3.10d) provides a simple way to construct a unique graph G_0 that is an I-map of M: starting with a complete graph, we delete every edge (α, β) for which $I(\alpha, Z, \beta)$ holds.

Proof:

1. The "necessary" part follows from the observation that all five axioms are satisfied by vertex separation in graphs. The logical independence of the five axioms can be demonstrated by letting U contain four elements and showing that it is always possible to contrive a subset I of triplets that violates one axiom and satisfies the other four.

2. To prove sufficiency, we must show that for any set I of triplets (X, Z, Y) closed under Eqs. (3.10a) through (3.10e), there exists a graph G such that (X, Z, Y) is in I iff Z is a cutset in G that separates X from Y. We show that $G_0 = (U, E_0)$ is such a graph, where $(\alpha, \beta) \notin E_0$ iff $I(\alpha, Z, \beta)$. In view of Remark 3 above, it is sufficient to show that

    $$I(\alpha, S, \beta) \implies \ <\alpha \mid S \mid \beta>_{G_0} \text{ where } \alpha, \beta \in U \text{ and } S \subseteq U,$$

    since the converse follows automatically from the construction of G_0.

This is proved by finite descending induction:

i. For $|S| = n - 2$, the theorem holds automatically, because of the way G_0 is constructed.

ii. Assume the theorem holds for all S of size $|S| = k \leq n - 2$. Let S' be any set of size $|S'| = k - 1$. For $k \leq n - 2$, there exists an element γ outside $S' \cup \alpha \cup \beta$, and using Eq. (3.10d), we have $I(\alpha, S', \beta) \implies I(\alpha, S' \cup \gamma, \beta)$.

iii. By Eq. (3.10e) we have either $I(\alpha, S', \gamma)$ or $I(\gamma, S', \beta)$.

iv. Assuming the first alternative in (iii) gives $I(\alpha, S' \cup \beta, \gamma)$, using (3.10d), the second alternative is treated symmetrically in (v) and (vi).

v. The middle arguments $S' \cup \gamma$ and $S' \cup \beta$ in (ii) and (iv) are both of size k, so by the induction hypothesis we have $<\alpha \mid S' \cup \gamma \mid \beta>_{G_0}$ and $<\alpha \mid S' \cup \beta \mid \gamma>_{G_0}$.

vi. By Eq. (3.10c), the intersection property for vertex separation in graphs, (iv) and (v) imply $<\alpha \mid S' \mid \beta>_{G_0}$. Q.E.D.

Having a complete characterization for vertex separation in graphs allows us to test whether a given model of dependency lends itself to graphical representation. In fact, it is now easy to show that probabilistic models may violate both of the last two axioms. Eq. (3.10d) is clearly violated in the coins and bell example of the preceding subsection. Transitivity (Eq. (3.10e)) is violated in the same example, for if one of the coins is not fair, the bell's response is dependent on the outcome of each coin separately; yet the two coins are independent of each other. Finally, Eq. (3.10c) is violated whenever Y and W logically constrain one another, as in the earlier water temperature example.

Having failed to provide isomorphic graphical representations for even the most elementary models of informational dependency, we settle for the following compromise: instead of complete graph isomorphism, we will consider only *I*-maps, i.e., graphs that faithfully display every dependency. However, acknowledging that some independencies will escape representation, we shall insist that their number be kept at a minimum—in other words, that the graphs contain no superfluous edges.

3.2 MARKOV NETWORKS

When a connection is drawn between such seemingly unrelated objects as probability distributions and graphs, it is natural to raise the following three questions:

1. Given a probability distribution *P*, can we construct an *I*-map *G* of *P* that has the minimum number of edges?

2. Given a pair (P, G), can we test whether *G* is an *I*-map of *P*?

3. Given a graph *G*, can we construct a probability distribution *P* such that *G* is a perfect map of *P*?

The theory of Markov fields provides satisfactory answers to Question 2 for strictly positive *P* [Isham 1981; Lauritzen 1982]. This treatment is rather complex and relies heavily on the numerical representation of probabilities. We shall start with Question 1 and show the following:

- Question 1 has a simple unique solution for strictly positive distributions.

- The solution to Question 2 follows directly from the solution to Question 1.

- The solutions are obtained by nonnumerical analysis, based solely on Eqs. (3.6*a*) through (3.6*e*) in Section 3.1.2.

Question 3 recently was answered affirmatively [Geiger and Pearl 1988a] and will be treated briefly in Section 3.2.3. Sections 3.2.3 and 3.2.4 focus on finding a probabilistic interpretation for a graph *G* such that the dependencies shown in *G* reflect empirical knowledge about a given domain.

3.2.1 Definitions and Formal Properties

DEFINITION: *A graph G is a **minimal** I-map of a dependency model M if deleting any edge of G would make G cease to be an I-map. We call such a graph a **Markov network** of M.*

THEOREM 3 [Pearl and Paz 1985]: *Every dependency model M satisfying symmetry, decomposition, and intersection (Eq. (3.6)) has a unique minimal I-map $G_0 = (U, E_0)$ produced by deleting from the complete graph every edge (α, β) for which $I(\alpha, U - \alpha - \beta, \beta)_M$ holds, i.e.,*

$$(\alpha, \beta) \notin E_0 \quad iff \quad I(\alpha, U - \alpha - \beta, \beta)_M. \tag{3.11}$$

The proof is given in Appendix 3-A.

DEFINITION: *A **Markov blanket** $BL_I(\alpha)$ of an element $\alpha \in U$ is any subset S of elements for which*

$$I(\alpha, S, U - S - \alpha) \quad and \quad \alpha \notin S. \tag{3.12}$$

*A set is called a **Markov boundary** of α, denoted $B_I(\alpha)$, if it is a minimal Markov blanket of α, i.e., none of its proper subsets satisfy Eq. (3.12).*

The boundary $B_I(\alpha)$ is to be interpreted as the smallest set of elements that shields α from the influence of all other elements. Note that $B_I(\alpha)$ always exists because $I(X, S, \varnothing)$ guarantees that the set $S = U - \alpha$ satisfies Eq. (3.12).

THEOREM 4 [Pearl and Paz 1985]: *Every element $\alpha \in U$ in a dependency model satisfying symmetry, decomposition, intersection, and weak union (Eq. (3.6)) has a unique Markov boundary $B_I(\alpha)$. Moreover, $B_I(\alpha)$ coincides with the set of vertices $B_{G_0}(\alpha)$ adjacent to α in the minimal I-map G_0.*

The proof of Theorem 4 is given in Appendix 3-B. Since $B_I(\alpha)$ coincides with $B_{G_0}(\alpha)$, the following two interpretations of *direct neighbors* are identical: neighborhood as a blanket that shields α from the influence of all other variables, and neighborhood as a permanent bond of mutual influence between two variables, a bond that cannot be weakened by other elements in the system. Models satisfying the conditions of Theorem 4 are called *pseudo-graphoids*, i.e., graphoids lacking the contraction property (Eq. (3.6d)).

Since every strictly positive distribution defines a pseudo-graphoid, we can derive two corollaries.

COROLLARY 1: *The set of Markov boundaries $B_I(\alpha)$ induced by a strictly positive probability distribution forms a **neighbor system**, i.e., a collection $B_I^* = \{B_I(\alpha) : \alpha \in U\}$ of subsets of U such that for all pairs $\alpha, \beta \in U$ we have*

    (i) $\alpha \notin B_I(\alpha)$ and

    (ii) $\alpha \in B_I(\beta)$ iff $\beta \in B_I(\alpha)$.

COROLLARY 2: *The Markov network G_0 of any strictly positive distribution can be constructed by connecting each variable α to all members of its Markov boundary $B_I(\alpha)$.*

Corollary 2 is useful because often it is the Markov boundaries $B_I(\alpha)$ that are given to us when we request the factors that affect α most directly. These factors may be the immediate consequences of an event, the justifications for an action, or the salient properties that characterize a class of objects or a concept. Moreover, since either construction will yield an *I*-map, many global independence relationships can be validated by separation tests on graphs constructed from local information.

TESTING I-MAPNESS
We are now in a position to answer Question 2 from the beginning of this subsection: can we test whether a given graph *G* is an *I*-map of a distribution *P* (i.e., test the *I-mapness* of *G*)? We assume that *P* is not given explicitly but is represented by a procedure that answers queries of the type "Is $I(X, Z, Y)$ true in *P*?"

THEOREM 5: *Given a strictly positive probability distribution P on U and a graph $G = (U, E)$, the following three conditions are equivalent:*

  i.   *G is an I-map of P.*

  ii. *G is a supergraph of the Markov network G_0 of P, i.e.,*

$$(\alpha, \beta) \in E \quad whenever \quad \neg I(\alpha, U - \alpha - \beta, \beta).$$

  iii. *G is locally Markov with respect to P, i.e., for every variable $\alpha \in U$ we have $I(\alpha, B_G(\alpha), U - \alpha - B_G(\alpha))$, where $B_G(\alpha)$ is the set of vertices adjacent to α in G.*

Proof: The implication (ii) => (i) follows from the *I*-mapness of G_0 (Theorem 3), and (i) => (iii) follows from the definition of *I*-mapness. It remains to show (iii) => (ii), but this follows from the identity of $B_I(\alpha)$ and $B_{G_0}(\alpha)$ (Theorem 4). Q.E.D.

Properties (ii) and (iii) provide local procedures for testing *I*-mapness without examining every cutset in *G*. To show the essential role played by the assumption of strict positivity let us demonstrate the insufficiency of local tests when variables are subjected to functional constraints. Imagine four random variables constrained by equality, i.e., $X = Y = Z = W$. Any single variable is a Markov boundary of any other, because knowing the first variable determines the value of the second. Consequently, the graph shown in Figure 3.3*a* would qualify under the Markov boundary condition (Property iii of Theorem 5). This graph is not an *I*-map of the distribution, however, because the pair (X, Y) is not independent of the pair (Z, W). Worse yet, since any pair of variables is rendered independent given the values of the other pair, $I(\alpha, U - \alpha - \beta, \beta)$ holds for every pair (α, β). Thus, were we to construct G_0 by the edge-deletion method of Eq. (3.11), we would get an empty graph (Figure 3.3*b*), which obviously is not an *I*-map of the distribution.

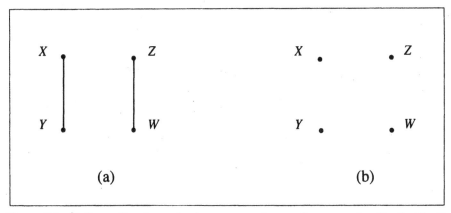

Figure 3.3. *Failure of local tests for I-mapness under equality constraints $X = Y = Z = W$. (a) A graph qualifying under the Markov boundary test. (b) An empty graph qualifying under the edge-deletion test (Eq. (3.11)).*

It can be shown that even if we connect each variable to the union of all its Markov boundaries, we will not get an *I*-map when categorical constraints are present. Thus, there appears to be no local test for *I*-mapness of undirected graphs that works for extreme probability distributions. We shall see in Section 3.3 that directed graphs do not suffer from this deficiency; local tests for *I*-mapness and minimal *I*-mapness exist even for distributions that reflect categorical constraints. It should be noted that the tests in (ii) and (iii), while local, still involve all the varibles in *U* and therefore may require exponentially complex procedures, especially when *P* is given as a table. Fortunately, in most practical applications we start with the graph representation *G* and use the probability model *P* merely as a theoretical abstraction to justify the operations conducted on *G*.

We see that representations of probabilistic independencies using undirected graphs rest heavily on the intersection and weak union axioms, Eqs. (3.6*e*) and (3.6*c*). In contrast, we shall see in Section 3.3 that directed graph representations rely on the contraction and weak union axioms, with intersection playing only a minor role.

3.2.2 Illustrations

GRAPHOIDS AND THEIR MARKOV NETWORKS

To see the roles of the various axioms of Eq. (3.6), consider a set of four integers $U = \{1, 2, 3, 4\}$, and let I be the set of twelve triplets listed below:

$$I = \{(1, 2, 3), (1, 3, 4), (2, 3, 4), (\{1, 2\}, 3, 4),$$

$$(1, \{2, 3\}, 4), (2, \{1, 3\}, 4) , \textit{symmetrical images}\}.$$

All other triplets are assumed to be dependent, i.e., outside I. It is easy to see that I satisfies the other axioms of Eq. (3.6) but does not satisfy contraction; I contains $(1, 2, 3)$ and $(1, \{2, 3\}, 4)$ but not $(1, 2, \{3, 4\})$. Thus, (from Theorem 1) I is supported by no probability model, but (from Theorem 3) it has a unique minimal I-map G_0, shown in Figure 3.4. Moreover, Theorem 4 ensures that G_0 can be constructed in two different ways, either by deleting the edges $(1, 4)$ and $(2, 4)$ from the complete graph, in accordance with Eq. (3.11), or by computing from I the Markov boundary of each element, in accordance with Eq. (3.12), yielding

$$B_I(1) = \{2, 3\}, \quad B_I(2) = \{1, 3\}, \quad B_I(3) = \{1, 2, 4\}, \quad B_I(4) = \{3\}.$$

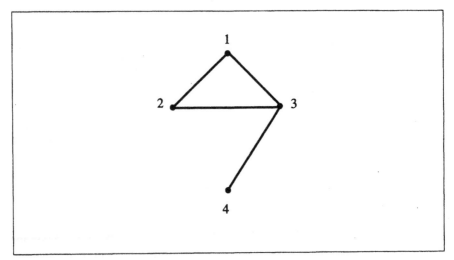

Figure 3.4. *The minimal I-map, G_0, of I.*

Now consider a modified list I' containing only the last two triplets of I (and their symmetrical images):

$$I' = \{(1, \{2, 3\}, 4), (2, \{1, 3\}, 4), symmetrical\ images\}.$$

I' is a semi-graphoid (it satisfies Eqs. (3.6a) through (3.6d)) but not a graphoid, because the absence of the triplet $(\{1,2\}, 3,4)$ violates the intersection axiom (Eq. (3.6e)). Hence, I' can represent a probability model but not a strictly positive one. Indeed, if we try to construct G_0 by the usual criterion of edge-deletion (Eq. (3.11)), we get the graph in Figure 3.4, but it is no longer an I-map of I'; it shows 3 separating 1 from 4, but (1, 3, 4) is not in I'. In fact, the only I-maps of I' are the three graphs in Figure 3.5, and the minimal I-map clearly is not unique.

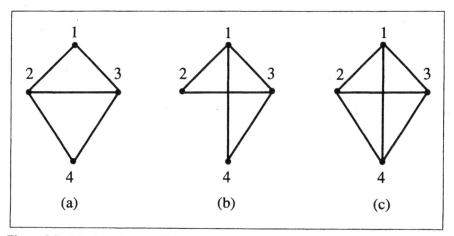

Figure 3.5. *The three I-maps of I'.*

Now consider the list

$$I'' = \{(1, 2, 3), (1, 3, 4), (2, 3, 4), (\{1, 2\}, 3, 4), symmetrical\ images\}.$$

I'' satisfies Eqs. (3.6a), (3.6b), and (3.6e), but not the weak union axiom (Eq. (3.6c)). From Theorem 3 we can still construct a unique I-map for I'' using the edge-deletion method, but because no triplet of the form $(\alpha, U - \alpha - \beta, \beta)$ appears in I'', the only I-map for this list is the complete graph. Moreover, the Markov boundaries of I'' do not form a neighbor set ($B_{I''}(4) = 3$, $B_{I''}(2) = \{1, 3, 4\}$, so $2 \notin B_{I''}(4)$ while $4 \in B_{I''}(2)$). Thus, we see that the lack of weak union prevents us from constructing an I-map by the Markov boundary method.

Since I does not obey the contraction property (Eq. (3.6d)), no probabilistic model can induce this set of independence relationships unless we add the triplet (1, 2, 4) to I. If I were a list of statements given by a domain expert, it would be possible to invoke Eq. (3.6*a*) through (3.6*e*) to alert the expert to the inconsistency caused by the absence of (1, 2, 4). The incompleteness of I' and I'' would be easier to detect by graphical means because they interfere with the formation of G_0 and could be identified by a system attempting to construct it.

CONCEPTUAL DEPENDENCIES AND THEIR MARKOV NETWORKS

Consider the task of constructing a Markov network to represent the belief about whether agent *A* will be late for a meeting. Assume the agent identifies the following variables as having influence on the main question of being late to a meeting:

1. The time shown on the watch of Passerby 1.

2. The time shown on the watch of Passerby 2.

3. The correct time.

4. The time it takes to travel to the meeting place.

5. The arrival time at the meeting place.

The construction of G_0 can proceed by one of two methods:

- The *edge-deletion* method.

- The *Markov boundary* method.

Following Eq. (3.11), the first method requires that for every pair of variables (α, β) we determine whether fixing the values of all other variables in the system will render our belief in α sensitive to β. We know, for example, that the reading on Passerby 1's watch (1) will vary with the actual time (3) even if all other variables are known. On that basis, we can connect node 1 to node 3 and, by proceeding this way through all pairs of variables, construct the graph of Figure 3.6. The unusual edge (3, 4) reflects the reasoning that if we fix the arrival time (5), the travel time (4) must depend on the current time (3).

The Markov boundary method requires that for every variable α in the system, we identify a minimal set of variables sufficient to render the belief in α insensitive to all other variables in the system. It is a commonsense task, for instance, to decide that once we know the current time (3), no other variable can affect what we expect to read on passerby 1's watch (1). Similarly, to estimate our arrival time (5), we need only know the current time (3) and how long it takes to travel (4), independent of the watch readings (1) and (2). On the basis of these considerations, we can connect 1 to 3, 5 to 4 and 3, and so on. After we find

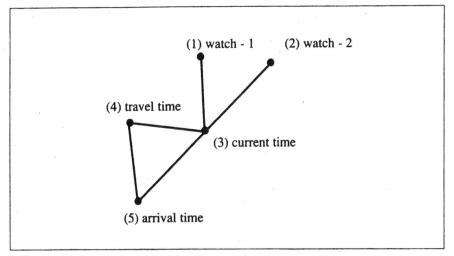

Figure 3.6. *The Markov network representing the prediction of A's arrival time.*

the immediate neighbors of any four variables in the system, the graph G_0 will emerge, identical to that of Figure 3.6.

Once established, G_0 can be used as an inference instrument. For example, we need not state explicitly that knowing the current time (3) renders the time on Passerby 1's watch (1) irrelevant for estimating the travel time (4) (i.e., $I(1,3,4)$); we can infer the information from the fact that 3 is a cutset in G_0, separating 1 from 4. Deriving such conclusions by syntactic manipulation of Eqs. (3.6a) through (3.6e) probably would be more complicated. Additionally, the graphical representation can help maintain consistency and completeness during the knowledge-building phase. One need ascertain only that the relevance boundaries identified by the expert form a neighbor system.

SUMMARY

The essential qualities of conditional independence are captured by five logical axioms: symmetry (Eq. (3.6a)), decomposition (Eq. (3.6b)), weak union (Eq. (3.6c)), contraction (Eq. (3.6d)), and intersection (Eq. (3.6e)). Intersection holds only for strictly positive distributions (i.e., reflecting no functional or definitional constraints) and is essential to the construction of undirected graphs. Symmetry, decomposition, and intersection enable us to construct a minimal graph G_0 (Markov network), in which every cutset corresponds to a genuine independence condition. The weak union axiom is needed to guarantee that the set of neighbors that G_0 assigns to each variable α is the smallest set required to shield α from the effects of all other variables.

The Markov network representation of conditional independence offers a sound inference mechanism for deducing, at any state of knowledge, which propositional variables are relevant to each other. If we identify the Markov boundaries associated with each proposition in the system and treat them as neighborhood relations defining a graph G_0, then we can correctly identify independence relationships by testing whether the set of known propositions constitutes a cutset in G_0.

Not all probabilistic dependencies can be captured by undirected graphs. For example, a dependency may be induced and non-transitive (see the coins and bell example of Section 3.1.3), but graph separation is strictly normal and transitive. For this reason directed graphs are finding wider application in reasoning systems [Duda, Hart, and Nilsson 1976; Howard and Matheson 1981; Pearl 1986c]. A systematic treatment of directed graph representations is given in Section 3.3.

3.2.3 Markov Network as a Knowledge Base

QUANTIFYING THE LINKS

So far, we have established the semantics of Markov networks in terms of the purely qualitative notion of conditional independence, i.e., a variable is proclaimed independent of all its non-neighbors once we know the values of its neighbors. However, if the network is to convey information useful for decisions and inference, we must also provide quantitative assessments of the strength of each link. In Figure 3.2, for example, if we know that the couple (M_1, F_2) meet less frequently than the couple (M_1, F_1), then the first link should be weaker than the second to show weaker dependency between the propositions m_1 and f_2.

The assigning of weights to the links of the graph must be handled with caution. If the weights are to be used in translating evidential data into meaningful probabilistic inferences, we must be certain that the model is both consistent and complete. Consistency guarantees that we do not overload the graph with too many parameters—overspecification can lead to contradictory conclusions, depending on which parameter is consulted first—and completeness protects us from underspecifying the model and thus guarantees that routines designed to generate conclusions will not get deadlocked for lack of information.

An attractive feature of the traditional joint-distribution representation of probabilities is the ease with which one can synthesize consistent probability models or detect inconsistencies in models. In this representation, to create a complete and consistent model, one need only assign to the elementary events (i.e., conjunctions of atomic propositions) nonnegative weights summing to one. The synthesis process in the graph representation is more hazardous. For example, assume that in Figure 3.2 we want to express the dependencies between the variables $\{M_1, M_2, F_1, F_2\}$ by specifying the four pairwise probabilities

$P(M_1, F_1)$, $P(F_1, M_2)$, $P(M_2, F_2)$, and $P(F_2, M_1)$. Unless the parameters given satisfy some nonobvious relationship, no probability model will support all four inputs, and we will get inconsistencies. Moreover, it is not clear that we can put all numerical inputs together without violating the qualitative dependency relationships shown in the graph. On the other hand, if we specify the pairwise probabilities of only three pairs, incompleteness will result; many models will conform to the input specification, and we will be unable to provide answers to many useful queries.

The theory of Markov fields [Isham 1981, Lauritzen 1982] provides a safe method (called *Gibbs' potential*) for constructing a complete and consistent quantitative model while preserving the dependency structure of an arbitrary graph G. The method consists of four steps:

1. Identify the cliques† of G, namely, the maximal subgraphs whose nodes are all adjacent to each other.

2. For each clique C_i, assign a nonnegative compatibility function $g_i(c_i)$, which measures the relative degree of compatibility associated with each value assignment c_i to the variables included in C_i.

3. Form the product $\prod_i g_i(c_i)$ of the compatibility functions over all the cliques.

4. Normalize the product over all possible value combinations of the variables in the system

$$P(x_1,...,x_n) = K \prod_i g_i(c_i), \qquad (3.13)$$

where

$$K = [\sum_{x_1,...,x_n} \prod_i g_i(c_i)]^{-1}.$$

The normalized product P in Eq. (3.13) constitutes a joint distribution that embodies all the conditional independencies portrayed by the graph G, i.e., G is an *I*-map of P (see Theorem 6, below).

To illustrate the mechanics of this method, let us return to the example of Figure 3.2 and assume that the likelihood of two members of the *i*-th couple having the same state of disease is measured by a compatibility parameter α_i, and the likelihood that exactly one partner of the couple will carry the disease is assigned a

---

† We use the term *clique* for the more common term *maximal clique*.

compatibility parameter β_i. The dependency graph in this case has four cliques, corresponding to the four edges

$$C_1 = \{M_1, F_1\}, C_2 = \{M_1, F_2\},$$
$$C_3 = \{M_2, F_1\}, \text{ and } C_4 = \{M_2, F_2\},$$

and the compatibility functions g_i are given by

$$g_i(x_{i_1}, x_{i_2}) = \begin{cases} \alpha_i & \text{if } x_{i_1} = x_{i_2} \\ \beta_i & \text{if } x_{i_1} \neq x_{i_2}, \end{cases} \tag{3.14}$$

where x_{i_1} and x_{i_2} are the states of disease associated with the male and female, respectively, of couple C_i. The overall probability distribution function is given by the normalized product

$$P(M_1, M_2, F_1, F_2) = K \, g_1(M_1, F_1) \, g_2(M_1, F_2) \, g_3(M_2, F_1) \, g_4(M_2, F_2)$$
$$= K \prod_i \beta_i^{|x_{i_1} - x_{i_2}|} \alpha_i^{1 - |x_{i_1} - x_{i_2}|}, \tag{3.15}$$

where K is a constant that makes P sum to unity over all states of the system, i.e.,

$$K^{-1} = \prod_i (\alpha_i + \beta_i) + \prod_i \alpha_i \sum_j \frac{\beta_j}{\alpha_j} + \prod_i \beta_i \sum_j \frac{\alpha_j}{\beta_j}. \tag{3.16}$$

For example, the state in which only the males carry the disease, $(m_1, \neg f_1, m_2, \neg f_2)$, will have a probability measure $K\beta_1\beta_2\beta_3\beta_4$ because the male and female of each couple are in unequal states of disease. The state $(m_1, f_1, \neg m_2, \neg f_2)$, on the other hand, has the probability $K\alpha_1\beta_2\beta_3\alpha_4$ because couples C_1 and C_4 are both homogeneous.

To show that P is consistent with the dependency structure of G, we note that any product of the form of Eq. (3.15) can be expressed either as the product $f(M_1, F_1, F_2) \, g(F_1, F_2, M_2)$ or as $f'(F_1, M_1, M_2) \, g'(M_1, M_2, F_2)$. Thus, invoking Eq. (3.5b), we conclude that $I(M_1, F_1 \cup F_2, M_2)_P$ and $I(F_1, M_1 \cup M_2, F_2)_P$.

The next theorem ensures the generality of this construction method.

THEOREM 6 [Hammersley and Clifford 1971]: *A probability function P formed by a normalized product of positive functions on the cliques of G is a Markov field relative to G, i.e., G is an I-map of P.*

Proof: G is guaranteed to be an I-map if P is locally Markov relative to G (Theorem 5). It is sufficient, therefore, to show that the neighbors in G of each variable α constitute a Markov blanket of α relative to P, i.e., that $I(\alpha, B_G(\alpha), U - \alpha - B_G(\alpha))$ or (using Eq. (3.5b)) that

$$P(\alpha, B_G(\alpha), U - \alpha - B_G(\alpha)) = f_1(\alpha, B_G(\alpha)) f_2(U - \alpha). \qquad (3.17)$$

Let J_α stand for the set of indices marking all cliques in G that include α, $J_\alpha = \{j : \alpha \in C_j\}$. Since P is in product form, we can write

$$P(\alpha, \beta, \ldots) = K \prod_j g_j(c_j) = K \prod_{j \in J_\alpha} g_j(c_j) \prod_{j \notin J_\alpha} g_j(c_j). \qquad (3.18)$$

The first product in Eq. (3.18) contains only variables that are adjacent to α in G; otherwise, C_j would not be a clique. According to the definition of J_α, the second product does not involve α. Thus, Eq. (3.17) is established. Q.E.D.

The converse of Theorem 6 also holds: any positive Markov field can be expressed in product form as in Eq. (3.13). The theorem, though not its converse (see Exercise 3.3), also holds for extreme probabilities. Theorem 6 still does not guarantee that *every* conditional *dependency* shown in the graph will be embodied in P if P is constructed by the product form of Eq. (3.13), but a more recent result gives us this guarantee, i.e., every undirected graph G has a distribution P such that G is a perfect map of P [Geiger and Pearl 1988a]. Thus, we can answer yes to Question 3 of the introduction to this section.

INTERPRETING THE LINK PARAMETERS

The preceding method of modeling guarantees consistency and completeness, but it leaves much to be desired. In particular, it is difficult to assign meanings to the parameters of the compatibility functions. If a model's parameters are to lead to meaningful inferences or decisions, they must come either from direct measurements or from an expert who can relate them to actual human experience. Both options encounter difficulties in the Markov network formulation.

Let us assume we have a huge record of medical tests conducted on homogeneous subjects, and the record includes a full account of their sexual habits. Can we extract from it the desired compatibility functions $g_i(M, F)$? The difficulty is that any disease pattern we observe on a given couple is a function not only of the relations between the male and female of this couple but also of interaction between this couple and the rest of the population. In other words, our measurements invariably are taken in a noisy environment; in our case, this means a large network of interactions surrounds the one that is tested.

To further appreciate the difficulties associated with context-dependent measurements, let us take an ideal case and assume that our record is based solely on groups of four interacting individuals (as in Figure 3.2), with each group isolated from the rest of the world and all groups having the same sexual pattern. In other words, we are given the joint probability $P(M_1, F_1, F_2, M_2)$, or a close approximation to it, and we are asked to infer the compatibility functions g_i. Clearly it is not an easy task, even in this ideal case; using the data provided by P we must solve a set of simultaneous nonlinear equations for g_i, such as Eq. (3.13) or Eq. (3.15). In addition, the solution we obtain for g_i will not be applicable to new situations in which, say, the frequency of interaction is different. Thus, we see why the compatibility parameters cannot be given meaningful experiential interpretation.

For a parameter to be meaningful, it must be an abstraction of some invariant property of one's experience. In our example, the relation between frequency of contact and transference of the disease from one partner to another, under conditions of perfect isolation from the rest of the world, is meaningful. In probabilistic terminology, the quantities $P(f_1 \mid m_1, \neg m_2)$ and $P(f_1 \mid \neg m_1, \neg m_2)$ and their relations to the frequency of interaction of couple $\{M_1, F_1\}$ are perceived as invariant characteristics of the disease, generalizable across contexts. It is with these quantities, therefore, that an expert would choose to encode experiential knowledge, and it is these quantities that an expert is most willing to assess. Moreover, were we conducting a clean scientific experiment, these are the quantities we would choose to measure.

Unfortunately, the Markov network formulation does not allow the direct specification of such judgmental input. Judgments about low-order conditional probabilities (e.g., $P(m_1 \mid f_1, \neg m_2)$) can be taken only as constraints that the joint probability distribution (Eq. (3.13)) must satisfy; from them, we might be able to calculate the actual values of the compatibility parameters. But this is a rather tedious computation, especially if the number of variables is large (imagine a group of n interacting couples), and the computation must be performed at the knowledge-acquisition phase to ensure that the expert provides a consistent and complete set of constraints.

3.2.4 Decomposable Models

Some dependency models do not suffer from the quantification difficulty described in the preceding section; instead, the compatibility functions are directly related to the low-order marginal probabilities on the variables in each clique. Such *decomposable* models have the useful property that the cliques of their Markov networks form a tree.

MARKOV TREES

To understand why tree topologies have this desirable feature, let us consider a distribution P having a Markov network in the form of a chain

$$X_1 - X_2 - X_3 - X_4.$$

From the chain rule of basic probability theory (Eq. (2.12)) we know that every distribution function $P(x_1,...,x_n)$ can be represented as a product:

$$P(x_1, ..., x_n) = P(x_1) P(x_2 | x_1) ... P(x_n | x_1, ..., x_{n-1}). \qquad (3.19)$$

Thus, if we expand P in the order dictated by the chain, we can write

$$P(x_1, x_2, x_3, x_4) = P(x_1) P(x_2 | x_1) P(x_3 | x_1, x_2) P(x_4 | x_1, x_2, x_3),$$

and using the conditional independencies encoded in the chain, we obtain

$$P(x_1, x_2, x_3, x_4) = P(x_1) P(x_2 | x_1) P(x_3 | x_2) P(x_4 | x_3).$$

The joint probability P is expressible in terms of a product of three functions, each involving a pair of adjacent variables. Moreover, the functions are the very pairwise conditional probabilities that should carry conceptual meaning, according to our earlier discussion. This scheme leaves the choice of ordering quite flexible. For example, if we expand P in the order (X_3, X_2, X_4, X_1), we get

$$P(x_3, x_2, x_4, x_1) = P(x_3) P(x_2 | x_3) P(x_4 | x_3, x_2) P(x_1 | x_3, x_2, x_4)$$
$$= P(x_3) P(x_2 | x_3) P(x_4 | x_3) P(x_1 | x_2),$$

again yielding a product of edge probabilities. The only requirement is this: as we order the variables from left to right, every variable except the first should have at least one of its graph neighbors to its left. The ordering (X_1, X_4, X_2, X_3), for example, would not yield the desired product form because X_4 is positioned to the left of its only neighbor, X_3.

Given a tree-structured Markov network, there are two ways to find its product-form distribution by inspection: *directed trees* and *product division*.

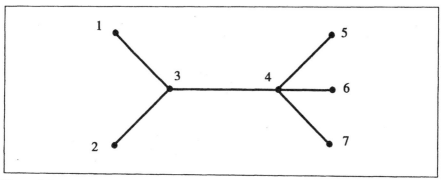

Figure 3.7. *An undirected tree of seven variables.*

Consider the tree of Figure 3.7, where the variables $X_1,..., X_7$ are marked 1,...,7 for short. If we arbitrarily choose node 3 as a root and assign to the links arrows pointing away from the root, we get the directed tree of Figure 3.8, where every non-root node has a single arrow coming from its unique parent. We can now write the product distribution by inspection, going from parents to children:

$$P(1,..., 7) = P(3)\,P(1\,|\,3)\,P(2\,|\,3)\,P(4\,|\,3)\,P(5\,|\,4)\,P(6\,|\,4)\,P(7\,|\,4). \qquad \textbf{(3.20)}$$

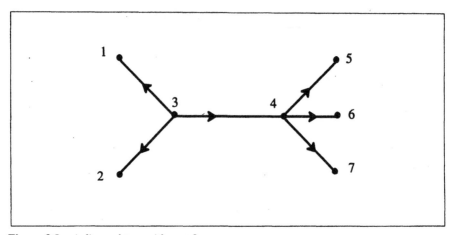

Figure 3.8. *A directed tree with root 3.*

The conditioning (right) variable in each term of the product is a direct parent of the conditioned (left) variable.

The second method for expressing the joint distribution is to divide the product of the marginal distributions on the edges (i.e., cliques) by the product of the distributions of the intermediate nodes (i.e., the intersections of the cliques). The distribution corresponding to the tree of Figure 3.8 will be written

$$P(1, ..., 7) = \frac{P(1, 3)\,P(2, 3)\,P(3, 4)\,P(4, 5)\,P(4, 6)\,P(4, 7)}{P(3)\quad P(3)\quad P(4)\quad P(4)\quad P(4)}, \qquad \textbf{(3.21)}$$

which is identical to Eq. (3.20). Each variable in the denominator appears one less time than it appears in the numerator.

JOIN TREES

Trees are not the only distributions amenable to product forms. Consider, for example, the structure of Figure 3.9a. Applying the chain rule in the order (A, B, C, D, E), and using the independencies embedded in the graph, we obtain

$$P(a, b, c, d, e) = P(a)\,P(b\,|\,a)\,P(c\,|\,a, b)\,P(d\,|\,a, b, c)\,P(e\,|\,a, b, c, d)$$

$$= P(a)\,P(b\,|\,a)\,P(c\,|\,a, b)\,P(d\,|\,b, c)\,P(e\,|\,c)$$

$$= \frac{P(a, b, c)\,P(b, c, d)}{P(b, c)}\cdot\frac{P(c, e)}{P(c)}. \qquad (3.22)$$

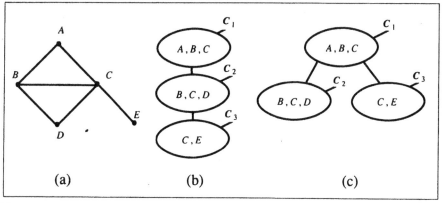

Figure 3.9. *Two join trees, (b) and (c), constructed from the cliques of the graph in (a).*

Eq. (3.22) again displays the same pattern as Eq. (3.21): the numerator is a product of the distributions of the cliques, and the denominator is a product of the distributions of their intersections. Note that C is a node common to all three cliques—$\{A, B, C\}$, $\{B, C, D\}$, and $\{C, E\}$— yet $P(c)$ appears only once in the denominator. The reason will become clear in the ensuing discussion, where we will justify the general formula for clique trees.

The unique feature of the graph in Figure 3.9a that enables us to obtain a product-form distribution is the fact that the cliques in this graph can be joined to form a tree, as seen in Figure 3.9b and Figure 3.9c. More precisely, there is a tree that is an *I*-map of *P*, with vertices corresponding to the cliques of *G*. Indeed, writing $C_1 = \{A, B, C\}, C_2 = \{B, C, D\}$, and $C_3 = \{C, E\}$, we see that C_3 and C_1 are independent given C_2, and we draw the *I*-map C_1—C_2—C_3 of Figure 3.9b. Since C_3 and C_2 are independent given C_1, we can also use the *I*-map C_2—C_1—C_3 of Figure 3.9c. This nonuniqueness of the minimal *I*-maps, an apparent contradiction to Theorem 3, stems from the overlapping of $C_1, C_2,$ and C_3, which induces equality constraints and occasionally leads to violation of the intersection axiom (Eq. (3.6e)).

Now we shall present a theorem about *chordal graphs* [Beeri et. al. 1983] in order to further articulate the concept of a clique tree.

DEFINITION: *An undirected graph* $G = (V, E)$ *is said to be* **chordal** *if every cycle of length four or more has at least one chord, i.e., an edge joining two nonconsecutive vertices along that cycle.*

THEOREM 7: *Let G be an undirected graph* $G = (V, E)$. *The following four conditions are equivalent:*

1. *G is chordal.*

2. *The edges of G can be directed acyclically so that every pair of converging arrows emanates from two adjacent vertices.*

3. *All vertices of G can be deleted by arranging them in separate piles, one for each clique, and then repeatedly applying the following two operations:*

   • *Delete a vertex that occurs in only one pile.*

   • *Delete a pile if all its vertices appear in another pile.*

4. *There is a tree T (called a join tree) with the cliques of G as vertices, such that for every vertex v of G, if we remove from T all cliques not containing v, the remaining subtree stays connected. In other words, any two cliques containing v are either adjacent in T or connected by a path made entirely of cliques that contain v.*

The four conditions of Theorem 7 are clearly satisfied in the graph of Figure 3.9a, and none are satisfied in the graph of Figure 3.2 (the diamond is the smallest nonchordal graph). Tarjan and Yannakakis [1984] offer an efficient two-step algorithm for both testing chordality of a graph and *triangulating* it (i.e., filling in the missing links that would make a non-chordal graph chordal).

GRAPH TRIANGULATION (FILL-IN) ALGORITHM

1. Compute an ordering for the nodes, using a *maximum cardinality search*, i.e., number vertices from 1 to $|V|$, in increasing order, always assigning the next number to the vertex having the largest set of previously numbered neighbors (breaking ties arbitrarily).

2. From $n = |V|$ to $n = 1$, recursively fill in edges between any two nonadjacent parents of n, i.e., neighbors of n having lower ranks than n

(including neighbors linked to n in previous steps). If no edges are added the graph is chordal; otherwise, the new filled graph is chordal.

Given a graph $G = (V, E)$ we can construct a join tree using the following procedure, whose correctness is insured by property 4 of Theorem 7.

ASSEMBLING A JOIN TREE

1. Use the fill-in algorithm to generate a chordal graph G' (if G is chordal, $G = G'$).

2. Identify all cliques in G'. Since any vertex and its parent set (lower ranked nodes connected to it) form a clique in G', the maximum number of cliques is $|V|$.

3. Order the cliques $C_1, C_2, ..., C_t$ by rank of the highest vertex in each clique.

4. Form the join tree by connecting each C_i to a predecessor C_j ($j < i$) sharing the highest number of vertices with C_i.

EXAMPLE: Consider the graph in Figure 3.9a. One maximum cardinality ordering is (A, B, C, D, E). Every vertex in this ordering has its preceding neighbors already connected, hence the graph is chordal and no edges need be added. The cliques are ranked C_1, C_2, and C_3 as shown in Figure 3.9b. $C_3 = \{C, E\}$ shares only vertex C with its predecessors C_2 and C_1, so either one can be chosen as the parent of C_3. These two choices yield the join trees of Figures 3.9b and 3.9c.

Now suppose we wish to assemble a join tree for the same graph with the edge (B, C) missing. The ordering (A, B, C, D, E) is still a maximum cardinality ordering, but now when we discover that the preceeding neighbors of node D (i.e., B and C) are nonadjacent, we should fill in edge (B, C). This renders the graph chordal, and the rest of the procedure yields the same join trees as in Figures 3.9b and 3.9c.

DECOMPOSABLE DISTRIBUTIONS

DEFINITION: *A probability model P is said to be **decomposable** if it has a minimal I-map that is chordal. P is said to be **decomposable relative** to a graph G if the following two conditions are met:*

i.   G is an I-map of P.

ii. G is chordal.

LEMMA 1: *If P is decomposable relative to G, then any join tree T of the cliques of G is an I-map relative to P. In other words, if C_X, C_Y, and C_Z are three disjoint sets of vertices in T, and X, Y, and Z are their corresponding sets of variables in G, then $I(X, Z, Y)_P$ whenever C_Z separates C_X from C_Y in T (written $< C_X \mid C_Z \mid C_Y >_T$).*

Proof: Since (X, Z, Y) may not be disjoint, we will prove $I(X, Z, Y)_P$ by showing that $I(X-Z, Z, Y-Z)_P$ holds the two assertions are equivalent, according to Remark 2 of Theorem 1. Moreover, since G is an I-map of P, it is enough to show that Z is a cutset in G, separating $X-Z$ from $Y-Z$. Thus, we need to show

$$< C_X \mid C_Z \mid C_Y >_T \implies < X - Z \mid Z \mid Y - Z >_G, \qquad (3.23)$$

which we shall prove by contradiction in two parts:

Part 1: If the right-hand side of Eq. (3.23) is false, then there exists a path $\alpha, \gamma_1, \gamma_2, ..., \gamma_n, \beta$ in G that goes from some element $\alpha \in X - Z$ to some element $\beta \in Y - Z$ without intersecting Z, namely,

$$(\alpha, \gamma_1) \in E \ (\gamma_i, \gamma_{i+1}) \in E, \ (\gamma_n, \beta) \in E \text{ and } \gamma_i \notin Z$$

for all $i = 1, 2, ..., n$.

Proof of Part 1: Let C_v denote the set of all cliques that contain some vertex v, and consider the set of cliques

$$S = \{C_\alpha \cup_i C_{\gamma_i} \cup C_\beta - C_Z\}.$$

We now argue that those vertices of T corresponding to the elements of S form a connected sub-tree. Indeed, T was constructed so that pulling out the variables in C_Z would leave the vertices of every C_{γ_i} connected. Moreover, the existence of an edge (γ_i, γ_{i+1}) in G guarantees that every clique containing γ_i shares an element (γ_i) with each clique containing (γ_i, γ_{i+1}); Each clique containing (γ_i, γ_{i+1}), in turn, shares an element (γ_{i+1}) with every clique containing γ_{i+1}. Consequently, the vertices corresponding to the elements of C_{γ_i} and $C_{\gamma_{i+1}}$ are connected in T, even after the variables in C_Z are deleted.

Part 2: Part 1 asserts the existence of a path in T from some vertex in $C_\alpha \subseteq C_X$ to some vertex in $C_\beta \subseteq C_Y$, bypassing all vertices of C_Z, thus contradicting the antecedent of Eq. (3.23). Q.E.D.

We are now in a position to demonstrate that decomposable models have joint distribution functions expressible in product form. Essentially, the demonstration relies on property iv of Theorem 7, which allows us to arrange the cliques of G as a tree and apply to them the chain rule formula (Eq. (3.19)), as we have done to the individual variables in Eq. (3.20).

THEOREM 8: *If P is decomposable relative to G, then the joint distribution of P can be written as a product of the distributions of the cliques of G divided by a product of the distributions of their intersections.*

Proof: Let T be the join tree of the cliques of G, and let $(C_1, C_2,..., C_i,...)$ be an ordering of the cliques that is consistent with T, i.e., for every $i > j$ we have a unique predecessor $j(i) < i$ such that $C_{j(i)}$ is adjacent to C_i in T. Clearly, $C_{j(i)}$ separates C_i from $C_1, C_2, ..., C_{i-1}$ in any such ordering. Applying the chain rule formula to the cliques of G, we obtain

$$P(x_1, x_2,..., x_n) = \prod_i P(c_i \mid c_1,..., c_{i-1}) = \prod_i P(c_i \mid c_{j(i)}) \tag{3.24}$$

$$= \prod_i P(c_i \mid c_i \cap c_{j(i)}) \tag{3.25}$$

$$= \prod_i \frac{P(c_i)}{P(c_i \cap c_{j(i)})}. \tag{3.26}$$

Eq. (3.24) follows from the *I*-mapness of T (Lemma 1), and Eq. (3.25) follows from the *I*-mapness of G, since the variables that $C_{j(i)}$ does not share with C_i are separated from those in C_i by the variables common to both C_i and $C_{j(i)}$. In Figure 3.9a, for example, A is separated from D by $\{B, C\}$. Q.E.D.

To render P decomposable relative to some graph G, it is enough that G be any *I*-map of P; it need not be minimal. Thus, if we wish to express P as a product of marginal distributions of clusters of variables, and the Markov network G_0 of P happens to be non-chordal, it is possible to make G_0 chordal by filling in the missing chords and expressing P as a product of distributions defined on the cliques of the resulting graph. For example, if the Markov network of a certain model is given by the graph of Figure 3.9a with edge (BC) missing (as in Figure 3.2), G_0 is not chordal, and we cannot express P as a product of the pairwise distributions $P(a, b)$, $P(a, c)$, $P(c, d)$, $P(d, b)$, and $P(e, d)$. However, by filling in the link (B, C) we create a chordal *I*-map G of P (Theorem 5), and we can express P as a product of distributions on the cliques of G, as in Eq. (3.22). It is true that the condition $I(B, AD, C)$ is not explicit in the expression of Eq. (3.22) and can be encoded only by careful numerical crafting of the distributions $P(a, b, c)$ and $P(b, c, d)$. However, once encoded, the tree structure of the cliques of G facilitates convenient, recursive updating of probabilities [Lauritzen and Spiegelhalter 1988], as will be shown in Section 4.4.1. Moreover, in situations where the cluster distributions are obtained by statistical measurements, the graph triangulation method can help the experimenter select the right variable clusters for measurement [Goldman and Rivest 1986]. For example, in the model depicted by Figure 3.2, graph triangulation would prompt the experimenter to tabulate measurements of variable triplets (such as $\{M_1, F_1, F_2\}$ and $\{M_2, F_1, F_2\}$) as well as variable pairs.

3.3 BAYESIAN NETWORKS

The main weakness of Markov networks is their inability to represent induced and non-transitive dependencies; two independent variables will be directly connected by an edge, merely because some other variable depends on both. As a result, many useful independencies go unrepresented in the network. To overcome this deficiency, Bayesian networks use the richer language of *directed* graphs, where the directions of the arrows permit us to distinguish genuine dependencies from spurious dependencies induced by hypothetical observations. Reiterating the example of Section 3.1.3, if the sound of a bell is functionally determined by the outcomes of two coins, we will use the network *coin 1 → bell ← coin 2*, without connecting *coin 1* to *coin 2*. This network reflects the natural perception of causal influences; the arrows indicate that the sound of the bell is determined by the coin outcomes, which are mutually independent.

These arrows endow special status on paths that traverse converging arrows, like the path leading from *coin 1* to *coin 2* through *bell*. Such a path should not be interpreted as forming a connection between the variables at the tails of the arrows; the connection should be considered nonexistent, or *blocked,* until the variable *bell* (or any of its descendents) is instantiated. This direction-dependent criterion of connectivity, called *d-separation,* captures the induced dependency relationship among the three variables: the outcomes of the two coins are marginally independent, but they become mutually dependent when we learn the outcome of the bell (or any external evidence bearing on that outcome). The *d*-separation criterion is replaced by the usual cutset criterion of Markov networks whenever the arrows are diverging (*height ← age → reading ability*) or cascaded (*weather → wheat crop → wheat price*).

A formal definition of the *d*-separation criterion for general directed acyclic graphs (DAGs) is given in Section 3.3.1. The criterion permits us to determine by inspection which sets of variables are considered independent of each other given a third set, thus making any DAG an unambiguous representation of dependency. In Section 3.3.2 we examine the possibility of using DAGs as minimal *I*-maps for probabilistic models, in much the same way that undirected graphs were used as minimal *I*-maps for Markov networks. Such minimal *I*-map DAGs will be called *Bayesian networks.*

In keeping with our treatment of Markov networks at the beginning of Section 3.2, we now address the following questions regarding Bayesian networks:

1. Given a probability distribution *P,* can we construct an edge-minimal DAG *D* that is an *I*-map of *P*?

2. Given a pair (*P, D*) can we test whether *D* is a (minimal) *I*-map of *P*?

3. Given a DAG *D,* can we construct a probability distribution *P* such that *D* is a perfect map of *P*?

Once again, the first two questions have simple solutions obtained by nonnumeric analysis and based solely on the axioms of conditional independence (Eq. (3.6)). This time, however, the semi-graphoid axioms, Eqs. (3.6a) through (3.6d), are used in the derivations, with the intersection axiom, Eq. (3.6e), playing only a minor role. Thus, the directionality of the arrows gives Bayesian networks another advantage over Markov networks; the requirement of strict positivity (i.e., the axiom of intersection) is no longer necessary for constructing an *I*-map from local dependencies. Hence, the network can serve as an inference instrument for logical and functional dependencies, too.

An even bigger advantage, perhaps, of the directed graph representations, is that they make it easy to quantify the links with local, conceptually meaningful parameters that turn the network as a whole into a globally consistent knowledge base. This feature is discussed in Section 3.3.2. Finally, in Section 3.3.3 we compare Bayesian networks with Markov networks for expressive power and range of applicability.

3.3.1 Dependence Semantics for Bayesian Networks

Bayesian networks are DAGs in which the nodes represent variables, the arcs signify the existence of direct causal influences between the linked variables, and the strengths of these influences are expressed by forward conditional probabilities.

The semantics of Bayesian networks demands a clear correspondence between the topology of a DAG and the dependence relationships portrayed by it. With Markov networks this correspondence was based on a simple separation criterion: If the removal of some subset Z of nodes from the network rendered nodes X and Y disconnected, then X and Y were proclaimed to be independent given Z, i.e.,

$$< X \mid Z \mid Y >_G \implies I(X, Z, Y).$$

DAGs use a slightly more complex separability criterion, called *d*-separation, which takes into consideration the directionality of the arrows in the graph.

DEFINITION: *If X, Y, and Z are three disjoint subsets of nodes in a DAG D, then Z is said to **d-separate** X from Y, denoted $< X \mid Z \mid Y >_D$, if along every path between a node in X and a node in Y there is node w satisfying one of the following two conditions: (1) w has converging arrows and none of w or its descendants are in Z, or (2) w does not have converging arrows and w is in Z.*

If a path satisfies the condition above, it is said to be *blocked*; otherwise, it is said to be *activated* by **Z**. In Figure 3.10, for example, $X = \{2\}$ and $Y = \{3\}$ are *d*-separated by $Z = \{1\}$; the path $2 \leftarrow 1 \rightarrow 3$ is blocked by $1 \in Z$, and the path $2 \rightarrow 4 \leftarrow 3$ is blocked because 4 and all its descendants are outside **Z**. *X* and *Y* are not *d*-separated by $Z' = \{1, 5\}$, however, because the path $2 \rightarrow 4 \leftarrow 3$ is rendered active: learning the value of the consequence 5 renders 5's causes, 2 and 3, dependent.

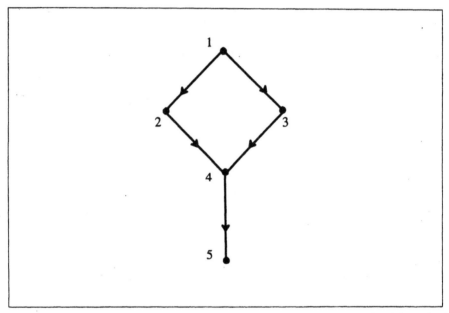

Figure 3.10. *A DAG depicting d-separation; node 1 blocks the path 2-1-3, while node 5 activates the path 2-4-3.*

The procedure for testing *d*-separation is only slightly more complicated than the conventional test for cutset separation in undirected graphs, and it can be handled by visual inspection. The only difference is that pathways along converging arrows, representing predicted events, are considered blocked until activated by evidential information. This is a basic pattern of diagnostic reasoning; for example, two inputs of a logic gate are presumed independent, but if the output becomes known, what we learn about one input has bearing on the other.

BAYESIAN NETWORKS AS I-MAPS

DEFINITION: *A DAG D is said to be an **I-map** of a dependency model M if every d-separation condition displayed in D corresponds to a valid conditional independence relationship in M, i.e., if for every three disjoint sets of vertices X, Y, and Z we have*

$$<X|Z|Y>_D \implies I(X, Z, Y)_M.$$

*A DAG is a **minimal** I-map of M if none of its arrows can be deleted without destroying its I-mapness.*

DEFINITION: *Given a probability distribution P on a set of variables U, a DAG $D = (U, \overrightarrow{E})$ is called a **Bayesian network** of P iff D is a minimal I-map of P.*

We now address the task of constructing a Bayesian network for any given distribution P.

DEFINITION: *Let M be a dependency model defined on a set $U = \{X_1, X_2,..., X_n\}$ of elements, and let d be an ordering $(X_1, X_2,..., X_i,...)$ of the elements of U. The **boundary strata** of M relative to d is an ordered set of subsets of U, $(B_1, B_2,..., B_i,...)$, such that each B_i is a Markov boundary of X_i with respect to the set $U_{(i)} = \{X_1, X_2,..., X_{i-1}\}$, i.e., B_i is a minimal set satisfying $B_i \subseteq U_{(i)}$ and $I(X_i, B_i, U_{(i)} - B_i)$. The DAG created by designating each B_i as parents of vertex X_i is called a **boundary DAG** of M relative to d.*

THEOREM 9: [Verma 1986]: *Let M be any semi-graphoid (i.e., any dependency model satisfying the axioms of Eqs. (3.6a) through (3.6d)). If D is a boundary DAG of M relative to any ordering d, then D is a minimal I-map of M.*

Theorem 9 is the key to constructing and testing Bayesian networks, as will be shown via three corollaries. The first corollary follows from the fact that every probability distribution P is a semi-graphoid (see Theorem 1).

COROLLARY 3: *Given a probability distribution $P(x_1, x_2,..., x_n)$ and any ordering d of the variables, the DAG created by designating as parents of X_i any minimal set Π_{X_i} of predecessors satisfying*

$$P(x_i | \Pi_{X_i}) = P(x_i | x_1,..., x_{i-1}) , \quad \Pi_{X_i} \subseteq \{X_1, X_2,..., X_{i-1}\} \qquad (3.27)$$

is a Bayesian network of P. If P is strictly positive, then all of the parent sets are unique (see Theorem 4) and the Bayesian network is unique (given d).

Although the structure of a Bayesian network depends strongly on the node ordering used in constructing it, each network nevertheless is an I-map of the underlying distribution P. This means that all conditional independencies portrayed in the network (via d-separation) are valid in P and hence are independent of the construction ordering. An immediate corollary of this observation yields an order-independent definition of Bayesian networks and a solution to Question 2 from the beginning of this section.

COROLLARY 4: *Given a DAG D and a probability distribution P, a necessary and sufficient condition for D to be a Bayesian network of P is that each variable X be conditionally independent of all its non-descendants, given its parents Π_X, and that no proper subset of Π_X satisfy this condition.*

The "necessary" part holds because every parent set Π_X d-separates X from all its non-descendants. The "sufficient" part holds because X's independence of all its non-descendants means X is also independent of its predecessors in a particular ordering d (as required by Corollary 3).

COROLLARY 5: *If a Bayesian network D is constructed by the boundary-strata method in some ordering d, then any ordering d´ consistent with the direction of arrows in D will give rise to the same network topology.*

Corollary 5 follows from Corollary 4, which ensures that the set Π_{X_i} will satisfy Eq. (3.27) in any new ordering as long as the new set of X_i's predecessors does not contain any of X_i's old descendants. Thus, once the network is constructed, the original order can be forgotten; only the partial ordering displayed in the network matters.

Another interesting corollary of Theorem 9 is a generalization of the celebrated *Markov chain* property, which is used extensively in the probabilistic analysis of random walks, time-series data, and other stochastic processes [Feller 1968; Meditch 1969; Abend, Hartley, and Kanal 1965]. The property states the following: if in a sequence of n trials $X_1, X_2, ..., X_n$ the outcome of any trial X_k (where $2 \le k \le n$) depends only on the outcome of the directly preceding trial X_{k-1}, then, given all its predecessors and successors, the outcome of X_k depends on its adjacent outcomes, X_{k-1} and X_{k+1}. Formally,

$$I(X_k, X_{k-1}, X_1 \cdots X_{k-2}) \implies I(X_k, X_{k-1} X_{k+1}, X_1 \cdots X_{k-2} X_{k+2} \cdots X_n).$$

(The converse holds only in strictly positive distributions, i.e., graphoids.) Theorem 9 generalizes the Markov chain property to non-probabilistic dependencies and to structures that are not chains, and, as the following corollary shows, the d-separation criterion uniquely determines a Markov blanket for any node X in a given Bayesian network (see Eq. (3.12)).

COROLLARY 6: *In any Bayesian network, the union of the following three types of neighbors is sufficient for forming a Markov blanket of a node X: the direct parents of X, the direct successors of X, and all direct parents of X's direct successors.*

Thus, if the network consists of a single path (i.e., is a Markov chain), the Markov blanket of any nonterminal node consists of its two immediate neighbors, as expected. In a tree, the Markov blanket consists of the (unique) father and the immediate successors. In Figure 3.10, however, the Markov blanket of node 3 is {1, 4, 2}. The reason the sets defined by Corollary 6 are Markov blankets but generally are not Markov boundaries is that alternative orderings might give X a different set of neighbors.

BAYESIAN NETWORKS AS A LOGIC OF DEPENDENCIES

A Bayesian network can be viewed as an inference instrument for deducing new independence relationships from those used in constructing the network. The topology of the network is assembled from a list of independence statements that comprise the boundary strata. This input list implies a host of additional statements, many of which can be deduced from the network by graphical criteria such as d-separation. For example, the network in Figure 3.10 was constructed from the boundary strata

$$(B_2 = \{1\}, B_3 = \{1\}, B_4 = \{2, 3\}, B_5 = \{4\}),$$

representing the independency list

$$L = \{I(2, 1, \varnothing), I(3, 1, 2), I(4, 23, 1), I(5, 4, 123)\}.$$

New independence relationships, all of them valid consequences of L, can be deduced from the network—e.g., $I(5, 23, 1)$ and $I(3, 124, 5)$. This raises the following questions:

1. Can d-separation be improved? Can a more sophisticated criterion reveal additional independencies that are valid consequences of the input information?

2. Are there valid consequences that escape graphical representation altogether?

The answer to both questions is no; every valid consequence of the input information L must show up as a d-separation condition in the DAG built from L. This follows from the next theorem.

THEOREM 10: [Geiger and Pearl 1988a]: *For any DAG D there exists a probability distribution P such that D is a perfect map of P relative to d-separation, i.e., P embodies all the independencies portrayed in D, and no others.*

Theorem 10 makes it impossible for some valid consequence σ of the input list to escape detection by *d*-separation. Any such σ is valid in all distributions that obey the input, and hence a probability *P* as specified in Theorem 10 (a probability that ought to violate σ) cannot exist.

COROLLARY 7: *Given a list L of independence relationships in the form of a boundary strata, a Bayesian network combined with the d-separation criterion constitutes a polynomially sound and complete inference mechanism relative to the closure of L, i.e., it identifies in polynomial time every conditional independence relationship that follows logically from those in L.*

Note, however, that a prerequisite of completeness is that the input be a boundary strata, i.e., that it identify recursively a Markov boundary for each element, in some order *d*. The tractability (and even the decidability) of the general membership problem, relative to an arbitrary noncausal input list of conditional independence statements, hinges upon the completeness conjecture stated in Section 3.1.2. Evidently, there are subtle computational advantages to organizing information in chronologically ordered strata. Whether this feature lends importance to causal schemata in knowledge organization is an interesting topic which we will leave for speculation.

3.3.2 Bayesian Network as a Knowledge Base

STRUCTURING THE NETWORK

In principle, given any joint distribution $P(x_1, ..., x_n)$ and an ordering d on the variables in U, Corollary 4 prescribes a simple recursive procedure for constructing a Bayesian network. We start by choosing X_1 as a root and assign to it the marginal probability $P(x_1)$ dictated by $P(x_1, ..., x_n)$. Next, we form a node to represent X_2; if X_2 is dependent on X_1, a link from X_1 to X_2 is established and quantified by $P(x_2 | x_1)$. Otherwise, we leave X_1 and X_2 unconnected and assign the prior probability $P(x_2)$ to node X_2. At the *i*-th stage, we form the node X_i, draw a group of directed links to X_i from a parent set Π_{X_i} defined by Eq. (3.27), and quantify this group of links by the conditional probability $P(x_i | \Pi_{X_i})$. The result is a directed acyclic graph that represents many of the independencies embedded in $P(x_1, ..., x_n)$, i.e., all the independencies that follow logically from the definitions of the parent sets (Eq. (3.27)).

Conversely, the conditional probabilities $P(x_i \mid \Pi_{X_i})$ on the links of the DAG should contain all the information necessary for reconstructing the original distribution function. Writing the chain rule formula in the ordering d and using Eq. (3.27), we get the product

$$P(x_1, x_2,..., x_n) = P(x_n \mid x_{n-1},..., x_1) \, P(x_{n-1} \mid x_{n-2},..., x_1)$$

$$\cdots P(x_3 \mid x_2, x_1) \, P(x_2 \mid x_1) \, P(x_1)$$

$$= \prod_i P(x_i \mid \Pi_{X_i}). \tag{3.28}$$

For example, the distribution corresponding to the DAG of Figure 3.11 can be written by inspection:

$$P(x_1, x_2, x_3, x_4, x_5, x_6) \tag{3.29}$$

$$= P(x_6 \mid x_5) \, P(x_5 \mid x_2, x_3) \, P(x_4 \mid x_1, x_2) \cdot P(x_3 \mid x_1) \, P(x_2 \mid x_1) \, P(x_1).$$

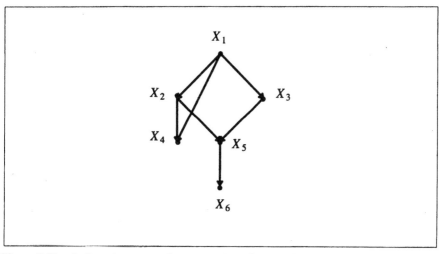

Figure 3.11. *A Bayesian network representing the distribution* $P(x_6 \mid x_5) \, P(x_5 \mid x_2, x_3)$ $P(x_4 \mid x_1, x_2) \, P(x_3 \mid x_1) \, P(x_2 \mid x_1) \, P(x_1).$

In practice, however, a numerical representation for $P(x_1,...,x_n)$ is rarely available. Instead we normally have only intuitive understanding of the major constraints in the domain. The graph can still be configured as before, but the parent sets Π_{X_i} must be identified by human judgment.

The parents of X_i are those variables judged to be *direct causes* of X_i or to have *direct influence* on X_i. The informal notions of causation and influence replace the formal notion of directional conditional independence as defined in Eq. (3.27). An important feature of the network representation is that it permits people to express directly the fundamental, qualitative relationships of direct influence; the network augments these with derived relationships of *indirect influence* and preserves them, even if the numerical assignments are just sloppy estimates. In Figure 3.11, for example, the model builder did not state that X_6 can tell us nothing new about X_1 once we know X_2 and X_3, but the relationship is logically implied by other inputs and will remain part of the model, regardless of the numbers assigned to the links.

The addition to the network of any new node Y requires that the knowledge provider identify a set Π_Y of variables that bear directly on Y, assess the strength of this relationship, and make no commitment regarding the effect of Y on variables outside Π_Y. Even though each judgment is performed locally, their sum is guaranteed to be complete and consistent, as we shall see next.

QUANTIFYING THE LINKS

Suppose we are given a DAG D in which the arrows pointing to each node X_i emanate from a set Π_{X_i} of parent nodes judged to have direct influence on X_i. To specify consistently the strengths of these influences, one need only assess the conditional probabilities $P(x_i \mid \Pi_{X_i})$ by some functions $F_i(x_i, \Pi_{X_i})$ and make sure these assessments satisfy

$$\sum_{x_i} F_i(x_i, \Pi_{X_i}) = 1 , \tag{3.30}$$

where $0 \le F_i(x_i, \Pi_{X_i}) \le 1$ and the summation ranges over the domain of X_i. This specification is complete and consistent because the product form

$$P_a(x_1, ..., x_n) = \prod_i F_i(x_i, \Pi_{X_i}) \tag{3.31}$$

constitutes a joint probability distribution that supports the assessed quantities. In other words, if we compute the conditional probabilities $P_a(x_i \mid \Pi_{X_i})$ dictated by $P_a(x_1, ..., x_n)$, the original assessments $F_i(x_i, \Pi_{X_i})$ will be recovered:

$$P_a(x_i \mid \Pi_{X_i}) = \frac{P_a(x_i, \Pi_{X_i})}{P_a(\Pi_{X_i})} = \frac{\displaystyle\sum_{x_j \notin (x_i \cup \Pi_{X_i})} P_a(x_1,..., x_n)}{\displaystyle\sum_{x_j \notin \Pi_{X_i}} P_a(x_1,..., x_n)} = F_i(x_i, \Pi_{X_i}). \tag{3.32}$$

Moreover, all the independencies dictated by the choices of Π_{X_i} (corresponding to those in Eq. (3.27)) are embodied in P_a.

Building models this way is much easier than quantifying Markov networks. The parameters requested from the model builder are the conditional probabilities that quantify many conceptual relationships in one's mind, e.g., cause-effect or frame-slot relations, they are psychologically meaningful and can be obtained by direct measurement. The thinking required for assessing the parameters of $P(x_i \mid \Pi_{x_i})$ is estimating the likelihood that the event $X_i = x_i$ will occur, given any instantiation of the variables in Π_{X_i} (for example, the likelihood that a patient will develop a certain symptom, assuming that he suffers from a given combination of disorders). These kinds of assessments are natural because they point to familiar frames (e.g., diseases) by which people organize empirical knowledge.

DAGs constructed by this method will be called *Bayesian belief networks* or *causal networks* interchangeably, the former emphasizing the judgmental origin and probabilistic nature of the quantifiers and the latter reflecting the directionality of the links. Such networks have a long and rich tradition, starting with the geneticist Sewal Wright in 1921. He developed a method called *path analysis* [Wright 1934], which later became an established representation of causal models in economics [Wold 1964], sociology [Blalock 1971; Kenny 1979], and psychology [Duncan 1975]. *Influence diagrams* represent another component in this tradition [Howard and Matheson 1981; Shachter 1986]; developed for decision analysis, they contain both event nodes and action nodes (see Chapter 6). *Recursive models* is the name given to such networks by statisticians seeking meaningful and effective decompositions of contingency tables [Lauritzen 1982; Wermuth and Lauritzen 1983; Kiiveri, Speed, and Carlin 1984].

In the strictest sense, Bayesian networks are not graphs but hypergraphs, because describing the dependency of a given node on its k parents requires a function of $k+1$ arguments; in general, it cannot be specified by k two-place functions on the individual links. Still, the directionality of the arrows and the fact that many parents remain unlinked convey important information that would be lost if we used the standard hypergraph representation and specified only the list of dependent subsets.

If the number of parents k is large, estimating $P(x \mid \Pi_{x_i})$ may be troublesome. In principle, it requires a table of size 2^k (for binary variables), but in practice (as noted in Section 2.2) people structure causal relationships into small prototypical clusters of variables; each requiring about k parameters. Common examples of such structures are noisy OR-gates (i.e., any variable is likely to trigger the effect), noisy AND-gates, and various enabling mechanisms (i.e., variables having no influence of their own except that they enable other influences to take effect). Detailed analysis of the noisy-OR-gate model is given in Section 4.3.2.

THE ROLE OF CAUSALITY

Note that the topology of a Bayesian network can be extremely sensitive to the node ordering d. What is a tree in one ordering might become a complete graph if that ordering is reversed. For example, if $X_1, ..., X_n$ stands for the outcomes of n independent coins, and X_{n+1} represents the output of a detector triggered when any coin comes up heads, then the Bayesian network will be an inverted tree of n arrows pointing from each of the variables $X_1, ..., X_n$ to X_{n+1}. On the other hand, if the detector's outcome is chosen to be the first variable, say X_0, then the resulting Bayesian network will be a complete graph.

This sensitivity to order may seem paradoxical at first; d can be chosen arbitrarily, whereas people have fairly uniform conceptual structures, e.g., they agree on whether two propositions are directly or indirectly related. This consensus about the structure of dependencies shows the dominant role causality plays in the formation of these structures. In other words, the standard ordering imposed by the direction of causation indirectly induces identical topologies on the networks that people adopt to encode experiential knowledge. Were it not for the social convention of adopting a standard ordering of events that conforms to the flow of time and causation, human communication as we know it might be impossible. Why, then, do we use temporal ordering to organize our memory? It may be because information about temporal precedence is more readily available than other indexing information, or it may be that networks constructed with temporal ordering are inherently more parsimonious (i.e., they display more independencies.) Experience with expert systems applications does not entirely rule out the second possibility [Shachter and Heckerman 1987]. More on this subject can be found in Chapter 8.

3.3.3 How Expressive Are Bayesian Networks?

One might expect the introduction of directionality into the language of graphs to render directed graphs more expressive, i.e., capable of portraying more conditional independencies. We saw, indeed, that the d-separation criterion permits us to display induced and non-transitive dependencies that were excluded from the Markov network vocabulary. So we might ask how DAGs compare for expressive power with undirected graphs and probability models. Two questions arise:

1.   Can all dependencies that are representable by a Markov network also be represented by a Bayesian network?

2.   How well can Bayesian networks represent the type of dependencies induced by probabilistic models?

The answer to the first question is clearly no. For instance, the dependency structure of a diamond-shaped Markov network (e.g., Figure 3.2) with edges (AB), (AC), (CD), and (BD) asserts two independence relationships: $I(A, BC, D)$ and $I(B, AD, C)$. No Bayesian network can express these two relationships simultaneously and exclusively. If we direct the arrows from A to D, we get

$I(A, BC, D)$ but not $I(B, AD, C)$; if we direct the arrows from B to C, we get $I(B, AD, C)$ but not $I(A, BC, D)$. In view of property iv of Theorem 7, it is clear that this difficulty will always be encountered in non-chordal graphs. No matter how we direct the arrows, there will always be a pair of nonadjacent parents sharing a common child, a configuration that yields independence in Markov networks and dependence in Bayesian networks.

On the other hand, property iv of Theorem 7 also asserts that every chordal graph can be oriented so that the tails of every pair of converging arrows are adjacent. Hence, every dependency model that is isomorphic to a chordal graph is also isomorphic to a DAG. We conclude that the class of probabilistic dependencies that can be represented by both a DAG and an undirected graph are those that form decomposable models, i.e., probability distributions that have perfect maps in chordal graphs. These relationships are shown schematically in Figure 3.12.

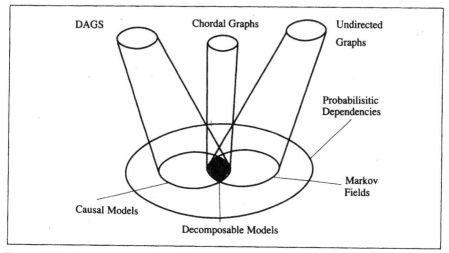

Figure 3.12. *Correspondence between probabilistic models and their graphical representations.*

The answer to Question 2 is also not encouraging. Clearly, no graphical representation can distinguish connectivity between sets from connectivity among their elements. In other word, in both directed and undirected graphs, separation between two sets of vertices is defined in terms of pairwise separation between their corresponding individual elements. In probability theory, on the other hand, independence of elements does not imply independence of sets (see Eq. (3.6b)), as the coins and bell example demonstrated. When the two coins are fair, any two variables are mutually independent, but every variable is (deterministically) dependent on the other two.

CAUSAL MODELS AND THEIR DEPENDENCY STRUCTURE

Despite these shortcomings, we will see that the DAG representation is more flexible than the undirected graph representation, and it captures a larger set of probabilistic independencies, especially those that are conceptually meaningful. To show this, we offer a partial axiomatic characterization of DAG dependencies that indicates clearly where they differ from undirected graph dependencies (Eq. (3.10)) and from probabilistic dependencies (Eq. (3.6)).

DEFINITION: *A dependency model M is said to be **causal**(or a DAG isomorph) if there is a DAG D that is a perfect map of M relative to d-separation, i.e.,*

$$I(X, Z, Y)_M \iff <X \mid Z \mid Y>_D. \tag{3.33}$$

THEOREM 11: *A necessary condition for a dependency model M to be a DAG isomorph is that $I(X, Z, Y)_M$ satisfies the following independent axioms (the subscript M is dropped for clarity):*

Symmetry:
$$I(X, Z, Y) \iff I(Y, Z, X). \tag{3.34a}$$

Composition/Decomposition:
$$I(X, Z, Y \cup W) \iff I(X, Z, Y) \& I(X, Z, W). \tag{3.34b}$$

Intersection:
$$I(X, Z \cup W, Y) \& I(X, Z \cup Y, W) \implies I(X, Z, Y \cup W). \tag{3.34c}$$

Weak union:
$$I(X, Z, Y \cup W) \implies I(X, Z \cup W, Y). \tag{3.34d}$$

Contraction:
$$I(X, Z \cup Y, W) \& I(X, Z, Y) \implies I(X, Z, Y \cup W). \tag{3.34e}$$

Weak transitivity:
$$I(X, Z, Y) \& I(X, Z \cup \gamma, Y) \implies I(X, Z, \gamma) \ or \ I(\gamma, Z, Y). \tag{3.34f}$$

Chordality:
$$I(\alpha, \gamma \cup \delta, \beta) \& I(\gamma, \alpha \cup \beta, \delta) \implies I(\alpha, \gamma, \beta) \ or \ I(\alpha, \delta, \beta). \tag{3.34g}$$

REMARKS:

1. Symmetry, intersection, weak union, and contraction are identical to the axioms governing probabilistic dependencies (Eq. (3.6)). Composition, weak transitivity, and chordality are constraints that go beyond Eq. (3.6). Thus, not every probabilistic model is a DAG isomorph.

2. Comparing Eq. (3.34) to the axioms defining separation in undirected graphs (Eq. (3.10)), we note that (Eq. (3.10)) implies all axioms in (Eq. (3.34)) except chordality (Eq. (3.34*g*)). Weak union is implied by strong union, composition and contraction are implied by intersection and strong union, and weak transitivity is implied by transitivity.

WEAK TRANSITIVITY

Weak transitivity (Eq. (3.34*f*)) means that if two sets of variables X and Y, are both unconditionally and conditionally independent given a singleton variable γ, it is impossible for both X and Y to be dependent on γ. Contrapositively, if X and Y are each dependent on γ, then they must be dependent on each other in some way, either marginally or conditionally given γ. This restriction, which may be violated in some probability models, remains in effect when we associate independence with d-separation in DAGs.

THEOREM 12: *d-separation in DAGs is weakly transitive.*

Proof: If both X and Y are d-connected to γ in some DAG, then there must be an unblocked path from X to γ and an unblocked path from Y to γ. These two paths form at least one bidirected path from X to Y via γ. If that path traverses γ along converging arrows, it should be unblocked when we instantiate γ, so X and Y cannot be d-separated given γ. Conversely, if the arrows meeting at γ do not converge, the path from X to Y is unblocked when γ is uninstantiated, so X and Y cannot be marginally d-separated. Q.E.D.

Probability theory does not insist on weak transitivity, as it allows the following four conditions to exist simultaneously:

$$I(X, \varnothing, Y)_P, \ I(X, \gamma, Y)_P, \ \neg I(X, \varnothing, \gamma)_P, \ \neg I(Y, \varnothing, \gamma)_P.$$

For example, let X and Y be singleton binary variables, $X, Y \in \{TRUE, FALSE\}$, and let γ be a ternary variable, $\gamma \in \{1, 2, 3\}$. Choosing

$$P(x, y, \gamma) = P(x \mid \gamma) \, P(\gamma \mid y) \, P(y),$$

$$P(X = TRUE \mid \gamma) = (1/2, 1/4, 3/8),$$

$$P(\gamma \mid Y = TRUE) = (1/3, 1/3, 1/3),$$

$$P(\gamma \mid Y = FALSE) = (1/2, 1/2, 0)$$

renders γ dependent on both X and Y, yet X and Y are mutually independent, both conditionally (given γ) and unconditionally. Thus, although DAGs seem more capable than undirected graphs of displaying non-transitive dependencies, even DAGs require some weak form of transitivity and cannot capture totally non-transitive probabilistic dependencies. It can be shown, however, that if all variables are either normally distributed or binary, all probabilistic dependencies must be weakly transitive (see Exercise 3.10).

CHORDALITY AND AUXILIARY VARIABLES

The chordality axiom (Eq. (3.34g)) excludes dependency models that are isomorphic to non-chordal graphs (such as the one in Figure 3.13a), since these cannot be completely captured by DAGs (see Figure 3.12). In essence, Eq. (3.34g) insists that we either add the appropriate chords to any long cycle (length ≥ 4), thus disobeying the antecedent of Eq. (3.34g), or nullify some of its links, thus satisfying the consequent of Eq. (3.34g).

Though DAGs cannot represent non-chordal dependencies, this deficiency can be eliminated by introducing auxiliary variables. Consider the diamond-shaped graph of Figure 3.13a, which asserts two independence relationships: $I(A, BC, D)$ and $I(B, AD, C)$.

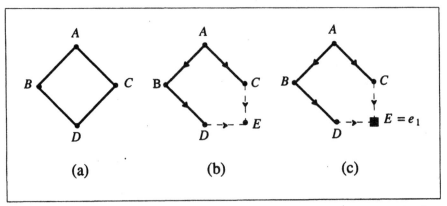

Figure 3.13. *The dependencies of an undirected graph (a) are represented by a DAG (c) using an auxilliary node E.*

Introducing an auxiliary variable E as shown in Figure 3.13b creates a DAG model of five variables whose dependencies are represented by the joint distribution function

$$P(a, b, c, d, e) = P(e \mid d, c) \, P(d \mid b) \, P(c \mid a) \, P(b \mid a) \, P(a).$$

Now imagine that we clamp the auxiliary variable E to some fixed value $E = e_1$, as in Figure 3.13c. The dependency structure that the clamped DAG induces on A, B, C, D is identical to the original structure (Figure 3.13a). Indeed, applying the d-separation criterion to Figure 3.12c uncovers the two original independencies: $I(A, BC, D)$ and $I(B, AD, C)$. The marginal distribution of the original variables conditioned upon $E = e_1$ is given by

$$P(a, b, c, d \,|\, E = e_1) = \frac{P(a, b, c, d, e_1)}{P(e_1)}$$

$$= K\, P(e_1 \,|\, d, c)\, P(d \,|\, b)\, P(c \,|\, a)\, P(b \,|\, a)\, P(a)$$

$$= g_1(d, c)\, g_2(d, b)\, g_3(a, c)\, g_4(a, b).$$

Using the analysis of Section 3.2.3, we see that this distribution is equivalent to the one portrayed by Figure 3.13a. Thus, the introduction of auxiliary variables permits us to dispose of the chordality restriction of Eq. (3.34g) and renders the DAG representation superior to that of undirected graphs; every dependency model expressible by the latter is also expressible by the former.

Weak transitivity and chordality are not the only dependencies that are sanctioned by probability theory but are not representable by DAGs. For example, one can show that the following axiom must hold in DAGs:

$$I(Y, X, Z)\ \&\ I(Z, Y, X)\ \&\ I(W, Z, X) \Longrightarrow I(X, \varnothing, W).$$

But its denial,

$$I(Y, X, Z)\ \&\ I(Z, Y, X)\ \&\ I(W, Z, X)\ \&\ \neg\, I(X, \varnothing, W),$$

is tolerated by probability theory (see Exercise 3.7). The question arises whether the class of properties specific to DAGs can be characterized axiomatically the way that of undirected graphs was (Theorem 2). The answer is probably no. The results of Geiger [1987] strongly suggest that the number of axioms required for a complete characterization of the d-separation in DAGs is unbounded.

3.4 BIBLIOGRAPHICAL AND HISTORICAL REMARKS

The idea of using graphical representations for probabilistic information can be traced to the geneticist Sewal Wright [1921], who developed the method of *path analysis* "as an aid in the biometric analysis of certain classes of data." The method came under severe attack (e.g., Niles [1922]) and was shunned by statisticians during the first half of the 20th century (an era ruled by hard data and quantitative analysis), until it was discovered by economists, psychologists, and sociologists (see Section 7.2). The 1960s saw a reversal of this outlook, with statisticians such as Vorobev [1962], Goodman [1970], and Haberman [1974] realizing that some decomposition properties of statistical tables (called log-linear models) can best be expressed in graphical terms. These explorations led to an appreciation of the desirable properties of join trees, which were later recognized by database researchers [Beeri et al. 1983]. Lemmer [1983] has suggested the use of trees of local events groups (LEGs) for Bayesian updating, and Spiegelhalter [1986] proposed the fill-in algorithm to transform Bayesian networks into join trees. Other mathematical properties of chordal graphs are given in Golumbic [1980].

The development of Markov fields progressed in parallel, but from an opposite direction. Here, the network topology was presumed to be given (usually a geometrical arrangement of physical elements in space), and the problem was to characterize the probabilistic behavior of a system complying with the dependencies prescribed by the network. A survey of Markov fields can be found in Isham [1981]. Lauritzen [1982] applied the theory of Markov fields to the analysis of statistical tables and derived Theorems 3, 4, and 5 for independencies embedded in strictly positive probability distributions. Application of Markov fields to pattern recognition and vision are reported in Abend, Hartley, and Kanal [1965], Kanal [1981], and Geman and Geman [1984].

Since graphoids are a central theme of this chapter, and since the theory is still in its embryonic stage, we take the liberty now of presenting an extended history of this development.

The theory of graphoids was conceived in the summer of 1985, when Azaria Paz visited UCLA and he and I began collaborating on the problem of graphical representations. Inspired by Lauritzen's lecture notes on contingency tables [Lauritzen 1982], I sought axiomatic conditions on a dependency model M that would include probabilistic dependencies as a special case, such that the graph construction of Eq. (3.11) would yield an I-map of M. I posed the problem to Professor Paz, we labored for a few weeks, and he came up with a proof of what later became Theorem 3. Surprisingly, only three axioms were needed: symmetry, decomposition, and intersection. These, unfortunately, were not sufficient for Corollary 4, which Lauritzen listed among the properties of Markov fields. We then set out to discover what additional axioms were needed to ensure that the graph obtained by the edge-deletion method be identical to that built by the Markov boundary method. This led to Theorem 4, and to the identification of weak union as the final axiom we needed to fully characterize the graphical properties of Markov fields. The prospects of providing similar characterization for graph separation led to Theorem 2.

Strangely, the contraction axiom was not needed for Theorem 3 or for Theorem 4, but when added to the other four axioms of Eq. (3.6) it enabled us to derive all properties of probabilistic dependencies that we managed to dream up. Hence, we posed the completeness of these axioms as a conjecture[1], and coined the name *graphoid*.

Around this time, Thomas Verma began examining the validity of d-separation in DAGs (Theorem 9). I had introduced this criterion without proof [Pearl 1986c], since my attempts to demonstrate its general validity got entangled in messy probability formulas. I therefore suggested that Tom try a "clean" proof, using the graphoid axioms only, and to our surprise he managed to do it without the intersection axiom [Verma 1986]. This led to semi-graphoids, and to directed graph representations of both probabilistic and logical dependencies; we finally understood how important the contraction property is for causal modeling. The generality of this result made us confident that dependency theorists dealing with databases and qualitative dependencies will eventually adopt DAGs as a representation scheme for their semi-graphoids, e.g., EMVD [Fagin 1977].

In December 1985, Glenn Shafer mentioned a possible connection between graphoids and previous work of A. P. Dawid. As it turned out, Dawid had presented axioms equivalent to Eqs. (3.6.a) through (3.6.d) as early as 1979 [Dawid 1979] but apparently was not concerned with their completeness or their relation to graphical representations. Smith [1989] has recognized the generality of Dawid's axioms and has used them to prove Corollaries 4 and 5 without resorting to probabilistic manipulations (unlike the treatment of Howard and Matheson [1981]).

The power of the d-separation criterion would have remained only partially appreciated without Geiger's proof of Theorem 10. Aside from showing that d-separation cannot be improved, the theorem legitimizes the use of DAGs as a representation scheme for probabilistic dependencies; a model builder who uses the language of DAGs to express dependencies is shielded from inconsistencies.

Recent advances in the theory of graphoids and Bayesian networks are reported in the references below.[2]–[6]

---

[1] The conjecture has recently been refuted by Studeny, M. "Conditional Independence Relations Have No Finite Complete Characterization," *Proc. of 11th Prague Conf. on Inf. Theory, Statist. Decision Funct. and Random Processes*, Prague, 1990. Also *Kybernetika*, 25(1-3), 1990, 72-79.

[2] R.M. Oliver and J.Q. Smith (Eds), *Influence Diagrams, Belief Nets and Decision Analysis*, Sussex, England: John Wiley & Sons, Ltd., 1990.

[3] D. Geiger, "Graphoids: A Qualitative Framework for Probabilistic Inference." Ph.D. Dissertation. University of California Los Angeles, Computer Science Dept. January 1990.

[4] Shachter, R., (ed.), Special Issue on Influence Diagrams, *Networks*, 20(5), 1990.

[5] D. Geiger, A. Paz, and J. Pearl, "Axioms and Algorithms for Inferences Involving Probabilistic Independence," *Information and Computation*, Vol. 91, No. 1, March 1991, 128-141.

[6] Geva, R., "Representation of Irrelevance Relations by Graphs," M.Sc. Thesis, Dept. of Computer Science, Technion, Haifa, Israel, 1989.

Exercises

3.1. Show that Eqs. (3.6*a*) through (3.6*d*) imply the chaining rule

$$I(X, Y, Z) \ \& \ I(XY, Z, W) \Longrightarrow I(X, Y, W)$$

and show that this rule cannot replace Eq. (3.6*d*) in the set of axioms.

3.2. Show which axioms of Eq. (3.6) are satisfied by the following dependency models:

a. Let U be the set of nodes in an undirected graph G, and let X, Y, and Z be three disjoint sets of nodes in G. $I(X, Z, Y)_{M_1}$ iff all shortest paths between a node $X \in X$ and a node $Y \in Y$ are intercepted by some node in Z.

b. Let U be the set of nodes in an undirected graph G, and let X, Y, and Z be three disjoint sets of nodes in G. $I(X, Z, Y)_{M_2}$ iff all shortest paths between the sets X and Y are intercepted by Z.

c. Let U be the set of points in a three-dimensional Euclidean space, and let X, Y, and Z be three disjoint regions of U. $I(X, Z, Y)_{M_3}$ iff every ray of light from a point in X to some point in Y is intercepted by Z.

d. Let U be the set of n-dimensional vectors, and let X, Y, and Z be three disjoint sets of such vectors. Denote by S_Z the linear subspace spanned by any set Z. $I(X, Z, Y)_{M_4}$ iff the closest distance between X and S_Z is equal to the closest distance between X and $S_{Z \cup Y}$.

e. Let U be a set of random variables, let P be a probability distribution on those variables, and let X, Y, and Z be three disjoint subsets of U. $I(X, Z, Y)_{M_5}$ iff

$$P(x, z) > 0 \ \& \ P(y, z) > 0 \Longrightarrow P(x, y, z) > 0.$$

3.3.   Let $U = \{X, Y, Z, W\}$, and let $P(x, y, z, w)$ be given by the following table:

X	Y	Z	W	P
1	1	1	1	⅓
1	2	2	2	⅓
2	2	1	3	⅓
all other tuples				0

a.   Show that the graph G given below is a minimal I-map of P.

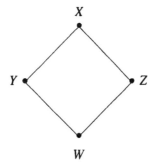

b.   Show that P cannot be expressed as a product of functions on the cliques of G.

c.   Find a tree I-map of P and express P as a product of functions on its edges.

d.   Draw all the Bayesian networks of P in the orderings (X, Y, Z, W) and (W, X, Y, Z) and compute their parameters.

3.4.   a.   Find the graphoid closure I^* of the set $I = \{(1, \varnothing, 2), (12, 3, 4)\}$.

b.   Construct the Markov network of I^*.

c.   Construct the Bayesian networks of I^* corresponding to the following 3 orderings: $(1, 2, 3, 4)$, $(4, 3, 2, 1)$, $(1, 4, 2, 3)$.

Note: The graphoid closure I^* is the smallest superset of I that is consistent with the axioms of Eqs. (3.6a) through (3.6e).

3.5.   We wish to construct a Bayesian network for a Markov field of an $N \times N$ grid in the plane. Find the set of parents of a typical node (e.g., row 3, column 5), in the following two orderings:

(a)   (b)

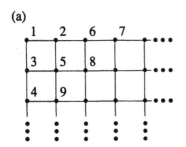   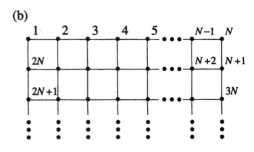

3.6.   **a.**   Find the Markov network G_0 of a probabilistic model P for which the following DAG is a perfect-map:

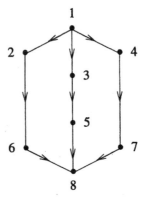

b.   Find an undirected graph G such that P (in problem (a)) is decomposable relative to G.

c.   Draw a join tree of G.

d.   Find an algebraic representation of P such that $P > 0$ for all events.

3.7.   (After D. Geiger)

a.   Prove that the following axiom holds for all DAGs:

$$I(\alpha_2, \alpha_1, \alpha_3) \ \& \ I(\alpha_3, \alpha_2, \alpha_4) \ \& \ I(\alpha_4, \alpha_3, \alpha_1) \Longrightarrow I(\alpha_1, \varnothing, \alpha_4)$$

(hint: use the definition of d-separation and prove by contradiction).

b. Generalize your arguments and prove that the following axiom holds as well:

$$I(\alpha_2, \alpha_1, \alpha_3) \& I(\alpha_3, \alpha_2, \alpha_4) \& \cdots \& I(\alpha_n, \alpha_{n-1}, \alpha_{n+1})$$
$$\& I(\alpha_{n+1}, \alpha_n, \alpha_1) \Longrightarrow I(\alpha_1, \varnothing \, \alpha_{n+1})$$

(where $n > 3$).

c. Construct a probability distribution that violates the axiom problem (a).

3.8. (After D. Geiger). Let P be a zero-mean normal distribution over n variables $X_1, ..., X_n$ with a covariance matrix $\Gamma = (\rho_{ij})$, where

$$\rho_{ij} = E[X_i \cdot X_j] \text{ and } E[X_i^2] = 1 \quad (1 \le i, j \le n).$$

a. Prove the following propositions:

$$I(X_i, \varnothing, X_j)_P \Longleftrightarrow \rho_{ij} = 0,$$
$$I(X_i, X_k, X_j)_P \Longleftrightarrow \rho_{ij} = \rho_{ik} \cdot \rho_{jk},$$

b. In light of Exercises **3.7a** and **3.8a** construct a normal distribution P such that no DAG is a perfect map of P.

3.9. a. Show that the axioms of Eqs. (3.34a) through (3.34g) do not preclude the occurrence of

$$I(X, \varnothing, Z) \& \neg I(X, Y, Z) \& I(Y, \varnothing, W) \& \neg I(Y, Z, W).$$

b. Show a DAG where Eqs. (3.34a) through (3.34g) hold (in *d*-separation) and X, Y, Z, and W are singleton nodes. (The DAG may have more than four nodes.)

c. Discuss the significance of problem (b) *vis a vis* the prospects of defining causal directionality in terms of dependencies.

3.10. Show that weak transitivity holds in
(a) every normal distribution, and
(b) every probability distribution over binary variables, relative to $Z=\varnothing$.

3.11. A *recursive diagram* [Wermuth and Lauritzen 1983] is a DAG constructed as follows: the elements of U are ordered $X_1, ..., X_n$ and the parents set S_i of each X_i is defined by $S_i = \{X_j : j < i$ and $\neg I(X_i, \{X_1, ..., X_{i-1}\} - X_j, X_j)\}$, namely, X_j is a parent of X_i if it remains dependent on X_i, given all other predecessors $\{X_1, ..., X_{i-1}\} - X_j$ of X_i.

a. Show that any recursive diagram constructed for a graphoid (i.e., a dependency model satisfying (3.6.*a*) to (3.6.*e*)) coincides with the Bayesian network constructed under the same ordering.

b. Show that for semi-graphoids (i.e., dependency models satisfying (3.6.*a*) to (3.6.*d*)) a recursive diagram is a subgraph of any Bayesian network constructed under the same ordering.

c. Find a probability distribution for which the Bayesian network is a chain but the recursive diagram has only one arc.

d. A recursive diagram R of a semi-graphoid M, has the shape of a linear chain of five nodes $1 \to 2 \to 3 \to 4 \to 5$. Using the same node ordering, draw all the DAGS that are guaranteed to be *I*-maps of M.

3.12. Given two DAGs, D_1 and D_2, on the same set of variables. Devise a polynomial time algorithm to test whether D_1 is an *I*-map of D_2 relative to *d*-separation.[1] What if D_2 contains a subset of the variables in D_1?[2]

3.13. A dag D is said to be a (causal) **model** of a probability function P if it is consistent with P, that is, the links of D can be annotated with conditional probabilities whose product equals P (see Eq. (3.28)). D is said to be a **minimal** model of P if the set of probabilities consistent with D is not a superset of those consistent with some other model of P.

a. Show that D is consistent with P iff it is an *I*-map of P.

Let a probability function P be isomorphic to a dag D:

b. Show that every minimal model of P must be a perfect map of D.

c. Show that every minimal model of P has the same arcs as D.

d. Identify the arcs in D whose orientation remains the same in all minimal models of P.[2]

[1] Pearl, J., D. Geiger & T. Verma, "The Logic and Influence Diagrams," in R.M. Oliver and J.Q. Smith (Eds.), *Influence Diagrams, Belief Nets and Decision Analysis*, Wiley, 1990, 67-87.

[2] T. Verma & J. Pearl, "Equivalence and Synthesis of Causal Models," in *Proc., Sixth Conf. on Uncertainty in AI*, Cambridge, Mass., 1990, 220-227. Also, North Holland, *UAI* 6, 1991, 255-268.

Appendix 3-A

Proof of Theorem 3

THEOREM 3 [Pearl and Paz 1985]: *Every dependency model M satisfying symmetry, decomposition, and intersection (see Eq. (3.6)) has a (unique) minimal I-map $G_0 = (U, E_0)$ produced by connecting only those pairs (α, β) for which $I(\alpha, U - \alpha - \beta, \beta)_M$ is FALSE, i.e.,*

$$(\alpha, \beta) \notin E_0 \quad \textit{iff} \ I(\alpha, U - \alpha - \beta, \beta)_M. \qquad (3.11)$$

Proof:

1. We first prove that G_0 is an I-map (i.e., $\langle X|S|Y\rangle_{G_0} \Rightarrow I(X, S, Y)$) using descending induction:

   i. Let $n = |U|$. For $|S| = n-2$ the I-mapness of G_0 is guaranteed by its method of construction, Eq. (3.11).

   ii. Assume the theorem holds for every S' with size $|S'| = k \leq n-2$, and let S be any set such that $|S| = k-1$ and $\langle X|S|Y\rangle_{G_0}$. We distinguish two subcases: $X \cup S \cup Y = U$ and $X \cup S \cup Y \neq U$.

   iii. If $X \cup S \cup Y = U$ then either $|X| \geq 2$ or $|Y| \geq 2$. Assume, without loss of generality, that $|Y| \geq 2$, i.e. $Y = Y' \cup \gamma$. From $\langle X|S|Y\rangle_{G_0}$ and obvious properties of vertex separation in graphs, we conclude $\langle X|S \cup \gamma|Y'\rangle_{G_0}$ and $\langle X|S \cup Y'|\gamma\rangle_{G_0}$. The two separating sets, $S \cup \gamma$ and $S \cup Y'$, are at least $|S| + 1 = k$ in size; therefore, by induction on the hypothesis,

   $$I(X, S \cup \gamma, Y') \ \& \ I(X, S \cup Y', \gamma).$$

   Applying the intersection property (Eq. (3.6e)) yields the desired result: $I(X, S, Y)$.

iv.   If $X \cup S \cup Y \neq U$, then there exists at least one element δ that is not in $X \cup S \cup Y$, and for any such δ two obvious properties of graph separation hold:

$$<X \mid S \cup \delta \mid Y>_{G_0}$$

and

$$\text{either} \ \ <X \mid S \cup Y \mid \delta>_{G_0} \ \ \text{or} \ \ <\delta \mid S \cup X \mid Y>_{G_0} \ \ \text{or both.}$$

The separating sets above are at least $|S| + 1 = k$ in size; therefore, by induction on the hypothesis,

$$I(X, S \cup \delta, Y) \quad \& \quad I(X, S \cup Y, \delta)$$

or

$$I(X, S \cup \delta, Y) \quad \& \quad I(\delta, S \cup X, Y).$$

Applying the intersection property (Eq. (3.6e)) to either case yields $I(X, S, Y)$, which establishes the I-mapness of G_0.

2.   Next we show that G_0 is edge-minimal and unique, i.e., that no edge can be deleted from G_0 without destroying its I-mapness. Indeed, deleting an edge $(\alpha, \beta) \in E_0$ leaves α separated from β by the complementary set $U - \alpha - \beta$, and if the resulting graph is still an I-map, we can conclude $I(\alpha, U - \alpha - \beta, \beta)$. However, from the method of constructing G_0 and from $(\alpha, \beta) \in E_0$ we know that $(\alpha, U - \alpha - \beta, \beta)$ is not in I. Thus, no edge can be removed from G_0, and its minimality and uniqueness are established. Q.E.D.

Note that the weak union property (Eq. (3.6c)) is not needed for the proof.

Appendix 3-B

Proof of Theorem 4

THEOREM 4: [Pearl and Paz 1985]: *Every element* $\alpha \in U$ *in a dependency model satisfying symmetry, decomposition, intersection, and weak union (Eq. (3.6)) has a unique Markov boundary* $B_I(\alpha)$. *Moreover,* $B_I(\alpha)$ *coincides with the set of vertices* $B_{G_0}(\alpha)$ *adjacent to* α *in the minimal I-map* G_0.

Proof:

i.   Let $BL^*(\alpha)$ stand for the set of all Markov blankets satisfying Eq. (3.12). $B_I(\alpha)$ is unique because the intersection property (Eq. (3.6e)) renders $BL^*(\alpha)$ closed under intersection. Moreover, $B_I(\alpha)$ equals the intersection of all members of $BL^*(\alpha)$.

ii. Conversely, every Markov blanket $BL \in BL^*(\alpha)$ remains in $BL^*(\alpha)$ after we add to it an arbitrary set of elements S' not containing α. This follows from the weak union property (Eq. (3.6c)). In particular, if there is an element β outside $B_I(\alpha) \cup \alpha$ then $U-\alpha-\beta$ is in $BL^*(\alpha)$.

iii. From (ii) we conclude that for every element $\beta \neq \alpha$ outside $B_I(\alpha)$, we have $I(\alpha, U-\alpha-\beta, \beta)$, meaning β cannot be connected to α in G_0. Thus,

$$B_{G_0}(\alpha) \subseteq B_I(\alpha).$$

iv. To prove that $B_{G_0}(\alpha)$ actually coincides with $B_I(\alpha)$ it is sufficient to show that $B_{G_0}(\alpha)$ is in $BL^*(\alpha)$, but this follows from the fact that G_0, as an I-map, must satisfy Eq. (3.12). Q.E.D.

Chapter 4

BELIEF UPDATING BY NETWORK PROPAGATION

Oh, would that my mind could let fall its dead ideas,
as the tree does its withered leaves.
— André Gide

This chapter deals with fusing and propagating the impact of new evidence and beliefs through Bayesian networks so that each proposition eventually will be assigned a certainty measure consistent with the axioms of probability theory. We start in Section 4.1 by arguing that any viable model of human reasoning should be able to perform this task with a self-activated propagation mechanism, i.e., with an array of simple and autonomous processors, communicating locally via the links provided by the network itself. The impact of each new piece of evidence is viewed as a perturbation that propagates through the network via message-passing between neighboring variables, with minimal external supervision. In Section 4.2 we show that these objectives can be fully realized with *causal trees,* i.e., Bayesian networks in which each node has at most one parent. In Section 4.3 we extend the result to *causal polytrees,* i.e., trees with arbitrary arrow orientation, and thus allow multiple roots and multiple parents. In both cases, we identify belief parameters, communication messages, and updating rules to guarantee that equilibrium will be reached in time proportional to the longest path in the network and that at equilibrium each proposition will be accorded a belief measure equal to its posterior probability, given all the available evidence. In Section 4.3.2, we illustrate this propagation method's evidence-pooling and credit-assignment policies with a canonical model, where multiple causes are assumed to interact disjunctively. Several approaches to achieving autonomous propagation in multiply connected networks are discussed in Section 4.4, including clustering, conditioning, and stochastic simulation. Finally, Section 4.5 extends the inferential repertoire of Bayesian networks to include answering Boolean queries under propositional constraints, with a special emphasis on conjunctive queries.

143

4.1 AUTONOMOUS PROPAGATION AS A COMPUTATIONAL PARADIGM

Since a fully specified Bayesian network constitutes a complete probabilistic model of the variables in a domain (i.e., it specifies a joint distribution over the variables), the network contains the information needed to answer all probabilistic queries about these variables. The queries might be requests to interpret specific input data or, if utility information is provided, requests to recommend the best course of action. Interpretation requires instantiating a set of variables corresponding to the input data, calculating their impact on the probabilities of variables designated as hypotheses, and finally, selecting the most likely combinations of these hypotheses.

In principle, once we have a joint distribution function P, the interpretation task can be performed mechanically using purely algebraic methods. For example, the impact of the observation $X_j = x_j$ on another variable X_i can be obtained from the conditional probabilities $P(x_i | x_j)$ for each value x_i in the domain of X_i. Using the textbook definition

$$P(x_i | x_j) = \frac{P(x_i, x_j)}{P(x_j)}$$

we compute $P(x_i, x_j)$ by summing the joint distribution $P(x_1, ..., x_n)$ over all variables except X_i and X_j. The summation can be executed in any order, but exponential savings can sometimes be realized by selecting a judicious ordering.

Network representations provide a valuable guide for making this selection. Summing over a variable, say X_k, amounts to eliminating X_k from the network while maintaining the proper dependencies among remaining variables—adding links between those neighbors of X_k that were d-separated by X_k and calculating the conditional probabilities associated with the new links. Since the size of a link matrix increases exponentially with the number of arrows that converge on a given variable, it is important to eliminate variables in an order that minimizes the number of converging arrows created throughout the process. Techniques for finding a good elimination ordering have been developed in the operations research literature [Bertelé and Brioschi 1972] and have been used for manipulating influence diagrams [Shachter 1986] (see Chapter 6). Such techniques do not, of course, avoid the exponential worst-case complexity of the interpretation task (the problem is *NP*-hard [Rosenthal 1975; Cooper 1987]), but they exploit the structural properties of sparse networks.

However, node elimination has several shortcomings. First, the process requires full supervision by a monitor that must access all parts of the network and use external computational facilities to decide, at any given stage, which variable should be eliminated next. The use of such a global supervisor is foreign to human reasoning because it requires faculties beyond most humans, e.g., comprehending the entire structure of the network and quickly diverting attention from one section of the network to another. Our limited short-term memory, narrow range of attention, and inability to shift rapidly between alternative lines of reasoning suggest that our reasoning process is fairly local, progressing incrementally along preestablished pathways. Second, elimination techniques literally cover their tracks; they provide the final impact of a piece of evidence on a single hypothesis, but do not calculate the impact of the evidence on the nodes eliminated in the process. In many applications, we wish to know the updated belief of every variable in the network. Third, and perhaps most important, the elementary steps in the process of node elimination often have no conceptual correlates. They create and calculate spurious dependencies among variables normally perceived to be independent, and the dependencies are hard to explain in qualitative terms. Finally, elimination techniques are basically sequential, and there is growing interest in reasoning models that permit unsupervised parallelism. The interest is motivated both by technological advances in parallel computation and by the need to develop viable models of human reasoning. The speed and ease with which people perform some low-level interpretive functions, such as recognizing scenes, reading text, and even understanding stories, strongly suggest that such processes involve a significant amount of parallelism and that most of the processing is done at the knowledge level itself [Shastri and Feldman 1984].

4.1.1 Constraint Propagation and Rule-based Computation

We can model such phenomena by viewing a belief network not merely as a passive code for storing factual knowledge but also as a computational architecture for reasoning about that knowledge. This means the links in the network should be treated as the only mechanisms that direct and propel the flow of data through the process of querying and updating beliefs. Accordingly, we assume that each node in the network is given a separate processor, which maintains the parameters of belief for the host variable and manages the communication links to and from neighboring, conceptually related variables. The communication lines are assumed to be open at all times, i.e., each processor may, at any time, interrogate its neighbors and compare their parameters to its own. If the compared quantities satisfy some local constraints, no activity takes place. However, if any constraint is violated, the responsible node is activated and the violating parameter corrected. This, of course, activates similar revisions at neighboring nodes and initiates a multidirectional propagation that will continue until equilibrium is reached.

EXAMPLE 1: To illustrate the process of constraint propagation, consider the graph coloring problem depicted by Figure 4.1. Each node in the graph must be assigned one of three colors, {1, 2, 3}, in such a way that no two adjacent nodes will have identical colors. The constraints in this problem are local; no node can assume a color seen at any of its neighbors. A local approach would be to assign a processor to each node and have it compare its current color to the colors of its neighbors. If equality is discovered, the processor should choose a new color, different (if possible) from the neighbors' colors. We assume there is no synchronization, so all possible activation schedules could be realized.

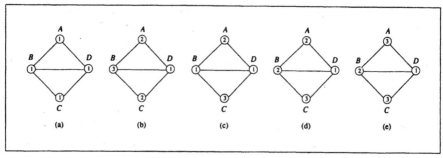

Figure 4.1. *Demonstrating constraint propagation in the graph coloring problem.*

Figure 4.1.*a* shows the initial state of the system: all nodes are colored 1. Figure 4.1*b* shows the configuration after the nodes are activated in the order A, B, C, D: a stable solution is established once C selects the color 2. If, instead, the activation schedule happens to be A, C, B, D, and if C selects the color 3, a deadlock occurs (Figure 4.1*c*): B cannot find a color different from all its neighbors. A way out of such deadlock is to instruct each processor to change its color arbitrarily if no better one can be found. Indeed, if B changes its color to 2 (temporarily conflicting with A, as in Figure 4.1*d*), it forces A to choose the color 3, thus realizing a global solution (Figure 4.1*e*).

Even if a global solution exists, there is no guarantee, in general, that it will be found by repeated local relaxations. However, if the escape from deadlock is totally random, the probability of reaching a solution within a given time t approaches 1 as t increases. Note also that if the node activation is both parallel and synchronous, the system can fall into an indefinite dynamic loop without reaching a solution. For example, starting with the state of Figure 4.1*a*, all processors may simultaneously choose the color 2, then 3, etc. Such pathological behavior will not occur in the networks that we shall deal with.

One of the main reasons for adopting this distributed computation paradigm in evidential reasoning tasks is that it automatically exploits the independencies embodied in the network, via subtask decomposition, to gain a substantial reduction in complexity. For example, if the Markov neighbors of some variable X have successfully computed their combined distribution function, X can compute its own distribution without interacting with any variable outside its neighborhood (see Eq. (3.12)). Moreover, if the network has a tree structure, then X can compute its distribution by consulting each of its neighbors separately. If any of X's neighbors undergo change, X updates its own distribution and reports the update to the other neighbors, and so on until, at the network's periphery, we meet evidential variables whose probabilities are predetermined and the process halts.

The second reason to adopt this distributed paradigm is that it leads to a "transparent" revision process, in which the intermediate steps can be given an intuitively meaningful interpretation. Because a distributed process allows each computational step to obtain input only from neighboring, semantically related variables, and because the activation of these steps proceeds along semantically familiar pathways, people find it easy to give meaningful interpretation to the individual steps and thus gain confidence in the final result. It is also possible to generate qualitative justifications mechanically by tracing the sequence of operations along the activated pathways and giving them causal or diagnostic interpretations using appropriate verbal expressions.

The ability to update beliefs by an autonomous propagation mechanism also has a profound effect on sequential implementations of evidential reasoning. Of course, when this architecture is simulated on sequential machines, the notion of autonomous processors working simultaneously is only a metaphor, but it signifies the complete separation of the stored knowledge from the control mechanism. This separation is the proclaimed, if rarely achieved, goal of rule-based systems. It guarantees the utmost flexibility for a sequential controller; the computations can be performed in any order, with no need to remember or verify which parts of the network have already been updated. Thus, belief updating may be activated by changes occurring in logically related propositions (*spreading activation*), by requests for evidence arriving from a central supervisor (*goal-directed activation*), by a predetermined schedule, or entirely at random. The communication and interaction among individual processors can be simulated using a blackboard architecture [Lesser and Erman 1977], where each proposition is designated specific areas of memory to access and modify.

Finally, the uniformity of this propagation scheme makes it easy to formulate in object-oriented languages: the nodes are objects of the same generic type, and the belief parameters are the messages by which interacting objects communicate. The programmer need only specify how a single object reacts to changes occurring at its neighbors; he need not provide timing information or say where to store partial results.

Constraint propagation mechanisms have a special appeal for AI researchers because they are similar in many respects to logical inference rules. We already have seen that an inference rule of the form "If premise A, then action B" constitutes a very attractive unit of computation for three reasons:

1. The triggering mechanism is local, i.e., it grants a license to initiate the action whenever the premise A is true in the knowledge base K, regardless of the other information that K contains.

2. The action is computationally simple and normally involves only a minor adjustment in the knowledge base.

3. Both the triggering mechanism and the action are conceptually meaningful and are therefore easy to program, modify, and explain.

Almost identical features hold in the constraint propagation formalism. Each processor receives a permanent license to act whenever a certain condition develops among its neighbors. The action is simple, since it involves only local perturbation of the processor's parameters. Both the activation and the action are meaningful because they engage semantically related propositions. Thus, whenever a problem can be solved by a constraint propagation mechanism, it is also easy to formulate in a pure production-rule formalism.

4.1.2 Why Probabilistic Reasoning Seems to Resist Propagation

While constraint propagation mechanisms have been essential to many AI applications, e.g., vision [Rosenfeld, Hummel, and Zucker 1976; Waltz 1972] and truth maintenance [McAllester 1980], their use in evidential reasoning, surprisingly, has been limited to non-Bayesian formalisms [Lowrance 1982; Quinlan 1983; Shastri and Feldman 1984]. There have been several reasons for this, all based on the essential difference between the probabilistic statement $P(A \mid B) = p$ and the logical rule $B \rightarrow A$ (see Sections 1.1.4, 1.3.1, and 2.3.1).

First, the conditional probabilities characterizing the links in the network do not seem to impose definitive constraints on the probabilities that can be assigned to the nodes. Consider a pair of nodes A and B linked by an arrow $B \rightarrow A$ and quantified by the conditional probabilities $P(a \mid b)$ and $P(a \mid \neg b)$. The quantifier $P(a \mid b)$ restricts the belief accorded to a only in a very special set of circumstances, namely, when b is known with absolute certainty to be true and when no other evidential data is available. Normally, all internal nodes in the network will be subject to some uncertainty. Thus, if processor A inspects its neighbor B and finds it in a state of uncertainty with $P(b) < 1$, it still cannot proceed with a definite action on $P(a)$. A natural recourse would be to compute the weighted average

$$P(a) = P(a \mid b) P(b) + P(a \mid \neg b) P(\neg b).$$

After the arrival of some evidence e, however, the posterior distributions A and B are no longer governed by $P(a \mid b)$ but rather by $P(a \mid b, e)$, via

$$P(a \mid e) = P(a \mid b, e) P(b \mid e) + P(a \mid \neg b, e) P(\neg b \mid e),$$

which may be a totally different relationship. (To take an extreme example, if e fully confirms or denies a, the overall probability of a becomes totally insensitive to $P(a \mid b)$.) The result is that any arbitrary assignment of beliefs to the propositions a and b can be consistent with the value of $P(a \mid b)$ that was initially assigned to the link connecting them; consequently, among these parameters, no violation of a constraint can be detected locally.

Second, the disparity between $P(a \mid b, e)$ and $P(a \mid b)$ suggests that once a new piece of evidence is introduced, the original weights on the link no longer retain their intended meaning; hence, they should not remain fixed but should undergo constant adjustment as new evidence arrives. This requires enormous computational overhead and an external unit to perform the adjustment, so it defeats the whole purpose of local propagation.

Finally, the presence of both top-down *(predictive)* and bottom-up *(diagnostic)* inferences in evidential reasoning has caused apprehensions that pathological instability, deadlock, and circular reasoning will develop once we allow the propagation process to run its course unsupervised [Lowrance 1982]. Indeed, if a stronger belief in a given hypothesis means a greater expectation of the occurrence of its various manifestations, and if, in turn, a greater certainty in the occurrence of these manifestations adds further credence to the hypothesis, how can one avoid infinite updating loops when the processors responsible for these propositions begin to communicate with one another?

EXAMPLE 2: You spread a rumor about person X to your neighbor N_1. A few days later, you hear the same rumor from N_1. Should you increase your belief in the rumor now that N_1 acknowledges it, or should you determine first whether N_1 heard it from another source besides you? It is clear that if you were N_1's only source of information, your belief should not change, but if N_1 independently confirmed the validity of the rumor, you have good reason to increase your belief in it.

Similar considerations apply to communicating processors that represent interdependent propositions. Imagine that a processor F, representing the event *Fire*, communicates asynchronously with a second processor S, representing the event *Smoke*. At time t_1, some evidence (e.g., the distant sound of a fire engine) gives a slight confirmation to F, thus causing the probability of *Fire* to increase from $P(F)$ to $P_1(F)$. At a later time, t_2, processor S may decide to interrogate F; upon finding $P_1(F)$, it revises the probability of *Smoke* from $P(S)$ to $P_2(S)$ in natural anticipation of smoke. Still later, at t_3, processor F is activated, and upon finding an increased belief $P_2(S)$ in *Smoke*, it increases $P_1(F)$ to an even higher value, $P_3(F)$. This feedback process may continue indefinitely, the two processors drawing steady mutual reinforcement void of any empirical basis, until eventually the two propositions, *Fire* and *Smoke*, appear to be firmly believed.

Such dangers are not unique to probabilistic reasoning, but should be considered in any hierarchical model of cognition where mutual reinforcement takes place between lower and higher levels of processing, e.g., connectionist models of reading [Rumelhart and McClelland 1982] and language production [Dell 1985].

To prevent these phenomena, we need a mechanism to keep track of the *sources* of belief, so that evidence is not counted twice and so that the impact of one piece of evidence is not fed back to its source. Unfortunately, source identification requires an overview of the entire network, and the question arises whether it can be represented and adjusted locally as an integral part of the propagation process.

This chapter demonstrates that in a large class of networks, coherent and stable probabilistic reasoning *can* be accomplished by local propagation mechanisms, keeping the weights on the links constant throughout the process. This is done by characterizing the belief in a proposition by a list of parameters, each representing the degree of support the host proposition obtains from one of its neighbors. In the next two sections we show that maintaining such a record of the sources of belief facilitates local updating of beliefs, and that the network relaxes to a stable equilibrium, consistent with the axioms of probability theory, in time proportional to the network diameter. Such a record of parameters is also postulated as a mechanism that permits people to retrace rationales and assemble explanations for currently held beliefs.

4.2 BELIEF PROPAGATION IN CAUSAL TREES

4.2.1 Notation

We shall first consider tree-structured causal networks, i.e., those in which every node except the one called *root* has exactly one incoming link. We allow each node to represent a multi-valued variable, comprising a collection of mutually exclusive hypotheses (e.g., the identity of an organism: $Org_1, Org_2, ...$) or observations (e.g., a patient's temperature: *High, Medium, Low*). Let variables be labeled by capital letters $(A, B,..., X, Y, Z)$ and their possible values by the corresponding lowercase letters $(a, b,..., x, y, z)$. In dealing with propositional variables, the symbols + and ¬ will be used to denote the affirmation and denial, respectively, of propositions. For example, $+a$ stands for $A = TRUE$, and $\neg a$ stands for $A = FALSE$. Each directed link $X \rightarrow Y$ is quantified by a fixed conditional probability matrix M, in which the (x, y) entry is given by

$$M_{y|x} \triangleq P(y|x) \triangleq P(Y = y | X = x) \tag{4.1}$$

$$
\begin{array}{c}
\rightarrow y \\[2pt]
\downarrow \\
x
\end{array}
=
\begin{bmatrix}
P(y_1|x_1) & P(y_2|x_1) & \cdots & P(y_n|x_1) \\
P(y_1|x_2) & P(y_2|x_2) & \cdots & P(y_n|x_2) \\
\vdots & \vdots & & \vdots \\
P(y_1|x_m) & P(y_2|x_m) & \cdots & P(y_n|x_m)
\end{bmatrix}
$$

Normally, the directionality of the arrow designates X as the set of causal hypotheses and Y as the set of consequences or manifestations of these hypotheses.

EXAMPLE 3: In a certain trial there are three suspects, one of whom has definitely committed a murder. The murder weapon, showing some fingerprints, was later found by police. Let X identify the last user of the weapon, namely, the killer. Let Y identify the last holder of the weapon, i.e., the person whose fingerprints were left on the weapon, and let Z represent the possible readings that may be obtained in a fingerprint laboratory.

The relations between these three variables normally would be expressed by the chain $X \to Y \to Z$; X generates expectations about Y, and Y generates expectations about Z, but X has no influence on Z once we know the value of Y.

To represent the commonsense knowledge that the killer is normally the last person to hold the weapon, we use a 3×3 conditional probability matrix:

$$M_{y|x} = P(y|x) = \begin{cases} 0.80 \text{ if } x = y \quad x, y = 1, 2, 3 \\ 0.10 \text{ if } x \neq y \quad x, y = 1, 2, 3. \end{cases} \tag{4.2}$$

To represent the reliability of the laboratory test, we use a matrix $M_{z|y} = P(z|y)$, satisfying

$$\sum_z P(z|y) = 1 \quad \text{for } y = 1, 2, 3 .$$

Each entry in this matrix represents an if-then rule of the following type: "If the fingerprint is of Suspect y, then expect a reading of type z, with certainty $P(z|y)$."

Note that this convention is at variance with that used in many expert systems (e.g., MYCIN), where rules point from evidence to hypothesis (e.g., if symptom, then disease), thus denoting a flow of mental inference. By contrast, the arrows in Bayesian networks point from causes to effects, or from conditions to consequences, thus denoting a flow of constraints attributed to the physical world. The reason for this choice is that people often prefer to encode experiential knowledge in causal schemata [Tversky and Kahneman 1977], and as a consequence, rules expressed in causal form are assessed more reliably.†

Incoming information may be of two types: *specific evidence* or *virtual evidence*. Specific evidence corresponds to direct observations that affect the belief in some variables in the network. Virtual evidence corresponds to judgments based on undisclosed observations that are outside the network but have

---

† It appears that frames used to index human memory by and large are organized to evoke *expectations* rather than *explanations*. The reason could be because expectation-evoking frames normally consist of more stable relationships. For example, $P(y|z)$ in Example 3 would vary drastically with the proportion of people who have type z fingerprints. $P(z|y)$, on the other hand, depends merely on the similarity between the type of fingerprint that Suspect y has and the readings observed in the lab; it is perceived to be a stable local property of the laboratory procedure, independent of other information regarding Suspect y.

bearing on variables in the network. Such evidence is modeled by dummy nodes representing the undisclosed observations, connected by unquantified (dummy) links to the variables affected by the observations. These links will carry information one way only, from the evidence to the variables affected by it.

For example, if it is impractical for the fingerprint laboratory to disclose all possible readings (in variable Z) or if the laboratory chose to base its finding on human judgment, Z will be represented by a dummy node, and the link $Y \rightarrow Z$ will specify the degree to which each suspect is likely to bear the fingerprint pattern examined. For example, the laboratory examiner may issue a report in the form of a list (0.80, 0.60, 0.50), stating that she is 80% sure that the fingerprint belongs to Suspect 1, 60% sure that it belongs to Suspect 2, and 50% sure that it belongs to Suspect 3. If the examiner was totally unbiased before the test, such a profile of belief can be established only if the likelihood ratio is

$$P(z_{observed} \mid y = 1) : P(z_{observed} \mid y = 2) : P(z_{observed} \mid y = 3) = 8 : 6 : 5,$$

which will be our standard way to characterize the impact of virtual evidence (see Sections 2.2.2 and 2.3.3). Because these numbers need not sum to unity, each judgment can be formed independently of the others—each suspect's fingerprints can be compared separately with those found on the weapon.

All incoming evidence, both specific and virtual, will be denoted by e and will be regarded as emanating from a set E of *instantiated* variables, i.e., variables whose values are known. For example, if the laboratory examination is the only evidence available in Example 3, we shall write $E = \{Z\}$ and $e = \{Z = z_{observed}\}$. If several facts become known, say, $A = TRUE$, $B = FALSE$ and $X = x$, then $E = \{A, B, X\}$ and $e = \{+a, \neg b, X = x\}$.

For the sake of clarity, we will distinguish between the fixed conditional probabilities that label the links, e.g., $P(y \mid x)$, and the dynamic values of the updated node probabilities, e.g., $P(x \mid e)$. The latter will be denoted by $BEL(x)$, which reflects the overall belief accorded to proposition $X = x$ by all evidence so far received. Thus,

$$BEL(x) \triangleq P(x \mid e),$$

where e is the value combination of all instantiated variables.

Since we will be dealing with discrete variables, functions such as $\lambda(x)$, $P(x)$, and $BEL(x)$ can be regarded as lists, or *vectors*, with each component corresponding to a different value of X. For example, if the domain of X is $D_X = \{Hot, Medium, Cold\}$, we can write

$$BEL(x) = (BEL(X = Hot), BEL(X = Medium), BEL(X = Cold))$$

$$= (0.1, 0.2, 0.7).$$

The product $f(x) g(x)$ of two such vectors will stand for term-by-term multiplication, e.g.,

$$(1, 2, 3)(3, 2, 1) = (1 \times 3, 2 \times 2, 3 \times 1) = (3, 4, 3).$$

Inner products (or *dot products*) will be denoted by a dot •, e.g.,

$$f(x) \bullet g(x) = (1, 2, 3) \bullet (3, 2, 1) = 1 \times 3 + 2 \times 2 + 3 \times 1 = 10.$$

The dot symbol • will also be used to indicate matrix products, e.g.,

$$f(x) \bullet M_{y|x} \triangleq \sum_x f(x) M_{y|x}.$$

The summation will always be taken over the repeated index, thus eliminating the need for transposing matrices or distinguishing between row and column vectors.

We shall use the symbol α to denote a *normalizing* constant, e.g.,

$$\alpha(1, 1, 3) = (0.2, 0.2, 0.6),$$

and the symbol β to denote an *arbitrary* constant, e.g.,

$$K\beta f(x) = \beta f(x) \quad \text{and}$$

$$\alpha\beta f(x) = \alpha f(x).$$

A vector of 1s will be written $\mathbf{1}$; for example,

$$BEL(x) = \alpha\mathbf{1} = \alpha(1, 1, 1, 1) = (0.25, 0.25, 0.25, 0.25).$$

4.2.2 *Propagation in Chains*

Consider the simplest of all tree-structured networks, namely, a network consisting of two nodes and a single link, $X \rightarrow Y$. If evidence $e = \{Y=y\}$ is observed, then from Bayes' Rule, the belief distribution of X is given by

$$BEL(x) = P(x \mid e) = \alpha P(x) \lambda(x), \tag{4.3}$$

where $\alpha = [P(e)]^{-1}$, $P(x)$ is the prior probability of X, and $\lambda(x)$ is the likelihood vector

$$\lambda(x) = P(e|x) = P(Y = y \mid x) = M_{y|x}. \tag{4.4}$$

In short, $\lambda(x)$ is simply the y's column of the link matrix M, as in Eq. (4.1). Since this matrix is stored at node Y, $\lambda(x)$ can be computed at Y and transmitted as a message to X, enabling X to compute its belief distribution $BEL(x)$.

If Y is not observed directly but is supported by indirect observation $e = \{Z = z\}$ of a descendant Z of Y, we have the chain $X \to Y \to Z$, and we can still write

$$BEL(x) \triangleq P(x \mid e) = \alpha P(x) \lambda(x).$$

The likelihood vector $\lambda(x)$ can no longer be directly obtained from the matrix $M_{y \mid x}$, however, but must reflect the matrix $M_{z \mid y}$ as well. Conditioning and summing on the values of Y, we can write

$$\lambda(x) = P(e \mid x) = \sum_{y} P(e \mid y, x) P(y \mid x) = \sum_{y} P(e \mid y) P(y \mid x)$$

$$= M_{y \mid x} \cdot \lambda(y), \qquad\qquad (4.5)$$

using the fact that Y separates X from Z. Thus, we have shown that node X can still calculate its likelihood vector $\lambda(x)$ if it somehow gains access to the vector $\lambda(y)$.

Generalizing to the chain of Figure 4.2, every node can calculate the correct current value of its λ vector if it learns the correct λ vector of its successor.

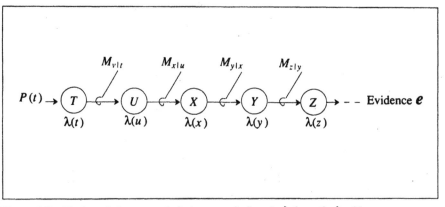

Figure 4.2. *Each node in a causal chain can calculate its λ from the λ of its successor.*

Since the chain ends with an observed variable whose value is determined externally, the λ vector of all variables can be determined recursively. If the chain ends with an unobserved variable Z and we set $\lambda(z) = 1$ for all z, Eqs. (4.3) and (4.5) are still valid, because every variable will obtain $\lambda = 1$ and all belief distributions will coincide with the prior distributions. Assuming that each node constantly inspects the λ of its child and updates its own λ accordingly, we are guaranteed that every variable along the chain will obtain its correct λ, properly reflecting any changes that might have occurred in e. This updating process is analogous to the way soldiers are counted.

EXAMPLE 4: A platoon of soldiers is marching at night in enemy territory. The leader wants to know how many soldiers remain under his command. He sends a "count" signal to the soldier behind him. This person, in turn, looks behind, and if someone is there, he passes on the "count" signal; if no one is left behind him, he returns the signal "1" to the soldier in front of him. The soldier in front receives the "1," adds 1 (for himself) and sends "2" to the soldier in front of him, and so on. The leader eventually receives the correct count. (See Figure 4.3.) In fact, the leader need not be at the head of the platoon. He can initiate a "count" command to both his front and his back, wait for responses from both sides, and add the values received (see Figure 4.4).

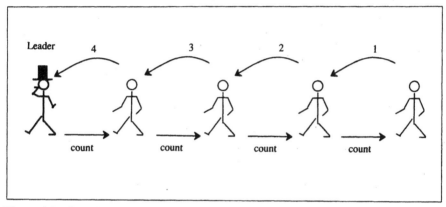

Figure 4.3. *Distributed soldier-counting.*

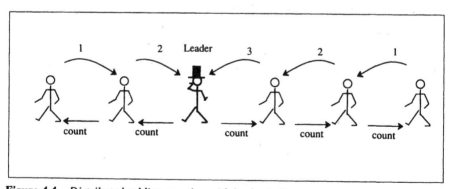

Figure 4.4. *Distributed soldier-counting with leader in line.*

This common procedure suffers because the leader may not be aware of any missing soldiers until he decides to count, and even then the count gets back to him only after communication delays to and from the end of the line. This problem can be overcome by instructing each soldier to constantly update and communicate the messages without waiting for the "count" signal, or more efficiently, to initiate communication as soon as a change is seen in the immediate environment. Thus, no communication takes place under normal conditions, but when any soldier suddenly finds himself at either the front or the end of the line, he will initiate a message-passing process that propagates toward the leader and eventually terminates at the leader (who is now passive) with the correct count (see Figure 4.5).

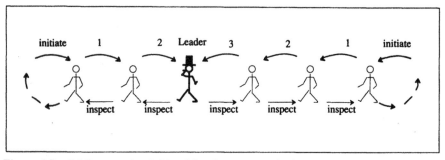

Figure 4.5. *Soldier-counting initiated by changes at endpoints.*

To draw the analogy closer to belief updating, let's remove the leader and force every soldier to be constantly aware of the current total count. In such a system, the messages, instead of stopping at any particular individual, should continue to propagate toward the periphery; the forward-moving messages should propagate all the way to the front of the line, and the backward-moving messages should propagate to the end of the line. Every soldier follows the same rule: receive a count from the person behind, add 1, and transmit the result to the person in front; receive a count from the person in front, add 1, and transmit to the one behind (see Figure 4.6). Note that each soldier must maintain and communicate two separate parameters, the back count and the front count; the overall count (the sum of the two) is not a message that can sustain the propagation.

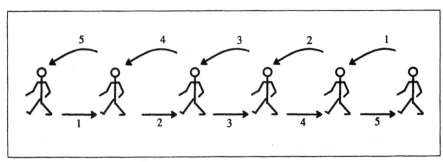

Figure 4.6. *Leaderless soldier-counting using dual-parameter communication.*

BIDIRECTIONAL PROPAGATION

The need for dual-parameter communication also exists in belief updating, where new evidence can emerge from both a descendant of a node and its ancestor. For example, in the chain of Figure 4.7, variables are instantiated at both the head and the tail of the chain, and we may wish to calculate $BEL(x)$ as a function of the values, e^+ and e^-, that these variables take.†

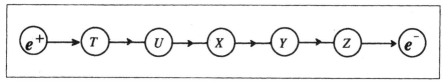

Figure 4.7. *A causal chain with evidential data at its head (e^+) and tail (e^-).*

In Eq. (4.3), $\lambda(x)$ was defined by $P(e|x)$, e being the total evidence available. We now find it more convenient to handle the impact of e^- and e^+ by two separate vectors,

$$\lambda(x) = P(e^- \,|\, x) \qquad\qquad (4.6a)$$

and

$$\pi(x) = P(x \,|\, e^+) . \qquad\qquad (4.6b)$$

Expressing the total belief distribution $BEL(x)$ in terms of $\lambda(x)$ and $\pi(x)$, with X separating e^+ from e^-, we have

$$BEL(x) \triangleq P(x \,|\, e^+, e^-) = \alpha\, P(e^- \,|\, x, e^+)\, P(x \,|\, e^+) = \alpha\, P(e^- \,|\, x)\, P(x \,|\, e^+)$$

$$= \alpha\, \lambda(x)\, \pi(x) ,$$

which is identical to Eq. (4.3) with $\pi(x)$ replacing $P(x)$.

To illustrate how information about $\pi(x)$ propagates from e^+ down the chain, let us condition Eq. (4.6b) on the values of the parent variable U:

$$\pi(x) = P(x \,|\, e^+) = \sum_u P(x \,|\, u, e^+)\, P(u \,|\, e^+) .$$

Since U separates X from e^+, we obtain

$$\pi(x) = \sum_u P(x \,|\, u)\, \pi(u) = \pi(u) \bullet M_{x \,|\, u} . \qquad\qquad (4.7)$$

---

† e^+ might represent the background knowledge one has about T, in which case the prior probability $P(t)$ will be identical to $P(t \,|\, e^+)$.

We see that the forward propagation of π's parameters is similar to the backward propagation of λ's parameters; both involve vector multiplication by the appropriate link matrix. Each node can now compute its own π and λ after obtaining the π of its parent and the λ of its child. (See Figure 4.8.)

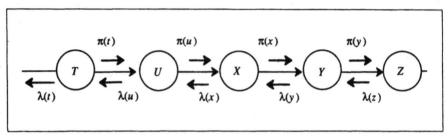

Figure 4.8. *Belief calculation using bidirected message passing in causal chains.*

EXAMPLE 5: Referring to the trial story of Example 3, let $e^- = \{Z = z\}$ represent the experience of examining the fingerprints left on the murder weapon, and let e^+ stand for all other testimony heard in the trial. So, $\pi(x) = P(x \mid e^+)$ stands for our prior certainty that the x-th suspect is the killer, $\pi(y) = P(y \mid e^+)$ stands for our prior certainty (before examining the fingerprints) that the y-th suspect was the last person to hold the weapon, and $\lambda(y) = P(e^- \mid y)$ represents the report issued by the fingerprint laboratory. Taking $\pi(x) = (0.8, 0.1, 0.1)$ and using the matrix of Eq. (4.2), we get

$$\pi(y) = (0.8, 0.1, 0.1) \bullet \begin{bmatrix} 0.8 & 0.1 & 0.1 \\ 0.1 & 0.8 & 0.1 \\ 0.1 & 0.1 & 0.8 \end{bmatrix} = (0.66, 0.17, 0.17).$$

Prior to inspection of the fingerprints, all λs are unit vectors 1 and the message profile on the chain is as shown in Figure 4.9.

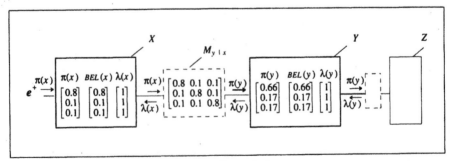

Figure 4.9. *Initial beliefs and messages in Example 5.*

Now assume that a laboratory report arrives, summarized by $\lambda(y) = \beta(0.8, 0.6, 0.5)$. Node Y updates its belief to read

$$BEL(y) = \alpha\, \lambda(y)\, \pi(y) = \alpha(0.8,\ 0.6,\ 0.5)\ (0.66,\ 0.17,\ 0.17)$$

$$= (0.738,\ 0.143,\ 0.119)$$

and delivers to X its $\lambda(y)$ vector. Upon receiving this message, node X computes its new $\lambda(x)$ vector,

$$\lambda(x) = M_{y\,|\,x} \bullet \lambda(y) = \beta \begin{bmatrix} 0.8 & 0.1 & 0.1 \\ 0.1 & 0.8 & 0.1 \\ 0.1 & 0.1 & 0.8 \end{bmatrix} \bullet \begin{bmatrix} 0.8 \\ 0.6 \\ 0.5 \end{bmatrix} = \beta \begin{bmatrix} 0.75 \\ 0.61 \\ 0.54 \end{bmatrix},$$

and its new belief distribution becomes

$$BEL(x) = \alpha\, \lambda(x)\, \pi(x) = \alpha(0.75,\ 0.61,\ 0.54)\ (0.8,\ 0.1,\ 0.1)$$

$$= (0.840,\ 0.085,\ 0.076)\,.$$

The messages are distributed as in Figure 4.10.

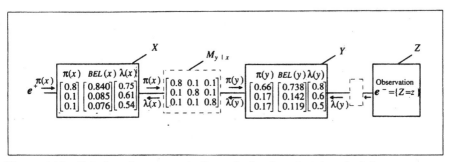

Figure 4.10. *Beliefs and messages in Example 5, after obtaining the laboratory report* $\lambda(y)$.

Now assume that Suspect 1 produces a very strong alibi, which (discounting fingerprint information) reduces the odds that he could have committed the crime from 0.80 to 0.28, thus yielding a revised prior probability of

$$\pi(x) = (0.28,\ 0.36,\ 0.36)\,.$$

This change propagates toward Y and results in a revised $\pi(y)$:

$$\pi(y) = \pi(x) \bullet M_{y\,|\,x} = (0.28,\ 0.36,\ 0.36) \bullet \begin{bmatrix} 0.8 & 0.1 & 0.1 \\ 0.1 & 0.8 & 0.1 \\ 0.1 & 0.1 & 0.8 \end{bmatrix} = (0.30,\ 0.35,\ 0.35)\,.$$

Each processor can now compute the revised total belief of its variable, taking into account the evidential impact of the fingerprint findings:

$$BEL(x) = \alpha\pi(x)\lambda(x) = \alpha(0.28, 0.36, 0.36)\,(0.75, 0.61, 0.54)$$

$$= \alpha(0.210, 0.220, 0.194)$$

$$= (0.337, 0.352, 0.311)\,,$$

$$BEL(y) = \alpha\pi(y)\lambda(y) = \alpha(0.30, 0.35, 0.35)\,(0.80, 0.60, 0.50)$$

$$= \alpha(0.240, 0.210, 0.175)$$

$$= (0.384, 0.336, 0.280)\,.$$

Thus, Suspect 2 now becomes the strongest candidate for being the killer (with $P(X = 2) = 0.349$), though Suspect 1 is still most likely to be the owner of the fingerprint (with $P(Y = 1) = 0.384$). The final message distribution is shown in Figure 4.11.

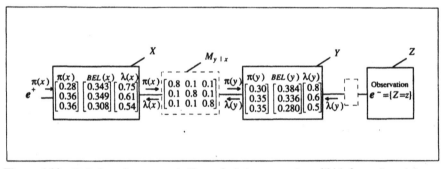

Figure 4.11. *Beliefs and messages in Example 5, incorporating alibi information $\pi(x)$.*

Note how the separation between causal and evidential support (i.e., between the πs and the λs) prevents feedback, circular reasoning, and indefinite relaxations of the type discussed in Section 4.1.1. Suspect 1's alibi renders him less likely (by a factor of $0.384/0.738$) to be the owner of the incriminating fingerprints, but this reduction is not fed back to further influence his likelihood of being the killer (this would amount to counting the alibi information twice) because $\lambda(x)$ and $\lambda(y)$ are unaffected by changes occurring in $\pi(x)$. Keeping these two modes of support orthogonal to each other ensures stable updating in a single pass.

The local computations performed by each processor are essentially constraint relaxations of the type discussed in Example 1, with two additional features: the constraints are equalities, and they can always be satisfied locally. If the state of each processor is defined by its associated π and λ vectors, then the updating procedure can be written as a collection of local inference rules, identical in form and spirit to those used in constraint relaxation and logical deduction. For example, assuming the content of π and λ is stored in two registers, called Π and Λ, the behavior of processor X in Figure 4.8 is specified by three inference rules:

$$\text{If } (X \rightarrow Y)_{M_{y|x}} \text{ and } \Lambda(Y) = \lambda(y) \quad \text{then } \Lambda(X) = \lambda(y) \cdot M_{y|x} , \tag{4.8}$$

$$\text{If } (U \rightarrow X)_{M_{x|u}} \text{ and } \Pi(U) = \pi(u) \quad \text{then } \Pi(X) = M_{x|u} \cdot \pi(u) , \tag{4.9}$$

$$\text{If } \Lambda(X) = \lambda(x) \text{ and } \Pi(X) = \pi(x) \quad \text{then } BEL(x) = \alpha\lambda(x)\,\pi(x) . \tag{4.10}$$

The first rule, for instance, reads:

If the rule "If $X = x$ then $Y = y$" was assigned the certainty $M_{y|x}$, **and** the current content of $\Lambda(Y)$ is $\lambda(y)$, **then** put $\sum_{y} \lambda(y)\, M_{y|x}$ into $\Lambda(X)$.

Eqs. (4.8) through (4.10) are depicted in Figure 4.12. The reasons for formulating simple updating equations like Eqs. (4.5) and (4.7) as *inference rules* is to demonstrate their similarity to logical deductions. Like deductive rules of inference, they can be invoked at any time and in any order; postponing the activation of a rule or invoking it repeatedly may delay equilibrium but will not alter the final result. Like deductive rules of inference, the actions specified by Eqs. (4.8) through (4.10) are determined solely by the premises, independent of the rest of the database. But these rules, unlike deductive rules, are non-monotonic in the sense that the conclusions (e.g., the belief measures $BEL(x)$) may undergo changes as new evidence arrives. Thus, Polya's aspirations of formulating patterns of plausible reasoning as rules of inference (see Section 2.3.1) are partially realized, and the pitfalls of his original patterns avoided, by distinguishing causal supports (π) from evidential supports (λ). Knowing that a neighboring proposition $Y = y$ has become "more credible" or "less credible" is insufficient to trigger an action in X; we must first ascertain whether it is $\lambda(y)$ or $\pi(y)$ that has changed. This distinction is expressed in logical terms in Section 10.3.

The scheme described in Figures 4.9 through 4.12 requires that each processor gain access to matrices of both incoming and outgoing links. This may be inconvenient both for hardware implementation and rule-based programming. An alternative scheme, depicted in Figure 4.13, requires that each processor store just one matrix corresponding to the incoming link. Here, each processor receives as input the π of its parent and the λ of its own variable. Upon activation, each processor computes its own π (to be delivered to its child) and the λ of its parent (to be delivered to the parent). This convention will be used throughout the rest of this chapter because it closely reflects the basic construction of Bayesian networks, whereby each node is characterized by its relation to its parents.

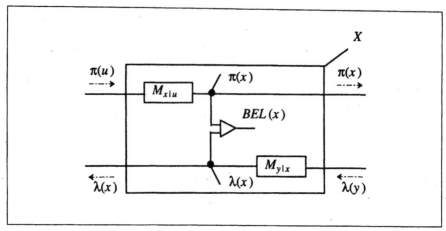

Figure 4.12. *Structure of individual processor, containing two link matrices.*

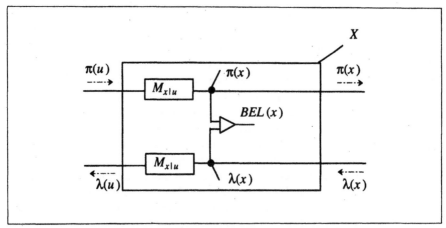

Figure 4.13. *Structure of individual processor, containing a single link matrix.*

4.2.3 *Propagation in Trees*

We now examine a general tree-structured network where a node might have several children and one parent. The propagation scheme in trees is very similar to that of chains, with two distinctions: Each node must combine the impacts of λ-messages obtained from several children, and each node should distribute a separate π-message to each of its children.

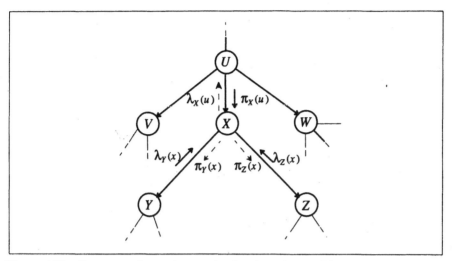

Figure 4.14. *Fragment of causal tree, showing incoming (solid arrows) and outgoing (broken arrows) messages at node X.*

Consider the tree fragment depicted in Figure 4.14. The belief in the various values of X depends on two distinct sets of evidence: evidence from the sub-tree rooted at X, and evidence from the rest of the tree. But the influence of the latter source of information on X is completely summarized by its effect on U, since U separates X from all variables except X's descendants. More formally, letting e_X^- stand for the evidence contained in the tree rooted at X and letting e_X^+ stand for the evidence contained in the rest of the network, we have

$$P(x \mid u, e_X^+) = P(x \mid u) \, . \tag{4.11}$$

This also leads to the usual conditional independence among siblings,

$$P(x, v \mid u) = P(x \mid u) P(v \mid u) \, , \tag{4.12}$$

since the proposition $V = v$ is part of e_X^+.

DATA FUSION

Assume we wish to find the belief induced on X by some evidence $e = e_X^- \cup e_X^+$. Bayes' Rule, together with Eq. (4.11), yields the product rule

$$BEL(x) = P(x \mid e_X^+, e_X^-) = \alpha \, P(e_X^- \mid e_X^+, x) \, P(x \mid e_X^+)$$

$$= \alpha \, P(e_X^- \mid x) \, P(x \mid e_X^+) \, , \tag{4.13}$$

where $\alpha = [P(e_X^- \mid e_X^+)]^{-1}$ is a normalizing constant.

Eq. (4.13) provides an interesting generalization of the celebrated Bayes product formula,

$$P(x \mid e) = \alpha P(e \mid x) P(x),\qquad\qquad(4.14)$$

by identifying a surrogate—$P(x \mid e_X^+)$—for the prior probability term $P(x)$—with every intermediate node in the tree. In recursive Bayesian updating (see Section 2.1.4), the posterior probability can be used as a new prior, relative to the next item of evidence, only when the items of evidence are conditionally independent, given the updated variable X. Such recursive updating cannot be applied to networks because only variables that are separated from each other by X are conditionally independent. In general, it is not permissible to use the total posterior belief, updated by Eq. (4.13), as a new multiplicative prior for the calculation. Eq. (4.13) is significant because it shows that a product rule analogous to Eq. (4.14) can be applied recursively to any node in the tree, even when the observations are not conditionally independent, but the recursive, multiplicative role of the prior probability has been taken over by that portion of belief contributed by evidence from the sub-tree above the updated variable, excluding the data collected from its descendants. The root is the only node that requires a prior probability estimation, and since it has no network above it, e_{root}^+ should be interpreted as the background knowledge remaining unexplicated.

Eq. (4.13) suggests that the probability distribution of every variable in the tree can be computed if the node corresponding to that variable contains the vectors

$$\lambda(x) = P(e_X^- \mid x)\qquad\qquad(4.15)$$

and

$$\pi(x) = P(x \mid e_X^+).\qquad\qquad(4.16)$$

Here, $\pi(x)$ represents the causal or *predictive* support attributed to the assertion "$X = x$" by all non-descendants of X, mediated by X's parent, and $\lambda(x)$ represents the diagnostic or *retrospective* support that "$X = x$" receives from X's descendants. The total strength of belief in "$X = x$" can be obtained by *fusing* these two supports via the product

$$BEL(x) = \alpha\lambda(x)\,\pi(x).\qquad\qquad(4.17)$$

To see how information from several descendants fuses at node X, we partition the data set e_X^- in Eq. (4.15) into disjoint subsets, one for each child of X. Referring to Figure 4.14, for example, the tree rooted at X can be partitioned into the root, X, and two sub-trees, one rooted at Y and the other at Z. Thus, if X itself is not instantiated, we can write $e_X^- = e_Y^- \cup e_Z^-$, and since X separates its children, we have

$$\lambda(x) = P(e_X^- \mid x)$$
$$= P(e_Y^-, e_Z^- \mid x)$$
$$= P(e_Y^- \mid x)P(e_Z^- \mid x) . \qquad (4.18)$$

So $\lambda(x)$ can be formed as a product of terms such as $P(e_Y^- \mid x)$, if these terms are delivered to X as messages from its children. Denoting these messages by subscripted λ's,

$$\lambda_Y(x) = P(e_Y^- \mid x) \qquad (4.19a)$$

and

$$\lambda_Z(x) = P(e_Z^- \mid x) , \qquad (4.19b)$$

we have the product rule:

$$\lambda(x) = \lambda_Y(x) \, \lambda_Z(x) . \qquad (4.20)$$

This product rule also applies when X itself is instantiated $(X = x')$ if we model the new data by adding to X a dummy child D that delivers the message

$$\lambda_D(x) = \delta_{x, x'} = \begin{cases} 1 & \text{if } x = x' \\ 0 & \text{if } x \neq x'. \end{cases}$$

EXAMPLE 6: In the fingerprint story of Example 5, imagine that we receive reports from two independent laboratories, $\lambda_{Z_1}(y) = \beta$ (0.80, 0.60, 0.50) and $\lambda_{Z_2}(y) = \beta$ (0.30, 0.50, 0.90). The overall diagnostic support $\lambda(y)$ attributable to the three possible values of Y is

$$\lambda(y) = \beta(0.80, 0.60, 0.50) \, (0.30, 0.50, 0.90) = \beta(0.24, 0.30, 0.45) ,$$

and this, combined with the previous causal support $\pi(y) = (0.30, 0.35, 0.35)$, yields an overall belief of

$$BEL(y) = \alpha(0.24, 0.30, 0.45) \, (0.30, 0.35, 0.35)$$
$$= \quad (0.215, 0.314, 0.471) .$$

What happens if Suspect 2 confesses, reliably, that he was the last weapon holder? We model this confession as a third report $\lambda_{Z_3}(y) = (0, 1, 0)$ which, by the product rule of Eq. (4.20), completely overrides the other two and yields $\lambda(y) = \beta(0, 1, 0)$ and $BEL(y) = (0, 1, 0)$.

Now we shall see if X can compute its $\pi(x)$ vector from information available at its parent U (see Figure 4.14).

Conditioning on the values of U we get

$$\pi(x) = P(x \mid e_X^+)$$
$$= \sum_u P(x \mid e_X^+, u)P(u \mid e_X^+)$$
$$= \sum_u P(x \mid u)P(u \mid e_X^+) .$$

$P(x \mid u)$ is the matrix stored on the link $U \to X$, and $P(u \mid e_X^+)$ can be calculated by U and delivered to X as the message

$$\pi_X(u) = P(u \mid e_X^+) , \tag{4.21}$$

yielding

$$\pi(x) = \sum_u P(x \mid u)\pi_X(u) = M_{x \mid u} \cdot \pi_X(u). \tag{4.22}$$

Substituting Eqs. (4.20) and (4.22) in Eq. (4.17) we have

$$BEL(x) = \alpha\lambda_Y(x)\lambda_Z(x)\sum_u P(x \mid u)\pi_X(u) . \tag{4.23}$$

Thus, node X can calculate its own beliefs if it has received the messages $\lambda_Y(x)$ and $\lambda_Z(x)$ from its children Y and Z and the message $\pi_X(u)$ from its parent U.

PROPAGATION MECHANISM

Our next task is to determine how the influence of new information will spread through the network. In other words, we imagine that each node eventually receives from its neighbors the π–λ messages needed to calculate its own belief, as in Eq. (4.23), and we must determine how that node calculates the π–λ messages that its neighbors expect to receive from it. If the calculations can be accomplished by local computations, and if we let each node perform the calculations often enough, then the proper belief distributions are guaranteed to be reached, eventually, at every node.

Consider first the message $\lambda_X(u) \triangleq P(e_X^- \mid u)$ that node X must send to its parent U (see Figure 4.14). If the value of X is known, say $X = x'$, then $\lambda_X(u)$ reduces to

$P(x'\mid u)$, which is column x' of the matrix $M_{x\mid u}$. If X is not known, we condition $P(e_X^-\mid u)$ on $X = x$ and get

$$\lambda_X(u) = \sum_x P(e_X^-\mid u, x)P(x\mid u)$$

$$= \sum_x P(e_X^-\mid x)\, P(x\mid u)$$

$$= \sum_x \lambda(x)P(x\mid u)$$

$$= M_{x\mid u} \cdot \lambda(x). \qquad (4.24)$$

Thus, the message going to the parent U can be calculated from the messages received from the children and the matrix stored on the link from the parent. Note that Eq. (4.24) also holds if X itself is instantiated (say to $X = x'$) because in such a case $\lambda(x) = \delta_{x,\,x'}$, and Eq. (4.24) yields $\lambda_X(u) = P(x'\mid u)$ as required.

Now, consider the message that node X should send to one of its children, say Y:

$$\pi_Y(x) \;=\; P(x\mid e_Y^+) \;=\; P(x\mid e_X^+, e_Z^-).$$

Using Bayes' Rule, we get

$$\pi_Y(x) = \alpha P(e_Z^-\mid x, e_X^+)P(x\mid e_X^+)$$

$$= \alpha P(e_Z^-\mid x)P(x\mid e_X^+)$$

$$= \alpha \lambda_Z(x)\pi(x)$$

$$= \alpha \lambda_Z(x)\sum_u P(x\mid u)\pi_X(u). \qquad (4.25)$$

The second equality follows from the fact that X separates e_Z^- from e_X^+, the third equality follows from the definition of $\pi(x)$ (Eq. (4.16)), and the fourth follows from Eq. (4.22). Thus, the message sent from X to Y is calculated using the message it receives from its *other child* Z (in general, the messages it receives from all its children, except Y) and the message X receives from its parent U. This is precisely how double-counting of evidence is prevented.

Figure 4.15 summarizes the calculations for node X.

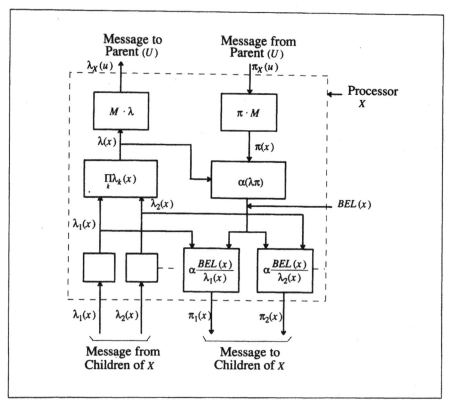

Figure 4.15. *The internal structure of a single processor performing belief updating for the variable X.*

By Eqs. (4.23) and (4.25),

$$\pi_Y(x) = \alpha \, \frac{BEL(x)}{\lambda_Y(x)} \, , \qquad\qquad (4.26)$$

so it might be advantageous for node X, instead of sending each child a different message, to send all its children the value of its current belief, $BEL(x)$, and let each child recover its respective π message by dividing $BEL(x)$ by the value of the last message sent to X (caution should be exercised whenever $\lambda(x)$ is zero or is very close to zero). There is no need, of course, to normalize the π messages prior to transmission; only the $BEL(\cdot)$ expressions require normalization. The sole purpose of the normalization constant α in Eqs. (4.25) and (4.26) is to preserve the probabilistic meaning of these messages. It is a good engineering practice to encode the π and λ messages so that the smallest component of each will attain the value 1.

SUMMARY OF PROPAGATION RULES FOR TREES

We shall now summarize the steps involved in tree propagation by specifying the activities of a typical node X having m children, $Y_1, Y_2,..., Y_m$, and a parent U. The belief distribution of variable X can be computed if three types of parameters are made available:

1. The current strength of the *causal* support, $\pi_X(u)$, contributed by the parent of X,

$$\pi_X(u) = P\ (u \mid e_X^+)\ .$$

2. The current strength of the *diagnostic* support, $\lambda_{Y_j}(x)$, contributed by the j-th child of X,

$$\lambda_{Y_j}(x) = P\ (e_{Y_j}^- \mid x)\ .$$

3. The fixed conditional probability matrix $P(x \mid u)$ that relates the variable X to its immediate parent U.

Using these parameters, local belief updating can be accomplished in three steps, to be executed in any order.

Step 1—Belief updating: When node X is activated to update its parameters, it simultaneously inspects the $\pi_X(u)$ message communicated by its parent and the messages $\lambda_{Y_1}(x)$, $\lambda_{Y_2}(x)$,... communicated by each of its children. Using this input, it updates its belief measure to

$$BEL(x) = \alpha\ \lambda(x)\ \pi(x), \qquad\qquad (4.27a)$$

where

$$\lambda(x) = \prod_j \lambda_{Y_j}(x), \qquad\qquad (4.27b)$$

$$\pi(x) = \sum_u P(x \mid u)\ \pi_X(u), \qquad\qquad (4.27c)$$

and α is a normalizing constant rendering $\sum_x BEL(x) = 1$.

Step 2—Bottom-up propagation: Using the λ messages received, node X computes a new message, $\lambda_X(u)$, which is sent to its parent U:

$$\lambda_X(u) = \sum_x \lambda(x)\ P(x \mid u)\ . \qquad\qquad (4.28)$$

Step 3—Top-down propagation: X computes new π messages to be sent to each of its children. For example, the new $\pi_{Y_j}(x)$ message that X sends to its j-th child Y_j is computed by

$$\pi_{Y_j}(x) = \alpha \, \pi(x) \prod_{k \neq j} \lambda_{Y_k}(x) \ . \tag{4.29}$$

The computations in Eqs. (4.27), (4.28), and (4.29) preserve the probabilistic meaning of the parameters. In particular,

$$\lambda_X(u) = P(e_X^- \mid u) \ , \tag{4.30}$$

$$\pi_Y(x) = P(x \mid e_Y^+) \ , \tag{4.31}$$

$$BEL(x) = P(x \mid e) \ . \tag{4.32}$$

Terminal and evidence nodes in the tree require special treatment. We must distinguish four cases:

1. *Anticipatory node*—a leaf node that has not been instantiated. For such variables, *BEL* should be equal to π, and we should therefore set $\lambda = (1,1,...,1)$.

2. *Evidence node*—a variable with instantiated value. Following Eq. (4.6a), if the j-th value of X is observed to be true, we set $\lambda(x) = (0,..., 0,1,0,..., 0)$ with 1 at the j-th position.

3. *Dummy node*—a node Y representing virtual or judgmental evidence bearing on X. We do not specify $\lambda(y)$ or $\pi(y)$ but instead post a $\lambda_Y(x)$ message to X, where $\lambda_Y(x) = \beta P(Observation \mid x)$, β being any convenient constant.

4. *Root node*—The boundary condition for the root node is established by setting π (root) equal to the prior probability of the root variable.

EXAMPLE 7: To illustrate these computations let us redo Example 5, using tree propagation on the network of Figure 4.16.

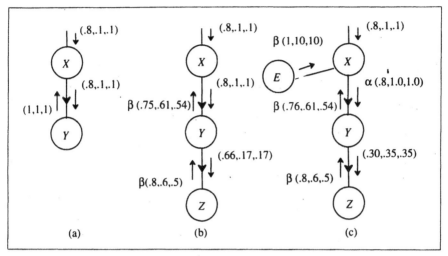

Figure 4.16. *Belief updating in Example 7 using tree propagation. The alibi is modeled as a dummy node E generating a λ message 1:10:10.*

As before, let us assume that our belief in the identity of the killer, based on all testimony heard so far, amounts to $\pi(x) = (0.8, 0.1, 0.1)$. Before we obtain any fingerprint information, Figure 4.16a shows Y as an anticipatory node with $\lambda(y) = (1, 1, 1)$, which means $\lambda_Y(x) = \lambda(x) = (1, 1, 1)$ and $BEL(x) = \pi(x)$. $\pi(y)$ can be calculated from Eq. (4.22) (using $\pi_Y(x) = \pi(x)$), yielding

$$\pi(y) = \pi_Y(x) \bullet M_{y\,|\,x} = (0.8, 0.1, 0.1) \bullet \begin{bmatrix} 0.8 & 0.1 & 0.1 \\ 0.1 & 0.8 & 0.1 \\ 0.1 & 0.1 & 0.8 \end{bmatrix}$$

$$= (0.66, 0.17, 0.17) = BEL(y).$$

Assume that a laboratory report arrives summarizing the test results (a piece of virtual evidence Z) by the message $\lambda_Z(y) = \lambda(y) = \beta(0.8, 0.6, 0.5)$, as in Figure 4.16b. Node Y updates its belief,

$$BEL(y) = \alpha\lambda(y)\pi(y) = \alpha(0.8, 0.6, 0.5)(0.66, 0.17, 0.17) = (0.738, 0.143, 0.119),$$

and based on Eq. (4.28), Y computes a new message, $\lambda_Y(x)$, for X:

$$\lambda_Y(x) = M_{y\,|\,x} \bullet \lambda(y) = \beta \begin{bmatrix} 0.8 & 0.1 & 0.1 \\ 0.1 & 0.8 & 0.1 \\ 0.1 & 0.1 & 0.8 \end{bmatrix} \bullet \begin{bmatrix} 0.8 \\ 0.6 \\ 0.5 \end{bmatrix} = \beta(0.75, 0.61, 0.54).$$

Upon receiving this message, node X sets $\lambda(x) = \lambda_Y(x)$ and recomputes its belief to

$$BEL(x) = \alpha\lambda(x)\pi(x) = \alpha(0.75,\ 0.61,\ 0.54)(0.8,\ 0.1,\ 0.1)$$

$$= (0.839,\ 0.085,\ 0.076)\ .$$

Now assume that Suspect 1 produces a very strong alibi, supporting his innocence ten times more than his guilt, i.e., $P(Alibi\ |X \neq 1) : P(Alibi\ |X = 1) = 10 : 1$. To fuse this information with all previous evidence, we link a new evidence node E directly to X and post the message $\lambda_E(x)=\beta(1,\ 10,\ 10)$ on the link (see Figure 4.16c). $\lambda_E(x)$ combines with $\lambda_Y(x)$ to yield

$$\lambda(x) = \lambda_E(x)\ \lambda_Y(x) = \beta(0.75,\ 6.10,\ 5.40)\ ,$$

$$BEL(x) = \alpha\lambda(x)\pi(x) = \alpha(0.75,\ 6.10,\ 5.40)(0.8,\ 0.1,\ 0.1)$$

$$= (0.343,\ 0.349,\ 0.308)\ ,$$

and generates the message $\pi_Y(x) = \alpha\lambda_E(x)\pi(x) = \alpha\ (0.8,\ 1.0,\ 1.0)$ for Y. Upon receiving $\pi_Y(x)$, processor Y updates its causal support $\pi(y)$ to (see Eq. 4.27)

$$\pi(y) = \pi_Y(x) \bullet M_{y\,|x} = \alpha(0.8,\ 1.0,\ 1.0) \bullet \begin{bmatrix} 0.8 & 0.1 & 0.1 \\ 0.1 & 0.8 & 0.1 \\ 0.1 & 0.1 & 0.8 \end{bmatrix} = (0.30,\ 0.35,\ 0.35)\ ,$$

and $BEL(y)$ becomes

$$BEL(y) = \alpha\lambda(y)\pi(y) = \alpha(0.8,\ 0.6,\ 0.5)(0.30,\ 0.35,\ 0.35)$$

$$= (0.384,\ 0.336,\ 0.280)\ .$$

Finally, since Y has only one child—Z—Eq. (4.29) reduces to $\pi_Z(y) = \pi(y)$ (see also Eq. (4.26)). The purpose of propagating beliefs top-down to sensory nodes such as Z is twofold: to guide data-acquisition strategies toward the most informative sources (see Section 6.4) and to facilitate explanations for the system's choices.

Note that $BEL(x)$ cannot be taken as an updated prior of x for the purpose of calculating $BEL(y)$. In other words, it is wrong to update $BEL(y)$ via the textbook formula

$$BEL(y) = \sum_x P(y\,|x)\,BEL(x) \tag{4.33}$$

(see discussion of Jeffrey's Rule, Section 2.3.3), because $BEL(x)$ was affected by information transmitted from Y, and feeding this information back to Y would amount to counting the same evidence twice. Only the $\pi_Y(x)$ portion of $BEL(x)$ is fed back to Y; it is based on evidence (E) not yet considered in $\lambda(y)$. Another way to view this is that once information is obtained from Z, the initial value of the link matrix $P(y\,|x)$ no longer represents the dependence between X and Y, so $P(y\,|x, z)$ should replace $P(y\,|x)$ in Eq. (4.33).

Note also that the activation steps need not be sequential but may be executed in parallel when several pieces of evidence arrive simultaneously. In the extreme case, we can imagine that all processors are activated simultaneously by a common clock. For example, if the lab report and the alibi arrive together, then in the first clock cycle X and Y will simultaneously update their beliefs to

$$BEL(x) = \alpha(0.08, 0.10, 0.10) = (0.286, 0.357, 0.357) \text{ and}$$

$$BEL(y) = (0.738, 0.142, 0.111)$$

and produce the messages

$$\pi_Y(x) = \alpha(0.08, 0.10, 0.10) \text{ and } \lambda_Y(x) = \beta(0.75, 0.61, 0.54),$$

respectively. In the second clock cycle, X and Y will simultaneously update their beliefs to

$$BEL(x) = (0.343, 0.349, 0.308) \text{ and } BEL(y) = (0.384, 0.336, 0.280)$$

and produce the same $\pi_Y(x)$ and $\lambda_Y(x)$ as before. From now on, the same beliefs and the same messages will be produced in every clock cycle unless additional evidence becomes available.

ILLUSTRATING THE FLOW OF BELIEF

Figure 4.17 shows six successive stages of belief propagation through a simple binary tree, assuming the updating is triggered by changes in the belief parameters of neighboring processors. Initially, the tree is in equilibrium, and all terminal nodes are anticipatory (Figure 4.17a). As soon as two data nodes are activated, white tokens are placed on the links from the nodes to their parents (Figure 4.17b). In the next phase, the parents, activated by these tokens, absorb them and manufacture enough tokens for their neighbors: white tokens for their parents and black ones for their children (Figure 4.17c). (The links from which the absorbed tokens originated do not receive new tokens because a π-message is not affected by a λ-message crossing the same link.) The root node now receives two white tokens, one from each of its descendants, triggering the production of two black tokens for top-down delivery (Figure 4.17d). The process continues in this fashion for six cycles, at which point all tokens are absorbed and the network reaches a new equilibrium. As soon as a leaf node posts a token for its parent, the leaf is ready to receive new data. If the new data arrives before the token was observed by the parent, a new token replaces the old one. In this fashion the inference network can track a changing environment and provide coherent interpretation of signals emanating simultaneously from multiple sources.

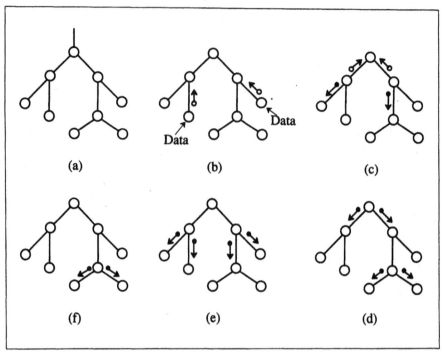

Figure 4.17. *The impact of new data propagates through a tree by a message-passing process.*

This updating scheme has the following properties:

1. The local computations it requires are efficient in both storage space and time. For a tree with m children per parent and n values per node, each processor should store $n^2+mn+2n$ real numbers and perform $2n^2+mn+2n$ multiplications per update.

2. The local computations and the final belief distribution are entirely independent of the control mechanism that activates the individual operations. These operations can be activated by either data-driven or goal-driven (e.g., requests for evidence) control strategies, by a central clock, or at random.

3. New information is diffused through the network in a single pass. Instabilities and indefinite relaxations are eliminated by maintaining a two-parameter system (π and λ) to decouple causal support from diagnostic support. The time required for completing the diffusion (in parallel) is proportional to the diameter of the network.

4.3 BELIEF PROPAGATION IN CAUSAL POLYTREES (SINGLY CONNECTED NETWORKS)

The tree structures treated in the preceding section require that exactly one variable be considered a cause of another given variable. This restriction simplifies computations, but its representational power is rather limited, since it forces us to form a single node from all causes sharing a common consequence. By contrast, when people see many potential causes for a given observation, they weigh one cause against another as independent variables, each pointing to a specialized area of knowledge. As an illustration, consider the situation discussed in Example 7 of Chapter 2:

> Mr. Holmes receives a phone call at work from his neighbor notifying him that she heard a burglar alarm sound from the direction of his home. As he is preparing to rush home, Mr. Holmes recalls that the alarm recently was triggered by an earthquake. Driving home, he hears a radio newscast reporting an earthquake 200 miles away.

Mr. Holmes perceives two episodes as potential causes for the alarm sound—an attempted burglary and an earthquake. Even though burglaries can safely be assumed independent of earthquakes, the radio announcement still reduces the likelihood of a burglary, as it "explains away" the alarm sound. Moreover, the two causal events are perceived as individual variables pointing to separate frames of knowledge (crime-related information seldom evokes associations of earthquakes), so it would be unnatural to lump the two events together into a single node.

Treating $E = Earthquake$ and $B = Burglary$ as two separate entities (as in Figure 2.2) allows us to relate each of them to a separate set of evidence without consulting the other. For example, if $R = The\ radio\ announcement$ and $S = The\ alarm\ sound$, we can quantify the relation between E and R by the probabilities $P(R \mid E)$ without having to consider the irrelevant event of burglary, as would be required if the pair (E, B) were combined into one variable. Moreover, if R is confirmed, a natural way to update the beliefs of E and B would be in two separate steps, mediated by updating S. E and B are presumed to be independent unless evidence supporting S is obtained (e.g., the neighbor's phone call); when this happens, E and B find themselves competing for a fixed amount of evidential support—information favoring one explanation (e.g., the radio report) would weaken the other explanation by undermining its connection with the mediator S.

This competitive interplay among multiple explanations is a prevailing feature of human reasoning and has been discussed in previous chapters (see Sections 1.2.2 and 2.2.4). When a physician discovers evidence in favor of one disease, it reduces the likelihood of other diseases that could explain the patient's symptoms, although the patient might well be suffering from two or more disorders simultaneously. When we find our driveway wet, the discovery that the sprinkler was on all night weakens the likelihood that it rained at night. The same maxim also governs the interplay of other frame-like (though not necesarily causal) explanations. For example, the sentence "Tweety tasted wonderful" provides a clue that Tweety, the celebrated non-flying bird from the AI literature (see Chapter 10), is not a penguin after all; a more likely explanation for Tweety's reluctance to fly is that she is broiled.

This section extends our propagation scheme to Bayesian networks where a node may have multiple parents, thus permitting "sideways" interactions via common successors. The networks are, however, required to be *singly connected*, namely, no more than one path exists between any two nodes, as in Figure 4.18a. We call such networks *causal polytrees* because they can be viewed as a collection of several causal trees fused together at the nodes where arrows converge head to head. The absence of loops in the underlying network permits us to develop a local updating scheme similar to that used for causal trees. The derivation of the propagation rules, likewise, will correspond to the derivation of Eqs. (4.27) through (4.29). The impatient reader is advised to skip directly to the Summary, Eqs. (4.47) through (4.53).

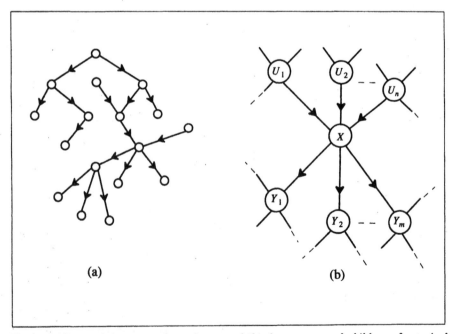

Figure 4.18. *(a) A fragment of a polytree and (b) the parents and children of a typical node X.*

4.3.1 Propagation Rules

Consider a typical fragment of a singly connected network (Figure 4.18*b*), consisting of a node X, the set of all X's parents, $U = \{U_1,..., U_n\}$, and the set of all X's children, $Y = \{Y_1,..., Y_m\}$. As before, let e be the total evidence obtained, e_X^- be the evidence connected to X through its children (Y), and e_X^+ be the evidence connected to X through its parents (U), so that

$$BEL(x) = \alpha P(e_X^- \mid x) P(x \mid e_X^+)$$

$$= \alpha \lambda(x) \pi(x). \qquad (4.34)$$

e_X^- and e_X^+ can be further decomposed into

$$e_X^- = \left\{ e_{XY_1}^-,..., e_{XY_m}^- \right\}$$

and

$$e_X^+ = \left\{ e_{U_1X}^+,..., e_{U_nX}^+ \right\},$$

where $e_{XY_j}^-$ stands for evidence contained in the subnetwork on the *head* side of the link $X \rightarrow Y_j$, and $e_{U_iX}^+$ stands for evidence contained in the subnetwork on the *tail* side of the link $U_i \rightarrow X$.

To avoid cumbersome notation, we will treat all evidence as virtual, i.e., obtained from dummy children of variables whose values are known. Thus, all instantiated nodes in the networks are assumed to be leaf nodes. Now,

$$\lambda(x) \triangleq P(e_X^- \mid x)$$

$$= P(e_{XY_1}^-,..., e_{XY_m}^- \mid x)$$

$$= P(e_{XY_1}^- \mid x) \cdot P(e_{XY_2}^- \mid x) \cdots P(e_{XY_m}^- \mid x)$$

$$= \prod_{j=1}^{m} \lambda_{Y_j}(x), \qquad (4.35)$$

where

$$\lambda_{Y_j}(x) = P(e_{XY_j}^- \mid x). \qquad (4.36)$$

Also,

$$\pi(x) \triangleq P(x \mid e_X^+)$$

$$= P(x \mid e_{U_1X}^+, \dots, e_{U_nX}^+)$$

$$= \sum_{u_1, \dots, u_n} P(x \mid u_1, \dots u_n) \, P(u_1, \dots, u_n \mid e_{U_1X}^+, \dots, e_{U_nX}^+)$$

$$= \sum_{u_1, \dots, u_n} P(x \mid u_1, \dots, u_n) \, P(u_1 \mid e_{U_1X}^+) \, P(u_2 \mid e_{U_2X}^+) \cdots P(u_n \mid e_{U_nX}^+) ,$$

because each pair $\{U_i, e_{U_iX}^+\}$ is independent of the other U's and their evidence sets.

Let

$$\pi_X(u_i) = P(u_i \mid e_{U_iX}^+). \tag{4.37}$$

Then

$$\pi(x) = \sum_{u_1, \dots, u_n} P(x \mid u_1, \dots, u_n) \pi_X(u_1) \pi_X(u_2) \cdots \pi_X(u_n)$$

$$= \sum_u P(x \mid u) \prod_{i=1}^n \pi_X(u_i) . \tag{4.38}$$

Substituting Eq. (4.36) and Eq. (4.38) in Eq. (4.34), we get

$$BEL(x) = \alpha \left[\prod_{j=1}^m \lambda_{Y_j}(x) \right] \left[\sum_u P(x \mid u) \prod_{i=1}^n \pi_X(u_i) \right] . \tag{4.39}$$

Thus, node X can calculate its own beliefs if it receives the messages $\lambda_{Y_j}(x)$ from its children and $\pi_X(u_i)$ from its parents.

To prescribe how the influence of new information will spread through the network, we need to specify how a typical node, say X, will compute its outgoing messages $\lambda_X(u_i)$, $i = 1, \dots, n$, and $\pi_{Y_j}(x)$, $j = 1, \dots, m$, from the incoming messages $\lambda_{Y_j}(x)$, $j = 1, \dots, m$ and $\pi_X(u_i)$, $i = 1, \dots, n$.

UPDATING λ

Consider the message $\lambda_X(u_i)$, which node X must send its parent U_i. By Eq. (4.36),

$$\lambda_X(u_i) = P(e_{U_iX}^- \mid u_i). \tag{4.40}$$

In deriving $\lambda_X(u_i)$ it is convenient temporarily to treat all parents (except U_i) as a single compound variable,

$$V = U - U_i = \{U_1, ..., U_{i-1}, U_{i+1}, ..., U_n\}, \tag{4.41}$$

connected to X via a single link $V \rightarrow X$, as in Figure 4.19.

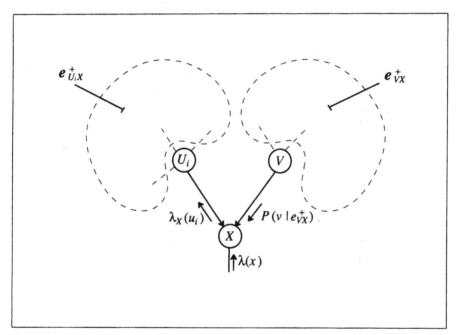

Figure 4.19. *Variables, messages, and evidence sets used in the derivation of* $\lambda_X(u_i)$.

The evidence $e_{\bar{U}_i X}$ governing $\lambda_X(u_i)$ can now be decomposed into two components:

$$e_{\bar{U}_i X} = \{e_{VX}^+, e_X^-\} \tag{4.42}$$

where

$$e_{VX}^+ = \bigcup_{k \neq i} e_{\bar{U}_k X}^+. \tag{4.43}$$

180

Substituting Eq. (4.42) into Eq. (4.40) gives

$$\lambda_X(u_i) = P(e^+_{VX}, e^-_X \,|\, u_i)$$

$$= \sum_x \sum_v P(e^+_{VX}, e^-_X \,|\, u_i, v, x)\, P(v, x \,|\, u_i)$$

(conditioning on x and v)

$$= \sum_x \sum_v P(e^-_X \,|\, x)\, P(e^+_{VX} \,|\, v)\, P(v, x \,|\, u_i)$$

(since X separates e^+_{VX} from e^-_X and V separates e^+_{VX} from U_i)

$$= \beta \sum_x \sum_v P(e^-_X \,|\, x)\, \frac{P(v \,|\, e^+_{VX})}{P(v)}\, P(x \,|\, v, u_i)\, P(v \,|\, u_i)$$

(by Bayes' Rule)

$$= \beta \sum_x \sum_v P(e^-_X \,|\, x)\, P(v \,|\, e^+_{VX})\, P(x \,|\, v, u_i)$$

(since U_i and V are marginally independent)

Restoring the meaning of V from Eqs. (4.41) and (4.43), we have

$$P(x \,|\, v, u_i) = P(x \,|\, u)\,,$$

$$P(v \,|\, e^+_{VX}) = \prod_{k \neq i} P(u_k \,|\, e^+_{VX}) = \prod_{k \neq i} P(u_k \,|\, e^+_{U_k X}) = \prod_{k \neq i} \pi_X(u_k),$$

and $\lambda_X(u_i)$ becomes

$$\lambda_X(u_i) = \beta \sum_x \lambda(x) \sum_{u_k:\, k \neq i} P(x \,|\, u) \prod_{k \neq i} \pi_X(u_k)\,, \tag{4.44}$$

where $\lambda(x)$ is given in Eq. (4.35). As before, $\lambda_X(u_i)$ is not affected by $\pi_X(u_i)$; the two messages pass along the same arc (in the opposite direction) without interacting.

In the derivation above we assumed that X itself is not instantiated and therefore is not part of the evidence set $e^-_{U_i X}$ in Eq. (4.42). This assumption does not affect the generality of Eq. (4.44) because the fact that X is an evidence node attaining the value x' can always be represented by instantiating a (dummy) child node Z, and thus delivering a message $\lambda_Z(x)$ to X, where

$$\lambda_Z(x) = \delta_{x,x'} = \begin{cases} 1 & x = x' \\ 0 & x \neq x'. \end{cases}$$

UPDATING π

Consider the message $\pi_{Y_j}(x)$, which node X must send to its child Y_j. By Eq. (4.37),

$$\pi_{Y_j}(x) = P(x \mid e_{XY_j}^+) .$$

$e_{XY_j}^+$ stands for the entire body of evidence e, excluding evidence found in the subnetwork on the head side of the link $X \rightarrow Y_j$,

$$e_{XY_j}^+ = e - e_{XY_j}^- .$$

Thus, $\pi_{Y_j}(x)$ is equal to $BEL(x)$ when the evidence $e_{XY_j}^-$ is suppressed. Equivalently, the expression for $\pi_{Y_j}(x)$ can be obtained from $BEL(x)$, Eq. (4.39), setting $\lambda_{Y_j}(x) = 1$. This leads to

$$\pi_{Y_j}(x) = \alpha \prod_{k \neq j} \lambda_{Y_k}(x) \, \pi(x) , \qquad (4.45)$$

where $\pi(x)$ is given in Eq. (4.38). Alternatively, $\pi_{Y_j}(x)$ can be obtained from $BEL(x)$, writing

$$\pi_{Y_j}(x) = \alpha \, \frac{BEL(x)}{\lambda_{Y_j}(x)} = BEL(x) \Big|_{\lambda_{Y_j}(x) \,=\, 1.} \qquad (4.46)$$

BOUNDARY CONDITIONS

The boundary conditions are established as follows:

1. *Root nodes:* If X is a node with no parents, we set $\pi(x)$ equal to the prior probability $P(x)$.

2. *Anticipatory nodes:* If X is a childless node that has not been instantiated, we set $\lambda(x) = (1,1,...,1)$.

3. *Evidence nodes:* If evidence $X = x'$ is obtained (X being any node in the network, not necessarily a leaf node), we set $\lambda(x) = \delta_{x,x'} = (0,...,0,1,0,...,0)$ with 1 at the x'-th position. Alternatively, the evidence $X = x'$ can be simulated by adding to X the auxiliary child node Z, directing a message $\lambda_Z(x) = \delta_{x,x'}$ toward X.

Eqs. (4.44) and (4.45) demonstrate that the outgoing messages, $\pi_{Y_j}(x)$ and $\lambda_X(u_i)$, are determined from the incoming messages available to X. They also demonstrate that perturbation of the causal parameter π does not affect the diagnostic parameter λ on the same link, and vice versa. The two are orthogonal to each other since they depend on two disjoint sets of data. Therefore, any perturbation of beliefs in response to new evidence propagates through the network and is absorbed at peripheral nodes without reflection.† A new equilibrium state will be reached after a finite number of updates—if they are conducted in parallel, the number will be equal to the diameter of the network.

Eq. (4.44) also reveals that if no data are observed below X (i.e., all λs pointing to X are unit vectors), then all λs emanating from X are unit vectors, regardless of the incoming π messages. So, evidence gathered at a particular node does not influence any of its spouses until their common child gathers diagnostic support. This reflects the d-separation conditions established in Section 3.3.2 and matches our intuition regarding multiple causes. In Mr. Holmes' case, for example, prior to the neighbor's telephone call, seismic data indicating an earthquake would *not* have influenced the likelihood of a burglary.

SUMMARY OF PROPAGATION RULES FOR POLYTREES

The steps involved in polytree propagation are similar to those used with trees. We shall now summarize these steps by considering a typical node X having m children, $Y_1,..., Y_m$, and n parents, $U_1,..., U_n$, as in Figure 4.18b.

The belief distribution of variable X can be computed if three types of parameters are made available:

1.   The current strength of the *causal* support π contributed by each incoming link $U_i{\rightarrow}X$:

$$\pi_X(u_i) = P(u_i \mid e^+_{U_iX}) . \qquad (4.47)$$

2.   The current strength of the *diagnostic* support, λ, contributed by each outgoing link $X \rightarrow Y_j$:

$$\lambda_{Y_j}(x) = P(e^-_{XY_j} \mid x) . \qquad (4.48)$$

3.   The fixed conditional-probability matrix $P(x \mid u_1,..., u_n)$ that relates the variable X to its immediate parents.

Using these parameters, local belief updating can be accomplished in three steps, to be executed in any order.

Step 1—Belief updating: When node X is activated, it simultaneously inspects the messages $\pi_X(u_i)$, $i = 1,..., n$ communicated by its parents and the messages

---

† A peripheral node is either a root with a single child or a leaf with a single parent. Every polytree must have at least two peripheral nodes.

$\lambda_{Y_j}(x)$, $j = 1,..., m$ communicated by its children. Using this input, it updates its belief measure to

$$BEL(x) = \alpha \, \lambda(x) \, \pi(x), \tag{4.49}$$

where

$$\lambda(x) = \prod_j \lambda_{Y_j}(x) , \tag{4.50}$$

$$\pi(x) = \sum_{u_1,..., u_n} P(x \mid u_1,..., u_n) \prod_i \pi_X(u_i) , \tag{4.51}$$

and α is a normalizing constant rendering $\sum_x BEL(x) = 1$.

Step 2—Bottom-up propagation: Using the messages received, node X computes new λ messages to be sent to its parents. For example, the new message $\lambda_X(u_i)$ that X sends to its parents U_i is computed by

$$\lambda_X(u_i) = \beta \sum_x \lambda(x) \sum_{u_k : k \neq i} P(x \mid u_1,..., u_n) \prod_{k \neq i} \pi_X(u_k) . \tag{4.52}$$

Step 3—Top-down propagation: Each node computes new π messages to be sent to its children. For example, the new $\pi_{Y_j}(x)$ message that X sends to its child Y_j is computed by

$$\pi_{Y_j}(x) = \alpha \left[\prod_{k \neq j} \lambda_{Y_k}(x) \right] \sum_{u_1,..., u_n} P(x \mid u_1,..., u_n) \prod_i \pi_X(u_i) \tag{4.53}$$

$$= \alpha \, \frac{BEL(x)}{\lambda_{Y_j}(x)} .$$

Numerical examples illustrating these propagation rules in polytrees are given in Section 4.5.3 (see also Section 5.2.1).

The presence of multiple parents introduces an added dimension of complexity; although the computations in Eqs. (4.51) through (4.53) are still local, the summation ranges over all value combinations of the parent variables, which are exponential in n. If the number of parents is small, the summation can be performed by enumeration. However, if there are more than four or five parents, approximation techniques must be invoked that make use of the special structure of the link matrix $P(x \mid u_1,..., u_n)$.

In Chapter 2, we remarked that when n is large, we must use prototypical models of child-to-parents interaction, involving disjunctions and conjunctions (noisy OR- and AND-gates), in order to specify the link matrix. Here we see that considerations of computational complexity also dictate such usage. In the next section, we shall see that some of these prototypical models enable us to compute Eqs. (4.51) through (4.53) in closed form, thus reducing the computation of the outgoing messages to simple products of about n parameters.

4.3.2 Canonical Models of Multicausal Interactions

The original formulation of Bayesian networks (Section 3.4) required, for each variable X, that one assess the conditional probability $P(x \mid u)$, where U is a set of variables judged to be direct causes of X. We have also noticed that the individual elements of U often point to disparate frames of knowledge, making it difficult to assess $P(x \mid u)$. If U_1 and U_2 represent frames of knowledge truly foreign to one another (e.g., burglaries and earthquakes) except that they share X_i as a common consequence (e.g., triggering the alarm), one cannot expect to find the matrix $P(x \mid u_1, u_2)$ prestored in memory. No reasoning system could spare the space required to permanently store the strength of connection between every conceivable event and every combination of conditions that might trigger that event. A more reasonable organization scheme would be to let each frame hold separately the weights associated with each of its likely consequences. Then, should a situation evoke more than one frame, the system can compute the weights of their common results "on the fly," using some *universal* combination rule. For example, in our burglary alarm scenario, it is reasonable to expect people to have some prestored idea of the likelihood that a burglary will trigger an alarm or that an earthquake will trigger it, but not of the likelihood that the combination, burglary and earthquake, will trigger it. A physician is expected to have prepackaged estimates of the chances that an individual disease will be accompanied by high fever, but when asked to estimate the likelihood of high fever given some rare combination of diseases, the physician cannot refer to prestored knowledge. Rather, she must resort to some canonical model of disease combinations in general, which most likely is also domain-independent, i.e., applicable to a wide class of interacting causes.

DISJUNCTIVE INTERACTION (THE NOISY OR-GATE)

One of the most common models of this type is *disjunctive interaction* (the "noisy OR-gate" of Chapter 2), which leads to a very convenient and widely applicable rule of combination. Disjunctive interaction occurs when any member of a set of conditions is likely to cause a certain event and this likelihood does not diminish when several of these conditions prevail simultaneously. For example, if each individual disease is likely to cause high fever, then a patient suffering from several of these diseases simultaneously would only be *more* likely to develop high fever. Moreover, if the patient is also suffering from a disease that in isolation is not normally accompanied by high fever, this added information does not reduce the patient's likelihood of developing high fever from the other diseases.

Disjunctive interactions can be approximated by an elegant mathematical model based on two assumptions: accountability and exception independence.

Accountability requires that an event E be presumed false (i.e., $P(E) = 0$) if all conditions listed as causes of E are false. In the burglary alarm example, this assumption requires that we list explicitly the main conditions likely to trigger the alarm and lump together all those conditions that we prefer to keep implicit under the heading "All other causes."

Exception independence asserts that if an event E is a typical consequence of either one of two causal conditions c_1 and c_2, then the mechanism that may inhibit the occurrence of E under c_1 is independent of the mechanism that may inhibit E under c_2. Each exception to normal behavior acts as an independent variable. For example, the mechanism that inhibits the activation of the alarm during an earthquake could be low vertical acceleration, while the mechanism acting during a burglary could be the burglar's skill and sophistication. Since these two can safely be presumed independent of each other, exception independence holds. A power failure, on the other hand, would inhibit the alarm activation in both frames and thus would violate exception independence if it is a likely event.

These two assumptions are represented schematically in Figure 4.20. The event X represents a prediction or a consequence and is viewed as the output of a logical OR-gate. Each input to the OR-gate is the output of an AND-gate representing the conjunction of a causal explanation of X, U_i, and the negation of its specific inhibitory mechanism I_i. (Readers familiar with the IN and OUT justifiers in truth maintenance systems [Doyle 1979] or with the *abnormal* predicate in circumscription [McCarthy 1986] should note their resemblance to the U_i and I_i variables in Figure 4.20.)

The inputs $U = (U_1, U_2,..., U_n)$ are the parents of X in the Bayesian networks, and they normally represent explanations, hypotheses, conjectures, causal factors, or enabling conditions that may account for the occurrence of X. The inhibitors $I_1,..., I_n$ represent exceptions or abnormalities that interfere with the normal relationship between U and X. These are normally not represented by nodes in Bayesian networks but are summarized implicitly by the link matrix $P(x \mid u_1,..., u_n)$. Here we explicate their structure and display them as root nodes in order to justify an especially useful form of the link matrix.

CONSTRUCTING THE LINK MATRIX

Denote by q_k the probability that the k-th inhibitor is active. If U_i is the only parent that is *TRUE*, X will be *TRUE* iff the inhibitor associated with U_i remains inactive. Hence, we have

$$P(X = TRUE \mid U_i = TRUE, U_k = FALSE \ \ k \neq i) = 1 - q_i .$$

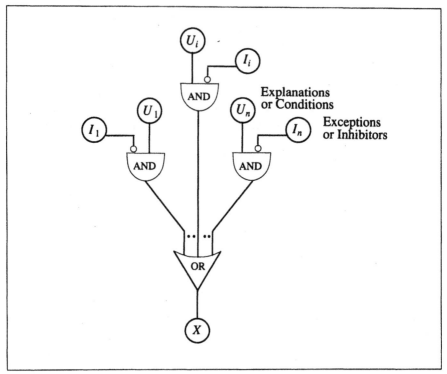

Figure 4.20. *The noisy OR-gate. A canonical model of disjunctive interactions among multiple causes $U_1 \ldots U_n$ predicting the same effect X.*

Thus, the parameter

$$c_i = 1 - q_i$$

represents the degree to which an isolated explanation $U_i = TRUE$ can endorse the consequent event $X = TRUE$.

   Let

$$u = (u_1, u_2, \ldots, u_n) \quad u_i \in \{0, 1\}$$

represent any assignment of truth values to the parent set U. The assumption of exception independence permits a closed-form calculation of the probability distribution of X given any assignment state u. If T_u represents the subset of parents that are $TRUE$,

$$T_u = \{i : U_i = TRUE\},$$

then X is *FALSE* iff all inhibitors associated with T_u are active. Thus, we can write

$$P(X = FALSE \mid u) = \prod_{i \in T_u} q_i,$$

or

$$P(x \mid u) = \begin{cases} \displaystyle\prod_{i \in T_u} q_i & \text{if} \quad x = 0 \\[2ex] 1 - \displaystyle\prod_{i \in T_u} q_i & \text{if} \quad x = 1, \end{cases} \tag{4.54}$$

where $x = 0$ and $x = 1$ represent the events $X = FALSE$ and $X = TRUE$, respectively. Eq. (4.54) constitutes a full specification for the link matrix. It also represents a general scheme for approximating a link matrix $P(x \mid u)$ from individual parent-child relationships, in cases with negligible cross-interaction.

COMPUTING BEL(x)

Following Eqs. (4.49) through Eq. (4.54), we write

$$BEL(x) = \alpha \, \lambda(x) \sum_{u} P(x \mid u) \prod_{i} \pi_X(u_i)$$

$$= \begin{cases} \alpha \, \lambda_0 \sum_{u} \left(\displaystyle\prod_{i \in T_u} q_i \right) \prod_{k} \pi_X(u_k) & \text{if} \quad x = 0 \\[2ex] \alpha \, \lambda_1 \sum_{u} \left(1 - \displaystyle\prod_{i \in T_u} q_i \right) \prod_{k} \pi_X(u_k) & \text{if} \quad x = 1, \end{cases} \tag{4.55}$$

where $\lambda(x) = (\lambda_0, \lambda_1)$ represents the combined evidential support contributed by X's children and $\pi_X(u_i)$ represents the message X receives from its i-th parent (i.e., the probability distribution of the i-th parent given all evidence from the subnetwork at the tail of the link $U_i \rightarrow X$).

The summation in Eq. (4.55) can be obtained in closed form by ecursive summation over the individual U's. Denoting by $+u_i$ and $\neg u_i$ the propositions $U_i = TRUE$ and $U_i = FALSE$, and letting

$$\pi_{iX} = \pi_X(+u_i) = 1 - \pi_X(\neg u_i),$$

we define

$$\Pi'_u \triangleq \sum_u (\prod_{i \in T_u} q_i) \prod_k \pi_X(u_k) = \sum_u \left[\prod_{i \in T_u} q_i \, \pi_{iX} \right] \left[\prod_{i \notin T_u} (1 - \pi_{iX}) \right],$$

and summing over the two states, $+u_j$ and $\neg u_j$, of one of the U's, say U_j, we obtain

$$\Pi'_u = \left[q_j \, \pi_X(+u_j) + \pi_X(\neg u_j) \right] \sum_{u - u_j} \prod_{i \in T_u - j} q_i \prod_{k \neq j} \pi_X(u_k)$$

$$= \left[q_j \, \pi_{jX} + 1 - \pi_{jX} \right] \Pi'_{u-u_j} = (1 - c_j \, \pi_{jX}) \, \Pi'_{u-u_j} .$$

Thus, summing over u_j has the effect of pulling out a factor $(1 - c_j \, \pi_{jX})$ and leaving behind the same form with $u - u_j$ instead of u, where

$$u - u_j = \{ u_1, ..., u_{j-1}, u_{j+1}, ..., u_n \} .$$

Applying this recursively† gives

$$\Pi'_u = \prod_i (q_i \pi_{iX} + 1 - \pi_{iX}) . \tag{4.56}$$

Hence,

$$BEL(x) = \begin{cases} \alpha \, \lambda_0 \prod_i (1 - c_i \, \pi_{iX}) & \text{if } x = 0 \\ \alpha \, \lambda_1 \, [1 - \prod_i (1 - c_i \, \pi_{iX})] & \text{if } x = 1. \end{cases} \tag{4.57}$$

Thus, we see that the overall belief distribution of a variable X can be formed by a multiplication over the individual contributions of X's parents (and X's children, via $\lambda(x) = (\lambda_0, \lambda_1)$). The product $c_i \, \pi_{iX}$ can be interpreted as the degree of *predictive endorsement* that the parent U_i lends to the proposition $X = TRUE$, hence the product $\prod_i (1 - c_i \, \pi_{iX})$ represents the overall *endorsement withheld* by all

---

† This derivation is due to Charles Kalme. Another way of verifying Eq. (4.56) is to use the formula $\prod_i (a_i + b_i) = \sum_u (\prod_{i \in T_u} a_i) (\prod_{i \notin T_u} b_i)$, substituting $a_i = q_i \pi_{iX}$ and $b_i = 1 - \pi_{iX}$.

parents. When each $c_i \, \pi_{iX}$ endorsement is small, Eq. (4.57) can be approximated by

$$\frac{BEL(x = 1)}{BEL(x = 0)} \approx \frac{\lambda_1}{\lambda_0} \sum_i c_i \, \pi_{iX} , \qquad (4.58)$$

demonstrating that the combined endorsement by all parents is additive over the individual endorsements.

COMPUTING THE λ's

Using Eq. (4.44) we write

$$\lambda_X(u_i) = \beta \sum_x \lambda(x) \sum_{u - u_i} P(x \mid u) \prod_{k \neq i} \pi_X(u_k) . \qquad (4.59)$$

The second summation in Eq. (4.59) is identical in form to that of Eq. (4.55), except that u_i is now excluded from the summation. Accordingly, using the formula Eq. (4.56) for Π'_u, we get

$$\lambda_X(u_i) = \beta \sum_x \lambda(x) \, F(x, u_i),$$

where

$$F(x, +u_i) = \begin{cases} q_i \prod\limits_{k \neq i} (1 - c_k \, \pi_{kX}) & \text{if} \quad x = 0 \\[2mm] 1 - q_i \prod\limits_{k \neq i} (1 - c_k \, \pi_{kX}) & \text{if} \quad x = 1 \end{cases}$$

and

$$F(x, \neg u_i) = F(x, +u_i) \Big|_{q_i = 1} .$$

Inserting this in Eq. (4.59) yields

$$\lambda_X(u_i) = \begin{cases} \beta \, [\lambda_0 \, q_i \, \Pi'_i + \lambda_1 \, (1 - q_i \, \Pi'_i)] & \text{if} \quad u_i = +u_i \\ \beta \, [\lambda_0 \, \Pi'_i + \lambda_1 \, (1 - \Pi'_i)] & \text{if} \quad u_i = \neg u_i, \end{cases} \qquad (4.60)$$

where

$$\Pi'_i = \prod_{k \neq i} (1 - c_k \, \pi_{kX}) \qquad (4.61)$$

represents the overall endorsement withheld by all parents except U_i. A more concise formula for encoding $\lambda_X(u_i)$ is

$$\lambda_X(u_i) = \beta \left[\lambda_1 - q_i^{u_i}(\lambda_1 - \lambda_0) \Pi'_i \right] \qquad u_i = 0, 1.$$

INTUITIVE INTERPRETATION AND CREDIT ASSIGNMENT POLICY

Since only the ratios

$$L_{XU_i} = \frac{\lambda_X(+u_i)}{\lambda_X(\neg u_i)} \quad \text{and} \quad L_X = \frac{\lambda_1}{\lambda_0}$$

enter the updating rules, we can write Eq. (4.60) as

$$L_{XU_i} = \frac{q_i \Pi'_i + (1 - q_i \Pi'_i) L_X}{\Pi'_i + (1 - \Pi'_i) L_X}$$

$$= 1 + \frac{\Pi'_i c_i (L_X - 1)}{1 + (1 - \Pi'_i)(L_X - 1)} . \tag{4.62}$$

Note that $L_X = 1$ implies $L_{XU_i} = 1$, so if X gathers no evidential support, U_i will neither receive evidential support from X nor be affected in any way by the other parents. This phenomenon is true in general (see Eq. (4.44)), and it reaffirms our intuition that causal frames should remain uncoupled until their common slots receive indication of empirical confirmation or denial. However, the noisy-OR-gate model has one more condition under which causal frames remain uncoupled, namely, when X is completely denied. This can be seen by substituting $L_X = 0$ in Eq. (4.62)), yielding

$$L_{XU_i} = 1 - c_i = q_i,$$

independent of c_k or π_{kX}, $k \neq i$. Thus, the denial of a common effect X results in each causal factor receiving a constant support $q_i \leq 1$, regardless of the existence of other factors (q_i is usually very small, so $L_{XU_i} = q_i$ means the withholding of support from U_i). From a network analysis viewpoint, this phenomenon means that any negatively instantiated variable X acts as an absorption barrier, similar to an anticipatory variable. The messages π_{kX} converging onto such a variable are totally absorbed and do not generate new λ messages. Negatively instantiated variables can even turn multiply connected networks into polytrees (see the example in Section 4.5.3, Figure 4.37).

There is another condition under which U_i receives no evidential support from X, namely, when at least one of the other parents, say U_k, extends a full endorsement to X by having $c_k \pi_{kX} = 1$. Under this condition $\Pi'_i = 0$, and again,

$\lambda_X(+u_i) / \lambda_X(\neg u_i) = 1$ regardless of c_i, meaning the connection between X and U_i is totally disrupted by U_k. This fits intuition; once we find a satisfactory explanation for a suspected symptom, that symptom no longer imparts confirmation to other explanations, no matter how sure we are of the symptom. For example, once I learn that the ignition wires in my car are disconnected, I no longer hypothesize a faulty battery no matter how sure I am that my car will not start. Explanations act as logical valves shutting off each other's flow of evidential support when they become confirmed. When two or more explanations achieve $c_k \pi_{kX} = 1$, none of them can receive evidential support from X because the Π'_i of each one, and of any other explanation of X, becomes zero. In fact, achieving $c_k \pi_{kX} = 1$ means the k-th explanations no longer need X's support; it is firmly established by other sources of information, and from that position its sole effect would be to undermine the flow of support from X to every other explanation. In Chapter 10, we shall formulate this undermining effect in the framework of default logic.

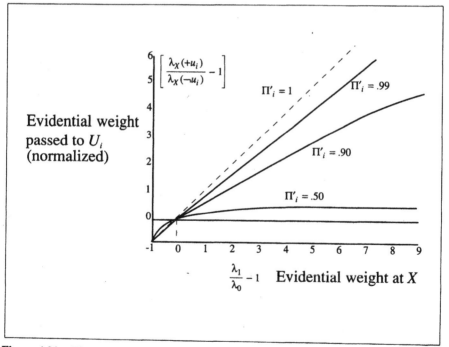

Figure 4.21. *The support that a partially confirmed event lends to its i-th explanation, U_i, as a function of the evidential weight accrued at X, and the amount of credit Π'_i left unclaimed by alternative explanations.*

Figure 4.21 depicts the relationship between the likelihood ratios L_{XU_i} and L_X for several values of Π'_i. It shows that for a given value of Π'_i, there is a maximum amount of evidential support that can be transferred from X to U_i. That amount (see Eq. (4.62)) is equal to

$$L_{XU_i} = 1 + \frac{c_i\,\Pi'_i}{1 - \Pi'_i}\,, \qquad (4.63)$$

and it is reached when $L_X = \infty$, namely, when $X = TRUE$ is confirmed with absolute certainty. Thus, Π'_i can be thought of as the maximum amount of *residual credit* left unclaimed by all alternative explanations combined.

An interesting situation develops when the a priori probabilities π_{kX} are extremely small. Under this condition, each cause individually provides only a small endorsement to the event $X = TRUE$. Yet when the truth of X is confirmed, the relative likelihoods of the various causes are determined by the relative magnitudes of their $c_k\pi_{kX}$ products. To see this, we write

$$\frac{BEL(+u_i)}{BEL(+u_j)} = \frac{\pi_{iX}}{\pi_{jX}}\,\frac{L_{XU_i}}{L_{XU_j}}\,.$$

Since $\pi_{kX} \ll 1$ renders $\Pi'_i \approx 1$ in Eq. (4.61), Eq. (4.63) yields

$$\frac{BEL(+u_i)}{BEL(+u_j)} \approx \frac{c_i\,\pi_{iX}}{c_j\,\pi_{jX}}.$$

If we make the further assumption that only one of the causes can be true (*single cause assumption*), we get the formula

$$BEL(+u_i) = \frac{c_i\,\pi_{iX}}{\displaystyle\sum_k c_k\,\pi_{kX}}\,.$$

Thus, the amount of credit deserved by explanation U_i is given by the product $c_i\pi_{iX}$, i.e., the endorsement offered by the explanation weighted by the probability that it is in fact *TRUE*.

To further demonstrate how parents compete for the evidential support provided by X let us assume that X is not confirmed with certainty, i.e., L_X is finite.

Making the rare-endorsement assumption

$$c_k \pi_{kX} \ll 1 \quad \text{for} \quad k \neq i$$

and expanding Eq. (4.62) in Taylor's series, we obtain

$$L_{XU_i} - 1 \approx \left[L_X - 1 \right] c_i \left[1 - \sum_{k \neq i} c_k \pi_{kX} \right]. \tag{4.64}$$

The term $L_X - 1$ can be identified with the overall *evidential weight* received by the proposition $X = TRUE$. Accordingly, Eq. (4.64) demonstrates that the evidential weight received from X by the i-th parent depends on three factors:

1. $L_X - 1$ = the total evidential weight accrued at X.

2. c_i = the degree to which U_i endorses X (if U_i is *TRUE*).

3. $1 - \sum_{k \neq i} c_k \pi_{kX}$ = the amount of *residual credit* left unclaimed by all other parents.

Thus, the struggle for a share of X's support is settled by the following policy: he who risks the strongest endorsement in a prediction earns the greatest credit when that prediction materializes. Note that while parents compete for credit from their child's success, the same is not true for children; the more a child endorses a parent, the greater the benefit to its brethren. This distinction is further examined in Section 10.3.

OTHER CANONICAL MODELS

The basic noisy-OR-gate model of the preceeding subsection is too restrictive in some applications, and more elaborate interactions among the causal conditions are sometimes needed. For example, conditions might interact conjunctively rather than disjunctively. The basic structure of such models remains the same, however: Boolean combinations of explicated conditions. The unexplicated conditions are summarized probabilistically under the assumption of exception independence.

The assumption of exception independence can easily be relaxed to represent global abnormality conditions, i.e., conditions that would inhibit the response event X even when several causal factors are triggered. For example, a power failure would inhibit the alarm from sounding under simultaneous burglary and earthquake conditions. To incorporate global inhibition in the model of Figure 4.20 we simply add another AND-gate between the OR-gate and the response variable X, as in Figure 4.22a. When the global inhibitor I_0 is ON, X will be OFF, regardless of other causal factors.

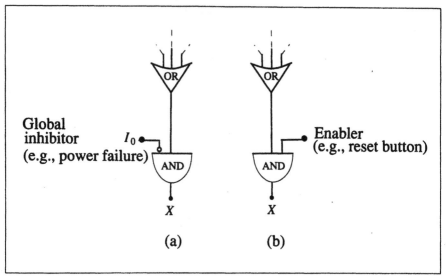

Figure 4.22. *Canonical models of global inhibition (a) and enabling mechanisms (b).*

In this fashion, we can also model various enabling mechanisms, i.e., conditions that have no influence of their own (on X) except to enable other influences to take effect. For example, if the alarm system has a reset button which Mr. Holmes occasionally forgets to push, setting this button is an enabling condition, as in Figure 4.22b.

SUMMARY

Canonical models can be thought of as default strategies for completing the specification of a Bayesian network whenever detailed interactions among causes are unavailable, too numerous to elicit, or too complex to be treated precisely. In particular, the disjunctive model of interacting causes has several advantages: it requires the specification of only n parameters (for a family of n parents), it executes the propagation routine in only n steps (for each node with n parents), and it leads to conclusions that match our intuition about how credit should be assigned among competing explanations. Having explicated the assumptions behind disjunctive interaction, i.e., accountability and exception independence, we can scrutinize the model's range of adequacy at a very basic level, and once this test is passed, the adequacy of the credit assignment policy is guaranteed.

4.4 COPING WITH LOOPS

Loops are undirected cycles in the *underlying* network, i.e., the network without the arrows.† When loops are present, the network is no longer singly connected, and local propagation schemes will invariably run into trouble. The reason is both architectural and semantic. If we ignore the existence of loops and permit the nodes to continue communicating with each other as if the network were singly connected, messages may circulate indefinitely around these loops, and the process may not converge to a stable equilibrium. This problem is usually encountered in non-probabilistic systems (such as Example 1), where each message can cause a discrete change in the state of the receiving processor (e.g., choosing a different color), a change that can be reversed each time its impact circulates around the loop. Such oscillations do not normally occur in probabilistic networks because of the stochastic nature of the link matrices, which tend to bring all messages toward some stable equilibrium as time goes on. However, this asymptotic equilibrium is not coherent, in the sense that it does not represent the posterior probabilities of all nodes of the network. The reason for this is simple: all of our propagation equations were based on some conditional independence assumptions that might be violated in multiply connected networks. For example, the product in Eq. (4.51) was based on the assumption that all parents of a node X are mutually independent as long as none of their common descendants is instantiated. This assumption will no longer be valid if some parents of X share a common ancestor. Even our basic fusion equation (Eq. (4.13)) was based on a clear distinction between causal and diagnostic evidence, the two being separated by X; the distinction gets blurred in multiply connected networks because e_X^- may influence X's parent via pathways that sidestep X. (Asymptotic relaxation can still be used as a method of approximation. See Exercise 4.7.)

This section introduces three coherent methods of handling loops while retaining some of the flavor of local computation: clustering, conditioning, and stochastic simulation. *Clustering* involves forming compound variables in such a way that the resulting network of clusters is singly connected. *Conditioning* involves breaking the communication pathways along the loops by instantiating a select group of variables. *Stochastic simulation* involves assigning each variable a definite value and having each processor inspect the current state of its neighbors, compute the belief distribution of its host variable, and select one value at random from the computed distribution. Beliefs are then computed by recording the percentage of times that each processor selects a given value.

---

† Directed cycles, like those representing feedback in electronic circuits or econometric models, are not allowed in Bayesian networks and will not be discussed in this book.

The operation of the three schemes will be illustrated with a simple example borrowed from Spiegelhalter [1986], originally by Cooper [1984]:

> Metastatic cancer is a possible cause of a brain tumor and is also an explanation for increased total serum calcium. In turn, either of these could explain a patient falling into a coma. Severe headache is also possibly associated with a brain tumor.

Figure 4.23 shows the Bayesian network representing these relationships. As in the preceeding sections, we use uppercase letters to represent propositional variables and lowercase letters for their associated propositions. For example, $C \in \{1, 0\}$ represents the dichotomy between having a brain tumor and not having one. $+c$ stands for the assertion $C = 1$ or "Brain tumor is present," and $\neg c$ stands for the negation of $+c$, i.e., $C = 0$.

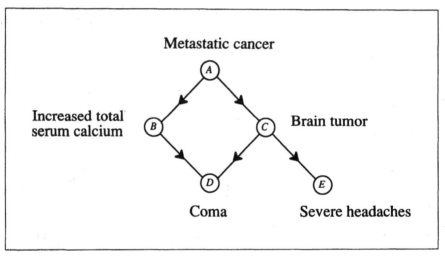

Figure 4.23. *A Bayesian network describing causal influences among five variables.*

Table 1 expresses the influences in terms of conditional probability distributions. Each variable is characterized by a *link matrix*, specifying the probability distribution of that variable given the state of its parents.† The root variable, having no parent, is characterized by its prior distribution.

---

† The probabilities are for illustration purposes only, and are not meant to realistically reflect current medical knowledge. Additionally, the variable "Coma" should be interpreted to mean "Lapsing occasionally into coma"; otherwise it would preclude headaches.

Table 1.

$P(a)$:	$P(+a) = .20$	
$P(b \mid a)$:	$P(+b \mid +a) = .80$	$P(+b \mid \neg a) = .20$
$P(c \mid a)$:	$P(+c \mid +a) = .20$	$P(+c \mid \neg a) = .05$
$P(d \mid b,c)$:	$P(+d \mid +b,+c) = .80$	$P(+d \mid \neg b,+c) = .80$
	$P(+d \mid +b,\neg c) = .80$	$P(+d \mid \neg b,\neg c) = .05$
$P(e \mid c)$:	$P(+e \mid +c) = .80$	$P(+e \mid \neg c) = .60$

Given this information, our task is to compute the posterior probability of every proposition in the system, given that a patient is suffering from severe headaches ($+e$) but has not fallen into a coma ($\neg d$), i.e., $e = \{E = 1, D = 0\}$.

4.4.1 Clustering Methods

A straightforward way of handling the network of Figure 4.23 would be to collapse B and C into a single node representing the compound variable $Z = \{B, C\}$ with the values

$$z \in \{(+b, +c), (\neg b, +c), (+b, \neg c), (\neg b, \neg c)\} . \tag{4.65}$$

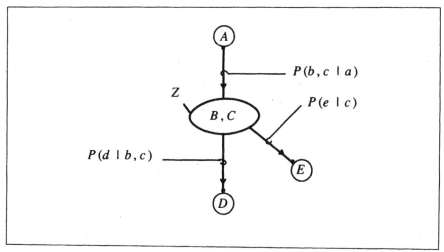

Figure 4.24. *Clustering B and C turns the network of Figure 4.23 into a tree.*

This results in the tree structure shown in Figure 4.24. Since the cardinality of variable Z is 4, the matrices on all three links must have either four rows or four columns. This does not mean, however, that the enlarged matrices should be stored explicitly at their corresponding nodes; often they can be generated from the smaller matrices of Table 1. For example, the matrix $P(z \mid a)$ can be generated as the product

$$P(z \mid a) = P(b, c \mid a) = P(b \mid a) \, P(c \mid a)$$

$$= \begin{cases} (0.16, \, 0.04, \, 0.64, \, 0.16) & \text{if} \quad A = 1 \\ (0.01, \, 0.04, \, 0.19, \, 0.76) & \text{if} \quad A = 0, \end{cases}$$

and $P(e \mid z)$ can be generated by simply ignoring the b component of z:

$$P(e \mid z) = P(e \mid b, c) = P(e \mid c).$$

Still, the process of belief updating will proceed as though the four components of Z were independent entities.

The propagation of belief updates is conducted in the same fashion as with ordinary trees. The only differences are the increased dimensionality of the π and λ messages and the need to reaggregate $BEL(z)$ in case we wish to find $BEL(b)$ or $BEL(c)$.

EXAMPLE: As an illustration, let us calculate the belief distribution of all variables in Figure 4.23, given the evidence $e = \{\neg d, +e\}$. Initially, the π messages are given by

$$\pi_Z(a) = \pi(a) = (0.20, \, 0.80),$$

$$\pi_D(z) = \pi_E(z) = \pi(z) = \sum_a P(z \mid a) \, \pi(a)$$

$$= \Big[(0.20 \cdot 0.16 + 0.80 \cdot 0.01), \, (0.20 \cdot 0.04 + 0.80 \cdot 0.04),$$

$$(0.20 \cdot 0.64 + 0.80 \cdot 0.19) \, (0.20 \cdot 0.16 + 0.80 \cdot 0.76) \Big]$$

$$= \Big[0.04, \, 0.04, \, 0.28, \, 0.64 \Big],$$

and the λ's are all unit vectors. Once D and E are instantiated, they generate

$$\lambda_D(z) = P(\neg d \mid z) = (0.20, \, 0.20, \, 0.20, \, 0.95),$$

$$\lambda_E(z) = P(+e \mid z) = (0.80, \, 0.80, \, 0.60, \, 0.60),$$

and these prompt node Z to compute

$$\lambda(z) = \lambda_D(z)\,\lambda_E(z) = (0.16, 0.16, 0.12, 0.57),$$

$$BEL(z) = \alpha\,\pi(z)\,\lambda(z)$$

$$= \alpha(0.04 \cdot 0.16, \; 0.04 \cdot 0.16, \; 0.28 \cdot 0.12, \; 0.64 \cdot 0.57)$$

$$= (0.0156, 0.0156, 0.0817, 0.887),$$

and generate

$$\pi_E(z) = \alpha\,\pi(z)\,\lambda_D(z) = \alpha(0.04 \cdot 0.20, \; 0.04 \cdot 0.20, \; 0.28 \cdot 0.20, \; 0.64 \cdot 0.95)$$

$$= (0.0118, 0.0118, 0.0823, 0.8941),$$

$$\pi_D(z) = \alpha\,\pi(z)\,\lambda_E(z) = \alpha(0.04 \cdot 0.80, \; 0.04 \cdot 0.80, \; 0.28 \cdot 0.60, \; 0.64 \cdot 0.60)$$

$$= (0.0519, 0.0519, 0.2727, 0.6233),$$

$$\lambda_Z(a) = \sum_z P(z\,|\,a)\,\lambda(z) = \Big[(0.16 \cdot 0.16 + 0.04 \cdot 0.16 + 0.64 \cdot 0.12 + 0.16 \cdot 0.57),$$

$$(0.01 \cdot 0.16 + 0.04 \cdot 0.16 + 0.19 \cdot 0.12 + 0.76 \cdot 0.57)\Big]$$

$$= \;(0.2, 0.464)\,.$$

Node A now computes its belief distribution,

$$BEL(a) = \alpha\,\pi(a)\,\lambda_Z(a) = \alpha(0.20 \cdot 0.20, \; 0.80 \cdot 0.464) = (0.097, 0.903),$$

and the propagation process halts. To find $BEL(b)$ and $BEL(c)$ we write

$$BEL(b) = \sum_c BEL[Z = (b, c)] = \Big[(0.0156 + 0.0817), \; (0.0156 + 0.887)\Big]$$

$$= (0.097, 0.903),$$

$$BEL(c) = \sum_b BEL[Z = (b, c)] = \Big[(0.0156 + 0.0156), \; (0.0817 + 0.887)\Big]$$

$$= (0.031, 0.969)\,.$$

SELECTING THE CLUSTERS

Every Bayesian network can be structured as a tree of clusters if we do not limit the size of the clusters. In the extreme case, we can lump together all non-leaf variables as one compound variable (see Figure 4.25a), which will yield a star structure as in Figure 4.25*b*. This approach was taken by Cooper [1984] and Peng and Reggia [1986] in their medical diagnosis systems, where each state of the compound variable was regarded as a possible explanation of the findings obtained. Unfortunately, the exponential cardinality and structureless nature of the compound variable make it difficult to compute, much less explain, the beliefs accrued by individual hypotheses within this variable.

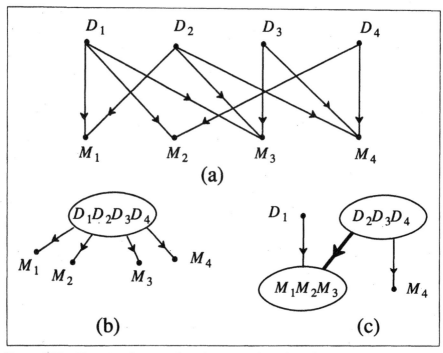

Figure 4.25.   *Clustering the network (a) into a tree (b) and a polytree (c).*

A less dramatic clustering scheme is shown in Figure 4.25*c*. Here, the formation of the two clusters

$$Z_1 = \{D_2, D_3, D_4\} \quad \text{and} \quad Z_2 = \{M_1, M_2, M_3\}$$

renders the network of Figure 4.25*a* a polytree, where the propagation techniques of Section 4.3 are applicable. Ad hoc techniques are currently being used to choose a clustering structure; little work has been done in the area of finding the optimal structure given some criterion of performance.

One of the most popular methods of clustering is based on *join trees* (see Section 3.2.4). If the clusters are allowed to overlap each other until they cover all the links of the original network, then the interdependencies between any two clusters are mediated solely by the variables they share. If we insist that these clusters continue to grow until their interdependencies form a tree structure, then the tree propagation scheme of Section 4.2 will be applicable.

We know from the discussion in Section 3.2.4 that if a probabilistic model P is decomposable with respect to a chordal graph G, the cliques of G can be arranged in a tree that is an I-map of P. This provides a simple, systematic method of forming clusters of variables for the purpose of propagating the impact of evidence in an arbitrary Bayesian network N_B:

1. Form the Markov network G of N_B by connecting all parents that share a common child and removing the arrows from the links (G is an I-map of N_B).

2. Form a chordal supergraph G' of G, using the graph-triangulation algorithm of Section 3.2.4 [Tarjan and Yannakakis 1984].

3. Identify the cliques of G' as compound variables, and connect them by links to form a join tree T.

4. Treat evidence nodes in N_B as dummy variables, transmitting λ-messages toward one of the clique nodes in T of which the evidence nodes are members.

5. Propagate the impact of these messages throughout T, and project the appropriate beliefs back to the individual variables of N_B.

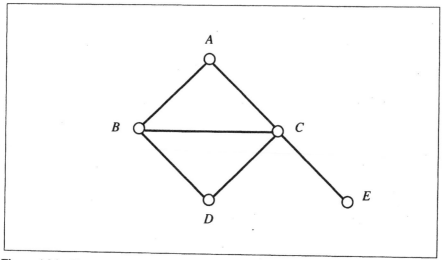

Figure 4.26. *The Markov network of the model in Figure 4.23.*

We illustrate this method on the model of Figure 4.23. The corresponding Markov network is formed by adding the link (B, C) between the two parents of D and removing all arrows (Figure 4.26). G is chordal and has three cliques:

$$Z_1 = \{A, B, C\}, \quad Z_2 = \{B, C, D\}, \quad Z_3 = \{C, E\}.$$

These cliques can be connected in two join tree structures (as in Figure 3.9), one of which is shown in Figure 4.27. The directionality of the arrows was chosen to match the directionality of the original network, Figure 4.23. The evidence variables D and E appear in Z_2 and Z_3, respectively, so dummy links are formed toward these two cliques, carrying λ-messages that exclude those states of Z_2 and Z_3 that are incompatible with $D = 0$ and $E = 1$.

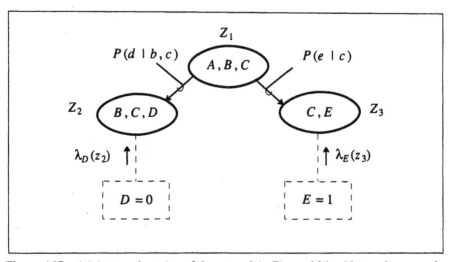

Figure 4.27. *A join tree clustering of the network in Figure 4.26, with two dummy nodes representing the observed findings.*

To facilitate the propagation we need to find the matrices that correspond to links between any two adjacent cliques in a join tree. Since the interdependencies between cliques Z_i and Z_j are mediated solely by the shared variable $Z_i \cap Z_j$, we have (see Eqs. (3.24) through (3.26))

$$M_{z_i | z_j} = P(z_i | z_j) = P(z_i | z_i \cap z_j).$$

Thus, if Z_j is a parent of Z_i in T, the link between the two cliques can be computed from the conditional probability of the group of variables unique to Z_i, conditioned on the variables that Z_i shares with its parent Z_j. In our example, since Z_2 shares $\{B, C\}$ with Z_1, we have

$$M_{z_2 | z_1} = P(z_2 | z_1) = P(b, c, d | b, c) = P(d | b, c). \tag{4.66}$$

Although the $M_{z_2|z_1}$ matrix should, in principle, measure 8 by 8, the requirement that the values assigned to B and C by Z_2 be identical to those assigned by Z_1 renders $M_{z_1|z_2}$ fully characterized by the four parameters in $P(d|b, c)$, as in Table 1. The computations will proceed as though the link matrix measured 8 by 8 and the messages traversing this link were eight-dimensional.

Let us demonstrate now how the evidence $\{\neg d, +e\}$ propagates its impact through the join tree of Figure 4.27. Before this evidence is observed the probabilities and π-messages are given by

$$\pi(z_1) = \pi_{Z_2}(z_1) = \pi_{Z_3}(z_1) = P(z_1) = P(a, b, c) = P(b|a)\, P(c|a)\, P(a). \quad (4.67)$$

The λ-messages are all unit vectors. Eq. (4.67) stands for the eight-component vector shown in the $\pi(z_1)$ column of Table 2.

Table 2.

a,	b,	c	$P(b|a)$	$P(c|a)$	$Pa)$	$\pi(z_1)$
1	1	1	0.80	0.20	0.20	0.032
1	1	0	0.80	(1 - 0.20)	0.20	0.128
1	0	1	(1 - 0.80)	0.20	0.20	0.008
1	0	0	(1 - 0.80)	(1 - 0.20)	0.20	0.032
0	1	1	0.20	0.05	(1 - 0.20)	0.008
0	1	0	0.20	(1 - 0.05)	(1 - 0.20)	0.152
0	0	1	(1 - 0.20)	(0.05)	(1 - 0.20)	0.032
0	0	0	(1 - 0.20)	(1 - 0.05)	(1 - 0.20)	0.608

In practice, these components can be generated upon demand, using the formula of Eq. (4.67), from the five parameters given in Table 1. The same applies to the prior probabilities of the other cliques:

$$\pi(z_2) = \sum_{z_1} P(z_2|z_1)\, P(z_1) = \sum_{a} P(d|b, c)\, P(a, b, c) = P(d|b, c)\, P(b, c),$$

$$\pi(z_3) = \sum_{z_1} P(z_3|z_1)\, P(z_1) = \sum_{a,b} P(e|c)\, P(a, b, c) = P(e|c)\, P(c).$$

$P(b, c)$ and $P(c)$ can be computed by summing over the appropriate terms of $\pi(z_1)$.

When the evidence $D = 0$ arrives, it sets up a λ-message for Z_2 which eliminates all states of Z_2 incompatible with $D = 0$, i.e.,

$$\lambda_D(z_2) = \begin{cases} 0 & \text{if} \quad z_2 = (b, c, +d) \\ 1 & \text{if} \quad z_2 = (b, c, \neg d). \end{cases}$$

Similarly, $E = 1$ generates

$$\lambda_E(z_3) = \begin{cases} 0 & \text{if} \quad z_3 = (c, \neg e) \\ 1 & \text{if} \quad z_3 = (c, +e). \end{cases}$$

These messages prompt Z_2 and Z_3 to generate corresponding λ messages for Z_1,

$$\lambda_{Z_2}(z_1) = M_{z_2 | z_1} \cdot \lambda_D(z_2) = P(\neg d \mid b, c),$$

$$\lambda_{Z_3}(z_1) = M_{z_3 | z_1} \cdot \lambda_E(z_3) = P(+e \mid c),$$

permitting Z_1 to compute its belief distribution:

$$BEL(z_1) = \alpha \, \lambda_{Z_2}(z_1) \, \lambda_{Z_3}(z_1) \, \pi(z_1)$$

$$= \alpha \, P(\neg d \mid b, c) \, P(+e \mid c) \, P(b \mid a) \, P(c \mid a) \, P(a).$$

The computation yields an eight-dimensional vector from which $BEL(a)$, $BEL(b)$, and $BEL(c)$ can be computed by the appropriate summations.

The close similarity between this computation and the one conducted using $Z = \{B, C\}$ as the only cluster should not be surprising. Although the new clusters have more dimensions, most of the computations within clusters are still conducted using the set $\{B, C\}$ as a mediator for A, D, and E. Taking advantage of this fact, Lauritzen and Spiegelhalter [1988] have suggested a variation of the join tree method whereby the compound variables used in the propagation phase are the intersection sets between any two adjacent cliques in the join tree.

4.4.2 The Method of Conditioning (Reasoning by Assumptions)

Conditioning is based on our ability to change the connectivity of a network and render it singly connected by instantiating a selected group of variables. In Figure 4.23, for example, instantiating A to any value would block the pathway $B—A—C$ and would render the rest of the network singly connected, so that the propagation techniques of Section 4.3 would be applicable. Thus, if we wish to propagate the impact of an observed fact, say $E = 1$, to the entire network, we first assume $A = 0$ (as in Figure 4.28a), propagate the impact of $+e$ to the variables B, C, and D, repeat the propagation under the assumption $A = 1$ (as in Figure 4.28b), and

finally, average the two results weighted by the posterior probabilities
$P(A = 1 | E = 1)$ and $P(A = 0 | E = 1)$. We can also execute the propagation in
parallel by letting each node receive, compute, and transmit two sets of
parameters, one for each value of the conditioning variable A. Conditioning
provides a working solution in many cases, but like clustering, if the network is
highly connected it may suffer from a combinatorial explosion—the message size
grows exponentially with the number of nodes required for breaking up the loops
in the network.

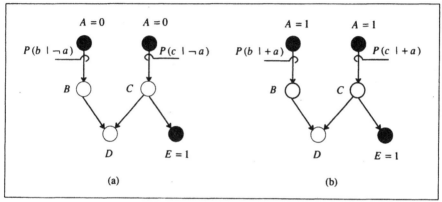

Figure 4.28. *The multiply connected network of Figure 4.23 is decomposed into two
polytrees corresponding to the two instantiations of A.*

The use of conditioning to facilitate propagation is not foreign to human
reasoning. When we find it hard to estimate the likelihood of a given outcome, we
often make hypothetical *assumptions* that render the estimation simpler, and then
negate the assumptions to see if the results vary substantially. One pervasive
pattern of plausible reasoning is the maxim that if two diametrically opposed
assumptions impart different degrees of confidence onto a proposition Q, then the
unconditional degree of confidence merited by Q should be somewhere between
them (see Section 1.4.2). The terms *hypothetical reasoning*, *assumption-based
reasoning*, *reasoning by cases*, and *envisioning* refer to the same basic mechanism
of selecting a key variable, binding it to some values, deriving the consequences of
each binding separately, and integrating the consequences.

Conditioning draws its legitimacy from the ever-faithful rule of total
probabilities, which for any three variables, X, Y, and Z, permits us to write

$$P(y | z) = \sum_{x} P(y | x, z) P(x | z).$$

In our example, if we wish to compute the belief distribution associated with the variable B given the evidence $E = e$, we can choose A as the conditioning variable and write

$$BEL(b) = P(b \mid e) = \sum_a P(b \mid a, e) \, P(a \mid e). \qquad (4.68)$$

The first term in the summation stands for the belief distribution of B that one would calculate by propagating the impact of $E = e$ through a network clamped at $A = a$. Since this clamping of A renders the network singly connected (see Figure 4.28), the computation can be performed swiftly. Note that C would be an equally good choice as a conditioning variable, but D would be a bad choice, since instantiating this variable would not block the pathway $A\!-\!D\!-\!C$ (by the *d*-separation criterion of Section 3.4).

The second term in the summation, $P(a \mid e)$, can be regarded as a *mixing weight*, because it is used to weigh the beliefs obtained under the two conditioning values of A and combine them additively into the correct belief distribution:

$$BEL(b) = BEL(b \mid a) \, P(+a \mid e) + BEL(b \mid \neg a) \left[1 - P(+a \mid e) \right].$$

This weight can easily be computed at the evidence node E using Bayes' Rule:

$$P(a \mid e) = \alpha \, P(e \mid a) \, P(a).$$

The first term on the right is the conditional probability associated with E prior to the observation; it can be obtained by propagating the impact of $A = a$ through a singly connected network onto E. The second term is simply the prior probability of A, which can be passed to every node of the network before any evidence arrives.

In general, if the evidence comprises several instantiated nodes E^1, E^2..., then the overall mixing weight $P(a \mid e^1, e^2, ...)$ can be computed recursively; every instantiated node E^i, in its turn, computes the new mixing weight $P(a \mid e^1, ..., e^{i-1}, e^i)$ from the old one $P(a \mid e^1, ..., e^{i-1})$ and passes it along to all the other variables. This computation is, again, best done by the product

$$P(a \mid e^1, ..., e^{i-1}, e^i) = \alpha \, P(e^i \mid a, e^1, ..., e^{i-1}) \, P(a \mid e^1, ..., e^{i-1}),$$

because the two terms on the right are available to E^i at the moment of its instantiation: the first stands for the current $BEL(e^i)$ distributions (corresponding to the two conditioning values of A), and the second is the previous mixing weight.

EXAMPLE: To show how conditioning works, let us return to the problem of Figure 4.23 and compute the belief distributions of A, B, and C given the evidence $\{\neg d, +e\}$. Initially, we compute the belief distribution for B, C, D, and E under the two conditions

$A = 1$ and $A = 0$ by propagating these two values down the polytrees of Figure 4.28. Denoting the two conditions above by superscripts 1 and 0, we write

$$\pi^1(b) = P(b \mid a) = (0.80, 0.20),$$
$$\pi^1(c) = P(c \mid a) = (0.20, 0.80),$$

$$BEL^1(+d) = \sum_{b,c} P(+d \mid b, c)\, \pi^1(b)\, \pi^1(c)$$

$$= \Big[0.80 \cdot 0.80 \cdot 0.20 + 0.80(1 - 0.80)\,0.20 + 0.80 \cdot 0.80(1 - 0.20)$$

$$+ 0.05(1 - 0.80)\,(1 - 0.20) \Big]$$

$$= 0.68,$$

$$BEL^1(+e) = \pi^1(+e) = \sum_c P(+e \mid c)\, \pi^1(c) = 0.80 \cdot 0.20 + 0.60 \cdot 0.80 = 0.64,$$
$$\pi^0(b) = P(b \mid \neg a) = (0.20, 0.80),$$
$$\pi^0(c) = P(c \mid \neg a) = (0.05, 0.95),$$

$$BEL^0(+d) = \pi^0(+d) = \sum_{b,c} P(+d \mid b, c)\, \pi^0(b)\, \pi^0(c)$$

$$= \Big[0.80 \cdot 0.20 \cdot 0.05 + 0.80 \cdot (1 - 0.20)\,0.05 + 0.80 \cdot 0.20(1 - 0.05)$$

$$+ 0.05(1 - 0.20)\,(1 - 0.05) \Big]$$

$$= 0.23,$$

$$BEL^0(+e) = \pi^0(+e) = \sum_c P(+e \mid c)\, \pi^0(c) = 0.80 \cdot 0.05 + 0.60 \cdot 0.95 = 0.61.$$

This initial message profile is shown in Figure 4.29. Each node stores its two belief distributions BEL^0 and BEL^1, together with the initial mixing weight

$$w = (w^1, w^0) = P(a) = (0.20, 0.80).$$

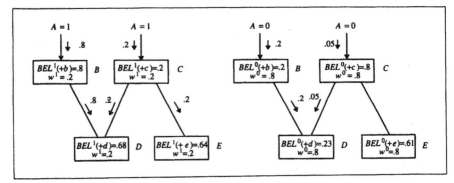

Figure 4.29. *Initial beliefs, messages, and weights under two assumptions.*

Now imagine the evidence $E = 1$ is observed. E computes and sends to all other nodes the new mixing weight:

$$w_E = P(a \mid +e) = \alpha\, P(+e \mid a)\, P(a)$$

$$= \alpha\, \Big[BEL^1(+e)\, w^1,\, BEL^0(+e)\, w^0 \Big]$$

$$= \alpha\, \Big[0.64 \cdot 0.20,\, 0.61 \cdot 0.80 \Big]$$

$$= (0.208,\, 0.792).$$

Simultaneously, E posts the messages $\lambda_E^1(c)$ and $\lambda_E^0(c)$ for C, where (since $P(e \mid c,a) = P(e \mid c)$)

$$\lambda_E^1(c) = \lambda_E^0(c) = P(+e \mid c) = (0.80,\, 0.60).$$

Node C now computes two $\pi_D(c)$ messages for D, $\pi_D^1(c)$ and $\pi_D^0(c)$, corresponding to the two conditioning values of A:

$$\pi_D^1(c) = BEL^1(c) = \alpha^1 \pi^1(c)\, \lambda_E(c) = \alpha^1 (0.20,\, 0.80)\, (0.80,\, 0.60)$$

$$= (0.25,\, 0.75),$$

$$\pi_D^0(c) = BEL^0(c) = \alpha^0 \pi^0(c)\, \lambda_E(c) = \alpha^0 (0.05,\, 0.95)\, (0.80,\, 0.60)$$

$$= (0.066,\, 0.934).$$

This results in the belief distributions

$$BEL^1(d) = \sum_{b,c} P(d \mid b,\, c)\, \pi^1(b)\, \pi_D^1(c) = (0.6875,\, 0.3125),$$

$$BEL^0(d) = \sum_{b,c} P(d \mid b,\, c)\, \pi^0(b)\, \pi_D^0(c) = (0.24,\, 0.76).$$

At this point, the propagation of these two sets of messages halts, because as long as D is an anticipatory node, the pathway C—D—B is blocked at D (see Figure 4.30).

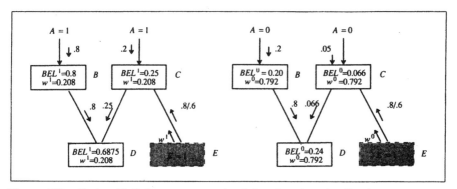

Figure 4.30. *Updated beliefs, messages, and weights after observing $E = 1$.*

The arrival of the next piece of evidence, $D = 0$, prompts D to compute the new mixing weight $w_{E,D}$ and then initiate a new message-passing process by generating $\lambda_D(b)$ and $\lambda_D(c)$:

$$w_{E,D} = P(a \mid +e, \neg d) = \alpha \, P(\neg d \mid a, +e) \, P(a \mid +e)$$

$$= \alpha \left[BEL^1(\neg d) \, w_E^1, \; BEL^0(\neg d) \, w_E^0 \right]$$

$$= \alpha \, (0.3125 \cdot 0.208, \; 0.76 \cdot 0.792) = (0.0975, 0.9025),$$

$$\left\{
\begin{aligned}
\lambda_D^1(c) &= \sum_b P(\neg d \mid b, c) \, \pi_D^1(b) = \left[(0.2 \cdot 0.8 + 0.2 \cdot 0.2), \; (0.2 \cdot 0.8 + 0.95 \cdot 0.2) \right] \\
&= (0.20, 0.35) \\
\lambda_D^0(c) &= \sum_b P(\neg d \mid b, c) \, \pi_D^0(b) = \left[(0.2 \cdot 0.2 + 0.2 \cdot 0.8), \; (0.2 \cdot 0.2 + 0.95 \cdot 0.8) \right] \\
&= (0.20, 0.8),
\end{aligned}
\right.$$

$$\left\{
\begin{aligned}
\lambda_D^1(b) &= \sum_c P(\neg d \mid b, c) \, \pi_D^1(c) = \left[(0.2 \cdot 0.25 + 0.2 \cdot 0.75), \; (0.2 \cdot 0.25 + 0.95 \cdot 0.75) \right] \\
&= (0.2, 0.76) \\
\lambda_D^0(b) &= \sum_c P(\neg d \mid b, c) \, \pi_D^0(c) = \left[(0.2 \cdot 0.066 + 0.2 \cdot 0.934), \; (0.2 \cdot 0.066 + 0.95 \cdot 0.934) \right] \\
&= (0.2, 0.9).
\end{aligned}
\right.$$

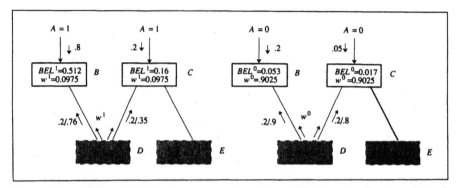

Figure 4.31. *Updated beliefs, messages, and weights after observing E = 1 and D = 0. Beliefs are computed by the combination BEL = w¹ BEL¹ + w⁰ BEL⁰.*

At this point, all belief distributions can be computed at their corresponding nodes, as in Figure 4.31:

$$BEL(b) = w^1_{E,D} \, BEL^1(b) + w^0_{E,D} \, BEL^0(b),$$

$$BEL(c) = w^1_{E,D} \, BEL^1(c) + w^0_{E,D} \, BEL^0(c),$$

where

$$BEL^1(b) = \alpha^1 \, \pi^1(b) \, \lambda^1_D(b) = \alpha^1(0.8 \cdot 0.2, \, 0.2 \cdot 0.76) = (0.512, \, 0.488),$$

$$BEL^0(b) = \alpha^0 \, \pi^0(b) \, \lambda^0_D(b) = \alpha^0(0.2 \cdot 0.2, \, 0.8 \cdot 0.9) = (0.053, \, 0.947),$$

$$BEL^1(c) = \alpha^1 \, \pi^1(c) \, \lambda^1_D(c) \, \lambda_E(c) = \alpha^1(0.2 \cdot 0.2 \cdot 0.80, \, 0.8 \cdot 0.35 \cdot 0.60)$$

$$= (0.16, \, 0.84),$$

$$BEL^0(c) = \alpha^0 \, \pi^0(c) \, \lambda^0_D(c) \, \lambda_E(c) = \alpha^0(0.05 \cdot 0.2 \cdot 0.80, \, 0.95 \cdot 0.8 \cdot 0.60)$$

$$= (0.017, \, 0.983).$$

These yield

$$BEL(b) = (0.096, \, 0.904),$$

$$BEL(c) = (0.031, \, 0.964).$$

$BEL(a)$, of course, is equal to the current mixing weight $w_{E,D} = (0.0975, \, 0.9025)$.

4.4.3 Stochastic Simulation

Stochastic simulation is a method of computing probabilities by counting how frequently events occur in a series of simulation runs. If a causal model of a domain is available, the model can be used to generate random samples of hypothetical scenarios that are likely to develop in the domain. The probability of any event or combination of events can then be computed by counting the percentage of samples in which the event is true.

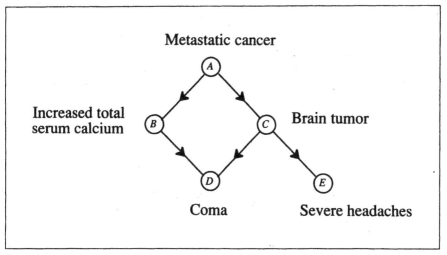

Figure 4.32. *The Bayesian network used to demonstrate stochastic simulation (same as in Figure 4.23).*

For example, in the causal model of Figure 4.32, we can generate hypothetical samples of patients by the following procedure: We draw a random value a_1 for A, using the probability $P(a)$. Given a_1, we draw random values b_1 and c_1 for the variables B and C, using the probabilities $P(b \mid a_1)$ and $P(c \mid a_1)$, respectively. Given b_1 and c_1, we draw random values d_1 and e_1 for D and E, using $P(d \mid b_1, c_1)$ and $P(e \mid c_1)$, respectively. The combination of values $(a_1, b_1, c_1, d_1, e_1)$ represents one sample of a patient scenario. The process now repeats from A down to D and E, each run generating a quintuple that represents one patient.

Stochastic simulation shows considerable potential as a probabilistic inference engine that combines evidence correctly but is computationally tractable. Unlike numerical schemes, the computational effort is unaffected by the presence of dependencies within the causal model; simulating the occurrence of an event given the states of its causes requires the same computational effort regardless of whether the causes are correlated. In our example above, simulating the event D given the states of events B and C was straightforward, even though B and C are correlated (via A). Thus, the presence of loops in the network does not affect the computation.

Stochastic simulation carries a special appeal for AI researchers in that it develops probabilistic reasoning as a direct extension of deterministic logical inference. It represents probabilities explicitly as "frequencies" in a sample of truth values, and these values, unlike numerical probabilities, can be derived by familiar theorem-proving techniques and combined by standard logical connectives. Nor is the technique foreign to human reasoning; assessing uncertainties by mental sampling of possible scenarios is a very natural heuristic and an important component of human judgment.

Another advantage offered by simulation techniques is their inherent parallelism. If we associate a processor with each of the propositional variables explicit in the model, then the simultaneous occurrence of events within each scenario can be produced by concurrently activating the processors responsible for these events. For example, the occurrence of the event $A = 1$, "The patient has metastatic cancer," could in one run trigger simultaneously events ($B = 1, C = 1$), while in a different run the combination ($B = 1, C = 0$) may occur. Though the propagation schemes developed in Sections 4.2 and 4.3 also provide parallelism, the simulation approach enjoys the added advantage of *message simplicity*. Instead of relaying probability distributions, the messages passing between processors are the actual values assigned to the corresponding variables.†

Henrion [1986a] has suggested a scheme, called *logic sampling*, which uses a Bayesian network as a scenario generator and assigns random values to all system variables in each simulation run in a top-down fashion. Belief distributions are calculated by averaging the frequency of events over those cases in which the evidence variables agree with the data observed. This scheme retains the merits of causal modeling in that it conducts the simulation along the flow of causation, so that each step can be given a conceptually meaningful interpretation. Since the simulation proceeds only forward in time, however, there is no way to account for evidence known to have occurred (e.g., $\neg d$, $+e$) until the variables corresponding to these observations are sampled. If they match the observed data, the run is counted; otherwise, it must be discarded. The result is that the scheme requires too many simulation runs. In cases comprising large numbers of observations (e.g., 20), all but a small fraction (e.g., 10^{-6}) of the simulations may be discarded, especially when a rare combination of data occurs.

A better way to account for the evidence would be to permanently clamp the evidence variables to the values observed, and then conduct a stochastic simulation on the clamped network. The question that remains is how to propagate the random values coherently through the network, now that boundary conditions are imposed on both the top and bottom nodes, i.e., on premises as well as consequences.

This section describes such a propagation method, involving a two-phase cycle: local numerical computation followed by logical sampling. The first

---

† . This conforms to the connectionist paradigm of reasoning [Rumelhart and McClelland 1986], in which processors are presumed to communicate by merely passing their levels of activity.

phase involves computing, for some variable X, the conditional distribution given the states of all its neighboring variables. The second phase involves sampling the computed distribution and instantiating X to the value selected by the sampling. The cycle then repeats itself by sequentially scanning all the variables in the system. We shall illustrate the simulation scheme using the medical example of Figure 4.32. Then we shall prove the correctness of the formula used in these computations and discuss methods for implementing the sampling scheme in parallel.

ILLUSTRATING THE SIMULATION SCHEME

Given the information in Table 1, our task is to compute the posterior probability of every proposition in the system, given that a patient is observed to be suffering from severe headaches ($+e$) but has not fallen into a coma ($\neg d$), i.e., $E = 1$ and $D = 0$. The first step is to instantiate all the unobserved variables to some arbitrary initial state, say $A = B = C = 1$, and then let each variable in turn choose another state in accordance with the variable's conditional probability, given the current state of the other variables. For example, if we denote by w_A the state of all variables except A (i.e., $w_A = \{ B=1, C=1, D=0, E=1 \}$), then the next value of A will be chosen by tossing a coin that favors 1 over 0 by a ratio of $P(+a \mid w_A)$ to $P(\neg a \mid w_A)$.

In the next subsection, we shall show that $P(x \mid w_X)$, the distribution of each variable X conditioned on the values w_X of all other variables in the system, can be calculated by purely local computations. It is given as the product of the link matrix of X and the link matrices of its children:

$$P(a \mid w_A) = P(a \mid b, c, d, e) = \alpha P(a) P(b \mid a) P(c \mid a), \qquad \textbf{(4.69a)}$$

$$P(b \mid w_B) = P(b \mid a, c, d, e) = \alpha P(b \mid a) P(d \mid b, c), \qquad \textbf{(4.69b)}$$

$$P(c \mid w_C) = P(c \mid a, b, d, e) = \alpha P(c \mid a) P(d \mid b, c) P(e \mid c), \qquad \textbf{(4.69c)}$$

where the α's are normalizing constants that make the respective probabilities sum to unity. The probabilities associated with D and E are not needed because these variables are assumed to be fixed at $D = 0$ and $E = 1$. Note that a variable X can determine its transition probability $P(x \mid w_X)$ by inspecting only *neighboring* variables, i.e., those belonging to X's *Markov blanket* (see Section 3.3.1, Corollary 6). For example, A must inspect only B and C, while B must inspect only A, C, and D.

EXAMPLE: For demonstration purposes, we will activate the variables sequentially, in the order A, B, C, acknowledging that any other schedule would be equally adequate.

ACTIVATING A

Step 1: Node A inspects its children B and C; finding both at 1, it computes (using Eq. (4.69a))

$$P(A = 1\mid w_A) = P(A = 1\mid B = 1, C = 1) = \alpha\, P(a)\, P(+b\mid+a)\, P(+c\mid+a)$$
$$= \alpha \times 0.20 \times 0.80 \times 0.20$$
$$= \alpha \times 0.032,$$
$$P(A = 0\mid w_A) = P(A = 0\mid B=1, C=1) = \alpha\, P(\neg a)\, P(+b\mid \neg a)\, P(+c\mid \neg a)$$
$$= \alpha \times 0.80 \times 0.20 \times 0.05$$
$$= \alpha \times 0.008,$$
$$\alpha = [0.032 + 0.008]^{-1} = 25,$$

yielding

$$P(A = 1\mid w_A) = 25 \times 0.032 = 0.80,$$
$$P(A = 0\mid w_A) = 25 \times 0.008 = 0.20.$$

Step 2: Node A consults a random number generator that issues 1s with 80% probability and 0s with 20% probability. Assuming the value sampled is 1, A adopts this value, and control shifts to node B.

ACTIVATING B

Step 1: Node B inspects its neighbors; finding them with values $A = 1, C = 1$, and $D = 0$, it computes (using Eq. (4.69b))

$$\frac{P(B = 1\mid w_B)}{P(B = 0\mid w_B)} = \frac{P(B = 1\mid A = 1, C = 1, D = 0)}{P(B = 0\mid A = 1, C = 1, D = 0)} = \frac{\alpha\, P(+b\mid+a)\, P(\neg d\mid+b, +c)}{\alpha\, P(\neg b\mid+a)\, P(\neg d\mid \neg b, +c)}$$
$$= \frac{0.80 \times (1 - 0.80)}{(1 - 0.80)(1 - 0.80)} = \frac{4}{1}.$$

Step 2:

As A did in its turn, B samples a random number generator favoring 1 by a 4 to 1 ratio. Assuming, this time, that the value sampled is 0, B adopts the value 0 and gives control to C.

ACTIVATING C

Step 1: The neighbors of C are at the state

$$w_C = \{A = 1, B = 0, D = 0, E = 1\}.$$

Therefore, from Eq. (4.69c):

$$\frac{P(+c \mid w_C)}{P(\neg c \mid w_C)} = \frac{P(+c \mid +a)\, P(\neg d \mid \neg b, +c)\, P(+e \mid +c)}{P(\neg c \mid +a)\, P(\neg d \mid \neg b, \neg c)\, P(+e \mid \neg c)}$$

$$= \frac{0.20 \times (1 - 0.80)\ 0.80}{(1 - 0.20)(1 - 0.05)\ 0.60} = \frac{1}{14.25}.$$

Step 2: C samples a random number generator favoring 0 by a 14.25 to 1 ratio. Assuming the value 0 is sampled, C adopts the value 0 and gives control to A.

ANSWERING QUERIES

The cycle now repeats itself in the order A, B, C until a query is posted, e.g., "What is the posterior distribution of A?" Such a query can be answered by computing the percentage of times A registered the value 1 or by taking the average of the conditional probabilities $P(A = 1 \mid w_A)$ computed by A. The latter method usually yields faster convergence.

To illustrate, the value of $P(A = 1 \mid w_A)$ computed in the next activation of A would be

$$P(A = 1 \mid B = 0, C = 0) = \alpha\, P(+a)\, (\neg b \mid +a)\, P(\neg c \mid +a)$$

$$= \alpha\ 0.20\ (1 - 0.80)\ (1 - 0.20)$$

$$= \alpha\ 0.032,$$

$$P(A = 0 \mid B = 0, C = 0) = \alpha\, P(\neg a)\, P(\neg b \mid \neg a)\, P(\neg c \mid \neg a)$$

$$= \alpha\ 0.80\ (1 - 0.20)\ (1 - 0.05)$$

$$= \alpha\ 0.608,$$

$$\alpha = (0.032 + 0.608)^{-1} = 1.5625,$$

$$P(A = 1 \mid B = 0, C = 0) = 0.05,$$

$$P(A = 0 \mid B = 0, C = 0) = 0.95.$$

If a query "$P(+a \mid \neg d, +e) = ?$" arrives at this point, A samples the computed distribution (i.e., $P(a) = 0.05$) and upon selecting a value 0 provides the estimate

$$\hat{P}(+a \mid \neg d, +e) = \frac{1 + 0}{2} = 0.5.$$

The second method gives

$$\hat{P}(+a \mid \neg d, +e) = \frac{0.80 + 0.05}{2} = 0.425.$$

The exact value of $P(+a \mid \neg d, +e)$ happens to be 0.097 (see the calculations in Sections 4.4.1 and 4.4.2); it takes over 100 runs for $\hat{P}$ to come within 1% of this value.

The convergence of $\hat{P}$ to the correct value of the posterior probability is guaranteed, under certain conditions, by a theorem of Feller [1950] regarding the existence of a limiting distribution for Markov chains. In each simulation run the system's configuration changes from state i to state j, and the change is governed by the transition probability $P(x \mid w_X)$ of the activated variable. The essence of Feller's theorem is this: if for any pair (i, j) of configurations there is a positive probability of reaching j from i in a finite number of transitions, then regardless of the initial configuration, the probability that the system will be found at a given state approaches a limit, which is determined by the *stationarity* condition

$$P(j) = \sum_i P(i)\, P(j \mid i),\qquad\qquad (4.70)$$

where $P(j \mid i)$ is the probability of reaching state j from state i in one transition. In our case, the reachability condition is guaranteed if all link probabilities are positive, because every configuration then has a positive probability of being realized in one run (over all variables). Thus, the fact that the transition probabilities $P(x \mid w_X)$ satisfy Eq. (4.70) relative to distribution P is sufficient to guarantee that the asymptotic probability distribution—and hence $\hat{P}$—will converge to P. In other words, as time progresses the system is guaranteed to reach a steady state, in the sense that regardless of the initial instantiation, the probability that the system will enter any global state w is given by the joint distribution $P(w_X)$ specified by the link matrices. The case where some link probabilities are zero corresponds to *reducible* Markov chains and limits the applicability of stochastic simulation schemes (see the concluding subsection).

This simulation scheme can also be used to find the *most likely interpretation* of the observed data, i.e., a joint assignment w^* of values to all variables that has the highest posterior probability of all possible assignments, given the evidence. This will be discussed in Chapter 5.

JUSTIFYING THE COMPUTATIONS

We shall now prove the correctness of the product formula (Eq. (4.69)) used for computing the transition probabilities $P(x \mid w_X)$. Clearly, the conditional distribution of X given the state of all remaining variables is sensitive not to every variable in the system but only to those in the *neighborhood* of X, namely, the variables that if known would render X independent of all other variables in the system. Such a neighborhood, called a *Markov blanket* B_X of X, was identified in Section 3.3.1 (Corollary 6) as comprised of three types of neighbors: direct parents, direct successors, and all direct parents of direct successors. In Figure 4.32, for example, the Markov blankets for each variable are given as follows:

$$\boldsymbol{B}_A = \{B, C\}, \quad \boldsymbol{B}_B = \{A, C, D\},$$
$$\boldsymbol{B}_C = \{A, B, D, E\}, \quad \boldsymbol{B}_D = \{B, C\}, \quad \boldsymbol{B}_E = \{C\}.$$

Yet, replacing $P(x \mid w_X)$ with $P(x \mid b_X)$ will not be very helpful unless the latter can be easily computed from the link matrices surrounding X. Next we shall show that $P(x \mid w_X)$ consists of a product of $m+1$ link matrices, where m is the number of X's children.

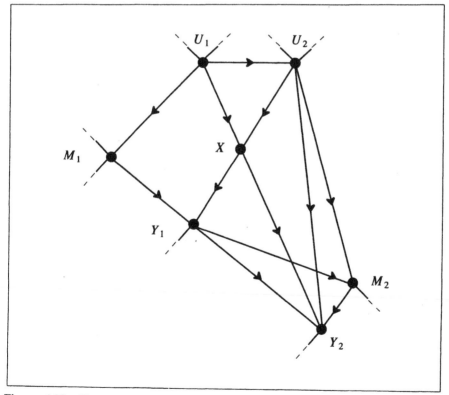

Figure 4.33. *The Markov neighborhood of* X, *including parents* (U_1, U_2), *children* (Y_1, Y_2), *and mates* (M_1, M_2).

Consider a typical neighborhood of variable X in some Bayesian network, as shown in Figure 4.33:   Define the following set of variables:

1. X's parents, $U_X = \{U_1,..., U_n\}$.

2. X's children, $Y_X = \{Y_1,..., Y_m\}$.

3. F_j, the set of parents of Y_j.

4. $W_X = W - X$, the set of all variables except X.

THEOREM 1: *The probability distribution of each variable X in the network, conditioned on the state of all other variables, is given by the product*

$$P(x \mid w_X) = \alpha\, P(x \mid u_X) \prod_j P[y_j \mid f_j(x)], \tag{4.71}$$

where α is a normalizing constant, independent of x, and x, w_X, u_X, y_j, and $f_j(x)$ denote any consistent instantiations of X, W_X, U_X, Y_j, and F_j, respectively.

Thus, $P(x \mid w_X)$ can be computed simply by taking the product of the instantiated link matrix stored at node X and those stored at X's children. In Figure 4.33, for example, we have

$$P(x \mid w_X) = \alpha\, P(x \mid u_1, u_2)\, P(y_1 \mid x, m_1)\, P(y_2 \mid x, u_2, y_1, m_2).$$

Proof: If we index the system's variables $W = \{X_1, X_2,..., X_i,....\}$ by an ordering consistent with the arrow orientation of the network, then the joint distribution of W can be written as a product (see Eq. (3.28), Chapter 3):

$$P(w) = P(x_1, x_2,..., x_i,...) = \prod_i P(x_i \mid \Pi_{X_i}),$$

where Π_{X_i} stands for the values attained by X_i's parents. Now consider a typical variable $X \in W$, having n parents U_X and m children $Y_X = \{Y_1,..., Y_m\}$. x appears in exactly $m+1$ factors of the product above; once in the factor $P(x \mid u_X)$ and once in each $P(y_j \mid f_j)$ factor corresponding to the j-th child of X. Thus, we can write

$$P(w) = P(x, w_X) = P(x \mid u_X) \prod_{j=1}^{m} P(y_j \mid f_j(x)) \prod_{k \in K} P(x_k \mid \Pi_{X_k}),$$

where

$$K = \{k: X_k \in W_X - Y_X\}.$$

Since x does not appear in the rightmost product (over k), this product can be regarded as a constant α' relative to x, and we can write

$$P(x, w_X) = \alpha' P(x \mid u_X) \prod_j (y_j \mid f_j(x)).$$

Moreover, since

$$P(w_X) = \sum_x P(x, w_X)$$

is also a constant relative to x, we have

$$P(x \mid w_X) = \frac{P(x, w_X)}{P(w_X)} = \alpha P(x \mid u_X) \prod_j P(y_j \mid f_j(x)),$$

which proves the theorem. Q.E.D.

The main significance of Theorem 1 is that $P(x \mid w_X)$ is computed as a product of parameters that are stored locally with the specification of the model. Thus, the parameters are readily available, and the computations are extremely simple.

CONCURRENT SIMULATION WITH DISTRIBUTED CONTROL

The simulation process can also be executed in parallel, but some scheduling is required to keep neighboring processors from operating at the same time. To see why this is necessary, imagine two neighboring processors, X and Y, entering the computation phase at the same time t_1. X observes the value y_1 of Y and calculates $P(x \mid y_1)$; at the same time, Y observes the value x_1 of X and calculates $P(y \mid x_1)$. At a later time, t_2, they enter the simulation phase with X instantiated to a sample x_2 drawn from $P(x \mid y_1)$ and Y instantiated to a sample y_2 drawn from $P(y \mid x_1)$. The new values x_2 and y_2 are not compatible with the distribution P. P was consulted to match y_2 with x_1 (and x_2 with y_1), but now that X has changed its value to x_2, y_2 no longer represents a proper probabilistic match to x.

To formalize this notion, note that a prerequisite to coherent relaxation is that the distribution of X and Y be stationary, as in Eq. (4.70). In other words, if at time t_1, X and Y are distributed by $P(x, y)$, then the values of X and Y at time t_2 must also be distributed by $P(x, y)$. This requirement is met when only one variable changes at any given time, because then we can write (assuming Y is the changing variable)

$$P(X_2 = x, \; Y_2 = y) = \sum_{x'y'} P(X_2 = x, Y_2 = y \mid X_1 = x', Y_1 = y') P(x', y')$$

$$= P(Y_1 = y \mid X_1 = x) P(X_1 = x)$$

$$= P(X_1 = x, Y_1 = y) = P(x, y), \tag{4.72}$$

which implies stationary distribution. If, however, X and Y change their values simultaneously, we have

$$P(X_2 = x, \; Y_2 = y) = P(Y_2 = y \mid X_2 = x) P((X_2 = x)$$

$$= \sum_{x'y'} P(X_2 = x, Y_2 = y \mid X_1 = x', Y_1 = y') P(x', y')$$

$$= \sum_{x'y'} P(X_1 = x \mid Y_1 = y') P(Y_1 = y \mid X_1 = x') P(x', y')$$

$$= \sum_{x'y'} \frac{P(x, y')}{P(y')} \; \frac{P(x', y)}{P(x')} \; P(x', y'), \tag{4.73}$$

which represents stationary distribution only in the pathological case where X_1 and Y_1 are independent.

This analysis, extended to the case of multiple variables, allows us to determine which variables can be activated simultaneously. Let the set of concurrently activated variables be $Z = \{Z_1, Z_2, ..., Z_n\}$, and assume that each Z_i variable chooses a new value z_i' by sampling the distribution $P(z_i \mid s_i)$, where S_i is the subset of variables inspected by Z_i prior to switching. If W_Z stands for the set of unchanged variables, then under the requirement of stationary distribution,

$$P(z', w_Z) = P(z, w_Z)$$

or

$$P(z' \mid w_Z) = P(z \mid w_Z), \tag{4.74}$$

because $P(w_Z)$ remains unchanged in the transition.

Since the values z' of the Z variables are drawn independently from $P(z_i \mid s_i)$, Eq. (4.74) translates to

$$\prod_{i=1}^{n} P(Z_i = z_i \mid s_i) = P(z_1, z_2, ..., z_n \mid w_Z). \tag{4.75}$$

This requirement is satisfied whenever each S_i is a Markov blanket of Z_i,

$$P(z_i \mid s_i) = P(z_i \mid w_{Z_i}), \tag{4.76}$$

and, simultaneously, each S_i shields Z_i from all other Z's,

$$P(z_i \mid s_i) = P(z_i \mid s_i \underset{j \neq i}{\wedge} z_j) \qquad i = 1, 2, ..., n. \tag{4.77}$$

To meet both Eq. (4.76) and Eq. (4.77), it is clear that if S_i contains any of the Z_j's, then $S_i - Z_j$ must also shield Z_i from all other Z's. However, if we assume that each S_i already is the smallest Markov blanket permitted by the network, we must conclude that no Z_j's should be a member of any of the S_i's. Thus, any set of variables licensed to be activated simultaneously must not contain a pair of variables belonging to the same Markov blanket.

A convenient way to enforce this requirement is to add dummy links between mates (i.e., nodes sharing a child), taking care that no two adjacent nodes in the augmented network are activated concurrently. The question now arises how to schedule the activation of the processors so that the following conditions hold:

1. No two adjacent processors are activated at the same time.

2. Every processor gets activated sufficiently often.

3. The activation commands are generated in distributed fashion, with no external supervision.

This problem is a version of the "dining philosophers" dilemma originally posed by Dijkstra [1972] and later solved independently by Gafni and Bertsekas [1981] and Chandy and Misra [1984]. The solution is a distributed control policy called *edge reversal*, involving the following steps:

1. The links of the network are assigned arbitrary acyclic arrow orientation. (This orientation bears no relation to the causal ordering governing the construction of Bayesian networks.)

2. Each processor inspects the orientation of the arrows on its incident links and waits until all arrows point inward, i.e., until the processor becomes a *sink*.

3. Once a processor becomes a sink, it is activated, and when it completes the computation, it reverses the direction of all its incident arrows (i.e., it becomes a *source)*.

It is easily seen that no two neighbors can be activated at the same time. What is more remarkable about this edge reversal policy, however, is that no processor ever gets "deprived"; every processor fires at least once before the orientation returns to its initial state and the cycle repeats itself. This feature is important because it constitutes a necessary condition for the convergence of the entire process [Geman and Geman 1984].

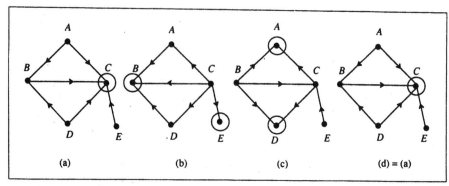

Figure 4.34. *Concurrent activation under the edge-reversal policy. Sinks fire and reverse their edges, thus ensuring that no two neighbors fire concurrently.*

Figure 4.34 applies this policy to the Bayesian network of Figure 4.32 by marking with circles the nodes activated at each step of the process. Initially, the dummy edge BC is added to designate these mates as neighbors, and the orientation of Figure 4.34a is assigned, where C is the only sink. Once C is activated, the arrows pointing to C are reversed (by C), whereupon B and E become sinks and fire. After three steps (Figure 4.34d), the orientation is back where it started, and the cycle repeats. Note that every processor fires once during the cycle and that we twice (Figures 4.34b and 4.34c) had two processors firing simultaneously. The problem of achieving maximum concurrency with edge reversal was analyzed by Barbosa [1986], who showed that the difference in the number of firings of any two nodes in the network cannot exceed a constant equal to the distance between them.

CONCLUSIONS

Stochastic simulation offers a viable inferencing technique for evidential reasoning tasks by virtue of its local and concurrent character. Although hundreds of runs may be necessary for achieving reasonable levels of accuracy, each run requires only $|V| + |E|$ computational steps, where $|V|$ is the number of vertices in the model and $|E|$ is the number of edges. Unlike purely numerical techniques, which sometimes entail exponential complexity, the length of computation is determined mainly by the required degree of accuracy, not by the dependencies embodied in the model. It is postulated, therefore, that stochastic simulation will be found practical in applications involving complex models with highly interdependent variables and in applications where "ballpark" estimates of probabilities will suffice.

The method has a drawback, however: the rate of convergence deteriorates when variables are constrained by functional dependencies. For example, if X and Y are a pair of adjacent variables constrained by equality, $X = Y$, then starting the simulation in a state where $X = Y = 0$ will leave X and Y clamped to 0 forever. Likewise, starting with $X = Y = 1$ will leave them clamped to 1 even though states having $X = Y = 0$ may be more probable. If we permit the equality to be violated with small probability p, this clamping phenomenon disappears, but the rate of convergence still seems to be proportional to $1/p$ [Chin and Cooper 1987]. While the theory of Markov chains [Feller 1950] guarantees that the simulation counts obtained by stochastic simulation will converge to the correct posterior probabilities associated with each proposition, the theory requires that every conceivable state has a nonzero probability of occurring, and this requirement is violated under logical or functional constraints.

One way to speed up the convergence rate is to treat clusters of tightly constrained elements as singleton variables, conduct the simulation runs on the clustered network, and then compute the internal distribution of the elements within each cluster. If such clusters cannot be identified in advance, the stochastic simulation method should be restricted to Henrion's scheme of forward simulation, i.e., each variable reacts only to the state of its direct parents, ignoring the states of other neighbors. This will render the method robust to functional dependencies but may necessitate a large number of runs to match rare sets of observations. A method combining the merits of both the forward-driven and the neighborhood-driven simulation schemes has not yet been identified.

4.5 WHAT ELSE CAN BAYESIAN NETWORKS COMPUTE?

4.5.1 Answering Queries

Since a quantified Bayesian network represents a complete probabilistic model of the domain, and since one can easily use such a network to derive the joint probability distribution $P(x_1,..., x_n)$ for all variables involved, it is clear that the network contains sufficient information for computing answers to all queries regarding the variables $X_1,..., X_n$. In other words, if $q(x_1,..., x_n)$ stands for any Boolean combination of the propositions $X_1 = x_1, X_2 = x_2,..., X_n = x_n$, then an answer of the form $P(q)$ can always be computed from the joint distribution represented by the network. For example, if all variables are propositional, and q stands for the truth value of $[(X_2 = TRUE) \wedge (X_3 = TRUE)] \vee (X_6 = TRUE)$, then $P(q)$ can be calculated by summing $P(x_1,..., x_n)$ over all elementary events $(x_1 \wedge x_2,..., \wedge x_n)$ entailed by the event q. Our goal is to find an efficient network representation for that calculation.

So far, the propagation scheme developed in this chapter has been aimed at computing the belief function BEL for each node in the network, which amounts to answering queries involving single propositions, e.g., $P(X_i = x_i)$. While a method of computing more elaborate probabilities can, in principle, be derived from the basic rules of probability theory, the focus of our discussion will be to answer queries at the knowledge level itself, i.e., using autonomous message-passing processes similar to those used for belief updating.

Consider the query $q = (x_2 \lor x_3) \land x_6$ being presented to the Bayesian network of Figure 4.35a, and assume that all variables are propositional. We can regard the partition $\{q, \neg q\}$ as another propositional variable Q and represent it by adding a seventh node to the network, with the set of parents $S_Q = \{X_2, X_3, X_6\}$. Alternatively, we can add two nodes, Q' and Q, to the network, with $Q' = X_2 \lor X_3$ and $Q = Q' \land X_6$, as in Figure 4.35.b.

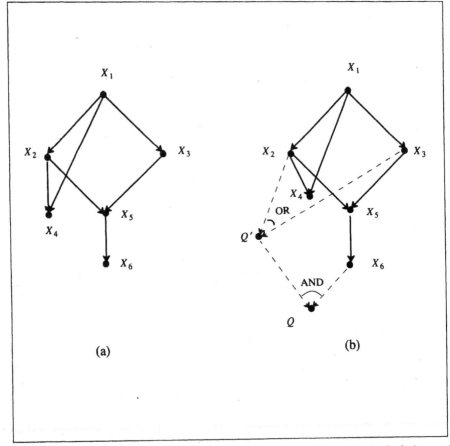

(a)   (b)

Figure 4.35. *Adding a query subnetwork to a) permits the calculation of* $P[(x_2 \lor x_3) \land x_6]$.

The conditional-probability assessments $P(x_i | S_i)$ required for the added links are simply the logical constraints represented by the Boolean formulae

$$P(q'|x_2, x_3) = \begin{cases} 1 & \text{if } q' = x_2 \lor x_3 \\ 0 & \text{if } q' \neq x_2 \lor x_3, \end{cases}$$

$$P(q|q', x_6) = \begin{cases} 1 & \text{if } q = q' \land x_6 \\ 0 & \text{if } q \neq q' \land x_6. \end{cases}$$

Computing an answer to the query "Is q true?" amounts to computing the belief distribution associated with the node Q and can be accomplished by the propagation techniques developed earlier in this chapter. Note that adding *query nodes* to the network does not alter its basic message-passing pathways. The joints at nodes Q' and Q of Figure 4.35*b* are "blocked," so they do not introduce new communication links between the original variables $X_1, ..., X_6$. Thus, while adding the query variable Q may require an extra computation for deriving $BEL(q)$, it does not perturb the belief parameters already computed. If the network is at equilibrium at query time, we can take the precomputed λ and π parameters and use them to assist the computation of $BEL(q)$.

4.5.2 *Introducing Constraints*

Queries presented to a reasoning system often include a "what if" question, where after the "if" we find a categorical constraint on the combination of values that some variables can attain. For example, "Would the project be completed in time, given the following limitation on resources?" The evidential information discussed in the preceding sections also represented a form of constraints, but these were of a very simple type, in which a group of variables were forced to assume a specific set of values. Constraints can be more elaborate, involving both disjunctions and conjunctions of events.

Such constraints can be introduced either as links among the variables involved or as auxiliary instantiated variables attached to the existing network. For example, the constraint

$$C: \text{ either } X_1 \text{ or } X_5 \text{ is true}$$

can be imposed on the network in Figure 4.35 by introducing an auxiliary variable $C = X_1 \lor X_5$ and permanently instantiating node C to the value *TRUE* (see Figure 4.36).

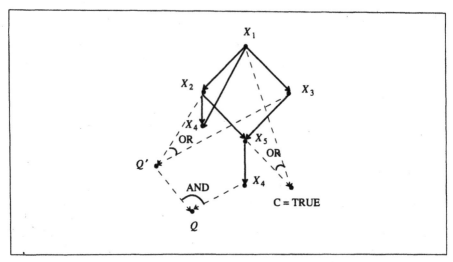

Figure 4.36. *Adding an instantiated node C permits the calculation of constrained queries*
P(Q | C).

These auxiliary *constraint nodes* play the same role as evidence nodes did in
Section 4.2. For example, to answer the conditional query "Is Q true, given that
either X_1 or X_5 is true?" we simply attach two auxiliary nodes to the original
network—a query node Q (as in Figure 4.35b) and a constraint node C (as in
Figure 4.36)—and compute the belief attributed to node Q under the hypothetical
evidence $e = \{C = TRUE\}$.

Note that constraint nodes, since they are instantiated, normally will perturb
the pathway topology of the original network and will therefore normally require
more elaborate computations than query nodes. In particular, the λ and π
parameters stored in the network at query time will have to be recomputed.

4.5.3 Answering Conjunctive Queries

Conjunctive queries play an important role in composite explanations (see Chapter
5), where it is required to compute the degree of belief that several events exist
concurrently. Such queries, characterized by the form

$$q = \bigwedge_{i \in I_Q} (X_i = x_i), \tag{4.78}$$

can be answered by the auxiliary node method described in Section 4.5.1, but
because of the special nature of the conjunctive connective, a more direct method
often may be preferred.

To compute the probability of a conjunctive query

$$q = (X_1 = x_1) \wedge (X_2 = x_2) \wedge \cdots \wedge (X_m = x_m), \quad (4.79)$$

it is convenient to use the chain rule

$$P(q) = P(x_m \mid x_{m-1}, \ldots, x_1) P(x_{m-1} \mid x_{m-2}, \ldots, x_1) \cdots P(x_2 \mid x_1) P(x_1). \quad (4.80)$$

Each factor in Eq. (4.80) amounts to the belief in a proposition $X_i = x_i$, treating all previous propositions $(X_1 = x_1) \cdots (X_{i-1} = x_{i-1})$ as evidence. Thus, $P(q)$ can be computed by taking the product of m belief measures, each being the result of an evidence-propagation exercise like the ones described in the preceding sections. Of course, there is no need to propagate the impact of each instantiation to the entire network; the π–λ messages should be transmitted only to those variables included in q.

As an illustration, let us consider the diagnosis network of Figure 4.37 (after Peng and Reggia [1986]), where the nodes at the top row, $\{D_1, D_2, D_3, D_4\}$, represent four hypothetical diseases and the nodes at the bottom row, $\{M_1, M_2, M_3, M_4\}$, represent four manifestations (or symptoms) of these diseases. The interaction among the possible causes of any given symptom is assumed to be of the "noisy-OR-gate" type (see Section 4.3.2), and the probability that a given symptom M_j will be observed in the presence of the disease set $D = \{D_i \mid i \in I_D\}$ is

$$P(+m_j \mid D) = 1 - \prod_{i \in I_D} q_{ij}, \quad (4.81)$$

where q_{ij} stands for

$$q_{ij} = P(M_j \text{ absent} \mid \text{Only } D_i \text{ present}). \quad (4.82)$$

The link parameters $q_{ij} = 1 - c_{ij}$ are shown in the network of Figure 4.37, together with the prior probabilities of the individual diseases, $\pi_i = P(D_i = TRUE)$.

Assume we wish to find the probability that a patient will contract disease D_1 and will simultaneously develop symptoms $\{M_1, M_3\}$ and *not* symptoms $\{M_2, M_4\}$. This amounts to computing $P(q)$ where q is a conjunctive query:

$$q = (d_1 = TRUE) \wedge (m_1 = TRUE) \wedge (m_3 = TRUE)$$

$$\wedge (m_2 = FALSE) \wedge (m_4 = FALSE)$$

$$= +d_1 \wedge +m_1 \wedge +m_3 \wedge \neg m_2 \wedge \neg m_4. \quad (4.83)$$

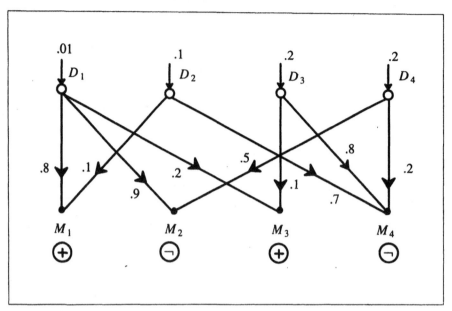

Figure 4.37. *A causal network representing four diseases and four symptoms. The parameters shown represent the probabilities of exceptions, q_{ij}.*

Since the network in Figure 4.37 becomes singly connected upon the instantiation of D_1, it is convenient to compute $P(q)$ in the following order:

$$P(q) = P(\neg m_4 \mid +m_3, \neg m_2, +m_1, +d_1)$$
$$P(+m_3 \mid \neg m_2, +m_1, +d_1)$$
$$P(\neg m_2 \mid +m_1, +d_1)\, P(+m_1 \mid +d_1)\, P(+d_1). \qquad (4.84)$$

After D_1 is instantiated to *TRUE*, the topology of the network is shown in Figure 4.38, where the links $D_1 \to M_i$ carry $\pi_{M_i}(d_1) = (1, 0)$ and all λ's are unit vectors. The link $D_2 \to M_1$ carries the message $\pi_{M_1}(d_2) = (\pi_2, 1 - \pi_2) = (0.1, 0.9)$, and $P(+m_1 \mid +d_1)$ is readily calculated as (see Eq. (4.55), Eq. (4.57) or the detailed derivation in Appendix 4-A)

$$P(+m_1 \mid +d_1) = (1 - q_{11}\, q_{21}) \cdot 1 \cdot \pi_2 + (1 - q_{11}) \cdot 1 \cdot (1 - \pi_2)$$
$$= (1 - 0.8 \cdot 0.1)\, 0.1 + (1 - 0.8)0.9 = 0.272. \qquad (4.85)$$

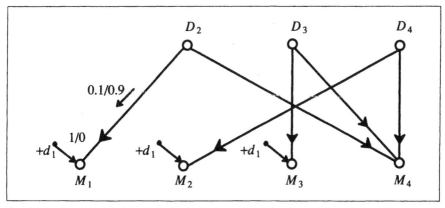

Figure 4.38. *The network of Figure 4.37 after instantiating* D_1 *and prior to instantiating node* M_1.

We now instantiate M_1 to *TRUE*, yielding the network of Figure 4.39, with all uninstantiated symptoms transmitting λ's that are unit vectors. Since the joints at M_3 and M_4 are blocked, this last instantiation has no effect on M_2; the link $D_4 \rightarrow M_2$ still carries $\pi_{M_2}(+d_4) = \pi_4 = 0.2$, and we get (see the detailed derivation in Appendix 4-A)

$$P(\neg m_2 \mid +m_1, +d_1) = q_{12}\, q_{42} \cdot 1 \cdot \pi_4 + q_{12} \cdot 1 \cdot (1 - \pi_4)$$

$$= 0.9 \cdot 0.5 \cdot 1 \cdot 0.2 + 0.9 \cdot 1 \cdot 0.8$$

$$= 0.81. \tag{4.86}$$

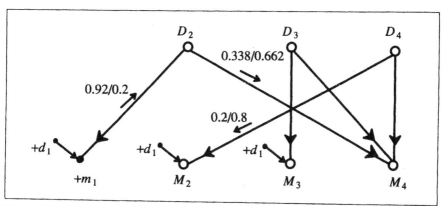

Figure 4.39. *Messages generated after instantiating node* M_1.

Setting $M_1 = TRUE$, however, also generates the messages $\lambda_{M_1}(d_2)$ and $\pi_{M_4}(d_2)$, which eventually will be needed at node M_4:

$$\lambda_{M_1}(d_2) = \left[(1 - q_{11} \, q_{21}), \, (1 - q_{11})\right]$$

$$= \left[(1 - 0.8 \cdot 0.1), \, (1 - 0.8)\right] = (0.92, \, 0.2),$$

$$\pi_{M_4}(d_2) = \alpha \left[\lambda_{M_1}(+d_2) \, \pi_2, \, \lambda_{M_1}(\neg d_2) \, (1 - \pi_2)\right]$$

$$= \alpha(0.92 \cdot 0.1, \, 0.2 \cdot 0.9) = (0.338, \, 0.662).$$

In a similar fashion, instantiating M_2 to *FALSE* and M_3 to *TRUE* yields

$$
\begin{aligned}
P(+m_3 \mid \neg m_2, +m_1, +d_1) &= P(+m_3 \mid +d_1) \\
&= (1 - \pi_3) \, (1 - q_{13}) + \pi_3 \, (1 - q_{13} \, q_{33}) \\
&= (1 - 0.2) \, (1 - 0.2) + 0.2 \, (1 - 0.2 \cdot 0.1) \\
&= 0.836 \qquad\qquad\qquad\qquad\qquad \textbf{(4.87)}
\end{aligned}
$$

and loads the network with the messages

$$\lambda_{M_2}(d_4) = \left[q_{12} \, q_{42}, \, q_{12}\right] = (0.9 \cdot 0.5, \, 0.9) = (0.45 \cdot 0.9),$$

$$\pi_{M_4}(d_4) = \alpha \left[\lambda_{M_2}(+d_4) \, \pi_4, \, \lambda_{M_2}(\neg d_4) \, (1 - \pi_4)\right]$$

$$= \alpha \left[0.45 \cdot 0.2, \, 0.9 \cdot 0.8\right] = (0.111, \, 0.889),$$

$$\lambda_{M_3}(d_3) = \left[(1 - q_{13} \, q_{33}), \, (1 - q_{13})\right] = \left[(1 - 0.2 \cdot 0.1), \, (1 - 0.2)\right] = (0.98, \, 0.8),$$

$$\pi_{M_4}(d_3) = \alpha \left[\lambda_{M_3}(+d_3) \, \pi_3, \, \lambda_{M_3}(\neg d_3) \, (1 - \pi_3)\right]$$

$$= \alpha \left[(0.98 \cdot 0.2, \, 0.8 \cdot 0.8\right] = \alpha \left[0.196, \, 0.64\right] = (0.23, \, 0.77),$$

as in Figure 4.40.

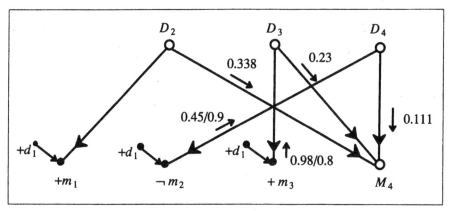

Figure 4.40. *Messages generated after instantiating M_1, M_2, and M_3.*

Having obtained all the π messages on the arrows pointing toward M_4, we can compute the last factor in the product of Eq. (4.84) (see Eqs. (4.55) and (4.56) in Section 4.3):

$$P\left[\neg m_4 \mid +m_3, \neg m_2, +m_1, +d_1\right]$$

$$= \prod_{i=2,3,4}\left[q_{i4}\,\pi_{M_4}(+d_i) + \pi_{M_4}(\neg d_i)\right]$$

$$= \prod_{i=2,3,4}\left[q_{i4}\,\pi_{i4} + 1 - \pi_{i4}\right]$$

$$= \left[0.7 \cdot 0.338 + 0.662\right] \times \left[0.8 \cdot 0.23 + 0.77\right] \times \left[0.2 \cdot 0.111 + 0.889\right]$$

$$= 0.781. \tag{4.88}$$

We now collect the factors from Eqs. (4.85) through (4.88) and, using Eq. (4.84), produce the final result:

$$P(q) = 0.781 \times 0.836 \times 0.81 \times 0.272 \times 0.01 = 1.439 \times 10^{-3}.$$

The belief attributable to a conjunctive query can also be computed in distributed fashion, with minimal external supervision. Once the order of instantiation is determined, we feed the network with the query list $Q = (\neg m_4, +m_3, +m_2, \neg m_1, +d_1)$ and an answer variable $BEL(Q)$, initially set at $BEL(Q) = 1$. Each node X inspects the Q list to see if the rightmost item is a proposition matched by X. When this happens, the matched node

1) is activated,

2) removes the rightmost item from the query list,

3) multiplies $BEL(Q)$ by the current belief in the removed proposition,

4) instantiates its value to that specified by the removed proposition, and

5) transmits to its neighbors the appropriate λ–π messages together with the shortened query list and the modified parameter $BEL(Q)$.

In our example, node D_1 will be the first to be activated. It will instantiate its value to $d_1 = TRUE$ and will transmit to M_1, M_2, and M_3 the parameters $\pi_{M_1}(d_1) = \pi_{M_2}(d_1) = \pi_{M_3}(d_1) = (1, 0)$, together with the shortened query list $Q = (\neg m_4, +m_3, \neg m_2, +m_1)$ and $BEL(Q) = BEL(+d_1) = \pi_1 = 0.01$. Nodes M_2 and M_3 are not activated by these messages, and they transmit the list to their neighbors unmodified. Node M_1, however, having found a match with the rightmost element on the query list, is activated. It truncates the query list to $Q = (\neg m_4, +m_4, \neg m_2)$, computes $BEL(+m_1) = 0.272$ as in Eq. (4.85), sets $BEL(Q)$ to $0.01 \times 0.272 = 2.72 \times 10^{-3}$, and transmits $\lambda_{M_1}(d_2)$ to D_2. The truncated Q list and $BEL(Q)$ travel in the network unmodified until they reach node M_2; thus, the process is repeated until at the last stage, node M_4 removes the last element $\neg m_4$ from Q. At this point, M_4 performs the last modification of $BEL(Q)$, multiplying it by $BEL(\neg m_4)$, and the process terminates with the correct value of $P(q)$.

4.6 BIBLIOGRAPHICAL AND HISTORICAL REMARKS

The analysis of evidence in a hierarchy of hypotheses can be traced to the prominent American jurist John H. Wigmore (1863 - 1943), who also developed a graphical representation for inference and argumentation in legal reasoning [Wigmore 1913]. Aided by Bayesian analysis, interest in cascaded inference has gained momentum both in judicial reasoning [Schum and Martin 1982; Friedman 1986] and in intelligence analysis [Kelly and Barclay 1973; Schum 1987]. Early attempts to formulate hierarchical inferences in causal networks can also be found in Good [1961], which studied networks of binary variables defined by Eq. (3.27) and having multiple causes that interact under a noisy-OR-gate model.

The propagation method for trees (Section 4.2) is based on Pearl [1982]. The method was extended to polytrees (Section 4.3.1) by Kim [Kim and Pearl 1983], and was used in a decision-aiding system named CONVINCE [Kim 1984; Kim and Pearl 1987]. CONVINCE handles loops by giving the network a polytree approximation in a manner similar to the maximum-weight spanning tree method of Section 8.2. The term *polytree* was suggested by George Rebane and is equivalent to *singly connected network* or *generalized Chow tree*, as used in Kim and Pearl [1983]. The term *influence diagrams* [Howard and Matheson 1981] denotes Bayesian networks that also contain decision and value nodes (see Chapter 6). Influence diagrams have traditionally been evaluated by the method of node elimination [Shachter 1986].

The noisy-OR-gate model of Section 8.3.2 was proposed in Pearl [1986c] and independently analyzed by Peng and Reggia [1986]. The method of clustering (Section 4.4.1) was inspired by Spiegelhalter [1986] and is further developed in Lauritzen and Spiegelhalter [1988] using propagation in the filled-in undirected graph. An adaptation of this method to constraint satisfaction problems is described in Dechter and Pearl [1987b]. The method of conditioning (Section 4.4.2) was reported in Pearl [1986b], and a similar method for constraint satisfaction problems is described in Dechter and Pearl [1987a, 1987c].

Section 4.4.3 is based on Pearl [1987a] and was motivated by Henrion [1986a]. The scheme for distributed control of concurrent simulation was adopted through discussions with Eli Gafni and Valmir Barbosa (who, during his oral examination, pointed out both the danger of concurrently activating neighboring variables and the remarkable features of the edge-reversal policy). Valmir has also pointed out that query nodes (see Figure 4.35) may remain "invisible" in the stochastic simulation process, namely, each query node may inspect its parents and compute its frequency count, but need not expose its state to its parents. The same applies to any node that is not an ancestor of an observed variable.

Hrycej[1] has pointed out the connection between stochastic relaxation, Gibbs sampling and simulated annealing. The method has been improved and analyzed by Chavez and Cooper[2], and Shachter and Peot[3]. Peot and Shachter[4] have described an improved method of conditioning which requires simple (rather than weighted) summation over the beliefs found in each cutset instantiation.

Heckerman[5] has developed an improved algorithm for diagnosing two-level networks of noisy-OR gates, and Spiegelhalter and Lauritzen[6] have described Bayesian methods of learning the link matrices from empirical data. A method of propagating probability bounds is described by Fertig and Breese[7].

---

[1] Hrycej, T., "Gibbs sampling in Bayesian networks" *Artificial Intelligence*, Vol. 46, No.3, 1990, 351-364.

[2] Chavez, M.R., and Cooper, G.F., "A Randomized Approximation Algorithm for Probabilistic Inference on Bayesian Belief Networks," *Networks*, Vol. 20, No. 5, 1990, 661-685.

[3] Shachter, R.D., and Peot, M.A., "Simulation Approaches to General Probabilistic Inference on Belief Networks," *Uncertainty in AI 5*, M. Henrion, R.D. Shachter, L.N. Kanal, and J.F. Lemmer (Editors). Elsevier Science Publishers B.V. (North Holland), 1990, 221-231.

[4] Peot, A., and Shachter, R. D., "Fusion and propagation with multiple observations in belief networks" *Artificial Intelligence*, Vol. 48, No. 3, 1991, 299-318.

[5] Heckerman, D., "A Tractable Inference Algorithm for Diagnosing Multiple Diseases," *Uncertainty in AI 5*, M. Henrion, R.D. Shachter, L.N. Kanal, and J.F. Lemmer (Editors). Elsevier Science Publishers B.V. (North Holland), 1990, 163-171.

[6] Spiegelhalter, D.J., and Lauritzen, S.L., "Sequential Updating of Conditional Probabilities on Directed Graphical Structures," *Networks*, Vol. 20, No. 5, 1990, 579-605.

[7] Fertig, K.W., and Breese, J.S., "Interval Influence Diagrams," *Uncertainty in AI 5*, Elsevier Science Publishers, 1990, 149-161.

Exercises

4.1.   A language L has a four-character vocabulary $V = \{\varepsilon, A, B, C\}$ where ε is the empty symbol. The probability that character v_i will be followed by v_j is given by the following matrix:

$$
P(v_j \mid v_i) =
\begin{array}{c|cccc}
 & \multicolumn{4}{c}{v_j} \\
v_i & \varepsilon & A & B & C \\
\hline
\varepsilon & \tfrac{1}{4} & \tfrac{1}{4} & \tfrac{1}{4} & \tfrac{1}{4} \\
A & \tfrac{1}{2} & 0 & \tfrac{1}{4} & \tfrac{1}{4} \\
B & \tfrac{1}{8} & \tfrac{1}{2} & \tfrac{1}{8} & \tfrac{1}{4} \\
C & \tfrac{1}{4} & \tfrac{1}{8} & \tfrac{1}{2} & \tfrac{1}{8}
\end{array}
$$

In transmitting messages from L, some characters may be corrupted by noise and be confused with others. The probability that the transmitted character v_j will be interpreted as v_k is given by the following confusion matrix:

$$
P_c(v_k \mid v_j) =
\begin{array}{c|cccc}
 & \multicolumn{4}{c}{v_k} \\
v_j & \varepsilon & A & B & C \\
\hline
\varepsilon & .9 & .1 & 0 & 0 \\
A & .1 & .8 & .1 & 0 \\
B & 0 & .1 & .8 & .1 \\
C & 0 & .1 & .1 & .8
\end{array}
$$

The string, $\varepsilon, \varepsilon, B, C, A, \varepsilon, \varepsilon$ is received, and it is known that the transmitted string begins and ends with ε.

a.   Find the probability that the i-th transmitted symbol is C, for $i = 1, 2,..., 7$.

b.   Find the probability that the string transmitted is the one received.

c.   Find the probability that no message (a string of ε's) was transmitted.

4.2.   Solve Exercise 2.3 of Chapter 2 by message propagation.

4.3. In the burglary story of Chapter 2, compute the reduction in *BEL (Burglary)* due to the radio announcement, assuming the following relations:

$$\lambda(+s) = 4{:}1,$$
$$P(+s \mid +b, \neg e) = .90,$$
$$P(+s \mid \neg b, +e) = .20,$$
$$P(+e) = 10^{-6},$$
$$\lambda_R(+e) = 10^7{:}1$$
$$P(+b) = 10^{-4}.$$

$(+b = Burglary)$
$(+e = Earthquake)$
$(R = Radio\ announcement)$
$(+s = Alarm\ sound)$

Assume a noisy-OR-gate model for $P(s \mid e, b)$.

4.4. Having observed the symptoms $(+m_1, \neg m_2, +m_3, +m_4)$ in the problem of Figure 4.37, find *BEL* (d_1) using the method of conditioning (condition on D_1).

4.5. Find a join-tree representation for the network in Figure 4.37, and solve Exercise **4.4** in that representation.

4.6. Continue the stochastic simulation process of Section 4.4.3 to 5,000 runs, and show that $P(+a \mid \neg d, +e)$ converges to 0.097.

4.7. Solve Exercise **4.4** by ignoring the loops, i.e., propagate the λ and π messages using the equations developed for singly connected networks, until you reach a stable equilibrium. Assess the merit of this technique as a possible approximation method.

4.8. The distributed algorithm described in Section 4.3.1 permits a variety of sequential implementations, some better than others. Devise a message-passing schedule (i.e., an algorithm that determines, at any given state of the network, which node should pass a message to which of its neighbors) for belief updating, such that every node will be activated at most twice, regardless of the number of observations[1]. Can this schedule be implemented by a purely distributed protocol?

---

[1] See Peot and Shachter (1991), footnote (4), page 233.

Appendix 4-A

Auxilliary Derivations for Section 4.5.3

DERIVATION OF EQ. (4.85)

Using $\pi_{M_1}(d_1) = (\pi_{11}, 1 - \pi_{11}) = (1, 0)$ in Eq. (4.55), we have

$$
\begin{aligned}
P(+m_1 \mid +d_1) = BEL(m_1 = 1) &= (1 - \pi_{11})(1 - \pi_{21})(1 - 1) \\
&\quad + (1 - \pi_{11})\pi_{21}(1 - q_{21}) \\
&\quad + \pi_{11}(1 - \pi_{21})(1 - q_{11}) + \pi_{11}\pi_{21}(1 - q_{11}q_{21}) \\
&= 0 + 0 + 1\,(1 - \pi_2)(1 - q_{11}) + 1\,\pi_2(1 - q_{11}q_{21}) \\
&= (1 - 0.1)(1 - 0.8) + 0.1(1 - 0.8 \times 0.1) = 0.272. \quad \textbf{(4.85)}
\end{aligned}
$$

DERIVATION OF EQ. (4.86)

Using $\pi_{M_2}(+d_1) = \pi_{12} = 1$ and $\pi_{M_2}(+d_4) = \pi_{42} = 0.2$ in Eq. (4.55), we have

$$
\begin{aligned}
P(\neg m_2 \mid +m_1, +d_1) = BEL(M_2 = 0) &= (1 - \pi_{12})(1 - \pi_{42})1 \\
&\quad + (1 - \pi_{12})\pi_{42}\,q_{42} \\
&\quad + \pi_{12}(1 - \pi_{42})\,q_{12} + \pi_{12}\,\pi_{42}\,q_{12}\,q_{42} \\
&= 0 + 0 + 1 \times (1 - \pi_4)\,q_{12} + 1 \times \pi_4\,q_{12}\,q_{42} \\
&= (1 - 0.2)\,0.9 + 0.2 \times 0.9 \times 0.5 = 0.81. \quad \textbf{(4.86)}
\end{aligned}
$$

DERIVATION OF $\lambda_{M_j}(d_i)$

From Eq. (4.60):

$$\lambda_X(u_i) = \begin{cases} \lambda_0 q_i \Pi_i' + \lambda_1(1 - q_i \Pi_i') & u_i = 1 \\ \lambda_0 \Pi_i' + \lambda_1(1 - \Pi_i') & u_i = 0, \end{cases}$$

where

$$\Pi_i' = \prod_{k \neq i} [1 - (1 - q_k)\pi_{kX}].$$

Rewriting in our notation for an instantiated node $X = M_j$, we have

$$\lambda_{M_j}(d_i) = \begin{cases} \prod_{k \neq i} [1 - (1 - q_{ki})\pi_{ki}] & M_j = 0 \quad u_i = 0 \\[2mm] q_{ij}\prod_{k \neq i} [1 - (1 - q_{ki})\pi_{ki}] & M_j = 0 \quad u_i = 1 \\[2mm] 1 - \prod_{k \neq i} [1 - (1 - q_{ki})\pi_{ki}] & M_j = 1 \quad u_i = 0 \\[2mm] 1 - q_{ij}\prod_{k \neq i} [1 - (1 - q_{ki})\pi_{ki}] & M_j = 1 \quad u_i = 1. \end{cases}$$

For example,

$$\lambda_{M_1}(d_2) = \{\, 1 - q_{21} [1 - (1 - q_{11}) \cdot 1]\,,\; 1 - [1 - (1 - q_{11})] \,\}$$
$$= (1 - q_{21}q_{11},\; 1 - q_{11}).$$

Chapter 5

DISTRIBUTED REVISION OF COMPOSITE BELIEFS

In the human mind, one-sidedness has always been the rule, and many-sidedness the exception. Hence, even in revolution of opinion, one part of the truth usually sets while another rises.

— John Stuart Mill

5.1 INTRODUCTION

People's beliefs normally are cast in categorical terms and often involve a set of propositions which, stated together, offer a satisfactory explanation of the observed data. For example, a physician might state, "This patient apparently suffers from two simultaneous disorders A and B which, due to condition C, caused the deterioration of organ D." Except for the hedging term "apparently," this composite statement conveys a sense of unreserved commitment to a set of four hypotheses. The individual components in the explanation are meshed together by mutually reinforced cause-effect relationships, forming a cohesive whole; the removal of any one component from the discourse would render the entire explanation incomplete.

Such cohesiveness suggests that a great amount of refuting evidence would have to be gathered before the current interpretation would require revision. Moreover, a revision, once activated, is likely to change the entire interpretation, not merely its level of plausibility. Another characteristic of coherent explanations is that they do not impute degrees of certainty to any individual hypothesis in the argument. Nor do they convey information about alternative, "second-best" combinations of hypotheses.

Rarely do we even consult the certainty of the accepted composite explanation; most everyday activities are predicated upon beliefs that, though provisional, do not seem to be muddled with varying shades of uncertainty. Consider for example the sentence "John decided to have a bowl of cereal, but when he found the cupboard empty, he figured out that Mary must have finished the cereal for breakfast." We normally perform routine actions, such as reaching for the cupboard, without the slightest hesitation or reservation, thus reflecting our adherence to firmly held beliefs, such as the belief that we will find cereal there. When we observe new facts that refute current beliefs, a process of belief revision takes place; new beliefs replace old ones and are firmly held until they, in turn, are refuted.

These behavioral features are somewhat at variance with the analysis in Chapter 4. There, we focused on the task of *belief updating*, i.e., assigning to each hypothesis in a network a degree of belief *BEL*, which changes smoothly and incrementally with each new item of evidence. This chapter applies Bayesian analysis and belief networks to another task: revision of belief commitments, where by *belief commitment* we mean the categorical but tentative acceptance of a subset of hypotheses that together constitute the most satisfactory explanation of the evidence at hand. In probabilistic terms, that task amounts to finding the most probable instantiation of all hypothesis variables, given the observed data. The resulting output is an optimal list of jointly accepted propositions, a list that may change abruptly as more evidence is obtained.

In pure form, this optimization task is intractable because enumerating and rating all possible instantiations is computationally prohibitive. Instead, heuristic techniques have been developed for various applications. In pattern recognition, the problem is known as the *multimembership problem* [Ben-Bassat 1980]; in medical diagnosis, it is known as *multiple disorders* [Ben-Bassat et al. 1980; Pople 1982; Reggia, Nau, and Wang 1983; Cooper 1984; Peng and Reggia 1986]; in circuit diagnosis, as *multiple faults* [Reiter 1987a; deKleer and Williams 1986]; and in truth maintenance, as *multiple extensions* [Doyle 1979].

Our approach is to introduce *distributed* computation as the basis for belief revision. As in belief updating (Chapter 4), we wish to view the impact of each new piece of evidence as a perturbation that propagates through the network from concept to neighboring concept with minimal external supervision. At equilibrium, each variable should be bound to a fixed value that together with all other value assignments is the best interpretation of the evidence. The reasons for adopting this distributed message-passing paradigm are the same as those introduced in our discussion of belief updating: to exploit the independencies embodied in sparsely constrained systems, to facilitate the use of object-oriented programming and the generation of meaningful verbal explanations, and to present a feasible model of the way humans revise their beliefs. We will seek idealized models in which distributed revision can be executed coherently, study in detail the propagation rules dictated by the models, and then posit these rules as universal strategies of belief revision.

We will show that in singly connected networks, the most satisfactory explanation can be found in linear time by a message-passing algorithm similar to the one used in belief updating. In multiply connected networks, the problem may be exponentially difficult, but if the network is sparse, clustering and conditioning methods can be used to render the interpretation task tractable. In general, assembling the most believable combination of hypotheses is no more complex than computing the degree of belief for any individual hypothesis.

This chapter contains seven sections. Section 5.2 compares belief updating with belief revision using a simple example from circuit diagnosis. Section 5.3 develops propagation rules for belief revision in singly connected networks and compares the rules to those governing belief updating. It then extends the propagation scheme to multiply connected networks using clustering, conditioning, and stochastic relaxation. Section 5.4 applies belief revision to the diagnosis of systems with multiple faults and demonstrates the advantages of distributed computation. Section 5.5 illustrates the method of conditioning with a simple medical diagnosis example, involving four diseases and four symptoms. Section 5.6 relates the revision process to previous philosophical work on belief acceptance and to current work on nonmonotonic reasoning. It discusses the adequacy of the "most probable" criterion and touches on the issue of consistency in belief revision.

5.2 ILLUSTRATING THE PROPAGATION SCHEME

The simple circuit of Figure 5.1 will be used to illustrate the nature of the propagation scheme, the semantics of the messages involved, and the difference between belief updating and belief revision. The circuit consists of three AND-gates in tandem. X_1, X_2, and X_3 are binary input variables ($X_i \in \{0, 1\}$), Y_3 is the circuit's output ($Y_3 = X_1 \wedge X_2 \wedge X_3$), and Y_1 and Y_2 are intermediate, unobserved variables ($Y_i = Y_{i-1} \wedge X_i$). Under normal operation all inputs are *ON*, and so is the output Y_3. A failure occurs ($Y_3 = 0$) when any of the inputs is *OFF* (the circuits are assumed to be operational). The problem is to infer which input is faulty, given the simultaneous observations $\{Y_3 = 0, X_2 = 1\}$ and assuming that failures are independent events with prior probabilities

$$q_i = 1 - p_i = P(X_i = 0), \qquad i = 1, 2, 3. \tag{5.1}$$

The Bayesian network corresponding to this circuit diagram is shown in Figure 5.1*b*. Since the output of each component is functionally determined by the state of its two inputs, X_i and Y_{i-1} are identified as the parents of Y_i, $i = 1, 2, 3$, and the conditional probabilities which characterize these child-parents relationships are given by

$$P(y_i \mid y_{i-1}, x_i) = \begin{cases} 1 & \text{if } y_i = y_{i-1} \wedge x_i \\ 0 & \text{otherwise.} \end{cases} \tag{5.2}$$

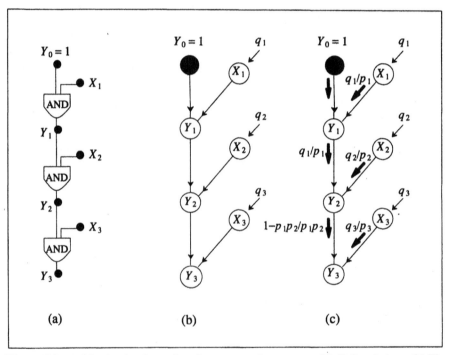

Figure 5.1. *(a) Logic circuit used to demonstrate the process of belief updating. (b) The Bayesian network corresponding to the circuit in (a). (c) Profile of π-messages in the initial state of the network; the λ-messages (not shown) are unit vectors.*

5.2.1 Belief Updating (A Review)

In the initial, quiescent state (Figure 5.1*c*), all λ's are unit vectors, $\lambda = (1, 1)$, since no variable has any observed descendant and there exists, therefore, no evidence favoring the state 1 over the state 0. The π messages on the links are computed from Eqs. (4.53), (5.1), and (5.2) and are given by

$$
\pi_{Y_i}(x_i) = \begin{cases} q_i & x_i = 0 \\ p_i & x_i = 1, \end{cases} \tag{5.3}
$$

$$
\pi_{Y_2}(y_1) = \begin{cases} q_1 & y_1 = 0 \\ p_1 & y_1 = 1, \end{cases} \tag{5.4}
$$

and

$$
\pi_{Y_3}(y_2) = \begin{cases} 1 - p_1 p_2 & y_2 = 0 \\ p_1 p_2 & y_2 = 1. \end{cases} \tag{5.5}
$$

These messages simply describe the prior probabilities of the corresponding variables. The belief measures can be computed using Eq. (4.49); they, too, stand for the prior probabilities associated with each variable. For example,

$$
BEL(x_2) = \begin{cases} q_2 & x_2 = 0 \\ p_2 & x_2 = 1 \end{cases} \tag{5.6}
$$

and

$$
BEL(y_3) = \begin{cases} 1 - p_1 p_2 p_3 & y_3 = 0 \\ p_1 p_2 p_3 & y_3 = 1. \end{cases} \tag{5.7}
$$

Now imagine that two observations are conducted simultaneously, yielding $Y_3 = 0$ and $X_2 = 1$. The first observation implies that at least one input is faulty, while the second exonerates X_2, leaving either X_1 or X_3—or both—as possible culprits. The problem is small enough to permit the global computation of all probabilities. For example, the probability that input X_1 is faulty is given by

$$
P(X_1 = 0 | e) = BEL(x_1 = 0) = \frac{q_1 p_3 + q_1 q_3}{q_1 q_3 + q_1 p_3 + p_1 q_3} = \frac{q_1}{1 - p_1 p_3}, \tag{5.8}
$$

while

$$
P(X_3 = 0 | e) = BEL(x_3 = 0) = \frac{q_1 q_3 + p_1 q_3}{q_1 q_3 + q_1 p_3 + p_1 q_3} = \frac{q_3}{1 - p_1 p_3}. \tag{5.9}
$$

These results can be derived through distributed computation, using the propagation equations of Chapter 4. Figure 5.2 illustrates three stages of the propagation process triggered by the two observations, assuming that a processor is assigned to each variable and that each processor is activated when a change occurs in its incoming messages. Each diagram displays the messages updated at the corresponding stage; the top-down arrows represent π-messages, and bottom-up arrows represent λ-messages.

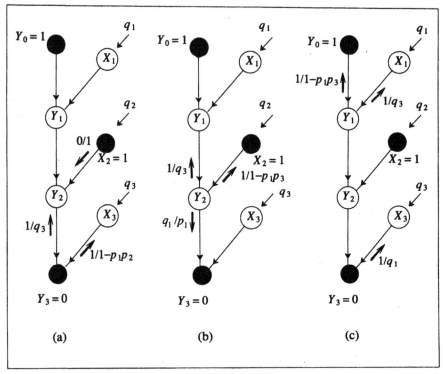

Figure 5.2. *Propagation of updated messages after observing $X_2 = 1$ and $Y_3 = 0$.*
(a) Messages generated immediately after the observations. (b) Messages
generated by the activation of Y_2. (c) Messages generated by the activation of
Y_1 and Y_3.

In Figure 5.2a the instantiation of Y_3 and X_2 triggers the updating of three
messages: $\lambda_{Y_3}(x_3)$, $\lambda_{Y_3}(y_2)$, and $\pi_{Y_2}(x_2)$. Their magnitudes are computed locally
from Eqs. (4.52) and (4.53), using the π-values in Eqs. (5.3) through (5.5), giving

$$\pi_{Y_2}(x_2) = (0, 1), \tag{5.10}$$

$$\lambda_{Y_3}(x_3) = (1, 1 - p_1 p_2), \tag{5.11}$$

and

$$\lambda_{Y_3}(y_2) = (1, q_3). \tag{5.12}$$

At the next phase of propagation (Figure 5.2b), Y_2 is activated, and it generates
three new messages: $\lambda_{Y_2}(y_1)$, $\lambda_{Y_2}(x_2)$, and $\pi_{Y_3}(y_2)$. The first message
incorporates the changes observed in both $\lambda_{Y_3}(y_2)$ and $\pi_{Y_2}(x_2)$, while the last two

reflect the recent changes in $\lambda_{Y_3}(y_2)$ and $\pi_{Y_2}(x_2)$, respectively. The magnitudes of these messages are given by

$$\lambda_{Y_2}(y_1) = (1, q_3), \tag{5.13}$$

$$\lambda_{Y_2}(x_2) = (1, 1 - p_1 p_3), \tag{5.14}$$

and

$$\pi_{Y_3}(y_2) = (q_1, p_1). \tag{5.15}$$

The final phase of propagation is depicted in Figure 5.2c. Processors Y_1 and Y_3 are activated simultaneously, and they generate the messages $\lambda_{Y_1}(y_0)$, $\lambda_{Y_1}(x_1)$, and $\lambda_{Y_3}(x_3)$. The first message is superfluous since Y_0 is "clamped" to 1. The last two are computed via Eq. (4.52), giving

$$\lambda_{Y_1}(x_1) = p_2 \lambda_{Y_2}(y_1) = p_2(1, q_3) \tag{5.16}$$

and

$$\lambda_{Y_3}(x_3) = p_2(1, q_1). \tag{5.17}$$

These equations represent the probabilities of the total evidence observed, conditioned on the two possible values, 0 and 1, of the variables X_1 and X_3, respectively. For example, under the assumption $X_1 = 0$ the probability of the total evidence $e = \{X_2 = 1, Y_3 = 0\}$ is p_2, while under the assumption $X_1 = 1$ that probability becomes $p_2 q_3$ (X_3 must be faulty if $Y_3 = 0$). The essential information conveyed by Eq. (5.16) is the ratio $p_2 / p_2 q_3 = 1 / q_3$.

From these final values of the λ–π messages the belief distribution BEL can be computed for each variable in the system (Eq. (4.49)). For example, for X_1 we obtain

$$BEL(x_1) = \alpha\, \pi_{Y_1}(x)\, \lambda_{Y_1}(x) = \alpha(q_1, p_1)\,(1, q_3)$$

$$= \alpha(q_1, p_1 q_3) = \left[\frac{q_1}{q_1 + p_1 q_3}, \frac{p_1 q_3}{q_1 + p_1 q_3} \right], \tag{5.18}$$

as in Eq. (5.8).

5.2.2 Belief Revision

The aim of belief revision is not to associate a measure of belief with each individual proposition, but rather to identify a composite set of propositions—one from each variable—that best explains the evidence at hand. In the example of Figure 5.1a, the aim is to find a consistent assignment of values to the set of uninstantiated variables, $\{X_1, X_3, Y_2\}$, that best explains the evidence $e = \{Y_3 = 0, X_2 = 1\}$. Since Y_2 is functionally dependent on X_1, the space of consistent assignments is determined by the values assigned to X_1 and X_3, but because $(X_1 = 1, X_3 = 1)$ is incompatible with $Y_3 = 0$, the choice is among three candidates:

$$I_1 = \{X_1 = 0, X_3 = 0\}, \quad I_2 = \{X_1 = 0, X_3 = 1\},$$

or

$$I_3 = \{X_1 = 1, X_3 = 0\}.$$

Such assignments will be referred to interchangeably as *explanations*, *extensions*, and *interpretations*.

Basic probabilistic considerations dictate

$$P(I_1 \mid e) = \frac{q_1 q_3}{1 - p_1 p_3}, \tag{5.19}$$

$$P(I_2 \mid e) = \frac{q_1 p_3}{1 - p_1 p_3},$$

and

$$P(I_3 \mid e) = \frac{p_1 q_3}{1 - p_1 p_3}.$$

If we assume for simplicity that

$$\tfrac{1}{2} > q_1 > q_2 > q_3, \tag{5.20}$$

then $I_2 = \{X_1 = 0, X_3 = 1\}$ is identified as the "best" explanation of the evidence e. However, this optimal assignment cannot be obtained simply by optimizing the belief distributions of the individual variables. For example, taking $q_1 = .45$ and $q_3 = .4$, we get (via Eqs. (5.8) and (5.9))

$$BEL(x_1 = 0) = .672 > BEL(x_1 = 1) = .328$$

and

$$BEL(x_3 = 0) = .597 > BEL(x_3 = 1) = .403.$$

Yet, choosing the most probable value of each variable separately yields the assignment $I_1 = \{X_1 = 0, X_3 = 0\}$, which is the *least* probable explanation— $P(I_1 \mid e) = .268$, while $P(I_2 \mid e) = .403$ and $P(I_3 \mid e) = .328$.

Now we shall demonstrate how the optimal explanation can be assembled by a distributed message-passing scheme similar to that used in belief updating (Figure 5.2). Clearly the messages used in this scheme should carry a summarized description of the entire network, sufficient to guarantee that locally optimal choices constitute a globally optimal explanation. For example, in Figure 5.1a, the final messages passed to processor X_1 should locally determine the choice $X_1 = 0$; simultaneously, those passed to X_3 should dictate $X_3 = 1$.

To meet this goal, we associate with each variable X a new function $BEL^*(x)$, which for each value x represents the probability of the *best interpretation* of the proposition $X = x$, i.e., an assignment of values to all variables that attains the highest probability, given $X = x$. For example, in Figure 5.1b, the best interpretation of the proposition $Y_2 = 0$ is the assignment $\{X_1 = 0, X_2 = 1, X_3 = 1\}$, with probability $q_1 p_2 p_3$, while the proposition $Y_2 = 1$ is best interpreted by the no-fault condition $\{X_1 = 1, X_2 = 1, X_3 = 1\}$, with probability $p_1 p_2 p_3$. Thus, the BEL^* function associated with Y_2 will be

$$BEL^*(y_2) = \begin{cases} q_1 p_2 p_3 & \text{if } y_2 = 0 \\ p_1 p_2 p_3 & \text{if } y_2 = 1, \end{cases} \tag{5.21}$$

and, since $q_1 < p_1$ (see Eq. (5.20)), the local choice $y_2 = 1$ is guaranteed to be part of the globally optimal explanation.

BEL^* can be computed using a local message-passing scheme similar to that of belief updating. The propagation dynamics are identical to those depicted in Figure 5.2, except that the information carried by the messages has different meaning and the computations paralleling those of Eqs. (4.52) and (4.53) involve maximization rather than summation.

The ability to assemble a globally optimal solution through local computation rests on the many conditional independence relations embodied in the system, as reflected in the network topology. These relations permit us to decompose the task of finding a best overall explanation into smaller subtasks of finding best explanations in subparts of the network, then combining them together. In Figure 5.1b, for example, the task of finding the best explanation for $Y_2 = 0$ can be decomposed into two independent subtasks:

1. Find a best sub-explanation for $Y_2 = 0$ in the *tail* subgraph of the link $Y_2 \rightarrow Y_3$ (i.e., comprising $\{X_1, Y_1, X_2\}$).

2. Find a best sub-explanation for $Y_2 = 0$ in the *head* subgraph of the link $Y_2 \rightarrow Y_3$ (i.e., comprising $\{Y_3, X_3\}$).

The fact that these two subgraphs are joined only by the link $Y_2 \rightarrow Y_3$ guarantees that the overall best explanation (for $Y_2 = 0$) is composed precisely of the two sub-explanations found in (1) and (2) above. Moreover, the degree of support that the overall best explanation extends to $Y_2 = 0$ can be computed locally from the degrees of support extended by the two sub-explanations. Thus, we can compute both $BEL^*(Y_2 = 0)$ and $BEL^*(Y_2 = 1)$ locally and decide the best value for Y_2 by choosing the one with the highest value of BEL^* (in this case $Y_2 = 1$).

The messages carrying these degrees of support across an arbitrary link $X \to Y$ will be denoted by $\lambda_Y^*(x)$ and $\pi_Y^*(x)$, formally defined as

$$\lambda_Y^*(x) = \max_{w_{XY}^-} P(w_{XY}^- \mid x) \tag{5.22}$$

and

$$\pi_Y^*(x) = \max_{w_{XY}^+} P(x, w_{XY}^+), \tag{5.23}$$

where w_{XY}^- and w_{XY}^+ stand, respectively, for any head-extension and tail-extension of $\{X = x, e\}$, relative to the link $X \to Y$. For example, in Figure 5.3a, $e = \varnothing$, and the best tail-extension of $Y_2 = 0$ is $w_{Y_2Y_3}^+ = \{X_1 = 0, Y_1 = 0, X_2 = 1\}$, with

$$\pi_{Y_3}^*(y_2 = 0) = P(Y_2 = 0, X_1 = 0, Y_1 = 0, X_2 = 1) = q_1 p_2, \tag{5.24}$$

while the best head-extension is $w_{Y_2Y_3}^- = \{Y_3 = 0, X_3 = 1\}$, with

$$\lambda_{Y_3}^*(y_2 = 0) = P(Y_3 = 0, X_3 = 1 \mid Y_2 = 0) = p_3. \tag{5.25}$$

By similar considerations we obtain

$$\pi_{Y_3}^*(y_2 = 1) = P(Y_2 = 1, X_1 = 1, Y_1 = 1, X_2 = 1) = p_1 p_2 \tag{5.26}$$

and

$$\lambda_{Y_3}^*(y_2 = 1) = P(Y_3 = 1, X_3 = 1 \mid Y_2 = 1) = p_3, \tag{5.27}$$

thus yielding the messages

$$\pi_{Y_3}^*(y_2) = p_2(q_1, p_1) \tag{5.28}$$

and

$$\lambda_{Y_3}^*(y_2) = p_3(1, 1). \tag{5.29}$$

In Section 5.3, we shall demonstrate the following:

1. The $\pi^*-\lambda^*$ messages defined above can be propagated by local computations, simply by replacing the summations in Eqs. (4.52) and (4.53) with maximizations over the same set of variables, as in Eqs. (5.44) and (5.47), Section 5.3.

2.   The BEL^* functions can be computed from the $\pi^*-\lambda^*$ messages using simple products, e.g.,

$$BEL^*(x) = \beta\, \pi_Y^*(x)\, \lambda_Y^*(x), \qquad (5.30)$$

or using a modification of Eqs. (4.49) and (4.51) with maximization replacing the summation (see Eq. (5.43)).

The rest of this section provides a qualitative description of how the best explanations in the Figure 5.1 example are found through a message-passing process. A quantitative account will be postponed until the propagation rules are established in Section 5.3 (see Eqs. (5.43), (5.45), and (5.47) or, more generally, Eqs. (5.50) through (5.52)).

Initially, all λ^*s are unit vectors, and the π^* messages are given in Figure 5.3a.

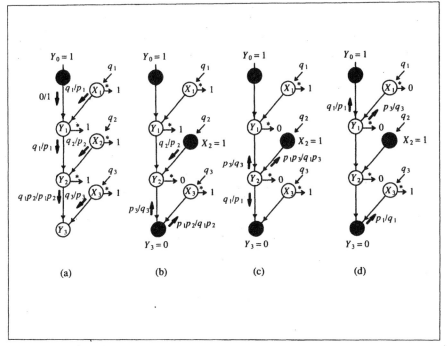

Figure 5.3. $\pi^* - \lambda^*$ *message propagation under belief revision. The observation* $\{Y_3 = 0, X_2 = 1\}$ *causes a switch from the initial default explanation* $\{X_1 = X_2 = X_3 = 1\}$ *in (a) to a new, stable (and maximally probable) explanation* $\{X_1 = 0, X_2 = 1, X_3 = 1\}$ *in (d). The intermediate states in (b) and (c) yield temporary belief commitments based on incomplete transient information.*

These π^* messages are almost identical to the π messages of Figure 5.1c, except for $\pi^*_{Y_3}(y_2)$ (see Eqs. (5.5), (5.24), and (5.26)). The difference stems from the fact that while $\pi_{Y_3}(y_2)$ represents the total probability of all tail-extensions of $Y_2 = y_2$, $\pi^*_{Y_3}(y_2)$ represents the probability of only one such tail-extension, namely, the most probable one. The pointers $\overset{*}{\rightarrow}$ indicate the current commitments made on the basis of BEL^* (see Eq. (5.30)), which at this stage represent the default state $\{X_1 = X_2 = X_3 = 1\}$. Note, however, that the initial π^* values represent not just the currently accepted explanation, but a whole set of possible system behaviors, each one a best explanation for some possible future observation of the form $Y = y$ or $X = x$.

When nodes Y_3 and X_2 are instantiated (Figure 5.3b), they set up new $\pi^*-\lambda^*$ messages, which temporarily lead to suboptimal and inconsistent belief commitments, such as $\{X_1 = 1, Y_1 = 1, Y_2 = 0, X_3 = 1\}$ in Figure 5.3b and $\{X_1 = 1, Y_1 = 0, Y_2 = 0, X_3 = 1\}$ in Figure 5.3c. Eventually, however, all messages are absorbed at the peripheral nodes, and a new consistent explanation emerges, $\{X_1 = 0, Y_1 = 0, Y_2 = 0, X_3 = 1\}$, which also is globally optimal. Furthermore, the propagation process can be activated concurrently. It subsides in time proportional to the network diameter, and at equilibrium the belief committed to every proposition $X = x$ is consistent with the overall best explanation.

5.3 BELIEF REVISION IN SINGLY CONNECTED NETWORKS

Let W stand for the set of all variables considered, including those in e. Any assignment of values to the variables in W that is consistent with e will be called an *extension*, *explanation*, or *interpretation* of e. Our problem is to find an extension w^* that maximizes the conditional probability $P(w|e)$. In other words, $W = w^*$ is the *most-probable-explanation (MPE)* of the evidence at hand if

$$P(w^*|e) = \max_w P(w|e). \qquad (5.31)$$

The task of finding w^* will be performed locally, by letting each variable X compute the function

$$BEL^*(x) = \max_{w'_X} P(x, w'_X|e), \qquad (5.32)$$

where $W'_X = W - X$. Thus, $BEL^*(x)$ stands for the probability of the most probable extension of e that also is consistent with the hypothetical assignment $X = x$. Unlike $BEL(x)$, $BEL^*(x)$ need not sum to unity over x.

The propagation scheme presented in the next subsection is based on the following philosophy: For every value x of a singleton variable X, there is a best extension of the complementary variables W'_X. Because there are so many independence relationships embedded in the network, the problem of finding the best extension of $X = x$ can be decomposed into finding the best complementary extension to each of the neighboring variables, then using this information to choose the best value of X. This process of decomposition—which resembles the principle of optimality in dynamic programming—can be applied recursively until, at the network's periphery, we meet evidence variables whose values are predetermined, and the process halts.

5.3.1 Deriving the Propagation Rules

We consider again a fragment of a singly connected network, as in Figure 5.4, and denote by W_{XY}^+ and W_{XY}^- the subset of variables contained in the respective subgraphs G_{XY}^+ and G_{XY}^-. The removal of any node X would partition the network into the subgraphs G_X^+ and G_X^- containing two sets of variables (W_X^+ and W_X^-) and possibly two sets of evidence (e_X^+ and e_X^-, respectively).

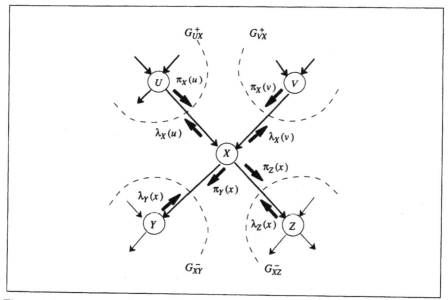

Figure 5.4. *Fragment of a singly connected network with multiple parents illustrating graph partitioning and message parameters.*

Using this notation, we can write

$$P(w^* \mid e) = \max_{x, w_X^+, w_X^-} P(w_X^+, w_X^-, x \mid e_X^+, e_X^-). \tag{5.33}$$

The conditional independence of W_X^+ and W_X^-, given X, and the entailments $e_X^+ \subseteq W_X^+$ and $e_X^- \subseteq W_X^-$, yield

$$P(w^* \mid e) = \max_{x, w_X^+, w_X^-} \frac{P(w_X^+, w_X^-, x)}{P(e_X^+, e_X^-)}$$

$$= \beta \max_{x, w_X^+, w_X^-} P(w_X^- \mid x) P(x \mid w_X^+) P(w_X^+), \tag{5.34}$$

where $\beta = [P(e_X^+, e_X^-)]^{-1}$ is a constant, independent of the uninstantiated variables in W and having no influence on the maximization in Eq. (5.34). From here on we will use the symbol β to represent any constant that need not be computed because it does not affect the choice of w^*.

Eq. (5.34) can be rewritten as a maximum, over x, of two factors:

$$P(w^* \mid e) = \beta \max_x [\max_{w_X^-} P(w_X^- \mid x)] [\max_{w_X^+} P(x \mid w_X^+) P(w_X^+)]$$

$$= \beta \max_x \lambda^*(x) \pi^*(x), \tag{5.35}$$

where

$$\lambda^*(x) = \max_{w_X^-} P(w_X^- \mid x) \tag{5.36}$$

and

$$\pi^*(x) = \max_{w_X^+} P(x, w_X^+). \tag{5.37}$$

Thus, if for each x an oracle could give us the MPE values of the variables in W_X^-, together with the MPE values of the variables in W_X^+, we would be able to determine the best value of X by computing $\lambda^*(x)$ and $\pi^*(x)$ and then maximizing their product, $\lambda^*(x) \pi^*(x)$.

We can express $\lambda^*(x)$ and $\pi^*(x)$ in such a way that they can be computed at node X from similar parameters available at X's neighbors. Writing

$$W_X^- = W_{XY}^- \cup W_{XZ}^- \qquad W_X^+ = W_{UX}^+ \cup W_{VX}^+$$
$$W_{U'X}^+ = W_{UX}^+ - U \qquad W_{V'X}^+ = W_{VX}^+ - V,$$

we obtain

$$\lambda^*(x) = \max_{w_{XY}^-} P(w_{XY}^- | x) \max_{w_{XZ}^-} P(w_{XZ}^- | x) = \lambda_Y^*(x)\lambda_Z^*(x) \tag{5.38}$$

and

$$\pi^*(x) = \max_{w_X^+} P(x, w_X^+),$$

$$= \max_{w_{UX}^+, w_{VX}^+} P(x, w_{UX}^+, w_{VX}^+)$$

$$= \max_{u, v, w_U^+, w_V^+} P(x, u, w_U^+, v, w_V^+)$$

$$= \max_{u, v, w_U^+, w_V^+} [P(x | u, v, w_U^+, w_V^+) P(u, v, w_U^+, w_V^+)]$$

$$= \max_{u, v, w_U^+, w_V^+} [P(x | u, v) P(u, v, w_U^+, w_V^+)]$$

$$= \max_{u, v} [P(x | u, v) \max_{w_{UX}^+} P(u, w_{UX}^+) \max_{w_{VX}^+} P(v, w_{VX}^+)]$$

(because U and W_{UX}^+ are independent of V and W_{VX}^+)

$$= \max_{u, v} P(x | u, v) \, \pi_X^*(u) \, \pi_X^*(v), \tag{5.39}$$

where $\lambda_Y^*(x)$ (and, correspondingly, $\lambda_Z^*(x)$) can be regarded as a message that a child Y sends to its parent X:

$$\lambda_Y^*(x) = \max_{w_{XY}^-} P(w_{XY}^- | x). \tag{5.40}$$

Similarly,

$$\pi_X^*(u) = \max_{w_{UX}^+} P(u, w_{UX}^+) \tag{5.41}$$

can be regarded as a message that a parent U sends to its child X. Note the similarities between λ^* (and π^*) and λ (and π) in Eqs. (4.47) and (4.48).

Clearly, if these λ^* and π^* messages are available to X, we can compute its best value x^* using Eqs. (5.35) through (5.37). What we must show now is that X, upon receiving these messages, can send back to its neighbors the appropriate $\lambda_X^*(u)$, $\lambda_X^*(v)$, $\pi_Y^*(x)$, and $\pi_Z^*(x)$ messages, while preserving their probabilistic definitions according to Eqs. (5.40) and (5.41).

UPDATING π^*

Rewriting Eq. (5.32) as

$$BEL^*(x) = P(x, w_X^{+*}, w_X^{-*} | e) \tag{5.42}$$

and using Eqs. (5.36) through (5.41), we have

$$BEL^*(x) = \beta\, \lambda^*(x)\, \pi^*(x)$$
$$= \beta\, \lambda_Y^*(x)\, \lambda_Z^*(x) \max_{u,v} P(x \mid u,\, v)\, \pi_X^*(u)\, \pi_X^*(v). \qquad (5.43)$$

Comparing this expression to the definition of $\pi_Y^*(x)$, we get

$$\pi_Y^*(x) = \max_{w_{X\cdot Y}^+} P(x,\, w_{X\cdot Y}^+) = \max_{w_X^+,\, w_{XZ}^-} P(x,\, w_X^+, w_{XZ}^-)$$
$$= \lambda_Z^*(x) \max_{u,v} P(x \mid u,\, v)\, \pi_X^*(u)\, \pi_X^*(v). \qquad (5.44)$$

Alternatively, $\pi_Y^*(x)$ can be obtained from $BEL^*(x)$ by setting $\lambda_Y^*(x) = 1$ for all x. Thus,

$$\pi_Y^*(x) = \beta\, BEL^*(x)\, \Big|_{\lambda_Y^*(x)=1} = \beta\, \frac{BEL^*(x)}{\lambda_Y^*(x)}. \qquad (5.45)$$

The division by $\lambda_Y^*(x)$ in Eq. (5.45) amounts to discounting the contribution of all variables in G_{XY}^-. Note that $\pi_Y^*(x)$, unlike $\pi_Y(x)$, need not sum to unity over x.

UPDATING λ^*

Starting with the definition

$$\lambda_X^*(u) = \max_{w_{\bar{U}X}^-} P(w_{\bar{U}X}^- \mid u), \qquad (5.46)$$

we partition $W_{\bar{U}X}^-$ into its constituents,

$$W_{\bar{U}X}^- = X \cup W_{\bar{X}Y}^- \cup W_{\bar{X}Z}^- \cup W_{\bar{V}\cdot X}^+ \cup V,$$

and obtain

$$\lambda_X^*(u) = \max_{x,\, w_{\bar{X}Y}^-,\, w_{\bar{X}Z}^-,\, w_{\bar{V}\cdot x}^+,\, v} P(x,\, w_{\bar{X}Y}^-,\, w_{\bar{X}Z}^-,\, v,\, w_{\bar{V}\cdot x}^+)$$

$$= \max_{x,v,w\text{'}s} P(w_{\bar{X}Y}^-,\, w_{\bar{X}Z}^- \mid w_{\bar{V}\cdot x}^+\, x,\, v,\, u)\, P(x,\, v,\, w_{\bar{V}\cdot x}^+ \mid u)$$

$$= \max_{x,v} [\lambda_Y^*(x)\, \lambda_Z^*(x)\, P(x \mid u,\, v) \max_{w_{\bar{V}\cdot x}^+} P(v,\, w_{\bar{V}\cdot x}^+ \mid u)].$$

Finally, using the marginal independence of U and W_{VX}^+, we have

$$\lambda_X^*(u) = \max_{x,v} [\lambda_Y^*(x) \, \lambda_Z^*(x) \, P(x \mid u, v) \, \pi_X^*(v)]. \qquad (5.47)$$

5.3.2 Summary of Propagation Rules

In general, if X has n parents, $U_1, U_2,..., U_n$, and m children, $Y_1, Y_2,..., Y_m$, then node X receives the messages $\pi_X^*(u_i)$, $i=1,..., n$ from its parents and $\lambda_{Y_j}^*(x)$, $j=1,..., m$ from its children.

$\pi_X^*(u_i)$ stands for the probability of the most probable tail-extension of the proposition $U_i = u_i$ relative to the link $U_i \rightarrow X$. This sub-extension is sometimes called an *explanation* or a *causal argument*.

$\lambda_{Y_j}^*(x)$ stands for the conditional probability of the most probable head-extension of the proposition $X = x$ relative to the link $X \rightarrow Y_j$. This sub-extension is sometimes called a *prognosis* or a *forecast*.

Using these $n+m$ messages together with the fixed probability $P(x \mid u_1, ..., u_n)$, X can identify its best value and further propagate these messages using the following three steps:

Step 1—Updating BEL^*: When node X is activated to update its parameters, it simultaneously inspects the $\pi_X^*(u_i)$ and $\lambda_{Y_j}^*(x)$ messages communicated by each of its parents and children and forms the product

$$F(x, u_1, ..., u_n) = \prod_{j=1}^{m} \lambda_{Y_j}^*(x) \, P(x \mid u_1, ..., u_n) \prod_{i=1}^{n} \pi_X^*(u_i). \qquad (5.48)$$

This F function enables X to compute its $BEL^*(x)$ function and simultaneously identify the best value x^* from the domain of X:

$$x^* = \max_x{}^{-1} BEL^*(x), \qquad (5.49)$$

where

$$BEL^*(x) = \beta \max_{u_k:1 \le k \le n} F(x, u_1,..., u_n) \qquad (5.50)$$

and β is a constant that is independent of x and need not be computed in practice.

Step 2—Updating λ^*: Using the F function computed in Step 1, node X computes the parent-bound messages by performing n vector maximizations, one for each parent:

$$\lambda_X^*(u_i) = \max_{x,\, u_k :\, k \neq i} [\, F(x,\, u_1,\, ...,\, u_n) \,/\, \pi_X^*(u_i) \,] \quad i = 1,...,\, n. \tag{5.51}$$

Step 3—Updating π^*: Using the $BEL^*(x)$ function computed in Step 1, node X computes the children-bound messages,

$$\pi_{Y_j}^*(x) = \beta\, \frac{BEL^*(x)}{\lambda_{Y_j}^*(x)}; \tag{5.52}$$

and posts these on the links to $Y_1,...,\, Y_m$.

These steps are identical to those governing belief updating (Eqs. (4.49) through (4.53)), with maximization replacing the summation. They can be viewed as tensor operations, using max for inner-product, i.e., $<AB>_{ik} = \max_{j} A_{ij} B_{jk}$; each outgoing message is computed by taking the max-inner-products of the tensor $P(x \mid u_1,..., u_n)$ with all incoming messages posted on the other links.†

The boundary conditions are identical to those of belief updating and are summarized below for the sake of completeness:

1. *Anticipatory node:* Representing an uninstantiated variable with no successors. For such a node X, we set $\lambda_{Y_j}^*(x) = (1,\, 1,...,\, 1)$.

2. *Evidence node:* Representing an instantiated variable. If variable X assumes the value x', we introduce a dummy child Z with

$$\lambda_Z^*(x) = \begin{cases} 1 & \text{if } x = x'. \\ 0 & \text{otherwise.} \end{cases}$$

This implies that if X has children, $Y_1,...,Y_m$, each child should receive the same message, $\pi_{Y_j}^*(x) = \lambda_Z^*(x)$, from X.

3. *Root node:* Representing a variable with no parents. For each root variable X, we introduce a dummy parent U, permanently instantiated to

---

† L. Booker, personal communication.

1, and set the conditional probability on the link $U \to X$ to the prior probability of X, i.e., $P(x \mid u) = P(x) = \pi^*(x)$.

These boundary conditions ensure that the messages defined in Eqs. (5.40) and (5.41) retain their correct semantics on peripheral nodes.

5.3.3 Reaching Equilibrium and Assembling a Composite Solution

To prove that the propagation process terminates, consider a parallel and autonomous control scheme whereby each processor is activated whenever any of its incoming messages changes value. Note that, since the network is singly connected, every path eventually must end at either a root node having a single child or a leaf node having a single parent. Such single-port nodes act as absorption barriers; updating messages received through these ports get absorbed and do not cause subsequent updating of the outgoing messages. Thus, the effect of each new piece of evidence subsides in time proportional to the longest path in the network.

To prove that at equilibrium, the selected x^* values indeed represent the most likely interpretation of the evidence at hand, we can reason by induction on the depth of the underlying tree, taking an arbitrary node X as the root. The λ^* or π^* messages emanating from each leaf node of such a tree certainly comply with Eqs. (5.40) and (5.41). Assuming that the λ^* (or π^*) messages at any node of depth k of the tree comply with their definitions of Eqs. (5.40) and (5.41), the derivation of Eqs. (5.42) through (5.47) guarantees that they will continue to comply at depth $k - 1$, and so on. Finally, at the root node, $\beta BEL^*(x^*)$ actually coincides with $P(w^* \mid e)$, as in Eq. (5.33), which means that $BEL^*(x)$ computed from Eq. (5.50) must give x the same rating as does $\max_{w'_x} P(x, w'_x \mid e)$ (see Eq. (5.32)). This proves that each local choice of x^* is part of some optimal extension w^*.

Had the choice of each x^* value been unique, the assembly of x^* values necessarily would constitute the (unique) most probable extension w^*. However, when several $X = x$ assignments yield the same optimal $BEL^*(x)$, a pointer system must be used to ensure that the tiebreaking rule is not arbitrary but coheres with choices made at neighboring nodes.

For example, in the circuit of Figure 5.1, had we assumed $q_1 = q_3 < \frac{1}{2}$, the optimal interpretations $\{X_1 = 1, X_3 = 0\}$ and $\{X_1 = 0, X_3 = 1\}$ would have been equally meritorious, yielding $BEL^*(X_3 = 0) = q_3 p_1 = BEL^*(X_3 = 1) = p_3 q_1$, as reflected in the $\pi^*(x_3)$ and $\lambda^*_{Y_3}(x_3)$ messages of Figure 5.3d; similarly, $BEL^*(X_1 = 0) = q_1 p_3 = BEL^*(X_1 = 1) = p_1 q_3$. Breaking the ties arbitrarily, in such cases, might result in choosing a suboptimal extension $\{X_1 = 0, X_3 = 0\}$, or even an inconsistent one $\{X_1 = 1, X_3 = 1\}$. To enforce a selection of values within the *same* optimal extension, local pointers should be saved to mark the neighbors' values at which the maximization is achieved. (In singly connected networks the relevant neighborhood consists of parents, children and spouses, i.e., parents of common children [see Chapter 3].) For example, in the maximization required for calculating $\lambda_{Y_3}^*(x_3)$ in Figure 5.3d we have (see Eq. (5.47))

$$\lambda_{Y_3}^*(x_3) = \max_{y_2, y_3} \lambda^*(y_3)\, P(y_3 \mid y_2, x_3)\, \pi_{Y_3}^*(y_2)$$

$$= \max_{y_2} \begin{cases} P(Y_3 = 0 \mid y_2, x_3)\, q_1 & \text{if } y_2 = 0 \\ P(Y_3 = 0 \mid y_2, x_3)\, p_1 & \text{if } y_2 = 1 \end{cases}$$

$$= \max_{y_2} \begin{cases} 1 \times q_1 & \text{if } y_2 = 0,\, x_3 = 0 \\ 1 \times q_1 & \text{if } y_2 = 0,\, x_3 = 1 \\ 1 \times p_1 & \text{if } y_2 = 1,\, x_3 = 0 \\ 0 \times p_1 & \text{if } y_2 = 1,\, x_3 = 1 \end{cases}$$

$$= \begin{cases} \max(q_1, p_1) = p_1 & \text{if } x_3 = 0 \quad (y_2^* = 1) \\ \max(0, q_1) = q_1 & \text{if } x_3 = 1 \quad (y_2^* = 0) \end{cases}$$

$$= (p_1, q_1) \quad \text{at} \quad y_2^* = (1, 0).$$

Establishing this correspondence between x_3 and y_2^* amounts to node Y_3 maintaining a pointer from $Y_2 = 1$ to $X_3 = 0$ and another pointer from $Y_2 = 0$ to $X_3 = 1$, to indicate that these two value pairs are compatible members of the same optimal extension.

When we face the choice of x_3^*, we compare the value of $BEL^*(x_3 = 0)$ with that of $BEL^*(x_3 = 1)$ and obtain the equality

$$BEL^*(x_3) = \lambda_{Y_3}^*(x_3)\, \pi^*(x_3) = (p_1 q_3, q_3 p_1) = p_1 q_3(1, 1).$$

However, the choice $x_3^* = 0$ must be accompanied by the choice $y_2^* = 1$, and the choice $x_3^* = 1$, by $y_2^* = 0$. By a similar analysis at node Y_1, such choices of y_2^* will be bound to the values of $x_1^* = 1$ and $x_1^* = 0$, respectively, thus ensuring that the choice $x_1^* = 1$ will always be accompanied by $x_3^* = 0$, and $x_1^* = 0$, by $x_3^* = 1$.

Having these pointers available at each node provides a simple mechanism for retrieving the overall optimal extension: we solve for x^* at some arbitrary node X and then recursively follow the pointers attached to x^*. Additionally, we can retrieve an optimal extension compatible with *any* instantiation (say, the second best) of some chosen variable Y and, by comparing the merits of several such extensions, can identify the globally second-best explanation [Geffner and Pearl 1987a]. Another use of the pointer mechanism is facilitating sensitivity analysis.

To determine the merit of testing an unknown variable, we can simply follow the links attached to each of its possible instantiations and examine the variable's impact on other propositions in the system.

5.3.4 Comparison to Belief Updating

The propagation procedure described in this section bears many similarities to that used in belief updating (Eqs. (4.49) through (4.53)). In both cases, coherent global equilibria are obtained by local computations in time proportional to the network's diameter. Additionally, the messages π^* and λ^* bear both formal and semantic similarities to their π and λ counterparts, and the local computations required for updating them are of roughly the same order of complexity.

There are, however, major differences between the two procedures. First, belief updating involves summation, whereas in belief revision, maximization is the dominant operation. Second, belief updating encounters more absorption centers than belief revision does. In the former process, every anticipatory node acts as an absorption barrier, blocking the passage of messages between its parents. This is clearly shown in Eq. (4.52); substituting $\lambda(x) = 1$ yields $\lambda_X(u) = 1$, which means that evidence in favor of one parent (V) has no bearing on another parent (U) as long as their common child (X) receives no evidential support ($\lambda(x) = 1$). This matches our intuition about how frames should interact; data about one frame (e.g., seismic data indicating an earthquake has occurred) should not evoke a change of belief in another unrelated frame (e.g., the possibility of a burglary in my home) merely because the two occurrences may give rise to a common consequence sometime in the future (e.g., triggering my burglar alarm). This frame-to-frame isolation does not hold for belief revision, as can be seen from Eq. (5.47). Even if $\lambda_Y^*(x) = \lambda_Z^*(x) = 1$, $\lambda_X^*(u)$ still is sensitive to $\pi_X^*(v)$.

Such endless frame-to-frame propagation raises psychological and computational problems. Psychologically, in an attempt to explain a given phenomenon, the mere act of imagining the likely consequences of the hypotheses at hand would conjure remotely related hypotheses that could also cause the imagined consequence. We *do not* ordinarily reason that way, though; in trying to explain the cause of a car accident, we do not raise the possibility of lung cancer merely because accidents and lung cancer both can lead to the same eventual consequence—death. Computationally, it appears that in large systems, the task of finding the most satisfactory explanation would require insurmountable effort; the propagation process would spread across loosely coupled frames until every variable in the system reexamined its selected value x^*.

These considerations, together with other epistemological issues (see Section 5.6), require that the set of variables w over which P is maximized be circumscribed in advance to a privileged set called *explanation corpus*. In addition to the evidence e, W should contain only those variables that are ancestors of e and have a significant impact on pending decisions. For example, if Y_2 is the only observed variable in Figure 5.1, then the explanation corpus will consist of $W = \{X_1, X_2, Y_2\}$; the variables X_3 and Y_3 will be excluded. If, in addition, X_1 and X_2 are outputs of two complex digital circuits and our only concern is to find out whether any of these circuits should be replaced, then the ancestors of X_1 and X_2 also should be excluded from W. In other words, if there is no practical utility in finding why a particular circuit is faulty, then it is both wasteful and erroneous to enter these ancestors into W (see Section 5.6).

Circumscribing an explanation corpus separates the variables in the system into two groups, W and its complement W'. The computation of w^* now involves both maximization over W and summation over W':

$$P(w^* \mid e) = \max_w P(w \mid e) = \max_w \sum_{w'} P(w \mid w', e)\, P(w' \mid e).$$

The propagation rules also should be mixed. Variables in W should follow the revision rules of Eqs. (5.48) through (5.52), while variables in W' should follow the updating rules of Eqs. (4.52) and (4.53). The interaction between the λ^*–π^* messages produced by W and the λ–π messages produced by W' should conform to the probabilistic semantics of these messages and will not be elaborated here.

5.3.5 Coping with Loops

When the network contains loops, i.e., cycles in the undirected network, the assumptions leading to the propagation equations (Eqs. (5.48) through (5.52)) are no longer valid, and one of the methods described in Section 4.4 should be employed, namely, *clustering, conditioning,* or *stochastic simulation.*

The adaptation of clustering to belief revision is straightforward; we form compound variables in such a way that the resulting network is singly connected, and then apply the propagation scheme of Section 5.3. The propagation rules for the clustered networks are identical to those derived in Eqs. (5.48) through (5.52).

An extreme example of clustering would be to represent all ancestors of the observed findings by a single compound variable. For example, if X_6 and X_4 are the observed variables in the network of Figure 5.5a, we can define the compound variable $Z = \{X_1, X_2, X_3, X_5\}$ and obtain the tree $X_4 \leftarrow Z \rightarrow X_6$. Assigning a value to the compound variable Z would constitute an explanation for the findings observed. Indeed, this is the approach taken by Cooper [1984] and by Peng and Reggia [1986]. Since finding the best explanation requires searching through the vast domain of possible values associated with the compound variable, admissible heuristic strategies had to be devised, similar to the A^* algorithm [Hart, Nilsson, and Raphael 1968]. Unfortunately, the complexity of such algorithms still is exponential [Pearl 1984], since they do not exploit the interdependencies among the variables in Z. Another disadvantage of this technique is the loss of conceptual flavor; the optimization procedure does not reflect familiar mental processes, so it is hard to construct meaningful arguments to defend the final conclusions. The join tree method discussed in Section 4.4.1 promises to overcome these shortcomings, especially in networks involving small loops.

The use of conditioning for belief revision is similar to the use discussed in Section 4.4.2. In Figure 5.5, for example, instantiating node X_1 to some value would block all pathways through X_1 and would render the rest of the network singly connected, amenable to the propagation technique of this section. Thus, if we wish to find the most likely interpretation of some evidence e, say $e = \{X_6 = 1\}$, we first assume $X_1 = 0$ (as in Figure 5.5b), propagate λ^* and π^* to find the best interpretation I_0 under this assumption, repeat the propagation to find the best interpretation I_1 under the assumption $X_1 = 1$ (as in Figure 5.5c), and finally, choose from the two interpretations the one with the highest probability. For example, if I_0 and I_1 are realized by the vectors

$$I_0 = (X_1 = 0, x_2^0, x_3^0, x_4^0, x_5^0) \quad \text{and} \tag{5.53}$$
$$I_1 = (X_1 = 1, x_2^1, x_3^1, x_4^1, x_5^1),$$

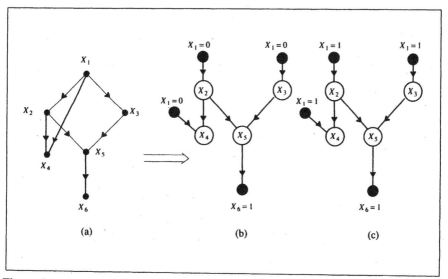

Figure 5.5. *Instantiating variable X_1 renders the network in (a) singly connected.*

then the best interpretation is determined by comparing the two products

$$P(I_0 \mid e) = \alpha P(X_6 = 1 \mid x_5^0) P(x_5^0 \mid x_2^0, x_3^0) P(x_4^0 \mid X_1 = 0, x_2^0)$$
$$P(x_3^0 \mid X_1 = 0) P(x_2^0 \mid X_1 = 0) P(X_1 = 0)$$

and

$$P(I_1 \mid e) = \alpha\, P(X_6 = 1 \mid x_5^1)\, P(x_5^1 \mid x_2^1, x_3^1)\, P(x_4^1 \mid X_1 = 1, x_2^1)$$
$$P(x_3^1 \mid X_1 = 1)\, P(x_2^1 \mid X_1 = 1)\, P(X_1 = 1),$$

where $\alpha = [P(e)]^{-1}$ is a constant. Since all the factors in the above product are available from the initial specification of the links' probabilities, the comparison can be conducted with simple computations.

Such globally supervised comparisons of products are the basic computational steps used in the search methods of Peng and Reggia [1986] and Cooper [1984]. However, we use them to compare only two candidates from the space of 2^5 possible value combinations. Most of the interpretation work is conducted by local propagation, selecting the appropriate match for each of the two assumptions $X_1 = 0$ and $X_1 = 1$. Thus, we see that even in multiply connected networks, local propagation provides a computationally effective and conceptually meaningful method of trimming the space of interpretations to a manageable size.

The effectiveness of conditioning depends heavily on the topological properties of the network. Since the amount of time each propagation phase takes varies linearly with the number of variables in the system (n), the overall worst-case complexity of the optimal interpretation problem is exponential with the size of the cycle cutset that we can identify. Identical complexity considerations apply to the task of belief updating (see Chapter 4), so finding the globally best explanation is no more complex than finding the degree of belief for any individual proposition.

A third method of sidestepping the loop problem is by using stochastic simulation, which amounts to generating a random sample of scenarios agreeing with the evidence, then selecting the most probable scenario from that sample. This is accomplished in distributed fashion by having each processor inspect the current state of its neighbors, compute the belief distribution of its host variable, and then randomly select one value from that distribution. The most likely interpretation is then found by identifying either the global state that has been selected most frequently or the one possessing the highest joint probability— which is computed by taking the product of n conditional probabilities, as in Eq. (3.28). Simulated-annealing methods can also be used to speed up the process of reaching the optimal state [Kirkpatrick, Gelatt, and Vechi 1983].

It is important to reemphasize that the difficulties associated with loops are not unique to probabilistic formulations but are inherent to any problem in which globally defined solutions are produced by local computations, whether the formulation is probabilistic, deterministic, logical, numerical, or a hybrid thereof. Identical computational issues arise in the Dempster-Shafer formalism [Shenoy and Shafer 1986], in constraint satisfaction problems [Dechter and Pearl 1985, 1987a], and in truth maintenance [Doyle 1979; de Kleer and Williams 1986], database management [Beeri et al. 1983], matrix inversion [Tarjan 1976], and distributed optimization [Barbosa 1986]. The importance of network representation is that it reveals the common core of these difficulties and provides an abstraction that encourages the exchange of solution strategies across domains.

5.4 DIAGNOSIS OF SYSTEMS WITH MULTIPLE FAULTS

5.4.1 An Example: Electronic Circuit

To illustrate the belief revision scheme, we will consider in detail an example treated by de Kleer and Williams [1986], Davis [1984], and Genesereth [1984]. The problem is, given the digital circuit depicted in Figure 5.6, to find the set of malfunctioning components that are most likely to have caused the observed behavior: $F = 10, G = 12$.

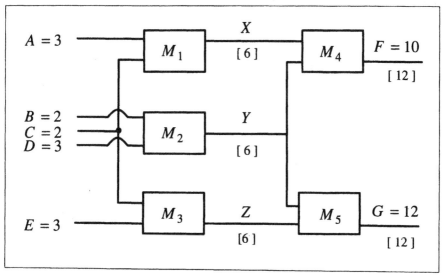

Figure 5.6. *A circuit containing three multipliers, M_1, M_2, and M_3, and two adders, M_4 and M_5.*

The causal network corresponding to this circuit is shown in Figure 5.7. The nodes of this network represent both observable points and the status of components. The circuit components appear as root variables constraining the relationship between input and output.

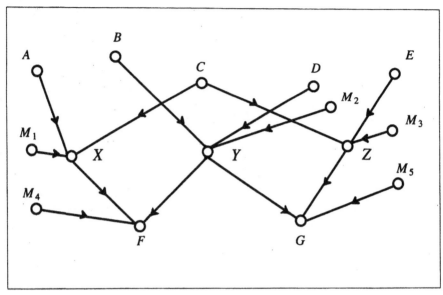

Figure 5.7. *The causal network representing the circuit of Figure 5.6.*

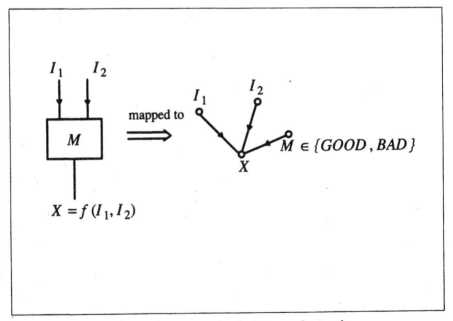

Figure 5.8. *The mapping used to convert circuits into causal networks.*

The link probabilities for the mapped circuit fragments depicted in Figure 5.8 are given by

$$P(x \mid I_1, I_2, M) = \begin{cases} 1 & \text{if } M = GOOD \text{ and } x = f(I_1, I_2) \\ 0 & \text{if } M = GOOD \text{ and } x \neq f(I_1, I_2) \\ \dfrac{1}{R_X} & \text{if } M = BAD \text{ and } x \text{ any value,} \end{cases} \quad \textbf{(5.54)}$$

where R_X is a constant representing the range of possible values of X, and f stands for the function computed by M.† This mapping conforms to the assumption normally made in circuit diagnosis that good behavior does not guarantee good components [de Kleer and Williams 1986].

5.4.2 Initialization

Initially, the value of the input is known, and no other observation has been made. Therefore, for every input $I \in \{A, B, C, D, E\}$ we have

$$\pi^*(I = \text{measured value}) = 1$$
$$\pi^*(I \neq \text{measured value}) = 0.$$

The status of the components is not known, but we assume a priori that

$$\pi^*(M_i = BAD) = q_i \quad \textbf{(5.55)}$$

and

$$\pi^*(M_i = GOOD) = q_i = 1 - q_i,$$

where q_i is some small value representing the prior probability of failure of the i-th component and p_i is simply an abbreviation for $1 - q_i$.

For the purpose of this example, we shall make the reasonable assumption that components of the same type have the same prior probability of failure, while the probability of failure for multipliers is greater than for adders. In other words, we assume that

$$q_1 = q_2 = q_3 > q_4 = q_5$$

and

$$R_X = R_Y = R_Z = R_F = R_G > 1 . \quad \textbf{(5.56)}$$

---

† In this example we use capital letters both for variable names and for variable values, writing $P(x \mid I_1, I_2, M)$ instead of $P(x \mid i_1, i_2, m)$, to facilitate a closer correspondence between the formulas and the diagrams.

We start by propagating downward the effects of the prior probabilities (with the arbitrary choice of $\lambda^* = 1$). For example, $\pi^*(x)$ is computed from Eq. (5.52):

$$\pi^*(x) = \max_{A,C,M_1} P(x \mid A, C, M_1) \, \pi_X^*(A) \, \pi_X^*(C) \, \pi_X^*(M_1). \tag{5.57}$$

Since A and C are fixed at $(A = 3, C = 2)$, $\pi^*(x)$ can be rewritten as

$$\pi^*(x) = \max_{M_1} P(x \mid A = 3, C = 2, M_1) \, \pi^*(A = 3) \, \pi^*(C = 2) \, \pi^*(M_1), \tag{5.58}$$

wherein we have replaced the π_X^* with π^*. For $x = 6$, assuming $p_1 >> q_1 / R_X$, the maximum is achieved with $M_1 = GOOD$. For $x \neq 6$, the maximum is achieved with $M_1 = BAD$, because according to the link probabilities, it is impossible to have a multiplier working correctly with inputs 3 and 2 and not have output of 6.

Using similar arguments, we compute the following parameters:

$$\pi^*(x) = \begin{cases} p_1 & x = 6 \\ q_1 / R_X & x \neq 6, \end{cases}$$

$$\pi^*(y) = \begin{cases} p_2 & y = 6 \\ q_2 / R_Y & y \neq 6, \end{cases}$$

$$\pi^*(z) = \begin{cases} p_3 & z = 6 \\ q_3 / R_Z & z \neq 6. \end{cases} \tag{5.59}$$

The rest of the messages are computed as follows. Since F and G are anticipatory nodes, we have

$$\lambda^*(F_i) = \lambda^*(G_i) = 1,$$

where F_i and G_i range over all possible values of F and G, respectively.

The message $\lambda_G^*(y)$ can be computed from Eq. (5.51):

$$\lambda_G^*(y) = \max_{G,z,M_5} P(G \mid y, z, M_5) \, \pi_G^*(M_5) \, \pi_G^*(z).$$

Regardless of the value of y, the maximum will always be achieved by choosing $G = y + z$, $z = 6$ and $M_5 = GOOD$. This yields

$$\lambda_G^*(y) = p_5 \, p_3,$$

which is equivalent to

$$\lambda_G^*(y_i) = 1,$$

for y_i ranging over all the possible values of y. The same holds for $\lambda_G^*(z)$, $\lambda_F^*(y)$, and $\lambda_F^*(x)$.

Returning to the top-down propagation, we can now compute $\pi^*(F)$:

$$\pi^*(F=12) = \max_{x,y,M_4} P(F=12 \mid x,y,M_4)\, \pi_F^*(x)\, \pi_F^*(y)\, \pi_F^*(M_4)$$

$$= \max_{x,y,M_4} P(F=12 \mid x,y,M_4)\, \pi^*(x)\, \pi^*(y)\, \lambda_G^*(y)\, \pi^*(M_4), \qquad (5.60)$$

where all the parameters are known. The maximum occurs at the normal-operation values of X, Y, and M_4 :

$$\pi^*(F=12) = P(F=12 \mid x=6, y=6, M_4=GOOD)\, \pi^*(x=6)\, \pi^*(y=6)\, \pi^*(M_4=GOOD)$$

$$= p_1\, p_2\, p_4.$$

For $F \neq 12$ we get

$$\pi^*(F \neq 12) = \max \left[p_1\, \frac{q_2}{R_Y}\, p_4 \,,\; \frac{q_1}{R_X}\, p_2\, p_4 \,,\, p_1\, p_2\, \frac{q_4}{R_F} \right], \qquad (5.61)$$

where the three alternatives correspond to the failure of M_2, M_1, and M_4, respectively. Since we are assuming $q_4 < q_1 = q_2$ and $R_X = R_Y = R_F$, we can eliminate the third alternative. A similar procedure is used to compute $\pi^*(G)$. To find out which extension is the best at this point, we compute $BEL^*(s)$ for each variable S and select the value s^* at which $BEL^*(s)$ peaks.† Of course, if there is no observed failure, the answer will be that all components are operating properly.

5.4.3 Fault Interpretation

Once the first two tests are made, finding $F = 10$ and $G = 12$, new messages begin to propagate concurrently along the links. For simplicity, we will follow only those messages that will affect the labeling of M_4, i.e., those passing through the path darkened in Figure 5.9. The message $\lambda_G^*(y)$ is computed from

$$\lambda_G^*(y) = \max_{M_5,\, z} P(G = 12 \mid y,\, z,\, M_5)\, \pi_G^*(z)\, \pi_G^*(M_5).$$

---

† For ways of dealing with multiple solutions, see Section 5.3.3.

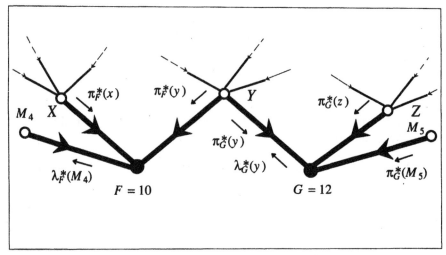

Figure 5.9. *Messages affecting the labeling of M_4, after G and F are observed.*

For $y = 6$, the maximum is achieved at $z = 6$ and $M_5 = GOOD$, so

$$\lambda_G^*(y = 6) = p_3\, p_5 .$$

If $y \neq 6$, then $z \neq 6$ or $M_5 = BAD$. Since $\pi_G^*(z \neq 6) = q_3$, $\pi_G^*\,(M_5 = BAD) = q_5$, and $q_3 > q_5$, we get

$$\lambda_G^*(y \neq 6) = q_3\, p_5 .$$

Now Y computes messages for its neighbors and sends to F the message $\pi_F^*(y)$, computed as

$$\pi_F^*(y) = \pi^*(y)\, \lambda_G^*(y).$$

The message that M_4 receives is computed from

$$\lambda_F^*(M_4) = \max_{x,\, y}\ P(F = 10 \mid x, y, M_4)\ \pi_F^*(x)\ \pi_F^*(y)$$

$$= \max_{x,\, y}\ P(F = 10 \mid x, y, M_4)\ \pi^*(x)\ \pi^*(y)\ \lambda_G^*(y).$$

For $M_4 = GOOD$, the maximum must occur when $x = 4$ and $y = 6$, or when $x = 6$ and $y = 4$. In other words,

$$\lambda_F^*(M_4 = GOOD) = \max \{\pi^*(x = 4) \, \pi^*(y = 6) \, \lambda_G^*(y = 6),$$

$$\pi^*(x = 6) \, \pi^*(y = 4) \, \lambda_G^*(y = 4) \}$$

$$= \max \left[\frac{q_1}{R_X} p_2 p_3 p_5 , p_1 \frac{q_2 q_3}{R_Y R_Z} p_5 \right]$$

which, under the assumptions in Eq. (5.56), becomes

$$\lambda_F^*(M_4 = GOOD) = \frac{q_1}{R_X} p_2 p_3 p_5 . \tag{5.62}$$

This reflects the fact that the most likely interpretation under $M_4 = GOOD$ pegs M_1 as the only faulty component.

For $M_4 = BAD$, the maximum is achieved with $x = y = 6$, resulting in

$$\lambda_F^*(M_4 = BAD) = \frac{1}{R_F} p_1 p_2 p_3 p_5 ,$$

since $M_4 = BAD$ explains the observed behavior by itself.

At this point, we can compute $BEL^*(M_4)$ to find M_4^*, i.e., the most probable status of M_4:

$$BEL^*(M_4) = [BEL^*(M_4 = GOOD), BEL^*(M_4 = BAD)]$$

$$= \beta [\lambda^*(M_4 = GOOD) \, \pi^*(M_4 = GOOD),$$

$$\lambda^*(M_4 = BAD) \, \pi^*(M_4 = BAD)], \tag{5.63}$$

so

$$M_4^* = \max_{M_4}^{-1} BEL^*(M_4)$$

$$= \max_{M_4}^{-1} \begin{cases} \dfrac{q_1}{R_X} p_2 p_3 p_4 p_5 & \text{if } M_4 = GOOD \\[2mm] \dfrac{q_4}{R_F} p_1 p_2 p_3 p_5 & \text{if } M_4 = BAD \end{cases}$$

$$= GOOD, \tag{5.64}$$

since q_1 was assumed to be greater than q_4.

Even at this early stage of the propagation, we already can label M_4 as *GOOD* and be confident that this label will remain part of the globally optimal solution. Apparently, the λ^* message arriving at M_4 already contains information (gathered during the initialization phase) that is sufficient to alert M_4 to the existence of a more likely culprit—the multiplier M_1.

Pursuing the propagation through the rest of the network, the optimal status of all the other components is determined. The resulting pattern of messages for all component nodes is depicted in the four leftmost columns of Figure 5.10. The

component status s	$\pi^*(s)$ priors	$\lambda^*(s)$ after observing $F=10$ and $G=12$	optimal label	$\lambda^*(s)$ after observing $F=10$, $G=12$, $X=6$, $Y=4$, and $Z=6$	optimal label
$M_1 = GOOD$	p_1	$\dfrac{q_4}{R_F} p_2 p_3 p_5$	$M_1^* = BAD$	$\dfrac{q_2 q_5}{R_Y R_G} p_3 p_4$	$M_1^* = GOOD$
$M_1 = BAD$	q_1	$\dfrac{1}{R_X} p_2 p_3 p_5$		$\dfrac{1}{R_X} \dfrac{q_2}{R_Y} \dfrac{q_5}{R_G} p_3 p_4$	
$M_2 = GOOD$	p_2	$\dfrac{q_1}{R_X} p_3 p_4 p_5$	$M_2^* = GOOD$	0	$M_2^* = BAD$
$M_2 = BAD$	q_2	$\dfrac{1}{R_Y} \dfrac{q_3}{R_Z} p_1 p_4 p_5$		1	
$M_3 = GOOD$	p_3	$\dfrac{q_1}{R_X} p_2 p_4 p_5$	$M_3^* = GOOD$	$\dfrac{q_2 q_5}{R_Y R_G} p_1 p_4$	$M_3^* = GOOD$
$M_3 = BAD$	q_3	$\dfrac{1}{R_Z} \dfrac{q_2}{R_Y} p_1 p_4 p_5$		$\dfrac{1}{R_Z} \dfrac{q_2 q_5}{R_Y R_G} p_1 p_4$	
$M_4 = GOOD$	p_4	$\dfrac{q_1}{R_X} p_2 p_3 p_5$	$M_4^* = GOOD$	$\dfrac{q_2 q_5}{R_Y R_G} p_1 p_3$	$M_4^* = GOOD$
$M_4 = BAD$	q_4	$\dfrac{1}{R_F} p_1 p_2 p_3 p_5$		$\dfrac{1}{R_F} \dfrac{q_2 q_5}{R_Y R_G} p_1 p_3$	
$M_5^* = GOOD$	p_5	$\dfrac{q_1}{R_X} p_2 p_3 p_4$	$M_5^* = GOOD$	0	$M_5^* = BAD$
$M_5 = BAD$	q_5	$\dfrac{1}{R_G} \dfrac{q_2}{R_Y} p_1 p_3 p_4$		1	

Figure 5.10. *The pattern of final messages at component nodes.*

optimal status of any component node is determined by simply comparing the $\lambda^* \cdot \pi^*$ product for each of its possible statuses. For example, to determine the optimal status of M_1, we compare the product $\dfrac{q_4}{R_F} p_2 p_3 p_5 p_1$ with $\dfrac{1}{R_X} p_2 p_3 p_4 p_5 q_1$ and conclude that M_1^*, the optimal status of M_1, is *BAD*, since the first term is greater than the second under the current assumptions about P and R.

For the sake of completeness, the fifth column of Figure 5.10 shows the λ^* messages resulting from the additional observations $X = 6$, $Y = 4$, and $Z = 6$. The π^* messages do not change. The reader may verify that with the new information, the best diagnosis establishes with certainty that components M_2 and M_5 are faulty.

5.4.4 Finding the Second-Best Interpretation

The parameters computed by the propagation process enable us to associate with every instantiation $X = x$ of any node X, a tree that encodes the best interpretation of the observations, consistent with that instantiation. The instantiation $X = x$ is also associated with a weight, $BEL^*(x)$, which stands for the probability of its best interpretation. As we suggested in the previous section, when a new measurement $Z = z$ is obtained, we can immediately obtain the best interpretation that accounts for the new enhanced set of observations, simply by retrieving the interpretation associated with the pointer structure rooted at $Z = z$. To assess that interpretation, we need not examine the messages that eventually emanate from Z; these are used only for updating the rest of the network to prepare it for accommodating future findings.

The first question that arises is whether the system can retrieve multiple optimal interpretations, i.e., multiple extensions with the same maximum weight. This can be accomplished in a straightforward way, as described in Section 5.3.3: While performing the maximizations for computing the messages, save pointers indicating all values at which the maximum is achieved. Subsequently, before committing to optimal labels, follow the pointers to ensure that the labels are consistent with the labels of the neighbors.

A second question of interest is whether other useful interpretations can be retrieved from the pointer structures stored in the network. We already have seen that this net contains all those interpretations that are optimal relative to individual node instantiations. It follows that every second-best interpretation also is retrievable, because each such interpretation constitutes the best extension of some variable that has a different value than it had in the best configuration.

For instance, given the observations of F and G in Figure 5.6, the best interpretation is $\{M_1 = BAD\}$, while the second-best is $\{M_4 = BAD\}$. These interpretations correspond to the pointer structures rooted at $M_1 = BAD$ and

$M_4 = BAD$, respectively. The root $M_4 = BAD$ is identified by selecting the proposition with the second highest BEL^* value, after $BEL^*(M_1 = BAD)$. In fact, a third-best interpretation, $\{M_2 = M_5 = BAD\}$, also is retrievable, either from $M_2 = BAD$ or from $M_5 = BAD$, but in general, it is not guaranteed that interpretations beyond the second-best will be retrievable. Indeed, another third-best interpretation, $\{M_1 = M_4 = BAD\}$, will not be retrievable, since it is the best extension of neither $M_1 = BAD$ nor $M_4 = BAD$. This interpretation, however, is nonminimal, because each of its two proper subsets perfectly explains the circuit behavior.

Notice that while the process for selecting an overall best interpretation is local (simply selecting the pointer structure rooted at the last observation), the retrieval of a second-best interpretation is not. It requires that we maintain a table storing the second-best value of each variable; then, when the "entry point" of a second-best interpretation is sought, the highest $BEL^*(\cdot)$ is looked up in the table, and its associated link is found.

5.5 APPLICATION TO MEDICAL DIAGNOSIS

The computational effectiveness of the propagation scheme developed in Section 5.3 becomes especially important when applied to nondeterministic systems, such as those used in medical diagnosis. Deterministic systems like the circuit analyzed in Section 5.4 can be diagnosed using set-covering [Reggia, Nau, and Wang 1983] or truth-maintenance [deKleer and Williams 1986] techniques. These identify sets of faults that are *minimal*, i.e., that contain no proper subset of faults that explain equally well the symptoms observed. Minimality helps limit the search to explanations that are not subsumed by others. However, when the system itself is nondeterministic, the notion of minimality is no longer helpful, because it is often possible to improve a given diagnosis by postulating a larger set of faults—the extent to which a diagnosis explains or "covers" a set of symptoms is a matter of degree.

Systems that take into account both probabilistic information about fault likelihood and uncertainty about system behavior and still return an optimal (most likely) diagnosis require substantially more computation [Cooper 1984; Peng and Reggia 1986]. Such systems normally employ a branch-and-bound search algorithm which often runs in exponential time and overlooks structural properties of the diagnosed system that could make the search significantly faster, if not superfluous. Also, though the outcome is globally optimal, it is hard to justify in meaningful terms because the global process of searching for that outcome is very different from the local mental process exercised by human diagnosticians.

To illustrate the effectiveness of message-passing schemes, let us reconsider the medical diagnosis example treated in Section 4.5.3.

5.5.1 The Causal Model

Consider the network of Figure 5.11, where the nodes at the top row, $\{D_1, D_2, D_3, D_4\}$, represent four hypothetical diseases, and the nodes at the bottom row, $\{M_1, M_2, M_3, M_4\}$, represent four manifestations (or symptoms) of those diseases. The numerical parameters shown on the links of Figure 5.11 represent the strengths of causal connections between diseases and symptoms:

$$c_{ij} = P(M_i \ observed \mid Only \ D_j \ present). \qquad (5.65)$$

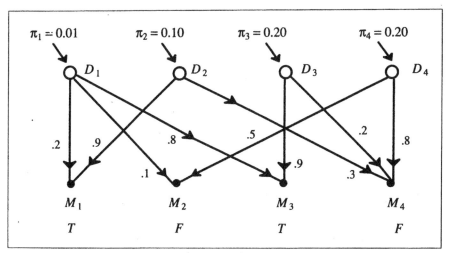

Figure 5.11. *A network representing causal relations between four diseases and four manifestations. The link parameters, c_{ij}, measure the strengths of causal connection.*

All four diseases are assumed to be independent. Their prior probabilities, $\pi_i = P(D_i = TRUE)$, are shown in Figure 5.11. When several diseases give rise to the same symptom, their combined effect is assumed to be governed by the noisy-OR-gate model analyzed in Section 4.3.2.

Given this model, we imagine a patient exhibiting the symptom set $\{M_1, M_3\}$ but not $\{M_2, M_4\}$. Our task is to find the disease combination that best explains the observed findings, namely, to find the *TRUE-FALSE* assignment for the variables D_1, D_2, D_3, and D_4 that constitutes the most probable extension of the evidence

$$e = \{M_1 = TRUE, M_2 = FALSE, M_3 = TRUE, M_4 = FALSE\}.$$

Let D_i and M_j denote the propositional variables associated with disease D_i and manifestation M_j, respectively; each may assume a *TRUE* or *FALSE* value.

For each propositional variable X, we let $+x$ and $\neg x$ denote the propositions $X = TRUE$ and $X = FALSE$, respectively. For example,

$$P(\neg m_j \mid +d_j) \triangleq P(M_j = FALSE \mid D_i = TRUE)$$

would stand for the probability that a patient with disease D_i will *not* develop symptom M_j.

Let X stand for some manifestation variable and let $\{U_1, ..., U_n\}$ represent its parents' set. The combined parent-to-child relationship $P(x \mid u_1, \ldots, u_n)$ is determined by the set of parameters c_{iX} on the individual links, as in Eq. (4.54). So,

$$P(\neg x \mid u_1, ..., u_n) = \prod_{i \in I_T} q_{iX} \qquad (5.66)$$

and

$$P(+x \mid u_1, ..., u_n) = 1 - \prod_{i \in I_T} q_{iX}, \qquad (5.67)$$

where

$$q_{iX} = 1 - c_{iX} \qquad (5.68)$$

and

$$I_T = \{i : U_i = TRUE\}. \qquad (5.69)$$

Substituting in Eq. (5.48), the function $F(x, u_1, ..., u_n)$ attains the form

$$F(+x, u_1, ..., u_n) = \left[1 - \prod_{i \in I_T} q_{iX}\right] \prod_{j=1}^{m} \lambda^*_{Y_j}(+x) \prod_{i=1}^{n} \pi^*_X(u_i), \qquad (5.70)$$

$$F(\neg x, u_1, ..., u_n) = \prod_{i \in I_T} q_{iX} \prod_{j=1}^{m} \lambda^*_{Y_j}(\neg x) \prod_{i=1}^{n} \pi^*_X(u_i). \qquad (5.71)$$

These product forms permit the calculation of the $\pi^* - \lambda^*$ messages according to Eqs. (5.49) through (5.52). In particular, for every negatively instantiated symptom node X we have

$$\frac{\lambda^*_X(+u_i)}{\lambda^*_X(\neg u_i)} = q_{iX}, \qquad (5.72)$$

independently of $\pi^*_X(u_k)$, for all $k \neq i$. For every disease node X, where $P(x \mid u_1, ..., u_n)$ coincides with the prior probability $\pi(x)$, Eq. (5.44) yields

$$\pi^*_{Y_j}(x) = \pi(x) \prod_{k \neq j} \lambda^*_{Y_k}(x). \qquad (5.73)$$

5.5.2 Message Propagation

For convenience, let us adopt the following notation:

$$\lambda_{ji} = \lambda^*_{M_j}(+d_i) / \lambda^*_{M_j}(\neg d_i), \tag{5.74}$$

$$\pi_{ij} = \pi^*_{M_j}(+d_i) / \pi^*_{M_j}(\neg d_i). \tag{5.75}$$

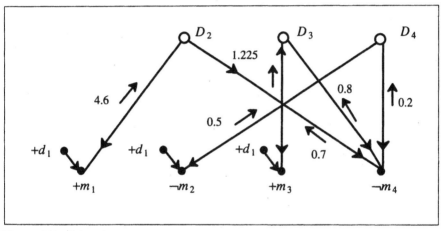

Figure 5.12. λ^* *messages after instantiating D_1 and all four symptoms.*

The network in Figure 5.11 becomes singly connected† upon the instantiation of D_1. We shall first instantiate D_1 to *TRUE*, find its best extension, and then repeat the process under the assumption $D_1 = FALSE$. Figure 5.12 shows the initial messages posted by the instantiated variables $\{+d_1, e\}$:

$$\lambda_{12} = (1 - q_{11}q_{21}) / (1 - q_{11}) = (1 - 0.8\,0.1) / (1 - 0.8) = 4.6,$$

$$\lambda_{33} = (1 - q_{13}q_{33}) / (1 - q_{13}) = (1 - 0.2\,0.1) / (1 - 0.2) = 1.225,$$

$$\lambda_{24} = q_{42} = 0.5, \qquad \lambda_{43} = q_{34} = 0.8,$$

$$\lambda_{44} = q_{44} = 0.2, \qquad \lambda_{42} = q_{24} = 0.7.$$

---

† Our particular pattern of evidence renders the network virtually singly connected, because all loops are blocked at M_2 and M_4. Conditioning on D_1 is done for illustrative purposes only.

The last four values are direct consequences of Eq. (5.72).

At the second phase, each D_i processor inspects the λ^* messages posted on its links and performs the operation specified in Eq. (5.73). This leads to the message distribution shown in Figure 5.13, with

$$\pi_{24} = \pi_2\lambda_{12} / (1 - \pi_2) = 0.511, \qquad \pi_{21} = \pi_2\lambda_{42} / (1 - \pi_2) = 0.077,$$

$$\pi_{34} = \pi_3\lambda_{33} / (1 - \pi_3) = 0.305, \qquad \pi_{33} = \pi_3\lambda_{43} / (1 - \pi_3) = 0.200,$$

$$\pi_{44} = \pi_4\lambda_{24} / (1 - \pi_4) = 0.125, \qquad \pi_{42} = \pi_4\lambda_{44} / (1 - \pi_4) = 0.050.$$

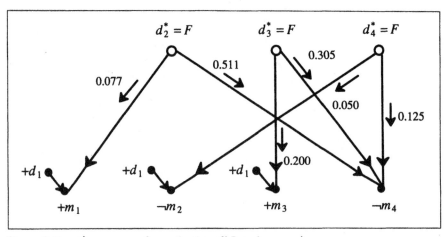

Figure 5.13. π^* *messages after activating all D nodes.*

The x^* value chosen by each of the D_i processors is *FALSE* (see Eq. (5.49)), because for each $i = 2, 3, 4$ we have

$$\frac{BEL^*(+d_i)}{BEL^*(\neg d_i)} = \prod_{j=1}^{4} \lambda_{ji} \frac{\pi_i}{1 - \pi_i} < 1.$$

For example, processor D_2 receives $\lambda_{12} = 4.6$ and $\lambda_{42} = 0.7$, so

$$\frac{BEL^*(+d_2)}{BEL^*(\neg d_2)} = \frac{\lambda_{12} \cdot \lambda_{42} \cdot \pi_2}{(1 - \pi_2)} = \frac{4.6 \cdot 0.7 \cdot 0.1}{0.9} = 0.358 < 1. \qquad (5.76)$$

The messages π_{21}, π_{33}, and π_{42} eventually will be absorbed at node D_1, while π_{24}, π_{34}, and π_{44} are now posted on the ports entering node M_4. Since M_4 is instantiated to $\neg m_4$, the λ^* messages generated by M_4 during the next activation phase remain unchanged (Figure 5.14), and the process halts with the current w^* values: $D_2 = D_3 = D_4 = FALSE$.

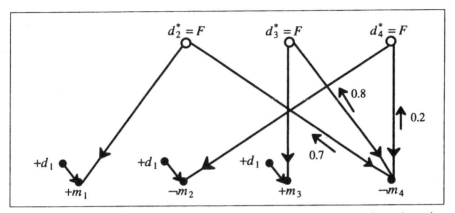

Figure 5.14. λ^* *messages after activating* M_4. *The best explanation is* $d_2^* = d_3^* = d_4^* =$ *FALSE.*

Let us now retract the assumption $D_1 = TRUE$ and posit the converse, $D_1 = FALSE$. The messages $\pi_{11} = \pi_{12} = \pi_{13} = 0$ are posted on all links emanating from node D_1 and are translated to $\lambda_{12} = \infty$, $\lambda_{33} = \infty$, and $\lambda_{24} = q_{42} = .5$. This means D_2 and D_3 will switch simultaneously and permanently to $TRUE$, while D_4, by virtue of

$$\frac{BEL^*(+d_4)}{BEL^*(\neg d_4)} = \lambda_{24} \cdot \lambda_{44} \cdot \pi_4 / (1 - \pi_4) \tag{5.77}$$

$$= 0.50 \cdot 0.20 \cdot 0.20 / 0.80 = .025 < 1,$$

tentatively remains *FALSE*, as illustrated in Figure 5.15.

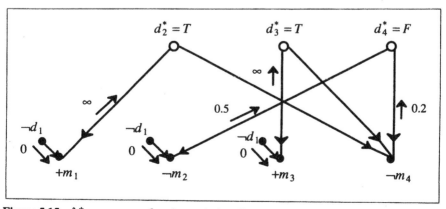

Figure 5.15. λ^* *messages after instantiating* D_1 *to FALSE. The best explanation is* $\{d_2^* = d_3^* = TRUE, d_4^* = FALSE\}$.

During the next activation phase (Figure 5.16), D_2 and D_3 post the messages $\pi_{24} = \pi_{34} = \infty$, which M_4 inspects for possible updating of λ_{44}. These new messages will not cause any change in λ_{44} because, according to Eqs. (5.51) and (5.66), the ratio λ_{44} remains

$$\lambda_{44} = \frac{P(\neg m_4 \mid +d_4, d_2, d_3)}{P(\neg m_4 \mid \neg d_4, d_2, d_3)} = q_{44},$$

independently of π_{24} and π_{34}. Thus, under the current premise $\neg d_1$, the best interpretation of the observed symptoms is $\{+d_2, +d_3, \neg d_4\}$, which, in view of the network topology, is to be expected.

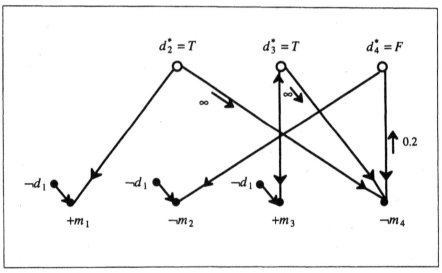

Figure 5.16. *Message profile after activating M_4. The best explanation remains* $\{d_2^* = d_3^* = TRUE, d_4^* = FALSE\}$.

5.5.3 Choosing the Best Interpretation

We have seen that the assumption $+d_1$ yields the interpretation $\{\neg d_2, \neg d_3, \neg d_4\}$, while $\neg d_1$ yields $\{+d_2, +d_3, \neg d_4\}$. Now we must decide which of the two interpretations is more plausible, i.e., which has the highest posterior probability given the evidence at hand, $e = \{+m_1, \neg m_2, +m_3, \neg m_4\}$. A direct way to decide between the two candidates is to calculate the two posterior probabilities, $P(I^+ \mid e)$ and $P(I^- \mid e)$, where $I^+ = \{+d_1, \neg d_2, \neg d_3, \neg d_4\}$ and $I^- = \{\neg d_1, +d_2, +d_3, \neg d_4\}$.

These calculations are quite simple, because instantiating the D variables separates the M variables from each other, so that the posterior probabilities involve only products of $P(M_j \mid Parents\ of\ M_j)$ over the individual symptoms and a product of the prior probabilities over the individual diseases. For example,

$$P(I^+ \mid e) = \alpha\, P(I^+)\, P(e \mid I^+)$$

$$= \alpha\, \pi_1 (1 - \pi_2)(1 - \pi_3)(1 - \pi_4)(1 - q_{11})\, q_{12}(1 - q_{13})$$

$$= \alpha\, 0.01 \cdot 0.90 \cdot 0.80 \cdot 0.80 \cdot 0.20 \cdot 0.90 \cdot 0.80$$

$$= \alpha\, 8.2944 \times 10^{-4}, \tag{5.78}$$

$$P(I^- \mid e) = \alpha\, P(I^-)\, P(e \mid I^-)$$

$$= \alpha\, (1 - \pi_1)\, \pi_2 \pi_3 (1 - \pi_4)(1 - q_{21})(1 - q_{33})\, q_{24} q_{34}$$

$$= \alpha\, 0.99 \cdot 0.10 \cdot 0.20 \cdot 0.80 \cdot 0.90 \cdot 0.90 \cdot 0.70 \cdot 0.80$$

$$= \alpha\, 7.186 \times 10^{-3}. \tag{5.79}$$

Since $\alpha = [P(e)]^{-1}$ is a constant, we conclude that I^- is the most plausible interpretation of the evidence e.

5.5.4 Generating Explanations

The propagation pattern of the λ^* and π^* messages can also be instrumental in generating verbal explanations mechanically. When belief in a certain proposition is supported (or undermined) from several directions, the π^* and λ^* messages can be consulted to determine the factors most influential in the selection of x^*. Tracing the most influential $\pi^* - \lambda^*$ messages back to the generating evidence yields a skeleton subgraph from which verbal explanation can be structured. For example, the messages of Figure 5.15 and Figure 5.16 could be summarized thus:

> Since we have ruled out disease D_1, the only possible explanation for observing symptoms M_1 and M_3 is that the patient suffers simultaneously from D_2 and D_3. The fact that M_2 and M_4 both came out negative indicates that disease D_4 is absent. Moreover, even if M_4 were positive, it would be completely explained away by D_2 and D_3.

The last sentence is a result of testing a positive instantiation of M_4 and realizing that the (∞) π^* messages from D_2 and D_3 are so strong that M_4 cannot deliver a λ_{42} high enough to switch D_4 to $TRUE$.

A special explanation might be warranted in cases of conflicting evidence, i.e., when strongly supporting and strongly opposing messages simultaneously impinge on the same proposition. For example, the proposition $D_2 = TRUE$ in Figure 5.12

receives strong support from $\lambda_{12} = 4.6$ and strong opposition from $\pi_2 = 0.1$. The two messages balance each other out and yield a $BEL^*(+d_2)$ that is very close to $BEL^*(\neg d_2)$ (see Eq. (5.76)). The following explanation is appropriate:

> Although symptom M_1 strongly suggests D_2, it is partly explained by D_1 (which we assumed to be *TRUE*), and in view of the rarity of D_2, this patient probably does not suffer from D_2.

5.5.5 *Reversibility vs. Perseverance*

It is interesting to note that there is a definite threshold value, $\pi_1 = 0.0804$, at which the interpretations I^+ and I^- are equiprobable. This means that as evidence in favor of $+d_1$ accumulates and π_1 increases beyond 0.0804, the system will switch abruptly from interpretation I^- to interpretation I^+. This abrupt change of view is a collective phenomenon characteristic of massively parallel systems and is reminiscent of the way people's beliefs undergo a complete reversal in response to a minor clue. Note, though, that the transition is reversible, i.e., as π_1 decreases, the system will switch back to the I^- interpretation at exactly the same threshold value, $\pi_1 = 0.0804$. No hysteresis occurs because w^* is globally optimal (although the computations are performed locally) and is therefore a unique function of all system parameters.

This perfect reversibility differs from human behavior. Once we commit our belief to a particular interpretation, it often takes stronger evidence to make us change our mind than it took to get us there in the first place. Simply discrediting a piece of evidence does not by itself make us abandon the beliefs that the evidence induced [Ross and Anderson 1982; Harman 1986]. This phenomenon is especially pronounced in perceptual tasks; once we adopt one view of Necker's cube or Escher's stairway, it takes a real effort to break loose our perceptions and adopt alternative interpretations. Hysteresis of this kind is characteristic of systems with local feedback, like the one responsible for magnetic hysteresis in metals. If the magnetic spin of one atom points to the north, it sets up a field that encourages neighboring atoms to follow suit; when the neighbors' spins eventually turn to the north, they generate a field that further locks the original atom in its northward orientation.

The hysteresis that characterizes human belief revision may have several sources. One possibility is that neighboring concepts create local feedback loops; if I suspect fire, I expect smoke, and the very expectation of smoke reinforces my suspicion of fire—as though I actually saw smoke. This is a rather poor explanation because it suggests that even in simple cases like the fire and smoke example, people will confuse hypothetical predictions with genuine evidence. A more reasonable explanation is that the message-passing process used is by and large feedback-free, resembling that of Section 5.3, where the π^* and λ^* on the same link are orthogonal to one another. However, in complex situations, where loops are rampant, people simply cannot afford the computational overhead required by conditioning or clustering. As an approximation, humans delegate the optimization task to local processes and continue to pass messages as though the belief network were singly connected. Interpretations made under these conditions are locally, not globally, optimal, and this yields irreversible belief revision.

Another possible source of belief perseverance is the difficulty of keeping track of all justifications of one's beliefs and tracing back all the evidence, past and present, upon which the beliefs are founded [Harman 1986]. For computational reasons, people simply forget the evidence and remember the conclusion. More formally, propositional networks such as those treated in this paper are not maintained as stable mental constructs, but are created and destroyed dynamically to meet temporary needs. Connections may be formed for the immediate purpose of explaining some strange piece of evidence or supporting a hypothesis of short-term importance. Once the evidence is imparted onto other propositions, we tend to break the mediating connection, forget the evidence itself, and retain only the conclusion. When that evidence is later discredited, the connection to the induced conclusions is a distant memory, while the discrediting information itself may not be perceived to be of sufficient practical importance to reestablish old connections.

5.6 THE NATURE OF EXPLANATIONS

5.6.1 Accepting vs. Assessing Beliefs

The method described in this chapter is a bridge between probabilistic reasoning and nonmonotonic logic. Like the latter, the method provides systematic rules that lead from a set of factual sentences (the evidence) to a set of conclusion sentences (the accepted beliefs) in a way that need not be truth-preserving. For example, in Figure 5.1, we start with the sentence ''All inputs are ON,'' obtain the sentence ''$Y_3 = $ OFF, $X_2 = $ ON,'' and yield the conclusion ''$X_1 = $ OFF, $X_3 = $ ON.'' True, the medium through which these inferences are made is probabilistic (the assumption $q_1 > q_3$ was critical to the conclusion, for example), but the input-output pairs are categorical. Seeking the most probable extension parallels the default logic aim of minimizing abnormal assumptions, and this chapter shows how and when the minimization can be realized by local computations.

In contrast to the scheme expounded here, the dominant AI paradigm for belief revision has been the logicist method. It formalizes belief revision as direct logical relationships between evidence and conclusions, unmediated by numerical measures of belief. The whole notion of degrees of belief plays only a minor role in these endeavors, and likelihood judgments are often regarded as mere by-products of the symbolic manipulation of categorical knowledge bases.

Many philosophers of science, especially those studying inductive logic, have taken a different tack. They hold that the bulk of human knowledge is probabilistic in nature, that there is a set Q of confirmation functions that measure the degree to which statements are confirmed by the evidence at hand. Some statements, however, enjoy a special status—they are accepted as true in almost every respect (though this status can be revoked at a later time, perhaps in light of new evidence). This corpus of statements K is called *accepted beliefs*. An agent is said to *accept K* if he behaves as though all statements in K were certain, e.g., the emergence of more evidence to support one of the statements does not change the behavior predicated on that statement [Loui 1986b].

In this view, accepted beliefs can be regarded as local, temporary crystallizations in a continuous stream of partial beliefs. Belief revision is viewed as the process that governs this crystallization, defining the conditions under which a statement is promoted to privileged membership in the corpus of accepted beliefs.

Philosophers disagree about what constitutes a good, rational rule of acceptance. At first glance it appears that knowledge of the confirmation functions in Q is, by itself, sufficient for defining acceptance rules. Not so, it turns out. One obvious rule of acceptance is the high probability or *thresholding* rule: Accept a statement h iff $P(h \mid e) > 1 - \varepsilon$, for some small ε. For any nonzero ε, this rule leads to knowledge bases that are grossly inconsistent. This problem has been described as the *lottery paradox* [Kyburg 1961]: A large number of people buy tickets for a lottery that will produce a single winner. The probability that the i-th person will win the lottery is clearly very small, and thresholding should lead us to accept the statement "Person i is not the winner" for every i. Yet, this collection of statements is inconsistent with the immutable fact that one person will win. Many other acceptance rules have been proposed, but none seem to satisfy both our requirement that behavior should remain invariant to evidence confirming an accepted statement and our desire that the acceptance corpus to some extent be deductively closed and consistent.

Levi [1980] argues that rules of acceptance cannot be formulated on the basis of confirmation functions alone but must take into account practical considerations as well, namely, what will be done with the statement once it is accepted. An extreme example of the importance of pragmatics can be found in betting behavior. No matter how sure a person is of the truth of a statement, if sufficiently heavy penalties are imposed on wrong decisions, the person will hesitate to act in accordance with his beliefs.

Harsanyi [1985] and Loui [1986b] include computational considerations as part of the pragmatics of belief acceptance. The crystallization of partial beliefs into a corpus of crisp logical statements has computational advantages which overshadow the incurred loss of detail. An obvious advantage is the economy gained in both storage and communication. A more subtle advantage is the ability to detect equivalent sets of beliefs in inferential schemata. In many reasoning tasks, use is made of prestored schemata that worked successfully in the past. These schemata must be matched to distinct classes of situations (e.g., the antecedent part of any decision rule identifies the situations to which the action part is applicable). Commitment to a categorical set of beliefs facilitates an efficient symbolic encoding of the classes of situations to which the inferential schemata are applicable.

Pragmatic considerations of this sort help explain the vast disparity between AI and the management sciences in the treatment of uncertainty. The reason the management sciences have embraced probabilistic approaches and have emphasized measures of beliefs and uncertainty is that the domain of management decisions involves a wide spectrum of critical payoffs and penalties. Thus, even very unlikely events cannot be automatically ignored but must be compared against the more likely (if less generously paid off) events.

In AI applications, on the other hand, the variability of the payoffs is often rather small and the number of decisions enormous, so even events that are merely likely can be treated as a sure thing. For example, John's walk to the cupboard for a box of cereal is an action involving no high risk; the cost of failure is a few extra steps. Had the stakes been higher, John might have embarked on lengthy deliberations before taking the action. For example, by recalling Mary's breakfast he could have assessed the chances that the cereal was finished. However, given the noncritical nature of the actions involved, there was no pressing need for such deliberation. John could safely proceed toward the cupboard without considering every piece of evidence, i.e., without propagating the evidence through the entire belief network. When contradictory evidence arrives, some statements switch abruptly from *ALMOST SURELY TRUE* to *ALMOST SURELY FALSE*, apparently without numerical evaluation. In summary, everyday activities are characterized by firmly held beliefs because (1) violated expectations involve relatively mild risks, (2) there is a definite computational advantage to accepting these expectations as firm beliefs, and (3) there is no practical danger in letting some of these beliefs turn inconsistent.

5.6.2 Is a Most-Probable Explanation Adequate?

The most-probable-explanation (MPE) criterion used in this chapter reflects the following acceptance rule:

A statement h is accepted iff h is entailed by I^*, where I^* is a conjunction of primitive sentences forming the most probable explanation of the available evidence.

An equivalent acceptance rule is:

Out of all world models consistent with the evidence, choose the one with the highest overall probability.

In the case of Kyburg's lottery, for example, the set of consistent world models consists of all choices of a single winner from the population of ticket holders. If the lottery is absolutely fair, all models are equally likely, and acceptance cannot be invoked. However, assuming that one person is known to have a higher chance of winning than the rest (say, by virtue of possessing a larger number of tickets), we fully commit our belief to the world model in which that person is the winner.

Like any acceptance rule based solely on confirmation, this one has its drawbacks. For example, if I were asked to bet $1,000 on a specific lottery contestant (with even payoffs), I would resist endorsing even the one holding dozens of tickets. Indeed, if payoff information is available, the MPE criterion loses its viability, and it should give way to maximum-utility or minimum-risk alternatives. However, when the payoffs are either unknown or insignificant, the MPE criterion offers a reasonable compromise. People tend to jump to conclusions on the basis of rather tenuous evidence. For example,

> h: "I am going to be the winner, because I feel I have a slightly better chance than anybody else."

> h: "Did you say my uncle bought a ticket too? I'll bet he is going to be the winner; he's been so damned lucky all his life."

Similarly, it is not uncommon for people to switch abruptly from one interpretation of Necker's cube to the opposite, as a result of a slight change in visual clues.

There are two situations in which the MPE criterion is justifiable even on pragmatic grounds:

1. When the difference between the best and the second-best explanation is appreciable.

2. When one is forced to choose a definite, terminal action, and the risks associated with wrong choices are all equal.

For example, in answering multiple-choice questions, the student's best strategy is to select the answer most likely to be correct. Similarly, technicians troubleshooting electronic circuits are doing well if at every phase of the diagnosis they test or replace the unit most likely to account for the faults observed. The truth-maintenance strategy of resolving contradictions by retracting the minimum number of assumptions is also a variant of the MPE criterion, where all assumptions are assumed to be equally probable.

When it comes to scientific or causal explanations, the MPE criterion carries the special advantage of yielding a neutral explanation, unbiased by practical considerations such as payoffs and risks. Still, even in purely scientific settings, an explanation is always translated into some action, and actions always lead to consequences and payoffs. It is desirable, therefore, that the most likely explanation not be issued in isolation but be accompanied by additional information, such as the absolute probability of the best explanation, the probability of the second-best explanations, and the likelihood that these measures will change in the face of future tests. Having an efficient method of propagating beliefs in causal networks is a necessary and often sufficient step toward computing these auxiliary measures (see Chapter 6).

5.6.3 Circumscribing Explanations

So far, we have assumed that every consistent instantiation of the variables in the system constitutes an explanation of the evidence; consequently, the optimization has been conducted over all nonevidence variables in the network. Unfortunately, this practice leads to computational and conceptual difficulties.

Computationally, the result is that every piece of evidence must be propagated to the entire network, and since unconfirmed consequences no longer serve as absorption centers—as they do in belief updating (see Section 5.3)—we are running the risk of expending valuable resources in totally irrelevant sections of our knowledge base. Conceptually, this unchecked frame-to-frame propagation might lead to paradoxical results.

Suppose, for example, that I am concerned about having a certain fatal disease, and by a stroke of good luck, a medical test reveals that there is an 80% chance that I am totally healthy. According to the MPE acceptance rule, I should commit all my belief to a world model in which I am healthy. So, I start imagining all kinds of possible scenarios associated with my newly adopted belief. For example, I imagine 10 mutually exclusive scenarios, $S_1, S_2, ..., S_{10}$ (a trip to the Bahamas, a trip to Afghanistan, etc.), each having a probability 0.1 of being realized. Now I repeat the MPE exercise, but this time on a larger scale, embracing the earlier facts about the disease and the newly imagined scenarios. Lo and behold, any world model in which I am healthy now receives only an 8% chance of being realized, so the most probable "explanation" of the evidence is that I *do* suffer from that horrible disease—and all for being a hasty daydreamer!

In everyday discourse we would exclude such scenarios from the explanation because they do not stand in causal relation to the observed evidence, i.e., the symptoms or the test outcome. This is, indeed, a form of circumscription that can easily be implemented in causal networks by insisting that an explanation of evidence e should consist only of ancestors of e, with all other variables excluded. Thus, the maximization exercise should range only over the set of variables that are ancestors of some observed facts.

This circumscription does not go far enough, however, as it does not insist that the relationship between e and its causal ancestors pass some test of strength or rationality. The spectrum of everyday observations is so rich that with a small stretch of the imagination one can always proclaim any proposition h to be supported by some observation e, however feeble the support. Thus, in theory, every proposition can qualify for admittance into the explanation corpus, and we are back where we started from.

The solution to this dilemma relies, again, on the notion of payoffs. In every practical situation, when we seek an explanation for some experience e, we have a fairly good idea about which hypotheses should be included in that explanation, namely, which set of variables should be submitted for optimization. This is determined by pragmatic considerations; we know which set of hypotheses would influence the consequences that stand at the center of our concern. For example, partitioning the hypothesis "I am healthy" into ten specific scenarios is a rational thing to do if I am pressed by my travel agent to pay for a plane ticket and must decide on a specific destination. It is not rational if my main concern is knowing whether or not I am sick.

In order to apply the MPE scheme described here, one must assume that the network contains only "interesting" partitions of world models, "interesting" meaning relevant to a set of consequences at the center of one's practical concerns. For example, if disease H_1 has ten equally likely and mutually exclusive prognoses, while a competing hypothesis H_2 has only one clear prognosis, should we partition H_1 prior to maximization, or should we maximize over the space H_1 vs. H_2, then maximize again over H_1's components if it turns out to be accepted? That depends on the circumstances. If the ten prognoses call for only minor variations in treatment, then we should do the latter, but if each prognosis calls for a drastically different action and any error can be devastating, then we should do the former. (Harsanyi [1985] calls it "the principle of small disparate risks.")

In conclusion, the MPE acceptance rule is justifiable only in small domains, compiled in advance by a fairly astute decision maker. Such compilation involves heuristic judgments gauging the trade-off between the gain in simplicity and the loss of utility associated with circumscribing these domains.

5.7 CONCLUSIONS

This chapter outlined a distributed scheme for finding the most probable composite explanation of a body of evidence.

We showed that in singly connected networks, globally optimal explanations can be configured by local, autonomous message-passing processes, similar to those used in belief updating; conceptually related propositions communicate with each other via a simple protocol, and the process converges to the correct solution in time proportional to the network diameter. In multiply connected networks, the propagation method must be assisted by clustering (into locally supervised groups of variables), conditioning (i.e., reasoning by assumptions), or stochastic simulation, each method exploiting different aspects of the network topology.

The implications of these results are several. First, from a psychological viewpoint, they provide a clear demonstration of how cognitive constructs exhibiting global coherence can be assembled by local, neuron-like processors, without external supervision. Second, on a more practical dimension, the message-passing method developed offers a substantial reduction in complexity as compared with previous optimization techniques, achieving linear complexity in singly connected networks and $exp(|cycle\ cutset|)$ complexity in general networks. This is accomplished through subtask decomposition, supervised solely by the network topology. Third, we have established a clear paradigmatic link between probabilistic and logical formalisms of nonmonotonic reasoning. We demonstrated how numerical probabilities can be used as a catalyst for coherent transformations from evidence sentences to conclusion sentences. We also identified the structures that allow such transformations to be executed by autonomous production rules and those that invite problems of intractability and instability unless treated with care.

5.8 BIBLIOGRAPHICAL AND HISTORICAL REMARKS

The revision method of Section 5.3 is based on Pearl [1987d], while the circuit diagnosis application of Section 5.4 was reported in Geffner and Pearl [1987a]. A diagnosis scheme that passes labels rather than numbers is described in Geffner and Pearl [1987d]. Portions of Section 5.6 are influenced by Harman [1986] and Loui [1986].

Belief revision and updating in general networks were shown to be NP-hard problems[1]. Connectionist approaches to finding the MPE are described in Peng and Reggia[2]. Systems for generating explanations in belief networks are described in Sember and Zukerman[3], and Henrion and Druzdzel[4]. Belief revision in temporal planning applications is described in Berzuini[5], and Kazanawa[6]. Qualitative probabilistic inferences are studied in Wellman[7].

---

[1]   Cooper, G.F. 1990. Computational Complexity of Probabilistic Inference Using Bayesian Belief Networks. *Artificial Intelligence*, 42(2):393-405. (See also Rosenthal (1975)).

[2]   Peng, Y., and Reggia, J.A. 1990. *Abductive Inference Models for Diagnostic Problem-Solving*, Springer-Verlag, New York.

[3]   Sember, P., and Zukerman, I. 1989. Strategies for Generating Micro Explanations for Bayesian Belief Networks, *Uncertainty in AI 5*, North Holland, 1990, 295-302.

[4]   Henrion, M., and Druzdzel, M.J. 1990. Qualitative propagation and scenario-based explanation of probabilistic reasoning, *Uncertainty in AI 6*, North Holland, 1991, 17-32.

[5]   Berzuini, C. 1990. Representing Time in Causal Probabilistic Networks, *Uncertainty in AI 5*, North Holland, 15-28.

[6]   Kanazawa, K., A Logic and Time Nets for Probabilistic Inference, *Proc. AAAI-91*, Anaheim, CA., 1991, 360-365.

[7]   Wellman, M.P., Fundamental Concepts of Qualitative Probabilistic Networks, *Artificial Intelligence*, 44(3), 1990, 257-305.

Exercises

5.1. Refer to Exercise **4.1**.

    a. Find the most likely seven-symbol string in L that starts and ends with ε.

    b. Find the message most likely to have been transmitted, given that the string $\varepsilon, \varepsilon, B, C, A, \varepsilon, \varepsilon$ is received.

5.2. Solve the diagnosis problem of Section 5.5.1 assuming that all four symptoms have been observed, i.e., $M_1 = M_2 = M_3 = M_5 = TRUE$.

5.3.   **a.** Solve Exercise **5.2** by ignoring the loops. In other words, activate all eight processors simultaneously and repeatedly through the updating rules of Eqs. (5.48) through (5.52) and determine if the d_1^*, d_2^*, d_3^*, and d_4^* stabilize to the correct diagnosis.

    b. Check if this process creates a hysteresis effect (e.g., vary the value of π_1 from zero to one, then back to zero, and plot the behavior of d_1^*, d_2^*, d_3^*, and d_4^* as a function of π_1).

5.4. Assuming that the AND-gates of Figure 5.1a have fault probability $f = q / 2$, and $q_1 = q_2 = q_3 = q$. Find all most-probable explanations for the observations $X_2 = 1$ and $Y_3 = 0$. (Assume the output of a faulty gate has equal probability of being 1 or 0.)

5.5. At time $t = 0$ you park your car illegally. At time $t = 10$ (minutes) you return to find that your car got towed away. The probability that a policeman will spot an illegally parked car in any given minute is 1/1000. You are trying to figure out **when** your car was towed away.

    a. Formulate the problem as that of finding the most-probable-explanation in a Bayesian network and compute the answer using a distributed message-passing process. Repeat the calculation assuming you return after a week (say $t = 10,000$).

    b. A friend of yours reports that he saw your parked car five minutes after you left it. Revise your beliefs, assuming that there is a 50% chance that your friend would mistake another car for yours but would never mistake your car for another.

Chapter *6*

DECISION AND CONTROL

In a minute there is time
For decisions and revisions which
a minute will reverse.
— T. S. Eliot

6.1 FROM BELIEFS TO ACTIONS: INTRODUCTION TO DECISION ANALYSIS

6.1.1 Rational Decisions and Quality Guarantees

Probabilistic methods provide coherent prescriptions for choosing actions and meaningful guarantees of the quality of these choices. The prescriptions are based on the paradigm that normative knowledge—that is, judgments about values, preferences, and desirability—represents a valuable abstraction of actual human experience, and that like its factual-knowledge counterpart it can be encoded and manipulated to produce useful recommendations. Whereas judgments about the likelihood of events is quantified by probabilities, judgments about the desirability of action consequences are quantified by utilities.

The set of actions available to an individual in any given situation can be represented by a variable or a group of variables that are under the full control of the decision-making individual, unlike the variables discussed so far. Choosing an action amounts to selecting a set of decision variables in a Bayesian network and fixing their values unambiguously. Such a choice normally alters the probability distribution of another set of variables, judged to be *consequences* of the decision variables. If to each configuration c of the consequence set C we assign a utility measure $U(c)$, representing its degree of desirability, then the overall expected utility associated with action a is given by

$$U(a) = \sum_c U(c)\, P(c \mid a, e)\,, \qquad (6.1)$$

where $P(c \mid a, e)$ is the probability distribution of the consequence configuration c, conditioned upon selecting action a and observing evidence e.†

Bayesian methodologies regard the expected utility $U(a)$ as a gauge of the merit of action a and therefore treat it as a prescription for choosing among alternatives. Thus, if we can choose either action a_1 or action a_2, we calculate both $U(a_1)$ and $U(a_2)$ and select the action that yields the highest value. Moreover, since the value of $U(a)$ depends on the evidence e observed until the time of decision, the outcome of the *maximum-expected-utility (MEU)* criterion will be an evidence-dependent plan (or decision rule) of the form "If e_1 is observed, choose a_1; if e_2 is observed, choose a_2,....."

The semantics of the utility measure $U(c)$ and the justification of the maximum-expected-utility rule will be outlined in the next few sections. We will see that this rule was not chosen purely for mathematical convenience; rather, it is based on pervasive psychological attitudes towards risk, choice, preference, and likelihood. These attitudes are captured by what is known as the *axioms of utility theory* [von Neumann and Morgenstern 1947], to be presented in Section 6.1.4. While textbook arguments for the expected-value criterion are normally based on a long-run accumulation of payoffs from a long series of repetitive decisions (e.g., gambling), we shall see that the expected-utility criterion is also justified in single-decision situations. The summation operation in Eq. (6.1) originates not with additive accumulation of payoffs but with the additive axiom of probability theory (Eq. (2.3)).

6.1.2 *Consequences, Payoffs, and Lotteries*

Consequences of actions are normally not associated with numerical payoffs but instead involve complex descriptions of world situations. For example, a consequence of purchasing a ticket to a ball game could be "You start watching the game, but it rains and you catch pneumonia" or "At the end of an enjoyable game you find that your car won't start but a beautiful stranger offers you a ride." Such descriptions we refer to as *consequences*, or *outcomes*. A rational method of choosing between two actions (say, buying or not buying the ticket) would be to

---

† We assume that each consequence C includes pertinent information about the actions that led to C; this permits us to write $U(c)$ instead of $U(c, a)$.

evaluate the *benefit* (or *value*, or *desirability)* of each of the various consequences and weigh the benefits with the probabilities that the consequences will occur. Consequences associated with familiar benefits are called *payoffs* or *prizes*, reminiscent of gambling, where consequences invariably involve winning or losing sums of money (the benefit of which is rarely disputed). In the absence of a firm association with familiar benefits, consequences must be further analyzed and reduced to simpler components which can be assessed more naturally. Thus, the elements of a rational theory of choice are pairs of the form

$$L = (C, P) , \qquad\qquad (6.2)$$

where $C = \{C_1, C_2, ... , C_n\}$ is a (finite) set of prizes or consequences and P is a probability distribution over C, satisfying $\sum_i P(C_i) = 1$. Each pair $L = (C, P)$ is called a *lottery* and can be represented either by a list of pairs,

$$L = [C_1, P(C_1); C_2, P(C_2); ... ; C_n, P(C_n)],$$

or by a treelike diagram, where each probability $P(C_i)$ labels an arc directed from L to the corresponding consequence node C_i. For example, the lottery of Figure 6.1 represents an agent's concern about undertaking a project having an uncertain completion time. The consequences shown represent the situations created when the project lasts one month, two months, and three months; these completion times are judged to have probabilities 0.60, 0.30, and 0.10., respectively. Consequences not shown in the diagram (e.g., a completion time of six weeks) are presumed to have zero probability.

Formally, lotteries are no different than the uncertain variables treated in previous chapters. Moreover, there is no clear distinction between consequences and lotteries; every consequence is a description of some situation and thus is a lottery relative to subsequent scenarios that might emerge from that situation. For example, the consequence C_1 in Figure 6.1, may represent both the monetary reward associated with completing the project ahead of schedule and the uncertainty—about whether the customer would appreciate the effort, about the nature of the next project assignment, and so on. Thus, the association with gambling-style lotteries, where the game ends the moment a player collects his payoff, is purely metaphoric. It does help emphasize the assumption that the probabilities associated with the consequences are known, and that at some point the process of generating hypothetical scenarios must stop for analysis. The stopping horizon should be signaled by familiar situations, such as getting a $10,000 raise, that accept reliable evaluation without further analysis. Note that although the actual benefits (or costs) of the three possible consequences in Figure 6.1 depend on future eventualities, it is clearly more convenient to assess the benefit associated with each individual consequence than to assess the benefit of the project lottery as a whole.

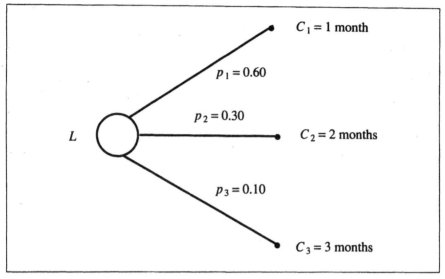

Figure 6.1. *A lottery representing uncertainty in the time required to complete a project.*

6.1.3 *Calibrating the Value of a Lottery*

A simple way to compare and evaluate lotteries would be to score their degree of desirability against some standard *calibration commodity,* such as money or time. For example, we could assess the smallest amount of money we would be willing to accept in lieu of participating in a given lottery, like the one shown in Figure 6.1, and use that amount as a measure of the desirability of the lottery. The question of choosing among actions then becomes one of comparing the calibrated scores of the lotteries emanating from each pending action and selecting the action with the highest value.

This simplistic calibration scheme meets two problems, however. First, direct assessment of the score means that every conceivable lottery must be spelled out for us to assess its trade-off value. Since the number of lotteries is infinite, some method must be found to deduce the scores of complex lotteries from those of more elementary lotteries, so that we would need to provide assessments only for the elementary ones. Second, a calibration commodity must be found that would be conducive to consistent assessments, i.e., it should not lead us to assess different trade-off values for the same lottery on successive days when we don't intend to.

The choice of an appropriate calibration commodity is a tricky one. Such a commodity should be commensurable with the prizes of the calibrated lotteries and should also maintain a stable value in the eyes of the assessor. For example, it would be hard for a project manager to assess how many bushels of frog legs he would be willing to trade for the lottery in Figure 6.1 because (1) the exchange is not realistic and (2) his attitude toward possessing large quantities of frog legs would not be stable—never having traded frog legs, his attitude would vary from moment to moment depending on whether the frog legs appear to be resellable for a reasonable price in a reasonable period of time. Calibrating consequences with a commodity of unstable value is like using rubber tape to measure distances. Even money, which is the most practical exchange mechanism, would fare poorly, because people's perception of their ability to use money, especially large quantities of it, varies widely over time and circumstance.

The calibration commodity chosen by decision theorists is an ingenious one: uncertainty itself. Rather than being subjected to hypothetical trade-offs between lotteries and some foreign commodity, the assessor is asked to compare lotteries containing prizes of the same type but with different degrees of uncertainty.

One standard of calibration is a two-prize lottery, L_s, producing the most desirable and the least desirable outcomes, C_B and C_W, with probabilities p_s and $1 - p_s$, respectively (the subscripts B and W connote "best" and "worst," respectively). For example, if the assessor feels that completing the project in one week's time is the best that can possibly be expected, while a year's delay is the worst that can be imagined, then the lottery of Figure 6.1 would be compared to L_s, as shown in Figure 6.2.

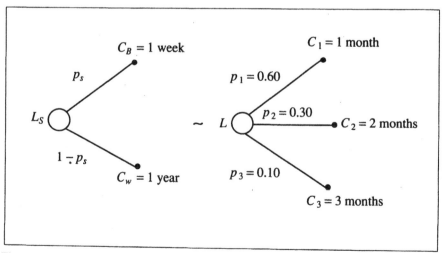

Figure 6.2. *Calibrating the lottery L of Figure 6.1 against a standard lottery L_s with two prizes and an adjustable probability p_s.*

The assessor is asked to determine what value of p_s would render him indifferent in choosing between the two lotteries. The chosen value of p_s is then taken as a measure of the desirability of lottery L, or its *utility*, $U(L)$. Formally, if L_s is a standard lottery

$$L_s = (p_s, C_B; 1 - p_s, C_W),\qquad\qquad (6.3)$$

then the utility of any lottery L is given by

$$U(L) = p_s \quad \text{iff} \quad L \sim L_s,\qquad\qquad (6.4)$$

where $\sim$ means indifference or willingness to exchange either way.

Having chosen a calibration standard, we now try to minimize the number of assessments required.

6.1.4 The Axioms of Utility Theory

The theory of utility rests on five axioms that constrain the patterns of preference an individual might exhibit toward the set of possible lotteries. These axioms can be regarded as a set of general strategies people accept as a basis for decision-making, or as patterns of behavior that people recall to have yielded beneficial results in the past.

AXIOM 1—Orderability: *A linear and transitive preference relation must exist between the prizes of any lottery.*

Using the symbol $A \geq^* B$ to denote "A is preferred or equivalent to B," Axiom 1 states that if C_1, C_2, and C_3 are any three prizes of some lottery then (a) (*linearity*) either $C_1 \geq^* C_2$ or $C_2 \geq^* C_1$ or both, and (b) (*transitivity*) if $C_1 \geq^* C_2$ and $C_2 \geq^* C_3$ then $C_1 \geq^* C_3$. If $A \geq^* B$ and not $B \geq^* A$, we say that A is *preferred* to B and write $A >^* B$. If $A \geq^* B$ and $B \geq^* A$, We say that A and B are *equivalent* and write $A \sim B$.

AXIOM 2—Continuity: *If $C_1 \geq^* C_2 \geq^* C_3$ then there exists a lottery L with only two prizes, C_1 and C_3, that is equivalent to receiving C_2 for sure, i.e.,*

$$L = [p, C_1; (1-p), C_3] \sim C_2.$$

The probability p at which equivalence occurs will be used to calibrate the merit of C_2 relative to the prizes C_1 and C_3.

AXIOM 3—Substitutability: *For any $0 < p \leq 1$ and any three lotteries L_1, L_2, and L_3,*

$$L_1 \sim L_2 \quad \text{iff} \quad [p, L_1; (1-p), L_3] \sim [p, L_2; (1-p), L_3].\qquad (6.5)$$

Axiom 3 asserts that adding the same prize (L_3) with the same probability $(1 - p)$ to two equivalent lotteries will not change the preference between the two. In other words, things equivalent when considered alone remain equivalent as part of a larger context.

AXIOM 4—Monotonicity: *In comparing two lotteries, each with the same two prizes, the lottery producing the better prize with the higher probability is preferred, i.e., if $C_1 >^* C_2$ then*

$$[p, C_1; (1 - p), C_2] \geq^* [p', C_1; (1 - p'), C_2] \quad \text{iff} \quad p \geq p'. \tag{6.6}$$

AXIOM 5—Reduction of compound lotteries: *Preferences are determined solely on the basis of the final outcomes and their associated probabilities, not on the way these outcomes are presented, i.e., for any two lotteries L_1 and $L_2 = [q, C_1; (1 - q), C_2]$,*

$$[p, L_1; (1 - p), L_2] \sim [p, L_1; (1 - p)q, C_1; (1 - p)(1 - q), C_2]. \tag{6.7}$$

In other words, the compound lottery $[p, L_1; (1 - p), L_2]$ with L_2 as a prize can be reduced to an equivalent lottery that lists explicitly L_2's prizes—C_1 and C_2—and, their associated probabilities. This axiom is sometimes called "no fun in gambling," since it places no value on the number of steps taken to achieve a given outcome.

THEOREM 1: *If a preference pattern $(\geq^*)$ on lotteries obeys Axioms 1 through 5, then there exists a real-valued function U on the set of prizes C and a rule for extending the function to the set of lotteries, such that for any two lotteries L_1 and L_2,*

$$L_1 \geq^* L_2 \quad \text{iff} \quad U(L_1) \geq U(L_2), \tag{6.8}$$

where

$$U[p_1, C_1; \ldots; p_n, C_n] = \sum_i p_i U(C_i). \tag{6.9}$$

In other words, every preference pattern obeying Axioms 1 through 5 can be faithfully encoded by specifying the utility measure of each individual consequence and deciding all preferences among lotteries on the basis of the expected-utility criterion. Alternatively, the policy of always choosing the lottery with the highest expected utility guarantees a choice that is consistent with Axioms 1 through 5, regardless of what utility is assigned to the consequences.

Proof: The essence of the proof rests on Axioms 2 and 4, which allow us to reduce any complex lottery to an equivalent two-prize standard lottery, then use the probability attached to the preferred prize as the criterion for deciding among standard lotteries. The proof will reveal how the expected-utility criterion and the arithmetic operations of multiplication and addition surface as factors in tasks involving qualitative, nonrepetitive choices among lotteries having nonnumeric consequences.

Let L and L' be two lotteries competing for preference. Axiom 1 allows us to arrange their combined set of prizes in a linear order such that

$$C_1 \geq^* C_2 \geq^* \cdots \geq^* C_n .$$

That is, C_1 is the most preferred prize, and C_n is the least preferred one. Ties can be broken arbitrarily, and we shall assume $C_1 >^* C_n$. The substitutability axiom further permits us to represent L and L' as simple lotteries with the same set of prizes, i.e.,

$$L = [p_1, C_1; p_2, C_2; \dots ; p_n, C_n] ,$$

$$L' = [p'_1, C_1; p'_2, C_2; \dots ; p'_n, C_n] .$$

If a prize C_i does not appear in a lottery, we simply set its probability p_i (or p'_i) to 0.

Now we choose a two-prize lottery $L_s = [p_s, C_1; (1-p_s), C_n]$ as a standard of calibration. The continuity axiom states that every prize C_i can be made equivalent to the standard lottery L_s by properly adjusting the probability p_s. Let the value of p_s needed to achieve $L_s \sim C_i$ be denoted by u_i, i.e.,

$$[u_i, C_1; (1-u_i), C_n] \sim C_i \qquad 0 \leq u_i \leq 1 . \tag{6.10}$$

We can now replace each prize in L and L' with its equivalent standard lottery (using the substitutability axiom), as shown in Figure 6.3, thus obtaining two-step lotteries containing only two prizes, C_1 and C_n. By applying the decomposability axiom, we can reduce these two-step lotteries to simple standard lotteries, where C_1 obtains probability $\sum_i p_i u_i$ in the lottery equivalent to L and probability $\sum_i p'_i u_i$ in the lottery equivalent to L', as shown in Figure 6.4. By the monotonicity axiom, since $C_1 >^* C_n$, the preference between L and L' should be determined by the magnitude of the probability attached to C_1. Thus,

$$L \geq^* L' \qquad \text{iff} \qquad \sum_i p_i u_i \geq \sum_i p'_i u_i , \tag{6.11}$$

which is equivalent to Eqs. (6.8) and (6.9). Q.E.D.

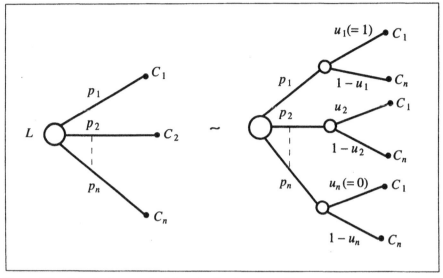

Figure 6.3. *Substituting standard lotteries for the prizes of lottery L.*

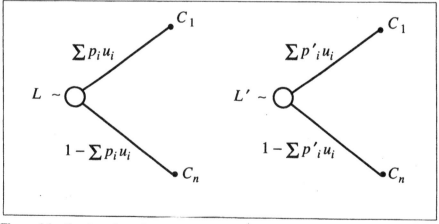

Figure 6.4. *Two lotteries reduced to standard form.*

6.1.5 Utility Functions

The utility function $U(C_i) = u_i$ defined in Eq. (6.10) requires comparison of each consequence C_i to a standard lottery having the best (C_B) and worst (C_W) consequences as the only possible prizes. Accordingly, we have $U(C_B) = 1$ and

$U(C_W) = 0$ as boundary conditions. On the other hand, it is clear from Eqs. (6.8) and (6.9) that uniformly adding a constant to $U(\cdot)$ or multiplying it by a positive factor would not change the preference pattern induced by the expected-utility criterion. Hence, we conclude that U is unique up to a positive linear transformation

$$u'_i = mu_i + b , \quad m > 0 . \tag{6.12}$$

In other words, if U is a utility function that faithfully encodes a preference pattern $\geq^*$, so will $U' = mU + b$. Thus, the boundary conditions can be adjusted by any convenient choice of two parameters. We can decide, for example, to assign a score of 1000 units called *utiles* to the best consequence C_B, and -1000 *utiles* to the worst consequence C_W; the other consequences will be scaled automatically by factoring the parameters m and b, as in Eq. (6.12).

When the consequences entail a continuous commodity X, such as money or time, the utility function can normally be described by a continuous curve $u(x)$, where $u(x)$ measures the merit of receiving quantity x of X. The literature on management decision-making contains many analyses of the shape of $u(x)$ (X being money), its significance, its measurement, and its correspondence with observed human behavior. For example, a concave-down $u(x)$ is said to represent *risk-averse* behavior because for any lottery L it satisfies

$$U[\textstyle\sum p_i x_i] \geq \sum p_i u(x_i) \tag{6.13}$$

or

$$U[E(L)] \geq U(L) , \tag{6.14}$$

where $E(L) = \sum p_i x_i$ is the *expected monetary value* (*EMV*) offered by L. In other words, an individual possessing a concave-down $u(x)$ will prefer to obtain in cash the expected monetary value of L rather than face L directly; hence the term *risk-averse*. In contrast, a convex-up $u(x)$ is said to represent a *risk-seeking* attitude, as the inequality in Eq. (6.14) is reversed.

The notion that people are averse to monetary risks goes back to Daniel Bernoulli (1700-1782), who used it to explain the St. Petersburg paradox, i.e., that people are willing to pay only moderate sums of money for lotteries offering infinite expected monetary rewards, e.g., $x_i = 2^i$, $p_i = 2^{-i}$. The concavity of $u(x)$ is also brought up to explain people's willingness to buy insurance protection despite the widely known fact that insurance companies have been making steady and enormous profits since the seventeenth century. However, people's fascination with gambling devices and state lotteries clearly indicates a risk-seeking attitude which cannot be reconciled with their attitude toward insurance.

While some researchers regard such irreconcilable cases as a failure of utility theory to capture human choice behavior, a more satisfactory explanation is that a typical person does not possess a stable utility curve for monetary rewards. Rather, the function $u(x)$ represents a person's tentative perception of her ability to convert an increment x of wealth to some meaningful gratification in a given context. In a gambling context, for example, one would attribute great importance to the feeling of "beating the machine" or "being lucky," even if the prizes are small. This perceived importance is not retained when the winning prize is an insurance claim.

6.2 DECISION TREES AND INFLUENCE DIAGRAMS

6.2.1 Decision Trees

A decision tree is an explicit representation of all scenarios that can possibly emanate from a given decision. The root of the tree represents the initial situation, while each path from the root corresponds to one possible scenario, involving a sequence of actions chosen by the decision-making agent, observations made by the agent, events that may occur in the agent's environment, and finally a consequence node expressing the utility of the situation created by the entire path.

The reason for explicating a decision problem with a tree is to facilitate a search for an optimal plan, where a *plan* is a prescription of responses to possible observations. An example follows.

A TYPICAL PLAN

If x_1 is observed, do a_1, and then $\begin{cases} \text{if } y_1 \text{ is observed, do } a_3, \text{ and then } \cdots \\ \text{else do } a_4, \text{ and then } \cdots \end{cases}$

If x_2 is observed, do a_2, and then $\begin{cases} \text{if } y_1 \text{ is observed, do } a_4, \text{ and then } \cdots \\ \text{else do } a_3, \text{ and then } \cdots \end{cases}$

else, do a_0.

The actions $a_0, a_1, a_2, \ldots$ include, of course, the options of waiting for something to happen, inspecting or activating a given measuring device, and gathering or investing physical resources to enable future actions.

A decision tree can be likened to a game played against nature, where the actions $a_0, a_1, \ldots$ are the moves taken by the agent, and the observations and final consequences are the moves taken by the opponent, i.e., nature. The agent's objective is to adopt a strategy that will maximize the expected utility. However, decision trees differ in several ways from perfect-information, zero-sum games such as chess and checkers. First, in perfect-information games we invariably assume that the final payoff is a known function of the game scenario (in most cases it is simply a function of the final game position). In decision problems the payoff function is given only probabilistically and implicitly, mediated by hidden events that we normally call *states of nature*. For example, the payoff associated with the scenario of operating on a patient after observing a given symptom S is normally mediated by the hypothetical variable *disease*, the true nature of which often remains unknown even after the operation is performed. The observed symptom helps shape the probability distribution of the possible diseases, but the payoffs themselves are more naturally associated with the hypothetical pair (disease, action), not with the observed pair (symptom, action).

A second difference between games and decisions is that in games we normally play against a hostile and intelligent adversary who benefits from our failure. Nature, on the other hand, is normally perceived as a neutral and somewhat stupid agent; her moves are presumed to be governed by a fixed probability distribution over states, observations, and payoffs, unaltered by the agent's intentions or benefits. Nature, for example, is not suspected of presenting the agent with misleading observations for the sheer purpose of inviting him to make a damaging move—a strategy common to human adversaries.

If the environment contains other intelligent agents, the neutrality of nature can no longer be assumed, and more sophisticated models of the opponents must be incorporated. For example, a probability distribution can be attached to the opponent's possible shades of character, ranging from hostile to neutral to benevolent. The role of observations, then, will be partly to determine the character of other agents and thus determine the strategy by which they choose their moves.

6.2.2 Planning with Decision Trees

The traditional approach to analyzing a decision problem has been to organize the elements of the problem in terms of a decision tree that depicts, in chronological order, the moves the decision-maker may choose and the moves governed by chance. This is very similar to the look-ahead scheme of analyzing a game of chess: explicating all possible moves available to the player, all possible responses of the opponent, all possible countermoves, and so on. Often, the decision-maker must pay a fee for acquiring information or enabling certain conditions along the way. Whenever a fee is to be paid, it is marked on the relevant branch, and so are the consequences or payoffs that eventually emanate from that branch.

A decision tree has two types of nodes: *decision nodes* and *chance nodes*. (We shall designate decision nodes graphically by squares and chance nodes by circles.) The branches emanating from a decision node represent options available to the agent; those emanating from a chance node represent uncontrollable events. At each chance node, each branch is assigned a conditional probability equal to the probability of the event represented by the branch, conditioned upon the knowledge available at that node. The leaves of the tree carry the numerical values of the utility associated with the scenario (path) leading to each leaf, or equivalently, the utility of the situation created by the sequence of events leading to the leaf.

The objective of finding the optimal strategy can be achieved by a *foldback* analysis: starting with the leaves and progressing recursively toward the root, we label each node by the utility of the situation it represents. Each chance node is labeled with the expected utility of its successors, and each decision node is labeled with the maximum utility of its successors. This is very similar to the "minimax" scheme used in the analysis of games [Pearl 1984] except that because of the neutrality of our adversary (nature) it now involves an expectation-maximization (*exp-max*) labeling procedure instead of the *min-max* procedure used in adversary games.

EXAMPLE 1 [Howard 1976a]: The buyer of a used car can decide to carry out various tests with various costs, and then, depending on the test results, decide which car to buy. The quality of the car purchased determines the payoff he gets, and since the amount of money involved is relatively small, we shall assume it has linear utility, i.e., the buyer's objective is to maximize the expected monetary value.

There are two possible tests, t_1 and t_2, though the buyer can decide to perform no tests, denoted by t_0. The cost of the tests are $50 for t_1 and $20 for t_2. There are two candidate cars, c_1 and c_2, and each can be of either good quality, q_1, or bad quality, q_2. Car c_1 costs $1,500, while its market value is estimated at $2,000, so the buyer stands to make $500 if the car is of good quality. If the quality is bad, the repair expenses might total $700, in which case the buyer would lose $200. Car c_2 costs $1,150, which is $250 below the market value. Even if it is in bad shape, however, the repairs will cost only $150. For simplicity, we shall assume that the buyer must buy either car c_1 or car c_2 and has time to perform one test at most.

The buyer knows from experience that the chances that car c_1 is of good quality are 0.70, while the chances that car c_2 is of good quality are 0.80. It is easy to verify that the EMV of car c_1 is $290 ($0.70 \times 500 + 0.30 \times (-200)$), while the EMV of car c_2 is $220 ($0.80 \times 250 + 0.20 \times 100$). So if no test is done, the buyer will choose car c_1, thus securing a perceived EMV of $290.

Test t_1 checks the quality of car c_1. If c_1 is of good quality, there is 0.90 probability that the test will confirm it. If the car is of bad quality, there is 0.65 probability that the test will discover it. (In another words, there is 0.10 probability that the test will disqualify the car when it is actually good, and 0.35 probability that the test will certify the car when it is bad.)

Test t_2 relates to the quality of car c_2 by the following conditional probabilities:

$$P(t_2 = pass \mid c_2 = q_1) = 0.75, \quad P(t_2 = pass \mid c_2 = q_2) = 0.30,$$

$$P(t_2 = fail \mid c_2 = q_1) = 0.25, \quad P(t_2 = fail \mid c_2 = q_2) = 0.70,$$

The decision tree corresponding to this situation is depicted in Figure 6.5. The tree is organized in chronological order of decisions being executed and information becoming available: a test (or no test) is chosen, the results are examined, the car is chosen, and finally, its quality is observed and its costs and benefits realized.

To compute the optimal strategy, we must assign a probability to every chance fork along this diagram. The probabilities along the t_0 branch are easy to calculate; with no test, we can simply use the prior probabilities of the quality of c_1 and c_2. However, to assign probabilities to the chance forks along the t_1 branch, we need to know the unconditional probability $P(t_1 = pass)$, as well as the posterior probabilities $P(c_1 \mid t_1 = pass)$, $P(c_1 \mid t_1 = fail)$, $P(c_2 \mid t_1 = pass)$, and $P(c_2 \mid t_1 = fail)$. Since these quantities are not provided explicitly, we call upon Bayes' Rule and compute

$$P(t_1 = pass, c_1 = q_1) = P(t_1 = pass \mid c_1 = q_1) \times P(c_1 = q_1) = 0.9 \times 0.7 = 0.63,$$

and, similarly,

$$P(t_1 = fail, c_1 = q_1) = 0.1 \times 0.7 = 0.07,$$

$$P(t_1 = pass, c_1 = q_2) = 0.35 \times 0.3 = 0.105,$$

$$P(t_1 = fail, c_1 = q_2) = 0.65 \times 0.3 = 0.195,$$

$$P(t_1 = pass) = 0.63 + 0.105 = 0.735,$$

$$P(t_1 = fail) = 0.07 + 0.195 = 0.265,$$

$$P(c_1 = q_1 \mid t_1 = pass) = 0.63 / 0.735 = 0.86,$$

$$P(c_1 = q_2 \mid t_1 = pass) = 0.105 / 0.735 = 0.14,$$

$$P(c_1 = q_1 \mid t_1 = fail) = 0.07 / 0.265 = 0.26,$$

$$P(c_1 = q_2 \mid t_1 = fail) = 0.195 / 0.265 = 0.74,$$

Since test t_1 applies only to car c_1, we have $P(c_2 \mid t_1) = P(c_2)$.

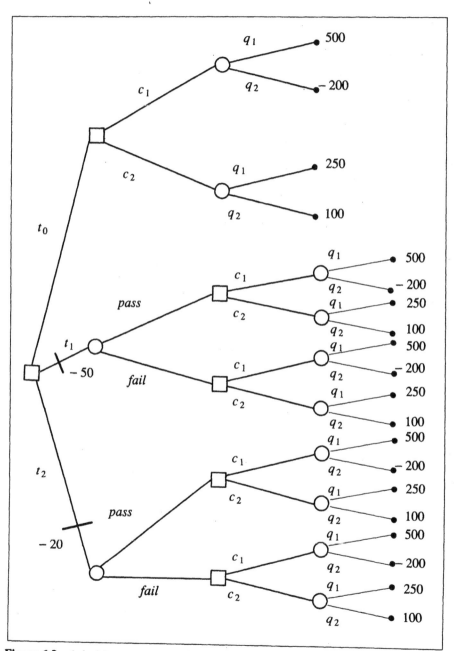

Figure 6.5. *A decision tree representing Example 1.*

In the same way we can compute the probabilities along the branch t_2, whereupon we can proceed with the exp-max foldback process:

1. Calculate the average utility at each chance node.

2. Calculate the maximum utility at each decision node, while marking the maximum branch.

3. Trace back the marked branches, from the root down, to find the desired optimal plan.

The results of applying this procedure to the tree of Figure 6.5 are shown in Figure 6.6, where the cost of the tests were subtracted from the payoffs of their respective consequences. The optimal plan, obtained by tracing back the maximum utility branch at every decision fork, is depicted by the darkened sub-tree of Figure 6.6. It calls for investing \$50 in test t_1, then buying car c_1 if the outcome is *pass* or buying car c_2 if the outcome is *fail*.

The decision-tree representation is convenient for plan optimization, as it contains explicit descriptions of complete strategies, i.e., prescriptions for actions to take in every conceivable situation. It is also a conceptually appealing representation when we have a naturally ordered sequence of decisions to be made, each decision being enabled by its predecessor. However, this representation often clashes with the natural way of modeling causal relationships in the environment. In our example, we assumed the agent (buyer) is comfortable estimating the probability of a particular test outcome conditioned on the actual quality of the car, but not the probability of that quality conditioned on the test results (see Figure 6.7). In other words, the chronological ordering of the tree might clash with the natural perception of influences among variables and hence with the natural way of assessing conditional probabilities. For this reason, decision analysts find it more convenient to assess probabilities using a device called a *probability tree* (see Figure 6.7a) and then convert this tree to the decision tree representation using Bayes' Rule.

Note that the probability tree shown in Figure 6.7b corresponds to the unfolding of a single link, $c_1 \rightarrow t_1$, in the Bayesian network representation. More generally, the problem of inferring the probabilities required for a decision tree representation is exactly the task handled by the Bayesian network formalism of Chapter 4. Finding the probability of a hypothesis $X = x$ given a sequence of observations amounts to computing $BEL(x)$, and finding the probability that we will make an observation y (given a sequence of previous observations) amounts to computing $BEL(y)$. Thus, causally organized belief networks can be used as a background knowledge base which is queried when the need arises to supply parameters for the temporary construction of a decision tree. The two components of knowledge, about beliefs and about actions, are integrated in a formalism called *influence diagrams* [Howard and Matheson 1981].

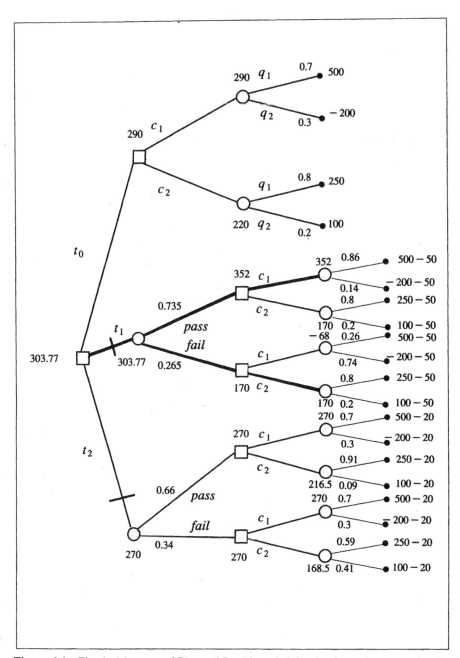

Figure 6.6. *The decision tree of Figure 6.5, with probability levels on the arcs and utility labels on the nodes. The darkened subtree represents the optimal plan.*

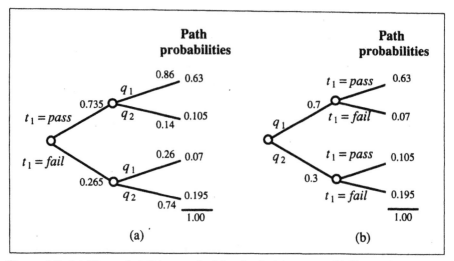

Figure 6.7 *(a) The probabilities required by the decision tree. (b) The probability tree supplied by the agent.*

6.2.3 *Influence Diagrams*

While a decision tree is a convenient representation for a search for an optimal plan, it is totally inadequate for representing domain knowledge, in the same way that knowledge about chess strategy cannot be represented by itemizing all possible moves: decision trees require an incredible amount of storage. Just imagine, for example, the size of the decision tree that would emerge if we lifted the restriction that the buyer is allowed at most one test. Two new branches would be added to the decision tree, representing the sequences (t_1, t_2, Buy) and (t_2, t_1, Buy), each sprouting a tree roughly the size of the tree in Figure 6.5. In general, if we can perform n tests before committing to a final decision, then the decision tree should display every possible sequence in which these tests can be performed. Casual inspection of the tree in Figure 6.5 also reveals that several sub-trees are duplicated. For example, the sub-tree rooted at the decision fork "c_1 or c_2" is displayed three times, albeit with different probability labels. Such duplication would pose insurmountable problems if the tree had to be elicited explicitly from an expert, stored in a computer's memory, and displayed to a user for possible modification.

Clearly, the only practical way of doing planning in uncertain domains is to generate portions of the decision tree *on the fly* from more economical forms of knowledge, in much the same way that game trees are partially generated from a brief description of the legal moves. The difficulty with such a scheme is that the construction of any decision tree requires three diverse sources of knowledge, each organized by a different set of principles:

1. Causal knowledge about how events influence each other in the domain.

2. Knowledge about what action sequences are feasible in any given set of circumstances.

3. Normative knowledge about how desirable the consequences are.

It is not coincidental that the chronology in which events occur during the actual execution of a plan often clashes with the directionality of causal relationships along which human knowledge is organized. Plan execution demands explicitness and immediacy of the kind provided by decision trees, whereas memory organization requires modularity and parsimony of the kind provided by causal networks. Influence diagrams are an attempt to capture all three knowledge sources in one graphical representation.

STRUCTURING AN INFLUENCE DIAGRAM

Influence diagrams are directed acyclic graphs with three types of nodes—*decision nodes, chance nodes,* and a *value node.* Decision nodes, shown as squares, represent choices available to the decision-maker. Chance nodes, shown as circles, represent random variables (or uncertain quantities). Finally, the value node, shown as a diamond, represents the objective (or utility) to be maximized.

The arcs in the graph have different meanings, based on their destinations. Arcs pointing to utility and chance nodes represent probabilistic or functional dependence, like the arcs in Bayesian networks. They do not necessarily imply causality or time precedence although in practice they often do. Arcs into decision nodes imply time precedence and are *informational,* i.e., they show which variables will be known to the decision-maker before the decision is made.

Formally speaking, an influence diagram can be viewed as a special type of Bayesian network, where the value of each decision variable is not determined probabilistically by its predecessors, but rather is imposed from the outside to meet some optimization objective. However, the decision task cannot be viewed as one of merely assigning values to a subset of variables, the way we found a best explanation in Chapter 5. Whereas the domains of the variables in a Bayesian network are fixed, the domain of each decision variable in an influence diagram varies according to previous decisions. For example, if a decision variable A has no predecessors, its domain is simply the set of actions available at that fork. If the decision variable has one chance node X as a parent, its domain is a set of pairs (a, x), each representing an action a in response to an observation x. If one of A's parents represents a decision T on whether or not to test variable X prior to taking action, then the domain of A will be either the set of (a, x) pairs or the set of unconditional actions $\{a\}$, depending on whether the decision to observe X was licensed by T.†

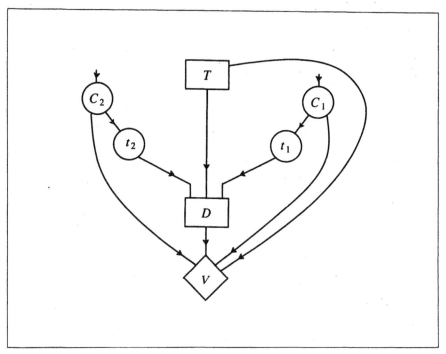

Figure 6.8. *An influence diagram representation of Example 1.*

Figure 6.8 shows the influence diagram representing the car-buyer example. T denotes the choice of test to be performed, $T \in \{t_0, t_1, t_2\}$, D stands for the decision of which car to buy, $D \in \{Buy\ 1, Buy\ 2\}$, C_i represents the quality of car i, $C_i \in \{q_1, q_2\}$, and t_i represents the outcome of the test on car i, $t_i \in \{pass, fail\}$.

As in Bayesian networks, the arcs specify dependencies of various types: those entering chance nodes are quantified by conditional probabilities, those entering D indicate which quantities and previous decisions can be consulted before we make the decision D, and those entering V indicate which quantities enter into the computation of the utility. The missing arcs signify conditional independencies; for example, the absence of a direct arc between C_1 and D asserts that given the

---

† Viewing decision modes as variables with varying domains is a purely formal device for matching the format of Bayesian networks. In practice, the pairs of conditional actions are not stored explicitly at the decision node but are generated during the process of optimization.

result of test t_1, the buying decision must remain the same, regardless of the actual quality of car 1.

Situation-specific knowledge is represented numerically as a set of functions relating each variable to its parent. Chance variables store the same conditional probabilities that quantify the links in Bayesian networks. For example, t_1 will store the conditional probability matrix $P(t_1 | C_1)$ for all values of C_1 and t_1, and C_1 will store the prior probability $P(C_1 = q_1)$ (hence the arc entering C_1 in Figure 6.8). Knowledge of feasibility of actions is stored as a set of functions relating decision variables to their parents. For example, the knowledge defining the options available at D is expressed in Table 1, showing how the test decision T permits the bifurcation of the buying decision into conditional strategies predicated upon the test results. These strategies are not stored explicitly, as in Table 1, but are encoded procedurally by prohibiting the bifurcation in case t_0 is chosen.

Table 1.

T	Options available at D
t_0	$\{Buy\ 1,\ Buy\ 2\}$
t_1	$\left\{ \begin{bmatrix} Buy\ 1 & \text{if } t_1 = pass \\ Buy\ 2 & \text{if } t_1 = fail \end{bmatrix},\ \begin{bmatrix} Buy\ 2 & \text{if } t_1 = pass \\ Buy\ 1 & \text{if } t_1 = fail \end{bmatrix},\ Buy\ 1,\ Buy\ 2 \right\}$
t_2	$\left\{ \begin{bmatrix} Buy\ 1 & \text{if } t_2 = pass \\ Buy\ 2 & \text{if } t_2 = fail \end{bmatrix},\ \begin{bmatrix} Buy\ 2 & \text{if } t_2 = pass \\ Buy\ 1 & \text{if } t_2 = fail \end{bmatrix},\ Buy\ 1,\ Buy\ 2 \right\}$

Normative knowledge likewise can be expressed as a set of functional relationships between the value node and its parents. For example, given the decision D, the quality of the car purchased, and the cost of test T (if any was performed), the value of V is specified unambiguously. Formally, being functionally determined by its parents, the value node is identical to a query node (Section 4.5.1). Once this functional relationship is available, the expected value of V can be calculated as well, given the distribution over its chance parents and the values of its decision parents.

Influence diagrams and decision trees contain the same amount of information, but the former are clearly more parsimonious and more conceptually appealing.

EVALUATING INFLUENCE DIAGRAMS

There are two methods for determining the optimal decision policy from an influence diagram. The first [Howard and Matheson 1981] consists of converting the influence diagram to a decision tree and solving for the optimal policy within the tree, using the exp-max labeling procedure. Note that if the diagram contains unordered decision variables, then the decision tree should enumerate all possible orderings of these variables. For example, if the car buyer can perform both t_1 and t_2 (in either order) then the domain of variable T should include the sequences $\{(t_0), (t_1), (t_2), (t_1 t_2), (t_2 t_1)\}$, and the corresponding decision tree should reflect these sequences by appending the appropriate sub-trees to Figure 6.7. The disadvantage of this method, of course, is the enormous amount of space required to store the tree.

The second approach to decision-making in influence diagrams consists of eliminating nodes from the diagram through a series of value-preserving transformations [Shachter 1986]. Each transformation leaves the expected utility intact, and at every step the modified graph is still an influence diagram. Two restrictions are imposed on the influence diagram to facilitate this method:

1. There is total ordering among the decision nodes.

2. Each decision node and its direct predecessors directly influence all successor decision nodes (this restriction is called "no forgetting," as it represents the agent's capability to recall past decisions).

There are four basic transformations allowed:

1. *Barren node removal*: Barren nodes are chance or decision nodes without successors (e.g., anticipatory leaf nodes in Bayesian networks). These can be removed from the diagram because their values do not affect other nodes. If the removal of a barren node causes other nodes to become barren, they can be removed as well.

2. *Arc reversal*: If there is an arc (i, j) between chance nodes i and j, but no other directed path from i to j, we can transform the influence diagram to a new influence diagram with an arc from j to i instead. First, to preserve *I*-mapness (see Section 3.3.1), each node inherits the other's conditional predecessors. Then new conditional probabilities are computed for i and j, using Bayes' Rule.

3. *Conditional expectation*: A chance node that directly precedes the value node can be removed in the following manner: First we add the predecessors of the chance node to the list of the value node's predecessors. Then we eliminate the chance node by conditional expectation.

4. *Maximization*: Once all barren nodes are removed, a decision node that directly precedes the value node can be removed by maximizing the

expected utility, provided that all direct predecessors of the value node are also direct predecessors of this decision node.

Shachter proved that each of these transformations is consistent with the original diagram and therefore does not affect the optimal decision strategy or the expected value of the optimal strategy. Moreover, at every step we can find some node to eliminate, perhaps after some arc reversals. Hence, the algorithm is guaranteed to terminate with the optimal value (i.e., decision) attached to the first decision variable. In Figure 6.8, for example, the algorithm will eliminate all nodes except T, and at termination T will be bound to its optimal value: t_1.

The node-elimination method overcomes some of the storage space problems inherent to decision-tree representations (it eliminates sub-tree duplication, for instance), but it still may require excessive storage space to support the intermediate steps. The reason is that arc reversal may direct a large number of arrows toward particular nodes, and the space required for storing the conditional probabilities of such nodes grows exponentially with the number of arrows pointing to them. Additionally, the method requires global supervision (to decide on the next transformation), and it hinders explanations; many intermediate chance nodes that play a central role in justifying the actions recommended (e.g., disease names) are eliminated from the diagram, thus preventing a natural explanation from being constructed mechanically (see the discussion in Section 4.1).

A hybrid method of evaluating influence diagrams naturally suggests itself, trading off time for storage. It is based on the realization that decision trees need not actually be generated and stored in their totality to produce the optimal policy. A decision tree can also be evaluated by *traversing* it in a depth-first, backtracking manner using a meager amount of storage space (proportional to the depth of the tree) (see Pearl [1984]). Moreover, branch-and-bound techniques can be employed to prune the search space and permit an evaluation without exhaustively traversing the entire tree.

Accordingly, an influence diagram can be evaluated by sequentially instantiating the decision and observation nodes (in chronological order) while treating the remaining chance nodes as a Bayesian network that supplies the probabilistic parameters necessary for tree evaluation. These parameters can be computed by any of the network propagation methods discussed in Chapter 4, or by the node elimination method of Shachter.

An example will serve to illustrate this hybrid method. Assume we wish to evaluate the diagram in Figure 6.8. We begin by instantiating the variable T to some value, say t_2, and proceed to D. Since $T = t_2$ permits D to be conditioned on the outcome of t_2 (see Table 1), we choose arbitrary values for t_1 and D, say $t_1 = fail$ and $D = Buy\ 2$, and proceed to the value node V. At this point we must compute the expected value of V, given the current values assigned to T, t_2, and D, as in Figure 6.9.

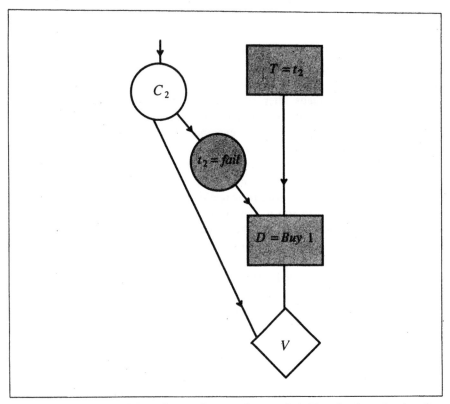

Figure 6.9. *A portion of the influence diagram during a hybrid evaluation, showing three nodes instantiated.*

The calculation can be performed by propagating the assumption $t_2 = fail$ (as evidence) onto the remaining network, computing $BEL(C_2)$ and then computing the expected utility

$$U = E(V) = V(Buy\ 2, C_2 = q_1, T = t_2)\ BEL(C_2 = q_1)$$
$$+ V(Buy\ 2, C_2 = q_2, T = t_2)\ BEL(C_2 = q_2).\qquad \textbf{(6.15)}$$

This is identical to the computation performed at the lowest branch of Figure 6.6, except that the parameter $BEL(C_2 = q_1) = P(C_2 = q_1 | t_2 = fail)$ can now be computed by network-based techniques rather than using the probability tree of Figure 6.7.

Upon receiving the value $E(V) = 168.5$, we backtrack to D and choose its next unexplored value, $D = Buy\ 1$. This new assignment yields a higher score, $E(V) = 270$ (see Figure 6.6), which we tentatively use to mark variable t_2 while we change its state to $t_2 = pass$. Continuing in this fashion, we traverse the tree of

Figure 6.6 from the bottom up until the root node T is evaluated and the optimal strategy extracted. Note that the tree is not generated explicitly; all instantiations and computations are performed directly on the variables in the influence diagram of Figure 6.8.

6.3 THE VALUE OF INFORMATION

6.3.1 Information Sources and Their Values

It is generally accepted that information is a useful commodity, that acting in an informed fashion is preferable to acting under ignorance. This is why people accumulate information when it is available and purchase information when it is scarce. People also possess strong intuition about whether one information source is more valuable (more reliable and pertinent) than another.

The analysis in the preceding sections permits the notion of *informational value* to be given a precise technical underpinning. The value of any information source is defined as the difference between the utilities of two optimal strategies, one providing the freedom of choosing different actions for different source outcomes, the other providing no such freedom. This criterion can be used to rate the usefulness of various information sources and to decide whether a piece of evidence is worth acquiring.

The merit of querying variable X can be decided before actually observing its value, using the following consideration: If we query X and find the value to be x, the utility of action a will be (see Eq. (6.1))

$$U(a \mid x) = \sum_c U(c)\, P(c \mid a, e, X = x) . \qquad (6.16)$$

At this point, we can choose the best among all pending alternatives and get the value

$$U(X = x) = \max_a U(a \mid x) . \qquad (6.17)$$

However, since we are not sure of the actual outcome of querying X, we must average $U(X = x)$ over all possible values of x, weighted by their probabilities. Thus, the utility of querying X calculates to

$$U_X = \sum_x P(X = x \mid e)\, U(X = x) , \qquad (6.18)$$

where e is the evidence acquired so far.

Example 1 should help illustrate this analysis. The information sources under evaluation are the two tests available, and the variables queried are the outcomes of these tests. The branches labeled t_1 and t_2 in Figure 6.6 represent decisions to consult those sources, and the branch t_0 represents the decision to refrain from using either source. The utility labels on these branches indicate that test t_1 is worth $56.42, because performing the test increases the utility of the root node by $296.42 − $290 = $6.42, even after paying $50 for the test. By the same consideration, test t_2 has zero informational value, because its utility ($270) is exactly $20 (the cost of t_2) below that of the uninformed strategy t_0. The reason t_2 adds no useful information is that it leads to the same decision—to buy c_1—regardless of whether the test outcome is $t_2 = pass$ or $t_2 = fail$.

This example highlights the information necessary for characterizing an information source and assessing its value. A source is characterized by a conditional probability function $P(x \mid z)$, where X is the output of the source and Z is the set of all variables that influence the utility of the consequences. A source can be assigned a value when we have full specification of $P(x \mid z)$ and when we have all the information required for calculating the expected utility $U(a \mid z)$ for every feasible action a. Note, however, that if several information sources are available and can be consulted in any order, the notion of informational value ceases to be a local characteristic of each source; in other words, one can no longer assess the value of any individual source independent of the other sources available and independent of the sequence in which they are to be consulted. For example, the value of test t_1 depends critically on whether t_2 is also available and on whether t_1 is conducted before or after t_2.

6.3.2 *Myopic Assessments of Information Sources*

In principle, decision theory's definition of informational value can be used to schedule many control functions in reasoning systems. For example, it can be used for deciding what to ask the user next, which test to perform next, which rule to invoke next, or which node to activate next. Unfortunately, the evaluation required by this definition is too cumbersome to be of any practical use. Before an information source can be evaluated, one must know the precise nature of all other sources that are available or that might become available in the future, all decisions that might be taken in the future, their consequences, their utilities, etc., ad infinitum. We are usually asked to choose among competing sources before having the detailed knowledge required for their evaluation, and before being able to run a full-fledged analysis of the entire problem under all possible orderings of the sources. In fact, once we have the facility to run a complete analysis of the problem, the need to evaluate and rank information sources vanishes, since the optimal strategies found already contain a precise prescription as to which information to consult and when.

To obtain a practical criterion for choosing among information sources, certain simplifications must be imposed on the decision problem at hand. The most popular ones are based on the following two assumptions:

1. *No competition*: Each information source is evaluated in isolation, as if it were the only source available for the entire decision.

2. *One-step horizon*: After consulting the source, we must make a terminal decision a, after which nature chooses a state z and a terminal utility is pronounced on the pair (z, a).

These assumptions result in a *myopic* policy for scheduling the selection of information sources. Instead of examining all possible sequences of pending sources, we evaluate each one independently, choose the one with the highest merit, observe its outcome, update all probabilities, resubmit the remaining information sources for evaluation, and repeat the process. The standard testing ground for evaluating sources is a four-tiered decision tree as shown in Figure 6.10. The first tier reflects the decision whether to consult the information source or act without it, the second tier reflects the potential reports (x) to be issued by the information source, the third tier reflects the choices (a) faced by the decision-maker, and the fourth tier reflects the possible states of nature (z).

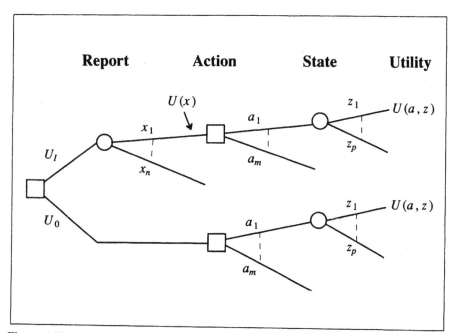

Figure 6.10. *The standard structure of a myopic assessment of information sources.*

The utility of the location marked $U(x)$ is given by

$$U(x) = \max_a \sum_z P(z \mid x) \, U(a, z) \,. \qquad (6.19)$$

This results in a utility U_I, for the informed choice, of

$$U_I = \sum_x P(x) \, U(x) = \sum_x \sum_z P(x \mid z) \, P(z) \, U(x) \,, \qquad (6.20)$$

which reflects both the probability of obtaining a report x and the utility of acting optimally after receiving it. The conditional probability $P(x \mid z)$ fully characterizes the nature of the information source,† as it measures the fidelity with which x mirrors z. The lower path, labeled U_0, reflects the utility the decision-maker expects when acting ignorantly, i.e., without consulting the information source.

The value of the information source $\eta = P(x \mid z)$ to the decision-maker is the difference between the upper and lower paths:

$$V(\eta) = U_I - U_0$$

$$= \sum_x \sum_z \max_a \cdot \left[\sum_{z'} P(z' \mid x) U(a, z') \right] P(x \mid z) P(z) - \max_a \sum_z P(z) U(a, z) \,. \qquad (6.21)$$

This difference can be shown to be always nonnegative, i.e.,

$$V(\eta) \geq 0 \,, \qquad (6.22)$$

stating that one can never be worse off by acquiring free information—because one always has the option of ignoring the information acquired and uniformly applying the action that optimizes the lower branch.

EXAMPLE 2: Let us assume that the report x reveals the precise state of nature z, i.e., $P(x \mid z) = P(z \mid x) = \delta_{z, x}$, where $\delta_{z, x}$ is the identity matrix. Substituting into Eq. (6.21), we get

$$V(\eta) = \sum_x \sum_z \max_a \left[\sum_{z'} \delta_{z', x} U(a, z') \right] \delta_{x, z} P(z) - \max_a \sum_z P(z) U(a, z)$$

$$= \sum_z P(z) \left[\max_a U(a, z) - U(a_r, z) \right] = \sum_z P(z) \Delta U(z) \,, \qquad (6.23)$$

---

† In the information theory literature, $P(x \mid z)$ has been termed an *information channel*, while the term *information source* applies to any mechanism that generates random sequences of symbols.

where a_r is the optimal action chosen without consulting the source. This is shown in Table 2.

Table 2.

state z	$P(z)$	$U(a, z)$ $a_1\ a_2\ a_3$	$\Delta U(z) =$ $\max_a U(a, z) - U(a_r, z)$	$P(z)\,\Delta U(z)$
z_1	$\frac{1}{4}$	1 2 3	$3 - 1 = 2$	$\frac{1}{2}$
z_2	$\frac{1}{4}$	2 3 1	$3 - 2 = 1$	$\frac{1}{4}$
z_3	$\frac{1}{2}$	3 1 2	$3 - 3 = 0$	0

Not knowing z, the best we can do is to choose the action $a_r = a_1$ across all states, yielding the utility U_0:

$$U_0 = \max_{i=1}^{3} \sum_{z=1}^{3} U(a_i, z)P(z) = \max\ (2.25;\ 1.75;\ 2) = 2.25\ . \tag{6.24}$$

With perfect information we get the highest utility in each row, because we can pick the action to fit the known state of nature. Hence, the value of perfect information is given by

$$V(\eta) = \sum_{z=1}^{3} P(z)\Delta U(z) = \tfrac{1}{2} + \tfrac{1}{4} + 0 = \tfrac{3}{4}\ . \tag{6.25}$$

EXAMPLE 3: Suppose we have imperfect information, and the action a consists of guessing the state of nature z. The utility is assumed to be 1 if the guess is correct and 0 otherwise, i.e., $U(a, z) = \delta_{a,z}$. Substituting in Eq. (6.21) gives

$$V(\eta) = \sum_x \sum_z \left[\max_a P(a\,|x)\right] P(x\,|z)\, P(z) - \max_a P(a)$$

$$= \sum_x P(x)\max_z P(z\,|x) - \max_z P(z)\ . \tag{6.26}$$

Once again, a numerical example, using the figures in Table 3.

Table 3.

state z	$U(a, z)$ a_1 a_2 a_3	$P(z)$	$P(x\mid z)$ x_1 x_2 x_3	report x	$P(x)$	$P(z\mid x)$ z_1 z_2 z_3
z_1	1 0 0	¼	½ ¼ ¼	x_1	$\dfrac{10}{48}$	$\dfrac{6}{10}$ $\dfrac{4}{10}$ 0
z_1	0 1 0	¼	⅓ ⅓ ⅓	x_2	$\dfrac{15}{48}$	$\dfrac{3}{15}$ $\dfrac{4}{15}$ $\dfrac{8}{15}$
z_3	0 0 1	½	0 ½ ⅔	x_3	$\dfrac{23}{48}$	$\dfrac{3}{23}$ $\dfrac{4}{23}$ $\dfrac{16}{23}$

$$U_I = \sum_{x=1}^{3} P(x)\max_{z=1}^{3} P(z\mid x) = \left[\frac{10}{48}\frac{6}{10} + \frac{15}{48}\frac{8}{15} + \frac{23}{48}\frac{16}{48}\right] = \frac{5}{8},$$

$$U_0 = \max_{z=1}^{3} P(z) = \max\left[¼; ¼; ½\right] = ½,$$

$$V(\eta) = \frac{5}{8} - \frac{1}{2} = \frac{1}{8}. \tag{6.27}$$

6.4 RELEVANCE-BASED CONTROL

6.4.1 Focusing Attention

Control is the process of scheduling the activation of information sources, both external (e.g., acquiring new input) and internal (e.g., invoking rules or updating beliefs). Decision analysis provides a framework for scheduling all computational activities so as to focus on specific goals—updating the belief in a *target set* of hypotheses, shifting attention to a new set, and terminating the activity once we reach an acceptable level of confidence in a hypothesis.

The main reason for focusing attention on a select set of target hypotheses is to economize the acquisition of new data. Let us imagine a subset S of the nodes (normally the leaves) that are known to be sensory or observable nodes for a given problem domain (e.g., laboratory tests in medical diagnosis). In general, the instantiation of any of these sensory nodes incurs a positive cost, and the utility of the information they convey might be insufficient to justify this cost. Thus, it is important to decide which node in S should be instantiated first, based on the information it contributes to the decision at hand, i.e., the target node. If utility information is available, then the value node naturally is the target. If we lack utility information, we assign priorities to pending information sources based on their degree of *informativeness*. This topic will be discussed in the next few subsections.

There is yet another reason for focusing attention on a target hypothesis: to confine inferences to pertinent regions of the network. In previous chapters we assumed that once a piece of evidence is obtained, its impact propagates to the entire network by appropriate updating of the π and λ messages. In many cases, there is a small set of hypotheses that stand at the center of one's concerns, so the reasoning task can focus on a narrow subset of variables, and propagation through the entire network is unnecessary.

In medical diagnosis, for example, the knowledge base may be comprised of hundreds of hypotheses and thousands of rules connecting them to symptoms, treatments, and observations. It would be wasteful to propagate the impact of allergy symptoms to regions of knowledge dealing with brain surgery or hearing impairment. Physicians, indeed, are notorious for exhibiting a narrow focus of attention, stubbornly pursuing a single hypothesis while ignoring evidence not bearing directly on the hypothesis pursued. While such behavior is clearly undesirable, it nevertheless reflects a pressing computational need to focus, at any given time, all reasoning activities on a manageable portion of one's knowledge base.

Instead of propagating all the information everywhere, it is possible to assess first the potential impact of every updating operation on the belief of the target node and to limit the updating process so that only relevant information is propagated. Doing so will decrease the amount of data traffic in the network and the amount of computation expended on inferencing. However, it is important that the information we choose not to propagate be allowed to accumulate at the boundaries and discharge its impact to new areas of knowledge once our current set of beliefs becomes stagnant. The ability occasionally to analyze a data item with respect to *all* conceivable causes (as in Chapter 5), ignoring the reason for which that item was requested, can lead to a generation of new alternatives and new goals.

6.4.2 Utility-Free Assessment of Information Sources

Decision theory considerations formally define the informational value associated with any computation or data-acquisition activity. The value $V(a)$ associated with an activity a having possible outcomes $a_1, a_2, ..., a_n$ is given by the difference between two utilities: the average utility of acting (optimally) upon learning the outcome of a, and the average utility of acting (optimally) before learning the outcome of a. Such a definition, although based on a myopic simplification (Section 6.3.2), could in principle be used to rank all pending computational activities and thus provide a solution to the problem of control.

Unfortunately, it suffers from some basic shortcomings. First, since the evaluation of $V(a)$ is itself a computational activity, we quickly run into a path of infinite regress: Which $V(a)$ should we consider next? Which consideration should we consider next? And so on ad infinitum. Second, the calculation of $V(a)$ requires that we know in advance the set of decision options available to us, their range of possible consequences, and the utilities of these consequences under all possible outcomes. We often must decide what is relevant or informative without having a definite purpose in mind. Third, even if utility information were available, ranking activities according to the myopic assessment $V(a)$ provides only a first-order heuristic; it does not guarantee that the resultant schedule will minimize the average time or cost of these activities. The reason is that the measure $V(a)$ considers only individual activities taken in isolation, not sequences of activities. It is quite possible that conducting two consecutive tests, each ranking poorly on the $V(a)$ scale, would be more valuable than conducting two other tests that individually score high on that scale. In such cases, strategies based on $V(a)$ will lead to suboptimal activity schedules.

In view of these considerations, an exact computation of $V(a)$ seems unwarranted, and approximation strategies should be adequate as long as they are based on reasonable measures of informativeness. Such measures, free of specific utility considerations, will be developed next.

SENSITIVITY MATRICES

The utility of any information source stems from the impact each of its outputs has on the belief measure of the target hypothesis. Let T be the variable corresponding to the target hypothesis, and let X be a *test variable*, i.e., an observable node whose impact on T is to be assessed. If the current belief in T is given by $BEL(t) = P(t \mid e)$, then the posterior belief $BEL(t \mid x) = P(t \mid e, x)$ will indicate how sensitive $BEL(t)$ is to each of the values that X may take. We therefore define the *sensitivity* of T to X by the matrix

$$S(t, x) \triangleq \frac{P(t \mid e, x)}{P(t \mid e)}$$

$$= \frac{BEL(t \mid x)}{BEL(t)}$$

$$= \frac{BEL(x \mid t)}{BEL(x)} \tag{6.28}$$

Note that $S(t, x)$ is a dynamic function, highly sensitive to the current evidence e, and is symmetric, i.e.,

$$S(t, x) = S(x, t) . \qquad (6.29)$$

Imagine now that a Bayesian network is at equilibrium. Belief measures are assigned to all nodes in the network, and we wish to evaluate the sensitivity of T to some node X. $S(t, x)$ can be calculated in two ways. First, there is the direct or *inward* way: Instantiate node X (temporarily) to each of its values, propagate the impact of each instantiation $X = x$ toward T, compute the resulting values of $BEL(t \mid x)$, and divide by the previous value $BEL(t)$. Second, there is the indirect or *broadcasting* way: Instantiate node T (temporarily) to each of its values, propagate the impact of each instantiation $T = t$ toward X, compute the resulting belief $BEL(x \mid t)$, and divide by the previous belief $BEL(x)$. $BEL(t)$ is available at T prior to instantiation while $BEL(x)$ is available at x prior to broadcasting.

There are several reasons why the broadcasting method of computation is better than the inward mode. First, target nodes normally represent causal explanations of some sort, so they normally will be higher in the causal hierarchy than test nodes. Thus, the instantiation of T will result in a network with fewer loops, allowing unsupervised propagation. Second, we normally have to deal with one or two target nodes and many test nodes. The inward method requires that we perform the evaluation sequentially, propagating separately the impact of each node that awaits evaluation. The broadcasting method, on the other hand, can perform this evaluation in parallel, propagating the impact of the target node instantiations in one wave toward the test nodes at the network's periphery.

MEASURES OF IMPACT

The sensitivity matrix itself, $S(t, x)$, is too detailed to serve as a score for prioritizing activities. It contains the influence of every conceivable value of X on every value of T but does not provide a concise summary of the overall contribution of the activities pending in X toward reducing the uncertainty in T. To achieve this we must translate the information contained in the matrix $S(t, x)$ into a single numerical quantity reflecting the value of X's contribution. Two such measures will be discussed next.

SHANNON'S MEASURE OF MUTUAL INFORMATION

Mutual information [Shannon and Weaver 1949] is one of the most commonly used measures for ranking information sources. It is based on the assumption that the uncertainty regarding any variable Z characterized by a probability distribution $P(z)$ can be represented by the entropy function

$$H(Z) = -\sum_{z} P(z) \log P(z) . \qquad (6.30)$$

Accordingly, the residual uncertainty regarding the true value of the target variable T, given that X is instantiated to x, can be written

$$H(T \mid x) = -\sum_t P(t \mid x) \log P(t \mid x) , \qquad (6.31)$$

and the average residual uncertainty in T, summed over all possible outcomes x, is

$$H(T \mid X) = \sum_x H(T \mid x) P(x)$$

$$= -\sum_x \sum_t P(t, x) \log P(t \mid x) . \qquad (6.32)$$

If we subtract $H(T \mid X)$ from the original uncertainty in T prior to consulting X, namely $H(T)$, we will obtain the total uncertainty-reducing potential of X. This potential is called Shannon's mutual information and is given by

$$I(T, X) = H(T) - H(T \mid X)$$

$$= -\sum_x \sum_t P(t, x) \log \frac{P(t, x)}{P(t) \, P(x)} . \qquad (6.33)$$

Clearly, $I(T, X)$ is symmetric with respect to X and T, so

$$I(T, X) = I(X, T) = H(X) - H(T \mid X). \qquad (6.34)$$

Additionally, $I(T, X)$ is a nonnegative quantity and is equal to 0 iff T and X are mutually independent [Gallager 1968].

$I(T, X)$ can be calculated in either an inward or a broadcast mode, substituting the appropriate belief expressions or sensitivity matrices into Eq. (6.31). These give

$$I(T, X) = -\sum_x \sum_t BEL(t, x) \log \frac{BEL(t, x)}{BEL(t) \, BEL(x)} , \qquad (6.35)$$

or

$$I(T, X) = -\sum_x \sum_t BEL(x) \, BEL(t) \, S(t, x) \log S(t, x) . \qquad (6.36)$$

The main weakness of Shannon's measure is that it does not reflect ordering or scale information relative to the values that a variable may take. For example, the uncertainty associated with the belief "The temperature is between 37° and 39°" would have the same entropy measure as the uncertainty associated with "The temperature is either between 0° and 1° or between 99° and 100°" (assuming uniform distributions over the intervals specified). Entropy is invariant to reordering or renaming the values in the domain, so it cannot reflect the fact that we perceive an error between 37° and 38° to be much less critical than an error between 0° and 100°. As a result, scheduling based on Shannon's measure of mutual information may occasionally exhibit peculiar behavior; it may spend precious resources on irrelevant tests, such as trying to distinguish between 37° and 38°, while neglecting more informative tests, capable of distinguishing between diverse hypotheses, say 1° and 100°.

The source of this peculiar behavior is that entropy, contrary to folklore, does not measure the harm caused by uncertainty; it measures the cost of *removing* the uncertainty (by querying an oracle and paying the same fee for all binary queries). This is why Shannon's mutual information measure endows equal penalty to all errors. A way to overcome this deficiency would be to adopt an alternative measure of uncertainty that more realistically reflects the risks of acting under ignorance.

ERROR-BASED MEASURES

While full disclosure of decisions, consequences, and utilities may be impractical, approximate canonical models can be used to capture some cost-benefit considerations by rating the severity of errors. For example, we can assume that a physician who acts on the premise that the patient's temperature is $\hat{t}$, while in reality it is t, may incur a cost described by some function of the error $t - \hat{t}$. The simplest and most commonly used function is the *square-error* cost criterion $(t - \hat{t})^2$. Using this criterion as an example, we shall demonstrate how it can be embedded into the impact parameters as a means for controlling tests and propagation.

Given a distribution $P(t)$ of a random variable T, it is well known that the best estimate of T in the mean-square-error sense is the mean, μ_T. In other words, if we need to guess a value $\hat{t}$ for T that will minimize the expected square-error $(t - \hat{t})^2$, then our best guess should be $\hat{t} = \mu_T$. Moreover, the expected cost associated with the best guess is equal to the variance σ_T^2. Thus, our criterion for prioritizing computational activities should be to activate first the variable X that promises the highest average reduction of σ_T^2. To define an impact measure reflecting these considerations, we can follow Eqs. (6.30) through (6.33) and substitute the cost σ_T^2 for the entropy $H(T)$.

Before X is consulted, the cost associated with the uncertainty in T is given by

$$C(T) = \sigma_T^2 . \tag{6.37}$$

Under the assumption $X = x$ the cost will be given by the variance of the posterior distribution $P(t \mid x)$,

$$C(T \mid x) = \sum_t P(t \mid x) (t - \mu_{T \mid x})^2 , \tag{6.38}$$

where $\mu_{T|x}$ is the posterior mean,

$$\mu_{T|x} = \sum_t P(t|x)\, t \,. \tag{6.39}$$

Averaging over all outcomes $X = x$, the expected posterior cost associated with the uncertainty in T after X is consulted is given by

$$C(T|X) = \sum_x P(x) \sum_t P(t|x)\, (t - \mu_{T|x})^2 \,. \tag{6.40}$$

Eq. (6.40) can be used as a gauge to rank the relevance of each candidate variable X.

In the sequential, inward mode of propagation, Eq. (6.40) will be calculated at the target variable T, using the updated beliefs $BEL(t|x)$ instead of $P(t|x)$. In the parallel, broadcasting mode of propagation, it will be calculated at each test variable X, using the updated $BEL(x|t)$ functions that result from broadcasting the instantiations $T = t$. Writing Eq. (6.40) in terms of $P(x|t)$ and using Eq. (6.39), we obtain, after some manipulations,

$$\begin{aligned} C(T|X) &= \mu_T^2 - E_x(\mu_{T|x}^2) \\ &= \mu_T^2 - \sum_x \left[\sum_t P(t|x)\, t \right]^2 P(x) \\ &= \mu_T^2 - \sum_x P(x) \left[\sum_t P(x|t)\, \frac{P(t)}{P(x)}\, t \right]^2 . \end{aligned} \tag{6.41}$$

Further substituting $BEL(\cdot)$ for $P(\cdot)$, we have

$$C(T|X) = \mu_T^2 - \sum_x BEL^{-1}(x) \left[\sum_t BEL(x|t)\, BEL(t)\, t \right]^2 . \tag{6.42}$$

All parameters necessary for computing Eq. (6.42) are available at the test node X. μ_T^2 is a constant. The values of t and $BEL(t)$ are broadcasted uniformly to all test nodes, $BEL(x|t)$ is propagated outward from T to X, and $BEL(x)$ is available at X prior to broadcasting.

6.4.3 Controlling Attention

Control is the process of activating information sources. *Attention* is the goal toward which we activate the sources. So far we have dealt with a fixed focus of attention—the set of target hypotheses—and our goal has been to schedule the activation of information sources in a way that will most economically refute or confirm the target hypotheses. It is toward this end that measures of impact were developed: to activate informative sources first and uninformative ones last.

Clearly, the target set itself should change as more data is obtained. The obvious case occurs when the current hypotheses are refuted by the evidence; alternative explanations must then be posited, by a process similar to that used in Chapter 5—identifying a new set of hypotheses that best explain the data at hand. However, there are reasons to temporarily change the focus of attention even before the current set of hypotheses goes sour. One reason is to posit a set of *subgoals* that if realized will help us determine whether the current set is still viable. For example, a lawyer might say, "The reason I asked this question is to determine whether the suspect was at the scene of the crime." Being at the scene of the crime is merely a subgoal, an auxiliary hypothesis that helps determine the value of the target hypothesis—whether the suspect actually committed the crime.

WHY SUBGOALS?

On the surface, positing subgoals (or *subgoaling*) seems superfluous; direct evaluation of information sources relative to the actual target hypothesis seems a more reasonable strategy to follow. The auxiliary hypotheses clearly should participate in the evaluation process, being the mediators between the target hypothesis and the candidate sources, but for them to be treated as the targets of subsequent evaluations, even on a temporary basis, seems superfluous and diversionary.

Subgoaling, however, remedies several drawbacks—some psychological and some computational—of centralized control strategies. The obvious drawback of centralized control is the difficulty of mentally computing measures of impacts through long chains of inference. It is much easier for a lawyer to assess the significance of a piece of evidence relative to the suspect's whereabouts than relative to the overall charge; the former is more direct and hence more reliable. Additionally, subgoaling narrows the set of information sources from which the most informative one is to be selected. A third advantage of subgoaling is that it leads to a more coherent line of questioning than does centralized control. Governed by criteria of maximal informativeness, the order of queries suggested by centralized control often looks peculiar or arbitrary to the person who is being queried, as it requires abrupt jumps across unrelated topics as soon as some leaf node becomes the most informative one on the network periphery.

Besides being psychologically pleasing, subgoaling also offers computational advantages. By considering aspects of scheduling that were neglected by the myopic assessment of information sources (Section 6.3.2), subgoaling can yield a more efficient data acquisition policy than centralized control can. Whereas myopic policies neglect to evaluate information sources in a context of groups or subsequences, subgoaling, by resolving to pursue a given subgoal, in effect treats those subsequences that pertain to that subgoal as single units. Assessed individually, each source might have a misleadingly small impact on the target hypothesis, yet as a group supporting the same subgoal, the impact can be significant and more accurately assessed.

NESTED SUBGOALING

The spectrum of heuristic strategies capable of controlling subgoals is very wide. After activating each information source (and propagating its impact) we must decide whether to keep or change the current target hypotheses (i.e., subgoals), and if a change is warranted, what the next subgoal ought to be. One straightforward subgoaling strategy is as follows: Start with the actual target hypothesis T_0 (i.e., the one that best explains the data) and examine its immediate successors. Treat each successor node as an information source, assuming that its precise value is about to be revealed, and select the most informative successor relative to T_0. Now posit the chosen successor, say T_1, as a subgoal, i.e., a new target hypothesis. Examine the successors of T_1 and select as a new subgoal the one most informative relative to T_1. Continue in this manner until an observable node is reached, in which case it is activated and its impact propagated to the entire network. At this point repeat the process, using T_0 (or a new best explanation) as the target node.

This control strategy has many variations. For example, instead of evaluating the immediate successors of the current subgoal one can go two steps ahead and examine its grandchildren. Also, instead of starting afresh at T_0, one can keep a subgoal active throughout a sequence of observations. Such variations have been formulated and investigated by Maler and Ben-Bassat [1986].

6.4.4 Summary

The task of controlling reasoning activities was formulated as that of finding an optimal schedule for activating information sources. Decision theory provides a framework for assessing the knowledge and computations needed to perform this optimization precisely. It turns out that the knowledge required is often unavailable, and the computation task is often intractable. Myopic policies sidestep the tractability problem by evaluating each information source in isolation, but they still require excessive knowledge about actions and utility. When utility information is unavailable, information sources can be ranked by relevance-based measures. Yet even this approximation may be too demanding, as it still requires that all pending sources be compared at each step. Subgoaling strategies emerge as a reasonable compromise; they are computationally tractable and psychologically appealing, but they still provide a focused way of acquiring information. These strategies are clearly suboptimal, yet the approximations and compromises are made explicit, and conceptual ties to the theoretical objectives are maintained.

6.5 BIBLIOGRAPHICAL AND HISTORICAL REMARKS

Statistical decision theory emerged in the 1940s with works by von Neumann and Morgenstern [1947] and Wald [1950], while the Bayesian approach to decision theory was pioneered by de Finetti [1937], Good [1950], and Savage [1954]. The axioms of utility theory also first appeared in von Neumann and Morgenstern [1947]. Savage developed utility and probability simultaneously, thus fusing de Finetti's pragmatic view of probability with von Neumann and Morgenstern's probabilistic view of utility.

A good introduction to decision analysis can be found in Raiffa [1968]. This paperback book is especially popular because of its lucid style and its abundance of examples. It also provides a historical survey of statistical methods and clarifies · the ties between decision analysis and the "normal" form of statistical decision theory. Papers on the practical aspects of decision analysis can be found in Howard, Matheson and Miller [1976]. Our exposition of utility theory follows that of Howard [1976b], with influence from the more formal approach of Chapter 1 in Ferguson [1967].

Advanced books on decision analysis include Raiffa and Schlaifer [1968], Kenney and Raiffa [1975], and von Winterfeldt and Edwards [1986]. This last book contains a comprehensive account of psychological research on human decision-making behavior. Another classic book on decision behavior is that of Kahneman, Slovic, and Tversky [1982], specializing in cognitive illusions, i.e., systematic deviations from normative theories. More computationally minded discussions on the normative vs. the conventionalistic approach to rational decisions can be found in Loui [1987] and Doyle [1988].

Myopic policies of scheduling tests were investigated by Ben-Bassat [1978], showing that performance is fairly insensitive to the choice of impact measure. de Kleer and Williams [1987] report the application of a myopic policy (based on Shannon's measure) to the diagnosis of electronic circuits with multiple faults. Error-based measures were studied in the pattern recognition literature under the classification-error criterion [Ben-Bassat 1978]. The treatment in Section 6.4.2 extends this measure to estimation tasks with the mean-square-error criterion. The use of impact measures to control network propagation is described in Pinto [1986].

Exercises

6.1. Let the relation ~ be the intersection of ≤* and *≥. Prove that ~ is an equivalence relation, i.e.,

(a) $p \sim p$,

(b) $p_1 \sim p_2 \implies p_2 \sim p_1$, and

(c) $p_1 \sim p_2, p_2 \sim p_3 \implies p_1 \sim p_3$

(reflexive, symmetric, and transitive).

6.2. Prove that $p_1 \leq^* p_2$ and $p_2 <^* p_3$ imply $p_1 <^* p_3$.

6.3. Defend the axiom of substitutability against the following criticism:

If you offer me a single shoe, I don't mind taking the left shoe or the right shoe. However, if I already have an extra left shoe at home, I will unquestionably prefer your right shoe, not your left. This shows that indifference in isolation should not imply indifference in every context; preferences are context-dependent.

6.4. A person is facing a choice of college classes characterized by the triplets

$$P_i = (\, q_i(A),\, q_i(B),\, q_i(C)\,),$$

where $q_i(A)$, $q_i(B)$, and $q_i(C)$ represent the probabilities of receiving the grades A, B, and C, respectively, if the i-th class is taken. The algorithm for choosing between two candidate classes, i and j, is as follows:

(a) If $q_i(A) > q_j(A)$, choose class i.
(b) If $q_j(A) > q_i(A)$, choose class j.
(c) If $q_i(A) = q_j(A)$, select the class with the highest $q(B)$.
(d) If $q_i(A) = q_j(A)$ and $q_i(B) = q_j(B)$, then the classes are equivalent.

Does the preference pattern generated by this algorithm have a corresponding utility function? If so, find $u(A)$, $u(B)$, and $u(C)$. If not, which axiom of Section 6.1.4 is violated?

6.5. Invent two algorithms for selecting college classes on the basis of the grade probabilities $q_i(A)$, $q_i(B)$, and $q_i(C)$; invent one that has an agreeing utility and one that does not. Make sure the first algorithm does not involve arithmetic operations (no additions or multiplications), while the second algorithm is rational enough to be adopted by some people you know.

6.6.   A person has a utility curve given by

$$U(x) = \begin{cases} x^2 & \text{for } x > 0 \\ x^3 & \text{for } x \leq 0, \end{cases}$$

where x is the monetary change from the present worth. This person is offered a lottery to bet a sum y with an equal chance of doubling the money or losing it.

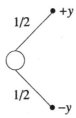

a.   At what range of y should betting be acceptable?

b.   What should be the optimal betting sum y?

c.   What is the minimal sum the person should be willing to accept in lieu of the option of participating in the optimal lottery of Problem **(b)**?

d.   Suppose the lottery is no longer balanced, but provides prizes y_1 and $-y_2$ with equal probability. Calculate the maximum value of y_2 (as a function of y_1) that would make the lottery attractive.

6.7.   Refer to the used car problem of Section 6.2.2. Suppose that in addition to the tests t_1 and t_2 the buyer has the option of performing both tests for a fee of $60.

a.   How does this additional option affect the decision tree? How is the buyer's strategy affected?

b.   Suppose that the buyer can decide not to buy a car. How does this affect the decision tree and the optimal strategy?

6.8.   Suppose you are hired as a decision analyst, and your client has just given you the first two layers of a decision tree representing the client's problem. The values on the leaf nodes represent the utility estimates (in utiles) given by the client, together with the client's uncertainty ranges for those estimates.

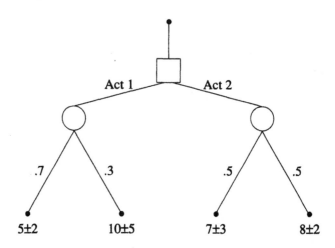

Assuming that the true utilities (those which one would obtain after an in-depth analysis) are uniformly distributed over the given ranges, and assuming that you can submit only one of the four consequences for further analysis, which of the four would you submit?

(Hint: for each leaf node, calculate the value of resolving the uncertainty at that node.)

6.9. You are asked to estimate the likelihood of a future event z_1, and your client decides to reward you by the following rule: If you report an estimate $P(z_1) = r$ $(0 < r < 1)$ and the event z_1 actually occurs, you will receive $C + \log r$; however, if z_1 does not occur, you will receive $C + \log(1 - r)$ (C is a constant).

a. If your true belief in the occurrence of z_1 is $\pi(z_1)$, what should you report to the client so as to maximize your expected return?

b. Imagine that before you make your report, you may consult another expert, who summarizes his opinion by the statement "z_1 will occur with probability π'." His reliability in your eyes can be described by the following distributions:

$$P(\pi' \le x \mid z_1) = x^2, \qquad 0 \le x \le 1,$$

$$P(\pi' \le x \mid \neg z_1) = 2x\left[1 - \frac{x}{2}\right], \qquad 0 \le x \le 1.$$

How will you modify your current belief $\pi(z_1) = \dfrac{1}{3}$ if the expert generates a report π'? Calculate the value of this expert as an information source (before receiving his report).

6.10. Refer to Exercise **2.3.** Suppose that only detectors E^1, E^2, and E^4 are connected. If the detector E^4 in your office turns on, you may wish to reduce your uncertainty about whether a burglary actually took place by reading one of the other two detectors, E^1 or E^2.

    a. Which detector should be read first using Shannon's measure of mutual information?

    b. Which detector should be read first using error-based measures?

Chapter 7

TAXONOMIC HIERARCHIES, CONTINUOUS VARIABLES, AND UNCERTAIN PROBABILITIES

At last the sailors said to each other,
'Come and let us cast lots to find out who
is to blame for this ordeal.' So they cast
lots and the lot fell on Jonah.
— Jonah 1,7

7.1 EVIDENTIAL REASONING IN TAXONOMIC HIERARCHIES

7.1.1 Taxonomic vs. Causal Hierarchies

The primary building blocks of the networks discussed in previous chapters were causal relationships; i.e., a node A was linked with an arrow to node B if the propositions comprising the variable A were perceived as having direct causal influence on those comprising B. In many applications, a variable may contain so many propositions that additional structure must be imposed on that space before it can be managed efficiently. As an extreme example consider a variable X that describes the position of some object in space. X is made up of an infinite number of mutually exclusive hypotheses of the form $X = x$, where x is a three-dimensional vector taking on real values from some region of space V. To manage such a huge hypothesis space, we partition the space into conceptually meaningful subspaces, e.g., {*On ground, Above ground*}, {*Near, Far*}, or {*Right, Left*}. Such an abstraction serves two purposes. It provides an efficient coding scheme for describing the approximate location of a singleton hypothesis, and it mirrors the evidence that the correct hypothesis is likely to produce. For example, we are not likely to find a piece of evidence supporting the singleton hypothesis $X = 1.01575$ but excluding its immediate neighbors. Nor are we likely to obtain evidence supporting the set of hypotheses $S = \{X = x \mid x$ is a prime number$\}$. However, it is reasonable to receive messages such as "The object seems to be moving off the ground, toward town Y." Thus, by coining names for the abstract subspaces,

$$S_1 = \textit{Off ground}, \qquad\qquad S_2 = \textit{Vicinity of Y},$$

we can interpret, correlate, and absorb each new piece of evidence in a direct and natural way.

An important class of abstraction spaces, called *taxonomic hierarchies,* involves subsets that are arranged hierarchically in a tree. An example of such a hierarchy is the diagnostic tree shown in Figure 7.1 [Shenoy and Shafer 1986]. In this example, a motorist is wondering why his car won't start, and we assume there is a single cause. The tree could be extended to take into account more and more detail, but as it stands there are nine terminal nodes corresponding to nine mutually exclusive hypotheses. Let this set of nine hypotheses be denoted by θ:

$\theta = \{$Fuel system at fault, Battery weak, Battery connections faulty, Transmission not in park or neutral, Some other aspect of starting system defective, Ignition switch defective, Starter relay defective, Some other switch defective, Other system at fault$\}$

The set θ is called the *frame of discernment* for the problem. The intermediate nodes $\{C, I, E\}$ represent meaningful groupings of the elements of θ. Each node in the tree corresponds to a subset of θ, and the children of each node represent a *partition* of the parent set, namely, a family of mutually exclusive subsets that comprises the parent set.

In principle, the taxonomic hierarchy of Figure 7.1 can be handled by the causal network formulation of Chapters 4 and 5. If we treat the various failure hypotheses as probable causes for the main finding ($\theta = \textit{Car won't start}$), the causal polytree of Figure 7.2 yields a structure identical to that of the tree in Figure 7.1, conveying the idea that if any of the parent nodes is true, its child is true as well. For instance, if the battery is weak (G) or the battery connections are faulty (H), we conclude that the battery system is at fault (C).

The causal network of Figure 7.2 is quite adequate for handling the diagnostic problem posed, and because the network is singly connected, the propagation techniques developed in Chapter 4 and 5 are directly applicable. In fact, this network is a more faithful model of the diagnosis problem than the tree of Figure

7.1, as it allows for multiple causes (see Section 5.4). However, this is precisely the weakness of causal models; it is difficult to incorporate constraints such as the single-fault assumption. Suppose the single-fault condition were not merely a

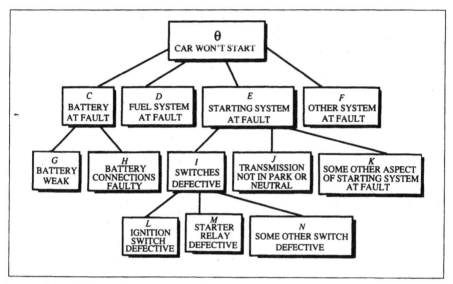

Figure 7.1. *A diagnostic tree representing a taxonomic hierarchy for the identification of the (single) cause of a car problem.*

convenient approximation to the problem but a genuine piece of knowledge (e.g., someone has checked the car and found the single fault but is keeping it secret). In order to incorporate this knowledge one needs to append auxiliary constraint nodes as in Section 4.5.2. For example, to make the parent hypotheses in Figure 7.2 mutually exclusive, one can tie each group of parents to an auxiliary child node via an exclusive-input gate and set the auxiliary node to *TRUE* (see Figure 7.3). Alternatively, one can tie the entire set of singleton hypotheses to one global exclusive-OR child and instantiate that child to *TRUE*.

These manipulations, however, would destroy the singly connected structure of the original network, thus rendering the propagation scheme more complex, and would destroy the natural taxonomic hierarchy of the original tree, where the only relationship used was PART-OF or IS-A. For these reasons, it is often advisable to leave an evidential reasoning task in the form of a taxonomic hierarchy (Figure 7.1), rather than converting it to an equivalent causal tree representation. Such considerations prevail whenever the discourse concerns properties of a single individual. For example, to process the sentence "Clyde is a gray elephant," it is convenient to use a knowledge base in which mutually exclusive constraints of the type "Gray is not white" and "An elephant is not a mouse" are built in, and need not be specified externally.

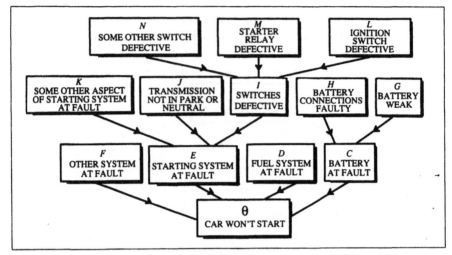

Figure 7.2. *A causal network representation of the diagnostic tree in Figure 7.1.*

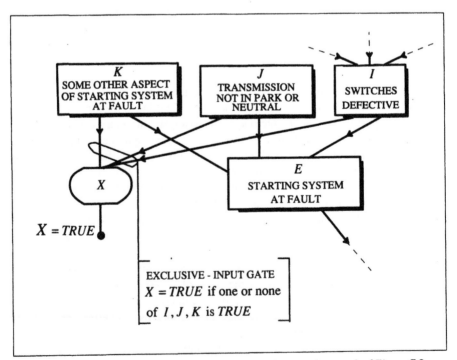

Figure 7.3. *Enforcing the single-fault assumption in the causal network of Figure 7.2.*

There are two ways to devise propagation rules for evidence in taxonomic hierarchies. First, we can regard each family consisting of a child and its parents (such as the family in Figure 7.3) as a single compound variable and (since these families are interconnected in a join tree fashion [see Section 3.2.4, Theorem 7]) apply the tree propagation technique developed in Section 4.2.3. Alternatively, we can derive propagation rules for individual nodes in the hierarchy to represent faithfully the class-subclass constraints embodied in each family. The first method is described in Chapters 4 and 5; here, we shall pursue the second approach.

7.1.2 Evidence Propagation in Taxonomic Hierarchies

Consider the diagnostic tree of Figure 7.1, and assume that each item of diagnostic evidence will bear most directly on a particular node of the tree, either supporting or refuting the hypothesis represented by that node. The challenge is to combine all of this diagnostic evidence. This problem was formulated in terms of belief functions (see Chapter 9) by Gordon and Shortliffe [1985], Shenoy and Shafer [1986], Kong [1986], and Shafer and Logan [1987], In this section we provide a probabilistic formulation of the problem and devise propagation rules which, like those developed for causal networks, allow evidence to be pooled through local computations, under local control.

THE DOMAIN

We start with a finite set $H = \{h_1, h_2, ...\}$ of hypotheses known to be exhaustive and mutually exclusive. Certain subsets of H have semantic interest, and these form a strict hierarchy; i.e., each subset is embraced by a unique parent set. The subsets can be viewed as nodes in a tree, with H as the root and the individual hypotheses as the leaves. Each intermediate node stands for the disjunction of its immediate successors. Initially, each singleton hypothesis h_i is quantified with a measure of belief $BEL(h_i)$, reflecting the prior probability that h_i is true given all previous evidence. By mutual exclusivity, the belief in each intermediate hypothesis is the sum of the beliefs given to its constituents. At this point, a new piece of evidence e arrives, which "bears directly" upon one of the subsets, say S, but says nothing about S's constituents.† The degree to which the evidence confirms or disconfirms S is determined either by having a human expert assess it directly or, if e is referenced explicitly in some knowledge base, by calculating the

---

† In this section we use S both as a set of hypotheses and as a sentence describing their disjunction. The truth of S means that exactly one of its constituents is true.

conditional probability of e given S. Either way, our task is to calculate the impact of e on the belief of every hypothesis in the hierarchy.

EVIDENCE AGGREGATION BY NORMALIZATION

A straightforward way of calculating the effect of evidence e would be the following three-step process:

1. *Estimation:* Determine the hypothesis set S upon which the evidence bears directly, and estimate the degree λ_S to which the evidence confirms or disconfirms S. λ_S is the likelihood ratio

$$\lambda_S = \frac{P(e \mid S)}{P(e \mid \neg S)} .$$ (7.1)

   Confirmation is expressed by $\lambda_S > 1$; disconfirmation, by $\lambda_S < 1$.

2. *Weight distribution:* Each singleton hypothesis $h_i \in S$ obtains the weight $W_i = \lambda_S$, while every hypothesis outside S receives a unity weight, $W_i = 1$.

3. *Belief updating:* The belief in each singleton hypothesis h_i is updated from the initial value of $BEL(h_i)$ to

$$BEL'(h_i) = P(h_i \mid e) = \alpha_S W_i BEL(h_i),$$ (7.2)

   where α_S is a normalizing factor:

$$\alpha_S = [\sum_i W_i BEL(h_i)]^{-1} .$$ (7.3)

   The belief in each intermediate hypothesis is computed from the sum of the beliefs of its singleton constituents.

This three-step process can be conducted recursively, where the updated beliefs calculated for the evidence e_k serve as prior beliefs for the next piece of evidence e_{k+1}. Also, weight distribution can be *postponed* until several pieces of evidence $e_1, e_2,..., e_n$ exert their impacts on their corresponding hypotheses $S_1, S_2, ..., S_n$. The weights are combined multiplicatively via

$$W_i(e_1, ..., e_n) = W_i^1 W_i^2 \cdots W_i^n ,$$ (7.4)

where

$$W_i^k = \begin{cases} \lambda_{S_k} & \text{if } h_i \in S_k \\ 1 & \text{if } h_i \in \neg S_k. \end{cases} \tag{7.5}$$

Eq. (7.4) assumes, of course, that each piece of evidence is conditionally independent of all previous evidence, given S_k or $\neg S_k$ (see Section 2.1.4).

PROPAGATION-BASED UPDATING

A method of updating beliefs that avoids the global summation of Eq. (7.3) is to start with the impacted node S and propagate the desired revisions up and down the tree by passing messages between neighboring nodes, as depicted in Figure 7.4.

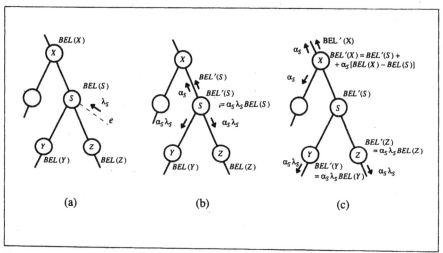

Figure 7.4. *Belief propagation through a taxonomic tree, initiated by a piece of evidence e bearing on an intermediate hypothesis S. λ_S is the likelihood ratio and $\alpha_S = [1 - BEL(S)(1 - \lambda_S)]^{-1}$.*

The message-passing process is defined by the following rules:

1. The impacted hypothesis S, with current belief $BEL(S)$, updates its belief to

$$BEL'(S) = \alpha_S \lambda_S BEL(S), \tag{7.6}$$

where

$$\alpha_S = [\lambda_S \; BEL(S) + 1 - BEL(S)]^{-1}, \qquad (7.7)$$

and transmits

i.   a single message, $m^- = \alpha_S \; \lambda_S$, to each of its successors, and

ii.   a pair of messages, $m_1^+ = BEL'(S)$ and $m_2^+ = \alpha_S$, to its father.

2.   Any node Y that receives a message m^- from its father passes m^- to all of its successors and modifies its belief by a factor m^-, i.e.,

$$BEL'(Y) = m^- \; BEL(Y) . \qquad (7.8)$$

3.   Any node X that receives the messages (m_1^+, m_2^+) from one of its successors (say X_1) passes m_2^+ to all of its other successors, updates its belief to

$$BEL'(X) = m_2^+ \; BEL(X) + m_1^+ - m_2^+ \; BEL(X_1), \qquad (7.9)$$

and passes to its father the message pair

$$(m_1^+)' = BEL'(X), \qquad (m_2^+)' = m_2^+.$$

The quantity $BEL(X_1)$ in Eq. (7.9) stands for the previous m_1^+ message that X received from X_1.

7.1.3 *Probabilistic Justification*

The operations described in the preceding paragraphs follow from attributing a specific probabilistic interpretation to the statement "Evidence e bears directly on S but says nothing about the individual elements of S." We take this statement to mean that the mechanism that gave rise to the observation e is a unique property of the subset S, common to all of its elements; therefore, it contributes no information to make us prefer one element over another. This understanding is captured by the notion of conditional independence:

$$P(e|S, h_i) = P(e|S) \qquad\qquad h_i \in S , \qquad (7.10)$$

which states that once we know S is true, identifying h_i makes e neither more likely nor less likely. Simultaneously, we also assume

$$P(e \mid \neg S, h_i) = P(e \mid \neg S) \qquad h_i \in \neg S , \qquad (7.11)$$

which states that the mechanism causing e in the absence of S could just as easily be present in each of the hypotheses outside S.

Eqs. (7.10) and (7.11) immediately give

$$P(e \mid h_i) = \begin{cases} P(e \mid S) & \text{if} \quad h_i \in S \\ P(e \mid \neg S) & \text{if} \quad h_i \in \neg S , \end{cases}$$

and together with Bayes' Rule lead to

$$P(h_i \mid e) = \begin{cases} \alpha_S \, \lambda_S \, P(h_i) & \text{if} \quad h_i \in S \\ \alpha_S \, P(h_i) & \text{if} \quad h_i \in \neg S , \end{cases} \qquad (7.12)$$

where λ_S is given by Eq. (7.1) and α_S is a normalizing factor assuring that $P(h_i \mid e)$ sum to 1:

$$\alpha_S = [\lambda_S \, P(S) + 1 - P(S)]^{-1} . \qquad (7.13)$$

Note that Eq. (7.12) holds not only when h_i is a singleton hypothesis but also for any subset of S, including S itself.

The correctness of Eqs. (7.1) through (7.5) follows by identifying $BEL(h_i)$ with $P(h_i)$ and $BEL'(h_i)$ with $P(h_i \mid e)$. Note that an identical weight-distribution process, followed by normalization, will be valid in any subclass-superclass hierarchy, even if sibling nodes are no longer mutually exclusive.

The legitimacy of propagation-based updating (Eqs. (7.6) through (7.9)) follows from the following considerations: The normalizing constant α_S in Eq. (7.13) can be computed directly at the impacted node S, yielding Eq. (7.7). Moreover, Eq. (7.12) states that each descendant of an impacted node S should modify its belief by the same factor $m^- = \alpha_S \, \lambda_S$, thus justifying the multiplication in Eq. (7.8). Since each class outside S should modify its belief by a constant factor α_S, and since every such class corresponds to a node that is neither a descendant nor an ancestor of S, the message $m_2^+ = \alpha_S$ is passed down to the siblings of S, to the siblings of its father, and so on, as in step 3. Next, the belief revision appropriate for the ancestors of S is determined by forcing each node to acquire a belief equal to the sum of the beliefs accrued by its immediate successors. This gives rise to Eq. (7.9) via

$$BEL'(Siblings\ of\ X_1) = \alpha_S\ BEL(Siblings\ of\ X_1)$$

$$= m_2^+\ [BEL(X) - BEL(X_1)].$$

Although the belief of every singleton hypothesis can be determined without updating the beliefs of S's ancestors, we still must perform this updating because subsequent evidence may directly impact any of these ancestors, and the magnitudes of the emerging messages depend upon the total belief that the impacted hypothesis merited just before the evidence arrived.

7.1.4 *Psychological and Computational Characteristics*

The updating scheme just described exhibits the following characteristics:

1. *Natural management of beliefs in a hierarchy of hypotheses:* Beliefs are combined coherently at whatever level of abstraction is appropriate for the evidence that has been gathered. To specify the effect of e on the entire knowledge base, the evidence interpreter need only quantify the relation between e and S (using λ_S) and is not required to consider other propositions in the system—that task is fully delegated to the background process of either normalization or propagation.

   This feature, together with the ability to postpone the weight-distribution step until appropriate conditions develop, is reminiscent of a popular metaphor of evidential reasoning whereby a quantity of uncommitted evidential mass is stored at S and distributed to its constituents when further evidence arrives. In the Dempster-Shafer formalism (see Chapter 9) the distribution of mass is dictated by the nature of the evidence, but in the Bayesian formalism it is a matter of choice and control. One retains the option of either keeping that mass at S (in the form of undistributed λ_S) or distributing it on a provisional basis to S's constituents, to be retracted and rerouted later if additional evidence so warrants.

2. *Distinction between confirmation and disconfirmation:* Shortliffe and Buchanan [1975] observed that experts who provide rules such as

$e \rightarrow h(0.7)$ (to read, "Evidence e suggests hypothesis h to a degree 0.7") may well agree that $P(h \mid e) = 0.7$, but become uneasy when confronted with the logical conclusion that $P(\neg h \mid e) = 0.3$. The experts would claim that the observations were evidence (to degree 0.7) in favor of h and should not be construed as evidence (to degree 0.3) against h. Such apprehensions were part of the reason the developers of early expert systems abandoned probabilistic reasoning and adopted less orthodox calculi.

This difficulty stems from an attempt to give the statement $e \rightarrow h(0.7)$ an absolute probability interpretation instead of extracting from it a likelihood ratio. Probability theory dictates that if the rule is to be treated as a stable, modular relationship between e and h, invariant to other information in the system, then it may convey only *changes* in probabilities, i.e., likelihood ratio information [Heckerman 1986b] (see also Section 2.2.2). The posterior probability $P(h \mid e)$, by contrast, is sensitive also to the prior probability $P(h)$ just before e is observed, so it cannot capture the intent of the rule.

The reason for the experts' unease with $P(\neg h \mid e) = 0.3$ is that the phrase "evidence in favor of a hypothesis" leads us to expect an *increase* in the probability of the hypothesis from $P(h)$ to $P(h \mid e)$ (with $P(h \mid e) > P(h)$), accompanied by the appropriate *decrease* in $P(\neg h)$. On the other hand, if $P(\neg h \mid e) = 0.3$ is viewed as the final product of the rule $e \rightarrow h(0.7)$, it may often mean an increase in $P(\neg h)$, say from 0.01 to 0.3, and that would violate the spirit of the rule.

The likelihood ratio formulation has a built-in protection against such confusion because it conveys only *change* information; evidence in favor of h is encoded by $\lambda > 1$ and will always produce $P(h \mid e) > P(h)$, while evidence opposing h is encoded by $\lambda < 1$ and will always result in $P(h \mid e) < P(h)$. Using the logarithm of λ makes the distinction even more pronounced by associating confirmation with a positive weight and disconfirmation with a negative weight. The logarithmic representation also provides a closer match to the distributed-mass metaphor, since masses combine additively, not multiplicatively.

3. *Clearly stated assumptions:* The assumptions behind the updating procedure are stated in familiar, meaningful terms. The evidence interpreter can readily judge whether the conditions of Eqs. (7.10) and (7.11) are satisfied in any given situation by answering basic qualitative queries of the type "Does X influence Y, given that we know Z?"

4. *Meaningful parameters:* The interpreter is required to assess only one type of numerical parameter, the likelihood ratio λ_S. The epistemological meaning of this parameter is clearly understood (in query form, "How much more likely would it be for e to occur under S

as opposed to not-S?"), and in principle the parameter can be derived from actual experiential data.

5. *Local computations:* As in the case of causal hierarchy, the main advantage of updating beliefs by message propagation instead of global normalization is that propagation is more *transparent,* i.e., the intermediate steps can be given intuitively meaningful interpretations. Every computation in the propagation process draws inputs only from neighboring, semantically related hypotheses, and the activation of these steps adheres to semantically familiar pathways. This facilitates both object-oriented programming and the mechanical generation of qualitative justifications. The latter involves tracing the sequence of operations along the activated pathways and casting each operation in linguistic terms that reflect the appropriate subclass-superclass relationship.

6. *Computational shortcomings:* The propagation method has two drawbacks. First, it is applicable only to trees, not to general class hierarchies, because when nodes share common descendants, the belief of any parent node may no longer equal the sum of its children's beliefs. Second, the propagation method does not properly handle multiple pieces of evidence that arrive simultaneously. The magnitude of the messages emerging from each impacted hypothesis S should reflect the stable updated belief of S given all previous evidence. If, however, the propagation begins as soon as multiple facts arrive, the emerging messages will reflect the state of belief that existed prior to the arrival of the new evidence, thus ignoring the presence of other messages traveling in the system. The correct way to handle multiple inputs is to process them sequentially, letting each piece of evidence impart its full impact to all nodes before processing the next piece of evidence (see Exercise 7.2).

7.2 *MANAGING CONTINUOUS VARIABLES*

7.2.1 *Plausible Reasoning about Uncertain Quantities*

The human environment contains many continuous quantities that affect normal, everyday activities. Problems involving time, distance, weight, and money often require trade-offs and adjustments that are too delicate to be handled by discrete variables. Although they fall far short of achieving the precision provided by numerical methods, people nevertheless manage to reason effectively about continuous quantities and to communicate convincing qualitative arguments about how an increase in one quantity causes an increase in another and how uncertainty about one amount translates into uncertainty about another.

While research in qualitative physics [Bobrow 1984] is aimed at uncovering how humans reason about continuous physical quantities, relatively little research has been done on how they process the uncertainties connected with those quantities. For example, while it is common knowledge that both temperature and time have a decisive effect on the quality of your barbecued hamburger, it is not quite clear how the color of the flame and the sound of sizzling translate into uncertainty about the temperature, and how this uncertainty translates into a decision about when to come back to inspect the progress of your dinner. Less esoterically, if the time shown on your car clock is different than that shown on your watch, how do you combine the two readings to determine if you have time to visit a friend on the way to work?

Obviously, people resort to gross approximations when dealing with continuous quantities. The most we can expect from people is to provide a vague estimate of the magnitude of each quantity, to have some idea of the range of uncertainty accompanying each estimate, to identify which quantity influences another, and to gauge the strength of these influences. With this pitiful state of knowledge, people seem to maneuver their way effectively in rather complicated situations. They smoothly combine information from different sources, each providing a different estimate and each carrying a different degree of reliability—a capability unmatched by any known machine. If we attempt to approximate such reasoning on a machine, representing each quantity by an estimated magnitude and a range of uncertainty, we quickly produce a computational mess. The intervals of uncertainty, instead of facilitating quick and dirty approximations, actually impose a computational tyranny of their own: they need to be stored, consulted, combined, propagated, and updated over and over again.

Take the simple example of two clocks displaying different readings. If we wish to take into account their estimated accuracies, we already have four numbers on our hands, delineating two time intervals. Now assume that you recall hearing the exact time (3:30 P.M.) on the radio fifteen minutes ago, give or take two minutes. How can we encode the overall information available, how can we combine it if someone asks us for the time, and how are we to assess the reliability of our reply (e.g., "Quarter to four, give or take three minutes")? Instead of articulating six numbers (for the three intervals obtained), people evidently manage to combine the three sources of information into a single interval. What is the calculus that governs such combinations?

To get clues about the cognitive processes invoked to handle uncertain quantities, we again examine what we believe is the main architectural constraint on human reasoning: local computation, namely, information about each quantity modifies the estimates and uncertainties associated with semantically related quantities, with little or no external supervision. We also assume that these interactions are executed by a few simple arithmetic operations and require a minimal amount of working memory. Identical architectural constraints were satisfied by the propagation techniques of Chapter 4, which were developed for networks of discrete variables. However, as the dimensionality of the variables increases beyond four or five, these techniques lose their appeal because they require the specification and manipulation of $N \times N$ matrices, where N is the dimensionality of the variables in the network. Clearly, if belief propagation is to be computationally feasible and psychologically meaningful, it must manage continuous quantities by a different method. An efficient encoding scheme must be employed to store and manipulate the belief distributions and the support messages, rather than storing these explicitly as in the case of discrete variables. One such encoding scheme is presented in this section. It is based on three assumptions:

1. All interactions between variables are linear;

2. The sources of uncertainty are normally distributed and are uncorrelated;

3. The causal network is singly connected.

We shall see that even though the mathematical derivations rely on these three assumptions, the propagation rules that emerge reflect familiar patterns of qualitative reasoning that often are applied to complex situations where these assumptions no longer hold. It is conjectured, therefore, that these assumptions constitute a canonical model which may reveal new patterns of plausible reasoning and which permits the processing of real quantities in ways that are meaningful to the human observer.

7.2.2 *Propagating Estimates and Ranges*

We will consider hierarchical systems of continuous random variables, like the network depicted in Figure 7.5. Each variable X has a set of parent variables $U_1, U_2,...,U_n$ and a set of children variables $Y_1, Y_2,...,Y_m$. The relation between X and its parents is given by the linear equation

$$X = b_1 U_1 + b_2 U_2 + \cdots + b_n U_n + w_X , \qquad (7.14)$$

where $b_1, b_2,...,b_n$ are constant coefficients representing the relative contribution made by each of the U variables to the determination of the dependent variable X, and w_X is a noise term summarizing other factors affecting X. w_X is assumed to be normally distributed with a zero mean, and uncorrelated with any other noise variable. Initially we shall assume that the network is singly connected, i.e., a

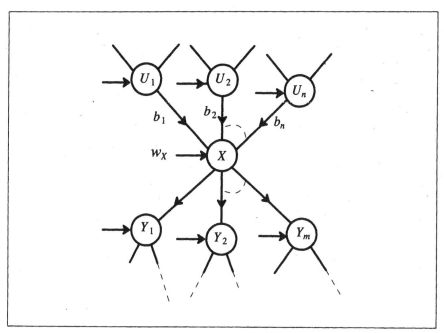

Figure 7.5. *A fragment of a singly-connected network showing the relationships between a continuous variable X, its parent variables U_1, ..., U_n and the noise w_X.*

polytree—at most one path connects any two variables. This implies that the U's are marginally uncorrelated but may become correlated once we know the value of X or any of its descendants.

The linear interaction of Eq. (7.14) has served as a standard for many causal models, including structural equations in psychology [Bentler 1980], path analysis in genetics and sociology [Wright 1921; Duncan 1975; Kenny 1979], and causal models in economics [Joereskog 1982]. Whereas the bulk of this work has focused on validating the model on the basis of empirical data, the emphasis here is on diagnosis and data interpretation. We are given the network topology, the link coefficients (b's), the variances (σ_{w_x}) of the noise terms, and the means and variances of the root variables (nodes with no parents). Our task is to devise a distributed scheme for updating the means and variances of every variable in the network to account for evidential data e, i.e., a set of variables whose values have been determined precisely.

Eq. (7.14) replaces the conditional probability matrices $P(x \mid u_1, ..., u_n)$, which were used in previous chapters to relate each variable to its parents. Whereas in networks of discrete variables these matrices were arbitrary and had to be stored explicitly, the current model is fully specified using $n + 1$ parameters per variable: the coefficients $b_1, ..., b_n$ and the variance σ_{w_x}. Moreover, the assumptions of linearity and normality now render all belief distributions normally distributed (see Appendix 7-A), so each π or λ message will be fully specified by just two parameters: the mean and the variance of its corresponding distribution. This makes the estimation task extremely simple, since each link is required to carry just two parameters in each direction.

In principle, since Eq. (7.14) completely specifies a correlation matrix for all variables in the system, the estimation task could be performed by familiar statistical estimation methods [Meditch 1969; Kenley 1986]. However, our added restriction is that the computation be conducted in *distributed* fashion, as though each variable were managed by a separate and remote processor communicating only with processors that are adjacent to it in the network. The reason for this restriction is, again, to achieve a humanlike revision process, in which the intermediate steps can be given an intuitively meaningful interpretation—a feature missing from methods based on matrix manipulations.

PROPAGATION RULES FOR SINGLY CONNECTED NETWORKS

As in the treatment of discrete variables (Section 4.3.1), the impact of each new piece of evidence will be viewed as a perturbation that propagates through the network via message-passing between neighboring processors. Each processor X has available to it the following set of parameters:

1. The link coefficients, $b_1, b_2, ..., b_n$;
2. The variance σ_{w_X} of the noise w_X that directly affects X;
3. The messages $\pi_X(u_i)$, $i = 1, 2, ..., n$ obtained from each parent of X;
4. The messages $\lambda_{Y_j}(x)$, $j = 1, 2, ..., m$ obtained from each child of X.

In the discrete case, $\pi_X(u_i)$ and $\lambda_{Y_j}(x)$ were vectors of dimensionalities matching those of U_i and X, respectively, but they are now characterized by the means and variances of the following Gaussian conditional densities:†

$$\pi_X(u_i) = f(u_i \mid e_i^+) = N(u_i; \sigma_i^+, \mu_i^+), \tag{7.15}$$

$$\lambda_{Y_j}(x) = f(e_j^- \mid x) = N(x; \sigma_j^-, \mu_j^-), \tag{7.16}$$

where e_i^+ and e_j^- stand for the values of all observed variables in the subnetworks connected to X via U_i and Y_j, respectively.

---

† We depart from most of the statistical literature by using the symbol σ to denote the variance and $s = \sigma^{1/2}$ to denote the standard deviation, i.e., $N(x;\sigma,\mu) = (2\pi\sigma)^{-1/2} \exp\{-(x-\mu)^2/2\sigma\}$.

Given this set of parameters, processor X must calculate the following quantities:

1. The belief distribution of variable X:

$$BEL(x) = f(x \mid e) = N(x; \sigma_X, \mu_X), \qquad (7.17)$$

where e stands for the set of all data observed so far.

2. The message $\pi_{Y_j}(x)$ to be sent to Y_j, the j-th child of X:

$$\pi_{Y_j}(x) = f(x \mid e - e_j^-)$$
$$= N(x; \sigma_j^+, \mu_j^+) \quad j = 1, 2, ..., m. \qquad (7.18)$$

3. The message $\lambda_X(u_i)$ to be sent to U_i, the i-th parent of X:

$$\lambda_X(u_i) = f(e - e_i^+ \mid u_i)$$
$$= N(u_i; \sigma_i^-, \mu_i^-) \quad i = 1, 2, ... \qquad (7.19)$$

Since all densities are Gaussian, it is clear that only the means and variances need be computed and transmitted. Accordingly, our task is to compute the quantities $\sigma_X, \mu_X, \sigma_j^+, \mu_j^+, \sigma_i^-, \mu_i^-$ from the available parameters $\sigma_{w_X}, b_i, \sigma_i^+, \mu_i^+, \sigma_j^-, \mu_j^-$, as shown schematically in Figure 7.6.

The derivations in Appendix 7-A show that the desired quantities can be computed using simple algebraic operations. Defining the parameters

$$\sigma_\lambda = \left[\sum_j \frac{1}{\sigma_j^-} \right]^{-1}, \qquad \mu_\lambda = \sigma_\lambda \sum_j \frac{\mu_j^-}{\sigma_j^-}, \qquad (7.20)$$

$$\sigma_\pi = \sigma_{w_X} + \sum_i b_i^2 \sigma_i^+, \qquad \mu_\pi = \sum_i b_i \mu_i^+, \qquad (7.21)$$

$BEL(x)$ and the messages emerging from X are given by the following formulas:

$$\mu_X = \frac{\sigma_\pi \mu_\lambda + \sigma_\lambda \mu_\pi}{\sigma_\pi + \sigma_\lambda}, \qquad \sigma_X = \frac{\sigma_\pi \sigma_\lambda}{\sigma_\pi + \sigma_\lambda}, \qquad (7.22)$$

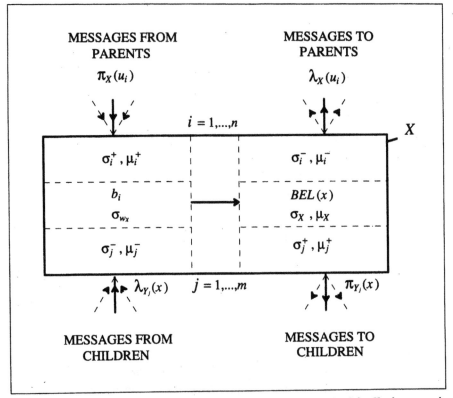

Figure 7.6. *The parameters on the left represent messages received by X, those on the right are computed and transmitted by X.*

$$\mu_j^+ = \mu_X \Big|_{\sigma_j^- \to \infty} = \frac{\displaystyle\sum_{k \neq j} \frac{\mu_k^-}{\sigma_k^-} + \frac{\mu_\pi}{\sigma_\pi}}{\displaystyle\sum_{k \neq j} \frac{1}{\sigma_k^-} + \frac{1}{\sigma_\pi}}, \quad \sigma_j^+ = \sigma_X \Big|_{\sigma_j^- \to \infty} = \left[\frac{1}{\sigma_\pi} + \sum_{k \neq j} \frac{1}{\sigma_k^-}\right]^{-1}, \quad (7.23)$$

$$\mu_i^- = \frac{1}{b_i}\left[\mu_\lambda - \sum_{k \neq i} b_k \mu_k^+\right], \qquad \sigma_i^- = \frac{1}{b_i^2}\left[\sigma_\lambda + \sigma_{w_X} + \sum_{k \neq i} b_k^2 \sigma_k^+\right]. \quad (7.24)$$

The boundary conditions appropriate for this propagation scheme can be established by assigning $\sigma = \infty$ (representing totally unknown inputs) and $\sigma = 0$ (representing observed inputs) to the peripheral nodes. In particular, every unobserved root node will be assigned $\sigma_\pi = \infty$ (representing no causal support), and every unobserved (anticipatory) leaf node will be assigned $\sigma_\lambda = \infty$ (representing no evidential support). Every observed node will receive a λ

message characterized by zero variance and a mean equal to the observed value. As in the case of discrete variables, evidence gathered at a given node does not influence its spouses until their common son gathers evidential support. This is reflected by the fact that if no descendant of X is observed, σ_λ will be infinite and all the $\lambda_X(u_i)$ messages emanating from X will have infinite σ_i^- variances as well (see Eq. (7.24)), regardless of the incoming π messages.

7.2.3 *Qualitative Patterns of Reasoning*

Some qualitative features of this updating scheme are worth noting:

1. In the absence of any evidential data ($e = 0$, $\sigma_\lambda = \infty$), the means and variances of all variables can be computed by a simple path-tracing method (using Eqs. (7.21) and (7.22)) called *predictive estimation*. For example, the mean of variable X, $\mu_X = \mu_\pi$, is equal to the weighted sum of the means of all of its root ancestors, and the weights are given by the products of the b coefficients along the corresponding paths, independent of the noise along those paths. The variance of X ($\sigma_X = \sigma_\pi$) is likewise given by a weighted sum of all the noise variances along the paths connecting X to its roots.

2. Calculating the impact of an observed variable Y on a given descendant X is equivalent to cutting off the network above Y and regarding Y as a zero-variance root, with mean equal to the observed value of Y. Again, this forward impact is unaffected by the noise along the path from Y to X.

3. The impact of an observed variable on its ancestors, to be termed *diagnostic estimation*, does depend on the noise along their connecting paths. For example, Eq. (7.20) describes μ_λ, the combined impact of X's children, as a weighted average of their individual contributions (i.e., the μ_j's), with the weights determined by the corresponding variances: the lower the variance, the higher the weight of influence. This will be termed a σ–*weighted* average rule.

4. Predictive and diagnostic estimations (i.e., μ_π and μ_λ) are also combined by a σ-weighted average rule (Eq. 7.22): the lower the variance, the higher the weight.

5. The minus sign in the specification of μ_i^- (Eq. (7.24)) captures the "explaining away" effect of interacting causes (see Chapter 4): the more evidence we have in favor of alternative causes (high μ_k, $k \neq i$), the less we are able to attribute an observed effect (say an increase of μ_λ) to any particular cause (say an increase of μ_i).

These patterns of reasoning will be illustrated using a problem of inferring wholesale prices, broken down into four subproblems.

EXAMPLE 1: Figure 7.7 illustrates a simple model of how the retail price of a given car is determined by the dealer's profit and the wholesale price, and how the latter depends on the production cost U_1, the marketing cost U_2, and the manufacturer's profit $U_3 + w_X$.

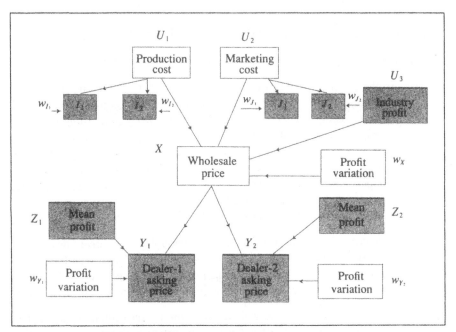

Figure 7.7. *A causal model used for estimating the wholesale price X of a car from the quantities shown in the shaded boxes.*

Our task is to estimate the wholesale price of the car X on the basis of the asking prices, Y_1 and Y_2, of two car dealers, and some additional indicators:

1. I_1 and I_2—two estimates of the production cost, given by two independent experts. The respective degrees of reliability of these experts are measured by the variances, σ_{I_1} and σ_{I_2}, of their errors, w_{I_1} and w_{I_2}.

2. J_1 and J_2—two independent estimates of the cost of marketing the car, given by two marketing experts with reliability measures σ_{J_1} and σ_{J_2}.

3. U_3—the mean profit of the industry and its associated variance σ_{w_X}.

4. Z_1 and Z_2—the mean profit per car realized by Dealer 1 and Dealer 2, respectively, in the past few years. The profit variations w_{Y_1} and w_{Y_2} are not known, but are characterized by the variances σ_{Y_1} and σ_{Y_2}.

Variables having known values are shown in shaded boxes; all others are unshaded. The value of every variable is equal to the sum of the values of its parents, i.e., all the b coefficients are 1. (The noise terms are represented explicitly, as parents of the perturbed variables.)

PROBLEM 1—diagnostic estimation: We are to estimate the wholesale price X, given only the asking prices of the two dealers, $Y_1 = y_1$, $Y_2 = y_2$, and their mean profits, $Z_1 = z_1$, $Z_2 = z_2$.

Solution: Before we get any information from the experts, U_1 and U_2 are totally unknown ($\sigma_{U_1} = \sigma_{U_2} = \infty$), since they have no parents. Therefore, X receives $\sigma_\pi = \infty$, and Eq. (7.22) yields $\mu_X = \mu_\lambda$ and $\sigma_X = \sigma_\lambda$. μ_λ is obtained from y_1 and y_2 via Eqs. (7.20) and (7.24):

$$\sigma_\lambda = \left[\frac{1}{\sigma_{Y_1}} + \frac{1}{\sigma_{Y_2}} \right]^{-1} , \qquad \mu_\lambda = \frac{\mu_1^- \sigma_{Y_2} + \mu_1^- \sigma_{Y_1}}{\sigma_{Y_1} + \sigma_{y_2}} ,$$

$$\mu_1^- = y_1 - z_1 , \qquad \mu_2^- = y_2 - z_2 ,$$

$$\mu_\lambda = \frac{(y_1 - z_1)\sigma_{Y_2} + (y_2 - z_2)\sigma_{Y_1}}{\sigma_{Y_1} + \sigma_{Y_2}} .$$

Clearly, the asking price of a dealer who varies his profits widely is a bad indicator of the wholesale price; this evidence is discounted proportionally with its variance relative to the variance of the other surveyed dealer. If, for example, $y_1 = \$8{,}000$, $y_2 = \$10{,}000$, $z_1 = z_2 = \$1{,}000$, $s_{Y_1} = \sigma_{Y_1}^{\frac{1}{2}} = \$300$, and $s_{Y_2} = \sigma_{Y_2}^{\frac{1}{2}} = \$1{,}000$, we obtain

$$\mu_X = \mu_\lambda = \frac{(8-1)1^2 + (10-1)0.3^2}{0.3^2 + 1^2} = \frac{7 + 0.81}{1.09} = \$7{,}165$$

and

$$\sigma_X = \sigma_\lambda = \frac{0.3^2 \times 1.0}{0.3^2 + 1.0} = \frac{0.09}{1.09} = 0.0826 , \quad s_X = \sigma_X^{\frac{1}{2}} = \$287 .$$

Thus, the final estimate of X is much closer to the estimate based on the more stable dealer ($\$7{,}000$) than it is to the estimate based on the less stable dealer ($\$9{,}000$). Likewise, the range of uncertainty ($\$287$) associated with the final estimate is only slightly lower than that associated with the more stable dealer ($\$300$); surveying the other dealer does not narrow this range very much. This justifies a commonly observed heuristic: if confronted by multiple indicators with widely varying degrees of reliability, one ignores all but the most reliable indicator.

PROBLEM 2—predictive estimation: Assume that experts I_1 and I_2 provide the estimates i_1 and i_2 of the production cost U_1, and simultaneously, experts J_1 and J_2 provide the estimates j_1 and j_2 of the marketing cost U_2. Assume further that the prevailing profit in the car industry is $U_3 = u_3$, and that the inaccuracies of the respective experts are measured by the variances σ_{I_1}, σ_{I_2}, σ_{J_2}, and σ_{J_3}. We must find the estimate μ_X of the car's wholesale price X and its variance σ_X, without knowing Y_1 or Y_2.

Solution: In this case, X receives no diagnostic information ($\mu_\lambda = \infty$), hence

$$\mu_X = \mu_\pi = \mu_{U_1} + \mu_{U_2} + u_3 \quad \text{and} \quad \sigma_X = \sigma_\pi = \sigma_{w_X} + \sigma_{U_1} + \sigma_{U_2},$$

where

$$\mu_{U_1} = \frac{i_1 \sigma_{I_2} + i_2 \sigma_{I_1}}{\sigma_{I_1} + \sigma_{I_2}}, \qquad \sigma_{U_1} = \frac{\sigma_{I_1} \sigma_{I_2}}{\sigma_{I_1} + \sigma_{I_2}},$$

$$\mu_{U_2} = \frac{j_1 \sigma_{J_2} + j_2 \sigma_{J_1}}{\sigma_{J_1} + \sigma_{J_2}}, \qquad \sigma_{U_2} = \frac{\sigma_{J_1} \sigma_{J_2}}{\sigma_{J_1} + \sigma_{J_2}}.$$

Thus, the estimate of X is the unweighted sum of the estimates of its parents U_1, U_2, and U_3.

PROBLEM 3—combining predictive and diagnostic estimates: Assume we have both the experts' estimates and the dealers' asking prices. We wish to find an estimate of X that incorporates all the available information.

Solution: Using Eq. (7.22), we have

$$\mu_X = \frac{\sigma_\pi \mu_\lambda + \sigma_\lambda \mu_\pi}{\sigma_\pi + \sigma_\lambda}, \qquad \sigma_X = \frac{\sigma_\pi \sigma_\lambda}{\sigma_\pi + \sigma_\lambda},$$

where μ_λ, σ_λ, μ_π, and σ_π are given in Problems 1 and 2, respectively. Thus, the predictive information μ_π and the diagnostic information μ_λ are combined by a σ-weighted average rule, i.e., the weights reflect the corresponding σ's.

PROBLEM 4—explaining away: How would the information about the dealers' asking prices and the marketing experts' reports affect the previous estimate of the production cost, μ_{U_1}?

Solution: Previously (in Problem 2), μ_{U_1} relied solely on the experts' estimates i_1 and i_2, giving

$$\mu_{U_1} = \left[\frac{i_1}{\sigma_{I_1}} + \frac{i_2}{\sigma_{I_2}} \right] \sigma_{U_1}.$$

With the added information (Y_1, and Y_2), μ_{U_1} is also influenced by μ_1^-, where (from Eq. (7.24))

$$\mu_1^- = \mu_\lambda - \mu_{U_2} - \mu_{U_3},$$

$$\sigma_1^- = \sigma_\lambda + \sigma_{w_X} + \sigma_{U_2}.$$

In other words, the added information is integrated as if it came from another expert, say I_3, who pronounced an estimate μ_1^- for U_1 with variance σ_1^-, where μ_1^- is the value of U_1 needed to satisfy the combining equation $X = U_1 + U_2 + U_3$, wherein μ_λ is a direct reading of X and μ_{U_2} and μ_{U_3} are direct readings of U_2 and U_3, respectively. Clearly, if μ_λ is high, the estimate of U_1 will also be high. However, if J_1 and J_2 report high marketing costs, the estimated production cost U_1 will go down, because high marketing costs "explain away" the high asking prices reflected in μ_λ.

7.2.4 Discussion

The propagation scheme described in the preceding section is based on the assumption that the parents of each variable are uncorrelated (see Appendix 7-A). This assumption breaks down when the underlying network contains loops, i.e., when two or more nodes possess both common descendants and common ancestors. As in the discrete case, if the existence of loops is ignored, messages will circulate indefinitely and the process normally will not converge to the correct equilibrium.

Multiply connected networks can be handled by the methods of *clustering* and *conditioning* described in Chapter 4, or by the method of *node elimination* [Shachter and Kenley 1987]. Alternatively, the entire correlation matrix of the network variables can be formed and new observations incorporated by well-known techniques of estimation or *Kalman filtering* [Meditch 1969]. These methods guarantee global coherence but lack the local computation of human reasoning. If the number of loops is small, then schemes based on conditioning offer a reasonable compromise between the requirements of coherence and local computation. The flavor of such schemes will be given next.

Assume that instantiating one variable, X_k, is enough to break all loops in the network. In other words, holding the value of X_k constant permits us to update all variables by applying the one-pass propagation scheme of the preceding section. Instead of propagating the usual set of λ and π parameters, we now require that two such sets be propagated, $\lambda^0-\pi^0$ and $\lambda^1-\pi^1$, corresponding to holding the value of X_k at two distinct values, say 0 and 1, respectively. (Remarkably, only two values are required, contrasted with N values—the domain size—for discrete random variables.) The computations are the same under both conditions, except that with $X_k = 0$ each son of X_k will receive the pair of messages $\sigma_k^+ = 0$ and $\mu_k = 0$, whereas with $X_k = 1$ the pair will be $\sigma_k^+ = 0$ and $\mu_k = 1$ (see Eq. (7.15)). Similarly, each parent of X_k will receive the usual σ^- and μ^- messages specified in Eq. (7.24), with two different settings of σ_λ and μ_λ; ($\sigma_\lambda = 0$, $\mu_\lambda = 0$) represents the case where $X_k = 0$ while ($\sigma_\lambda = 0, \mu_\lambda = 1$) represents the case where $X_k = 1$. The two sets of estimates are later combined by a weighted average rule.

If the network requires the removal of K nodes ($K > 1$) to break up all loops, the updating equations become more complicated; they involve operations on $K \times K$ matrices and the transmission of K-dimensional vectors as messages. When K is large we lose the transparency provided by the message-passing scheme, and global matrix-manipulation techniques may be the only coherent inferencing tool applicable.

Clustering techniques likewise offer a reasonable approach when the network is sparse—especially methods based on join trees (see Section 4.4). After triangulating the graph and forming the join tree, we treat each clique in the tree as a compound (multivariate) Gaussian variable, completely characterized by the correlation matrix formed from variables participating in that clique. The links between cliques will likewise be characterized by cross-correlation matrices of variables in the adjacent cliques. The π and λ messages will now take the form of m-dimensional vectors, where m is the number of variables in the parent clique. The number of parameters participating in the propagation is clearly more manageable than the number required for discrete random variables, where the marginal distribution of an m-variable clique requires $\exp(m)$ storage.

Matrix techniques clearly outperform local propagation methods if precise updating is required in multiply connected networks. Moreover, the complexity of these techniques is only polynomial (n^3) in the number of variables, so they are not hindered by the exponential explosion that can plague networks with discrete variables. Thus, no substantial run-time computational benefits are gained by the use of message-passing schemes (except in singly connected networks). However, message-passing schemes possess the desirable features of locality, autonomy, and low storage requirements and therefore are more akin to human knowledge processing: Partial results are stored exactly where they will be useful, computational steps can be performed in any order, and there is no need to remember which part of the network has been updated and which part has not.

CONCLUSIONS

There is a vast difference in the way humans and machines process continuous quantities. Humans manage to do it with minimal arithmetic, very little short-term memory storage, and local and autonomous computation, and still produce estimates that are acceptable, defensible, and meaningful. Human performance is far better than that produced by any known machine subject to similar architectural constraints. The question then is, what are the rules of approximation that guide human reasoning? One way to search for these rules is to reason backward and ask what idealized models of reality lend themselves to *exact* solutions, given the computational constraints we wish to satisfy? If we find such a model, we can examine the rules by which quantities combine and posit them as the basic building blocks of approximate reasoning. The advantages of following this philosophy are that the rules extracted are guaranteed to be consistent, that they are known to produce exact results on at least a subset of problem domains, and that it is possible to determine in advance when the environment lies outside their range of applicability.

The assumptions of linear interaction, normal noise, and singly connected networks represent an idealized model of reality where message-passing's desirable features are fully realized and the scheme produces exact solutions. No other model is known that admits these computational features. This suggests that the fragments of qualitative reasoning extracted from this idealized model are the basic building blocks of the strategies by which people process continuous quantities under uncertainty. It also suggests that even if one resorts to full matrix techniques, the conclusions obtained should be explained using the following reasoning patterns:

1. Unweighted sums for predictive estimation;

2. A σ-weighted average for diagnostic estimation;

3. A σ-weighted average for combining predictive and diagnostic estimates;

4. Subtraction for "explaining away."

7.3 *REPRESENTING UNCERTAINTY ABOUT PROBABILITIES*

There is no doubt that people make a distinction between sure and unsure probabilistic judgments. For example, everyone would agree that a typical coin has a 50% chance of turning up "heads," but most people would hesitate to assign a definite probability to a coin produced in a gambler's basement if they suspect the coin has been tampered with. For that reason we sometimes feel more comfortable assigning a range, rather than a point estimate, of uncertainty, thus expressing our ignorance, doubt, or lack of confidence about the judgment required. We may say, for example, that the probability of the coin turning up "heads" lies somewhere between 60% and 40%, having no idea whether or how the coin was biased.

The apparent failure of individual probabilistic expressions to distinguish between uncertainty and ignorance, between certainty and confidence, has swayed many researchers to seek alternative formalisms, where confidence measures are given explicit notation [Shafer 1976]. In this section, we shall first describe the difficulties of representing confidence measures in classical probability theory, using "higher-order probabilities" or "probabilities of probabilities." We shall then demonstrate, using an interpretation advanced by de Finetti [1977], how the causal-network formulation of probabilities facilitates the representation of confidence measures as an integral part of one's knowledge system, requiring neither specialized notation nor the use of higher-order probabilities.

7.3.1 The Semantics of Probabilities of Probabilities

Traditional probability theory insists that probabilities be assigned only to propositions about factual events, namely, to sentences whose truth value can in principle be verified unequivocally by empirical tests. Following this tradition, it is hard to justify assigning probabilities to probability distributions themselves. The truth of probabilistic statements about any specific event cannot be confirmed or refuted empirically; once we observe the uncertain event, i.e., the object of the statement, its probability becomes either 1 or 0, trivially ruling out all intermediate values. If a first-order probability is the proportion of times that a given event occurs, to define second-order probabilities we must count the proportion of times that a given proportion occurs—a hopeless task by any standard.

The difficulty is somewhat mitigated in cases where it is natural to associate probabilities with verifiable properties of physical objects. Thus, in the standard classroom example of a pair of urns with different proportions of black and white balls inside, the verification consists of counting the balls and shaking the urns well. In this setting, the inference from "The proportion of black balls is p, and the urn was shaken vigorously" to the statement "The probability of drawing a black ball is p" is almost universally accepted as sound. In the same way, if a fair coin is flipped to determine which urn to draw a ball from, it seems sound to say, "The probability is .5 that the probability of drawing a black ball is p." Thus, we have a straightforward case of a probability of a probability, with solid verifiability—the assertion that the coin is fair can be based on as many practice tosses as seems necessary.

Still, such remedies are not applicable to the subjective interpretation of probability, which is the standard interpretation in this book. If the statement $P(A) = p$ stands for one's state of certainty regarding the truth of A, then there is only one such state at any given time, and what do we mean by a state of certainty in a state of certainty? If our mental machinery is equipped with some thermometer with which we measure the certainties of various statements, then presumably the thermometer is designed to take as inputs truths of propositions. How then can we ask it suddenly to take as inputs degrees of certainty, namely, outputs of some other thermometers? Or do we have two types of thermometers, one for measuring the certainty of propositions and the other for measuring the reliability of thermometers?

While it is possible to construct mathematical theories of higher-order probabilities that exhibit some desirable properties [Fisher 1957; Good 1950; Dempster 1967; Shafer 1976; Domotor 1981; Gaifman 1986], the utility of such theories depends on how well they account for the origin of partial confidence and how well they predict systematic fluctuations in perceived confidence levels as new information arrives. Therefore, a theory of confidence measures may remain purely tautological until a clear empirical semantics is attributed to its primitive parameters or until the theory provides clear predictions of how different streams of raw observations would give rise to different confidence intervals.† Thus, the questions remain: What do people mean when they assign confidence intervals to probabilistic sentences? What empirical and procedural information is conveyed by such intervals? How do these intervals expand and contract in light of new information? Should we embrace these intervals in AI systems or simply dismiss them as computationally insignificant human peculiarities?

We shall now cast the semantics of second-order probability statements within the framework of classical, first-order probability theory.

Our starting point is the claim that probabilistic statements such as $P(A) = p$ are themselves empirical events, of no lesser stature than other sentences reporting empirical observations. While not referring to events that are open to full public scrutiny, these statements do nevertheless report outcomes of genuine experiments, namely, the mental procedures invoked in assessing the belief of a given proposition A. Thus, stating, "Event A has a chance p of occurring" is equivalent to stating, "The mental event of computing the likelihood of A has produced the outcome p."

Endowing probabilistic statements with event status neutralizes the syntactic objection to sentences such as $P[P(A) = p]$. The square brackets and the parentheses enclose arguments of the same type, namely empirical events. True, the event A is external while the event $P(A) = p$ is personal. However, in the post-behaviorist era of cognitive psychology this distinction no longer acts as a barrier to useful semantics: adopting a computational model of knowledge representation (e.g., rule-based systems, semantic networks, or causal networks) often permits us to specify the mental procedures involved in belief assessments with the same clarity and precision that we specify experimental procedures in a laboratory setting. Two things still remain to be done. First, we must explain what renders the event $P(A) = p$ an unknown, random event, rather than a fixed outcome of a stable procedure. Second, we must explicate more precisely the mental procedures involved in making the assessments $P(A)$ and $P[P(A) = p]$, identify their empirical content, and specify their computational role.

---

† The Dempster-Shafer theory, for example, predicts that all confidence intervals should disappear whenever we possess a precise probabilistic model of a domain or whenever the available evidence consists of confirmations and denials of events defined in the model. Thus, the theory fails to capture the obvious lack of confidence in the judgment "The coin will turn up heads with probability 50%" if the coin was produced by a defective machine—precisely 49% of its output consists of double-headed coins, 49% are no-headed coins, and the rest are fair. Nor will the theory explain why we normally regain confidence in the 50% judgment as soon as we are told that in the past two trials the coin's outcome was tails and then heads. Apparently, the belief intervals encoded in the Dempster-Shafer theory have a totally different semantics than the confidence measures portrayed by the example above (see Section 9.1.4).

7.3.2 De Finetti's Paradigm of Uncertain Contingencies

A paradigm answering the first question has been suggested by de Finetti [1977] and has been guiding the Bayesian interpretation of confidence measures for over a decade (most recently, Spiegelhalter [1986] and Heckerman and Jimison [1987]). The basic idea is that the event $P(A) = p$ is perceived as a random variable whenever the assessment of $P(A)$ depends substantially on the occurrence or nonoccurrence of some other event(s) modeled by the system. In the words of de Finetti:

> The information apt to modify the probability assessed for an event E—in so far as the observation of H_i makes us change from $P(E)$ to $P(E \mid H_i)$—can make us view the H_i's as sort of "noisy" signals concerning the occurrence and nonoccurrence of the event E.

Adopting this interpretation, we shall further show that the procedure involved in the assessment of $P[P(A) = p]$ is no different than that involved in the assessment of $P(A)$; moreover, the information used for calculating $P(A)$ is sufficient for calculating the confidence interval associated with the statement $P(A) = p$. Thus, the notions of ignorance and doubt are intrinsic and indigenous to classical probabilistic formulations; no second-order probabilities or specialized notational machinery are required to reintroduce them to their natural habitat.

We shall first illustrate the basic idea using the two-coin example, coin 1 being a typical, legal coin, and coin 2 having been minted in the basement of a notoriously unscrupulous gambler. Let E_i, $i = 1, 2$ stand for the statement "Coin i is about to turn up heads." To say that we are unsure about the probability of E_2 means that our belief in it is extremely susceptible to change in light of further evidence. More specifically, being unsure about the probability $P(E_2)$ means that we are aware of a set of contingencies, each of which is likely to be true and each of which, if true, would substantially alter our assessment of the probability that the coin will turn up heads on the next toss. For example, since coin 2 comes from a disreputable source, we might entertain the following contingencies: †

$C_1 =$ "The coin is fair ($p = 0.50$)."
$C_2 =$ "The coin is loaded for heads ($p = 0.60$)."
$C_3 =$ "The coin is loaded for tails ($p = 0.40$)."

---

†   The three contingencies listed are only coarse abstractions of a spectrum of possible coin-loadings. They do, however, express genuine limitations on one's ability to bias a coin more than 10% off center. Also, the gambler would not bother with the coin unless he could achieve at least 10% bias.

If we attribute a 20% probability to the possibility that the coin has been tampered with, and if we have no reason to believe that the gambler prefers heads to tails, then our assessment of the likelihood of these three conditions can be summarized by a probability vector $P(C_1) = 0.80$, $P(C_2) = 0.10$, $P(C_3) = 0.10$ (see Figure 7.8a), and the distribution of $P(E_2)$ will assume the form given in Figure 7.8b. This distribution can be thought of as the result of a mental simulation of possible scenarios emanating from the contingency set, with each scenario weighted and its impact assessed in light of the total evidence available. In some applications it might also be useful to characterize this distribution with several of its attributes—for example, the range [0.40, 0.60], the mean 0.50, and the variance $\sigma^2 = 0.002$.

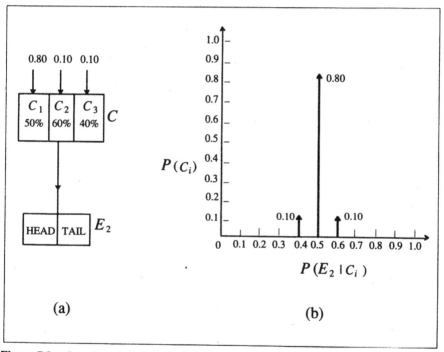

Figure 7.8. *Causal model (a) and belief distribution (b) for the two-coin example.*

The point to notice is that by specifying a causal model for predicting the outcome E_2, we automatically specified the variance of that prediction. In other words, when humans encode probabilistic knowledge as a causal model of interacting variables, they automatically specify not only the marginal and joint distributions of the variables in the system, but also a particular procedure by which each marginal is to be computed, which in turn determines how these marginals may vary in the future. It is this implicitly encoded dynamic that makes probabilistic statements random events, admitting distributions, intervals, and other confidence measures.

Why, then, is our confidence in $P(E_1) = 0.50$ higher than our confidence in $P(E_2) = 0.50$? True, each of the contingencies mentioned might also hold for a typical coin pulled out of our pocket, but because the probabilities associated with contingencies C_2 and C_3 are negligibly small, the resultant distribution of the assessment $P(E_1)$ would be focused sharply about its mean, 0.5. Thus, our confidence in $P(E_1) = 0.5$ stems from not finding in our knowledge base a set of conditions that are likely to happen and that would substantially sway the assessment of $P(E_1)$ one way or the other.

There is, of course, a whole spectrum of conditions we can draw from physics that would make the outcome of the coin sway in favor of either heads or tails. For example, we can specify a narrow range of initial conditions (e.g., position, orientation, and linear and rotational momentum) under which the outcome of the coin toss is almost sure. Such conditions do not qualify as meaningful contingencies, however, because short of complex scientific experimentation, the granularity and vocabulary required to specify these conditions lie beyond the level of abstraction common to everyday discourse. Abstraction levels are adopted to match the sort of evidence one expects to find under various circumstances, and since in normal coin-tossing settings one cannot make or envision the fine physical distinctions necessary for determining the outcome of the toss, such distinctions are glossed over and summarized in probabilistic terms. On the other hand, eventualities such as "The coin was loaded" lie within the boundaries of normal discourse because they involve common actions and intentions that can be understood, envisioned, and revealed by ordinary means (e.g., the coin producer may confess to his action or intention).

The granularity of the model chosen for predicting an event E plays a major role in determining the balance between confidence and certainty. For example, had we chosen to explicate all of our knowledge about Newtonian mechanics and molecular physics within the knowledge base, there would hardly be room for probabilistic predictions. Instead, most predictions would be deterministic, but because of missing boundary conditions they would be issued with zero confidence. In other words, $P(E \mid c)$ would oscillate between 0 and 1 depending on the particular boundary condition assumed for c. Once we decide to exclude trajectory calculations from our knowledge base and summarize them with variables of coarse grain, probabilistic predictions become feasible and our confidence in each prediction is reflected by a narrow distribution such as that shown in Figure 7.8b.

Language granularity is not the only factor governing the level of confidence reflected in a model. The mechanism connecting E and c plays no less a role. Take, for example, the network of Figure 7.8a. Its topology specifically proclaims C_1, C_2, and C_3 to be causal factors of E and not the other way around, indicating that information should flow from the former to the latter and hence that C_1, C_2, and C_3 should serve as contingencies for E and not vice versa. If we choose to express the identical joint probability distribution with a different graphical model, a different set of contingencies will be designated and different levels of confidence will result. For example, reversing the arrow between E and C and labeling the arrow with the conditional probabilities $P(C_i | E)$ instead of $P(E | C_i)$ will designate E as a contingency for the C_i's; the assessment $P(E) = 50\%$ will be issued with full confidence, while the confidence in $P(C_i)$ will be measured by the variation between $P(C_i | E = TRUE)$ and $P(C_i | E = FALSE)$. Thus, besides specifying the joint distribution of the variables in the systems and depicting their interdependencies, the choice of network structure carries semantics of its own. It reveals the knowledge organization adopted by the model builder while encoding experiential data and the mental procedures intended to be used in the retrieval of this data. In other words, the network structure designates which variables should constitute the *frame* (or *context* or *reference*) on the basis of which belief in other variables should be assessed. Cause-effect relationships are a special case of this asymmetric frame-based organization.

We are ready now to give this interpretation of confidence intervals a more formal underpinning, using $BEL(E)$ to denote $P(E \mid$ all evidence obtained so far).

7.3.3 A Formal Definition of Network-Induced Confidence Measures

Having agreed to associate partial confidence in $BEL(E)$ with the susceptibility of $BEL(E | c)$ to the various contingencies in C, we need a definition of the contingency set C, relative to E. Once C is defined, we will be able to calculate the confidence in any probabilistic statement, say $BEL(E) = b$, directly from the network model in which E is embedded. For example, we will be able to "simulate" the events in C by instantiating various combinations of its variables, weighted by their appropriate probabilities, and then measure the resulting fluctuations in $BEL(E | c)$.

Obviously, not every proposition qualifies for membership in the set C of contingencies. De Finetti [1977] was careful to point out that by cleverly manipulating C one can fabricate any arbitrary distribution of $BEL(E | c)$, thus producing any desired confidence measure while maintaining the same uncertainty, $BEL(E)$. In the extreme case, if C contains evidential variables that bear decisively on the truth of E, then the distribution of $BEL(E | c)$ will fluctuate between 0 and 1, indicating a total loss of confidence in the assessment of $BEL(E)$. Such behavior is not supported by introspective analysis. For example, suppose we are told that there is a bell hidden somewhere in the room, and it will ring if and only if the coin turns up heads; will this news alter our confidence in $P(E_1) = 0.5$? It should if the bell's sound B is proclaimed to be a contingency relative to E_1. Yet despite the fact that the conditional probability $P(E_1 | B)$ is substantially different than $P(E_1 \mid \neg B)$, most people would agree that the story about the bell has no effect whatsoever on our confidence in $P(E_1) = 0.5$. Why? Apparently, causal consequences of events do not qualify as contingencies for those events. If the story were reversed—namely, the outcome of the coin toss is by some magical means influenced by the sound of a bell—we would no doubt consider the bell to be part of the contingency set, affecting the confidence of $P(E_1)$.

Is it reasonable, then, to exclude consequences categorically from the contingency set? Doing so seems to conflict with another mode of behavior, in which anticipated consequences play a dominant role in judging confidence. Consider an example given by Spiegelhalter [1986]:

> ... a patient presented to a specialist may have a 10% chance of gastric cancer just from the known incidence in that referral clinic. However, one may be unwilling to make a decision until many further questions were asked, after which it may well be reasonable to perform an endoscopy even on the basis of the same 10% belief, since no further interrogation will substantially alter our belief.

Surely, the answers a patient gives to the specialist's questions are causal consequences of the patient's conditions, and the latter are causal consequences of the target event *Gastric cancer*. Yet the very potential of obtaining answers to these questions renders the belief less sure before the interrogation than after it. Why? Spiegelhalter's explanation—"since no further interrogation will substantially alter our belief"—may cause us to conclude that the set of possible answers are the very contingencies upon which our confidence rests. Is it adequate, then, to make C the set of observations one is likely to obtain?

Suppose a particular patient from the same referral clinic stubbornly refuses to answer any questions. His refusal is so adamant, in fact, that we are absolutely sure that no further interrogation will alter our belief. Does this make us more confident in stating "$P(Gastric\ cancer) = 10\%$" for this patient, compared with patients who will be more cooperative during their interrogation? The answer is, of course, no. It is the diversity of beliefs about the patient's conditions, not the availability of future observations, that governs our confidence judgments.

The reason we are so sure in this case that interrogation will increase our confidence in the assessment of $P(Gastric\ cancer)$ is that interrogations often reveal alternative mechanisms that "explain away" previously observed symptoms and complaints, thus exonerating the target event $E = Gastric\ cancer$ from direct responsibility. Since such alternative explanations play a dominant role in the assessment of $P(Gastric\ cancer)$, they too (but not the anticipated answers) should be included in the contingency set.

To summarize where we now stand on the issue of contingencies, the following features have been identified:

1. Partial confidence in the belief assessment for event E is caused by anticipated fluctuations in a set C of other events called *contingencies* and by the susceptibility of $BEL(E \mid c)$ to such fluctuations.

2. Consequences of E are excluded from C.

3. Observing some consequences of E often strengthens our confidence in the belief of E. Yet knowing whether or not we are about to gain access to such observations does not alter our confidence.

4. After observing consequences of E our confidence in estimating $BEL(E)$ depends on whether we can articulate alternative explanations—not involving E—for such observations.

Joining these features with causal network terminology, the following coherent picture emerges:

1. C contains direct parents of E and all variables that could influence the relation between E and past observations. These include the direct parents of past observations and the direct parents of all nodes lying on paths between past observations and E.†

2. Our confidence in the assessment of $BEL(E)$ is measured by the (narrowness of the) distribution of $BEL(E \mid c)$ as c ranges over all combinations of contingencies, and each combination c is weighted by its current belief $BEL(c)$.

3. The effect of observations on the confidence attributed to $BEL(E)$ is threefold:

    i.   Normally, the evidence observed leaves $BEL(c)$ focused on a smaller number of combinations, thus minimizing the fluctuations of $BEL(E \mid c)$.

    ii. Normally, the evidence observed renders $BEL(E \mid c)$ less sensitive to c (e.g., $BEL(E \mid c)$ may rely more on the likelihood ratio $\lambda(E)$ and less on the prior probability $\pi(E)$).

    iii. New observations may introduce into C new contingencies (e.g., their direct parents), made up of alternative, uncertain

---

† The need to include parents of intermediate nodes was pointed out by David Heckerman, in personal communication.

explanations of the observations, which previously had no effect on *BEL(E)*.

The reason *C* is composed of direct parents rather than more remote ancestors of the target events is that the influence of the remote ancestors is summarized by the direct parents. This is the essence of the conditional independence criterion by which direct parents were identified (see Section 3.3.1). In other words, direct parents point to the most specific *reference classes* from which the belief in an event is to be determined [Kyburg 1983]. The reason we must qualify points i and ii ("normally") is that observational data may occasionally have the effect of weakening our confidence. For example, evidence showing that the gambler definitely has attempted to tamper with the fairness of the coin would undoubtedly weaken our confidence in the statement $P(E_2) = .5$.

7.3.4 The Effect of Evidence on Confidence: An Example

To illustrate this approach, let us take an example from Heckerman and Jimison [1987], originally given by de Finetti [1977]. Suppose we ask a person for his opinion on the probability that a given football team will win an upcoming game. We discover that he is uncomfortable supplying a point value because the probability of a win depends on three factors: (1) whether a star player, recently threatened with suspension by league authorities, will be able to play; (2) whether the playing field will be dry or muddy because of rain; and (3) whether the rumored promise of a bonus to the winning players will be confirmed. We will label these events *Suspension*, *Dry*, and *Bonus*, and assuming they are independent, we can represent their respective influence on the event *Win* by the causal network of Figure 7.9. The contingency set *C* consists of the direct parents of *Win*, namely the variables {*Suspension, Dry, Bonus*}.

Suppose the individual is able to assess point values for each of the influencing events, say $P(Suspension) = .6$, $P(Dry) = .7$, and $P(Bonus) = .2$, as well as the probability of a win conditioned on each of the possible outcomes of these influencing events. A hypothetical set of assessments are shown in the second column of Table 1. This completes the specification of the causal network and allows us to compute both the belief in the event *Win* and the confidence in that belief.

The probability of each combination of outcomes is shown in the third column of Table 1. A plot of the third column versus the second column of Table 1 is shown in Figure 7.10. This plot graphically depicts the nature of partial confidence in the individual's assessment of $P(Win)$. The quantity $P(Win)$ varies as a function of the outcomes of the influencing events in the contingency set; in general, the wider the curve in such a plot, the lower the confidence in the assessment.

The overall belief in a win is given by the mean of the distribution of Figure 7.10,

$$P(Win) = \sum P(Win \mid Suspension, Dry, Bonus) \, P(Suspension, Dry, Bonus)$$
$$= .53 \,,$$

where the sum ranges over all possible outcomes of the influencing events. The confidence interval can be measured by the range [.4, .7] or, better yet, by the standard deviation

$$\sigma = \left\{ \sum \left[P(Win \mid Suspension, Dry, Bonus) - .53 \right]^2 P(Suspension, Dry, Bonus) \right\}^{\frac{1}{2}}$$

$$= \left[(.4 - .53)^2 \, .14 + (.50 - .53)^2 \, .48 + (.6 - .53)^2 \, .32 + (.7 - .53)^2 \, .06 \right]^{\frac{1}{2}}$$

$$= .0781 \,.$$

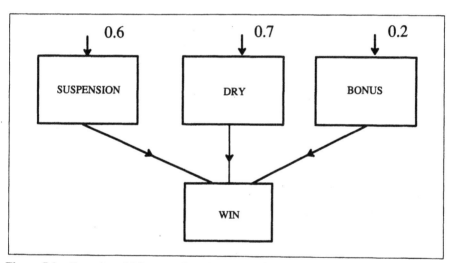

Figure 7.9. *Causal model for event E = Win.*

Table 1.

Conditioning events			$P(Win \mid Events)$	$P(Events)$
¬Suspension	Dry	Bonus	.7	(.4)(.7)(.2) = .06
¬Suspension	Dry	¬Bonus	.6	(.4)(.7)(.8) = .22
¬Suspension	¬Dry	Bonus	.6	(.4)(.3)(.2) = .02
¬Suspension	¬Dry	¬Bonus	.5	(.4)(.3)(.8) = .10
Suspension	Dry	Bonus	.6	(.6)(.7)(.2) = .08
Suspension	Dry	¬Bonus	.5	(.6)(.7)(.8) = .34
Suspension	¬Dry	Bonus	.5	(.6)(.3)(.2) = .04
Suspension	¬Dry	¬Bonus	.4	(.6)(.3)(.8) = .14

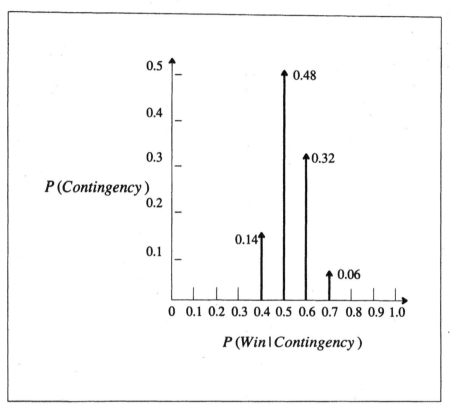

Figure 7.10. *Belief distribution associated with the model of Figure 7.9.*

Now let us examine the effect of new evidence on the individual's belief and confidence. Assume that the individual is given the option of consulting a member of the committee deciding the suspension of the star player. Additionally, he can call the weather bureau to get the weather forecast for the day of the game. These potential sources of information are represented by the two leaf nodes added to the network in Figure 7.11*a*. Before these sources are consulted, however, the distribution of $P(Win)$ remains the same as in Figure 7.10; the mere availability of information sources should not change the individual's confidence, since these sources do not belong to the contingency set C. On the other hand, assuming the committee member states that the star player will not be suspended and the weather report generates a likelihood ratio of 4:1 in favor of $\neg Dry$, the belief distribution of the contingency set changes to $BEL(Suspension) = 0$, $BEL(Dry) = \dfrac{.7}{.7 + .3 \times 4} = .368$, $BEL(Bonus) = .2$, and the probabilities of a win are given by Table 2 and Figure 7.11*b*.

Notably, the new distribution of $BEL(Win)$ is narrower, having the standard deviation .0627 about the mean .556. This demonstrates the narrowing of confidence intervals by evidence that prunes and dampens the range of possible combinations in the contingency set C (point ii in the previous subsection).

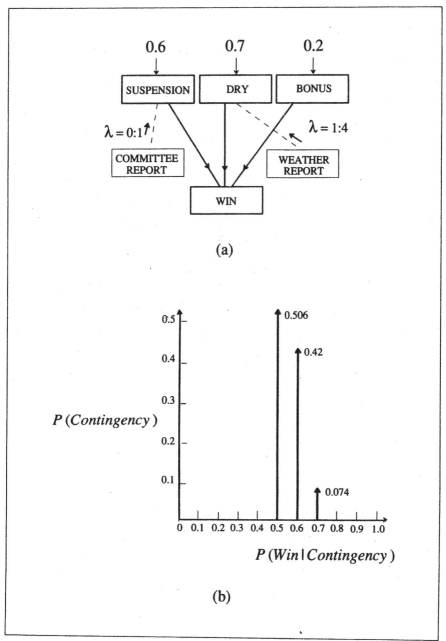

Figure 7.11. *Causal model (a) and belief distribution (b) after obtaining reports.*

Table 2.

Conditioning events			$BEL(Win \mid Event)$	$BEL(Event)$
¬Suspension	Dry	Bonus	.7	(1) (.368) (.2) = .074
¬Suspension	Dry	¬Bonus	.6	(1) (.368) (.8) = .294
¬Suspension	¬Dry	Bonus	.6	(1) (.632) (.2) = .126
¬Suspension	¬Dry	¬Bonus	.5	(1) (.632) (.8) = .506

To demonstrate the effect of a piece of evidence that is a consequence of the central event *Win* (point i), imagine that the individual making the prediction could not attend the match, having to leave town that day, and he asked his brother to call him if the home team wins. It is now two hours after the ending time of the game and his brother has not called. This new piece of evidence, *No call*, is shown as a successor (i.e., consequence) of the variable *Win* in the causal network of Figure 7.12a. Again, we allow the influencing events to range over the four possible value combinations shown in Table 2, but both the belief in each combination and the conditional belief in *Win* given that combination are now influenced by the evidence *No call*.

Assuming that the new evidence *No call* imparts a likelihood ratio of $\lambda = 3{:}1$ against *Win*, the resulting beliefs are shown in Table 3.

Table 3.

Conditioning events			$BEL(Win \mid Event)$	$BEL(Event)$
¬Suspension	Dry	Bonus	.437	.063
¬Suspension	Dry	¬Bonus	.333	.281
¬Suspension	¬Dry	Bonus	.333	.120
¬Suspension	¬Dry	¬Bonus	.250	.536

For example, $BEL(Win \mid Dry, Bonus)$ was calculated by

$$BEL(Win \mid Dry, Bonus) = \frac{.7}{.7 + .3 \times 3} = .437,$$

and

$$BEL(Dry, Bonus) = \alpha\, \pi(Dry, Bonus)\, \lambda(Dry, Bonus)$$
$$= \alpha\, .074(.7 \times 1 + .3 \times 3) = \alpha\, .1184$$
$$= (.1184 + .5292 + .2268 + 1.012)^{-1}\, .1184 = .063 .$$

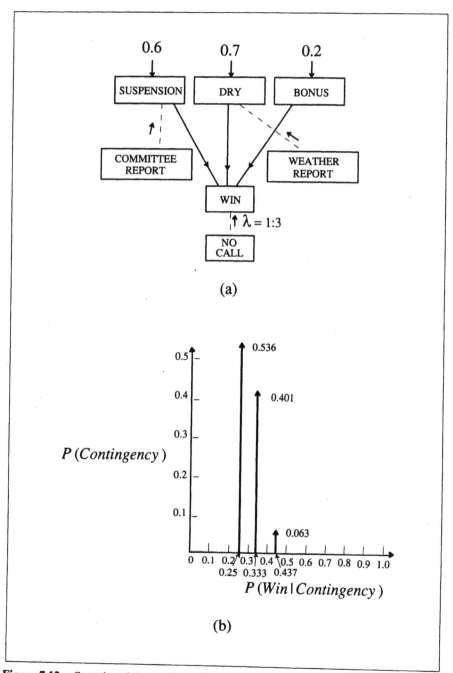

Figure 7.12. *Causal model (a) and belief distribution (b) after obtaining No call.*

We see that the new evidence tends to diminish the likelihood of *Win* for every combination of influencing events, and it simultaneously tends to put the blame on the combination $\{\neg Dry, \neg Bonus\}$. The resulting distribution of $BEL(Win)$ is given in Figure 7.12b, having mean .2953 and standard deviation .0542.

To illustrate the introduction of new contingencies into C (point iii), imagine that the individual involved feels uncomfortable with the assessed likelihood ratio of $\lambda = 3{:}1$. Generally, such an assessment would summarize a large number of possibilities explaining why a phone call might not materialize despite the event *Win*. This numerical summary would normally be adequate, except that in this particular situation, the individual is disturbed by the real possibility that he gave his brother the phone number of the wrong hotel. This new possibility should be described as a direct parent of the observation *No call* and treated as a new contingency. Under the assumption that the wrong phone number was given, the likelihood ratio will be 1:1 and the spread of $BEL(E \mid C_i)$ will be the same as in Figure 7.11b. Under the assumption that the right phone number was given, the likelihood ratio will of course be higher—perhaps 5:1 against *Win*. The average over these two assumptions should coincide with Figure 7.12b, but the overall spread of $BEL(E \mid c)$ can be much higher, depending on the probability attached to the event *Wrong number*. It is not uncommon for one's sense of confidence to vary depending on what assumptions are made explicit at any given time.

In larger networks, $BEL(c)$ can be computed using the chain-product rule for conjunctive queries (Section 4.5), instantiating the variables in C one at a time. A reasonable way to approximate the distribution of $BEL(E \mid c)$ would be to calculate only the three or four most likely combinations of contingencies from C and examine how susceptible $BEL(E \mid c)$ is to these combinations. This parallels people's tendency to justify lack of confidence by imagining a few likely scenarios leading to diverse consequences.

7.3.5 Conclusions

The need to express ignorance about probabilities has led to a proliferation of new calculi of probability intervals and higher-order probabilities. Kyburg [1987] recently argued that "so-called second order probabilities have nothing to contribute conceptually to the analysis and representation of uncertainty," because "'information about the accuracy of P can be expressed by a probability density function over P' [Cheeseman 1985]." This section offers even stronger support to Kyburg's claim, showing that some basic information about accuracy of P need not even be expressed by a probability density function over P; it is a built-in feature of the very same model that provides the information about P. The meaning of the probability intervals encoded in the Dempster-Shafer formalism will be discussed in Section 9.1.4.

7.4 BIBLIOGRAPHICAL AND HISTORICAL REMARKS

Taxonomic hierarchies like those treated in Section 7.1 represent the simplest of semantic networks, since they are based solely on binary relations such as IS-A,

IS-PART-OF, or IS-COMPOSED-OF. Such networks have a long tradition in AI [Woods 1975; Schubert 1976] and in cognitive psychology [Quillian 1968], and have also been used in PROSPECTOR (Duda et al. 1978). An application of the method of Section 7.1 to image segmentation is reported in Chou and Brown [1987].

The treatment in Section 7.1 was motivated by Gordon and Shortliffe [1985], who studied the application of the Dempster-Shafer (D-S) theory to a hierarchy of hypotheses and stated that they were aware of no other model that could allow inexact reasoning at any level of abstraction. Gordon and Shortliffe developed an approximate algorithm for computing the D-S belief functions on tree hierarchies, an algorithm which was later improved by Shafer and Logan [1987] and Shenoy and Shafer [1986]. Shafer and Logan showed that an exact solution can be obtained in time proportional to the number of nodes in the tree, and Shenoy and Shafer showed that it can be obtained by local computations, similar to the propagation method of Section 7.1.2. Chapter 9 compares the meaning of the beliefs computed by the D-S method to those computed by Bayesian methods.

Section 7.3 was inspired by Spiegelhalter [1986] and Kyburg [1987a]. David Heckerman has pointed out that the idea of defining confidence by the presence of uncertain contingencies can be traced back to Tribus [1969].

Exercises

7.1.   Consider the car diagnosis problem of Figure 7.1 and assume that, initially, each of the nine hypotheses is equally likely. Calculate the effect of finding that the battery connections are good and that the transmission is in neutral

   (a) by normalization,

   (b) by message passing,

   (c) by message passing, given that the two findings are not entirely accurate, $\lambda = 9:1$.

7.2.   The propagation scheme described in Section 7.1.2 cannot handle simultaneous evidence. Can new propagation rules be devised to rectify this deficiency? (Hint: if we view the system as clusters of parents, constrained by an exclusive-input gate as in Figure 7.3, we get an ordinary Bayesian network, which can handle simultaneous evidence.)

7.3.   In the example of Figure 7.7:

   a.   Calculate the sensitivity of the estimate of X to variations in Z_2.

   b.   Calculate the sensitivity of Z_2 to variations in X.

   c.   Explain the difference.

7.4.   In the example of Section 7.3.4, what is the distribution of $BEL(Win)$ after we introduce the event "*Wrong number*"?

Appendix 7-A

Derivation of Propagation Rules For Continuous Variables

Eqs. (7.22) through (7.24) are derived using the following seven formulas, which facilitate the manipulation of normal distributions:

$$N(x; \sigma, \mu) = \beta \exp\left\{-\frac{1}{2\sigma}(x-\mu)^2\right\}, \qquad (7.25)$$

where β is some arbitrary constant that does not necessarily normalize N,

$$N(x; \sigma, \mu) = N(\mu; \sigma, x), \qquad (7.26)$$

$$N(ax + b; \sigma, \mu) = N\left[x; \frac{\sigma}{a^2}, \frac{\mu - b}{a}\right], \qquad (7.27)$$

$$N(x; \sigma_1, \mu_1) \cdot N(x; \sigma_2, \mu_2) = N\left[x; \frac{\sigma_1\sigma_2}{\sigma_1 + \sigma_2}, \frac{\sigma_2\mu_1 + \sigma_1\mu_2}{\sigma_1 + \sigma_2}\right], \qquad (7.28)$$

$$\prod_i N(x; \sigma_i, \mu_i) = N\left[x; \left[\sum_i \frac{1}{\sigma_i}\right]^{-1}, \frac{\sum_i \frac{\mu_i}{\sigma_i}}{\sum_i \frac{1}{\sigma_i}}\right], \qquad (7.29)$$

$$\int N(y; \sigma_1, \mu_1) N(y; \sigma_2, x)\, dy = N(x; \sigma_1 + \sigma_2, \mu_1), \qquad (7.30)$$

$$\int_{x_1} \cdots \int_{x_n} \prod_{i=1}^{n} N(x_i; \sigma_i, \mu_i) N\left[\sum_{i=1}^{n} b_i x_i; \sigma, \mu\right] dx_1 \cdots dx_n$$

$$= N\left[0; \sigma + \sum_{i=1}^{n} b_i^2 \sigma_i, \mu - \sum_{i=1}^{n} b_i \mu_i\right]. \qquad (7.31)$$

To compute $BEL(x)$ we divide the evidence e into two components, e_X^+ and e_X^-, representing data in the subnetworks above X and below X, respectively:

$$BEL(x) = f(x \mid e_X^+, e_X^-) = \alpha\, f(x \mid e_X^+)\, f(e_X^- \mid x)$$

$$= \alpha\, \pi(x) \cdot \lambda(x) ,$$

$$\pi(x) = f(x \mid e_X^+) = \int_{u_1} \cdots \int_{u_n} f(x \mid e_X^+, u_1, ..., u_n)\, f(u_1, ..., u_n \mid e_X^+)\, du_1 \cdots du_n$$

$$= \int_{u_1} \cdots \int_{u_n} f(x \mid u_1, ..., u_n) \prod_{i=1}^{n} f(u_i \mid e_i^+)\, du_1 \cdots du_n$$

$$= \int_{u_1} \cdots \int_{u_n} N\left[x; \sigma_{w_X}, \sum_{i=1}^{n} b_i\, u_i\right] \prod_{i=1}^{n} N(u_i; \sigma_i^+, \mu_i^+)\, du_1 \cdots du_n ,$$

and, using Eq. (7.31),

$$\pi(x) = N\left[0; \sigma_{w_X} + \sum b_i^2\, \sigma_i^+, x - \sum_{i=1}^{n} b_i\, \mu_i^+\right]$$

$$= N\left[x; \sigma_{w_X} + \sum_{i}^{n} b_i^2\, \sigma_i^+, \sum_{i=1}^{n} b_i\, \mu_i^+\right]$$

$$= N(x, \sigma_\pi, \mu_\pi) ,$$

where σ_π and μ_π are defined in Eq. (7.21). Similarly, for $\lambda(x)$ we have

$$\lambda(x) = f(e_X^- \mid x) = f(e_1^-, e_2^-, ..., e_m^- \mid x) = \prod_j f(e_j^- \mid x) = \prod_j \lambda_j(x)$$

$$= N(x; \sigma_\lambda, \mu_\lambda) ,$$

where σ_λ and μ_λ are defined in Eq. (7.20). Combining these two results, and using Eq. (7.28), we obtain

$$BEL(x) = N(x; \sigma_\pi, \mu_\pi)\, N(x; \sigma_\lambda, \mu_\lambda) = N\left[x; \frac{\sigma_\pi \sigma_\lambda}{\sigma_\pi + \sigma_\lambda}, \frac{\sigma_\pi \mu_\lambda + \sigma_\lambda \mu_\pi}{\sigma_\pi + \sigma_\lambda}\right] ,$$

which proves Eq. (7.22).

To find $\pi_{Y_j}(x)$, we note that it is conditioned on all data except a subset $\mathbf{e}_j^-$ of variables that connect to X via Y_j. Therefore,

$$\pi_{Y_j}(x) = f(x \mid \mathbf{e} - \mathbf{e}_j^-) = BEL(x \mid \mathbf{e}_j^- = \varnothing)$$

$$= BEL(x) \Big|_{\sigma_j \to \infty} = BEL(x) \Big|_{\sigma_\lambda^- = \left[\sum_{k \neq j} \frac{1}{\sigma_k^-}\right]^{-1}} = N(x; \sigma_{Y_j}^+, \mu_{Y_j}^+),$$

where

$$\sigma_{Y_j}{}^+ = \frac{\sigma_\pi \left[\sum_{k \neq i} \frac{1}{\sigma_k^-}\right]^{-1}}{\sigma_\pi + \left[\sum_{k \neq j} \frac{1}{\sigma_k^-}\right]^{-1}} = \left[\frac{1}{\sigma_\pi} + \sum_{k \neq j} \frac{1}{\sigma_k^-}\right]^{-1}$$

and

$$\mu_{Y_j}^+ = \frac{\displaystyle\sum_{k \neq j} \frac{\mu_k^-}{\sigma_k} + \frac{\mu_\pi}{\sigma_\pi}}{\displaystyle\sum_{k \neq j} \frac{1}{\sigma_k^-} + \frac{1}{\sigma_\pi}}.$$

This establishes Eq. (7.23).

To compute $\lambda_X(u_i)$ we divide the evidence $\mathbf{e}$ into its disjoint components $\mathbf{e}_i^+$, $i=1, ..., n$ and $\mathbf{e}_j^-$, $j=1, ..., m$, and condition $\lambda_X(u_i)$ on all parents of X. For notational convenience we temporarily denote U_i by U and b_i by b, and let the other parents be indexed by k, ranging from 1 to some n:

$$\lambda_X(u) = f(\mathbf{e} - \mathbf{e}_U^+ \mid u)$$

$$= \int_{u_1} \cdots \int\!\!\int_{u_n x} f(\mathbf{e}_1^+, ..., \mathbf{e}_n^+, \mathbf{e}_1^-, ..., \mathbf{e}_m^- \mid u_1, ..., u_n, x, u)$$
$$\cdot f(u_1, ..., u_n, x \mid u)\, dx\, du_1 \cdots du_n$$

$$= \int_{u_1} \cdots \int_x \prod_j \lambda_{Y_j}(x) \prod_k f(\mathbf{e}_k^+ \mid u_k)\, f(x \mid u, u_1, ..., u_n)$$
$$\cdot f(u_1, ..., u_n \mid u)\, dx\, du_1 \cdots du_n$$

$$= \int_{u_1} \cdots \int_{u_n}\!\!\int_x \lambda(x) \prod_k \frac{f(u_k \mid \mathbf{e}_k^+)\, f(\mathbf{e}_k^+)}{f(u_k)} \cdot$$
$$\cdot \prod_k f(u_k)\, f(x \mid u, u_1, ..., u_n)\, dx\, du_1 \cdots du_n$$

$$= C \int_{u_1} \cdots \int_{u_n}\!\!\int_x \lambda(x) \prod_{k=1}^n \pi_X(u_k)\, f(x \mid u, u_1, ..., u_n)\, dx\, du_1 \cdots du_n,$$

where

$$\lambda(x) = N(x; \sigma_\lambda, \mu_\lambda), \qquad \pi_X(u_k) = N(u_k; \sigma_k^+, \mu_k^+),$$

$$f(x \mid u, u_1, ..., u_n) = N(x; \sigma_{w_x}, bu + \sum_{k=1}^{n} b_k \mu_k).$$

Using Eqs. (7.26) through (7.31) we write

$$\lambda_X(u) = \int_{u_1} \cdots \int_{u_n} \int_x N(x; \sigma_\lambda, \mu_\lambda) \prod_{k=1}^{n} N(u_k; \sigma_k^+, \mu_k^+)$$

$$\cdot N(x; \sigma_{w_x}, bu + \sum_{k=1}^{n} b_k u_k)\, dx\, du_1 \cdots du_n$$

$$= \int_{u_1} \cdots \int_{u_n} \prod_{k=1}^{n} N(u_k; \sigma_k^+, \mu_k^+)\, N(bu + \sum_{k=1}^{n} b_k u_k; \sigma_\lambda + \sigma_{w_x}, \mu_\lambda)\, du_1 \cdots du_n$$

$$= \int_{u_1} \cdots \int_{u_n} \prod_{k=1}^{n} N(u_k; \sigma_k^+, \mu_k^+)\, N\left[\sum_{k=1}^{n} b_k u_k; \sigma_\lambda + \sigma_{w_x}, \mu_\lambda - bu\right] du_1 \cdots du_n$$

$$= N(0; \sigma_\lambda + \sigma_{w_x} + \sum_k b_k^2 \sigma_k^+, \mu_\lambda - bu - \sum_k \mu_k^+ b_k)$$

$$= N\left[b\mu; \sigma_\lambda + \sigma_{w_x} + \sum_{k=1}^{n} b_k^2 \sigma_k^+, \mu_\lambda - \sum_{k=1}^{n} b_k \mu_k^+\right]$$

$$= N\left[u; \frac{1}{b^2}\left[\sigma_\lambda + \sigma_{w_x} + \sum_{k=1}^{n} b_k^2 \sigma_k^+\right], \frac{1}{b}\left[\mu_\lambda - \sum_{k=1}^{n} b_k \mu_k^+\right]\right].$$

Therefore, for the i-th parent, U_i, we have

$$\lambda_X(u_i) = N\left[u_i; \frac{1}{b_i^2}\left[\sigma_\lambda + \sigma_{w_x} + \sum_{k \neq i} b_k^2 \sigma_k^+\right], \frac{1}{b_i}\left[\mu_\lambda - \sum_{k \neq i} b_k \mu_k^+\right]\right]$$

$$= N(u_i; \sigma_X^-(u_i), \mu_X^-(u_i)).$$

This confirms Eq. (7.24), and substituting Eq. (7.20) we obtain

$$\sigma_X^-(u_i) = \frac{1}{b_i^2} \left[\sigma_{w_x} + \sum_{k \neq i} b_k^2 \, \sigma_k^+ + \left[\sum_j \frac{1}{\sigma_j^-} \right]^{-1} \right],$$

$$\mu_X^-(u_i) = \frac{1}{b_i} \left[\frac{\displaystyle\sum_{j=1}^{m} \frac{\mu_i^-}{\sigma_j^-}}{\displaystyle\sum_{j=1}^{m} \frac{1}{\sigma_j^-}} - \sum_{k \neq i} b_k \mu_k^+ \right].$$

Chapter *8*

LEARNING STRUCTURE FROM DATA

Do two men travel together unless they have agreed?
Does a lion roar in the forest if he has no prey?
Does a young lion growl in his den if he has caught nothing?
Does a bird fall into a trap on the ground if the striker is
not set for it?
— *Amos, 3*

In studying belief networks we have thus far assumed that the structure and conditional probabilities necessary for characterizing the network were provided externally, say by an expert or an intelligent agent capable of encoding real-world experience in such terms. Our task has been to draw inferences from the network but not to challenge its authenticity. This chapter deals with the problem of constructing a network automatically from direct empirical observations, thus bypassing the human link in the process known as *knowledge acquisition*. We shall see that this problem produces some interesting challenges.

The task of finding a generic model of empirical data usually falls under the category of *learning* or *induction*. In contrast, the task of interpreting or explaining a specific pattern of observations is known as *abduction*, a term coined by the philosopher Charles Peirce (1839-1914). Learning can be thought of as the process of acquiring an effective internal representation for the persistent constraints in the world, i.e., generic facts and rules, as well as assembling the computational facilities by which predictions and explanations are produced. Routine diagnosis tasks involving fixed-domain knowledge (e.g., medicine) require abduction, while acquiring the knowledge necessary to perform an adequate diagnosis requires learning. The latter is comprised of two subtasks: extracting generic hypothesis-evidence relationships from records of medical experience and organizing such relationships in a data structure to facilitate quick response using a minimal amount of memory.

Taking Bayesian belief networks as the basic scheme of knowledge representation, the learning task separates nicely into two additional subtasks: learning the numerical parameters (i.e., the conditional probabilities) for a given network topology and identifying the topology itself—specifically, the missing links and the directionality of the arrows. These subtasks are clearly not independent because the set of parameters needed depends largely on the topology assumed, and conversely, the structure of the network is formally dictated by the joint distribution function (see Section 3.3.2). Still, it is more convenient to execute the learning process in two separate phases: *structure learning* and *parameter learning*. The reason is that the amount of data required for achieving any degree of confidence in the parameters learned increases substantially with the number of parameters. Moreover, a model with too many links is computationally useless, as it consumes too much storage space and requires lengthy procedures to produce predictions or explanations. Thus, for the representation to be of any use, it is vital that we give the learning process a built-in preference toward *simple* structures, i.e., sparse networks—those that have the fewest possible parameters and embody the fewest possible dependencies. The two-phase approach to learning permits us to introduce this Occam's razor in a natural way: we start with the simplest possible structure (i.e., the one with the minimum number of links) and try to find parameters that fit the data; if this attempt fails, we try more complex structures, and so on.

Our focus in this chapter will be on learning structures rather than parameters; the topic of parameter learning is fairly well covered in the literature on estimation techniques [Raiffa and Schlaifer 1968; Meditch 1969; Duda and Hart 1973], but relatively little work has been done on structure learning. Moreover, in many applications the exact values of the parameters play only a minor role; most of the knowledge needed for reasoning plausibly about a domain lies in its structure.

We shall focus on causal structures and in particular on causal trees and polytrees, where the computational role of causality as a modularizer of knowledge achieves its fullest realization. The next section elaborates on the nature of causation, reiterating the thesis that causation is not a property of nature but rather a mental construct devised for the efficient organization of knowledge. Subsequent sections will present more technical material and will develop techniques for discovering causal structures in empirical data.† Section 8.2 deals with the task of configuring causal structures for a set of observed variables, and Section 8.3 will introduce fictitious "dummy" variables to facilitate such configuration.

---

† We use the term *discovery* rather loosely. Following the paradigm of Section 8.1, a more accurate phrase would be "finding effective causal structures that fit empirical data."

8.1 CAUSALITY, MODULARITY, AND TREE STRUCTURES

Human beings exhibit an almost obsessive urge to mold empirical phenomena conceptually into cause-effect relationships. This tendency is, in fact, so strong that it sometimes comes at the expense of precision and often requires the invention of hypothetical, unobservable entities (such as the ego, elementary particles, and supreme beings) to make theories fit the mold of causal schemata. When we try to explain the actions of another person, for example, we invariably invoke abstract notions of mental states, social attitudes, beliefs, goals, plans, and intentions. Medical knowledge, likewise, is organized into causal hierarchies of invading organisms, physical disorders, complications, syndromes, clinical states, and only finally, the visible symptoms.

What are the merits of these fictitious variables called *causes* that make them worthy of such relentless human pursuit, and what makes causal explanations so pleasing and comforting once they are found? We take the position that human obsession with causation, like many other psychological compulsions, is computationally motivated. Causal models are attractive mainly because they provide effective data structures for representing empirical knowledge—they can be queried and updated at high speed with minimal external supervision.

The effectiveness of causal models stems from their *modular architecture*, i.e., an architecture in which dependencies among variables are mediated by a few central mechanisms. If I ask n persons in the street what time it is, the answers will undoubtedly be very similar. Yet instead of suggesting that the persons surveyed or the answers evoked somehow influenced each other, we postulate both the existence of an invisible central cause, the correct time, and the commitment of each person to adhere to that standard. If I wish to predict the response of the $(n + 1)$-th person I do not need to go back and consult each of the previous n responses; it is enough to consult the previously computed estimate of the actual time, then guess the next person's response while accounting for possible inaccuracies. Conversely, after hearing the $(n + 1)$-th answer, if I need to identify the individual owning the most accurate watch, it is sufficient for me to update the estimate of the correct time, then find the person whose answer lies closest to that estimate. Thus, instead of being a complex n-ary relation among the individuals involved, the causal model in this example consists of a network of n binary relations, all connected in a starlike pattern to one central variable (the correct time), which serves to dispatch information to and from the connecting variables. Psychologically, this modular architecture is much more pleasing than one that entails communication between variables. Since each variable is affected by only one source of information (i.e., the central cause), no conflict arises; any assignment of belief that is consistent with the central source will also be consistent with the beliefs assigned to other variables, and a change in any of the variables can communicate its impact to all other variables in just two steps.

Computationally speaking, such invisible causes are merely names given to storage places, which, by holding partial results, facilitate efficient manipulation of the visible variables in the system. They encode a summary of the interactions among the visible variables and, once calculated, permit us to treat the visible variables as though they were mutually independent.

With its dual role, summarizing and decomposing, a causal variable is analogous to an orchestra conductor: It achieves coordinated behavior through central communication and thereby relieves the players of having to communicate directly with one another. In the physical sciences, a classic example of such coordination is the contruct of a *field* (e.g., gravitational, electric, or magnetic). Although there is a one-to-one mathematical correspondence between the electric field and the electric charges in terms of which it is defined, nearly every physicist takes the next step and ascribes physical reality to the electric field, imagining that in every point of space there is some real physical phenomenon taking place which determines the potential of ultimately generating a force at that point. This psychological construct had a huge impact on the historical development of electrical science. It decomposed the complex phenomena associated with interacting electrical charges into two independent processes: The creation of the field at a given point by the surrounding charges and the conversion of the field into a physical force once another charge passes near that point.

The advantages of centrally coordinated architectures are not unique to star-structured networks but are also present in tree structures, since every internal node in the tree centrally coordinates the activities of its neighbors. Trees are the only graph structures whose links can be oriented in such a way that each node will receive input from at most one source—its parent—thus ensuring conflict-free communication. In a management hierarchy, for example, where employees can communicate with each other only through their immediate superiors, the passage of information is swift, economical, conflict-free, and highly parallel. The propagation techniques developed in Chapters 4 and 5 demonstrate clearly the computational advantages of trees when the relationships constraining the variables are probabilistic in nature. Similar advantages occur in systems subject to hard, externally imposed constraints (e.g., graph coloring, Section 4.1); if the constraints on a set of variables can be represented by a tree of binary relations, then globally consistent solutions can be found in linear time, using local relaxations [Frueder 1982; Dechter and Pearl 1985].

In probabilistic formalisms, the topological concepts of modularity and central coordination are embodied in the notion of conditional independence. The answers to the question "What time is it?" in the previous example would be viewed as random variables that are bound together by a *spurious correlation* [Simon 1954; Suppes 1970]; they become independent of each other once we know the state of the mechanism causing the correlation, i.e., the correct time. Conditional independence thus captures both functions of our orchestra conductor: coordination and decomposition.

The most familiar connection between causality and conditional independence is reflected in the scientific notion of a *state*, which was devised to nullify the influence that the past exerts on the future by providing a sufficiently detailed description of the present. In probabilistic terms this came to be known as a Markov property: Future events are conditionally independent of past events, given the current state of affairs. This is precisely the role played by the set of parents Π_X in the construction of Bayesian networks (Section 3.3); they screen each variable X from the influence of all other predecessors of X.

Causal labeling creates modularity not only by separating the past from the future, but also by decoupling events occurring at the same time. Knowing the set of immediate causes Π_X renders X independent of all other variables except X's descendant; many of these variables may occur at the same time as X, or even later. In fact, this sort of independence is causality's most universal and distinctive characteristic. In medical diagnosis, for example, a group of co-occurring symptoms often become independent of each other once we identify the disease that caused them. When some of the symptoms directly influence each other, the medical profession invents a name for that interaction (e.g., *syndrome, complication,* or *clinical state*) and treats it as a new auxiliary variable, which again assumes the modularization role characteristic of causal agents—knowing the state of the auxiliary variable renders the interacting symptoms independent of each other. In other words, the auxiliary variable constitutes a sufficient summary for determining the likely development of each individual symptom in the group; additional knowledge regarding the states of the other symptoms becomes superfluous.

The continuous influx of such auxiliary concepts into our languages shows the role of conditional independence in probabilistic modeling. Contrary to positions often found in the literature, conditional independence is not a "restrictive assumption" made for mathematical convenience; nor is it an occasional grace of nature for which we must passively wait. Rather, it is a mental construct that we actively create, a psychological necessity that our culture labors to satisfy.

The decompositional role of causal variables attains its ultimate realization in tree-structured networks, where every pair of nonadjacent variables becomes independent given a third variable on the path connecting the pair. Only in a tree structure can a node be sure that the information provided by each of its neighbors originates from an independent source, so that a local combination rule can be applied without fear of conflict, feedback, or correlation (counting information twice). Only in a tree structure can a node be sure that the information received from one node (the father) renders all other nodes except its descendants irrelevant, thus providing a license to activate local rules without fear that some remote piece of information will render the rules inapplicable. Indeed, the updating scheme described in Section 4.2 draws its speed, stability, and autonomy from the high degree of decomposition provided by the tree structure. These computational advantages, we postulate, give rise to the satisfying sensation called in-depth understanding, which people experience when they discover causal models consistent with their observations.

Given that tree-structured networks capture the main feature of causation and provide a convenient computational medium for performing interpretations and predictions, we now ask whether it is possible to reconfigure, or at least approximate, every belief network as a tree. The pioneering step in this direction was taken by Chow and Liu [1968], who showed that an arbitrary joint distribution can be optimally approximated by a tree-dependent distribution, using the marginal probabilities of pairs of variables. This technique is described in Section 8.2.1, and an extension to polytrees is given in Section 8.2.2. The latter is shown to be a much harder problem; we can find a causal polytree if the data fits exactly into such a structure, but we do not know how to construct the *best* polytree approximation to data that has no polytree representation.

Section 8.3 explores the possibility of constructing tree representations by introducing invisible "dummy" variables. That dummy variables should be capable of facilitating tree representations is clear from the following consideration: Imagine that the intermediate nodes of some tree T cannot be observed, so that one can measure the leaf variables only. Analyzing the dependencies between the leaves, we realize that no two of them can be separated by the others; therefore, if we were to construct a Bayesian network based on the leaf variables alone, a complete graph would result. Yet when considered with the intermediate variables the interactions among the leaf variables form a tree, clearly demonstrating that some multiply connected networks can inherit all the advantages of tree representations through the introduction of a few dummy variables. To characterize this class of networks, we first ask what conditions on the observed probability distribution would guarantee the existence of dummy variables that could decompose the network into a tree. Then we ask whether the internal structure of such a tree can be determined from observations made solely on the leaves. If it can, then the structure found will constitute an operational definition for the hidden causes often found in causal models. Additionally, if we take the view that learning entails the acquisition of computationally effective representations of nature's regularities, then such procedures for configuring trees may reflect an important component of human learning.

We will show that the introduction of dummy variables marks a significant departure from the structuring task treated in Section 8.2. In Chow's trees all nodes denote observed variables, so the conditional probability for any pair of variables can be measured directly. By contrast, when only the leaves are accessible to empirical observation, we know none of the conditional probabilities that link the internal nodes to the leaves or to other internal nodes—these we must infer by indirect methods. The method described in Section 8.3 offers a solution to this problem, but it assumes some restrictive conditions: All variables must be either bi-valued (Section 8.3.1) or normally distributed (Section 8.3.2). In addition, the method works only when a solution tree exists. Finding the best tree approximation for arbitrary data turns out, again, to be an intractable problem, admitting only heuristic, suboptimal solutions.

8.2 STRUCTURING THE OBSERVABLES

8.2.1 Chow's Method of Constructing Trees

Chow and Liu [1968] were concerned with the enormous storage space required for representing a probability distribution function of n discrete random variables. If each variable X_i takes on r values, then the random vector $x = (x_1, x_2,..., x_n)$ can take on as many as r^n values. If P is unknown and if independent samples $x^1,..., x^s$ with the distribution P are observed, then one normally estimates $P(x)$ by calculating the relative frequency of x among the observations $x^1,..., x^s$. In general this requires calculating and storing r^n values for a complete specification of P. However, if the components $X_1,..., X_n$ are independent, so that

$$P(x) = \prod_i P(x_i),$$

then each $P(x_i)$ can be calculated by observing the relative frequency of $X_i = x_i$, and only $n \cdot r$ calculations must be stored to obtain the estimate of $P(x)$. For any value combination x, $P(x)$ could then be calculated from a multiplication of n of the stored numbers. Since the assumption of total independence is often unrealistic, it is desirable to examine models that lie somewhere in between; they capture interdependencies among the variables yet require a modest amount of storage space. A distribution with tree dependence is one such model.

We saw in Chapter 3 that any tree-dependent distribution $P^t(x)$ (i.e., P^t is a Markov field relative to the tree t) can be written as a product of $n - 1$ pair-wise conditional probability distributions,

$$P^t(x) = \prod_{i=1}^{n} P(x_i \mid x_{j(i)}), \qquad (8.1)$$

where $X_{j(i)}$ is the variable designated as the parent of X_i in some orientation of the tree. The root X_1 can be chosen arbitrarily, and having no parents, it is characterized by the prior probability $P(x_1 \mid x_0) = P(x_1)$. Thus, the number of parameters needed for specifying a tree-dependent distribution is $(r - 1) r(n - 1) + (r - 1)$, namely, $r(r - 1)$ parameters for each of the $n - 1$ link matrices and $r - 1$ parameters for the root node.

The advantages of tree representation, of course, go beyond its storage economy. With trees, the required parameters $P(x_i \mid x_j)$ can be estimated reliably from sample data, since there will normally be enough samples matching any specified value combination of x_i and x_j. Additionally, as argued in Section 8.1, tree representations have a distinct computational advantage in data interpretation, since trees are the only structures that permit coherent inferencing through local computations.

Chow and Liu asked the following question: If we measured (or estimated) a distribution P, what is the tree-dependent distribution P^t that best approximates P? In other words, among all spanning trees that one can draw on n variables, each yielding a product form P^t as in Eq. (8.1), which P^t will be closest to P? As a distance criterion between two distributions, P and P', Chow and Liu chose the Kullback-Leibler cross-entropy measure [Kullback and Leibler 1951; Shore 1986]:

$$D(P, P') = \sum_x P(x) \log \frac{P(x)}{P'(x)} . \qquad (8.2)$$

This measure is nonnegative and attains the value 0 if and only if P' coincides with P.

The optimization task can be performed in two steps. First, we fix the structure of some tree t and ask what conditional probabilities $P^t(x_i | x_j)$ would render P^t the best approximation of P. We call this best distribution the *projection* of P on t, P_P^t. Second, we vary the structure of t over all possible spanning trees, and among all the projections of P on these spanning trees we seek the one that is closest to P. These two tasks are surprisingly simple.

THEOREM 1: *The projection of P on t is characterized by the equality*

$$P_P^t(x_i | x_{j(i)}) = P(x_i | x_{j(i)}) . \qquad (8.3)$$

In other words, by forcing the conditional probabilities along the branches of the tree t to coincide with those computed from P, we get the best t-dependent approximation to P.

THEOREM 2 [Chow and Liu 1968]: *The distance measure of Eq. (8.2) is minimized by projecting P on any maximum weight spanning tree (MWST), where the weight on the branch (X_i, X_j) is defined by the mutual information measure*

$$I(X_i, X_j) = \sum_{x_i, x_j} P(x_i, x_j) \log \frac{P(x_i, x_j)}{P(x_i) P(x_j)} \geq 0 . \qquad (8.4)$$

The proof of Theorems 1 and 2 is given in Appendix 8-A.

With these results, our minimization problem can be solved without considering every single possible tree; the MWST can be found in $O(n^2)$ steps using well-known algorithms [Even 1979]. Furthermore, the solution requires only second-order component distributions; it is based on evaluating the mutual information for pairs of variables, hence higher-order distributions are not needed.

The Chow and Liu MWST algorithm is summarized in the following steps:

1. From the given (observed) distribution $P(x)$, compute the joint distributions $P(x_i, x_j)$ for all variable pairs.

2. Using the pairwise distributions (step 1), compute all $n(n-1)/2$ branch weights and order them by magnitude.

3. Assign the largest two branches to the tree to be constructed.

4. Examine the next-largest branch, and add it to the tree unless it forms a loop, in which case discard it and examine the next-largest branch.

5. Repeat step 4 until $n - 1$ branches have been selected (at which point a spanning tree has been constructed.)

6. $P^t_P(x)$ can be computed by selecting an arbitrary root node and forming the product in Eq. (8.1).

While the projection of P on any given tree is unique, the structure of the MWST may not be unique if several branches have equal weight. For example, if $P(x, y, z)$ is invariant to permutations of variables, then the three branches (X, Y), (Y, Z), and (Z, X) have equal weights and the MWST algorithm might produce any one of three spanning trees,

$$X—Y—Z, \quad Z—X—Y, \quad \text{or} \quad Y—Z—X,$$

depending on the tie-breaking rule used. Each of these MWSTs yields a distribution that is equidistant from P, however. In particular, since Eq. (8.2) yields zero only if $P = P'$, we have the following corollary.

COROLLARY 1: *If the underlying distribution P is itself tree-dependent, then its projection on every MWST must coincide with P.*

The merits of the MWST algorithm are several. First, it uses only second-order statistics, which are easily and reliably measured from sample data and are economical to store. The tree is developed in $O(n^2)$ steps using only weight comparisons, thereby avoiding expensive tests for conditional independence. Finally, it can be shown that if the branch weights are computed from sampled data, then P^t_P will be a maximum likelihood estimate of P. The consequence of this is that if the underlying distribution is indeed one of tree-dependence, the approximating probability constructed by the MWST algorithm converges with probability 1 to the true underlying distribution [Chow and Wagner 1973].

It is worth noting that these advantages are unique to tree structures and do not apply to general multiply connected graphs. Even if we could afford to enumerate all graphs in a given class, the task of finding the projection of P on other product forms might involve enormous computations (see Chapter 3) unless that graph could be embedded in a suitable join tree. Product forms based on join trees can inherit some of the advantages of tree structuring if the cliques are not too large. Still, efficient algorithms such as the MWST are applicable only to join trees of pairs (i.e., trees of singletons); optimal higher-order structures can be found only by exhaustive enumeration or heuristic approximation [Malvestuto 1986].

The next subsection presents an exceptional join tree—a *polytree*, which, though it allows us to describe higher-order interactions, enjoys many of the computational advantages of simple trees. Even more remarkably, its structure can be identified by second-order distributions using an MWST algorithm similar to that of Chow and Liu.

8.2.2 *Structuring Causal Polytrees*

Assume we are given a distribution $P(x)$ of n discrete-value variables, and we are told that $P(x)$ can be represented by some unknown polytree F_0, called a *generating polytree*, in the sense that F_0 is an I-map of $P(x)$. We seek to recover the structure of F_0, i.e., the set of branches and hopefully their directionality, by examining the properties of $P(x)$. To be supported by a polytree, $P(x)$ must have the form

$$P(x) = \prod_{i=1}^{N} P(x_i \mid x_{j_1(i)}, x_{j_2(i)}, ..., x_{j_m(i)}) , \qquad (8.5)$$

where $\{x_{j_1(i)}, x_{j_2(i)}, ..., x_{j_m(i)}\}$ is the (possibly empty) set of direct parents of variable x_i in F_0, and the parents of each variable are mutually independent, i.e.,

$$P(x_{j_1(i)}, x_{j_2(i)}, ..., x_{j_m(i)}) = \prod_{k=1}^{m} P(x_{j_k(i)}) \quad \text{for all } i . \qquad (8.6)$$

That the structure of F_0 may not always be recoverable uniquely is apparent from examining the dependencies induced by the three possible types of adjacent triplets allowed in polytrees:

1. $X \rightarrow Y \rightarrow Z$

2. $X \leftarrow Y \rightarrow Z$

3. $X \rightarrow Y \leftarrow Z$

Since type 1 and type 2 represent the same dependency model, they are indistinguishable. Type 3, however, can be uniquely identified, since X and Z are marginally independent and all other pairs are dependent. Thus, while the *skeletons* (the graphs stripped of arrows) of these three triplets are identical, the directionality of the arrows is partially identifiable.

The algorithm described next will recover the skeleton of F_0 uniquely and will determine its directionality to the maximum extent permitted by $P(x)$.

The dependency structure that governs all descendants of a given node X in a polytree is identical to a simple tree, and the subgraphs containing the parents of X are marginally independent of each other. Thus, a tree-structuring algorithm like the MWST should be able to recover the skeleton tree of F_0. Given this skeleton, the dependency structure of type 3 can be used to determine if a variable has multiple parents and, once the first two parents have been found, to resolve the directionality of all branches touching their child. Specifically, we note that a partially directed triplet $X \rightarrow Y - Z$ can be completed by testing for the mutual independence of X and Z; if X and Z are independent, Z is a parent of Y, else Z is a child of Y.

We first restrict the analysis to *nondegenerate* distributions.

DEFINITION: *A distribution $P(x)$ is said to be **nondegenerate** if it has a connected, perfect-map, i.e., if there exists a connected DAG that displays all the dependencies and independencies embedded in P.†*

The purpose of this restriction is to guarantee, as shown in the next lemma, that any F_0 that is an I-map of P will also be both connected and a perfect-map of P. If P is represented by several unconnected DAGs, two or more subsets of variables must be independent of each other, so that the algorithm can be applied separately to each of these subsets.

LEMMA: *If P has a perfect-map D, then every I-map of P contains all the arcs of D.*

Proof: Let D' be an I-map of P, and let E_D and $E_{D'}$ stand for the set of undirected edges of D and D', respectively. If $(X, Y) \in E_D$, then for every subset S of variables, X and Y are dependent given S. If $(X, Y) \notin E_{D'}$, however, then there must exist some subset S' that renders X and Y independent given S', e.g., the parents of X together with those of Y. This contradicts the premise that D is a perfect-map of P. Q.E.D.

COROLLARY 2: *If P has a perfect-map D and an I-map F_0 that is a polytree, then*

1) *P has a polytree F that is a perfect-map of P,*

2) *$E_F \subseteq E_{F_0}$, and*

3) *if D is connected, then $E_F = E_{F_0} = E_D$.*

---

†   All I-maps and perfect-maps in this section refer to DAGs. Nondegenerate distributions were called "DAG isomorph" in Section 3.3.

We see that if P is nondegenerate, then F_0 must be a perfect-map of P, meaning that all unblocked paths correspond to genuine dependencies in P. Clearly, any other polytree representation of $P(x)$ must have the same set of branches as F_0, albeit different orientations.

In terms of the information measure I, nondegeneracy implies that for any pair of variables (X_i, X_j) that do not have a common descendant we have

$$I(X_i, X_j) > 0 , \tag{8.7}$$

and that if X_k does not block the path between X_i and X_j, then

$$I(X_i, X_j \mid X_k) > 0 , \tag{8.8}$$

where

$$I(X_i, X_j \mid X_k) = \sum_{x_i, x_j, x_k} P(x_i, x_j, x_k) \log \frac{P(x_i, x_j \mid x_k)}{P(x_i \mid x_k) P(x_j \mid x_k)} . \tag{8.9}$$

In addition, by Eq. (8.6), the parents of any variable are mutually independent, hence

$$I(X_{j_1(i)}, X_{j_2(i)}) = 0 , \tag{8.10}$$

and if X_k blocks the path between X_i and X_j, then (from Eq. (8.5))

$$I(X_i, X_j \mid X_k) = 0 . \tag{8.11}$$

Recall that in polytrees, a node X blocks a path p iff X is an intermediate node that is a source of some arrow along p.

The inequalities of Eqs. (8.7) and (8.8) and the equalities of Eqs. (8.10) and (8.11) will permit the precise recovery of the skeleton of F_0 and the partial but fullest possible recovery of its directionality.

POLYTREE RECOVERY ALGORITHM

The recovery algorithm [Rebane and Pearl 1987] consists of the following steps:

1. Generate a maximum-weight undirected spanning tree (a skeleton), using the MWST procedure (steps 1 through 5) of Section 8.2.1.

2. Search the internal nodes of the skeleton, beginning with the outermost layer and working inward, until a multi-parent node is found using the $X \rightarrow Y \leftarrow Z$ test described at the beginning of this section.

3. When a multi-parent node n is found, determine the directionality of all of its branches using the $X \rightarrow Y \leftarrow Z$ test.

4. For each node having at least one incoming arrow, resolve the directionality of all of its remaining adjacent branches using the $X \rightarrow Y \leftarrow Z$ test.

5. Repeat steps 2 through 4 until no further directionality can be discovered.

6. If there remain undirected branches, label them "undetermined" and supply external semantics needed for completion.

7. From $P(x)$ compute the conditional probabilities prescribed in Eq. (8.5).

The assignment of directions to the branches of the tree skeleton (steps 4 and 5) is best illustrated using the notion of a *causal basin*. A causal basin starts with a multi-parent cluster (a child node and all of its direct parents) and continues in the direction of causal flow to include all of the child's descendants and all of the direct parents of those descendants. Figure 8.1 shows an example of a polytree with two disjoint causal basins. As will become apparent, the directionality of a branch can be recovered if and only if the branch falls within some causal basin of F_0.

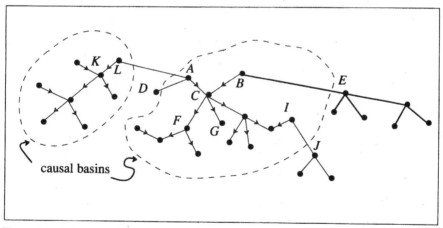

Figure 8.1. *Two causal basins rooted as nodes K and C. The arrows in each causal basin can be determined uniquely, while the directions of branches outside the basins are undetermined.*

The algorithm works best if F_0 is rich in multi-parent clusters, because these clusters provide the information needed for determining directionality in their associated basins. Branches outside these basins cannot be oriented by the information that $P(x)$ provides. Thus, a direct benefit of the algorithm is its ability to pinpoint precisely the minimum (if any) external semantics required to determine the causal relationships among the variables considered.

The theoretical justification for the recovery algorithm stands on two theorems.

THEOREM 3: *If a nondegenerate $P(x)$ is representable by a polytree F_0, then the MWST algorithm of Section 8.2.2 unambiguously recovers the skeleton of F_0.*

Proof: Nondegeneracy implies that all branches of F_0 have nonzero weight, as in Eq. (8.7), and that the conditional weights $I(X, Z|Y)$ are also nonzero for any pair (X, Z) not mediated by Y (as in Eq. (8.8)). If X, Y, and Z are any three variables obeying conditional independence,

$$P(x|y,z) = P(x|y), \qquad (8.12)$$

then it is well known [Gallager 1968] that

$$I(X, Y) = I(X, Z) + I(X, Y|Z) \qquad (8.13)$$

and

$$I(Y, Z) = I(X, Z) + I(Z, Y|X) . \qquad (8.14)$$

Consequently, for any triplet (X, Y, Z) satisfying Eq. (8.12) (e.g., $X \to Y \to Z$ and $X \leftarrow Y \to Z$ triplets) we have

$$\min[I(X, Y), I(Y, Z)] > I(X, Z). \qquad (8.15)$$

Eq. (8.15) also holds for $X \to Y \leftarrow Z$ triplets, since X and Z are marginally independent. Thus, it holds for any triplet X, Y, Z such that Y lies on the path connecting X and Z in F_0. Consequently, step 2 of the MWST algorithm will never list a branch weight of an unlinked pair (X_i, X_j) higher than the branch weight of any legitimate branch on the path connecting X_i and X_j. Any attempt to select the unlinked pair (X_i, X_j) would form a loop with already-selected branches, and that would cause (X_i, X_j) to be discarded. Therefore, the skeleton recovered from $P(x)$ exactly matches that of F_0.

THEOREM 4: *The directionality of a branch can be recovered if and only if it is contained within some causal basin of the generating polytree F_0.*

Proof: In the derived skeleton of F_0 each node with multiple neighbors is examined. The neighbors are tested in pairs to determine if at least two of them are marginally independent. Finding the first pair of parents allows us to specify the remaining members of the multi-parent cluster. Parent or descendant identities are determined for all members using the test for partially directed triplets.

The succeeding generations of descendants are resolved similarly using the partially directed triplet test. This process is continued in the direction of causal flow, thus sweeping out the causal basin of the discovered multi-parent cluster. In similar fashion we can identify all parents of any descendant, but further "upstream" orientation of these parents is not possible unless they themselves have multiple parents.

COROLLARY 3: *In simple trees (having no multi-parent clusters) it is not possible to assign direction to any of the links.*

This follows directly from the inability to identify any $X \rightarrow Y \leftarrow Z$ triplet and from the indistinguishability of $X \rightarrow Y \rightarrow Z$ and $X \leftarrow Y \rightarrow Z$ triplets.

THE DEGENERATE CASE

Under conditions of degeneracy, $P(x)$ can be represented by several polytrees, each having a different skeleton or a different branch orientation, or both. There is no way to guarantee then that the orientation produced by the recovery algorithm, even within the causal basins, will agree with any particular polytree from the set. For example, let Z stand for the sound of a bell that rings whenever the outcomes, X and Y, of two fair coins are equal. Any one of these variables is functionally dependent on the other two, while any two variables are marginally independent. Such a dependency structure has no perfect-map in DAGs. For example, any of the following three polytrees is an *I*-map of P, but none represents *all* of P's dependencies:

$$X \rightarrow Y \leftarrow Z, \qquad Z \rightarrow X \leftarrow Y, \qquad Y \rightarrow Z \leftarrow X.$$

Indeed, since all branch weights are equal to zero, the recovery algorithm might generate and orient any one of the polytrees above, depending on the tie-breaking rule used while constructing the skeleton. Obviously, the causal directionality discovered in this case is not dictated by the probability distribution; the same branch, say X—Y, may obtain either orientation depending on which skeleton is produced by the MWST procedure. Thus, while the structure $X \rightarrow Z \leftarrow Y$ is the one reflecting the causal influences related in the story, all three polytrees are in fact valid when we lack temporal information, since each permits a faithful representation of P via the product expansions of Eqs. (8.5) and (8.6).

In general, while we are not guaranteed that every skeleton produced by the MWST algorithm will permit a faithful representation of P, we are guaranteed that at least one of these skeletons will do so. This is because if P can be represented by a set of k distinct skeletons $T = (T_1,...,T_k)$, then each of these skeletons (and perhaps others) must have maximum weight. The proof is similar to that of Theorem 3, except that Eqs. (8.7), (8.8), and (8.15) now permit equalities.

Once a skeleton tree is found, however, the process of identifying and orienting its causal basins (steps 3 and 4 of the polytree recovery algorithm) must now employ higher-order statistics. For example, parents can no longer be identified merely by having *I* measures of 0, because children, too, may be marginally independent. Hence, the criterion $I(X, Z \mid Y) > 0$ should be invoked to distinguish $X \rightarrow Y \leftarrow Z$ triplets from $X \rightarrow Y \rightarrow Z$ and $X \leftarrow Y \rightarrow Z$ triplets, for which the equality $I(X, Z \mid Y) = 0$ holds.

8.2.3 Conclusions: Causation or Covariation?

Polytrees represent much richer dependency models than trees, as they support products of higher-order distributions. It is remarkable, therefore, that they can be identified by the same MWST algorithm that was used by Chow and Liu (Section 8.2.1) to find tree structures. Even better, the method requires only second-order statistics to establish the branch weights. The transition from trees to polytrees is not without losses, however. While Chow's method is guaranteed to find a *best* tree-dependency approximation to an arbitrary distribution $P(x)$, no such guarantee exists for polytrees; the structure of F_0 can be found only if $P(x)$ has a perfect-map in DAGs. Otherwise, there is no guarantee that the distribution found by the MWST method (or by any other known method) will be the best polytree-dependency approximation to $P(x)$.

An interesting philosophical question is whether any method based on probabilities can identify causal directionality among observable variables. Do the arrows discovered by the MWST method point unequivocally to a particular causal mechanism and exclude others? Do the arrows stand for genuine physical influences between connected variables? Or could the algorithm produce influences that conflict grossly with our intuition (e.g., an arrow drawn from a future event toward some event in the past)?

There are several answers. Formally speaking, probabilistic analysis is indeed sensitive only to covariations, so it can never distinguish genuine causal dependencies from spurious correlations, i.e., variations coordinated by some common, often unknown causal mechanism. But what is the operational meaning of a genuine causal influence? How do humans distinguish it from spurious correlation? Our instinct is to invoke the notion of *control*; e.g., we can cause the ice to melt by lighting a fire but we cannot cause fire by melting the ice. Yet the element of control is often missing from causal schemas. For example, we say that the rain caused the grass to become wet despite our being unable to control the rain. The only way to tell that wet grass does not cause rain is to find some other means of getting the grass wet, clearly distinct from rain, and to verify that when the other means is activated, the ground surely gets wet while the rain refuses to fall.

Thus, the perception of voluntary control is in itself merely a by-product of covariation observed on a larger set of variables [Simon 1980], including, for example, the mechanism of turning one's sprinkler on. In other words, whether X causes Y or Y causes X is not something that can be determined by running experiments on the pair (X, Y), in isolation from the rest of the world. The test for causal directionality must involve at least one additional variable, say Z, to test if by activating Z we can create variations in Y and none in X, or alternatively, if variations in Z are accompanied by variations in Y while X remains unaltered.

This is exactly the meaning of causality that the polytree recovery algorithm attributes to the arrows on the branches. The meaning relates not to a single branch in isolation but to an assembly of branches heading toward a single node. An arrow is drawn from X to Y and not the other way around when a variable Z is found that correlates with Y but not with X (see Figure 8.2a). More generally, we can define X as a direct cause of Y, if there exists an ordering of the variables in which X is a free parent of Y (non-adjacent to at least one other parent of Y) and no ordering in which Y is a free parent of X.

The discovery of the third variable Z, however, does not necessarily mean that X and Z are the ultimate causes of Y. The relationship among the three could change entirely upon the discovery of new variables. In Figure 8.2b, for example, the dependencies among variables X, Y, and Z are identical to those in Figure 8.2a; still, by postulating two auxiliary variables, U and V, we seem to have destroyed the causal connection between X and Y (as well as between Z and Y). However, the information provided by the variable Z is not completely useless, as it reveals that Y could not be a cause of X. Some causal inferences, however, can be ascertained with greater confidence, as they are robust to the discovery of hidden variables. For example, if a fourth variable W is found satisfying $I(W, Y, XZ)$ and no other independency, we can conclude that Y is most likely a genuine cause of W— any configuration of hidden variables that accounts for these independencies must contain an arrow pointing from Y to W or violate stability (see Pearl and Verma [1991] and exercises 8.10 - 8.12).

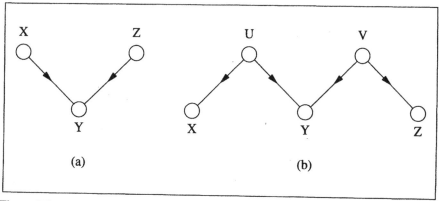

Figure 8.2. *(a) The direction of the causal relationship between X and Y is determined by the presence of a third variable Z that correlates with Y, but not with X. (b) Hypothesizing two auxiliary variables, U and V, alters the causal relationships between X, Y and Z, although all their dependencies remain the same.*

8.3 LEARNING HIDDEN CAUSES

8.3.1 Problem Definition and Nomenclature

Consider a set of n binary-valued random variables $X_1,..., X_n$ with a given probability mass function $P(x_1,..., x_n)$. First we examine whether P can be represented as the marginal probability of an $(n+1)$-variable distribution $P_s(x_1,..., x_n, w)$ in which $X_1,..., X_n$ are conditionally independent given W, i.e.,

$$P_s(x_1,..., x_n, w) = \prod_{i=1}^{n} P_s(x_i \mid w) P_s(w), \tag{8.16}$$

$$P(x_1,..., x_n) = \alpha \prod_{i=1}^{n} P_s(x_i \mid w=1) + (1-\alpha) \prod_{i=1}^{n} P_s(x_i \mid w=0). \tag{8.17}$$

The functions $P_s(x_i \mid w)$, $w=0, 1$, $i=1,..., n$ can be viewed as 2 by 2 stochastic matrices relating each X_i to the central hidden variable W (see Figure 8.3a); hence, we call P_s a *star-distribution* and call P *star-decomposable*. Each matrix contains two independent parameters, f_i and g_i, where

$$f_i = P_s(x_i =1 \mid w=1),$$

$$g_i = P_s(x_i= 1 \mid w=0), \tag{8.18}$$

and the central variable W is characterized by its prior probability $P_s(w=1) = \alpha$ (see Figure 8.3).

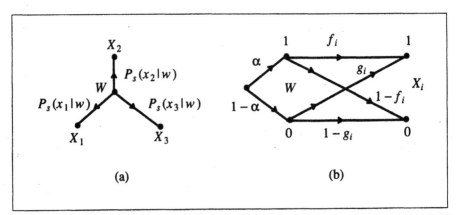

Figure 8.3. *(a) Three random variables, X_1, X_2, X_3, connected to a central variable W by a star network. (b) The three parameters, α, f_i, g_i, associated with each link.*

Star-decomposable distributions represent an extreme form of causal modularity, and its advantages are illustrated by the time-survey example of Section 8.1. First, the product form of P_s in Eq. (8.16) makes it very easy to compute the probability of any combination of variables. More importantly, the product form is extremely convenient for evidential reasoning tasks; the impact of any observation $X_j = x_j$ on any other variable can be computed with just two vector multiplications.

Unfortunately, when the number of variables exceeds three the conditions for star-decomposability become very stringent and are not likely to be met in practice. Indeed, a star-decomposable distribution for n variables has $2n + 1$ independent parameters, while the specification of a general distribution requires $2^n - 1$ parameters. Lazarfeld [1966] considered star-decomposable distributions where the hidden variable W is permitted to range over λ values, $\lambda > 2$. Such an extension requires the solution of $\lambda n + \lambda - 1$ nonlinear equations to find the values of the $\lambda n + \lambda - 1$ independent parameters. Letting $\lambda = 2^n - 1$ yields a trivial, unconstrained solution, where each value of W corresponds to one entry of the joint distribution function.

Aiming at the assembly of tree structures, we pursue a different approach, allowing a larger number of hidden binary variables but insisting that they form a treelike structure (see Figure 8.4), i.e., each triplet forms a star, but the central variables may differ from triplet to triplet.

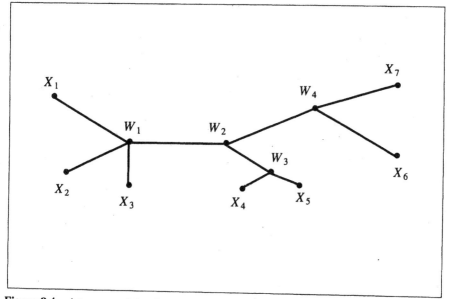

Figure 8.4. *A tree containing four dummy variables and seven visible variables.*

We shall say that a distribution $P(x_1, x_2,..., x_n)$ is *tree-decomposable* if it is the marginal probability of a tree-dependent distribution

$$P_T(x_1, x_2,..., x_n, w_1, w_2,..., w_m) \quad m \le n-2,$$

such that $W_1, W_2,..., W_m$ correspond to the internal nodes of a tree T and $X_1, X_2,..., X_n$ correspond to its leaves. We say that P_T is a *tree-extension* of P, and P is the *leaf-marginal* of P_T.

Clearly, one can create an arbitrary number of tree-extensions for any tree-decomposable P simply by placing new internal nodes on the links of one such extension or—even worse—by adding sub-trees of W variables, totally disconnected from the X variables. To eliminate such ambiguities, we therefore define a *minimal* tree-extension P_T to be a tree-extension of P such that no variable or link can be deleted from the tree T without P_T ceasing to be tree-extension of P. Clearly, every internal node W in a minimal tree-extension P_T must be connected to at least three neighbors; if it has only two neighbors, it can simply be replaced by a direct link between the two. Also, all of the link matrices in a minimal extension must be nonsingular, representing genuine dependencies between the linked variables; otherwise, the tree could be decomposed into disconnected sub-trees.

To simplify our discussion we shall restrict our analysis to tree-decomposable distributions on *connected* trees. If the minimal extension supports a set of disconnected trees (i.e., a forest) then the X variables can be partitioned into two or more mutually independent subsets of variables, in which case the analysis applies to each such subset.

Recall that if P_T supports a tree T, it can be written in product form (see Eq. (8.1)) using the following procedure: First choose an arbitrary node as a root. This will define a unique parent $Y_{j(i)}$ for each node $Y_i \in \{X_1,..., X_n, W_1, ..., W_m\}$ in T, except the chosen root, Y_1. The joint distribution is simply given by the product

$$P_T(x_1,..., x_n, w_1,..., w_m) = \prod_{i=1}^{m+n} P(y_i | y_{j(i)}), \qquad (8.19)$$

where $P(y_1 | \varnothing)$ stands for $P(y_1)$. For example, if in Figure 8.4 we choose W_2 as the root, we obtain

$$P_T(x_1,..., x_7, w_1,..., w_4) = P(x_7 | w_4) P(x_6 | w_4) P(x_5 | w_3) P(x_4 | w_3)$$
$$P(x_3 | w_1) P(x_2 | w_1) P(x_1 | w_1) P(w_1 | w_2)$$
$$P(w_3 | w_2) P(w_4 | w_2) P(w_2).$$

If we are given $P_T(x_1,..., x_n, w_1,..., w_m)$, then we clearly can obtain $P(x_1,..., x_n)$ by summing over the w's. We now ask whether the inverse transformation is possible, i.e., given a tree-decomposable distribution $P(x_1,..., x_n)$, can we recover its underlying minimal extension $P_T(x_1,..., x_n, w_1,..., w_m)$? We shall show that

(1) the minimal tree extension P_T is unique up to renaming of the variables or their values, (2) P_T can be recovered from P using $n\log n$ computations, and (3) the structure of T is uniquely determined by the second-order probabilities of P. The construction method depends on the analysis of star-decomposability for triplets, which is presented next. (Impatient readers may skip this analysis and go directly to Section 8.3.3.)

8.3.2 Star-Decomposable Triplets

In order to test whether a given three-variable distribution $P(x_1, x_2, x_3)$ is star-decomposable, we first solve Eq. (8.17) and express the parameters α, f_i, g_i as a function of the parameters specifying P. This task was carried out by Lazarfeld [1966] in terms of the seven joint-occurrence probabilities

$$p_i = P(x_i=1) ,$$
$$p_{ij} = P(x_i=1, x_j=1) , \qquad \textbf{(8.20)}$$
$$p_{ijk} = P(x_i=1, x_j=1, x_k=1) ,$$

the variances

$$\sigma_i = [p_i (1-p_i)]^{1/2} , \qquad \textbf{(8.21)}$$

and the correlation coefficients

$$\rho_{ij} = \frac{p_{ij} - p_i p_j}{\sigma_i \sigma_j} . \qquad \textbf{(8.22)}$$

The derivation, presented in Appendix 8-B, yields the following theorem.

THEOREM 5: *A necessary and sufficient condition for three binary random variables to be star-decomposable is that they satisfy the inequalities*

$$\frac{p_{ik}p_{ij}}{p_i} \le p_{ijk} \le \frac{p_{ik}p_{ij}}{p_i} + \sigma_j\sigma_k (\rho_{jk} - \rho_{ij}\rho_{ik}) \qquad \textbf{(8.23)}$$

for all $i, j, k \in \{1, 2, 3\}$ and $i \neq j \neq k$. When these conditions are satisfied, the parameters of the star-decomposed distribution can be determined uniquely, up to a complementation of the hidden variable W, i.e., $w \to (1-w), f_i \to g_i, \alpha \to (1-\alpha)$.

Obviously, in order to satisfy Eq. (8.23), the term $(\rho_{jk} - \rho_{ij}\rho_{ik})$ must be nonnegative. This introduces a simple necessary condition for star-decomposability that may be used to quickly rule out many candidates.

COROLLARY 4: *A necessary condition for a distribution $P(x_1, x_2, x_3)$ to be star-decomposable is that all correlation coefficients obey the triangle inequality*

$$\rho_{jk} \geq \rho_{ji}\rho_{ik} \quad i, j, k \in \{1, 2, 3\} \quad i \neq j \neq k . \qquad (8.24)$$

Eq. (8.24) is satisfied with equality if W coincides with X_i, i.e., if X_j and X_k are independent given X_i. Thus, an intuitive interpretation of this corollary is that the correlation between any two variables must be stronger than that induced by their dependencies on the third variable; a mechanism accounting for direct dependencies must be present. Moreover, Eq. (8.24) requires that the three variables $\{X_1, X_2, X_3\}$ be *positively correlated*, i.e., that all three correlation coefficients be nonnegative:

$$\rho_{ij} \, \rho_{jk} \, \rho_{ki} \geq 0. \qquad (8.25)$$

(If two of them are negative, we can rename two variables by their complements; the newly defined triplet will have all of its pairs positively correlated.)

Having established the criterion for star-decomposability, we can address a related problem. Suppose P is *not* star-decomposable. Can it be approximated by a star-decomposable distribution $\hat{P}$ that has the same second-order probabilities?

The preceding analysis contains the answer to this question. Note that the third order statistics are represented only by the term p_{ijk}, and this term is confined by Eq. (8.23) to a region whose boundaries are determined by second-order parameters. Thus, if we insist on keeping all second-order dependencies of P intact and are willing to change p_{ijk} so as to yield a star-decomposable distribution, we can find such a p_{ijk} only if the region circumscribed by Eq. (8.23) is nonempty.

THEOREM 6: *A necessary and sufficient condition for the second-order dependencies within the triplet X_1, X_2, X_3 to support a star-decomposable extension is that the six inequalities*

$$\frac{p_{ij}p_{ik}}{p_i} \leq p \leq \frac{p_{ij}p_{ik}}{p_i} + \sigma_j\sigma_k \, (\rho_{jk} - \rho_{ij}\rho_{ik}) \quad i = 1, 2, 3 \quad i \neq j \neq k \qquad (8.26)$$

possess a solution for p.

8.3.3 A Tree-Reconstruction Procedure

We are now ready to confront the central problem of this section: given a tree-decomposable distribution $P(x_1, ..., x_n)$, can we uncover its minimal tree-extension $P_T(x_1, ..., x_n, w_1, ..., w_m)$ and the topology of its underlying tree?

The construction method presented here is based on the observation that any three leaves in a tree have one and only one internal node that can be considered their *center*, i.e., it lies on all the paths connecting the leaves to each other. If one removes the center, the three leaves become disconnected from one another. This means that if P is tree-decomposable, then the joint distribution of any triplet of leaf variables X_i, X_j, X_k is star-decomposable, and based on Theorem 5, $P(x_i, x_j, x_k)$ uniquely determines the parameters α, f_i, g_i. Moreover, if one computes any of these parameters by choosing different leaf triplets, identical values should emerge.

Consider a quadruplet X_1, X_2, X_3, X_4 of leaves in T. These leaves are interconnected through one of the four possible topologies shown in Figure 8.5. The topologies differ in the identity of the triplets that share a common center. For example, in the topology of Figure 8.5a, $(1,2,3)$ and $(1,2,4)$ share a common center, and so do $(1,3,4)$ and $(2,3,4)$. In Figure 8.5b, on the other hand, the sharing pairs are $[(1,2,4), (2,4,3)]$ and $[(1,3,4), (2,1,3)]$, and in Figure 8.5d all triplets share the same center. We shall now show that the correlations between the leaves enable us to prune away some of these topologies, which helps configure the entire tree.

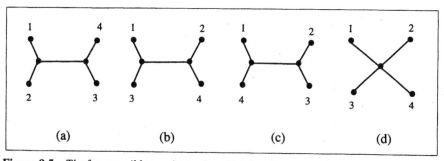

(a)   (b)   (c)   (d)

Figure 8.5. *The four possible topologies by which four leaves can be related.*

The conditional independence relationships displayed by the topologies in Figure 8.5 impose distinct constraints on the correlation coefficients $\rho_{i,j}$, $i, j = 1, 2, 3, 4$. It is easy to show that the correlation coefficient between any two variables in a tree is equal to the product of the correlation coefficients on the links connecting the two variables (Exercise 8.5). For instance, denoting by r and s respectively the left and right intermediate nodes in Figure 8.5a, we have

$$\rho_{13} = \rho_{1r}\, \rho_{rs}\, \rho_{s3}, \quad \rho_{42} = \rho_{4s}\, \rho_{sr}\, \rho_{r2}, \quad \text{etc.}$$

This yields the equality

$$\rho_{13}\rho_{42} = \rho_{14}\rho_{32} \tag{8.27}$$

relative to the topology of Figure 8.5*a*. Similarly, the topology of Figure 8.5*b* dictates

$$\rho_{12}\rho_{43} = \rho_{14}\rho_{23} \,, \qquad\qquad (8.28)$$

and that of Figure 8.5*c* dictates

$$\rho_{12}\rho_{34} = \rho_{13}\rho_{24} \,. \qquad\qquad (8.29)$$

Thus, we see that each of these three topologies is characterized by its own distinct equality, and the topology of Figure 8.5*d* is distinguished by compliance with all three equalities. This provides the necessary second-order criterion for deciding the topology of any quadruplet tested: if the equality $\rho_{ij}\rho_{kl} = \rho_{ik}\rho_{jl}$ holds for some permutation of the indices, we decide on the topology

If it holds for two permutations with distinct topologies, the entire quadruplet is star-decomposable. Note that the equality $\rho_{ij}\rho_{kl} = \rho_{ik}\rho_{jl}$ must hold for at least one permutation of the variables if the quadruplet is to be tree-decomposable.

Now we shall show how the topology of each quadruplet of leaves can be used to configure the entire tree.

We start with any three variables X_1, X_2, and X_3, connect them in a star, choose a fourth variable X_4, and ask which branch of the star X_4 should be joined to. We can answer this question easily by determining the appropriate topology of the quadruplet and connecting X_4 accordingly. Similarly, if we already have a tree structure T_i with i leaves and we wish to know where to join the $(i+1)$-th leaf, we can choose any triplet of leaves from T_i with a central variable W and test which branch of $W X_{i+1}$ should be joined to. This, in turn, identifies a sub-tree T_i' of T_i that should receive X_{i+1} and permits us to remove from further consideration the sub-trees emanating from the unselected branches of W. Repeating this operation on the selected sub-tree T_i' will eventually reduce it to a single branch, to which X_{i+1} is joined.

It is possible to show [Pearl and Tarsi 1986] that if we choose, in each state, a central variable that splits the available tree into sub-trees of roughly equal size, the joining branch of X_{i+1} can be identified in at most $\log(i)$ tests, to the base $\frac{k}{k-1}$, where k is the maximal degree of the tree T_i. This amounts to $O(n\log n)$ tests for constructing an entire tree of n leaves.

So far, we have shown that the structure of the tree T can be uncovered uniquely. Next we show that the distribution P_T can be determined uniquely from P, i.e., that we can determine all the functions $P(x_i \mid w_j)$ and $P(w_j \mid w_k)$ in Eq. (8.19), for $i = 1, \dots, n$ and $j, k = 1, 2, \dots, m$. The functions $P(x_i \mid w_j)$ assigned to the peripheral branches of the tree are determined directly from the star-decomposition of triplets involving adjacent leaves. In Figure 8.4, for example, the star-decomposition of $P(x_1, x_2, x_5)$ yields $P(x_1 \mid w_1)$ and $P(x_2 \mid w_1)$. The conditional probabilities $P(w_j \mid w_k)$ assigned to interior branches are determined by solving matrix equations. For example, $P(x_1 \mid w_2)$ can be obtained from the star-decomposition of $\{X_1, X_5, X_7\}$, and it is related to $P(x_1 \mid w_1)$ via

$$P(x_1 \mid w_2) = \sum_{w_1} P(x_1 \mid w_1) P(w_1 \mid w_2) .$$

This matrix equation has a solution for $P(w_1 \mid w_2)$ because $P(x_1 \mid w_1)$ must be nonsingular. It is singular only when $f_1 = g_1$, i.e., when X_1 is independent of W_1 and therefore of all other variables, a condition excluded from our analysis. Hence, we can determine the parameters of the branches next to the periphery, use them to determine more interior branches, and so on until all the interior conditional probabilities $P(w_i \mid w_j)$ are determined.

8.3.4 Extensions to Normal Variables

In this subsection, we extend the dummy-variable scheme of structuring causal trees from binary to continuous variables. Paralleling the treatment of Sections 8.3.1 through 8.3.3, we show that if all the variables are normally distributed and if the activities of the visible variables are governed by a tree-decomposable, normal joint distribution, then the tree can be structured from the observed correlations between pairs of variables. Moreover, the conditions for normally distributed variables to be tree-decomposable are less restrictive than the corresponding conditions for bi-valued variables.

Let $X_1, X_2, ..., X_n$ be random variables from an n-dimensional normal joint distribution:

$$f(x_1, x_2, ..., x_n) = (2\pi)^{-\frac{n}{2}} (det \textstyle\sum_n)^{-\frac{1}{2}} \exp[-\tfrac{1}{2}(x_n - \mu_n)^t \textstyle\sum_n^{-1}(x_n - \mu_n)] , \quad \textbf{(8.30)}$$

where $x_n = (x_1, x_2, ..., x_n)^t$, $\mu_n = Ex_n$ is the mean vector, and $\sum_n = E(x_n - \mu_n)(x_n - \mu_n)^t$ is the covariance matrix of x_n.

As in Section 8.3.2, we can ask if $f(x_1, x_2, ..., x_n)$ can be represented as a marginal distribution of an $(n + 1)$- dimensional normal distribution of $n + 1$ variables, $X_1, ..., X_n, W$, such that the X_i's are conditionally independent given W, i.e.,

$$f(x_1, x_2, ..., x_n) = \int_{-\infty}^{+\infty} f_s(x_1, x_2, ..., x_n, w) dw , \quad \textbf{(8.31)}$$

$$f_s(x_1, x_2, ..., x_n, w) = \prod_{i=1}^{n} f_s(x_i \mid w) f(w) . \quad \textbf{(8.32)}$$

If the decomposition in Eq. (8.31) is possible, we call f_s a *star-distribution* and call f *star-decomposable*.

Using the correlation coefficients defined as

$$\rho_{ij} = \sigma_{ij} / (\sigma_{ii}\sigma_{ij})^{\frac{1}{2}}, \tag{8.33}$$

the conditional independence embedded in Eq. (8.32) yields

$$\rho_{ij} = \rho_{iw}\rho_{jw}, \quad \text{for all } i, j, \tag{8.34}$$

which merely reaffirms the product rule for paths in trees. In the case of three variables, we can solve Eq. (8.34) for ρ_{iw} and obtain

$$\rho_{1w} = (\rho_{12}\rho_{13} / \rho_{23}^{\frac{1}{2}}), \quad \rho_{2w} = (\rho_{12}\rho_{23} / \rho_{13}),^{\frac{1}{2}} \quad \rho_{3w} = (\rho_{13}\rho_{23} / \rho_{12})^{\frac{1}{2}}. \tag{8.35}$$

These, together with the requirement that the ρ_{iw}'s must be real numbers with magnitude not exceeding 1, yield another theorem.

THEOREM 7 [Xu and Pearl 1987]:

1. *A necessary and sufficient condition for three random variables with a joint normal distribution to be star-decomposable is that the correlation coefficients satisfy the inequalities*

$$\rho_{jk} \geq \rho_{ji}\rho_{ik} \tag{8.36}$$

   for all $i, j, k \in \{1, 2, 3\}$ and $i \neq j \neq k$.

2. *The conditional densities $f(x_i \mid w) \sim N(\mu_{i \mid w}, \sigma_{i \mid w})$, $i = 1, 2, 3$ are specified by the parameters*

   $$\sigma_{i \mid w} = \sigma_{ii}(1 - \rho_{iw}^2) = \sigma_{ii}(1 - \rho_{ji}\rho_{ik} / \rho_{jk}),$$

   $$\mu_{i \mid w} = \mu_i - \sigma_{wi}(w - \mu_w) / \sigma_{ww} = \mu_i - \rho_{wi}\frac{\sqrt{\sigma_{ij}}}{\sigma_{ww}}(w - \mu_w),$$

   and $f(w) \sim N(\mu_w, \sigma_w)$, where $\sigma_{ww} > 0$ and μ_w may be chosen arbitrarily.

Comparing Theorems 5 and 7, we see that the conditions for a normally distributed triplet to be star-decomposable are less restrictive than those for bi-valued variables; there is no restriction corresponding to the third-order constraint imposed on p_{ijk} in Theorem 5. Additionally, unlike with bi-valued variables (see Appendix 8-B), the link parameters can be obtained in closed form. The densities $f(w), f(x_i \mid w)$ are readily determined by the selection of μ_w and σ_w, which one may conveniently set to $\sigma_w^2 = 1$ and $\mu_w = 0$. To ensure that $n(>3)$ variables of a joint normal distribution be star-decomposable, Eq. (8.34) must lead to a consistent solution for all of the ρ_{iw}'s.

The tree construction method for normal variables proceeds just like that of bi-valued variables: Eqs. (8.27) through (8.29) determine the topology of each leaf quadruplet, and these topologies are used to uncover the tree structure. The link parameters, likewise, are computed from the leaves inward, ensuring that at each stage the μ_w, σ_w parameters of the intermediate nodes are selected in a consistent way.

8.3.5 Conclusions and Open Questions

This section provides an operational definition for entities called "hidden causes," which are not directly observable but which facilitate the formation of effective causal models of empirical data. Hidden causes are viewed as dummy variables which, if held constant, induce probabilistic independence among sets of visible variables. In contrast to the methods described in Section 8.2, the introduction of dummy variables can decompose strongly coupled sets of visible variables, even those that reflect no conditional independencies. It is shown that if all variables are either bi-valued or normal, and if a tree decomposition of the visible variables is feasible, then the topology of the tree can be uncovered uniquely from the observed correlations between pairs of variables. Moreover, the structuring algorithm requires only $n\log n$ steps.

The method introduced in this section has two major shortcomings: it requires precise knowledge of the correlation coefficients, and it works only when the underlying model is tree-decomposable. In practice, we often have only sample estimates of the correlation coefficients; therefore, it is unlikely that criteria based on equalities (as in Eq. (8.27)) will ever be satisfied exactly. It is possible, of course, to relax these criteria and make topological decisions by seeking proximities rather than equalities. For example, instead of searching for an equality $\rho_{ij}\rho_{kl} = \rho_{ik}\rho_{jl}$, we can decide the quadruplet topology on the basis of the permutation of indices that minimizes the difference $|\rho_{ij}\rho_{kl} - \rho_{ik}\rho_{jl}|$. Experiments show, however, that the structure that evolves from such a method is sensitive to inaccuracies in the estimates of ρ_{ij}, because no mechanism is provided to retract erroneous decisions made in the early stages of the structuring process. Ideally, the placement of the $(i+1)$-th leaf should be decided not merely by its relation to a single triplet of leaves chosen to represent an internal node W but also by its relations to all previously structured triplets sharing W as a center. This, of course, will substantially increase the complexity of the algorithm.

Similar difficulties plague the task of finding the best tree-structured *approximation* for a distribution that is not tree-decomposable. Even though we argued that natural data lending itself to causal modeling should be representable as tree-decomposable distributions, these distributions may contain internal nodes with more than two values. The task of determining the parameters associated with such nodes is much more complicated, and it rarely yields unique solutions. In view of these difficulties, extending the dummy-variable method from trees to polytrees seems hopeless. A similar problem of configuring probabilistic models with hidden variables is mentioned by Hinton, Sejnowski, and Ackley [1984] as one of the tasks that a Boltzmann machine should be able to solve. However, it is not clear whether the relaxation techniques employed by the Boltzmann machine can easily escape local minima and whether they can readily accept the constraint that the resulting structure be a tree.

We leave open the question of explaining how approximate causal modeling, an activity humans seem to perform with relative ease, can be embodied in computational procedures that are both sound and efficient. Though it is basic to man's ability to comprehend his environment, causal modeling has defied mechanization. As Einstein once mused, "The most incomprehensible thing about the world is that it is comprehensible."

8.4 BIBLIOGRAPHICAL AND HISTORICAL REMARKS

The tree structuring method of Chow and Liu [1968] was originally applied to problems of character recognition. Dechter [1987] has used a similar method to decompose general *n*-ary relations into trees of binary relations. The polytree recovery algorithm of Section 8.2 was developed by George Rebane and reported in Rebane and Pearl [1987], together with an earlier version of Theorem 3. An earlier version of Section 8.3 was included in Pearl [1986c]. Norm Dalkey has called my attention to the work of Lazarsfeld [1966], on which Appendix 8-B is based. Section 8.3.4 was derived by Xu Lei and reported in Xu and Pearl [1987]. A system designed to fit causal structures to statistical data is described in Glymour et al. [1987]. The system, called TETRAD, suggests alternative structures together with their measures of fit, but does not employ a systematic procedure of finding a structure which in some sense is a best fit.

Our probabilistic treatment of causation is influenced by that of Simon [1954, 1980], and it stresses non-temporal causal ordering. Suppes [1970] provides a probabilistic account of causation which is based on temporal ordering. A logic-based account of causation and temporal reasoning is given in Shoham [1988]. A contrast between two conceptions of causal ordering, in the context of representing device behavior in AI systems, is described by Iwasaki and Simon [1986] and de Kleer and Brown [1986].

A general probabilistic account of causation has recently been developed, based on minimal-model semantics (Exercise 3.13.), where a variable X is said to have a causal influence on a variable Y if there is a directed path from X to Y in *all minimal causal models* (DAGs) consistent with the data [Pearl and Verma 1991]. The theory provides criteria for detecting genuine and spurious causes, with and without temporal information (Exercises 8.10 - 8.12), and yields algorithms for recovering general causal networks (with hidden variables) from statistical data.[1]

----

[1]   See Verma and Pearl (footnote (2), page 138) and Spirtes, P. and Glymour, C., An Algorithm for Fast Recovery of Sparse Causal Graphs, *Social Science Computer Review*, Spring 1991, 9(1):62-72.

Exercises

8.1. **a.** Apply Chow's method to the distribution of Exercise **3.3**, draw the maximal-weight spanning-tree, and represent P^t in product form.

b. Repeat problem (**a**) on the distribution described in Exercise **4.3**.

c. Repeat problem (**a**) on the distribution underlying Figure 4.37.

8.2. Given a covariance matrix Σ of multivariate normal distribution $f(x)$, devise a test procedure for deciding if $f(x)$ can be represented by a tree, and if it can, devise a procedure for finding the structure of the tree from Σ (see Dempster [1972]).

8.3. Apply the polytree recovery algorithm to the distributions described in Exercise **4.3** and Figure 4.37. Check if the arrows' directionalities match that of the original model. Explain.

8.4. Give an example of a probability distribution P under each of these conditions:

a. P has a unique polytree representation.

b. P has multiple polytree representations which share a unique skeleton.

c. P has exactly two polytree representations with different skeletons.

8.5. A distribution is *3-tree-dependent* if it is a Markov field relative to a *3-tree*. A *3-tree* is a tree of size-3 cliques, such that no two cliques have more than one node in common.

Explore the feasibility of finding the best 3-tree-dependent approximation to a given distribution P, i.e., generalize Chow's method of maximal-weight spanning-trees from standard trees to 3-trees.

8.6. Repeat Exercise **8.2** for polytrees.

8.7. Devise an algorithm for unique recovery of bipartite DAGs (i.e., DAGs of depth 2, such as the one in Figure 4.37).

8.8. Prove that the correlation coefficient between any two variables in a tree is equal to the product of the correlation coefficients on the links connecting the two variables.

8.9. Seven binary variables are distributed by a tree-decomposable distribution. Their correlation coefficients are given in the table below.

	1	2	3	4	5	6	7
1	1	0.81	0.81	0.4032	0.4032	0.3456	0.3456
2		1	0.81	0.4032	0.4032	0.3456	0.3456
3			1	0.4032	0.4032	0.3456	0.3456
4				1	0.49	0.18816	0.18816
5					1	0.18816	0.18816
6						1	0.36
7							1

Find the topology of the underlying tree and the correlation coefficients on all its branches using the method of Section 8.3.3.

8.10. Show that, barring functional dependencies, the minimal-model semantics of causation[1] sanctions the following criterion whenever temporal information is available:

"X has a causal influence on Y if there exists a third variable Z, preceding X, such that Z and Y are dependent and Z and Y are independent given X."

In other words, show that finding such Z guarantees that there must be a dependence between X and Y that is not due to hidden variables acting as common causes for both.

8.11. Devise a criterion for testing spurious causation, i.e., dependence between a variable X and a later variable Y that is attributed solely to the influence of other causal factors, common to both.

8.12. Generalize the criterion in Exercise 8.10 to cases lacking temporal information, showing that the existence of an intransitive triplet $\{X, Z, Z'\}$, satisfying $I(Z, S, Z')$, $\neg I(Z, S, X)$ and $\neg I(Z', S, X)$, can be substituted for the temporal relation "Z precedes X."

---

[1] See definition on page 408 or Pearl, J., and Verma, T., 1991, A Theory of Inferred Causation. *Proceedings of KR-91*, Morgan Kaufmann, 441-452.

Appendix 8-A

Proof of Theorems 1 and 2

Let $P'(x)$ be a tree-dependent distribution based on some fixed tree t. From Eq. (8.1) and (8.2) we have

$$D(P, P') = -\sum_x P(x) \sum_{i=1}^n \log P'(x_i \mid x_{j(i)}) + \sum_x P(x) \log P(x) \tag{8.37}$$

$$= -\sum_{i=1}^n \sum_{x_i, x_{j(i)}} P(x_i, x_{j(i)}) \log P'(x_i \mid x_{j(i)}) - H(X)$$

$$= -\sum_{i=1}^n \sum_{x_{j(i)}} P(x_{j(i)}) \sum_{x_i} P(x_i \mid x_{j(i)}) \log P'(x_i \mid x_{j(i)}) - H(X) .$$

It is well known that when P is kept constant, the expression $\sum_x P(x) \log P'(x)$ is maximized by the choice $P'(x) = P(x)$. Therefore, for any value of $x_{j(i)}$, the term

$$\sum_{x_i} P(x_i \mid x_{j(i)}) \log P'(x_i \mid x_{j(i)})$$

achieves its maximal value with

$$P'(x_i \mid x_{j(i)}) = P(x_i \mid x_{j(i)}). \tag{8.38}$$

Likewise, the entire sum in Eq. (8.37) will attain its maximal value when Eq. (8.38) is enforced for every value of $x_{j(i)}$ and all i. This proves Theorem 1.

To prove Theorem 2, we substitute Eq. (8.38) into Eq. (8.37) and obtain

$$D(P, P') = -\sum_{i=1}^n \sum_{x_i, x_{j(i)}} P(x_i, x_{j(i)}) \left[\log \frac{P(x_i, x_{j(i)})}{P(x_i) P(x_{j(i)})} + \log P(x_i) \right] - H(X)$$

$$= -\sum_{i=1}^n I(X_i, X_{j(i)}) - \sum_{i=1}^n \sum_{x_i} P(x_i) \log P(x_i) - H(X) .$$

Since the second and third terms are independent of the tree t, and since $D(P, P')$ is nonnegative, minimizing the distance measure $D(P, P')$ is equivalent to maximizing the sum of branch weights $\sum_{i=1}^n I(X_i, X_{j(i)})$.

Appendix 8-B

Conditions for Star-Decomposability
(After Lazarfeld [1966])

Make the following assignments:

$$p_i = P(x_i=1),$$

$$p_{ij} = P(x_i=1, x_j=1), \qquad\qquad\qquad (8.39)$$

$$p_{ijk} = P(x_i=1, x_j=1, x_k=1).$$

The seven joint-occurrence probabilities, $p_1, p_2, p_3, p_{12}, p_{13}, p_{23}, p_{123}$, uniquely define the seven parameters necessary for specifying $P(x_1, x_2, x_3)$.

For example,

$$P(x_1 = 1, x_2 = 1, x_3 = 0) = p_{12} - p_{123},$$

$$P(x_1 = 1, x_2 = 0) = p_1 - p_{12},$$

and so on. These probabilities will be used in the following analysis.

Assuming P is star-decomposable (Eqs. (8.16) and (8.17)), we can express the joint-occurrence probabilities in terms of α, f_i, g_i and obtain seven equations for these seven parameters:

$$p_i = \alpha f_i + (1 - \alpha) g_i, \quad i = 1,2,3, \qquad\qquad (8.40)$$

$$p_{ij} = \alpha f_i f_j + (1 - \alpha) g_i g_j, \quad i \ne j, \qquad\qquad (8.41)$$

$$p_{ijk} = \alpha f_i f_j f_k + (1 - \alpha) g_i g_j g_k, \quad i \ne j \ne k. \qquad\qquad (8.42)$$

These equations can be manipulated to yield product forms on the right-hand sides:

$$p_{ij} - p_i p_j = \alpha(1 - \alpha)(f_i - g_i)(f_j - g_j), \qquad\qquad (8.43)$$

$$p_i p_{ijk} - p_{ij} p_{ik} = \alpha(1 - \alpha) f_i g_i (f_j - g_j)(f_k - g_k). \qquad\qquad (8.44)$$

Eq. (8.43) contains three equations which can be solved for the differences $f_i - g_i$, $i = 1, 2, 3$, giving

$$f_i - g_i = S_i [\alpha(1 - \alpha)]^{-\frac{1}{2}}, \qquad\qquad (8.45)$$

where

$$S_i = \pm \left[\frac{[ij][ik]}{[jk]} \right]^{1/2} \tag{8.46}$$

and the term $[ij]$ stands for the determinant

$$[ij] = p_{ij} - p_i p_j . \tag{8.47}$$

These, together with Eq. (8.40), determine f_i and g_i in terms of S_i and α (still unknown):

$$f_i = p_i + S_i \left[\frac{1-\alpha}{\alpha} \right]^{1/2}, \tag{8.48}$$

$$g_i = p_i - S_i \left[\frac{\alpha}{1-\alpha} \right]^{1/2}. \tag{8.49}$$

To determine α, we invoke Eq. (8.44) and obtain

$$\left[\frac{\alpha}{1-\alpha} \right]^{1/2} = t \quad (\text{or } \alpha = \frac{t^2}{1+t^2}), \tag{8.50}$$

where t is the solution to

$$t^2 + Kt - 1 = 0 \tag{8.51}$$

and K is defined by

$$K = \frac{S_i}{p_i} - \frac{p_i}{S_i} + \frac{\mu_i}{S_i p_i}, \tag{8.52}$$

$$\mu_i = \frac{[jk, i]}{[jk]} = \frac{p_i p_{ijk} - p_{ij} p_{ik}}{[jk]}. \tag{8.53}$$

It can easily be verified that K (and therefore α) obtains the same value regardless of which index i provides the parameters in Eq. (8.52).

From Eq. (8.52) we see that the parameters S_i and μ_i of P govern the solutions of Eq. (8.51), which in turn determine whether P is star-decomposable via the resulting values of α, f_i, g_i. These conditions are obtained by requiring that

a) S_i be real",
b) $0 \leq f_i \leq 1$, and
c) $0 \leq g_i \leq 1$.

Requirement a) implies that of the three bracketed terms in Eq. (8.46), either all three are nonnegative or exactly two are negative. These terms are directly related to the correlation coefficient via

$$\rho_{ij} = [ij] \, [p_i \, (1-p_i)]^{-\frac{1}{2}} \, [p_j \, (1-p_j)]^{-\frac{1}{2}} = \frac{[ij]}{\sigma_i \sigma_j} , \qquad (8.54)$$

so requirement a) is equivalent to the condition that all three correlation coefficients be nonnegative. If two of them are negative, we can rename two variables by their complements; the newly defined triplet will have all of its pairs positively correlated.

Now attend to requirement b). Equation (8.48) shows that f_i can be negative only if S_i is negative, i.e., if S_i is identified with the negative square root in Eq. (8.46). However, the choice of negative S_i yields a solution (f_i', g_i', α') that is symmetrical to (f_i, g_i, α) stemming from a positive S_i, with $f_i' = g_i$, $g_i' = f_i$, $\alpha' = 1-\alpha$. Thus, S_i and f_i can be assumed to be nonnegative, and it remains to examine the condition $f_i \leq 1$, or equivalently, $t \geq \dfrac{S_i}{1-p_i}$ (see Eqs. (8.48) and (8.50)). Imposing this condition in Eq. (8.51) translates to

$$p_{ijk} \leq \frac{p_{ij}p_{ik}}{p_i} + \sigma_k \sigma_j [\rho_{jk} - \rho_{ij}\rho_{ik}] . \qquad (8.55)$$

Similarly, inserting requirement c, $g_i \geq 0$, in Eq. (8.51) yields the inequality

$$\frac{p_{ik}p_{ij}}{p_i} \leq p_{ijk} , \qquad (8.56)$$

which, together with Eq. (8.55), leads to Theorem 5.

Chapter *9*

NON-BAYESIAN FORMALISMS FOR MANAGING UNCERTAINTY

> *When you have eliminated the impossible, what-*
> *ever remains, however improbable, must be the*
> *truth.*
>
> — *Sherlock Holmes (A. Conan Doyle)*

Pure Bayesian theory requires the specification of a complete probabilistic model before reasoning can commence. In causal modeling, for example, this means determining for each variable X the conditional probabilities of the values of X, given the factors perceived as causes of those values. When a full specification is not available, Bayesian practitioners use approximate methods of completing the model, methods that match common patterns of human reasoning. The noisy-OR-gate model of Section 4.3.2 is one such approximation; rather than specifying the conditional probabilities associated with each combination of causes, we quantify the individual cause-effect relationships, then combine them disjunctively (provided that exception-independence is a reasonable assumption to make). A more familiar method of model completion is provided by the maximum entropy principle [Jaynes 1979; Cheeseman 1983], wherein the available specifications are treated as constraints, and the model selected is the probability distribution attaining the highest entropy under these constraints.

An alternative method of handling partially specified models is provided by the Dempster-Shafer theory [Dempster 1968; Shafer 1976], which is the main topic of this chapter. Rather than completing the model, the Dempster-Shafer (D-S) theory sidesteps the missing specifications and computes probabilities of *provability* rather than computing probabilities of truths. The partially specified model is used only for representing qualitative relationships of compatibility (or possibility) among the propositions involved; these qualitative relationships are then used as a logic for assembling proofs that lead from evidence to conclusions. The stronger the evidence, the more likely it is that a complete proof will be assembled.

The current popularity of the D-S theory stems both from its willingness to admit partially specified models and its compatibility with the classical, proof-based style of logical inference, sharing the syntax of deductive databases and logic programming. However, inattentive use of this similarity with logic may cause reasoning based on the D-S theory to inherit many of the problems associated with monotonic logic, as demonstrated in Section 9.1.

Section 9.2 presents two additional formalisms for dealing with uncertainty: truth-maintenance systems (Sections 9.2.1 and 9.2.2) and incidence calculus (Section 9.2.3). Although developed independently and with different motivations, these approaches are seen as cousins to the Dempster-Shafer theory because they, too, use provability as the basic relationship connecting evidence with a conclusion. Truth maintenance systems provide a symbolic mechanism for identifying the set of assumptions needed to assemble the desired proofs, so when we assign probabilities to these assumptions, the systems can be used as symbolic engines for computing the belief functions sought by the D-S theory. Incidence calculus (Section 9.1.3) suggests a stochastic simulation approach to computing these belief functions—subjecting a theorem prover to randomly sampled assumptions and counting how often a proof can be assembled.

A third way to deal with partially specified models is to consider the space of all models consistent with the specifications available, and compute bounds instead of point values for the probabilities required. Nilsson's probabilistic logic (Section 9.3) uses this approach. It differs from the D-S approach in that it uses complete probabilistic models to make the basic inferences, while using logical relationships between sentences to define the bounds on the probabilities computed.

9.1 THE DEMPSTER-SHAFER THEORY

9.1.1 Basic Concepts

We introduce the Dempster-Shafer (D-S) theory of belief functions using the Three Prisoners puzzle discussed in Section 2.3.2. To recapitulate briefly, three prisoners, A, B, and C, await their verdict, knowing that one of them will be declared guilty and the other two released. Prisoner A asks the jailer, who knows the verdict, to pass a letter to another prisoner—to one who is to be released; later, the jailer tells Prisoner A that he gave the letter to prisoner B. The problem is to assess Prisoner A's chances of being declared guilty. The problem can be formulated in terms of three exhaustive and mutually exclusive propositions,

G_A, G_B, and G_C, where G_i stands for "Prisoner i will be declared guilty." We also have the jailer's testimony, which could have been either "B" or "C," and thus can be treated as a bi-valued variable L (connoting *letter recipient*) taking on the values $\{L_B, L_C\}$.

In our Bayesian treatment of the problem we made two tacit assumptions. First, we assumed that lack of prior knowledge regarding the verdict translates to equal prior probabilities on the components of G, namely, $\pi(G_A) = \pi(G_B) = \pi(G_C) = \frac{1}{3}$. Second, we assumed that if G_A were true, the jailer would choose a letter recipient at random, giving equal probabilities to B and C. These two assumptions yield the Bayesian network of Figure 9.1a, where Figure 9.1b depicts the link matrix $M_{L|G}$ necessary for full characterization of the information source L. This model yields the answer $P(G_A \mid L_B) = \frac{1}{3}$, meaning that the jailer's testimony is totally irrelevant to A's prospects of being released. If, on the other hand, the jailer does not deliver the letter at random but prefers B (or C), then $P(G_A \mid L_B)$ will vary smoothly from 0 (if B is avoided) to $\frac{1}{2}$ (if C is avoided).

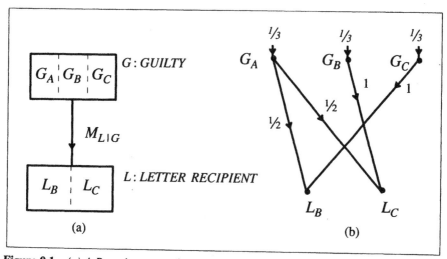

Figure 9.1. (a) A Bayesian network representation of the Three Prisoners puzzle and (b) the conditional probability matrix characterizing the link $G \to L$.

Having no idea what sort of trial the prisoners were given, we know only that any one of the prisoners can be the guilty one, i.e., none can be ruled out conclusively. Similarly, not knowing the process by which the letter recipient was chosen, all we can assert with certitude is that L_B is *compatible* with both G_A and G_C and is incompatible with G_B (assuming the jailer is honest). Thus, following the testimony L_B, the only possible states of affairs are the two combinations $\{(G_A, L_B), (G_C, L_B)\}$; all others are ruled out. These legal states are called *extensions* or *models* or *worlds* in the language of logic, *solutions* in the language of constraint processing [Montanari 1974], *tuples* in the language of relational databases, *possibilities* in fuzzy logic [Zadeh 1981], and *frame of discernment* in the Dempster-Shafer theory. The constraints that determine which extensions are legal are called *compatibility relations* (e.g., that exactly one prisoner will be found guilty), representing items of information that one chooses to cast in hard, categorical terms because a more refined model is unavailable (e.g., regarding the unlikely circumstances under which all three prisoners will be pardoned).

Clearly, not having the parameters $\pi(G_i)$ and $P(L_j | G_i)$ keeps us from constructing a complete probabilistic model of the story and keeps us from answering probabilistic queries of the type "How certain is G_A in light of the jailer's testimony?"—previously encoded as $P(G_A | L_B)$. In the partial model available, the probability $P(G_A | L_B)$ could be anywhere from 0 to 1, depending on the prior probability π. On the other hand, if by *certainty* we mean the assurance that G_A can be *proved* true, then the certainty of G_A, logically speaking, is zero.

The Dempster-Shafer theory stands between these two extremes, claiming that even in the logical interpretation of certainty, the assurance that there exists a proof for a proposition A can take on various strengths, depending on the strength of the evidence available (namely, how close it is to inducing a logical proof of A). This degree of assurance is called a *belief function* and is denoted by $Bel(A)$.† In our story, both $Bel(G_A)$ and $Bel(\neg G_A)$ are zero, because having total ignorance regarding the trial and verdict process means we have no evidence capable of enabling a logical proof of either G_A or $\neg G_A$.

Under what conditions will these belief functions be anything but zero? One obvious condition is when the negation of a proposition becomes incompatible with the evidence. For example, since G_B is incompatible with L_B, we have $Bel(\neg G_B) = 1$, stating that $\neg G_B$ is compelled by the evidence. But the more interesting condition occurs when *partial* evidence becomes available in favor of some propositions. For example, if the jailer says, "Gee, I forgot who got the letter—I think it was B, but I am only 80 percent sure," we can no longer prove $\neg G_B$. Yet, taking the jailer's testimony literally, we could say that there is an 80% chance that his memory is correct, compelling the truth of $\neg G_B$, so $Bel(\neg G_B) = 0.80$. Similarly, if we have good reason to believe that the witnesses in the trial gave equal support to each prisoner's guilt and that the verdict reflects this testimony fairly, then (and only then) we can take the liberty of assigning equal *weights* to the components of G.

Let us first focus on the case of equal weights, ignoring for the moment the jailer's information. The weight distribution process can be modeled as a chance event: Imagine a switch that oscillates randomly among three positions, G_A, G_B,

---

† $Bel(A)$ is to be distinguished from $BEL(A)$, which, following Chapters 4 and 5, is defined by $BEL(A) \triangleq P(A | \text{all evidence})$.

and G_C, and in each of these positions assigns the value *TRUE* to the corresponding proposition and no value to the others (Figure 9.2a). The other propositions in the system are affected by the switch only indirectly, via compatibility relations they must satisfy with G_A, G_B, and G_C. These relations are shown schematically by the graph in Figure 9.2a. For example, the link connecting G_B and $\neg G_C$ indicates that the two may coexist, while the absence of a link between G_A and G_B means those two are incompatible. (Not all of the compatible pairs are shown in the graph; for example, $\neg G_A$ and $\neg G_B$ are compatible whenever G_C is true.)

If we are asked now about the chance of G_A being provable, the answer will be ⅓, because the switch spends one-third of the time in position G_A, where the truth of G_A is established externally. During this time G_B and G_C can be proved false by virtue of being incompatible with G_A. Thus, averaging over all three positions of the switch,

$$Bel(G_A) = Bel(G_B) = Bel(G_C) = ⅓$$

and

$$Bel(\neg G_A) = Bel(\neg G_B) = Bel(\neg G_C) = ⅔,$$

exactly as in the Bayesian treatment.

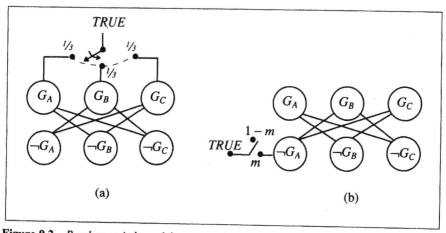

Figure 9.2. *Random switch model representing (a) equal prior probabilities, and (b) an alibi weakly supporting A's innocence.*

The departure from the Bayesian formalism comes when we devise fancier mechanisms for the weight-distribution switch so as to form more faithful models of how (according to D-S philosophy) people reason with partial evidence.

Assume, for example, that the evidence gathered during the trial is not available to us in its entirety, but rather we have access to a small portion of it, namely, an alibi weakly supporting Prisoner A's innocence. Assume, further, that the alibi bears exclusively on A's whereabouts at the time of the crime and has no direct bearing on B's or C's involvement. The D-S theory will model this case by the switch shown in Figure 9.2*b*: a fraction m of the time, the switch will force the truth of $\neg G_A$, while the remaining $1 - m$ of the time it will stay in a neutral position, lending support to no specific hypothesis or, equivalently, supporting the universal hypothesis $\theta = G_A \vee G_B \vee G_C$.

To calculate the belief functions $Bel(G_A)$ and $Bel(\neg G_A)$ we first identify the positions of the switch in which G_A can be proved true, then calculate the percentage of time spent in these positions. In the first position, representing a convincing alibi, the switch forces the truth of $\neg G_A$, while in the neutral position it is compatible with both G_A and $\neg G_A$ so nothing can be proved. Hence, $Bel(\neg G_A) = m$ and $Bel(G_A) = 0$. The belief acquired by the other elementary propositions is zero (prior to the jailer's testimony) because even in the first position the switch is compatible with each of the four propositions: G_B, G_C, $\neg G_B$, and $\neg G_C$.

The parameter $m(A)$, measuring the strength of the argument in favor of a proposition A, is called the *basic probability assignment,* and the proposition A upon which an argument bears directly is called the *focal element.* If there is only one focal element A, then the weight $1 - m(A)$ is assigned to the universal proposition θ, and the belief in any other proposition B is given by

$$Bel(B) = \begin{cases} 1 & \text{if} \quad B = \theta \\ m(A) & \text{if} \quad A \supset B \\ 0 & \text{otherwise .} \end{cases} \qquad (9.1)$$

A complex piece of evidence may be represented by a switch with more than two positions, each position forcing a different constraint on the knowledge base for a certain fraction of the time. For example, if evidence was found suggesting that the guilty person was either left-handed (with weight m_1) or black-haired (with weight m_2) but not both, and if Prisoners A and B are left-handed while B and C have black hair, the constraint $G_A \vee G_B$ will be imposed a fraction m_1 of the time, $G_B \vee G_C$ will be imposed a fraction m_2 of the time, and the rest of the time, $1 - m_1 - m_2$, no external constraint will be imposed.

In general, if there are several focal elements A, the total weight still sums to unity,

$$\sum_A m(A) = 1 , \qquad (9.2)$$

and $Bel(B)$ may be affected by all the A's, via

$$Bel(B) = \sum_{A:\, A \supset B} m(A). \qquad\qquad (9.3)$$

The summation reflects the fact that if B can be proved from several distinct sets of assumptions (represented by several positions of the switch) then $Bel(B)$, the probability that B is provable, is the total weight assigned to those assumptions (corresponding to the time that the switch spent in those positions).

The measure $1 - Bel(\neg A)$ is called the *plausibility* of A, denoted

$$Pl(A) = 1 - Bel(\neg A), \qquad\qquad (9.4)$$

representing the probability that A is compatible with the available evidence, i.e., that it cannot be disproved and is therefore *possible*. In our example, $Pl(G_A) = 1 - m$, while G_B and G_C have plausibility 1. The interval

$$Pl(A) - Bel(A) = 1 - [Bel(A) + Bel(\neg A)] \geq 0$$

represents the probability (fraction of time) that both A and $\neg A$ are compatible with the available evidence.

9.1.2 Comparing Bayesian and Dempster-Shafer Formalisms

We see that the D-S theory differs from probability theory in several aspects. First, it accepts an incomplete probabilistic model when some parameters (e.g., the prior or conditional probabilities) are missing. Second, the probabilistic information that is available, like the strength of evidence, is interpreted not as likelihood ratios but rather as random epiphenomena that impose truth values to various propositions for a certain fraction of the time. This model permits a proposition and its negation simultaneously to be compatible with the switch for a certain portion of the time, and this may permit the sum of their beliefs to be smaller than unity. Finally, given the incompleteness of the model, the D-S theory does not pretend to provide full answers to probabilistic queries but rather resigns itself to providing partial answers. It estimates how close the evidence is to forcing the truth of the hypothesis, instead of estimating how close the hypothesis is to being true.

BEL vs. Bel

This last point is the most important departure between the two formalisms and is best illustrated, in the Three Prisoners puzzle, by trying to incorporate the jailer's information L_B into the equal-weight model $m(G_A) = m(G_B) = m(G_C) = \frac{1}{3}$ (see Figure 9.3). Starting with $Bel(G_A) = \frac{1}{3}$, we now ask for the revised value of $Bel(G_A)$ given L_B, i.e., the proportion of the time that proposition G_A is provable, considering all of the available evidence. Clearly, the time spent by the switch in position G_B is incompatible with the evidence L_B, so we exclude this time from the calculation. The remaining $\frac{2}{3}$ of the time is divided equally between G_A and G_C, hence G_A is forced to be true with probability $\frac{1}{2}$, yielding $Bel(G_A) = Bel(\neg G_A) = \frac{1}{2}$. The Bayesian analysis of Chapter 2 gives $P(G_A \mid L_B) = \frac{1}{3}$, assuming a random choice model ($P(L_B \mid G_A) = \frac{1}{2}$, as in Figure 9.1). For a partial model with unknown $P(L_B \mid G_A)$, the Bayesian result may be anywhere between $P(G_A \mid L_B) = 0$ and $P(G_A \mid L_B) = \frac{1}{2}$.

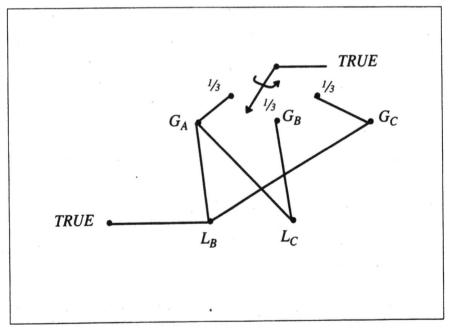

Figure 9.3. *The D-S representation of the Three Prisoners story, incorporating equal prior probabilities and the evidence L_B = TRUE.*

This disparity is not surprising in view of the fact that we still have an incomplete probabilistic model on our hands, as the process by which B was selected remains unspecified. It is quite possible that the jailer's choice was not random but was marked by a deliberate attempt to avoid choosing C whenever possible. Under such extreme circumstances, the jailer's answer L_B could be avoided only ⅓ of the time (when B is guilty), indeed leaving A and C with equal chances of being the condemned prisoner. What may sound somewhat counterintuitive is that from all the scenarios that could be used to complete the model, D-S theory appears to select a rather extreme and unlikely one, which also happens to be the one that puzzle books warn us to avoid [Gardner 1961].†

Actually, the D-S theory never attempts to complete the model, and if it appears to be doing so, it is only as an occasional by-product of the way weights are distributed. Prior to the jailer's answer, all four extensions {(G_A, L_B), (G_A, L_C), (G_B, L_C), (G_C, L_B)} are compatible with the evidence, each of the last two receiving $m = ⅓$ while the remaining weight (⅓) is assigned to the disjunction of the first two, with no preference for one or the other. The strategy of keeping some weight uncommitted (often associated with the notion of postponing judgment) is a distinct feature of the D-S theory and does not correspond to any probabilistic model. This uncommitted weight gets distributed only when we receive the jailer's answer, which excludes the extensions (G_A, L_C) and (G_B, L_C) and routes all the uncommitted weight (⅓) to the remaining member of the first pair, (G_A, L_B). At this point the weight happens to be distributed fully to the individual extensions, and the model resembles a complete probabilistic model, but this is where the resemblance ends.

The disparity between the answers produced by the two formalisms stems from the semantics of the answers. While the probabilistic approach interprets ''belief in A'' to mean the conditional probability that A is true, given the evidence e, the D-S approach calculates the probability that the proposition A is *provable* given the evidence e and given that e is consistent. Due to the inconsistency of L_B with the evidence we previously had in favor of G_B, e is consistent ⅔ of the time, and within this time, G_A can be proved with probability ½. Thus, instead of the conditional probability $P(A \mid e)$, the D-S theory computes the probability of the logical entailment $e \models A$. The entailment $e \models A$ is not a proposition in the ordinary sense, but a meta-relationship between e and A, requiring a logical, object-level theory by which a proof from e to A can be constructed. In the D-S scheme the object-level theory consists of categorical *compatibility* relations among the propositions, stating, for example, that L_B is compatible with G_A but incompatible with G_B. Compatibility constraints are the only form of knowledge that remains once we refrain from committing numbers to certain probabilities. The choice of these constraints is rather arbitrary and can make Bayesian and D-S formalisms appear as far apart as one wishes. For example, introducing the possibility, however slight, that the jailer may be lying suddenly makes G_B and L_B compatible

---

† An even stranger result obtains in the Thousand Prisoner story of Section 2.3.2 (see Exercise 9.7).

and renders $Bel(G_A) = \frac{1}{3}$ (unless one decides to model the jailer's reliability by another random switch).

Remarkably, whereas calculating the probability $P(A \mid e)$ (as well as the probability of the material conditional, $P(e \supset A)$) requires a complete probabilistic model, calculating $P(e \models A)$ does not. For example, in the incomplete model of Figure 9.3, $P(L_B \models G_A)$ can be calculated as $\frac{1}{2}$ without any assumption about the process by which the letter recipient was selected; we simply take 1 minus the (normalized) weight assigned to all propositions compatible with both L_B and the negation of G_A—namely, 1 minus the (normalized) time the switch spends at G_C.

At this point, it is natural to ask whether conditional probability information, if available, can be incorporated in the D-S model, and whether it will lead to the same answer as the Bayesian model. The answer is a qualified yes; it will, provided that the information is sufficient for forming a complete probabilistic model. Instead of dealing with individual propositions, we now create the set of all feasible extensions and attach to each extension a weight m equal to the appropriate joint probability dictated by the probabilistic model. To illustrate, if in the Three Prisoners example we accept the equal-prior random-selection model, then the four feasible extensions $\{(G_A, L_B), (G_A, L_C), (G_B, L_C), (G_C, L_B)\}$ initially receive the weights $\{\frac{1}{6}, \frac{1}{6}, \frac{1}{3}, \frac{1}{3}\}$ (see Figure 9.1b). This assignment can be modeled by a four-position switch whose contacts represent extensions rather than atomic propositions. When the evidence $e = L_B$ is obtained, it rules out two extensions, (G_A, L_C) and (G_B, L_C), and forces the switch to spend $\frac{1}{3}$ of its time at (G_C, L_B) and $\frac{1}{6}$ of the time at (G_A, L_B). Thus,

$$Bel(G_A) = \frac{\frac{1}{6}}{\frac{1}{3} + \frac{1}{6}} = \frac{1}{3}, \quad Bel(\neg G_A) = \frac{\frac{1}{3}}{\frac{1}{3} + \frac{1}{6}} = \frac{2}{3},$$

as in the Bayesian analysis.

We see from this example that any complete probabilistic model can be encoded in the D-S formalism, albeit in a somewhat clumsy manner. Probabilities are encoded as weights assigned to individual extensions, instead of conditional probabilities among propositions. This might not seem a severe limitation when we are processing complete models, but it hinders the handling of partial models. Large fragments of empirical knowledge cast in the form of conditional probabilities (such as the relation between symptoms and diseases) cannot be incorporated into the D-S compatibility frame until we have sufficient information to form a complete probability model and to calculate the weights of individual extensions. In the Three Prisoners story, for example, even if we obtain ample evidence that the jailer acts randomly (i.e., $P(L_B \mid G_A) = \frac{1}{2}$), we cannot incorporate this evidence so as to affect $Bel(G_A)$ as long as we are missing the prior probability $P(G_A)$. This is because conditional probabilities cannot be modeled as switches that constrain the set of possible extensions. In other words, the statement

$P(A \mid B) = p$ cannot be converted into an equivalent statement of the form $P[f(A, B)] = q$, where f is some Boolean function of A and B [Goodman 1987].

To a certain degree this limitation also applies to Bayesian methods; we can begin drawing inferences only when the model is complete. However, in cases where we have acquired a large body of knowledge and are missing just a few parameters, the Bayesian approach encourages us to assume *any* reasonable values for the missing parameters, so that the knowledge acquired will not be totally wasted. For example, assuming equal priors in the Three Prisoners story enables us to deploy the information about the jailer's behavior $P(L_B \mid G_A) = q$, and conclude $P(G_A \mid L_B) = q / (1 + q)$. The D-S analysis continues to conclude $Bel(G_A) = 0$, regardless of the jailer's behavior, as long as the prior $P(G_A)$ remains unspecified.

Thus, while the D-S approach has the capability to tolerate total ignorance, it lacks flexibility to accommodate partial information.

META-REASONING WITH PROBABILITIES

It is also natural to raise the converse question: Can probability theory answer the kind of queries that the D-S theory is concerned with, namely, how close the evidence comes to rendering a proposition provable? In principle, the answer should be yes, because a complete model should do everything that can be done with a partial model and perhaps more. Let us examine this point in detail.

Let us assume that we possess the complete probabilistic model specified in Figure 9.1, including the evidence $e = L_B$, and we now ask for the probability that G_A can be proved true. At first, the question sounds odd, if not meaningless. Obviously, after calculating $P(G_A \mid L_B) = \frac{1}{3}$, the answer ought to be 0; there is no way to prove a proposition true if that proposition has only $\frac{1}{3}$ probability of being true. A proposition can be proved only if its probability is 1, so why not ask directly whether the proposition has a probability 1 or not? Thus, before probability theory can answer queries of this sort, the process of proving or disproving propositions must be separated from the process of drawing probabilistic inferences—or else the query is vacuous.

This was precisely the reason for invoking the random-switch metaphor in the D-S formalism (alternative metaphors, using random codes [Shafer 1981], databases [Zadeh 1986], or voting models [Hummel and Manevitz 1987], can serve the same purpose). The function of the switch is to summarize the available probabilistic knowledge and separate it from the task of proving or disproving a proposition. Once the position of the switch is determined and the compatibility relations agreed upon, the existence of a proof becomes a testable event that is similar to the output of a physical device (we exclude from this discussion any questions of decidability) and about which we can reason probabilistically. Thus, the random switch together with the compatibility constraints constitute a complete probabilistic model that can be interrogated to answer any probabilistic query within its vocabulary, e.g., what is the probability of the event "A is provable"? It is, in a way, an autoepistemic model, as it involves hypothetical reasoning about what one ought to consider true if certain facts (constraints) become known (i.e., forced by the switch).

Such hypothetical exercises are not foreign to probabilistic theories. We saw in Chapter 6 that the value of information sources was computed by envisioning, hypothetically, what the impact of an outcome would be on the belief in some hypothesis. This was computed by simulating the propagation of potential evidence through a knowledge base represented as a Bayesian network. Similarly, in Section 7.3 we measured the confidence level of our beliefs by predicting how they would vary in the face of hypothetical events called contingencies. It stands to reason, therefore, that meta-reasoning similar to that used in the D-S approach could very well be formulated in purely probabilistic terms, e.g., by taking Bayesian networks instead of compatibility constraints as the object-level knowledge base.

Assume that our object-level model is given by the Bayesian network of Figure 9.1 and that instead of giving a categorical answer, the guard replies, "Gee, I think I gave the letter to B, but I am only 80 percent sure." Taking this testimony literally, we subject the model of Figure 9.1 to the influence of a random switch, forcing the truths of L_B and L_C with probabilities 0.80 and 0.20, respectively. Conceptually, this amounts to submitting the object-level model to a hypothetical meta-reasoner who observes the model's behavior under two different pieces of evidence, $L_B = TRUE$ and $L_C = TRUE$.

We know the answer to this exercise; the Bayesian analysis of either $e = L_B$ or $e = L_C$ gives $BEL(G_A) \triangleq P(G_A | e) = \frac{1}{3}$, hence if someone asks for the value of $Bel(G_A)$, the probability of G_A being provable, the answer is of course zero. Provability means $BEL = 1$. Less trivial is calculating $Bel(G_C)$ and $Bel(\neg G_C)$. Under $e = L_B$, the object-level model returns the probabilities $P(G_C | e) = \frac{2}{3}$ and $P(\neg G_C | e) = \frac{1}{3}$, while under $e = L_C$ these probabilities become $P(G_C | e) = 0$ and $P(\neg G_C | e) = 1$. This amounts to having zero chance of proving G_C and a 20% chance of proving $\neg G_C$, i.e., $Bel(G_C) = 0$ and $Bel(\neg G_C) = 0.20$. Note that these answers were totally different when we used the D-S model, which yielded $Bel(G_A) = \frac{1}{2}$ even under $e = L_B$ and even with $P(L_B | G_A)$ unknown. The reason is that there, we modeled the trial process ($\pi(G_A) = \frac{1}{3}$) as part of the meta-reasoner, in the form of a random switch oscillating between G_A, G_B, and G_C, whereas in the Bayesian analysis this information is included as part of the object-level theory, in order to retain its completeness.

We now address the question raised earlier—whether one can do more with a complete model than with a partial model. As anticipated, the answer is yes. Having a complete model at our disposal permits us to answer sophisticated queries, about more than just the provability of certain propositions. For instance, we could ask for the probability that the posterior probability $BEL(G_C) = P(G_C | e)$

will not exceed some constant α. The answer would be a parameterized belief function:

$$Bel_\alpha(G_C) = P(e \mid = \text{``} BEL(G_C) \le \alpha \text{''}) = \begin{cases} 0.2 + 0.9\alpha & 0 \le \alpha \le \dfrac{2}{3} \\ 1 & \alpha > \dfrac{2}{3}. \end{cases}$$

This may sound like computing probabilities of probabilities, a notion rejected in Chapter 7 as being ill-defined. But the separation between object-level reasoning and meta-reasoning now endows this notion with clear semantics—the semantics of hypothetical envisioning, like the one used to reason about confidence levels in Chapter 7.

Why, then, has nobody incorporated such parameterized belief functions or confidence levels into the D-S formalism? It turns out that to calculate these functions, we must have a complete probabilistic model at the object level, when such a model is not available, primitive queries about provability are really all that we can hope to answer.

TRUTH, POSSIBILITY, AND PROVABILITY

Compatibility constraints represent a simplified black-and-white abstraction of a world that is ridden with exceptions. The notion of provability normally reflects mathematical artifice rather than empirical reality. Thus, the preceding discussion might leave the erroneous impression that the D-S theory deals with a totally unrealistic model of the world and provides answers to contrived, uninteresting queries about such a model. There are, however, cases where compatibility relations are natural representations of world knowledge, and where queries concerned with the probability of provability rather than the probability of truth are the ones that we wish to ascertain.

For example, suppose we face the problem of scheduling classes; we have a set of teachers, a set of topics, a set of classrooms, and a set of time slots, and our task is to cover all of the topics with the available resources. Before we actually select an assignment (if one exists), our knowledge is represented in the form of constraints: some teachers cannot teach certain topics, some classrooms are unavailable at certain times, etc. On the basis of this knowledge, all we can answer are questions about possibilities, e.g., whether it is possible to take topic x in time slot y, whether it is feasible to get teacher z for topic w, etc. To answer such queries, we need to search the space of feasible assignments (i.e., those satisfying all of the constraints) and test whether there is an assignment that satisfies the query. If a query Q is satisfied by at least one feasible assignment, we say that Q is *possible;* if it is satisfied by all feasible assignments, we say it is *necessary* or *provable.*

Probabilistic measures enter in the form of partial constraints. For example, suppose one of the teachers states, "Due to a medical problem, there is an 80 percent chance that I will be unable to teach Mondays and Thursdays." This information imposes on the problem an additional constraint—this time probabilistic in nature, similar to the action of the switch in Figure 9.3. It assigns a weight of $m = 0.80$ to a narrower set of feasible assignments and a weight of $m = 0.20$ to the original set, in which the teacher was presumed to be available on Mondays and Thursdays. It is natural now for some other teacher to ask, "What are the chances that I will be able to teach mathematics?" or, "What are the chances that I will be forced to teach on Tuesday evening?" These queries, concerning possibilities and necessities, translate directly into the D-S measures of $Pl(Q)$ and $Bel(Q)$, respectively. To answer such queries, we must solve the assignment problem for each state of the switch, determine for each state whether the query is provable, possible, or impossible, and then compute the desired probability using the weight m.

Can such answers be computed by a pure, single-level Bayesian model? Not really. We could of course assume a uniform distribution over the feasible assignments in each state, combine the two distributions with the appropriate weights—0.20 and 0.80—and then calculate the resultant probability of the query sentence Q (e.g., that teacher x will be assigned to teach on Tuesdays). However, this is not the same as the probability that Q is possible, or the probability that it is necessary, and the difference might be significant. For example, the inquirer might have a strong aversion to teaching on Tuesdays and hence be determined to talk his way out of any such assignment if a feasible alternative exists. He is, therefore, concerned not with the probability of being assigned a Tuesday time slot, but rather with the probability that such an assignment will be necessary for lack of an alternative. In such cases, the purely probabilistic approach will not provide the desired answer. Queries regarding probability of possibility (or necessity) require two levels of knowledge and hence cannot be answered by treating the compatibility constraints as probability statements having value 0 or 1. Rather, the compatibility constraints must remain outside the probabilistic model and serve as object-level theories which, in themselves, are assigned probabilistic measures.

9.1.3 Dempster's Rule of Combination

When several pieces of evidence are available, their impacts are combined by assuming that the corresponding switches act independently of each other. For example, if in addition to Prisoner A's alibi (Figure 9.2b) the trial records include testimony supporting A's guilt to a degree m_2, one can imagine two random switches operating simultaneously and asynchronously, the first as described in Figure 9.2b and the second spending a fraction m_2 of the time constraining G_A to the value *TRUE* and staying neutral the rest of the time (see Figure 9.4a).

Clearly, for a fraction $m_1 m_2$ of the time the two switches are in conflict with each other—one is constraining G_A to *TRUE*, and the other is constraining $\neg G_A$ to *TRUE*—thus permitting no consistent extension. For a fraction $(1 - m_1)m_2$ of the time G_A is true while switch 2 is neutral, rendering G_A, $\neg G_B$, and $\neg G_C$ provable. Similarly, for a fraction $m_1(1 - m_2)$ of the time $\neg G_A$ is true while switch 1 is

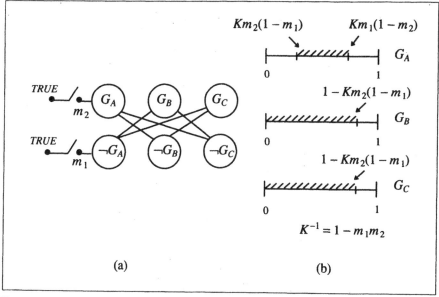

Figure 9.4. *Combination of two sources of evidence in the Three Prisoners puzzle. (a) m_1 and m_2 represent the percentage of time each switch is closed. (b) Belief intervals for the three propositions G_A, G_B, and G_C.*

neutral, rendering $\neg G_A$ (but no other proposition) provable. Summing up and normalizing by the time of no conflict, $1 - m_1 m_2$, we have

$$Bel(G_A) = Bel(\neg G_B) = Bel(\neg G_C) = \frac{m_2(1 - m_1)}{1 - m_1 m_2},$$

$$Bel(\neg G_A) = \frac{m_1(1 - m_2)}{1 - m_1 m_2},$$

$$Bel(G_B) = Bel(G_C) = 0.$$

These measures are shown schematically in Figure 9.4*b*. The assumption of evidence independence, coupled with the normalization rule above, leads to an evidence-pooling procedure known as *Dempster's rule of combination*. The combined impact of several pieces of evidence can be calculated, again, by computing the fraction of time that a given proposition A is compelled to be true by the combined action of all switches, assuming that they operate independently. Thus, the analysis of belief functions amounts to analyzing the set of extensions permitted by a network of static constraints (representing generic knowledge), subject to an additional set of externally imposed, fluctuating constraints (representing the impact of the available evidence). For any combination of the evidential constraints, we need to decide whether the proposition A is entailed by that combination; i.e., whether every extension contains A and none contains $\neg A$. The total time that a system spends under constraint combinations that compel A, divided by the total time spent in no-conflict combinations, yields $Bel(A)$.

The constraint-network formulation of Dempster's combination rule is illustrated schematically in Figure 9.5. It shows a static network of variables

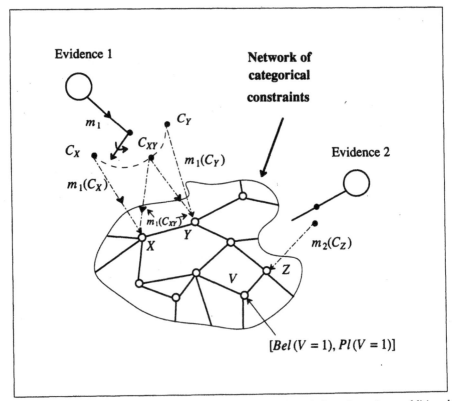

Figure 9.5. *Multiple evidence modeled as random switches imposing additional constraints on a static network of compatibility relations.*

$X, Y, Z, V...$ (the nodes) interacting via local constraints (the arcs), subject to the influence of two switches that impose additional, fluctuating constraints on various regions of the network. To illustrate the analysis of the extension sets, let us assume that the static network represents the classical graph-coloring problem: Each node may take on one of three possible colors, 1, 2, or 3, but no two adjacent nodes may take on identical colors. The positions of the switches represent additional constraints, e.g., C_{XY} means either X or Y must contain the color 1, while C_Z means Z cannot be assigned the color 2. The relative time that a switch spends enforcing each of the constraints is indicated by the weight measures $m_1(C_X)$, $m_1(C_{XY})$, $m_2(C_Z)$, etc. Our objective is to compute $Bel(A)$ and $Pl(A)$, where A stands for the proposition $V = 1$, namely, variable V is assigned the color 1.

Figure 9.6 represents typical sets of solutions to the coloring problem under different combinations of the switches (the values shown are fictitious).

Each row represents one extension (or solution), where the entries indicate the values assigned to the variables (columns). The first set of solutions is characterized by having the value 1 assigned to V in every row. If the system spends a fraction α of the time in such combinations of switches, we say that $P[e \models V = 1] = \alpha$, namely, the proposition $A:V = 1$ can be proved true with probability α, given the evidence e. A type-2 position is characterized by the column of V containing 1's as well as alternative values, e.g., 2 and 3. Each such position (or position combination) is compatible with both A and $\neg A$. Similarly, a type-3 position permits only extensions that exclude $V = 1$, while a type-4 position represents a conflict situation: There exists no extension consistent with all the constraints. $Bel(A)$ and $Pl(A)$ are computed from the time spent in each type of constraint combination:

$$Bel(A) = \frac{\alpha}{\alpha + \beta + \gamma} ,$$

$$Pl(A) = 1 - Bel(V \neq 1) = 1 - \frac{\gamma}{\alpha + \beta + \gamma} = \frac{\alpha + \beta}{\alpha + \beta + \gamma} .$$

These are illustrated as a belief interval in Figure 9.6b.

The preceding analysis can be rather complex. The graph-coloring problem, even with only three colors, is known to be NP-complete. Moreover, if each piece of evidence is modeled by a two-position switch and we have n such switches, then a brute force analysis of $Bel(A)$ will require solving 2^n graph-coloring problems. Listing the solutions obtained under all switch combinations and identifying the combinations that yield $e \models A$ seems hopeless. Fortunately, two factors help alleviate these difficulties: the sequential nature of Dempster's rule and the ability to exploit certain topological properties of the constraint network. The latter is done by decomposing the network into a tree (a join tree, as in Chapter 3), where solutions can be obtained in linear time [Dechter and Pearl 1987b]. Adaptations of

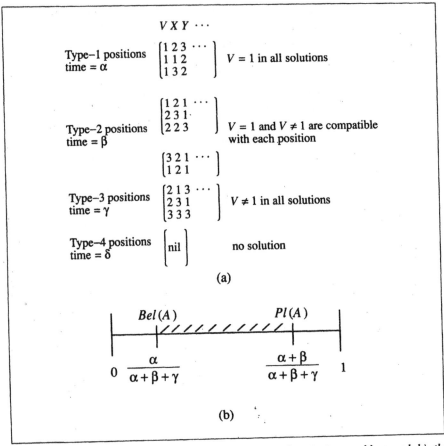

Figure 9.6. (a) Four types of constraints in the graph coloring problem and b) the resulting belief interval for the proposition $A : V = 1$.

tree decomposition to belief function computations are reported in Shafer, Shenoy, and Mellouli [1986] and Kong [1986].

Dempster's rule, being associative and commutative, permits us to combine multiple evidence sequentially without enumerating all switch combinations encountered in the past. It is based on the fact that if two distinct switch combinations give rise to the same set of solutions, we can replace the two by a single equivalent constraint that allows exactly that set of solutions, for the total amount of time that the two combinations lasted. Thus, instead of recording all distinct switch combinations it is sufficient to record all distinct solution sets induced by the combinations, and keep track of their weights.

This scheme sometimes requires much less space, especially under conditions of tight constraints where many switch combinations would yield no solution.

Metaphorically, the set of recorded solution sets and their associated weights is equivalent to a single giant switch, with one position for each distinct solution set. The impact of each new piece of evidence e'' can be calculated by first calculating the constraints accumulated by all the previous evidence e', then combining it with the constraints created by e'' itself, as if no other evidence existed. If e' induces a belief function Bel' and e'' induces Bel'', the result of combining the two by Dempster's rule is denoted by $Bel' \oplus Bel''$ and is called the *orthogonal sum* of Bel' and Bel''. Mathematically, for any proposition B, $Bel' \oplus Bel''(B) = Bel(B)$ can be computed from $m(A) = m' \oplus m''(A)$, using Eq. (9.3), where $m(A)$, reflecting the constraints imposed by both e' and e'', is given by

$$m(A) = m' \oplus m''(A) = K \sum_{A_1 \wedge A_2 = A} m'(A_1)\, m''(A_2) \qquad A \neq \emptyset \qquad \textbf{(9.5)}$$

and

$$K^{-1} = \sum_{A_1 \wedge A_2 \neq \emptyset} m'(A_1)\, m''(A_2). \qquad\qquad \textbf{(9.6)}$$

In other words, the weight $m(A)$ assigned to the solution set A is the summation over all pairs of solution sets A_1, A_2 whose intersection is A. Multiplying $m'(A_1)$ by $m''(A_2)$ reflects the independence assumption; the probability that the two constraints will be enforced together is equal to the product of the probabilities that each holds separately. The intersection $A_1 \wedge A_2$ reflects the fact that the solution set resulting from the simultaneous imposition of two constraints is the intersection of the two solution sets obtained under the individual constraints. K is a normalizing factor guaranteeing that

$$\sum_A m(A) = 1,$$

and it serves to discount the weight assigned to conflicting constraints (i.e., $A_1 \wedge A_2 = \emptyset$) and redistribute it equally among the remaining solution sets.

Figure 9.7 illustrates the essence of Dempster's rule using the two-switch model of Figure 9.6. Assume that the evidence e', represented by the two switches in Figure 9.6, permits the following set of four distinct solution sets:

$$A'_1 = \begin{bmatrix} 1 & 2 & 3 \\ 1 & 1 & 2 \\ 1 & 3 & 2 \end{bmatrix}, \quad A'_2 = \begin{bmatrix} 1 & 2 & 1 \\ 2 & 3 & 1 \\ 2 & 2 & 3 \end{bmatrix}, \quad A'_3 = \begin{bmatrix} 1 & 2 & 1 \\ 3 & 2 & 1 \end{bmatrix}, \quad A'_4 = \begin{bmatrix} 2 & 1 & 3 \\ 2 & 3 & 1 \\ 3 & 2 & 3 \end{bmatrix},$$

$A'_4 = \begin{Bmatrix} 2 & 1 & 3 \\ 2 & 3 & 1 \\ 3 & 2 & 3 \end{Bmatrix}$ (m'_4)	$\varnothing$	$\varnothing$	$\varnothing$
$A'_3 = \begin{Bmatrix} 1 & 2 & 1 \\ 3 & 1 & 1 \end{Bmatrix}$ (m'_3)	$\left\{ 1 \quad 2 \quad 1 \right\}$ $(m'_3 \, m''_1)$	$\varnothing$	$\varnothing$
$A'_2 = \begin{Bmatrix} 1 & 2 & 1 \\ 2 & 3 & 1 \\ 2 & 2 & 3 \end{Bmatrix}$ (m'_2)	$\left\{ 1 \quad 2 \quad 1 \right\}$ $(m'_2 \, m''_1)$	$\left\{ 2 \quad 2 \quad 3 \right\}$ $(m'_2 \, m''_2)$	$\varnothing$
$A'_1 = \begin{Bmatrix} 1 & 2 & 3 \\ 1 & 1 & 2 \\ 1 & 3 & 2 \end{Bmatrix}$ (m'_1)	$\left\{ \begin{matrix} 1 & 3 & 2 \\ 1 & 1 & 2 \end{matrix} \right\}$ $(m'_1 \, m''_1)$	$\left\{ 1 \quad 2 \quad 3 \right\}$ $(m'_1 \, m''_2)$	$\varnothing$
	$A''_1 = \begin{Bmatrix} 1 & 3 & 2 \\ 1 & 1 & 2 \\ 1 & 2 & 1 \end{Bmatrix}$ (m''_1)	$A''_2 = \begin{Bmatrix} 1 & 2 & 3 \\ 2 & 2 & 3 \end{Bmatrix}$ (m''_2)	$A''_3 = \left\{ 2 \quad 3 \quad 2 \right\}$ (m''_3)

Figure 9.7. *Illustrating Dempster's rule of combination using the graph coloring problem of Figure 9.6.*

with corresponding weights (m'_1, m'_2, m'_3, m'_4). As before, the columns represent the variables V, X, Y (with the other variables ignored for convenience), and the entries stand for the colors assigned to these variables. Set A'_1 is of type 1 relative to the proposition A: $V = 1$; A'_2 and A'_3 are of type 2, and A'_4 is of type 3. Now assume that a new piece of evidence e'' is obtained, represented by a three-position switch which, in isolation, gives rise to the following three sets of solutions

$$A''_1 = \begin{bmatrix} 1 & 3 & 2 \\ 1 & 1 & 2 \\ 1 & 2 & 1 \end{bmatrix}, \quad A''_2 = \begin{bmatrix} 1 & 2 & 3 \\ 2 & 2 & 3 \end{bmatrix}, \quad A''_3 = \begin{bmatrix} 2\,3\,2 \end{bmatrix},$$

with corresponding weights (m''_1, m''_2, m''_3). The combined effect of e' and e'' is shown in Figure 9.7. It displays the intersections of all pairs of solution sets (A'_i, A''_j), where A'_i is taken from e' and A''_j from e''. A total of four distinct solution sets survive the intersection, while seven intersections turn up empty sets. The weight destined for these empty subsets is equal to

$$1 - K^{-1} = m'_4(m''_1 + m''_2 + m''_3) + m''_2 m'_3 + m''_3(m'_1 + m'_2 + m'_3)$$

$$= m'_4 + m''_2 m'_3 + m''_3 - m''_3 m'_4$$

(using $\sum m(A) = 1$), and will serve to normalize the weights of the surviving solution sets.

To calculate $Bel(V = 1)$, we combine the weights of the three type-1 subsets,

$$\{1\,2\,1\}, \begin{bmatrix} 1 & 3 & 2 \\ 1 & 1 & 2 \end{bmatrix}, \text{ and } \{1\,2\,3\},$$

and divide by K^{-1}:

$$Bel(V = 1) = \frac{m''_1(m'_1 + m'_2 + m'_3) + m''_2 m'_1}{1 - (m'_4 + m''_2 m'_3 + m''_3 - m''_3 m'_4)}.$$

Figure 9.8 displays the types of solution sets that emerge from Dempster's rule. The solution sets of each piece of evidence are grouped into four types, and the type of the intersection is indicated in the table. In principle, the intersection of any two subsets can be empty, i.e., type 4. In addition, a type-1 set combined with either a type-1 or a type-2 set can yield only a type-1 set (solutions compatible with $\neg A$ are ruled out by type 1). Similarly, the intersection of type 3 with either type 3 or type 2 must yield a type-3 set (or nil). However, the intersection of two type-2 subsets may be of any type. Manifestly, type-2 solution sets can emerge only from the intersection of two type-2 sets. Hence, once type-2 sets become extinct (i.e., by exposure to zero-interval evidence) they remain extinct forever.

Dempster's rule assumes a particularly convenient form when several pieces of evidence bear on the same proposition (or its negation). This is illustrated in Figure 9.9, using, again, the two-switch model. Each switch is characterized by three parameters (α, β, γ), indicating the fraction of the time that the switch spends in each state. In the first state, called *TRUE*, *A* is forced to *true*; in the *UNDETERMINED* state, the evidence is compatible with both *A* and ¬*A*, and the third state *FALSE* forces *A* to *FALSE*. The semantics of these states determine what state is created by any combination of them. For example, a *FALSE* state combined with an *UNDETERMINED* state yields a *FALSE* state because all extensions compatible with *A* would be excluded by the former. The weights assigned to the combined states are indicated by their corresponding areas in the

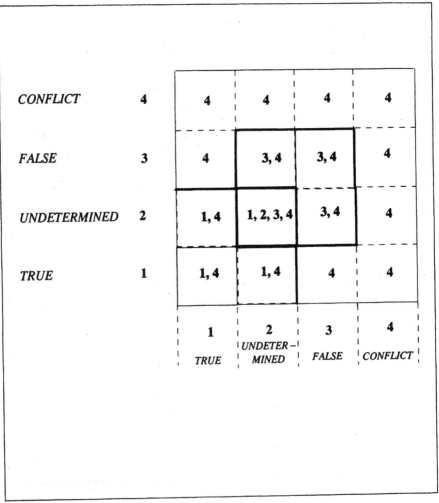

Figure 9.8. *Set intersection in Dempster's rule of combination.*

diagram of Figure 9.10. For example, $Bel' \otimes Bel''(A)$ is given by the sum of the three areas labeled α, divided by the active areas $\alpha + \beta + \gamma$:

$$Bel(A) = Bel' \oplus Bel''(A) = \frac{\alpha}{\alpha + \beta + \gamma} = \frac{\alpha'\alpha'' + \alpha'\beta'' + \alpha''\beta'}{1 - \alpha'\gamma'' - \alpha''\gamma'} ,$$

$$Pl(A) = Pl' \oplus Pl''(A) = 1 - \frac{\gamma}{\alpha + \beta + \gamma} = 1 - \frac{\gamma'\gamma'' + \gamma'\beta'' + \beta'\gamma''}{1 - \alpha'\gamma'' - \alpha''\gamma'} .$$

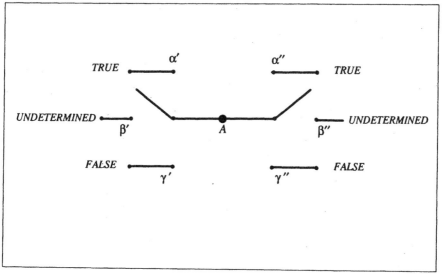

Figure 9.9. *A two-switch model for two pieces of evidence bearing on the same proposition A.*

Expressed in terms of the belief parameters *Bel* and *Pl*, we use

$$b' = Bel'(A), \qquad\qquad p' = Pl'(A),$$
$$b'' = Bel''(A), \qquad\qquad p'' = Pl''(A),$$

and obtain

$$Bel(A) = \frac{p'p'' - (p' - b')(p'' - b'')}{1 - [b'(1 - p'') + b''(1 - p')]} ,$$

$$Pl(A) = \frac{p'p''}{1 - [b'(1 - p'') + b''(1 - p')]} . \qquad\qquad (9.7)$$

This combination rule constitutes a convenient calculus for D-S intervals [Ginsberg 1984; Hájek 1987]. To compute the interval [*Bel*, *Pl*] of proposition *A*, it is necessary only to compute the parameters [*Bel* and *Pl*] associated with each separate piece of evidence, then combine them incrementally using Eq. (9.7). Note, however, that this combination rule is applicable only when A is the focal point of all the evidence available. A more complicated computation is required when pieces of evidence impinge on different propositions, as in Eq. (9.5).

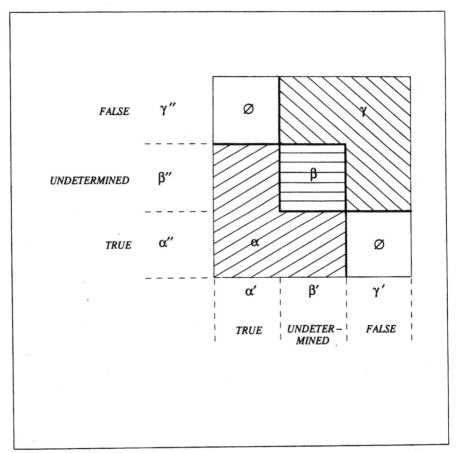

Figure 9.10. *Dempster's rule of combination for the two-switch model of Figure 9.9.*

9.1.4 More on the Nature of Probability Intervals

At this point, it is worthwhile to reflect on the significance of the interval $Pl(A) - Bel(A)$ in the D-S formalism. This interval is often interpreted as the degree of ignorance we have about probabilities, namely, the range where the "true" probability should fall if we had a complete probabilistic model. Such intervals might be a useful supplement to Bayesian methods, which always provide point probabilities and thus can give a false sense of security in the model.

Unfortunately, the D-S intervals have little to do with ignorance; nor do they represent bounds on the probabilities that might ensue once ignorance is removed. This was already demonstrated in the Three Prisoners puzzle (Section 9.1.1). We saw that despite our total ignorance regarding the process by which the jailer chose the letter recipient, the interval $Pl(G_A) - Bel(G_A)$ was zero, thus giving the false impression that the answer $Bel(G_A) = \frac{1}{2}$ was based on a complete model (with the jailer avoiding C whenever possible). At the same time, knowledge of the selection process could sway the posterior probability $P(G_A \mid e)$ all the way from 0 to $\frac{1}{2}$.

Figure 9.8 and Eq. (9.7) reveal that the disappearance of the "ignorance" interval is not an isolated incident but will occur whenever a piece of evidence imparts all of its weight to a proposition and its negation. In other words, if e'' induces $Pl''(A) = Bel''(A)$, then regardless of the ignorance we possessed before (i.e., $Pl'(A) - Bel'(A)$) and regardless of any ignorance that might be conveyed by future evidence, $Pl(A) - Bel(A)$ will remain zero forever. In particular, whenever we start with a complete probabilistic model (where all belief intervals are zero), no amount of conflicting evidence will ever succeed in widening that interval so that it reflects the conflict.

The upshot is that many sources of ignorance or uncertainty about probabilities are not represented in the D-S formalism. In particular, the uncertainty caused by high sensitivity to unknown contingencies (Section 7.3) cannot be represented by belief intervals. Reiterating our example from Chapter 7, suppose we know that a given coin was produced by a defective machine—precisely 49% of its output consists of double-headed coins, 49% are no-headed coins, and the rest are fair. This description constitutes a complete probabilistic model which predicts that the outcome of the next toss will be heads with probability 50% and warns us that the prediction is extremely susceptible to new information regarding the coin. Though most people would hesitate to commit a point estimate of 50% to the next outcome of the coin, the D-S theory nevertheless assigns it a belief of 50%, with zero belief interval. Now imagine that we toss the coin twice and observe tails and then heads. This immediately implies that the coin is fair, and most people would regain confidence that the next toss has a 50% chance of turning up heads. Yet this narrowing of the confidence interval remains unnoticed in the D-S formalism; the theory will again assign the next outcome a belief of 50%, with zero belief interval.

The disappearance of the difference $Pl\!-\!Bel$ in the Three Prisoners puzzle is a by-product of the normalization used in Dempster's rule. Avoiding this normalization would have yielded an interval $[\frac{1}{3}, \frac{2}{3}]$ for G_A, reflecting the fact that G_A and $\neg G_A$ can each be proved only one-third of the time (assuming no proposition is truly provable from a contradiction). Indeed, normalization by the time-without-conflict stands at odds with the basic definition of *Bel* as the probability of enabling a proof. Instead of this intended probability, the normalized version of *Bel* reflects the conditional probability of enabling a proof given that the set of extensions is nonempty. Valuable information is sometimes lost in this conditionalization process. After all, a state of conflict represents an inadequacy in our model of the world (e.g., that the jailer is reliable, or that only two prisoners will be released), not a major flaw in the world itself. So the support that a proposition receives in conflicting situations depends on how we plan to extend or refine the model once a contradiction is found. A more reasonable approach would be to keep two intervals, the one measuring the degree of conflict and the other measuring the degree of evidence not committed. That would entail characterizing each proposition by four parameters corresponding to the four types of solution sets (see Figure 9.10). (Similar criticism of the normalization used in the D-S approach was advanced by Zadeh [1984].)

9.1.5 Applications to Rule-based Systems

Representing knowledge in the Dempster-Shafer theory is more natural when the compatibility relations are expressed in rule form. A rule, r, is a constraint among a group of propositions, expressed in *IF-THEN* format:

$$r: a_1 \wedge a_2 \wedge \cdots \wedge a_n \implies c . \tag{9.8}$$

Propositions a_1, ..., a_n are called the *antecedents* (or *justifications*) of the rule, and c is its *consequent*. The semantics of the rule lies in forbidding any extension in which the antecedents are all true while the consequent is false; in other words, a rule is equivalent to the constraint

$$r: \neg[a_1 \wedge a_2 \wedge \cdots \wedge a_n \wedge \neg c] . \tag{9.9}$$

Normally, rules are based on tacit *assumptions,* the failure of which (called *exceptions*) may invalidate the rule. For example, I may assert the rule r: "If it is Sunday John will go to the baseball game," tacitly assuming the prerequisites "John still holds season tickets," "John is not sick," etc. Since such assumptions are too numerous to explicate, they are often summarized by giving the rule a measure of strength, m. For example, the rule above might be given a strength of $m = 0.80$, indicating 80% certainty that none of the implicit exceptions will materialize.

One of the attractive features of the D-S formalism is that it allows rules with exceptions to be treated much the same as rules of inference in deductive logic. A rule is treated as just another compatibility constraint in the knowledge base, while *m* measures the strength with which the constraint is enforced.† Using our random switch metaphor, the strength *m* translates to a switch that spends a fraction *m* of the time imposing the constraint conveyed by the rule. The activity of the switch during the time remaining depends on the nature of the exceptions anticipated. Some exceptions (e.g., "John is sick") lead to the negation of the conclusion while others (e.g., "John has no season tickets this year") render the conclusion unknown or uncommitted. In the first case the switch will force the negation of the conclusion while in the second case it will spend its remaining time in a neutral position. Thus, the rule author must be aware of the type of assumptions summarized by the rule strength. For the sake of simplicity we will characterize rules with a simple switch model that supports the consequence *c* but not its negation. More sophisticated models, such as the three-position switches in Figure 9.9, yield essentially the same results.

COMBINING BELIEF FUNCTIONS IN RULE NETWORKS

Assume we have a system of rules and a list *F* of observed facts called *premises*, and we wish to find the belief $Bel(\cdot)$ attributable to some proposition *c*. This amounts to computing the probability that a proof exists from the premises in *F* to the conclusion *c*. Each proof consists of a sequence of rules $r_1, r_2,..., r_m$ such that the antecedents in each r_i are either premises or are proved and the consequence of r_m is the desired conclusion *c*. Graphically, a proof can be represented by a directed graph like the one shown in Figure 9.11*a*, where the root nodes are all premises, the leaf node is *c*, and each bundle of converging arrows represents a given rule. The arcs connecting the arrows represent the logical AND function between the antecedents of each rule.

The collection *R* of all rules available to a system can be represented by an AND/OR graph like the one in Figure 9.11*b*, where an OR function is understood to exist between any two parent bundles converging toward the same node. The graph in Figure 9.11*b* contains two proofs for *c*, (r_1, r_2) and (r_3, r_4). If *t* can no longer be asserted as a premise, the proof (r_1, r_2) is no longer valid, but *c* can still be proved via (r_3, r_4).

We are now in a position to calculate $Bel(c)$, namely, the probability that *c* is provable in a system of uncertain rules, where each rule r_i is characterized by a strength measure m_i. A system of such rules is equivalent to an AND/OR graph whose links are interrupted by random switches, as shown in Figure 9.12. The task of computing $Bel(c)$, then, amounts to calculating the percentage of time that some

---

† Since this treatment of rules is the prevailing view among D-S practitioners, we shall call it the *D-S approach*. An alternative treatment, viewing rules as conditional probability statements, is in theory also permitted within the D-S formalism, but because it is identical to the Bayesian treatment we shall call it the *Bayesian approach*.

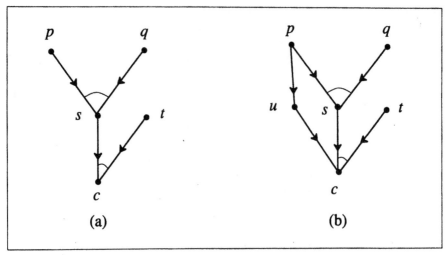

Figure 9.11. *(a) A proof graph for proposition c, representing two rules $p \wedge q \to s$,*
$s \wedge t \to c$ and the premises p, q, t. (b) An AND/OR graph representing four
rules.

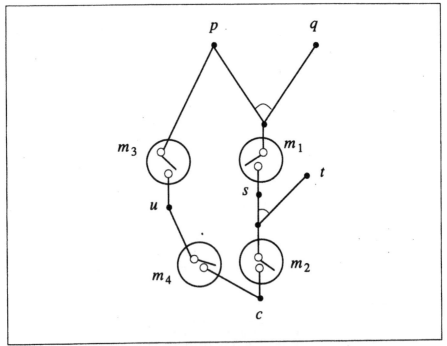

Figure 9.12. *Random switch model for the rule network of Figure 9.11b.*

proof graph of c remain uninterrupted. In the special case where every rule has a single antecedent, the problem can be reduced to finding the percentage of time that an uninterrupted path exists between some premise and the conclusion. Such problems have been studied extensively in the area of network reliability, and in general they turn out to be rather complex, even under the assumption that the interruptions are independent of each other [Rosenthal 1975].

A brute-force way of calculating $Bel(c)$ would be to enumerate all switch combinations, test each combination to see if a proof exists for it, and then total the time the switches spend in combinations that pass the test. For a system with n rules, this would require the enumeration of 2^n combinations. Fortunately, the simple nature of the network in Figure 9.12 permits the calculation to be done without enumerating all combinations. Since the network contains two disjoint proofs, the active times of the two proof graphs are mutually independent; hence, the time that c is unprovable is equal to the product of the amounts of time that each proof graph is inactive, i.e., $(1 - m_3 m_4)(1 - m_1 m_2)$. The rest of the time c is provable, hence

$$Bel(c) = 1 - (1 - m_3 m_4)(1 - m_1 m_2). \qquad (9.10)$$

Note that instead of enumerating all $2^4 = 16$ switch positions, we had to enumerate only the two proof paths (in general, proof graphs) (r_1, r_2) and (r_3, r_4), calculate the active time t_i of each path, and then calculate $Bel(c)$ using the formula

$$Bel(c) = 1 - \prod_i (1 - t_i). \qquad (9.11)$$

Such shortcuts are not feasible in general rule networks. For example, if we add the rule $r_5{:}s \rightarrow u(m_5)$ to the system of Figure 9.11b, an additional proof graph is added, $\{r_1, r_5, r_4\}$, whose activation time is dependent on the other proof graphs, and we can no longer calculate $Bel(c)$ by multiplying the inactive times of each separate proof graph. Rather, we must enumerate all of the distinct ways that one or more proof graphs remain active, i.e.,

$$Bel(c) = [1 - (1 - m_3 m_4)(1 - m_1 m_2)] + m_1 m_5 m_4 (1 - m_2)(1 - m_3). \qquad (9.12)$$

The first term represents the condition that at least one of the proofs, (r_1, r_2), (r_3, r_4), is active, and the second represents the proof remaining under the complementary condition.

What permits shortcuts such as the one taken in Figure 9.11b is a topological feature called *series-parallel*. This feature allows recursive solution of many graph problems including network flow, network reliability, belief functions, and probabilities. Formally, a rule network is said to be series-parallel if it can be reduced to a single rule by repeated application of the following two operations:

1. Series reduction:

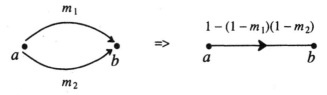

2. Parallel reduction:

It is clear from this definition that series-parallel rule networks permit the calculation of belief functions in time proportional to the number of rules (as opposed to the number of switch combinations), since each reduction operation reduces the number of rules by one. For example, the network of Figure 9.13 can be reduced in three operations, yielding

$$Bel(c) = m_1(m_2\|m_3\,m_4) = m_1[1 - (1 - m_2)(1 - m_3m_4)] . \qquad (9.13)$$

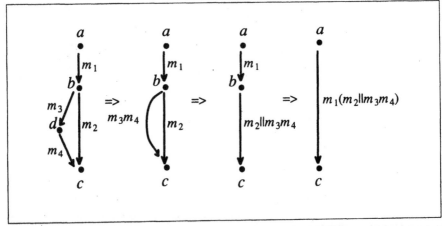

Figure 9.13. *Reducing a series-parallel rule network to a single rule*
  ($m_1\|m_2$ stands for $1 - (1 - m_1)(1 - m_2)$).

In general networks, however, the calculation of $Bel(c)$ may require exponential time.

THE LIMITS OF EXTENSIONAL ANALYSIS

Though it involves only simple graph operations, the foregoing analysis is at variance with most uncertainty management techniques used in rule-based systems. These techniques are based on extensional analysis, where the uncertainty associated with the consequent of each rule is presumed to be solely a function of the uncertainties of the antecedents of the rule and the uncertainty of the rule itself (see Figure 1.1). In the D-S formulation of extensional techniques these uncertainties are represented by a pair of supports $[b, p]$, so the pair associated with the consequent of each rule is presumed to be a sole function of the pair that characterizes the rule and the pairs that characterize the antecedents [Ginsberg 1984; Falkenhainer 1986; Baldwin 1987]. Moreover, when two rules converge toward the same conclusion, the pair associated with the conclusion is determined via the interval calculus of Eq. (9.7) from the pairs associated with the individual rules. This is precisely where extensional systems deviate from the principles dictated by the D-S theory. The combination rule of Eq. (9.7) was derived under the assumption that the two items of evidence would be independent of each other (i.e., the two switches in Figure 9.9 would work independently). Applying this combination rule to every pair of converging arrows in a large network may violate this independence assumption, especially if proof paths overlap. For example, given the truth of a in the initial network of Figure 9.13, an extensional analysis will compute $Bel(c)$ as follows:

$$Bel(b) = m_1 \, ,$$

$$Bel(d) = m_3 \, Bel(b) = m_3 \, m_1 \, ,$$

$$Bel(c) = m_4 \, Bel(d) \, \| \, m_2 \, Bel(b) = m_4 \, m_3 \, m_1 \, \| \, m_2 \, m_1$$

$$= 1 - (1 - m_4 m_3 m_1)(1 - m_2 m_1)$$

$$= m_1(m_4 m_3 + m_2 - m_4 m_3 m_2 m_1) \, . \qquad (9.14)$$

The correct result is

$$Bel(c) = m_1(m_2 \| m_3 m_4) = m_1(m_2 + m_3 m_4 - m_2 m_3 m_4),$$

as in Eq. (9.13). The difference between the two expressions is equal to $m_2 m_3 m_4(m_1 - m_1^2)$, and it clearly stems from counting the arc m_1 twice. An extensional system is too local to realize that the beliefs at b and d originate from the same source.

It is easy to find conceptual examples that amplify the discrepancy between the two approaches and thus highlight the conditions under which extensional systems lead to paradoxical conclusions. To maximize the difference $m_1 - m_1^2$, we let $m_1 = \frac{1}{2}$ and $m_2 = m_3 = m_4 = 1$, and assemble the following system of rules:

r_1: If I flip the coin (a), then it will turn up heads (b) $(m_1 = \frac{1}{2})$

r_2: If the coin turns up heads (b), then you win (c) $(m_2 = 1)$,

r_3: If the coin turns up heads (b), then I lose (d) $(m_3 = 1)$,

r_4: If I lose (d), then you win (c) $(m_4 = 1)$.

Suppose I flip the coin ($a = TRUE$); what is the belief attributable to your victory (c)? The correct answer is clearly $\frac{1}{2}$, since the path $b \rightarrow d \rightarrow c$ is superfluous. Yet the answer computed by an extensional system is $Bel(c) = \frac{3}{4}$, as if my loss contributes an extra piece of evidence toward your winning.

In general, extensional techniques are easier to program and faster to run, as they require no network supervision and permit each rule to fire independently. The problem is that they violate the independence assumption when two or more proof paths share a common origin; in rule networks that are tree structured, this error condition disappears. Thus, we conclude that D-S analysis, like the Bayesian formulation (Chapter 4), admits extensional techniques only when the rules form a tree structure [Hájek 1987].

Interestingly, a Bayesian analysis will produce the same result as Eqs. (9.10) and (9.11) under the following assumptions:

1.   A rule $r: a \rightarrow b \; (m)$ is interpreted as two conditional probability statements: $P(b \mid a) = m$ and $P(b \mid \neg a) = 0$;

2.   Converging rules interact disjunctively, via the noisy-OR model of Section 4.3.2.

These two assumptions permit the construction of a complete probabilistic model (i.e., a Bayesian network) for any acyclic rule network. The probabilities $BEL(A) = P(A \mid e)$ calculated from such models are identical to the belief functions $Bel(A)$ calculated from the D-S model, for any proposition A in the rule set. However, the negations of these propositions get the probabilities $BEL(\neg A) = 1 - BEL(A)$ whereas in the D-S model they are assigned zero $Bel(\cdot)$ values ($\neg A$ cannot be proved by any rule set unless $\neg A$ appears as a consequent of at least one rule).

9.1.6 Bayes vs. Dempster-Shafer: A Semantic Clash

The essential difference between the Bayesian and D-S interpretations of the rules shows up in systems that have a mixture of conflicting rules, some supporting a proposition A and some supporting its negation, $\neg A$. In such systems the semantic gap between the two approaches leads to qualitatively different conclusions. Whereas the D-S scheme resolves conflicts by Dempster's normalization (see Figure 9.9), the Bayesian approach resolves them by a more cautious mechanism, appealing to their conditional probability interpretation. As a result, the D-S approach will inherit all of the problems of classical monotonic logic when applied to situations requiring belief revision. We shall demonstrate these problems using a simple three-rule example, the so-called penguin triangle.

Consider the rule set R:

r_1: $p \to \neg f$ (m_1), meaning "Penguins normally don't fly;"

r_2: $b \to f$ (m_2), meaning "Birds normally fly;"

r_3: $p \to b$ $(m_3 = 1)$, meaning "Penguins are birds."

To emphasize our strong conviction in these rules, we make m_1 and m_2 approach unity and write

$$m_1 = 1 - \varepsilon_1 , \quad m_2 = 1 - \varepsilon_2 ,$$

where ε_1 and ε_2 are small positive quantities. Assume we find an animal called Tweety that is categorically classified as a bird and a penguin, and we wish to assess the likelihood that Tweety can fly. In other words, we are given the premises p and b, and we need to compute $Bel(f)$ using the D-S approach or $P(f|p, b)$ using the Bayesian approach.

The Bayesian approach, treating rules as conditional probabilities, immediately yields the expected result—that Tweety's "birdness" does not render her a better flyer than an ordinary penguin. The reason is that the entailment $p \supset b$ permits us to replace $P(f|p, b)$ by $P(f|p)$, giving

$$P(f|p, b) = P(f|p) = 1 - P(\neg f|p) = 1 - m_1 = \varepsilon_1 . \tag{9.15}$$

In the D-S approach, on the other hand, if we treat the rules as a system of uncertain compatibility constraints (see Eqs (9.8) and (9.9)), a counterintuitive result emerges: birdness seems to endow Tweety with extra flying power. This is shown in Table 1, where the four states of the rules r_1 and r_2 are enumerated along with the associated probabilities and the provability state of the proposition Fly.

Table 1.

Probabilities	r_1	r_2	*Fly*	$\neg Fly$
$\varepsilon_1 \varepsilon_2$	inactive	inactive	not provable	not provable
$(1 - \varepsilon_1)\varepsilon_2$	active	inactive	not provable	provable
$\varepsilon_1(1 - \varepsilon_2)$	inactive	active	provable	not provable
$(1 - \varepsilon_1)(1 - \varepsilon_2)$	active	active	conflict	conflict

Summing over the states where *Fly* is provable, and normalizing, we obtain

$$Bel(Fly) = \frac{\varepsilon_1(1 - \varepsilon_2)}{1 - (1 - \varepsilon_1)(1 - \varepsilon_2)} = \frac{\varepsilon_1 - \varepsilon_1\varepsilon_2}{\varepsilon_1 + \varepsilon_2 - \varepsilon_1\varepsilon_2} \approx \frac{\varepsilon_1}{\varepsilon_1 + \varepsilon_2}. \qquad (9.16)$$

We see that the belief attributable to Tweety's flying critically depends on whether she is a penguin-bird or just a penguin. In the latter case, rule r_1 dictates $Bel(Fly) = \varepsilon_1$, which is negligibly small. In the former case, adding the superfluous information that all penguins are birds and birds normally fly makes $Bel(Fly)$ substantially higher, as in Eq. (9.16). It does not go to zero with ε_1 and ε_2, but depends on the relative magnitudes of these quantities. If the proportion of nonflying birds (ε_2) is smaller than the proportion of flying penguins (ε_1), Tweety's flying will be assigned a belief measure greater than 0.50. Using switches with *FALSE-TRUE* positions or with *FALSE-NEUTRAL-TRUE* positions to model rules yields essentially identical results.

Identical results are also obtained when rule r_3 is not asserted with absolute certainty ($m_3 = 1$) but is subject to exceptions, i.e., $m_3 = 1 - \varepsilon_3 < 1$. The Bayesian analysis yields

$$P(f \mid p, b) \leq \frac{\varepsilon_1}{1 - \varepsilon_3}, \qquad (9.17)$$

meaning that as long as ε_3 remains small, penguin-birds have very little chance of flying, regardless of how many birds cannot fly (ε_2). The D-S analysis, on the other hand, still yields the paradoxical result

$$Bel(f) \cong \frac{\varepsilon_1}{\varepsilon_1 + \varepsilon_2}, \qquad (9.18)$$

meaning that if nonflying birds are very rare, i.e., $\varepsilon_2 \approx 0$, then penguin-birds have a very big chance of flying.

The clash with intuition revolves not around the exact numerical value of $Bel(f)$ but rather around the unacceptable phenomenon that rule r_3, stating that penguins are a subclass of birds, plays no role in the analysis. Knowing that

Tweety is both a penguin and a bird renders *Bel*(*Tweety flies*) solely a function of m_1 and m_2, regardless of how penguins and birds are related. This stands contrary to common discourse, where people expect class properties to be overridden by properties of more specific subclasses.

While in classical logic the three rules in our example would yield an unforgivable contradiction, the uncertainties attached to these rules, together with Dempster's normalization, now render them manageable. However, they are managed in the wrong way whenever we interpret if–then rules as randomized logical formulas of the material-implication type, instead of statements of conditional probabilities. As we stated in Chapter 1, the material-implication interpretation of if–then rules is so fundamentally wrong that it cannot be rectified by allowing exceptions in the form of randomization. The real source of the problem is the property of transitivity, $(a \rightarrow b, b \rightarrow c) \Rightarrow a \rightarrow c$, which is basic to the material-implication interpretation. There are occasions when rule transitivity must be totally suppressed, not merely weakened, to avoid getting strange results. One such occasion occurs in property inheritance, where subclass specificity should override superclass properties. Randomization, in this case, weakens the flow of inference through the chain but does not bring it to a dead halt, as it should.

This phenomenon also arises outside the realm of property inheritance. For example, consider these rules:

r_1: If I am sick, then I can't answer the door (m_1),

r_2: If I am home, then I can answer the door (m_2),

r_3: If I am sick, then I stay home ($m_3 \approx 1$).

Rule r_3 tells us that exceptions to rule r_2, due to sickness, are already reflected in the measure m_2, and exceptions to rule r_1, including those emanating from staying home, have been summarized in the measure m_1. Thus, given that I am sick, the conclusion is that I cannot answer the door, with confidence m_1; given that I am both sick and at home, the same conclusion applies, and the same confidence, too.

In abductive tasks, rule transitivity can lead to even stranger results. Consider the example from Chapter 1:

r'_1: If the ground is wet, then it rained last night (m'_1),

r'_2: If the sprinkler was on, then the ground is wet ($m'_2 \approx 1$).

If we find that the ground is wet, rule r'_1 tells us that $Bel(Rain) = m'_1$. Now, suppose we learn that the sprinkler was on. Instead of decreasing $Bel(Rain)$ by explaining away the wet ground, the new evidence leaves $Bel(Rain)$ the same. More seriously, suppose we first observe the sprinkler. Rule r'_2 will correctly predict that the ground will get wet, and without even inspecting the ground, r'_1 will conclude that it rained last night, with $Bel(Rain) = m'_1 m'_2$.

These difficulties have haunted nonmonotonic logic for years (see Chapter 10 for more details) and will be inherited by the D-S analysis whenever it treats if–then rules as material implications, however much weakened by randomization. The problems can be circumvented by two methods, neither of which is truly satisfactory. One method requires the rule author to state explicitly the exceptions (or assumptions) underlying each rule. For example, rule r'_2 will be phrased "If I am at home, I can answer the door, unless I am sick, or asleep, or under a gun threat ... in which case I will not be able to answer the door." This method works well under the D-S analysis, but the enormous number of potential exceptions to each rule prevents it from being practical. The second method, used in inheritance systems [Touretzky 1986; Etherington 1987], is to use extra logical criteria to decide when transitivity is applicable. For example, Ginsberg has proposed the meta-rule "Never apply a rule to a set when there is a corresponding rule which can be applied to a subset" [Ginsberg 1984]. In Chapter 10 we will show that such priorities among rules emerge automatically if the rules are simply given their proper interpretation, namely, conditional probability statements with probabilities close to 1.

9.2 TRUTH MAINTENANCE SYSTEMS

Truth maintenance systems [Doyle 1979; McAllester 1980] provide a way to keep track of beliefs and belief justifications developed during an inference session. Since knowledge and beliefs are built largely on default assumptions and educated guesses, a reasoning system must be able to retract some of these assumptions in the light of new information. All conclusions that were derived from these assumptions would have to be retracted as well, unless they could be supported by new arguments. To manage this retraction process, a truth-maintenance system maintains a dependency record for each inferred fact, indicating its justification in terms of both the presence and absence of information.

This retraction task is similar to the belief revision of Chapter 5, with two exceptions: First, the relationships between propositions are logical, not probabilistic; a conclusion is either justified or not justified by a set of facts, with no intermediate levels of support strength. As a result, the abductive task of finding the "most likely explanation" cannot be accomplished by numerical means, as in Chapter 5, but relies on explicit diagnostic rules suggesting hypotheses that account for observations. Second, uncertainty in these systems is represented not by numerical degrees of belief but rather by symbolic annotations called *assumptions*, which identify by name those uncertain facts that, if true, would justify our belief in a given proposition (we referred to such entities as *contingencies* in Section 7.3). In other words, instead of being associated with a numerical quantity, the truth value of a proposition is represented by a Boolean expression that identifies the assumptions needed for believing in that proposition.

Although lacking numerical criteria for deciding among opposing hypotheses, these systems are nevertheless popular because they are compatible with the style of logical inference, and because unlike monotonic logic they do not dispose of the inferences once the conclusion is established. On the contrary, by recording the history of inferences, these systems can retrace the sources of beliefs, a feature necessary for generating explanations and for resolving contradictions.

The reason for introducing truth maintenance systems in this chapter is twofold. First, these systems can be viewed as symbolic engines for computing D-S belief functions. Second, like the D-S theory, truth-maintenance systems generate inferences through hard, categorical compatibility relations and hence base the notion of evidential support on *provability*.

9.2.1 Naming the Assumptions

A truth maintenance systems (TMS) uses rules as its elementary units of knowledge and, similar to our treatment in Section 9.1.5, draws conclusion by piecing together rules to form proofs. Once again, rules may have exceptions that can cause the expected conclusion of the proof to clash with observed facts or with other deductions. However, whereas in Section 9.1.5 the exceptions and assumptions were summarized numerically, using the rule weight m, the generic TMS approach maintains an explicit list of the main assumptions or exceptions associated with each rule. For example,

$$Turn\ key\ \rightarrow\ Start\ engine \qquad (m) \qquad\qquad \textbf{(9.19)}$$

will be written

$$Turn\ key \wedge [Good\ starter,\ Battery\ not\ dead,\ etc.\ ]\ \rightarrow\ Start\ engine\ , \qquad \textbf{(9.20)}$$

where the terms in the square brackets are the assumptions behind the rule in Eq. (9.19). Thus, each rule in a TMS consists of two types of antecedents— *preconditions* (e.g., *Turn key*) and *assumptions* (e.g., *Battery not dead*). The difference between the two is only that assumptions are presumed to be true under normal conditions while preconditions may be true or false, depending on whether they can be proved or refuted from observed facts, called *premises* in TMS terminology.†

This distinction introduces a bias that should allow us temporarily to ignore the assumptions altogether; proofs constructed from preconditions alone are considered legitimate, and their conclusions are tentatively adopted as firmly held beliefs. Indeed, in a version of TMS proposed by Doyle [1979], assumptions are manipulated only when an observation is made that conflicts with proofs based on previously held assumptions, at which time the TMS produces an alternative set of

---

† In Doyle's TMS the preconditions are called *IN-justifiers* and the assumptions are represented by exceptions, called *OUT-justifiers*, which are presumed to be false, e.g., *Battery dead*.

assumptions consistent with the observation. For example, if in addition to the rule in Eq. (9.20), we also have the facts (premises) that the key is turned and the engine does not start, then the TMS will issue a new assumption set, either {*Bad starter*} or {*Battery dead*}, rendering the observation consistent with the premises.

In a subsequent version of TMS, called *assumption-based TMS* or *ATMS* [de Kleer 1986], the system maintains not just one but a whole collection of assumption sets (called *environments*), any of which, if realized, could support our currently held beliefs. Each assumption set is *minimal,* or nonredundant, in the sense that no assumption can be moved from the set without destroying the set's support of the current belief. Minimality corresponds to the notion of most-probable-explanation (see Chapter 5) if exceptions (i.e., negations of assumptions) are assumed to be rare, equiprobable and independent events.

Let us illustrate ATMS using the example of Figure 9.11*b*, with a fifth rule added, $r_5 : s \to u$. Instead of switches and rule weights as in Figure 9.12, exceptions are formulated in terms of propositional symbols $A_1, A_2, ...,$ connoting assumptions that are added to the antecedents of the corresponding rules. Altogether, we have a five-rule system, as shown in Figure 9.14:

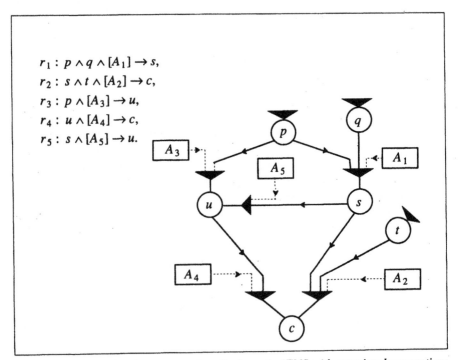

$$r_1 : p \wedge q \wedge [A_1] \to s,$$
$$r_2 : s \wedge t \wedge [A_2] \to c,$$
$$r_3 : p \wedge [A_3] \to u,$$
$$r_4 : u \wedge [A_4] \to c,$$
$$r_5 : s \wedge [A_5] \to u.$$

Figure 9.14. *A graphical representation of a five-rule ATMS with associated assumptions, $A_1, ..., A_5$ and premises p, q and t.*

Note the striking similarity between Figure 9.14 and Figure 9.12; the switches and their weights $m_1, m_2, ...$ are merely replaced by the proposition labels $A_1, A_2, ...,$ representing assumptions. Accordingly, each assumption A_i can be viewed as a valve that controls the position of a switch and asserts, "The switch corresponding to rule r_i is on." However, unlike the switches in the D-S formalism, each A_i can be a complex Boolean formula of propositions, which can be consequents of other rules.

Under normal operation, the ATMS is given a set of premises, e.g., $\{p, q, t\}$, and it maintains for each propositional symbol in the system a list of minimal sets of assumptions under which the corresponding proposition can be proven. Such a list is called a *label*. In our example, the label of u would be $L(u) = \left\{ \{A_3\}, \{A_1, A_5\} \right\}$. The set $\{A_3\}$, for instance, indicates that assumption A_3 (together with the premises) is sufficient to activate rule r_3; so, A_3 supports a proof of u. Proposition c, however, will have a more extensive label:

$$L(c) = \left\{ \{A_3, A_4\}, \{A_1, A_5, A_4\}, \{A_1, A_2\} \right\}, \qquad \textbf{(9.21)}$$

where each set corresponds to the assumptions that lead to one distinct proof-graph for c.

An ATMS keeps separate labels for the negations of the propositions in the system. In our system these labels will be empty because there is no rule with either $\neg s$, $\neg u$, or $\neg c$ as a consequent, and so there is no way to prove any of these propositions. Had the system been augmented with the rule

$$r_6 \colon \neg u \wedge [A_5] \to \neg c,$$

we would then label $\neg c$ with

$$L(\neg c) = \{A_5 \wedge L(\neg u)\} \qquad \textbf{(9.22)}$$

Labels represent the *contexts* or *environments* under which propositions can safely be believed. The purpose of maintaining these labels explicitly is to propagate them quickly from one proposition to another and to keep the ability to retract the proper set of assumptions when a contradiction arises. For example, if $\neg c$ is asserted as a premise, assumptions that underlie c are no longer consistent with the premise set, and at least one assumption must be retracted from each of the three sets of $L(c)$. Any minimal set of retracted assumptions (called a *minimal candidate* in de Kleer and Williams [1986]) can be regarded as a plausible *explanation* for the conflict. In our example, if $\neg c$ is observed, the set of minimal candidates will be

$$\left\{ \{\neg A_1, \neg A_3\}, \{\neg A_3, \neg A_5, \neg A_2\}, \{\neg A_4, \neg A_2\}, \{\neg A_1, \neg A_4\} \right\}.$$

These sets come from negating the disjunction of the sets in $L(c)$, and they correspond, as the reader may have expected, to the four (minimal) cutsets of the network in Figure 9.14.

In addition to labels and candidate sets, the ATMS also keeps a global database of "no-good" assumption sets to be removed from any label in which they appear. In our example, the "no-good" assumption sets resulting from observing $\neg c$ would simply be the sets contained in $L(c)$. These, as well as their supersets, should be removed from the label of every proposition in the system, especially those propositions derived prior to the observation of $\neg c$.

In summary, the ATMS can be viewed as a symbolic algebra system that produces a Boolean expression $L(c)$ for every given proposition c. $L(c)$ contains a list of nonredundant sets of assumptions called environments, each of which is sufficient to support a proof of c, given the available premises. In logical terms, $L(c)$ enumerates the prime implicants entailing c [Reiter and de Kleer 1987]. In graphical terms, assuming that each rule contains a single justification and a single assumption, $L(c)$ enumerates all the paths (proofs) leading from the premises to c.

9.2.2 Uncertainty Management in an ATMS

From a purely logical viewpoint, the label $L(c)$ that the ATMS attaches to a proposition yields only three possible truth values for c: *BELIEVED*, *DISBELIEVED*, and *UNKNOWN*. If any environment in $L(c)$ is believed, then c is *BELIEVED*; if we believe any environment in $L(\neg c)$, then c is *DISBELIEVED*. If we can confirm neither $L(c)$ nor $L(\neg c)$, then c is *UNKNOWN*.†

This three-value logic cannot rate the degree of uncertainty attributable to unknown propositions, and thus may lead to a stalemate whenever a decision is to be made whose outcome depends critically on the truth of these propositions. However, there are three very useful functions that one can perform, even within this limitation:

1. *Producing Explanations*: Once a proposition c is *BELIEVED*, the ATMS can retrace the justification paths and identify the argument (proof) justifying that belief, as well as the assumptions upon which it is founded. This is similar to tracing back the π and λ messages in probabilistic belief networks and is facilitated by recording the antecedent part of the rules next to each datum – which essentially amounts to keeping the network structure in memory.

2. *Managing conflicts*: Contradictions between expectations and reality are viewed as signals that the currently held set of assumptions should be modified. New sets of assumptions that are consistent and maximal

---

† The terms IN and OUT are used to denote *BELIEVED* and *UNKNOWN*, respectively.

(i.e., containing a minimal set of exceptions) are generated automatically.

3. *Guiding the acquisition of new information*: If a certain proposition is in an unknown state, then the label $L(c)$ provides clues as to the information required to render it known, i.e., *BELIEVED* or *DISBELIEVED*. For example, if a confirmation of assumption A is all that is missing from one set in $L(\neg c)$, while the confirmation of $\neg A$ is missing from some set in $L(c)$, then a test leading to the confirmation or denial of A should be devised.

INTRODUCING NUMERICAL UNCERTAINTIES

These three features do not fully replace the facilities provided by numerical measures of uncertainty. For example, a pending decision may depend crucially on the likelihood that a given *UNKNOWN* proposition c will become *BELIEVED*, and this, in turn, depends on our relative certainty in the assumption sets of $L(c)$ compared with those of $L(\neg c)$. Likewise, there might be several diagnostic tests that one can perform, each having the potential of confirming or denying a crucial proposition c, yet some tests might be judged more likely than others to yield that determination. It is for these reasons that several attempts have been made to augment ATMS with numerical measures of uncertainty [Falkenhainer 1986; D'Ambrosio 1987; de Kleer and Williams 1987].

In principle, the introduction of numerical measures of uncertainty within the ATMS setting requires only that we assess the relative likelihood of the various assumptions in the system. The ATMS provides a symbolic facility to translate these assessments into a certainty measure for any conclusion. This certainty measure will represent exactly what belief functions did in the D-S formalism, i.e., the probability of establishing a proof for the conclusion.

Since $L(c)$ constitutes a Boolean expression whose truth signifies the existence of a proof for c, $Bel(c)$ can be obtained simply by computing the probability of $L(c)$,† i.e.,

$$Bel(c) = P[L(c)]. \qquad (9.23)$$

Moreover, since the atoms that make up $L(c)$ are all assumption-type propositions, $P[L(c)]$ can be computed from the probabilities assigned to the assumptions. In particular, if one assumes that assumptions are independent of each other, the computation of $P[L(c)]$ can be done symbolically; it amounts to the same computation we have conducted for belief functions in rule-based systems (see Section 9.1.4).

---

† If the "no-good" set is non-empty conditional probabilities are required, conditioned on the consistency of the label.

Consider Figure 9.14, and let p_i stand for the probability that assumption A_i is true. To calculate $Bel(c)$, the ATMS provides the label $L(c)$ from Eq. (9.21), and we have

$$Bel(c) = P[L(c)] = P[A_3 A_4 \vee A_1 A_4 A_5 \vee A_1 A_2] . \qquad (9.24)$$

Probability calculus permits us to calculate the probability of a disjunction or conjunction of any two expressions (in terms of the probabilities of the individual expressions) if the expressions are either mutually exclusive or independent. Unfortunately, the sub-expressions in Eq. (9.24) are neither, because they share common elements. We therefore substitute

$$A_3 A_4 = A_3 A_4 (A_1 \vee \neg A_1)$$

and obtain

$$Bel(c) = P[A_3 A_4 \neg A_1 \vee A_1 (A_2 \vee A_4 (A_3 \vee A_5))] . \qquad (9.25)$$

The first term in the square bracket is disjoint of the second term, which is in series-parallel form. This yields

$$
\begin{aligned}
Bel(c) &= p_3 p_4 (1 - p_1) + p_1 [p_2 \| p_4 (p_3 \| p_5)] \\
&= p_3 p_4 (1 - p_1) + p_1 [p_2 + p_4 (p_3 \| p_5) - p_2 p_4 (p_3 \| p_5)] \\
&= p_3 p_4 (1 - p_1) + p_1 [p_2 + p_4 (1 - p_2)(p_3 + p_5 - p_3 p_5)] . \qquad (9.26)
\end{aligned}
$$

This expression is identical to the one in Eq.(9.12), identifying p_i with m_i. Mechanical procedures for computing the probability of an arbitrary Boolean expression (assuming that propositional symbols stand for independent binary random variables) have been reported in the literature on network reliability [Grnarov, Kleinrock, and Gerla 1979] and can easily be applied to the labels returned by the ATMS.

9.2.3 Incidence Calculus

Incidence calculus [Bundy 1985], a mechanism proposed for managing uncertainty in expert systems (see Section 9.4), suggests an alternative method of computing belief functions, similar in spirit to the method of logical sampling (stochastic simulation) presented in Section 4.4.3. Consider again the rule network of Figure 9.14, where it is required to compute $Bel(c)$ given the probabilities of the assumptions $A_1,..., A_5$. Instead of computing a symbolic expression for $Bel(c)$ in terms of $p_1,..., p_5$, as in the preceding subsection, one can actually simulate the behavior of the network under a random assignment of truth values to the assumptions, then count the frequency with which c is proved true. The truth value of each assumption A_i will be represented by a random bit string of ones and zeros, in which the frequency of ones is p_i. In every time step, each assumption selects the next bit from its bit string and sets its truth value accordingly, and a theorem in which the frequency of ones is p_i. In every time step, each assumption selects the next bit from its bit string and sets its truth value accordingly, and a theorem prover attempts to prove the truth of c. The frequency with which a proof is established is equal to $Bel(c)$.

This scheme is an embodiment of the random switch model described in Section 9.1.3. The random position of each switch is replaced by the random bit string assigned to each proposition (i.e., assumption) whose degree of certainty we wish to assert. The advantage of this scheme is that the theorem prover can be general purpose (e.g., first-order logic), not limited to propositional constraints. Moreover, the scheme can simulate dependencies among items of evidence, provided the bit strings are generated by a complete probabilistic model (e.g., a causal network) that embodies these dependencies.

9.3 PROBABILISTIC LOGIC

While Bayesian theory requires the specification of a complete probabilistic model and the D-S theory sidesteps the missing specifications by compromising its inferences, *probabilistic logic* [Nilsson 1986] considers the space of all models consistent with the specifications that are available and computes bounds instead of point values for the probabilities required.† Probabilistic logic (*PL*) addresses the following problem: Suppose we are given a collection S of logical sentences, some representing facts (e.g., "Socrates is a dog") and some representing generic laws (e.g., "All dogs bark"), and suppose someone attaches probability measures to some of the sentences, representing degrees of belief in their truth. Our task is to deduce the probability of other sentences whose probabilities were not specified explicitly (e.g., "Socrates barks").

In some ways this problem resembles the evidential reasoning tasks of Chapters 4 and 5. There, too, we started with probabilistic assessments on a small set of sentences (i.e., those used in the construction of the Bayesian network), and we were able to deduce the probability of every query phrased in propositional form (see Section 4.5). In Bayesian networks, however, the probabilities were assigned in a principled way, guaranteeing consistency and completeness; merely assigning probabilities to a set of logical sentences does not, in general, define a complete probabilistic model, even when the assignment is consistent. The logical relationships between the sentences in S will, in general, admit a high number of truth value assignments, called *extensions,* (or *worlds*), and unless one assigns a probability rating to each such extension, the model remains incomplete, in a

---

† Uncertainty formalisms based on probability bounds originate with Good [1950], Fisher [1957], and Smith [1961].

To illustrate this point, let us examine a simple example involving the following three sentences:

$$S_1 = p,$$
$$S_2 = p \supset q,$$
$$S_3 = q.$$

If we regard these sentences as binary variables that may take on Boolean values, then out of the $2^3 = 8$ value combinations, the four consistent ones are extensions. These are given by the rows of Table 2.

Table 2.

Extensions	$S_1 = p$	$S_2 = p \supset q$	$S_3 = q$
W_1	*TRUE*	*TRUE*	*TRUE*
W_2	*TRUE*	*FALSE*	*FALSE*
W_3	*FALSE*	*TRUE*	*TRUE*
W_4	*FALSE*	*TRUE*	*FALSE*

Assigning probability measures to any two sentences does not fully specify a model and does not yield a unique probability measure for the third sentence. The best way to see this, using the Bayesian method of model construction, is to view S_1 and S_3 as parent variables of S_2. Since S_2 is a Boolean function of S_1 and S_3, its value is completely determined by the values assigned to S_1 and S_3. This means that a complete probabilistic model can be defined by assigning arbitrary weights to each of the four possible truth values of (S_1, S_3), making sure that they sum to unity. This requires a specification of three parameters, e.g., $P(p, q)$, $P(p, \neg q)$, and $P(\neg p, q)$. If we specify only $P(p)$ and $P(q)$, the model remains underspecified.

More interesting difficulties surface when someone assigns probability measures to S_1 and S_2 and seeks to deduce the probability of S_3. This is a typical occurrence in rule-based systems, where S_2 is (falsely) taken to be the logical representation of the English sentence "If p then q." Since S_3 is not a Boolean function of S_1 and S_2 (for $S_1 = FALSE$ and $S_2 = TRUE$, S_3 can attain either value), even specifying the joint probability of the pair (S_1, S_2) will not suffice; one still must assess $P(S_3 = TRUE \mid S_1 = FALSE, S_2 = TRUE)$ before the model is completely specified. Moreover, since S_2 and S_1 cannot both be *FALSE*, one cannot specify the joint probability of (S_1, S_2) by an arbitrary selection of three parameters; caution must be exercised to ensure that the selection is consistent with the requirement

$$P(S_1 = FALSE) + P(S_2 = FALSE) \leq 1 . \tag{9.27}$$

Violations of such consistency requirements can be prevalent in rule-based expert systems [Duda et al. 1976]. $P(S_2 = FALSE)$ is often perceived as measuring one's doubt in the validity of some generic rule (e.g., exceptions to the rule S_2: "Dogs bark"), and hence is kept constant. At the same time, since $P(S_1 = FALSE)$ is allowed to vary depending on the amount of support that S_1 receives from other rules, the consistency requirement of Eq. (9.27) will occasionally be violated. It is also common to find an expert providing the assessments $P(S_2 = FALSE) = 0.1$, reflecting a rule $p \supset q$ with 10% exceptions, and $P(S_1 = TRUE) = 0.001$, reflecting some rare event p. The two assessments are clearly inconsistent because S_2 must be true whenever S_1 is false, i.e., at least 99.9% of the time. Aside from the obvious conclusion that the material implication $S_2 = p \supset q$ is the wrong interpretation of the conditional sentence "If p then q," the example shows how easy it is to introduce inconsistencies while assigning probability measures to individual logical sentences.

Probabilistic logic provides a formal way of testing whether probability assignments are consistent with each other. Once we have a criterion for testing consistency, we also possess a device for determining bounds on the permissible probabilities that any given sentence may assume, given the probabilities assigned to other sentences. Such bounds are said to be *probabilistically entailed* by the other assignments.

Conceptually, probabilistic consistency and entailment have simple semantics: The probability $P(S_i) = \pi_i$ associated with a sentence S_i in S constitutes a *constraint* on the probability distribution P that can be assigned to the extensions of S. Since the constraints are not sufficient to determine one unique distribution, we seek a description of the set P of all probability distributions that comply with the given constraints. Each distribution $P \in P$ defines a probability value $P(\phi)$ for any arbitrary sentence ϕ; $P(\phi)$ is simply the sum total of the probabilities of those extensions in which ϕ is true. Given P, we can determine the range of admissible $P(\phi)$ values, letting P span the entire set P.

Let $W = \{W_1, W_2, ...\}$ stand for the set of all extensions of S, let $P(W_i)$ be the weight assigned to W_i by some distribution $P \in P$, and let w_{ij} be a binary variable taking the value 1 if sentence S_j is in extension W_i, and 0 otherwise. The constraints that the assignments $P(S_j) = \pi_j$ impose on the distribution P are given in the form of linear equations:

$$\pi_j = P(S_j) = \sum_{W_i \supset S_j} P(W_i) = \sum_i w_{ij} P(W_i) \quad j = 1, 2, ... \qquad (9.28)$$

In our three-sentence example above, we had four feasible extensions, each corresponding to a row in the truth table, so w_{ij} is given by the (i, j)-th entry of the table. If we demand that our three sentences be given the probability vector $\Pi = (P(S_1), P(S_2), P(S_3))$, then the three equations in Eq. (9.28) constitute constraints on the distributions $P = (P(W_1), P(W_2), P(W_3), P(W_4))$ that could be assigned to our extensions. Given any P satisfying Eq. (9.28) and an arbitrary sentence ϕ, $P(\phi)$ can be computed simply by adding the weights $P(W_j)$ of the extensions where ϕ holds.

Eq. (9.28) also constitutes a description of the set Π of consistent probabilities that can be assigned to the sentences in S. Consistency means that Eq. (9.28) should have at least one solution for $P(W_j)$. Since it is a linear mapping between $P(W_j)$ and $P(S_i)$, Eq. (9.28) maps extreme distributions $P(W_j)$ to extreme assignments $P(S_i)$, and the convex hull of these extreme assignments defines the set of consistent assignments Π. Moreover, since each extreme distribution on W selects one row from the w_{ij} table, we conclude that the set of consistent assignments Π to the sentences in S is bounded by the convex hull generated by the extensions of S.

To illustrate how probability bounds are entailed, let us assume that we start with a single sentence S_2, to which we attribute the probability $P(S_2) = \pi_2$, and we wish to know what values are permitted for either $P(S_1)$ or $P(S_3)$. (For more elaborate examples, together with geometrical representations of the convex hull, see Nilsson [1986].)

There are three feasible extensions permitted for S_1 and S_2, given by Table 3, which shows that the three extreme distributions on these extensions, (1, 0, 0), (0, 1, 0), and (0, 0, 1), map into the following values for the pair $[P(S_1), P(S_2)]$: (0, 1), (1, 0), and (1, 1). Each extension defines an extreme point in the space $[P(S_1), P(S_2)]$, and the convex hull generated by these points defines the permissible range for the pair of probability assignments $[P(S_1), P(S_2)]$ (see Figure 9.15a). Clearly, if $P(S_2)$ is set to π_2, then $P(S_1)$ is bounded by the inequality

$$1 - \pi_2 \leq P(S_1) \leq 1 .\qquad\qquad \textbf{(9.29)}$$

The bounds on $P(S_3)$ can be found in the same way. The three legitimate extensions are shown in Figure 9.15b, which yields

$$0 \leq P(S_3) \leq \pi_2 . \qquad\qquad \textbf{(9.30)}$$

Table 3.

Extensions	$S_1 = p$	$S_2 = p \supset q$
W_1	0	1
W_2	1	0
W_3	1	1 ·

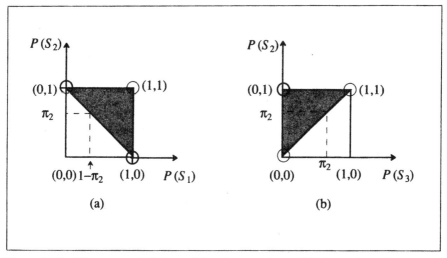

Figure 9.15. *The convex hull formed by the extensions of S determines the range of consistent probability assignments to the sentences in S.*

SUMMARY

Probabilistic logic is a method of dealing with partially specified probabilistic models, where the specification is in the form of probability assignments to a select set of logical sentences. Any such assignment defines a range of permissible complete models, and by describing the boundaries of this range one can deduce bounds on the probabilities of new sentences.

The way probabilistic logic deals with partially specified models is opposite to the way the D-S theory does it. Both methods accept specifications in the form of logical sentences and allow a probability assignment to a subset of these sentences. However, whereas probabilistic logic treats probabilistic models as object-level theories and treats logical relations as meta-constraints on such theories, the D-S theory reverses these roles: Logical constraints serve as the object-level theory, within which deductions take place, and probabilistic information is treated as meta-constraints that modify (randomly) these theories. The two systems represent two different ways of viewing the mixture of soft (probabilistic) and hard (logical) information items in our possession. Probabilistic logic views this mixture as a layer of hard restrictions imposed on a set of soft models, while the D-S theory views it as a layer of soft restrictions imposed on a set of hard models.

Since the two paradigms produce different numerical responses to what appears to be the same set of queries, the choice between the two is clearly not arbitrary; it depends on the nature of the problem we wish to solve. When our task is one of sythesis (e.g., the class scheduling problem), the constraints are externally imposed, and our concern really centers on issues of possibility and necessity—so the D-S theory offers a better representation for the anticipated queries. However, when we face a task of analysis (e.g., diagnosis, as in the Three Prisoners dilemma), where we are trying to piece together a model of physical reality, the constraints are merely by-products of our ignorance, and the probabilistic approach is more suitable, whether in the probabilistic logic or the Bayesian manifestation.

9.4 BIBLIOGRAPHICAL AND HISTORICAL REMARKS

Belief functions were introduced by Dempster [1967] as a generalization of Bayesian inference wherein probabilities are assigned to sets rather than to individual points. In Dempster's formulation, $Bel(A)$ and $Pl(A)$ are interpreted as lower and upper probabilities induced on A by a restricted family of probability distributions – those that are "maximally supportive" of the observations at hand.† In this interpretation, however, it is hard to justify the exclusion of models that are perfectly consistent with the information available but that take into account the possibility that the observations *could have* turned out differently (e.g., the random selection model in the Three Prisoners problem).

   Shafer [1976] has reinterpreted Dempster's theory as a model of evidential reasoning including two interacting frames: a probabilistic frame representing the evidence, and a frame of possibilities over which categorical compatibility relations are defined. Shafer's reinterpretation abandons the idea that belief functions arise as lower bounds of some family of ordinary probability distributions; rather, it views belief functions as the fundamental components in reasoning about uncertain evidence. The relations between belief functions, possibility theory, and possible-worlds semantics are discussed in Shafer [1987] and Ruspini [1987]. Our interpretation of belief functions as probabilities of provability reflects a translation of Shafer's formulation into a language more familiar to an AI audience, appealing to the notions of proofs and constraints. It was prepared for a survey on evidential reasoning which I presented at the AAAI-87 conference (in Shrobe [1988, pp. 402–409]). Similar interpretations were pursued by D'Ambrosio [1987] and Laskey and Lehner [1988].

   Shafer [1976] (Chapter 3), Kyburg [1987b], and Smets [1988] describe methods of incorporating conditional probability information into the D-S formalism. It is not clear, though, how this can be accomplished without modifying the basic semantics of belief functions as probabilities of provability.

---

†   This was pointed out to me by Ted Seidenfeld, in conversation.

The observation that the D-S theory gives ½ in the Three Prisoners Problem, and that it has no natural explanation, was also made in Diaconis and Zabell [1986].

Truth-maintenance systems incorporating measures of uncertainty include Falkenhainer [1986], D'Ambrosio [1987], and de Kleer and Williams [1987]. De Kleer and Williams applied an ATMS to circuit diagnosis, where the normal operation of each component is expressed in terms of functional constraints and the evidence is comprised of a set of measurements together with probabilistic judgments about components' failure rates. The output of each faulty component was assumed uniformly distributed over its feasible range (as in Section 5.4), which permitted them to rate explanations (called candidates) using Bayesian analysis. If no assumptions were made about the behavior of faulty components, the model would remain incomplete, and the probabilities computed by the ATMS would be exactly the D-S belief functions (see Exercise 9.1). Falkenhainer and D'Ambrosio's systems employ local approximations, closer in spirit to the extensional scheme discussed in Section 9.1.5. Laskey and [1988] present an ATMS formalism for exact calculation of belief functions, including a correct account of dependencies among propositions due to shared antecedents.

In the original presentation of incidence calculus [Bundy 1985], propositions were not assigned numerical degrees of belief but instead were given a list of labels called *incidences*, representing a set of situations in which the propositions are true. Attaching such labels to some propositions should enable us to compute lower-bounding and upper-bounding labels for every other proposition in the system – lower bounds representing situations in which the proposition is definitely true and upper bounds representing situations in which the proposition could be true. Thus, incidences are semantically equivalent to the ATMS notion of "environments", and it is in this symbolic form that incidence calculus was first implemented by Bundy. Our treatment of incidence calculus as a simulation method for computing belief functions (Section 10.2.3) was reconstructed from Bundy's representation of incidences as bit strings, which amounts to replacing the space of environments (or switch positions) by a representative sample.

Our treatment of probabilistic logic in Section 9.3 follows that of Nilsson [1986], although the basic idea of using probabilistic bounds goes back to Good [1950] and was also studied by Smith [1961] and de Finetti [1974]. A mechanism for propagating probabilistic bounds on sentences has been implemented in INFERNO [Quinlan 1983], which can be regarded as a local approximation to Nilsson's probabilistic logic.

In addition to generating bounds and verifying consistency, Nilsson also aspires to represent the set of constrained distributions by a single distribution function attaining *maximum entropy* (ME) (see Section 10.2.3). However, computational techniques for finding a maximum-entropy distribution [Cheeseman 1983] are usually intractable, and the resulting distribution is often at odds with our perception of causation. For example, if we first find an ME distribution for a set of n variables $X_1, ..., X_n$ and then add one of their consequences, Y, we find that the ME distribution $P(x_1, ..., x_n, y)$ constrained by the conditional probability $P(y \mid x_1, ..., x_n)$ changes the marginal distribution of the X variables (see Exercise 10.2), and introduces new dependencies among them. This is at variance with the common conception of causation, whereby hypothesizing the existence of unobserved future events is presumed to leave unaltered our beliefs about past and present events. This phenomenon was communicated to me by Norm Dalkey and is discussed in Hunter [1989].

Chapter 9 includes no treatment of fuzzy sets and fuzzy logic [Goodman and Nguyen 1985; Yager et al. 1987]. This omission reflects a decision to limit the scope of this book to probabilistic formalisms and their derivatives. Fuzzy logic is orthogonal to probability theory – it focuses on the ambiguities in decribing events, rather than the uncertainty about the occurrence or nonoccurrence of events.

The author's personal preferences among competing uncertainty formalisms are expressed in the summary of Section 9.3.

The role of belief functions in reasoning systems is discussed in Chapter 6 of Shafer and Pearl [*Readings in Uncertain Reasoning*, Morgan Kaufmann, 1990] and in a special issue of the *International Journal of Approximate Reasoning* [Vol. 4, 5/6, 1990].

The probability of provability interpretation of the D-S theory (alternatively, the sampled-assumptions interpretation[1]) turned out useful to many researchers. It facilitated numerical assessments of ATMS conclusions[2], as well as symbolic[3] and Monte Carlo[4] methods of calculating belief functions. It also provides the basis for extending the theory to dependent evidence and nonpropositional logics[4] (see Section 9.2.3.). Thus, it appears that the probability of provability interpretation will become the canonical AI model for understanding belief functions.

The major focus of current debates is on whether generic domain knowledge (e.g., if-then rules) can adequately be encoded as a single belief function, rather than constraints over a family of such functions. Encoding if-then rules as randomized material implications seems to produce the desired behavior in some cases (see Exercise 9.5.e.) but fails to handle specificity (see top of page 449), reasoning-by-cases (Exercise 9.5.a.) and causal relations (Exercise 9.5.c.). Additional concerns revolve around the compatibility of belief functions with rational decisions (see Exercises 9.3., and 9.5.d., for violation of the hypothetical middle rule) and their insensitivity to repeated independent observations (Exercise 9.5.b.).

---

[1] Pearl, J. 1990a. Which is more believable, the probably provable or the provably probable? In *Proceedings, CSCSI-90, Eighth Canadian Conference on Artificial Intelligence*, Ottawa, Canada, May 23-25, 1-7.

[2] Laskey, K.B. and Lehner, P.E. 1989. Assumptions, beliefs and probabilities. *Artificial Intelligence*, 41(1):65-77.

[3] Provan, G. 1989. An analysis of ATMS-based techniques for computing Dempster-Shafer belief functions. In *Proc. Int. Joint Conf. on AI, (IJCAI-89)* 1115-1120.

[4] Wilson, N. 1990. Rules, belief functions and default logic. In Bonissone, P., and Henrion, M., Eds. *Proc. 6th Conference on Uncertainty in AI*, MIT, Cambridge, Mass., August, 443-449.

Exercises

9.1.   **a.**   Under the assumptions of Exercise **5.4**, compute $Bel(X_1 = 0)$ and *Bel (Gate 1 is faulty)*, and compare your results to the posterior probabilities obtained by Bayesian analysis.

       b.   Repeat question **(a)** under the assumption that the behavior of a faulty gate is totally unknown, i.e., cannot be specified probabilistically.

       c.   Repeat question **(b)** under the assumption that the failure rate of the gates is also unknown.

9.2.   **a.**   Draw a rule network for Problem **9.1.b** and compute $Bel(x_1 = 0)$ by extensional analysis.

       b.   Draw a rule network for Problem **9.1.b** and compute *Bel (Gate 1 is faulty)* by extensional analysis.

9.3.   **a.**   Treat the normal behavior of the inputs and gates of Exercise **5.4** as assumptions in an ATMS. Find an expression for the labels of the propositions "$X_1 = 0$" and *"Gate 1 is faulty"*.

       b.   Compute the belief functions associated with the two labels of question **(a)**.

9.4.   (After Smets [1988], pp. 284). Peter, Paul and Mary are three suspects in a murder case, exactly one of them has committed the crime. Evidence 1 provides equal support for the murderer being a male or a female, i.e., $m_1(Peter \vee Paul) = m_1(Mary) = 0.5$. Evidence 2 is "Peter cannot be the killer" (he was in Africa), i.e., $m_2(Paul \vee Mary) = 1$.

       a.   Combine the two pieces of evidence and calculate *Bel* and *Pl* for each of the three suspects.

       b.   Solve the problem probabilistically, assuming equal prior probabilities for each of the suspects and translating the two pieces of evidence into likelihood ratios (as in Sections 2.2 and 7.1).

       c.   Discuss the differences between and plausibility of the answers to (*a*) and (*b*), and explain why some researchers (falsely) consider this an example where a probabilistic approach leads to paradoxical results.

9.5. For each of the following problems, compute the corresponding belief function and probability interval. Discuss the plausibility of your answers.

    a. (After Smets) Suppose we have 3 potential killers, A, B or C. First, a killer is chosen by some undisclosed criterion, then the chosen killer selects his weapon by an independent random process with $P(gun) = 0.2$ and $P(knife) = 0.8$. What is your "belief" that the killer will use a gun.

    b. Referring to the 3-prisoners story, imagine Prisoner A handing the same letter to each of 1000 different jailers, none knowing about the others, and all naming B as one who will be spared. What is A's "belief" that he will be executed.

    c. We are given the following rules:

        1. If a person is intelligent then he is popular, with certainty m=.90.

        2. If a person is bold then he is not popular, with certainty m=.90.

    John is bold, what is your "belief" that John is not-intelligent?

    d. What is the "belief" that the output Y of an exclusive-OR gate is ON, given that one of the inputs, X_1, has a 50% chance of being ON, while the other input, X_2, is known only to be independent of X_1.

    e. We are given the following rules:

        1. Typically birds fly, with certainty m=.99

        2. Typically flying animals are light, with certainty m=.99

    What is the "belief" that a yellow bird flies? What is the "belief" that a bird is light? What is the "belief" that a non-flying animal is not a bird?

9.6. Devise a rule network containing $2n$ rules, n propositions, and one premise, such that a proposition c has at least 2^n environments.

Chapter *10*

LOGIC AND PROBABILITY: THE STRANGE CONNECTION

> *Life is the art of drawing sufficient conclusions from insufficient premises.*
> — *Samuel Butler*

10.1 INTRODUCTION TO NONMONOTONIC REASONING

One universal feature of commonsense reasoning is people's readiness to "jump to conclusions" and act on imperfect information. We constantly adopt tentative beliefs about the world, use them as though they were true, then retract them if necessary when new observations arrive. For example, the reader of this book is surely ready to act as though the rest of this chapter is written in English, by the same author and about the same subject, rather than religion or astrology. These expectations are plausible yet not provable from the facts available. If any of these expectations fail to match subsequent observations, the reader's beliefs will undergo revision (perhaps doubting the seriousness of the author or the publisher), and new expectations will take their place to be firmly held until retracted.

In Chapter 5, we modeled the process of belief commitment (i.e., belief acceptance and revision) as part of a policy to adopt a most probable explanation for a body of evidence. There, however, the knowledge base within which the optimization took place was assumed to be probabilistic; the aim of nonmonotonic

467

logic is to give a symbolic, nonnumeric account of the dynamics of belief commitment. Commitment is viewed as a direct transformation between information sentences (e.g., facts and rules) and belief sentences, unmediated by probabilistic considerations. *Nonmonotonic* is a term chosen to emphasize the retraction part of the revision process, contrasting it with classical monotonic logic, where the set of deducible conclusions always grows with added information and new axioms can never overrule previously established theorems.

One common means of jumping to conclusions is by deriving *default assumptions* from "typicality" information: given a commonsense fact of the form "Typically, A's are B's" and an individual x which is an A, conclude "This particular A is B." Because some A's are not B's, this conclusion must be treated as a default assumption or tentative belief about the world, since subsequent observations may yield "This particular A is not a B." The derivation of the belief "This particular A is a B" is a form of plausible reasoning that is often required when conclusions must be drawn from incomplete information. The objective of default logic is to provide a representation for commonsense facts of the form "Typically, A's are B's" and to articulate an appropriate logic to characterize correct reasoning using such facts.

In classical logic, the sentence "If A then B" can be given two interpretations: an *empirical* interpretation, stating that a world in which A and $\neg B$ coexist is an impossibility, and a *procedural* interpretation, stating, "Whenever the truth of A is established, the label *TRUE* can safely and permanently be attached to B." Strictly speaking, a default rule such as "Typically, birds fly," written $Bird(x) \rightarrow Fly(x)$, embodies neither of these interpretations—a world in which some birds do not fly is certainly a possibility, and any license to tag a given bird by a label "fly" may be proven premature by subsequent observations. Still, the formal similarity between hard rules and default rules has prompted researchers to attribute empirical and procedural interpretations to the latter. Researchers in the logicist school have focused on procedural interpretations, viewing $A \rightarrow B$ as a *qualified* license to assert B if certain conditions (e.g., consistency) are met. Researchers in the probabilistic camp have focused on the empirical interpretation, viewing $A \rightarrow B$ as an *elastic* constraint on worlds that does not completely rule out all worlds in which $A \wedge \neg B$ is true but proclaims such worlds to be much less likely than others.

10.1.1 *Reiter's Default Logic*

The default logic proposed by Reiter [1980] is an example of the procedural approach. The approach taken is to distinguish between prototypical facts, such as "Typically, birds fly," and "hard" facts about the world, such as "All birds are animals" or "Tweety is a bird." The former are viewed as ''quasi-rules'' of inference, called *default rules*, which apply to the hard facts and help produce plausible conclusions, using deductive strategies. Since the set of all hard facts cannot completely specify the world, we are left with gaps in our knowledge; the purpose of the default rules is to help fill in those gaps with plausible (though not infallible) conclusions [Reiter and Criscuolo 1983].

Formally, this default logic is based on two types of sentences, D and W, where D is a set of default rules applying to some world being modeled and W is a set of hard facts about that world. The pair $T = (D, W)$ is called a *default theory*. The set(s) of beliefs sanctioned by a default theory is called an *extension* and is interpreted as an acceptable set of beliefs that one may entertain about the world being represented. Default statements are treated not as formulas in a theory, but as procedural rules of inference. For example, the flying bird default is represented by the rule of inference†

$$\frac{Bird(x):Fly(x)}{Fly(x)} . \qquad \textbf{(10.1)}$$

This may be read, "If x is a bird and it can consistently be assumed to fly, then you can infer that x flies." More generally, rule schematas of the following form are permitted:

$$\frac{\alpha(x):\beta(x)}{\gamma(x)} , \qquad \textbf{(10.2)}$$

meaning, "If $\alpha(x)$ holds and $\beta(x)$ can consistently be assumed, then you can infer $\gamma(x)$."

Reiter's approach is to begin with the set of logical sentences W, which represent incomplete knowledge about the world, and use the default rules to create a more complete extension of the theory. For example, if such an incomplete theory contains $Bird(Tweety)$, and if $Fly(Tweety)$ is consistent with the theory, then by the above default schemata for flying birds we can extend this theory by adding $Fly(Tweety)$ to it.

Reiter defines an *extension* of a logical theory as a new logical theory containing W, such that

1) none of the default rules can consistently be applied to obtain a conclusion not already in the extension, and

2) the extension is minimal subject to the first condition.

The first condition guarantees that we have drawn all the consistent default conclusions we can, and the second ensures that we haven't added something to our logical theory for no reason [Ginsberg 1987].††

---

† Actually a set of rules or *rule schemata*, because of the variable x.

†† Reiters' definition is, in fact, more complicated [V. Lifschitz, in conversation]. The conditions above are sufficient for most normal defaults and better illustrate the main idea.

The following example [Reiter 1987b] illustrates the notion of extension. Let a theory $T = (W, D)$ be given by

$$W = \{E, E \supset F\},$$

$$D = \left\{ \frac{E:C}{\neg B} , \frac{F:B}{\neg C} \right\}. \qquad \qquad (10.3)$$

Here E and $E \supset F$ are the two things we know about a world W. The first default can be invoked since C is consistent with W, so we infer $\neg B$. $\neg B$ prevents the second default from applying, so no further inferences are possible. This yields an extension $(W \cup \{\neg B\})^*$. The * symbol indicates that the extension also includes all the logical implications of the sentences in brackets, e.g., $F, E \wedge \neg B$, and all tautologies. The second (and only other) extension $(W \cup \{\neg C\})^*$ is obtained similarly by invoking the second default.

This example demonstrates that extensions are (minimal) *fixed points* of the operator D, namely, that further application of the default rules in D to the sentences in an extension has no effect. It also demonstrates that multiple extensions are possible, each representing different, sometimes even conflicting, sets of beliefs. The perspective adopted on these [Reiter 1980] is that any such extension is a possible belief set for an agent, although one could, as do McDermott and Doyle [1980], insist that an agent's beliefs be defined by the intersection of all extensions.

10.1.2 Problems with Default Logics

It turns out that the general class of default theories is mathematically intractable and that many desirable features of the logic can be obtained only for the class of so-called *normal* default theories, namely, theories in which all defaults have the form

$$\frac{\alpha(x):w(x)}{w(x)}. \qquad \qquad (10.4)$$

Such defaults are extremely common; for example, "Typically, birds fly" would be written

$$\frac{Bird(x) : Fly(x)}{Fly(x)} \qquad \qquad (10.5)$$

without explicating specific conditions $\beta(x)$ under which the inference should be blocked.

MULTIPLE EXTENSIONS

While most naturally occurring defaults are normal, the interactions among such defaults lead to anomalous conclusions. For example, suppose we use normal defaults to express the facts that Tweety is a penguin, that penguins are birds, and that birds typically fly but penguins typically do not. We have

$$W = \{Bird(Tweety), Penguin(x) \supset Bird(x)\}, \qquad (10.6)$$

$$D = \left\{ \frac{Bird(x) : Fly(x)}{Fly(x)}, \frac{Penguin(x) : \neg Fly(x)}{\neg Fly(x)} \right\}. \qquad (10.7)$$

This theory has two extensions,

$$E_1 = (W \cup Fly(Tweety))^* \qquad (10.8)$$

and

$$E_2 = (W \cup \neg Fly(Tweety))^*, \qquad (10.9)$$

depending on which default rule is applied first. The theory provides no machinery for preferring the intended extension E_2 over the anomalous extension E_1, so it encounters the same problem seen in the Dempster-Shafer analysis (Section 9.1.6)—inability to translate the information that penguins are a subclass of birds into preference among extensions. The source of the problem is, again, that the transitivity of the chain $Tweety \rightarrow Bird \rightarrow Fly$ should be blocked in order to endow Tweety with the specific properties of penguins.

To avoid this sort of problem, Reiter and Criscuolo [1981] (and later Etherington and Reiter [1983]) proposed the use of *semi-normal* default rules, i.e., rules of the form

$$\frac{\alpha(x) : \beta(x) \wedge w(x)}{w(x)}. \qquad (10.10)$$

In our example, the first default rule in D should be replaced by

$$\frac{Bird(x) : \neg Penguin(x) \wedge Fly(x)}{Fly(x)}, \qquad (10.11)$$

stating that in the absence of information to the contrary, birds fly unless they are penguins. This rule will be blocked by $Penguin(Tweety)$, thus preventing extension E_1 from evolving. This remedy requires the enumeration of all exceptions within the default rules themselves and might result in unwieldy descriptions when large problems are considered.

Touretzky [1984] noticed that the use of semi-normal defaults is unnecessary when there is enough information in the system to guarantee a preference for one extension over another. Touretzky argued that a more natural approach to this problem is to prioritize the default rules based on a concept he called *inferential distance*. The essential idea is that default rules about subclasses should override default rules about the superclasses that contain them. More generally, if one describes property inheritance rules as directed arcs in a network (called an *inheritance network*), the inferential distance criterion states (recursively) that a chain of rules $x_1 \to x_2 \to x_3 \to \cdots \to x_{n-1} \to x_n$ is *certified* if it *preempts* all its opposing chains $x_1 \to y_1 \to y_2 \to \cdots \to y_k \to \neg x_n$, i.e., if there is a chain from x_{n-1} to some y such that $x_1 \to \cdots \to x_{n-1} \to \cdots \to y$ is certified by the theory. In our example, the chain *Tweety* $\to$ *Bird* $\to$ *Fly* will be preempted by the chain *Tweety* $\to$ *Penguin* $\to$ $\neg$*Fly*, because the inference *Penguin* $\to$ *Bird* is certified by the theory. The application of this criterion amounts to automatically replacing normal default rules by semi-normal rules when the information is available.

REASONING BY CASES

Another problem with the procedural approach represented by Reiter's logic is that it is incapable of reasoning "by cases." For example, suppose we obtain the empirical rule that male birds fly (written $b \wedge m \to f$) and a separate empirical rule that female birds fly (written $b \wedge \neg m \to f$). Suppose further that we know Tweety is a bird (written b) of unspecified gender. This gives rise to the default theory

$$W = \{b\} \quad D = \{b \wedge m \to f, b \wedge \neg m \to f\}, \quad (10.12)$$

which has no extensions aside from W because none of the rules' prerequisites ever gets satisfied in isolation. Thus, the natural conclusion that Tweety flies ($b \to f$) is not in *any* extension.

This, together with the tolerance to anomalous conclusions (e.g., Eq. (10.8)), brings into question the adequacy of extensions as representatives of "acceptable sets of beliefs that one may hold about an incompletely specified world" [Reiter 1980]. One argument supporting the notion of extensions is that they do not presume to capture *all* conclusions implicit in the logic, but only those that emanate from limited, simple modes of reasoning. Inferences based on disjunctions or counterfactual or conditional proofs are hard for people and machine alike to integrate and thus are not the focus of default theories.† In Section 10.2, we will show that reasoning by cases can be incorporated as an integral part of the default logic.

REASONING ABOUT DEFAULTS

Because the defaults are treated as inference rules rather than object-level formulas, defaults cannot be reasoned about. That is, one cannot deduce new

---

† Jon Doyle and Ronald Loui, in conversation.

defaults from old ones. For example, from "Normally, canaries are yellow" and "Yellow things are never green," we cannot conclude "Normally, canaries are never green" [Reiter 1987b]. The result is that many patterns of reasoning need to be explicated in detail if we are to draw plausible conclusions. For example, from "Normally, birds fly" and "Tim does not fly," we cannot conclude that Tim is not likely to be a bird, unless one states explicitly, "Normally, nonflying objects are nonbirds."

An immediate consequence of this weakness of Reiter's logic, as well as other procedure-based nonmonotonic theories, is that it does not provide a means for checking the internal consistency of the knowledge base. For example, if we add to the basic rule "Birds fly" the contrary statement "Birds do not fly," together with the fact that Tweety is a bird, two legitimate extensions emerge. In one extension Tweety appears as a bird that flies; in the second, as a bird that does not fly— similar extensions are obtained if Tweety is a penguin. Thus, the logic does not distinguish between exceptions (e.g., "Penguins are birds that do not fly") and contradictions (e.g., "Typically, birds do and do not fly"). While such obvious contradictions can easily be removed from the database, more subtle ones might escape detection (e.g., "Birds fly," "Birds are feathered animals," "Feathered animals are birds," "Feathered animals do not fly)." Section 10.2 provides a criterion for detecting inconsistencies, as distinct from exceptions.

10.1.3 Empirical vs. Procedural Semantics in Default Reasoning

Researchers in nonmonotonic logic are adamant about disassociating default reasoning from any statistical or empirical interpretation. Reiter and Criscuolo [1983], for example, were careful to distinguish two senses of the sentence "Most A's are B's":

> It is important to note that not all senses of the word "most" lead to default assumptions. One can distinguish two such senses:
>
> 1. A purely statistical connotation, as in "Most voters prefer Carter". Here, "most" is being used exclusively in the sense of "the majority of". This setting does not lead to default assumptions: given that Maureen is a voter one would not want to assume that Maureen prefers Carter.† Default logic makes no attempt to represent or reason with such statistical facts.

---

† Reiter and Criscuolo's example reminded this author of a personal experience in a Parisian bookstore a few years ago. One of the book browsers asked curiously, "Where are you from?" Upon receiving the reply "From America," he said with disgust, "You Reagan hoodlum...." Thus, it appears that the statistical and prototypical senses are not easily distinguishable when it comes to default reasoning.

2. A prototypical sense, as in "Most birds fly". True, there is a statistical connotation here—the majority of birds do fly—but in addition a characteristic of a prototypical or normal bird is being described in the following sense: given a bird Polly, one is prepared to assume that it flies unless one has reasons to the contrary. It is towards such prototypical settings that default logic is addressed.

Before getting into the formal probabilistic interpretation of such sentences, it should be made very clear that probability theory, too, is concerned only with the second, prototypical sense of the sentence: given a bird Polly, lacking more specific properties, it is highly likely that Polly flies. The sentence "The majority of birds fly" represents factual information that is observably either true or false but is outside the probability model itself. Counting information of this sort may help decide what properties we dare attribute to individual objects in the domain but is not what the sentences in the language are about.

In Section 10.2 we shall show that the two senses of the word *most* share many interesting properties; in fact, the empirical or statistical sense may provide the semantic coherence that theories based on purely prototypical settings lack. While prototypical interpretations model the conventions used in human communication and knowledge organization, the statistical interpretation accounts for the empirical forces that help shape these conventions. In some sense, the relation between the two interpretations resembles the interplay between medieval astronomy and modern physics. The astronomers labored to provide a phenomenological account of celestial observations, while the physicist attempts to trace these observations to some underlying physical principles, such as gravitational fields and the laws of motion.

IS EVERY BIRD A TYPICAL BIRD?

What, then, is the probabilistic interpretation of "Typically, birds fly"? Does it refer to *all* birds? Most birds? This particular bird? Or some mythical "typical" bird? The interpretation expounded in this chapter (to be further elaborated in Section 10.2) is that the sentence translates directly into the universal formula

$$\forall(x) \ P[Fly(x)\,|\,Bird(x)] = HIGH. \qquad (10.13)$$

Thus, the referent of the sentence is every *individual* bird in the universe and, in fact, each and every object x that we care to talk about.

This might sound a bit paradoxical when we think of dead birds, baby birds, or even more disturbingly, our good friend Tweety who—for no apparent reason—simply cannot fly. However, when we read carefully what Eq. (10.13) actually asserts about Tweety, it seems quite reasonable. Substituting $x = Tweety$ in Eq. (10.13) yields

$$P[Fly(Tweety) \mid Bird(Tweety)] = HIGH, \tag{10.14}$$

which means that Tweety is likely to fly, given that all we know about Tweety is that she is a bird. Should we have any other information about Tweety, say that she is broiled or just plain moody, we are obliged to include this information in the conditioning context; Eq. (10.14) would then become invalid and $P(Fly(Tweety) \mid Bird(Tweety), Broiled(Tweety))$ would be evaluated instead.

This treatment of the universal quantifier is at variance with its classical use as a syntactic license to substitute any object for x, regardless of what else we know about the object (Schubert, personal communication). However, since classical logic does not possess an operator equivalent to the conditioning bar (|) in probability, we are at liberty to modify the traditional treatment of the universal quantifier, whenever it contains a conditioning bar within its scope.

Another way to reconcile this difference is to redefine the referent of the sentence in Eq. (10.13) to be, not the individuals in the domain, but rather the properties *Fly* and *Bird* themselves. In other words, the sentence asserts that a certain relationship holds between the *outcomes of two procedures*: One designed to test the birdness of x, the other testing its Flying abilities. Outcomes of tests are events in the best tradition of probability theory, and x, in this case, does not stand for actual objects in the world but for any conceivable object, past and future. This interpretation is more in the spirit of Pollock's notion of "nomic" probabilities [Pollock 1974].

Probability theory, unlike default logics, exhibits an almost paranoid aversion toward extending class properties to subclasses. For example, given that Tweety is a red bird and that birds fly, we cannot automatically infer that Tweety can fly, because $P(f \mid b, r)$ cannot be derived from (or even constrained by) $P(f \mid b)$. While default logics normally presume that red birds fly unless it is proven otherwise, probability theory reserves all judgment unless assurances are given that redness is irrelevant to flying.

Yet despite this skeptical attitude toward subclasses, probability theory extends full inheritance rights to individuals, as shown in Eqs. (10.13) and (10.14). Although the substitution $x = Tweety$ in Eq. (10.13) can be construed as a change of context prompted by an added property

$$P[Fly(x) \mid Bird(x), NAME(x) = Tweety], \tag{10.15}$$

the property *NAME* is treated differently than all other properties, e.g., *Color*. While the arrival of color information would require a reevaluation of

$$P[Fly(x) \mid Bird(x), Color(x) = Red], \tag{10.16}$$

NAME is presumed to be a "faceless" property, permitting substitution without change of context.

This feature can in fact be taken as a *definition* of a name, i.e., a limitation on the types of properties with which we are allowed to distinguish individual objects. $NAME(x) = a$ is a proposition that is true for exactly one object in the domain and that satisfies

$$\forall Q, \ \forall (x) \ P[Q(x) | NAME(x) = a] = P[Q(x)] \,, \qquad \textbf{(10.17)}$$

where Q is every predicate that obtains probability values. With this understanding, the substitution

$$x = a, \ \text{if} \ NAME(x) = a,$$

licensed by Eq. (10.13), should no longer be objectionable.

Schubert [1988] has provided an interesting argument against the universal interpretation (Eq. (10.13)) of probabilistic statements. His argument involves an experiment in which a card is drawn at random from an ordinary deck, thus giving the ace of spades a 1/52 probability of being chosen. According to Schubert, this probability statement cannot be interpreted as a universal sentence

$$\forall (x) \ P(Ace \ of \ spades(x) | In\text{-}deck(x)) = 1/52 \qquad \textbf{(10.18)}$$

because it obviously does not hold for $x = $ the ace of spades (or for any other card in the deck).

Eq. (10.18) appears strikingly paradoxical because we normally identify cards by their suit, using the phrase "ace of spades" to denote both the property *ace of spades* and the individual card having this property. In principle, however, the paradox should hold also when we identify cards by other means, say by their serial number, weight, or current position in the deck. After all, each card either is or is not the ace of spades, so Eq. (10.18) should yield either 1 or 0, but not 1/52. Still, the sentence $P(Ace \ of \ spades(x) \ | \ Top\text{-}of\text{-}deck \ (x)) = 1/52$ appears more benign, possibly because *Top-of-deck* is only a temporary property of a card, and as such will seldom be used for card identification.

The ace of spades paradox is resolved by adhering to the rule of context-dependent substitutions. The license to substitute $x = a$ in Eq. (10.18) calls for augmenting the context by everything else we know about a and, if *Ace of spade(a)* is true, we must evaluate a new formula,

$$P(Ace \ of \ spades(a) | In\text{-}deck(a), \ Ace \ of \ spade \ (a)) \,,$$

which yields the correct answer, 1 (see also [Cheeseman 1988]).

CONVENTIONS VS. NORMS

Conventions, as opposed to statistical *norms* , are currently being touted as the defining character of default assumptions in the logic-based literature. McCarthy [1986], for example, writes:

> Neither (1) [communication conventions] nor (2) [data retrieval conventions] requires that most birds can fly. Should it happen that most birds that are subject to the communication or about which information is requested from the database cannot fly, the convention may lead to inefficiency but not incorrectness.

Reiter [1987] makes a similar disclaimer:

> Now, in certain settings a statistical reading is warranted. Regardless of my concept of a prototypical bird, if I find myself lost and hungry in a remote part of the world, my design of a bird-catching trap will depend upon my observation of the frequency with which the local birds fly. But to appeal exclusively to a statistical reading for plausible inference is to misunderstand the intended purpose of nonmonotonic reasoning.
>
> In a wide variety of settings, nonmonotonic reasoning is necessary precisely because the information associated with such settings requires that certain *conventions* be respected. Such conventions may be explicit, as in the closed world assumption for the representation of negative information in databases. More commonly, these conventions are implicit, as in various principles of cooperative communication of information where it is understood by all participants that the informant is conveying all of the relevant information. Any relevant item of information not so conveyed is justifiably (and nonmonotonically) assumed false ...
>
> It would seem that with respect to such conventions, statistical reasoning has *no role to play* whatsoever [italics added].

McCarthy and Reiter seem to be emphasizing that default sentences such as "Typically, birds fly" are used for many different purposes, the least significant of which is to report what proportion of birds fly. The more significant usage, at least in AI, lies in the context of communication agreements that go something like this: "You and I agree that whenever I want you to conclude that some bird does not fly, I will say so explicitly; otherwise you can presume it does fly." Here the purpose of the agreement is to guarantee that in subsequent conversations, the informed draws correct conclusions, i.e., matching those intended by the informer.

The multifunctional nature of default reasoning is clearly beyond dispute, yet diversity of use does not imply diversity of means. To suggest that a logic serving one use be exempt from the norms imposed by another use amounts to suggesting that each use be served by a separate logic. We would have one logic for hunting birds, one for talking about birds, and, perhaps a few more (one for storing information about birds, one for checking how much we know about birds, etc.) Given that we still do not have an adequate logic for even one nonmonotonic use, a more productive approach would be to first focus on the commonality among the various uses and conventions and only when this becomes well-formed and understood to attend to their specific peculiarities.

While the word *convention* connotes an element of arbitrariness and choice, most man-made conventions do respect certain norms of coherence, reflecting the statistical reality that compelled the design and use of these conventions. There is a compelling economical advantage, for example, to the convention of printing airline schedules with flights that do exist, as opposed to flights that do not exist. It is a simple consideration of economy, or "efficiency" in McCarthy's terms, in a world that provides much fewer flights than nonflights. In other words, since our environment plays the major role in determining the conventions we adopt, the statistical structure of the former should provide valuable information about the logical structure of the latter. The mere acknowledgement of this empirical origin dictates that certain universal *norms* be respected by all conventions of reasoning, norms that tell us, for example, when one convention is incompatible with another, not because they lead to contradictions (those can presumably be resolved by meta-conventions or some other means), but because there could be no environment in which the two conventions together would make economical sense.

For example, suppose we are drafting an agreement on how to communicate about birds. We could conceivably come up with the following three-part convention:

1. Each time I mention a raven, you can presume it is black; if it is not black, I will say so explicitly.

2. Each time I mention a black raven, you can presume it can fly; if it cannot fly, I will say so explicitly.

3. Each time I mention a raven, you can presume it does not fly; if it does fly, I will say so explicitly.

This convention corresponds to the following default rules:

$$R_1: \quad r \to b.$$
$$R_2: \quad r \land b \to f.$$
$$R_3: \quad r \to \neg f. \tag{10.19}$$

McCarthy is right: there is nothing about any item of this agreement that requires that most ravens can fly or that most ravens do not fly—conventions, remember, are not bound by the laws of proportions. Yet there is something clearly irrational in the agreement above, and assuming we wish to capture ordinary human discourse, the agreement should be forbidden by any logic of common sense. At the very least, our logic should be allowed to fail or err given pathological agreements of that sort.

What, precisely, is wrong with the agreement? At first glance it appears that the trouble is that the third item, $r \to \neg f$, is contrary to what one would naturally tend to infer from the first two items: from r and (R_1) we can infer $r \wedge b$, then using (R_2) we conclude f. Thus, from r we can conclude f, contrary to R_3. But that cannot be where the trouble lies, because every rule that conveys an exception stands, by definition, contrary to inferences that would otherwise be drawn from other rules, and exceptions are at the heart of commonsense reasoning. For example, had R_2 been changed to $b \to f$, we would also infer (chaining (R_1) and (R_2)) that ravens fly $(r \to f)$, contrary to (R_3). Yet the agreement as a whole would appear perfectly rational, reflecting a world in which black things normally fly while ravens, being a special kind of black thing, do not fly.

What makes our original agreement appear so irrational is exactly the presumption that communication conventions are designed for economy and efficiency. It so happens that there is no conceivable environment in which it would make economical sense to agree on all three items together. Assuming we gain communication efficiency by agreeing on any two items from the list, we can always increase our efficiency by reversing the policy described by the third item (this will be proved in Section 10.2).

What does this have to do with commonsense reasoning? After all, we are not in the business of designing communication equipment, so why should we concern ourselves so much with efficiency? Supposedly, we should care not about the design of the conventions but about how to interpret messages *correctly*, in compliance with a given convention. The purpose of nonmonotonic logic, in this view, is only to provide a criterion for deciding whether messages are interpreted according to the habits and conventions adopted in ordinary discourse, no matter how inefficient or capricious they appear to be.

Unfortunately, we are still at a stage of research where we do not have a formal description of the habits that govern natural discourse. All we have are isolated instances of such habits (as revealed by consulting intuition), from which we attempt to extract general laws and principles. At this stage, any information regarding the origin or purpose of these habits should be carefully exploited to add a new piece to the general picture. Consideration of economy and efficiency offers such information.

A metaphor might help illustrate this point. Assume you are trying to discover the algorithm that controls traffic lights in some foreign city. You could try several random algorithms and check them against observations, or you could make your job easier and assume that the traffic lights, instead of being wired arbitrarily, were designed by thoughtful individuals for the purpose of transporting vehicles quickly and safely. This assumption may be wrong in some cities, but it will help put a sense of coherence into a collection of rules that otherwise might appear chaotic and capricious. For instance, it may help you discover quickly that no two lights at any given intersection may turn green at the same time.

The traffic lights of default reasoning have also been designed with a purpose in mind. Moreover, since the environment that default conventions were designed to serve is governed by the laws of proportions, the logic of defaults can be expected to mirror the logic of proportions, i.e., probability theory. Since probability theory is accessible, coherent, and well understood, it should be consulted to reveal the intricacies of the logic of defaults.

Even if one takes literally Reiter's statement that "it would seem that with respect to such conventions, statistical reasoning has no role to play whatsoever," it would still be counterproductive to ignore statistical considerations altogether. Statistical analysis can provide the precise criteria for determining which patterns of nonmonotonic reasoning are dictated by normality considerations and which are products of cultural conformity or, perhaps, arbitrary habits.

It is also hard to believe that the human mind would adopt two types of logics, one for hunting birds (statistic-based defaults) and the other for talking about birds (convention-based defaults). A decade of AI debate on whether the sentence "Birds fly" should be interpreted statistically or procedurally attests to the obscurity of this distinction. It is more reasonable to assume that reasoning patterns designed to handle communication conventions have evolved *on top* of those designed to handle empirical needs, and if this is the case, the axioms governing the latter should be adopted as canonical norms for all nonmonotonic logics.

In Section 10.2 we shall see that these norms can be encapsulated in just three simple axioms. For mnemonic purposes we shall describe these axioms using our black raven example:

1. *Triangularity*—if ravens are black and ravens fly, then black ravens fly:

$$r \rightarrow b, \; r \rightarrow f \implies b \wedge r \rightarrow f. \qquad \textbf{(10.20}a\textbf{)}$$

2. *Bayes*—if ravens are black and black ravens fly, then ravens fly:

$$r \rightarrow b, \; r \wedge b \rightarrow f \implies r \rightarrow f. \qquad \textbf{(10.20}b\textbf{)}$$

3. *Disjunction*—if black ravens fly and non-black ravens fly, then ravens fly:

$$r \wedge b \rightarrow f, \; r \wedge \neg b \rightarrow f \implies r \rightarrow f. \qquad \textbf{(10.20}c\textbf{)}$$

These axioms, or rules of inference, are sound and complete if one interprets the default statement $a \rightarrow b$ to mean "Almost all a's are b's," where by "almost all" we mean that the conditional probability $P(b \mid a)$ is arbitrarily close to 1, short of actually being 1.

The triangularity axiom tells us that a subclass (black ravens) is authorized to inherit the properties of its superclass (ravens) when the subclass is dominant. We satisfied such an axiom in Section 9.1.6 when we noticed that Dempster-Shafer analysis (as well as truth-maintenance systems) can endow Tweety the penguin with flying capability, on account of Tweety being a bird. The triangularity axiom now exempts penguin-birds from inheriting any of the flying habits of typical birds, exactly because penguin-birds are the dominant group of penguins.

The Bayes axiom asserts that a superclass (ravens) may inherit the properties of its dominant subclasses (black ravens). The disjunction axiom corresponds to what we called *reasoning by cases* in Section 10.1.2.

It is not hard to see that each of these axioms is sound in the sense that whenever their premises hold with high (conditional) probability, so do their consequences. What is remarkable, though, is that the three axioms are also *sufficient,* namely, there is no general almost-all law that is not derivable from the three axioms [Adams 1975]. A formal definition of the almost-all semantics and further elaboration of its logic and applications are given in the next section. We shall also see that these axioms constitute only the very basic norms of plausible reasoning and should be augmented by additional inference rules expressing the notion of relevance (or independence). Because of the soundness property, every communication convention that violates any of these axioms is bound to exhibit irrational behavior, the reason being that if any of the axioms is violated, then regardless of the statistical environment in which the convention is to be used, at least one of the convention components could be reversed to yield substantial gains in efficiency. This was demonstrated earlier using a convention that violated the triangularity axiom, but one can easily imagine conventions that would violate the other axioms or any combination thereof.

10.2 PROBABILISTIC SEMANTICS FOR DEFAULT REASONING

We consider a default theory $T = <F, \Delta>$ in the form of a database containing two types of sentences: factual sentences (F) and default statements (Δ). The factual sentences assign properties to specific individuals; for example, $p(a)$ asserts that individual a has the property p. The default statements are of the type "p's are typically q's," written $p(x) \rightarrow q(x)$ or simply $p \rightarrow q$, which is short for saying, "Any individual x having property p typically has property q." The properties $p, q, r, ...$ can be complex Boolean formulas of some atomic predicates $p_1, p_2, ..., p_n$, with x as their only free variable, but no ground default statements (e.g., $p(a) \rightarrow q(a)$) are allowed in F and no compound defaults (e.g., $p \rightarrow (q \rightarrow r)$) are allowed in Δ. Generic facts, e.g., $\forall(x)\, p(x)$, will be written as default statements $T \rightarrow p(x)$, where T is the universal-truth symbol. The default statement $S' : p \rightarrow \neg q$ will be called the *denial* of $S : p \rightarrow q$.

The exclusion of ground defaults from F somewhat restricts our language, but in prototypical reasoning these restrictions are not too severe. Defaults pertaining to a specific individual, e.g., $p(a) \rightarrow q(a)$, can in effect be sanctioned by instantiating some generic rule schemata $c(x) \wedge p(x) \rightarrow q(x)$ to $x = a$, where $c(a)$ is a predicate specifying any unique properties of a. For example, the normal behavior $Bird(a) \rightarrow Fly(a)$ can clearly be expressed as an instantiation of $Bird(x) \rightarrow Fly(x)$, and the more individualistic behavior $Happy(a) \rightarrow Cry(a)$ can be expressed as a combination of a generic default schemata, $Strange(x) \wedge Happy(x) \rightarrow Cry(x)$, and a ground formula, $Strange(a)$.

For clarity, no distinction will be made between "soft" statements such as "Typically, birds fly" and "hard" statements such as "All birds are animals."† We shall see that the essential characteristics of default (e.g., preference toward subclass specificity) are common to both hard and soft statements.

Our task is to draw plausible but defeasible conclusions from the database T. For example, from $T_1 = \langle Bird(a), Bird(x) \rightarrow Fly(x) \rangle$ we wish to conclude $Fly(a)$, and from $T_2 = \langle Penguin(a), Bird(a), Penguin(x) \rightarrow Bird(x), Penguin(x) \rightarrow \neg Fly(x), Bird(x) \rightarrow Fly(x) \rangle$ we expect to conclude $\neg Fly(a)$. For that purpose, we now establish probabilistic semantics for what is meant by *plausible*.

10.2.1 ε-semantics

The language within which we phrase input facts and conclusions is purely propositional: the propositions in F provide a partial description of an individual a, and the conclusions provide propositional extensions of a's description. The default statements in Δ are nonpropositional, as they involve the arrow $\rightarrow$ connecting two propositional formulas. Following Adams [1975], we shall call the language of propositional formulas the *factual language* (L) and the set of default statements the *conditional extension* of L.

Every sentence in L corresponds to a set of possible *worlds*, where a world is a complete description of a typical individual in the domain, i.e., a conjunction of all the atomic properties. For example, the sentence $Bird(a) \wedge \neg Fly(a)$ denotes the set of worlds in which both $Bird(a)$ and $\neg Fly(a)$ hold. Since some worlds are obviously more typical than others, we can express the differences by assigning probability weights to the set of possible worlds; this, in turn, defines a probability distribution P over the formulas of L.

We view Δ as a set of specifications for P, and F as a body of evidence (about the actual description of a) upon which P is to be conditioned. Instead of a complete specification, Δ imposes restrictions on P, in the form of extreme conditional probabilities, infinitesimally distant from 0 or from 1. Thus, the

---

† For a full treatment of this distinction, see Goldszmidt and Pearl (footnote (5), p. 517).

sentence $Bird(x) \rightarrow Fly(x)$ stands for $P(Fly(x) \mid Bird(x)) \geq 1 - \varepsilon$; namely, for every x in the domain, if all we know about x is that it-is a bird, then x is very likely to have flying ability. ε is understood to stand for a quantity that can be made arbitrarily small, short of actually being zero.

The conclusions we wish to draw from Δ are formulas in L that, given the input F and the restrictions Δ, are forced to acquire extremely high probabilities if ε is made very small. In particular, if F contains the sentences $\{f_1, f_2, ..., f_n\}$, then a propositional formula r qualifies as a plausible conclusion of T whenever the restrictions in Δ force P to exhibit $P(r \mid f_1, f_2, ..., f_n) = 1 - O(\varepsilon)$.†

DEFINITION: *Let Δ_ε stand for the set of ε-bound conditional probability interpretations of the defaults in Δ, i.e.,*

$$\Delta_\varepsilon = \{P(q \mid p) \geq 1 - \varepsilon : p \rightarrow q \in \Delta\}. \qquad (10.21)$$

*A sentence r is a **plausible conclusion** of a theory $T = <F, \Delta>$, written $F \models_\Delta r$, if every P that satisfies Eq. (10.21) also satisfies*

$$P(r \mid F) \geq 1 - O(\varepsilon), \qquad (10.22)$$

*An alternative way of reading $F \models_\Delta r$ is "r is a plausible conclusion of F **in the context** of Δ."*

For example, we shall demonstrate how accepting

$$\Delta = \{Penguin \rightarrow \neg Fly, \, Bird \rightarrow Fly, \, Penguin \rightarrow Bird\} \qquad (10.23)$$

renders $\neg Fly(Tweety)$ a plausible conclusion of

$$F = \{Penguin(Tweety), Bird(Tweety)\}. \qquad (10.24)$$

Our problem is to determine the range of $P(Fly \mid Bird, Penguin)$ permitted by the sentences in Δ_ε. More abstractly, we wish to examine the degree to which the probability $P(f \mid b, p)$ is constrained by the inputs

$$\Delta_\varepsilon = \{P(f \mid b) \geq 1 - \varepsilon, \, P(f \mid p) \leq \varepsilon, \, P(b \mid p) \geq 1 - \varepsilon\}. \qquad (10.25)$$

---

† $O(\varepsilon)$ stands for any function $g(\varepsilon)$ such that $\lim_{\varepsilon \to 0} g(\varepsilon) = 0$; in other words, for every $\delta > 0$ there exists a $\varepsilon > 0$ such that $g(\varepsilon) \leq \delta$.

Conditioning $P(f|p)$ on both b and $\neg b$, we obtain

$$P(f|p) = P(f|p, b)\, P(b|p) + P(f|p, \neg b)\, [1 - P(b|p)]$$
$$\geq P(f|p, b)\, P(b|p)\,.$$

Thus,

$$P(f|p, b) \leq \frac{P(f|p)}{P(b|p)} \leq \frac{\varepsilon}{1-\varepsilon} = O(\varepsilon),$$

hence

$$P(\neg f|p, b) = 1 - O(\varepsilon). \qquad \qquad \textbf{(10.26)}$$

We see that the conclusion *Penguin* $\wedge$ *Bird* $\rightarrow$ $\neg Fly$ is entailed by Δ even if penguins are not regarded as a strict subclass of birds—the "soft" condition $P(b|p) \geq 1 - \varepsilon$ suffices.

Note the nonmonotonicity permitted by the conditional probability interpretation of default statements. Whereas in monotonic logic $p \wedge b \supset f$ is a logical consequence of $b \supset f$, it is now perfectly consistent for *Bird* $\rightarrow$ *Fly* and *Penguin* $\wedge$ *Bird* $\rightarrow$ $\neg Fly$ to coexist. From *Bird*(a) alone we can conclude *Fly*(a), and upon learning that a is also a penguin, *Bird*(a) $\wedge$ *Penguin*(a), we can retract the conclusion and assert $\neg Fly(a)$. Unlike interpretations based on the material implication, the conditional probability interpretation of the default statement $p \rightarrow q$ permits a total reevaluation of the probability of q whenever the context p is enriched by new properties. Note also that the desired conclusion is obtained without having to state (as in circumscription) that penguins are *abnormal* birds; this can be derived from the input (see Eq.(10.33) and Example 2).

It is convenient to characterize the set of conclusions sanctioned by a theory $T = \langle F, \Delta \rangle$ in terms of the set of default statements that are ε-*entailed* by Δ.

DEFINITION: *Let* $\mathcal{P}_{\Delta, \varepsilon}$ *stand for the set of distributions licensed by* Δ *for any given* ε, *i.e.*,

$$\mathcal{P}_{\Delta, \varepsilon} = \left\{ P : P(v|u) \geq 1 - \varepsilon \quad \text{and} \quad P(u) > 0 \ \text{ if } \ u \rightarrow v \in \Delta \right\}. \qquad \textbf{(10.27)}$$

A default statement $S: p \rightarrow q$ *is said to be* ε-**entailed**† *by* Δ, *written* $\Delta \vdash_\varepsilon S$, *if every distribution* $P \in \mathcal{P}_{\Delta, \varepsilon}$ *satisfies* $P(q|p) = 1 - O(\varepsilon)$ *(i.e., for every* $\delta > 0$ *there exists an* $\varepsilon > 0$ *such that every* $P \in \mathcal{P}_{\Delta, \varepsilon}$ *would satisfy* $P(q|p) \geq 1 - \delta$).

---

† Adams [1975] called this *p-entailed*, but ε-*entailed* distinguishes this better from weaker forms of probabilistic entailment (see Section 10.4). The restriction $P(u) > 0$ ensures that defaults refer to nonempty classes and is used in the proof of Theorem 4.

In essence, this definition guarantees that an ε-entailed statement S is rendered highly probable whenever all the defaults in Δ are highly probable. The connection between ε-entailment and plausible conclusions (Eq. (10.22)) now reads

$$F \mathrel{\vdash_{\Delta}} r \quad \text{iff} \quad \Delta \mathrel{\vdash_{\varepsilon}} (F \to r) . \tag{10.28}$$

10.2.2 Axiomatic Characterization and a System of Defeasible Inference

A logic developed by Adams [1966, 1975] faithfully represents these semantics with qualitative inference rules, thus facilitating the derivation of new sound sentences by direct symbolic manipulations on Δ. The essence of Adams's logic is summarized in the following theorem.

THEOREM 1: [Adams 1975]: *Let L be a factual language, let p, q, and r be formulas of L, let S be a (conditional) statement of the conditional extension of L, and let Δ be a finite set of such statements. Δ ε-entails S if and only if S is derivable from Δ using the following rules of inference:†*

1.	*Triangularity:*	$p \to q, p \to r \implies (p \wedge q) \to r.$	**(10.29a)**
2.	*Bayes:*	$p \to q, (p \wedge q) \to r \implies p \to r.$	**(10.29b)**
3.	*Disjunction:*	$p \to r, q \to r \implies (p \vee q) \to r.$	**(10.29c)**

The intuition behind these three axioms was discussed in Section 10.1.3 (see Eq. (10.20)), and their operational significance will be shown shortly. The soundness of the triangularity rule was proved in the penguin example (Eq. (10.23)), and the soundness of Eq. (10.29b) follows directly from Bayes' Rule (hence the name). These three rules are sufficient, i.e., no other statement is forced by Δ and the ε-semantics unless that statement is derivable using the rules above. Note that neither transitivity, $p \to q, q \to r \implies p \to r$, nor contraposition, $p \to q \implies \neg q \to \neg p$, are theorems of the logic.

Theorem 1, together with Eq. (10.28), constitutes the basis of an inference system proposed by Geffner and Pearl [1987b] that is capable of deriving all plausible conclusions of a given theory $T = \langle F, \Delta \rangle$. At the core of the system are the rules that form the next theorem.

---

† Adams's theorem in fact contains seven inference rules; the other four are of technical character (such as interchanging p with $T \to p$ or with any logical equivalent of p) and were omitted here for clarity. The symbol $\implies$ stands for derivational if-then license.

THEOREM 2: *Let $T = <F, \Delta>$ be a default theory, where F is a set of ground proposition formulas and Δ is a set of default rules. r is a plausible conclusion of F in the context of Δ, written $F \mathrel{\vert\kern-0.4em\raise0.3ex\hbox{\tiny$\Delta$}} r$, iff r is derivable from F using the following rules of inference:*

1.	*Defaults:*	$(p \to q) \in \Delta \implies p \mathrel{\vert\!\raise0.3ex\hbox{\tiny$\Delta$}} q.$	**(10.30a)**
2.	*Logic theorems:*	$p \supset q \implies p \mathrel{\vert\!\raise0.3ex\hbox{\tiny$\Delta$}} q.$	**(10.30b)**
3.	*Triangularity:*	$p \mathrel{\vert\!\raise0.3ex\hbox{\tiny$\Delta$}} q, p \mathrel{\vert\!\raise0.3ex\hbox{\tiny$\Delta$}} r \implies (p \wedge q) \mathrel{\vert\!\raise0.3ex\hbox{\tiny$\Delta$}} r.$	**(10.30c)**
4.	*Bayes:*	$p \mathrel{\vert\!\raise0.3ex\hbox{\tiny$\Delta$}} q, (p \wedge q) \mathrel{\vert\!\raise0.3ex\hbox{\tiny$\Delta$}} r \implies p \mathrel{\vert\!\raise0.3ex\hbox{\tiny$\Delta$}} r.$	**(10.30d)**
5.	*Disjunction:*	$p \mathrel{\vert\!\raise0.3ex\hbox{\tiny$\Delta$}} r, q \mathrel{\vert\!\raise0.3ex\hbox{\tiny$\Delta$}} r \implies (p \vee q) \mathrel{\vert\!\raise0.3ex\hbox{\tiny$\Delta$}} r.$	**(10.30e)**

Rule 1 permits us to conclude the consequent of a default when its antecedent is all that has been learned. Rule 2 states that theorems that logically follow from a set of formulas can be concluded in any theory containing those formulas. Rule 3 permits the attachment of a set of established conclusions (q) to the current set of facts (p), without affecting the status of any other derived conclusions (r). Rule 4 says that any conclusion (r) that follows from a fact set (p) augmented by a derived conclusion (q) also follows from the original fact set alone. Finally, rule 5 says that a conclusion that follows from two facts also follows from their disjunction.

Some meta-theorems:

1.	Logical closure:	$p \mathrel{\vert\!\raise0.3ex\hbox{\tiny$\Delta$}} q, p \wedge q \supset r \implies p \mathrel{\vert\!\raise0.3ex\hbox{\tiny$\Delta$}} r.$	**(10.31)**
2.	Equivalent contexts:	$p \equiv q, p \mathrel{\vert\!\raise0.3ex\hbox{\tiny$\Delta$}} r \implies q \mathrel{\vert\!\raise0.3ex\hbox{\tiny$\Delta$}} r.$	**(10.32)**
3.	Exceptions:	$p \wedge q \mathrel{\vert\!\raise0.3ex\hbox{\tiny$\Delta$}} r, p \mathrel{\vert\!\raise0.3ex\hbox{\tiny$\Delta$}} \neg r \implies p \mathrel{\vert\!\raise0.3ex\hbox{\tiny$\Delta$}} \neg q.$	**(10.33)**

Some nontheorems:

1.	Transitivity:	$p \supset q \text{ and } q \mathrel{\vert\!\raise0.3ex\hbox{\tiny$\Delta$}} r \nRightarrow p \mathrel{\vert\!\raise0.3ex\hbox{\tiny$\Delta$}} r.$	**(10.34)**
2.	Positive conjunction:	$p \mathrel{\vert\!\raise0.3ex\hbox{\tiny$\Delta$}} r \text{ and } q \mathrel{\vert\!\raise0.3ex\hbox{\tiny$\Delta$}} r \nRightarrow p \wedge q \mathrel{\vert\!\raise0.3ex\hbox{\tiny$\Delta$}} r.$	**(10.35)**
3.	Contraposition:	$p \mathrel{\vert\!\raise0.3ex\hbox{\tiny$\Delta$}} r \nRightarrow \neg r \mathrel{\vert\!\raise0.3ex\hbox{\tiny$\Delta$}} \neg p.$	**(10.36)**

The reason transitivity, positive conjunction, and contraposition are not sanctioned by the ε-semantics is clear: There are worlds in which they fail. For instance, transitivity fails in the penguin example—all penguins are birds, birds typically fly, yet penguins do not. Positive conjunction fails when p and q create a new condition unshared by either p or q. For example, if you marry Ann (p) you will be happy (r), if you marry Nancy (q) you will be happy as well (r), but if you marry both ($p \wedge q$), you will be miserable ($\neg r$). Contraposition fails in situations where $\neg p$ is incompatible with $\neg r$. For example, let $p \to r$ stand for *Birds $\to$ Fly*. Now imagine a world in which the only nonflying objects are a few sick birds. Clearly, $Bird \rightarrow Fly$ holds, yet if we observe a nonflying object we can safely conclude that it is a bird, hence $\neg r \rightarrow p$, defying contraposition.

THEOREM 3 (Δ-monotonicity): *The inference system defined in Theorem 2 is monotonic relative to the addition of default rules, i.e.,*

$$\text{if } p \mathrel{\vdash_{\!\Delta}} r \text{ and } \Delta \subseteq \Delta', \text{ then } p \mathrel{\vdash_{\!\Delta'}} r . \qquad (10.37)$$

The proof follows directly from the fact that $\mathcal{P}_{\Delta', \, \varepsilon} \subseteq \mathcal{P}_{\Delta, \, \varepsilon}$, because each default statement imposes new constraints on $\mathcal{P}_{\Delta, \, \varepsilon}$. Thus, the logic is monotonic relative to the addition of new properties to individuals (in F). Full nonmonotonicity will be demonstrated in Section 10.2.3, where we consider weaker forms of entailment.

CONSISTENCY AND AMBIGUITY

An important feature of the system defined by rules 1 through 5 of Theorem 2 is its ability to distinguish theories conveying inconsistencies (e.g., $<p \rightarrow q, p \rightarrow \neg q>$) from those conveying ambiguity (e.g., $<p(a) \wedge q(a), p \rightarrow r, q \rightarrow \neg r>$) and those conveying exceptions (e.g., $<p(a) \wedge q(a), p \rightarrow \neg q>$).

DEFINITION: Δ *is said to be* ε-*consistent if* $\mathcal{P}_{\Delta, \, \varepsilon}$ *is non-empty for every* $\varepsilon > 0$; *otherwise* Δ *is* ε-*inconsistent. Similarly, a set of default statements* $\{S_{\alpha}\}$ *is said to be* ε-*consistent with* Δ *if* $\Delta \cup \{S_{\alpha}\}$ *is* ε-*consistent.*

DEFINITION: *A default statement S is said to be* **ambiguous** *given* Δ *if both S and its denial are* ε-*consistent with* Δ.

THEOREM 4 [Adams 1975]: *If* Δ *is* ε-*consistent, then a statement* $S : p \rightarrow q$ *is* ε-*entailed by* Δ *iff its denial* $S' : p \rightarrow \neg \, q$ *is* ε-*inconsistent with* Δ.

In addition to rules 1 through 5, the logic also possesses a systematic procedure for testing ε-consistency (and hence ε-entailments), similar to the method of truth-table proofs in propositional calculus.

DEFINITION: *Given a truth-valuation t respecting the usual Boolean connectives, a default statement* $p \rightarrow q$ *is said to be* **verified** *under t if t assigns the value TRUE to both p and q.* $p \rightarrow q$ *is said to be* **falsified** *under t if p is assigned TRUE and q is assigned FALSE.*

THEOREM 5 [Adams 1975]: *Let Δ be a finite set of default statements. Δ is ε-consistent iff for every nonempty subset Δ' of Δ there exists a truth valuation t such that no statement of Δ' is falsified under t and at least one is verified under t.*

When Δ can be represented as a network of default rules, the criterion of Theorem 5 becomes a simple graphical test for consistency:

THEOREM 6 [Pearl 1987c]: *Let Δ be a default network, i.e., a set of default statements $p \to q$ where both p and q are atomic propositions (or negations thereof). Δ is consistent iff for every pair of conflicting arcs $p_1 \to q$ and $p_2 \to \neg q$*

1) p_1 and p_2 are distinct, and

2)   there is no cycle of positive arcs that embraces both p_1 and p_2.

Theorem 6 generalizes Touretzky's consistency criterion [Touretzky 1986] to networks containing cycles as well as arcs emanating from negated propositions (e.g., $\neg p \to q$). Exercise 10.11 provides a general test for consistency.

ILLUSTRATIONS

We now present two examples to show how plausible conclusions are derived from both the ε-semantics and the system of rules 1 through 5 (Theorem 2).

A classic example of a statement left ambiguous by Δ is the "Nixon diamond" shown in Figure 10.1. Here,

$$F = \{Quaker\ (Nixon),\ Republican\ (Nixon)\}$$

$$\Delta = \{Quaker \to Pacifist,\ Republican \to \neg Pacifist\}$$

Since $P(Pacifist \mid Republican,\ Quaker)$ is not sufficiently constrained by either $P(Pacifist \mid Republican)$ or $P(Pacifist \mid Quaker)$, there exists a P in $\mathcal{P}_{\Delta,\,\varepsilon}$ that yields $P(Pacifist \mid Republican,\ Quaker) \geq 1 - \varepsilon$ and another $P' \in \mathcal{P}_{\Delta,\,\varepsilon}$ yielding $P'(Pacifist \mid Republican,\ Quaker) < \varepsilon$, thus rendering the statement $Pacifist(Nixon)$ ambiguous. For instance, if Quaker-Republicans are a negligible minority of Quakers or of Republicans, we can make $P(Pacifist \mid Republican,\ Quaker)$ equal 1 or 0, while still complying with the constraints imposed by Δ.

Unlike Reiter's default logic, the system described here does not generate multiple extensions. Rules 1 through 5 do not sanction the conclusion $Pacifist\ (Nixon)$ (or its negation) because no information is available regarding the enriched context of Quaker-Republicans.

The real power of ε-semantics lies in resolving rather than merely detecting conflicts of property inheritance. A perfect example is the "Penguin triangle" of Figure 10.2, which was semantically analyzed in Eq. (10.26). Here we wish to examine the syntactic and graphical derivations sanctioned by Theorems 2, 4, and 6.

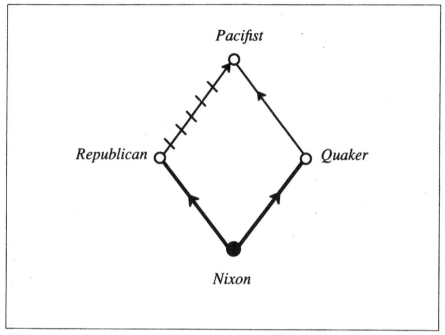

Figure 10.1. *An inheritance network depicting ambiguity. Heavy arcs represent factual information about individuals, thin arcs represent default statements among properties, slashed arcs represent denials.*

Early inheritance systems (e.g., FRL [Roberts and Goldstein 1978] and NETL [Fahlman 1979]) have resolved the conflict between $Penguin \rightarrow \neg Fly$ and $\{Penguin \rightarrow Bird, Bird \rightarrow Fly\}$ by appealing to the "shortest path" criterion, which correctly prefers the direct conclusion $Penguin \rightarrow \neg Fly$ over the inferred sentence $Penguin \rightarrow Fly$. However, as observed by Etherington [1982] and Touretzky [1984], the "shortest path" criterion does not always provide the desired preference for more specific defaults. For example, adding the property *White penguin* between *Tweety* and *Penguin* in Figure 10.2 would render the distance between *Tweety* and *Fly* shorter than that between *Tweety* and $\neg Fly$, thus yielding the anomalous conclusion that white penguins fly. We shall now demonstrate, without referring to intuition about subclass specificity, how the desired conclusion follows directly from rules 1 through 5.

T comprises the sentences

$$F = \{Penguin(Tweety), Bird(Tweety)\}$$

$$\Delta = \{Penguin \rightarrow \neg Fly, Bird \rightarrow Fly, Penguin \rightarrow Bird\}. \quad \textbf{(10.38)}$$

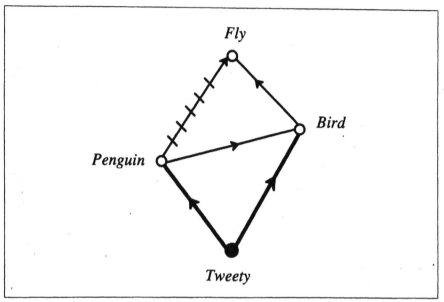

Figure 10.2. *The arc between Penguin and Bird sanctions the conclusion "Tweety does not fly."*

Although Δ does not specify explicitly any properties of penguin-birds, these can be derived in three steps, using rules 1 and 3 of Theorem 2:

1. *Penguin (Tweety)* $\mathrel{\vdash_{\Delta}}$ *¬Fly (Tweety)*.   (from rule 1)
2. *Penguin (Tweety)* $\mathrel{\vdash_{\Delta}}$ *Bird (Tweety)*.   (from rule 1)
3. *Penguin (Tweety)*, *Bird(Tweety)* $\mathrel{\vdash_{\Delta}}$ *¬Fly (Tweety)*.
                                                              (applying rule 3 to lines 1 and 2)

Translated to the graphical descriptions of Figures 10.1 and 10.2, this result states that ambiguities among conflicting defaults are resolved if a direct arrow exists between the tails of the corresponding conflicting arrows. Whenever such an arrow exists (e.g., *Penguin → Bird* in Figure 10.2), ambiguities are resolved in favor of the property labeling the tail of the arrow (e.g., *Penguin* in Figure 10.2). Whenever the two tails, b and p, are not connected directly, the ambiguity can be resolved if the required condition $p \to b$ (or $b \to p$), can be inferred from indirect paths between b and p, applying the criterion recursively. If neither $p \to b$ nor $b \to p$ can be derived, the ambiguity remains, whereas if both can be derived, Δ is inconsistent. This criterion lends probabilistic support to Touretzky's inferential distance (see Section 10.1.2), which rectifies the deficiencies of the shortest-path heuristic.

Applying the Exceptions Theorem (Eq. 10.33) to the network of Figure 10.2 yields another plausible conclusion, *Bird* → ¬ *Penguin*, stating that when one talks about birds one does not have penguins in mind, i.e., penguins are an exceptional kind of bird. It is a valid conclusion of Δ because every P in $\mathcal{P}_{\Delta,\varepsilon}$ must yield $P(p \mid b) = O(\varepsilon)$. Of course, if the statement *Bird* → *Penguin* is artificially added to Δ, inconsistency results; as ε diminishes below a certain level (1/3 in our case), $\mathcal{P}_{\Delta,\varepsilon}$ becomes empty. This can be predicted from purely topological considerations (Theorem 6), since adding the arc *Bird* → *Penguin* would create a cycle of positive arcs embracing *Bird* and *Penguin*, and these sprout two conflicting arcs toward *Fly*. Moreover, Theorem 4 implies that if the addition of S makes the network inconsistent, then that network ε-entails S's denial, S'. Hence, the network of Figure 10.2 ε-entails *Bird* → ¬*Penguin* (as well as *Fly* → ¬ *Penguin*).

10.2.3 Relevance-based Conventions

Default reasoning requires two facilities, one that forces conclusions to be retracted in light of new refuting evidence and another that protects conclusions from retraction in light of new but irrelevant evidence. Rules 1 through 5 excel on the first requirement but fail on the second (the opposite is true for default logics). For instance, in Fig. 10.2, if we were told that Tweety is also a blue penguin, the system would retract all previous conclusions as ambiguous, even though there is no rule that in any way connects color to flying ability.

The reason for this conservative behavior is our insistence that any conclusion issued attain high probability in *all* probability models licensed by Δ—one such model is a world in which blue penguins do fly. Clearly, if we want the system to respect the communication convention that properties are presumed to be *irrelevant* to each other unless stated otherwise, we need to restrict the family of probability models relative to which a given conclusion must be checked for soundness. In other words, we should consider only distributions that minimize dependencies relative to Δ (i.e., they embody dependencies that are absolutely implied by Δ), and no others.

THE MAXIMUM-ENTROPY (ME) APPROACH

A traditional way of defining a minimal dependency extension to a given set of constraints is to invoke the *maximum-entropy (ME)* principle [Jaynes 1979; Grosof 1986]. The principle amounts to selecting from $\mathcal{P}_{\Delta,\varepsilon}$ a single-distribution, $P^*_{\Delta,\varepsilon}$, defined by

$$H(P^*_{\Delta,\varepsilon}) \geq H(P) \quad \forall P \in \mathcal{P}_{\Delta,\varepsilon}, \tag{10.39}$$

where $H(P)$ is the entropy function

$$H[P(x)] = -\sum_x P(x) \log P(x) . \qquad \textbf{(10.40)}$$

We can now define a weak form of entailment by invoking $P^*_{\Delta, \varepsilon}$ instead of $\mathcal{P}_{\Delta, \varepsilon}$.

DEFINITION: *A theory* $T = <F, \Delta>$ *weakly entails a conclusion* r, *written* $F \models^{\cdot}_{\Delta} r$, *iff*

$$P^*_{\Delta, \varepsilon}(r \,|\, F) \geq 1 - O(\varepsilon) \qquad \textbf{(10.41)}$$

(i.e., if for every $\delta > 0$ *there is an* $\varepsilon > 0$ *such that* $P^*_{\Delta, \varepsilon}(r \,|\, F) \geq 1 - \delta$*).*

ε-entailment clearly subsumes weak entailment, because $P^*_{\Delta, \varepsilon} \in \mathcal{P}_{\Delta, \varepsilon}$.

When applied to small default systems, the *ME* method yields patterns of reasoning that parallel common discourse. For example, if a theory T involves only three primitive propositions, p, q, and r, the *ME* approach gives rise to the following patterns of reasoning:

1. Accepting irrelevant properties (strengthening the antecedents):

$$\text{if} \quad \Delta = \{q \to r\} \quad \text{then} \quad q \wedge p \models^{\cdot}_{\Delta} r . \qquad \textbf{(10.42)}$$

2. Mediated Inheritance (Weak Transitivity):

$$\text{if} \quad \Delta = \{p \to q, q \to r\} \quad \text{then} \quad p \models^{\cdot}_{\Delta} r . \qquad \textbf{(10.43)}$$

3. Positive Conjunction:

$$\text{if} \quad \Delta = \{p \to r, q \to r\} \quad \text{then} \quad p \wedge q \models^{\cdot}_{\Delta} r . \qquad \textbf{(10.44)}$$

4. Contraposition:

$$\text{if} \quad \Delta = \{p \to r\} \quad \text{then} \quad \neg r \models^{\cdot}_{\Delta} \neg p . \qquad \textbf{(10.45)}$$

Applying the *ME* principle to larger systems reveals intriguing phenomena and challenging possibilities. For example, taking

$$\Delta' = \{p \to s, s \to q, p \to r, q \to \neg r\}$$

yields

$$p \wedge q \models^{\cdot}_{\Delta'} r .$$

In other words, the intermediate property s seems not to weaken the triangularity rule (Eq. (10.30c)), which gives priority to the subclass p over q.

This is in line with Touretzky's inferential distance criterion, which allows preemption through long chains of default rules. For example, if the link in Figure 10.2 between *Penguin* and *Bird* is mediated by an intermediate property, say *Winged animal*, the conclusion ¬*Fly(Tweety)* still follows from *F* = {*Penguin(Tweety)*, *Bird(Tweety)*}. Strangely, however, the conclusion *Bird(Tweety)* no longer follows from *F* = {*Penguin(Tweety)*}. Two competing arguments (paths) now lead from *Penguin* to *Bird*; transitivity sanctions the path *Penguin* → *Winged animal* → *Bird*, and contraposition sanctions *Penguin* → ¬*Fly* → ¬*Bird*. As a result, Tweety's "birdness" becomes ambiguous, as Nixon's pacifism was in Figure 10.1 (see Exercise 10.7).

SYNTACTIC APPROACHES

The *ME* approach has several shortcomings, the biggest being its computational complexity; nobody yet has been able to extract from this semantics a complete system of qualitative axioms similar to those encapsulating the ε-semantics. Instead, several attempts have been made to extrapolate syntactically the reasoning patterns of Eqs. (10.42) through (10.45) to more complex systems, involving long chains of interacting defaults. The systems of Horty, Thomason, and Touretzky [1987], Loui [1987], and Geffner and Pearl [1987b] are examples of such extrapolations.

In the Geffner and Pearl system, for example, rules 1 through 5 of Theorem 2 (Eq. (10.30)) are augmented by a sixth rule, incorporating explicitly a predicate of *irrelevance* $I_\Delta(q, \neg r \,|\, p)$ (to be read "*q* is irrelevant to ¬*r*, given *p*"):

6. *Irrelevance*:

$$\text{if } (p \to r) \in \Delta \text{ and } I_\Delta(q, \neg r \,|\, p) \text{ then } p \land q \mathrel{\vdash_{\Delta}^{\pm}} r . \qquad \textbf{(10.46)}$$

Rule 6 reflects the intuition that *q* should not be allowed to interfere with the conclusion $p \mathrel{\vdash_{\Delta}^{\pm}} r$ if *q* is found to be incapable of swaying an argument for ¬*r*, once we know *p*. The definition of $I_\Delta(q, \neg r \,|\, p)$ is formed by constructing arguments from the defaults in Δ and ensuring that no argument for ¬*r* will rest critically on *q* (see Exercises 10.8 and 10.9). Having retained rules 1 through 5 as the basis for its inference mechanism, the system enjoys the consistency guarantees provided by these rules.

It is still unclear whether any of these syntactic extrapolations conforms to the dictates of the *ME* method or some other dependence-minimizing principle.

10.2.4 Do People Use the Logic of Extreme Probabilities?

Probabilities that are infinitesimally close to 0 and 1 are very rare in the real world. Most default rules used in ordinary discourse maintain a certain percentage of exceptions, simply because the number of objects in every meaningful class is finite. Thus, a natural question to ask is, why study the properties of a logic that applies only to extreme probabilities? Why not develop a logic that characterizes moderately high probabilities, say probabilities higher than 0.5 or 0.9—or more ambitiously, higher than α, where α is a parameter chosen to fit the domains of the predicates involved?

The answer is that any such alternative logic would be extremely complicated and probably would need to invoke many of the axioms of arithmetic. Take, for example, the logic of "majority," namely, interpreting the default rule $a \rightarrow b$ to mean "The majority of a's are b's," or $P(b\,|\,a) > 0.5$. None of the three axioms of Theorem 1 (Eq. (10.29)) remain sound in this interpretation. For example, the triangularity axiom is violated by the following proportions: 51% of students are males ($s \rightarrow m$), 51% of all students will receive the grade A ($s \rightarrow A$), yet contrary to the triangularity axiom it does not follow that the majority of male students will receive A's. It is even possible that only 2% of the male students will receive the grade A (if all females receive A's), yielding $s \wedge m \rightarrow \neg A$. Even the disjunction axiom can be violated (see the proportions in Figure 10.3); it holds only for disjoint sets, where it is called *reasoning by cases*:

$$A \supset \neg B, A \rightarrow C, B \rightarrow C \implies (A \vee B) \rightarrow C. \qquad (10.47)$$

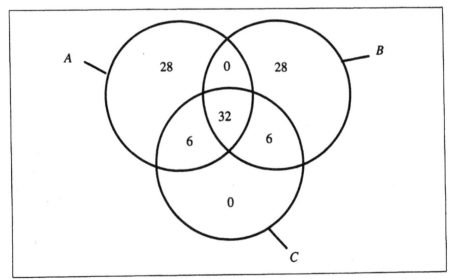

Figure 10.3. *Violation of the disjunction axiom: the majority of A's are C's (38/66) and the majority of B's are C's (38/66), yet only 44% of (A $\cup$ B)s are C's.*

In general, given an arbitrary Boolean formula F, the only way to guarantee that the majority of objects in the class corresponding to F possess some property p is to partition F into a set of disjoint subclasses, obtain a full account of the relative number of individuals in each subclass, obtain the proportion of p's in each subclass, and then use arithmetic procedures to verify that the overall proportion exceeds 50%. No logic is known that can faithfully replace arithmetic in reasoning about majorities. Moreover, it appears that every logic capable of producing sound and complete inferences about majorities (let alone other thresholds of proportions) is bound to have the complexity of arithmetic inequalities.

How, then, do people reason qualitatively about proportions, majorities, great majorities, and overwhelming majorities? It appears that the machinery invoked by people for such tasks amounts to approximating the calculus of proportions by some expedient abstraction. The machinery may be adequate for an idealized model of these proportions but would not respond to all their fine details.

The logic of extreme probabilities provides such an approximation. It captures precisely those relations involving overwhelming majorities, but when applied to situations involving moderate proportions it may lead to unfounded conclusions. For example, from the sentences "Most students are males" and "Most students will get an A," the logic would infer "Most male students will get an A." This conclusion can be grossly incorrect, as shown in the example above, yet it is a rather common inference made by people, given these two inputs. As a matter of fact, when these inputs are accompanied by the statement "Most male students will receive a B," some explanation is usually required, e.g., that "most" meant only 51% and that all females will receive an A.

The disparity between the semantics of proportions and the logic chosen by people to reason about those proportions is best exemplified by the celebrated Simpson's Paradox [Simpson 1951]. Simpson's Paradox has been discussed at length in the statistical literature [Dawid 1979], but it continues to trap the unwary. It involves a hypothetical test of the effectiveness of a certain drug on a population consisting of males and females, as shown in the following table:

	Male		Female		Overall	
	R	$\neg R$	R	$\neg R$	R	$\neg R$
D	15	40	90	50	105	90
$\neg D$	20	40	20	10	40	50

The entries show the number of individuals that recovered (R) and the number that did not recover ($\neg R$), with (D) and without ($\neg D$) taking the drug. We see that the drug appears to increase the recovery ratio in the total population from 40/50 to 105/90, but the effect on each subpopulation is the opposite; the recovery ratio of males has diminished from 20/40 to 15/40 and that of females has gone from 20/10 to 90/50.

The remarkable feature of Simpson's Paradox is that when it is phrased verbally, people refuse to believe it and invariably insist on "seeing the numbers." Imagine your family physician saying, "This drug seems to work on the population as a whole, but it has an adverse effect on males ... and an adverse effect on females." Your first reaction would probably be, "Wait a minute, let me see that data!" Only when you look at the numbers and agree to interpret the phrase "seems to have an effect" as a statement about a change in proportions do you begin to see that the calculus of proportions clashes with our intuitive predictions. In other words, the approximate symbolic representation people have adopted for reasoning about how drugs affect various populations yields predictions that are occasionally unsound relative to the calculus of proportions. In particular, Simpson's Paradox seems to violate the axiom of disjunction, even on disjoint sets (i.e., reasoning by cases):

$$m \supset \neg f, \, m \rightarrow a, \, f \rightarrow a \Longrightarrow m \vee f \rightarrow a \, ,$$

where $x \rightarrow a$ stands for the expression "If x, then the drug effect is adverse." Simpson's table seems to show that a drug may have an adverse effect on males ($m \rightarrow a$), adverse on females ($f \rightarrow a$), yet positive on the population as a whole ($m \vee f \rightarrow \neg a$). But this is utterly impossible—a table such as Simpson's cannot be obtained in any controlled (randomized) experiment designed to test the efficacy of a drug, where the drug is assigned independently of gender. The surprise with which people react to Simpson's Paradox suggests that the disjunction axiom has been adopted as one of the canons of causal reasoning, and rightly so. While this axiom is not sound relative to the semantics of increased proportions, it is sound relative to the semantics of causation (as well as the semantics of overwhelmingly high proportions, i.e., ε-semantics). In conclusion, it appears that the machinery of plausible reasoning is more in line with the rules of causal logic (and "almost-all" logic) than with those of "majority" logic.

CONCLUSIONS

This section has explored the use of probability theory as a semantic basis for default reasoning. The system presented, an adaptation of Adams's logic of conditionals, interprets defaults as conditional probability statements, infinitesimally removed from 0 or 1. This interpretation yields a system of defeasible inference with rather unique features:

1. The system makes a formal distinction between exceptions, ambiguities, and inconsistencies and offers systematic methods of maintaining consistency in databases containing defaults.

2. Multiple extensions do not arise, and preferences among arguments (e.g., toward higher specificity) are derived by natural deduction.

3. There is no need to specify abnormality relations in advance (as in circumscription); such relations (e.g., that penguins are abnormal birds) are automatically inferred from the input.

10.3 EMBRACING CAUSALITY IN DEFAULT REASONING

Almost every default rule falls into one of two categories: *expectation-evoking* or *explanation-evoking*. Rules of the first type describe associations among events in the *outside* world (e.g., "Fire is typically accompanied by smoke"); rules of the second type describe how *we* reason about the world (e.g., "Smoke normally suggests fire"). This distinction is consistently recognized by people and serves as a tool for controlling the invocation of new default rules. This section explores ways that the computational benefits of causal organization can be reaped within the formal framework of default logic.

10.3.1 How Old Beliefs Were Established Determines Which New Beliefs Are Evoked

Let A and B stand for the following propositions:

$$A = \text{"Joe is over seven years old."}$$
$$B = \text{"Joe can read and write."}$$

CASE 1: Consider a reasoning system with the default rule
$$def_B: \quad B \to A.$$

A new fact now becomes available,

$$e_1 = \text{"Joe recites passages from Shakespeare,"}$$

together with a new default rule,

$$def_1: \quad e_1 \to B.$$

CASE 2: Consider a reasoning system with the same default rule,
$$def_B: \quad B \to A.$$

A new fact now becomes available,

$$e_2 = \text{"Joe is a child prodigy"}$$

together with a new default rule,

$$def_2: \quad e_2 \to B.$$

A graphical representation of these two cases is given in Figure 10.4.

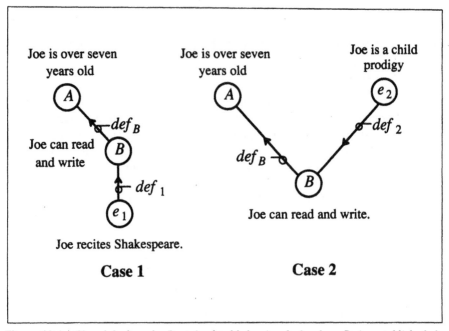

Figure 10.4. *The default rule B → A should be invoked when B is established by evidential information (Case 1) and inhibited when B is established by prediction (Case 2). Causal rules point downward and evidential rules, upward.*

Common sense dictates that Case 1 should lead to conclusions opposite to those of Case 2. Learning that Joe can recite Shakespeare should evoke belief in Joe's reading ability (B) and consequently belief in his correspondingly mature age (A). On the other hand, learning of his prodigy reputation, while still inspiring belief in Joe's reading ability, should *not* trigger the default rule B→A because it does not support the hypothesis that Joe is older than seven. On the contrary, any evidence we had of Joe's literary skills could now be attributed to his unique talents rather than to Joe's natural state of development. Thus, if a belief were previously committed to A, and if measures of belief were permitted, it would not seem unreasonable for e_2 to *weaken* somewhat the belief in A.

From a purely syntactic viewpoint, Case 1 is identical to Case 2. In both cases we have a new fact triggering B by default. Yet, in Case 1 we wish to encourage the invocation of B→A whereas in Case 2 we wish to suppress it. Can a default-based reasoning system distinguish between the two cases?

A straightforward way of suppressing A in Case 2 would be to employ a more elaborate default rule, where more exceptions are stated explicitly. For example, rather than $B \rightarrow A$, the proper default rule should be $B \rightarrow A \mid UNLESS\ e_2$. Such exceptions can be encoded as semi-normal defaults in Reiter's logic (see Section 10.1) or as OUT justifiers in truth-maintenance systems [Doyle 1979]. Unfortunately, this cure is inadequate on two grounds. First, it requires that every default rule be burdened with an unmanageably large number of conceivable exceptions. Second, it misses the intent of the default rule def_B: $B \rightarrow A$, the primary aim of which is to evoke belief in A whenever the truth of B can be ascertained; it would be very disturbing for the rule author to have to dream up farfetched exceptions instead of simply articulating the everyday knowledge that children with reading ability are typically over seven years old.

To summarize, what we want is a mechanism that is sensitive to the way B was established. If B was established by direct observation or by strong supporting evidence (Case 1), the default rule $B \rightarrow A$ should be invoked. If, on the other hand, B was established by expectation, anticipation, or prediction (Case 2), then $B \rightarrow A$ should not be invoked, no matter how strong the expectation.

The asymmetry between expectation-evoking and explanation-evoking rules is based less on chronological ordering than on human memory organization. For example, age evokes expectations of certain abilities not because it precedes them in time (in many cases it does not) but because the concept called "child of age seven" was chosen by the culture as a bona fide frame, while the abilities were chosen as slots within that frame, representing typical expectations. Similar asymmetries can be found in object-property, class-subclass and action-consequence relationships.

10.3.2 More on the Distinction Between Causal and Evidential Support

Consider the following two sentences:

1. Bill seemed unable to stand up, so I believed he was injured.

2. Harry seemed injured, so I believed he would be unable to stand up.

Any reasoning system that does not take into account the direction of causality, or at least the source and mode by which beliefs are established, will conclude that Harry is as likely as Bill to be drunk (see Figure 10.5). Our intuition, however, dictates that Bill is more likely than Harry to be drunk because Harry's inability to stand up—the only indication of drunkenness mentioned in his case—is portrayed as an expectation-based property emanating from injury, and injury is a perfectly acceptable alternative to drunkenness. In Bill's case, on the other hand, inability to stand up is described as a primary property supported by direct observation, while injury is brought up as an explanatory property, inferred by default.

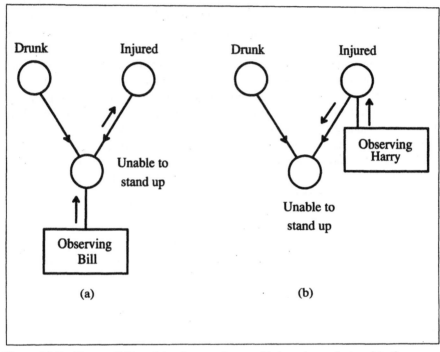

Figure 10.5. *The possibility of drunkenness is more likely to be conjectured in the case of Bill (a) than in that of Harry (b).*

Note that the perceived difference between Bill and Harry does not stem from a difference in our confidence in each man's ability to stand up. Harry will still appear less likely than Bill to be drunk if we rephrase the sentences:

1. Bill showed slight difficulties standing up, so I believed he was injured.

2. Harry seemed injured, so I was sure he would be unable to stand up.

Notice the important role played by the word *so*. It clearly designates the preceding proposition as the primary source of belief in the proposition that follows. Natural languages contain many connectives for indicating how conclusions are reached (e.g., *therefore, thus, on the other hand*, and *nevertheless*). Classical logic and all known versions of default logic appear to ignore this vital information by treating as equals all beliefs, whether they were established by external means (e.g., observations), by presumptuous expectations, by a quest for explanations, or by logical derivation.

But even if we are convinced of the importance of the sources of one's belief, the question remains how to store and use such information. In the Bayesian analysis of belief networks (Chapters 4 and 5), this is accomplished with numerical parameters: Each proposition is assigned two parameters, π for its accrued *causal* support and λ for its accrued *evidential* support. These parameters then play decisive roles in guiding the impact of new evidence throughout the network as embodied in the propogation rules of Section 4.3.1. For example, Harry's inability to stand up accrues some causal support, emanating from injury, and zero evidential support, while Bill's situation produces the opposite support profile. As a result, observing bloodstains on the floor would reduce the overall belief that Bill is drunk but would have no impact on the belief that Harry is drunk. Similarly, finding a whiskey bottle nearby would weaken the belief in Bill's injury but have no impact on the belief in Harry's.

Can a nonnumeric logic capture and exploit these nuances? True, it cannot accommodate the notions of "weak" and "strong" expectations, or the notion of accrued support, but this limitation may not be too severe in some applications, e.g., those in which belief or disbelief in a proposition is triggered by just a few decisive conditions. We can still maintain an indication of how a given belief was established—by expectational or evidential considerations, or both—and use these indications to decide which default rules can be activated in any given state of knowledge.

10.3.3 The C-E System: A Coarse Logical Abstraction of Causal Directionality

Commonsense reasoning evidently involves two types of default rules: expectation-evoking (e.g., "If fire then smoke") and explanation-evoking (e.g., "If smoke then fire"). We call the first type *causal* rules, and the second type *evidential* rules. The meaning that default logics associate with a default rule $A \rightarrow B$ is usually given in terms of a license to presume B if A is believed, as long as B is consistent with currently held beliefs (see Section 10.1). This interpretation fits the nature of causal rules but not of evidential rules. Rules of the type "If observation A then hypothesis B" should be blocked not only when B is inconsistent with current beliefs, but also whenever an alternative explanation is available for the observation A, even if B is perfectly consistent with current beliefs. The problems described in the preceding sections stem from subjecting the two types of defaults to the same operational semantics: Presume B unless it is contradictory.

There are two ways of handling these problems. One way is to admit default rules of only one kind, and the other is to admit a mixture of causal and evidential rules, label each rule by its type, and manage them accordingly. The first method is certainly easier to implement. The MYCIN system [Shortliffe 1976], for example, admits only evidential rules (always pointing from evidence to hypothesis); it can perform simple diagnoses but cannot combine diagnosis with prediction (see Chapter 1). Alternatively, one might admit as input only causal rules, as is indeed the prevailing practice in Bayesian analysis: Input information is given in an "If cause then effect" format, while diagnoses are *derived* by explanation-seeking procedures (e.g., minimization), rather than by explicit diagnostic rules (see Chapter 5). Poole [1987] has likewise devised a logic-based system where default rules are restricted to the causal variety, and reasoning from evidence to hypotheses is accomplished by specialized "theory formation" procedures. Such causal-based systems (often called *model-based* or *first-principles-based*) enjoy the features of parsimony, stability, and modularity and facilitate a more natural, declarative representation of world knowledge.

In practice, however, most default-handling systems in AI admit a mixture of causal and evidential rules. For example, truth-maintenance systems accept both causal justifiers, as in (IS FRED PROFESSOR) → (POOR FRED), and evidential justifiers as in (PAIN FRED SIDE) → (HAS FRED APPENDICITIS) [Charniak, Riesbeck, and McDermott 1980]. The reason for the mixture is that despite the advantages of causal systems, it is hard for rule-writers to resist the temptation of articulating compiled procedural knowledge leading from familiar situations to previously successful actions or guesses (e.g., that smoke suggests fire, that symptoms suggest diseases.) The C-E logic described in this section was devised to maintain plausibility in a mixed system, where causal and evidential rules reside side by side, each labeled by its type name.

Let each default rule in the system be labeled as either C-*def* ("causal") or E-*def* ("evidential"). The former will be distinguished by the symbol $\to_C$, as in *Fire $\to_C$ Smoke*, (read fire causes smoke), and the latter by $\to_E$, as in *Smoke $\to_E$ Fire*, (read smoke is evidence for fire). Correspondingly, let each believed proposition be labeled by a distinguishing symbol, E or C. A proposition P is E-*believed,* written $E(P)$, if it is a direct consequence of only E-*def* rules. If P can be established as a direct consequence of a C-*def* rule, it is said to be C-*believed,* written $C(P)$. The semantics of the C-E distinction are captured by the following three inference rules:

$$
\text{a)} \quad \frac{\begin{array}{c} P \to_C Q \\ C(P) \end{array}}{C(Q)} \qquad \text{b)} \quad \frac{\begin{array}{c} P \to_C Q \\ E(P) \end{array}}{C(Q)} \qquad \text{c)} \quad \frac{\begin{array}{c} P \to_E Q \\ E(P) \end{array}}{E(Q)}.
$$

$$(10.48)$$

Note that we purposely omitted the inference rule

$$P \rightarrow_E Q$$
$$C(P)$$
$$\overline{\qquad\qquad}\quad,$$
$$Q \qquad\qquad\qquad\qquad\qquad\qquad\text{(10.49)}$$

which led to counterintuitive conclusions in Case 2 of Joe's story.

Inference rules (a), (b), and (c) imply that conclusions can attain E-*believed* status only by a chain of purely E-*def* rules. C-*believed* conclusions, on the other hand, can be obtained from a mixture of C-*def* and E-*def* rules. For example, an E-*def* rule may (via rule (c)) yield an E-*believed* conclusion, which can feed into a C-*def* rule (via rule (b)) and yield a C-*believed* conclusion. Note also that (a), (b), and (c) can license the use of $A \rightarrow B$ and $B \rightarrow A$ without falling into the circular reasoning trap. Iterative application of these two rules will never cause a C-*believed* proposition to become E-*believed*, because at least one of the rules must be a C-*def* rule.

The distinction between the two types of rules can be demonstrated using the "wet grass" example of Section 2.3.1 (see Figure 10.6).

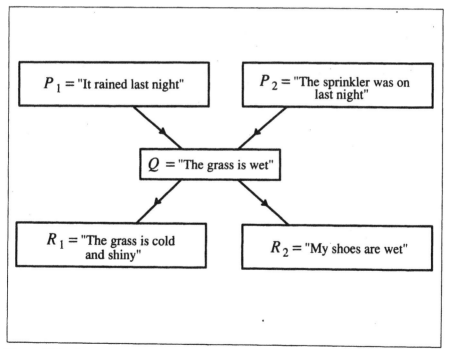

Figure 10.6. P_1 *is invoked as an explanation when* Q *is established by observing* R_1 *or* R_2, *but not by observing* P_2.

Let P_1, P_2, Q, R_1, and R_2 stand for the following propositions:

P_1 = "It rained last night."
P_2 = "The sprinkler was on last night."
Q = "The grass is wet."
R_1 = "The grass is cold and shiny."
R_2 = "My shoes are wet."

The causal and evidential relationships between these propositions would be written:

$$P_1 \rightarrow_C Q, \qquad Q \rightarrow_E P_1,$$
$$P_2 \rightarrow_C Q, \qquad Q \rightarrow_E P_2,$$
$$Q \rightarrow_C R_1, \qquad R_1 \rightarrow_E Q,$$
$$Q \rightarrow_C R_2, \qquad R_2 \rightarrow_E Q.$$

If Q is established by an E-*def* rule such as $R_1 \rightarrow_E Q$, then it can trigger both P_1 as explanation and R_2 as prediction. However, if Q is established merely by a C-*def* rule, say $P_2 \rightarrow_C Q$, then it can trigger R_2 (and R_1) but *not P_1*.

The essence of the asymmetry stems from the fact that two causes of a common consequence interact differently than two consequences of a common cause; in the absence of direct interactions, the former compete with each other, whereas the latter support each other. Moreover, the former interact when their connecting proposition is confirmed, whereas the latter interact only when their connecting proposition is unconfirmed. In our example, the state of the sprinkler influences our belief in rain only when the grass wetness is confirmed by observation. However, knowing whether the shoes are wet or dry can influence the prediction "The grass is cold" only prior to the wetness of the grass being confirmed. This asymmetry is the basis of constructing and interpreting Bayesian networks in Section 3.3, and it served as the defining characteristic of causal directionality in Section 8.2.

Let us see how this C-E system resolves the problem of Joe's age (see Figure 10.4). def_B and def_1 will be classified as E-*def* rules, while def_2 will be proclaimed a C-*def* rule. All provided facts (e.g., e_1 and e_2) will naturally be E-*believed*. In Case 1, B will become E-*believed* (via rule (c)), and subsequently, after invoking def_B in rule (c), A, too, will become E-*believed*. In Case 2, however, B will only become C-*believed* (via rule (b)); as such, it cannot invoke def_B, and A is left undetermined, as expected.

To handle retraction we can employ a mechanism of *justification maintenance*, similar to that used in truth-maintenance systems [Doyle 1979]. We define an *extension* to be an assignment of $C$$-$$E$$-$$OUT$ status to the propositions in the system that is closed under rules (a), (b), and (c), Eq. (10.48). An extension X is said to be *well founded** if all of its labels can be justified by the three inference rules above with the provision that being C-*believed* supercedes being E-*believed*. In other words, every C-*believed* proposition Q in X is a conclusion of some C-*def*

---

* In cyclic databases extensions need to be *grounded*, i.e., based on the available facts.

rule $P \rightarrow_C Q$, where P is labeled either E or C; every E-*believed* proposition Q in X is one that cannot be labeled C-*believed* and is either given as a fact or is a conclusion of some E-*def* rule $P \rightarrow_E Q$, where P is labeled E. New facts propagate their impact on the beliefs of other propositions by maintaining the well-foundedness of the extension. For example, if in Joe's story we first learn fact e_1, then the only well-founded extension is $X_1 = \{E(e_1), E(B), E(A)\}$, namely, all propositions are E-*believed*. If we later learn a new fact, e_2, then extension X_1 gives way to $X_2 = \{E(e_1), E(e_2), C(B), OUT(A)\}$. Thus, e_2 causes B to become C-*believed* (explained by the truth of e_2), which suppresses the rule def_B and retracts the belief in A—that Joe is over seven years old.

The merits of this definition of *well-foundedness* can be demonstrated by applying it to the so-called Yale shooting problem [Hanks and McDermott 1987]. In its simplest version (see Figure 10.7), the problem involves shooting a person known to be alive at time t_1 ($Alive(t_1)$) with a gun known to be loaded at time t_0 ($Loaded(t_0)$). Normally, we would expect the gun to remain loaded at t_1 and the victim to be dead at time t_2. Yet, if we express the natural tendency of things to persist over time by the default rules

$\quad$ 1) $Loaded(t_0) \rightarrow Loaded(t_1)$

and $\quad$ 2) $Alive(t_1) \rightarrow Alive(t_2)$,

and express the impact of shooting a loaded gun by the rule

$\quad$ 3) $Loaded(t_1) \rightarrow Dead(t_2)$,

an anamolous extension ensues, whereby the victim is alive at t_2 and the gun is unloaded at t_1. The extension is assembled by applying rule 2 to the fact $Alive(t_1)$, followed by the contrapositive form of rule 3,

$\quad$ 3´) $Alive(t_2) \rightarrow \neg Loaded(t_1)$.

The C-E system would handle this problem by labeling (1), (2), and (3) as causal rules and (3´) as an evidential rule. Starting with the facts $Loaded(t_0)$ and $Alive(t_1)$, if we first apply rules 1 and 3, we get the intended well-founded extension

$$X_1 = \{E[Loaded(t_0)], E[Alive(t_1)], C[Loaded(t_1)], C[Dead(t_2)]\},$$

while applying rules 1 and 2 yields an anomalous well-founded extension:

$$X_2 = \{E[Loaded(t_0)], E[Alive(t_1)], C[Loaded(t_1)], C[Alive(t_2)]\}.$$

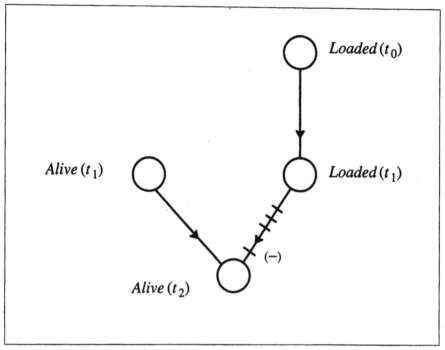

Figure 10.7. *Graphical representation of the Yale shooting problem.*

The anomalous extension of Hanks and McDermott, entailing $\neg Loaded(t_1)$, would not be well-founded, because $Alive(t_2)$ is C-*believed* and hence cannot serve as a justification for an E-*def* rule like (3′).

Although the C-E system yields an anomalous extension X_2, it is not an unreasonable extension considering the syntax of the rules used. Indeed, exchanging $Alive(t_1)$ with the predicate *Wearing-bulletproof-vest* (t_1) would satisfy rules 1, 2, 3, and 3′ and would render X_2 a more acceptable extension than X_1. In other words, there is no syntactic way of inferring from rules 1 through 3 that being alive at t_1 does not constitute protection against gunfire (if there were, then the purpose of rule 3 would be to assert that dead people cannot be revived by being shot). To convey the disruptive effect of gunfire on the persistence of life, one can use, for example, the rule $Alive(t_1) \wedge Loaded(t_1) \rightarrow Dead(t_2)$ in place of (3) (see Section 10.4). However, unlike the reasoning presented by Hanks and McDermott, the C-E logic will never allow the hypothetical prediction $Alive(t_1) \rightarrow Alive(t_2)$ to turn backwards and trigger doubts about whether the gun is loaded at t_1, regardless of the mechanism one chooses to represent the volatility of life under gunfire. On the other hand, were the victim actually seen alive at t_2, the natural explanation $Unloaded(t_1)$ would be activated. Again, this asymmetry is not unique to chronological ordering but is applicable to property inheritance and class-subclass relationships in general [Morris 1987].

10.3.4 Implicit Suppressors and the Need for Finer Abstractions

E-believed status enjoys some advantages over *C-believed* status. The former can trigger both *C-def* and *E-def* rules, whereas the latter, no matter how strong the belief, triggers only *C-def* rules. On the other hand, *C-def* rules are more powerful than *E-def* rules, since the former can be applied to both *E-believed* and *C-believed* propositions, whereas *E-def* rules can be applied only to *E-believed* propositions. More generally, *E-def* rules are weaker because they can be undermined by propositions that do not themselves contradict or oppose the conclusion of the rules, but only offer alternative explanations for the antecedent. In Figure 10.6, for example, P_2 deactivates the rule $Q \rightarrow P_1$ despite the fact that it is perfectly consistent for a sprinkler (P_2) to turn on during a rainy night (P_1). This suppression reflects the natural tendency of people to prefer simpler explanations (i.e., involving fewer assumptions) and hence can be regarded as a local filtering scheme, serving some global minimization policy.

The computational advantages of such suppression can be demonstrated in the context of the frame problem associated with the *E-def* rule "If the car does not start, assume the battery is dead." Obviously, there are many exceptions to this rule, e.g., "...unless the starter is burned out," "...unless someone pulled the spark plugs," and "...unless the gas tank is empty," and if any of these conditions is believed to be true, people will *suppress* the invocation of the battery as an explanation for having trouble starting the car. What is equally obvious is that people do not store all these hypothetical conditions explicitly with each conceivable explanation of car-starting problems but treat them as unattached *implicit suppressors*, namely, conditions that exert their influence only upon becoming actively believed and that uniformly suppress every *E-def* rule having "car won't start" as its sole antecedent.

But if the list of suppressors is not prepared in advance, how do people distinguish a genuine suppressor from a bogus one. In other words, by what criterion can people discriminate between the suppressor "The starter is burned out" and the candidate suppressor "I hear no motor sound"? Both of these inspire strong belief in "The car won't start" and "I'll be late for the meeting," yet the burned-out starter is licensed to suppress the conclusion "The battery is dead," while the motor's silence is licensed to evoke it. We can only conclude that it is the *causal directionality* of the suppressor-suppressed relationship that provides the identification criterion: The antecedents of causal rules qualify as suppressors, and those of evidential rules do not. It is hard to see how implicit suppression could be realized if people were not blessed with the ability to distinguish clearly between *explanation-evoking* and *expectation-evoking* rules. So why stifle this distinction in formal reasoning systems?

Formally, implicit suppression can be defined in terms of a meta-rule that qualifies the viability of every E-*def* rule $P \rightarrow_E Q$ in the system:

$$P \rightarrow_E Q \ | \ \text{unless} \ \exists (Q') : (Q' \rightarrow_C P) \ \text{and} \ [E(Q') \ \text{or} \ C(Q')] . \qquad (10.50)$$

The rule says that the default rule $P \rightarrow_E Q$ can be invoked only when no alternative explanation Q' is available for P. One may, in fact, turn things around and take this vulnerability to implicit suppression as the defining criterion for evidential rules. Accordingly, a rule $P \rightarrow Q$ will be said to be evidential if there exists another rule $Q' \rightarrow P$, such that $Q' \wedge P$ is a reason to believe $\neg Q$, while Q' alone is not a reason to believe $\neg Q$. Otherwise, the rule will be called causal.

The main benefit of this suppression scheme is that we no longer need to attach the name of each potential suppressor to every potentially suppressed rule; the connection between the two will be formed "on the fly" once the suppressor becomes actively believed. The mere fact that belief in a proposition P can be justified by some explanation Q' will automatically and precisely block all the rules we wish to have suppressed. More ambitiously, it should also cause the retraction of all conclusions drawn from premature activation of such rules, as demonstrated in Section 10.3.3. This is one of the computational benefits offered by the organizational instrument called causation. It has in fact been realized in the belief revision method of Chapter 5, but since human reasoning is mostly qualitative, it would be useful to embody implicit suppression in nonnumerical systems as well.

Unfortunately, implicit suppression is hindered by some fundamental issues, and it is not clear how it might be realized in purely categorical systems, which preclude any representation for the degree of support that a premise imparts to a conclusion. Treating *all* C-*def* rules as implicit suppressors would be inappropriate: Only facts (e.g., a burned starter) that have strong predictive influence over other facts (e.g., the car not starting) should inhibit all E-*def* rules emanating from the realization of such predictions (e.g., a dead battery). Others (e.g., having an old starter) do not deserve that power. Apparently there is a sharp qualitative difference between *strong* C-*def* rules such as

$$\text{Has burned starter } (x) \rightarrow_C \text{Won't start } (x)$$

and *weak* C-*def* rules such as

$$\text{Has old starter } (x) \rightarrow_C \text{Won't start } (x).$$

A strong C-*def* rule, when invoked, should inhibit all E-*def* rules emanating from its consequence. On the other hand, weak C-*def* rules should allow these E-*def* rules to fire (via rule (c)).

This distinction is exactly the role played by the numerical parameters in Bayesian inference; they measure the accrued strength of causal support and serve to distribute the impact of newly observed facts among those propositions that had predicted the observations. Normally, those propositions that generated strong prior expectations of the facts observed would receive the major share of support imparted by the observation. This plausible credit-assignment policy emerges naturally from the probabilistic analysis of causal interactions (see Section 4.3.2) but seems hard to realize in nonnumeric systems.

SUMMARY

The distinction between causal and evidential defaults allows us to distinguish properly rules that should be invoked from rules that should not be invoked. While the full power of this distinction can be unleashed only in systems that are sensitive to the relative strengths of the default rules, there is still much that causality can offer to systems lacking this sensitivity. Moreover, it is quite feasible that the major computational benefits of causal reasoning could be tapped with just a rough quantification of rule strength. Bayesian analysis should be consulted as a standard for abstracting more refined logical systems.

10.4 A PROBABILISTIC TREATMENT OF THE YALE SHOOTING PROBLEM

The Yale shooting problem discussed in the last section (see Figure 10.7) has triggered disenchantment with the logicist perspective in AI and has served as a focal point for discussions on the merit of this perspective [McDermott 1987]. This section presents a probabilistic treatment of the problem with the following objectives in mind:

1. To show that probability theory is more than number-crunching. Taken as a system for manipulating contexts, the theory provides a methodology for constructing sound qualitative arguments.

2. To show that pure probability theory is insufficient for handling commonsense reasoning. It can overcome some of the hurdles faced by the logicist approach only by invoking the auxiliary notions of causation and relevance, in their appropriate probabilistic interpretations.

10.4.1 The Problem and its Solution

A simplified version of the Yale shooting problem goes like this: Suppose you load a gun at time t_0, wait awhile, then shoot someone at time t_1. The shooting is supposed to make the victim dead at time t_2, despite the normal tendency of *Alive* to persist over long time periods. Surprisingly, the logical formulation of the episode reveals an alternative, perfectly symmetrical version of reality, whereby the persistence of *Alive* is retained but the persistence of *Loaded* is interrupted, yielding the unintended conclusion that the victim is alive at time t_2. The question ·is, what information do people extract from the story that makes them prefer the persistence of *Loaded* over the persistence of *Alive*?

Our analysis of the shooting episode will be facilitated by the following definitions:

LD_0 = "The gun is loaded at time t_0,"

LD_1 = "The gun is loaded at time t_1,"

SH_1 = "You pull the trigger at time t_1,"

AL_1 = "The victim is alive at time t_1,"

AL_2 = "The victim is alive at time t_2."

The story contains three known facts, LD_0, AL_1, and SH_1, and the problem is to infer the truth of $\neg AL_2$ (and of LD_1). Domain knowledge is given by four default rules (see Figure 10.8):

d_1: $LD_0 \rightarrow LD_1$, d_3: $AL_1 \wedge SH_1 \wedge LD_1 \rightarrow \neg AL_2$,

d_2: $AL_1 \rightarrow AL_2$, d_4: $AL_1 \wedge SH_1 \wedge \neg LD_1 \rightarrow AL_2$.

Rule d_1, for example, states that under normal circumstances a gun is expected to remain loaded; d_2 asserts the natural tendency of life to persist over time. These rules can be given the following probabilistic interpretation:

d'_1: $P(LD_1 \mid LD_0) = HIGH = 1 - \varepsilon_1$,

d'_2: $P(AL_2 \mid AL_1) = HIGH = 1 - \varepsilon_2$,

d'_3: $P(AL_2 \mid AL_1, SH_1, LD_1) = LOW = \varepsilon_3$,

d'_4: $P(AL_2 \mid AL_1, SH_1, \neg LD_1) = HIGH = 1 - \varepsilon_4$,

where the ε's are small positive quantities whose exact values turn out to be insignificant.

Using these inputs, our task is to derive the conclusion that given the stated facts $\{LD_0, AL_1, SH_1\}$, the victim is unlikely to remain alive at t_2, namely,·

$$P(AL_2 \mid LD_0, AL_1, SH_1) = LOW. \tag{10.51}$$

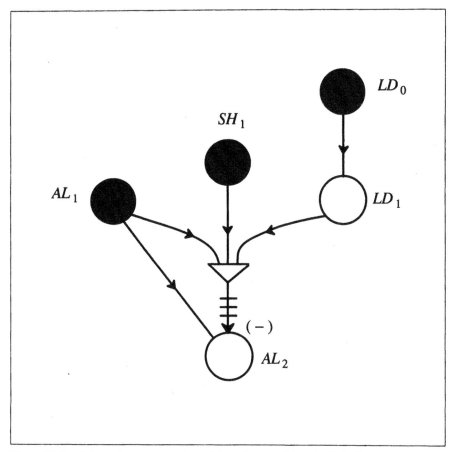

Figure 10.8. *Schematic representation of the rules specifying the Yale shooting problem.*

Probabilists will realize immediately that the information given does not specify a complete probabilistic model and therefore is insufficient for deriving the intended conclusion (Eq. (10.51)) or its negation. The assumptions needed for completing the model involve the notions of causality and dependency and can be precisely formulated within the language of conditional probabilities.

Since the context of Eq. (10.51) differs from that of d'_3, the natural first step is to refine the former by expansion over the two possible cases of LD_1:

$$P(AL_2 \mid LD_0, AL_1, SH_1)$$

$$= P(AL_2 \mid LD_1, LD_0, AL_1, SH_1) \, P(LD_1 \mid LD_0, AL_1, SH_1)$$

$$+ P(AL_2 \mid \neg LD_1, LD_0, AL_1, SH_1) \, P(\neg LD_1 \mid LD_0, AL_1, SH_1) . \quad \textbf{(10.52)}$$

Clearly, before we can use the given default rules, the first and last terms in Eq. (10.52) must undergo the following two transformations of context:

$$P(AL_2 \mid LD_1, LD_0, AL_1, SH_1) = P(AL_2 \mid LD_1, AL_1, SH_1) = \varepsilon_3 \qquad \textbf{(10.53)}$$

and

$$P(\neg LD_1 \mid LD_0, AL_1, SH_1) = P(\neg LD_1 \mid LD_0) = \varepsilon_1 . \qquad \textbf{(10.54)}$$

The first states that the effect of the shooting depends only on the state of the gun at time t_1, not on its previous history. The second asserts that the truth of AL_1 and SH_1 does not diminish the likelihood that the gun will be loaded at t_1, given that it is loaded at t_0.

Assuming that Eqs. (10.53) and (10.54) are permissible (justification will follow), the desired conclusion, Eq. (10.51), can be reached immediately. Substituting Eq. (10.53) and Eq. (10.54) in Eq. (10.52) yields

$$P(AL_2 \mid LD_0, AL_1, SH_1) = \varepsilon_3(1 - \varepsilon_1) + P(AL_2 \mid \neg LD_1, LD_0, AL_1, SH_1)\, \varepsilon_1$$

$$\leq \varepsilon_3 + \varepsilon_1$$

$$= LOW ,$$

which confirms Eq. (10.51).

One can easily imagine situations where Eq. (10.53) or Eq. (10.54) is violated, e.g., the gun user is known to be a meticulous individual who would not pull the trigger (SH_1) before making sure that the gun is loaded at t_1. However, the main point is not to dream up possible violations of expectations but rather to formulate the general principles that govern our normal expectations—in other words, the principles that allow us to posit the validity of Eq. (10.53) and Eq. (10.54) while rejecting the alternative symmetrical assumption

$$P(AL_2 \mid LD_0, AL_1, SH_1) = P(AL_2 \mid AL_1) = 1 - \varepsilon_2 , \qquad \textbf{(10.55)}$$

which affirms the persistence of life under all conditions. Such principles have not been explicated in the probabilistic literature, where it is often assumed that all conditional probabilities are either available or derivable from a complete distribution function.

Cast in probabilistic terms, three general principles can be identified:

1. Propositions not mentioned explicitly in the default rules represent possibilities summarized by the numerical values of the probabilities involved; e.g., the possibility that somebody has emptied the gun between t_0 and t_1 is summarized by ε_1.

2. Dependencies not mentioned explicitly are presumed to be independencies (provided that they are consistent with mentioned

dependencies); e.g., AL_2 is presumed to be independent of LD_0, given LD_1, AL_1, and SH_1 (thus justifying Eq. (10.53)), because no direct influence between LD_0 and AL_2 is given explicitly. The two cannot be assumed to be unconditionally independent, because that would violate the dependencies embodied in d_1 and d_3.

3. The directionality of the default rules is presumed to represent a *causal structure*. Interpreted probabilistically, this means that there exists some total ordering θ of the propositions in the system, consistent with the orientation of the default rules, such that propositions mentioned as direct justifiers (antecedents) of an event E render E conditionally independent of all its predecessors in θ. θ can be thought of as a temporal precedence, along which the present is presumed to be sufficiently detailed to render the future independent of the past. An identical interpretation also applies to nontemporal hierarchies of property inheritance.

This third principle has far-reaching ramifications, stemming from the logic of conditional independence developed in Chapter 3. One of its corollaries (Corollary 5 in Section 3.3.1) states that the existence of one ordering θ satisfying the independence conditions of principle 3 guarantees that the conditions are satisfied in *every* ordering consistent with the directions of rules. In other words, we need not know the actual chronological order of events in the system; given the truth of all propositions mentioned as antecedents of event E, the probability that E will materialize is not affected by any other proposition in the system (except, of course, by E's own consequences). For example, LD_1 is presumed to be independent of AL_1 and SH_1, given LD_0, because LD_0 is mentioned as the only cause (justifier) of LD_1 and because AL_1 and SH_1 are not mentioned as consequences of LD_1. On the other hand, AL_2 is not independent of SH_1 given AL_1, because SH_1 is mentioned as a direct cause of $\neg AL_2$ in rule d_3. Thus, the transformations in Eqs. (10.53) and (10.54) are licensed by principles 1, 2, and 3, but the transformation in Eq. (10.55) is rejected.

10.4.2 Concluding Dialogue

Logicist: I am quite intrigued by the $P(* \mid *)$ notation you employ to keep track of varying contexts—it reminds me of the way truth-maintenance systems keep track of justifications. But getting to the bottom of things, what really makes your system prefer the persistence of *Loaded* over the persistence of *Alive*?

Probabilist: Honestly, my system hates to interrupt the persistence of life; after all, it tries to minimize all abnormal events. But as you well know, simply minimizing the number of abnormal events is a bad policy; what needs to be minimized is *conditional* abnormality—abnormality in the context of all known facts. Under usual circumstances, clipping one's life is indeed abnormal. But we are not dealing here with usual circumstances because two facts are known to have occurred— *Shoot* and *Gun loaded at* t_0—and there is no rule stating that life tends to persist in this refined context.

Logicist:

But circumstances are hardly ever "normal"; with any reasoning activity we are always going to have new facts floating around that were not spelled out in the rules. How do you ever get to use any of the rules if their context does not exactly match the context created by all the new facts? Suppose you have a rule $a \rightarrow b$, and you know facts a and c; can you invoke the rule?

Probabilist:

Offhand, I can't. I would worry that "a and c" represents an exception to the rule.

Logicist:

Well, I am more courageous. I would apply the rule without a second thought, unless someone told me that "a and c" is an exception.

Probabilist:

By then it might be too late! Actually, I am not that helpless either. Using the logic of probabilistic independence, I would attempt to judge if c is irrelevant to b (given a), in which case the rule could be invoked. The logic permits me to identify and prune away irrelevant facts from the current context so that it matches the context specified by the rules. This is how I managed to show that *Shoot* is irrelevant to the persistence of *Loaded* (Eq. (10.54)). But I could not show that *Shoot* is irrelevant to the persistence of *Alive* because the rules (rule d_3, for instance) tell me that *Shoot* (when combined with *Loaded*) is capable of interfering with *Alive*.

Logicist:

I meant to ask you about this biased treatment. The rules also tell you that *Shoot* (when combined with other facts) is capable of interfering with *Loaded*; if we find the victim alive at t_2, then by knowing *Shoot* we can conclude *Unloaded*. So it seems to me, contrary to Eq. (10.54), that *Shoot* and *Loaded* are not entirely independent. Now, since we have no rule stating that guns tend to remain loaded in contexts involving *Shoot*, shouldn't the persistence of *Loaded* be questioned the way the persistence of *Alive* was?

Probabilist: Here is where causality comes in. Writing rule d_3 with *Shoot* and *Loaded* as antecedents makes me assume that the two causally affect *Alive*. Now, we have strict laws on how to interpret causal information in terms of independence relations. One of these laws tells us that an event with no antecedents is independent of all other events except its own consequences. This means that *Shoot* and *Loaded* are independent events while *Shoot* and *Alive* are not.†

Logicist: You mean to tell me that you draw all causality information from the directions of the rules? This means they must be acyclic, and you would have to be very careful about using contraposition.

Probabilist: I would much rather extract causal information directly from temporal precedence, as you folks are doing; it would make things much easier for me. But if temporal information is not available, I rely on the directionality of the rules, as most people would do, and then, yes, I must be careful. For example, had you written rule d_3 in its contrapositive form,

$$Alive(t_1) \wedge Alive(t_2) \wedge Shoot(t_1) \rightarrow \neg Loaded(t_1),$$

   without warning me that the rule now conveys diagnostic rather than causal information, I would be led to believe that *Shoot* has some causal influence over *Loaded*. Finding no arrow from *Shoot* to *Alive*, I would also conclude that those two are independent events, that *Shoot* cannot clip *Alive*.

Logicist: When you come down to it, the real reason you ruled out *Shoot* as a potential interference with *Loaded* is because the two interact only if the victim was seen alive at t_2, and one of your independence laws says that interactions mediated by unconfirmed future events can be discounted. Isn't this equivalent to Shoham's scheme of *chronological ignorance*,†† whereby one sweeps forward in time and minimizes the number of abnormal events while ignoring, as much as possible, the effect of future events.

Probabilist: Yes. The right to ignore unconfirmed future events is definitely a common feature of both schemes, but I am not sure at this

---

† Figure 10.8 shows SH_1 *d*-separated from LD_1 but not from AL_2.
†† Shoham 1986.

point whether chronological ignorance captures *all* the context transformations licensed by the probabilistic interpretation of causality; the probabilistic scheme also teaches us how to manage facts that can't be "ignored" by chronological considerations. Nevertheless, the logic of probabilistic independence does give Shoham's scheme its operational and probabilistic legitimacy. In general, probabilistic analysis can give many innovative but poorly understood developments in the logicist camp the empirical semantics they need.

10.5 BIBLIOGRAPHICAL AND HISTORICAL REMARKS

A good overview of various approaches to default reasoning can be obtained from Genesereth and Nilsson [1987] and the articles collected in Ginsberg [1987] and Smets et al. [1988].

Attempts to treat defaults with various uncertainty formalisms have been reported in Rich [1983], Ginsberg [1984], Michalski and Winston [1986], Yager [1987], and Dubois and Prade [1988]. However, these schemes do not take advantage of the conditioning device offered by probability theory, and exceptions therefore must be mentioned explicitly in the antecedent part of the rules. This requirement, which is similar to that of semi-normal default logic [Reiter and Criscuolo 1981], defies the very purpose of nonmonotonic reasoning [Touretzky 1984].

My interest in providing a coherent probabilistic semantics for defaults was kindled by Hector Geffner, who called my attention to the semantic gaps in inheritance networks with exceptions, as described in Brachman [1985] and Sandewall [1986]. Immersed as we were in Bayesian network techniques, the possibility that defaults could mean something other than statements of high conditional probabilities did not even cross our minds.

The discovery of Ernst Adams's work [Adams 1966] came as a revelation to both of us, though Hector had already developed independently an equivalent set of axioms. The axioms in Theorem 2 are tailored after Adams [1975] and are complete only for "soft" defaults. Complete axiomatization of mixed hard and soft statements can be obtained from the logic developed in Adams [1966], at the price of weakening the connection between entailment and consistency (Theorem 4). Rules 3 and 4 in Eq. (10.29) also appear in Gabbay [1985] as relations among sentences to be satisfied by any reasonable nonmonotonic logic.

The treatment of Section 10.2 is based on Pearl [1987b], Pearl and Geffner [1988] and Geffner and Pearl [1987b]. Additional features of the framework advanced in Geffner and Pearl [1987b] are a syntactic account of the conditions under which certain irrelevance assumptions can be postulated (see Exercises 10.7 and 10.8), and a distinction between evidential statements and model-specification statements (see Exercises 10.1 and 10.2). Further refinements along these lines are reported in Geffner [1988].

Section 10.3 is based on Pearl [1988b], while Section 10.4 on Pearl [1988a].

Recently, systems based on probabilistic semantics have been developed at a rapid pace, and have come closer to those stemming from the logical approach. A comprehensive summary of this progress can be found in a recent survey by the author.[1] Among these developments one should mention the unification of ε-semantics and ranked-models semantics[2] (Exercise 10.12.), a natural prioritization of default rules[3] (Exercise 10.11.a.), bridging the dispositional and conditional interpretations of defaults[4], efficient algorithms for deciding consistency and ε-entailment[5] (Exercise 10.11), a system based on the maximum entropy approach[6], systems incorporating causal relationships[4], systems accepting variable-strength defaults[7] and strict conditional statements[5], a logic for reasoning about statistical data[8], and a graph-based logic for inferring "support" relationships ("p supports q" if $P(q \mid p) > P(q)$)[9].

[1] J. Pearl, "Probabilistic Semantics for Nonmonotonic Reasoning: A Survey." *Proc. 1st Intl. Conf. on Principles of Knowledge Representation and Reasoning*, Toronto, Canada, May 1989, 505-516. Expanded version in *Philosophical AI: Computational Approaches to Reasoning*, eds. Robert Cummins and John Pollock, Bradford Books/MIT Press. 1991.

[2] Lehmann, D. What does a conditional knowledge base entail? *Proc. 1st Intl. Conf. on Principles of Knowledge Representation and Reasoning*, Toronto, Canada, May 1989, 212-222.

[3] J. Pearl, "System Z: A Natural Ordering of Defaults with Tractable Applications to Nonmonotonic Reasoning." In *Theoretical Aspects on Reasoning about Knowledge*, R. Parikh (ed), San Mateo: Morgan Kaufmann, 1990, 121-135.

[4] H. Geffner, "Default Reasoning: Causal and Conditional Theories." Ph.D. Dissertation, Computer Science Dept., University of California, Los Angeles, November 1989. Forthcoming, Cambridge, MA: The MIT Press.

[5] M. Goldszmidt & J. Pearl, "Deciding Consistency of Databases Containing Defeasible and Strict Information," in *Uncertainty in AI 5*, M. Henrion, R.D. Shachter, L.N. Kanal, and J.F. Lemmer (Eds.). Elsevier Science Publishers B.V. (North Holland), 1990, 87-97. Expanded version forthcoming in *Artificial Intelligence*.

[6] M. Goldszmidt, P. Morris, & J. Pearl, "A Maximum Entropy Approach to Nonmonotonic Reasoning." In *Proceedings, AAAI-90*, Boston, MA, 1990, 646-652.

[7] Goldszmidt, M. and Pearl, J. System Z^+: A Formalism for Reasoning with Variable Strength Defaults. *Proceedings, AAAI-91*, Anaheim, CA., July 1991, 399-404.

[8] Bacchus, F. *Representing and reasoning with probabilistic knowledge*, Cambridge, MA: The MIT Press, 1990.

[9] Neufeld, E., 1991. Notes on "A clash of intuitions," *Artificial Intelligence*, 48, (2):225-240.

Exercises

10.1. (After H. Geffner) A party is about to take place and, usually, most of your friends participate in such affairs. Before the party you meet your friend Tom and he tells you that if John goes, he will definitely not go.

    a.   Describe what your 'justified' beliefs are about Tom and John, before and after you met Tom.

    b.   Formulate the problem in terms of Reiter's default logic. Do the expected conclusions follow from the formulation?

    c.   Describe the nature of the problem and relate it to the Yale Shooting problem.

10.2. Solve Exercise **10.1** probabilistically starting with a reasonable probability distribution over the variables that concern us.

    a.   Assimilate the information received from Tom as a constraint on your original distribution and calculate your revised beliefs.

    b.   Treat the information received from Tom as an item of evidence, condition the original distribution on this evidence and compute your revised beliefs. Compare to the beliefs calculated in (**a**). Explain.

    c.   Solve problem **10.1** by the maximum entropy approach, assuming you have no prior knowledge about the behavior of Tom and John. Compute the maximum entropy distributions before and after receiving the information from Tom, treating the latter as a constraint. Compare to (**a**) and (**b**).

10.3. Prove the soundness of Eqs. (10.29b) and (10.29c) relative to ε-semantics.

10.4. Prove the Exceptions Theorem, Eq. (10.33) using

    a.   The five rules of Theorem 2.

    b.   Theorems 4 and 5.

10.5. Show that contraposition (Eq. 10.36) is not sanctioned by ε-semantics.

10.6. Show that if a theory T involves only three primitive propositions p, q and r, the maximum entropy approach sanctions Eqs. (10.42) through (10.45).

10.7. (After M. Goldszmidt) Consider the following set of defaults:

> $Penguin \rightarrow \neg Fly$ $\quad\quad$ $Penguin \rightarrow Winged\ animal$
> $Bird \rightarrow Fly$ $\quad\quad\quad\quad$ $Winged\ animal \rightarrow Bird$

Test if ε-semantics together with maximum entropy sanction the statements

a. $Penguin \wedge Bird \rightarrow Fly$

b. $Penguin \rightarrow Bird$

c. $Winged\ animal \wedge \neg Fly \rightarrow Bird$

10.8. (After H. Geffner). Assume that the predicate $I_\Delta(q, \neg r \,|\, p)$ in Eq. (10.40) is true if every directed path from q to $\neg r$ goes through p (in the graph which corresponds to Δ).

Prove, using rules 1-6, that Squeaky flies, given that: Squeaky is a winged mammal, bats are mammals, most bats fly, most mammals don't fly, and most winged mammals are bats.

(Hint: First prove that the conclusion follows from $Bat(Squeaky)$, $Mammal(Squeaky)$ and $Winged(Squeaky)$, then eliminate $Bat(Squeaky)$ from the premises).

10.9. (After H. Geffner). In Exercise **10.8**, a simple graph theoretic definition of predicate $I(\cdot)$ was given. In order to deal with more general cases, define $I_\Delta(r, \neg q \,|\, p)$ to be true only when every directed path that connects r to $\neg q$ is blocked by some consequence s of p that is not undermined by r (i.e., s satisfies $p \,\vert_{\overline{\Delta}}\, s$ and p, $r \,\vert_{\overline{\Delta}}\, s$).

a. Using rules 1-6 and this definition of $I(\cdot)$, show that Tom is likely not to be married, given that he is a university student and a worker, and that typically working people and university students are adults, and that while most adults are married, most university students are not.

b. Show that Jim, who is known to be a worker, is likely not to be a university student.

c. Discuss the relationship between this last definition of $I(\cdot)$ (in the context of rules 1-6) and Touretzky's inferential distance criterion (see Section 10.1.2 or [Touretzky 84]). Can you find examples in which the two criteria lead to different conclusions?

10.10. **a.** Convert the causal network of Figure 4.37 into a system of causal and diagnostic rules. Find all well-founded extensions of the observation $M_1 = TRUE, M_4 = TRUE$.

      b. Repeat question (a) for the observation $M_1 = M_2 = M_3 = TRUE$

      c. Assuming that causal rules contrapose (i.e., $A \rightarrow_C B$ is accompanied by $\neg B \rightarrow_E \neg A$) and that conflicting rules do not yield believed propositions, repeat question (a) for the observation $M_1 = FALSE, M_2 = M_3 = TRUE$.

10.11. We say that a default statement s is **tolerated** by Δ if there exists a truth valuation t that verifies s and does not falsify any statement in Δ.

      a. Show that Theorem 5 yields the following procedure for testing whether a knowledge base Δ is ε-consistent: Identify every statement that is tolerated by Δ, and remove those from Δ. Identify every statement that is tolerated by the remaining ones, remove those from the knowledge base, and so on. Δ is ε-consistent iff this removal procedure terminates with an empty set.

      b. Estimate the complexity of the procedure in **a** for the case in which all statements in Δ are Horn type.

      c. Use the procedure in **a** to prove the Exception Theorem, Eq. (10.33).

10.12. Let $P(t, \varepsilon)$ be a probability function, parameterized by ε, such that for each model (or truth valuation) t, $P(t, \varepsilon)$ is a polynomial function of ε. Define the rank of a model t as the lowest power of epsilon in $P(t, \varepsilon)$.

      a. Translate the probabilistic interpretation of defaults, Eq. (10.21), to the language of ranked models, by showing that as $\varepsilon \rightarrow 0$, each statement $p \rightarrow q$ in Δ imposes the following constraints on the ranks of models:
         i. q holds in every minimally-ranked model satisfying p, and
         ii. there should be at least one model satisfying p.

      b. Show that the procedure of Exercise 10.11.a guarantees the existence of a ranking (mapping of models to integers) that simultaneously satisfies all these constraints in 10.12.a.

Bibliography

Abend, K., Hartley, T. J., and Kanal, L. N. 1965. Classification of binary random patterns. *IEEE Trans. on Info. Theory* IT-11 (no. 4):538-44.

Adams, E. 1966. Probability and the logic of conditionals. In *Aspects of inductive logic,* ed. J. Hintikka and P. Suppes. Amsterdam: North Holland.

Adams, E. 1975. *The logic of conditionals.* Dordrecht, Netherlands: D. Reidel.

Aleliunas, R. A. 1988. A new normative theory of probabilistic logic. *Proc., 7th Biennial Conf. of the Canadian Society for Computational Studies of Intelligence* (CSCSI-88), Edmonton, Alta., 67-74.

Andreassen, S., Woldbye, M., Falck, B., and Andersen, S. K. 1987. MUNIN: A causal probabilistic network for interpretation of electromyographic findings. *Proc., 10th Intl. Joint Conf. on AI* (IJCAI-87), Milan, 366-72.

Baldwin, J. F. 1987. Evidential support logic programming. *Fuzzy Sets and Systems* 24:1-26.

Barbosa, V. C. 1986. Concurrency in systems with neighborhood constraints. Ph.D. diss., Computer Science Department, University of California, Los Angeles.

Bayes, T. 1763. An essay towards solving a problem in the doctrine of chances. *Phil. Trans. 3:370-418.* Reproduced in *Two papers by Bayes,* ed. W.E. Deming. New York: Hafner. 1963.

Beeri, C. 1980. On the membership problem for functional and multivalued dependencies in relational databases. *ACM Trans. on Database Systems* 5 (no. 3):241-49.

Beeri, C., Fagin, R., Maier, D., and Yannakakis, M. 1983. On the desirability of acyclic database schemes. *JACM* 30 (no. 3):479-513.

Ben-Bassat, M. 1978. Myopic policies in sequential classification. *IEEE Trans. Comput.* 27:170-74.

Ben-Bassat, M. 1980. Multimembership and multiperspective classification: Introduction, applications and a Bayesian model. *IEEE Trans. SMC* 10:331-36.

Ben-Bassat, M. 1982. Use of distance measures, information measures and error bounds in feature evaluation. In *Handbook of statistics,* ed. P. R. Krishnaiah and L. N. Kanal, vol. 2, 773-91. Amsterdam: North Holland.

Ben-Bassat, M., Carlson, R. W., Puri, V. K., Lipnick, E., Portigal, L. D., and Weil, M. H. 1980. Pattern-based interactive diagnosis of multiple disorders: The MEDAS system. *IEEE Trans. on Pattern Analysis and Machine Intelligence* PAMI-2:148-60.

Bentler, P. N. 1980. Multivariate analysis with latent variables. *Review of Psychology* 31: 419-56.

Bertelé, U., and Brioschi, F. 1972. *Nonserial dynamic programming.* New York: Academic Press.

Blalock, H. M. 1971. *Causal models in the social sciences.* London: Macmillan.

Bobrow, D. G., ed. 1984. Special volume on qualitative reasoning about physical systems. *Artificial Intelligence* 24:1-5.

Bobrow, D. G., and Winograd, T. 1977. An overview of KRL, a knowledge representation language. *Cognitive Science* 1 (no. 1):3-46.

Bonissone, P. P., Gans, S. S., and Decker, K. S. 1987. RUM: A layered architecture for reasoning with uncertainty. *Proc., 10th Intl. Joint Conf. on AI* (IJCAI-87), Milan, 891-98.

Brachman, R. J. 1985. I lied about the trees, or defaults and definitions in knowledge representation. *AI Magazine* 6 (no. 3):80-93.

Brown, F. M., ed. 1987. *The frame problem in artificial intelligence. Proceedings of the 1987 workshop* (Lawrence, Kansas). Los Altos: Morgan Kaufmann.

Buchanan, B. G., and Duda, R. O. 1983. Principles of rule-based expert systems. In *Advances in computers,* ed. M. C. Yovits, vol. 22, 164-216. New York: Academic Press.

Buchanan, B. G., and Shortliffe, E. H. 1984. *Rule-based expert systems.* Reading, Mass.: Addison-Wesley.

Bundy, A. 1985. Incidence calculus: A mechanism for probabilistic reasoning. *Journal of Automated Reasoning* 1:263-83.

Chandrasekaran, B., and Mittal, S. 1983. Conceptual representation of medical knowledge for diagnosis by computer: MDX and related systems. In *Advances in computers,* ed. M. C. Yovits, vol. 22., 217-93. New York: Academic Press.

Chandy, K. M., and Misra, J. 1984. The drinking philosophers problem. *ACM Trans. on Programming Languages and Systems* 6 (no. 4):632-46.

Charniak, E., Riesbeck, C. K., and McDermott, D. V. 1980. *Artificial intelligence programming.* Hillsdale, N.J.: Lawrence Erlbaum.

Cheeseman, P. 1983. A method of computing generalized Bayesian probability values for expert systems. *Proc., 6th Intl. Joint Conf. on AI* (IJCAI-83), Karlsruhe, W. Germany, 198-202.

Cheeseman, P. 1985. In defense of probability. *Proc., 8th Intl. Joint Conf. on AI* (IJCAI-85), Los Angeles, 1002-9.

Cheeseman, P. 1988. An inquiry into computer understanding. *Computational Intelligence* 4 (no. 1):58-66.

Chin, H. L., and Cooper, G. F. 1987. Stochastic simulation of Bayesian belief networks. *Proc., 3rd Workshop on Uncertainty in AI,* Seattle, 106-13.

Chou, P. B., and Brown, C. M. 1987. Probabilistic information fusion for multi-model image segmentation. *Proc., 10th Intl. Joint Conf. on AI* (IJCAI-87), Milan, 779-82.

Chow, C. K., and Liu, C. N. 1968. Approximating discrete probability distributions with dependence trees. *IEEE Trans. on Info. Theory* IT-14:462-67.

Chow, C. K., and Wagner, T. J. 1973. Consistency of an estimate of tree-dependent probability distributions. *IEEE Trans. on Info. Theory* IT-19:369-71.

Clancey, W. J. 1985. Heuristic classification. *Artificial Intelligence* 27 (no. 3):289-350.

Cohen, P. R. 1985. *Heuristic reasoning about uncertainty: An artificial intelligence approach.* Boston: Pitman.

Cohen P., Day, D., Delisio, J., Greenberg, M., Kjeldsen, R., Suthers, D., and Berman, P. 1987. Management of uncertainty in medicine. *Intl. Journal of Approximate Reasoning* 1 (no. 1):103-16.

Cohen, P. R., Shafer, G., and Shenoy, P. P. 1987. Modifiable combining functions. *Proc., 3rd Workshop on Uncertainty in AI,* Seattle, 10-21.

Cooper, G. F. 1984. NESTOR: A computer-based medical diagnostic aid that integrates causal and probabilistic knowledge. Ph.D. diss., Department of Computer Science, Stanford University.

Cooper, G. F. 1990. The computational complexity of probabilistic inferences. *Artifical Intelligence* 42:393-405.

Cox, R. 1946. Probability frequency and reasonable expectation. *American Journal of Physics* 14 (no. 1):1-13.

D'Ambrosio, B. 1987. Truth maintenance with numeric certainty estimates. *Proc., 3rd IEEE Conf. on AI Applications,* Orlando, Fla., 244-49.

David, F. N. 1962. *Games, gods and gambling.* London: Griffin.

Davis, R. 1984. Diagnostic reasoning based on structure and behavior. *Artificial Intelligence* 24:347-410.

Davis, R., Buchanan, B. G., and Shortliffe, E. H. 1977. Production rules as a representation for a knowledge-based consultation system. *Artificial Intelligence* 8 (no. 1):15-45.

Dawid, A. P. 1979. Conditional independence in statistical theory. *J. Royal Statist. Soc.,* ser. B 41 (no. 1):1-31.

de Finetti, B. 1937. Foresight: its logical laws, its subjective sources. *Ann. Inst. H. Poincaré* 7:1-68. Translated by H. E. Kyburg in Kyburg and Smokler [1980], 55-118.

de Finetti, B. 1974. *Theory of probability.* New York: Wiley.

de Finetti, B. 1977. Probabilities of probabilities: A real problem or a misunderstanding? In *New developments in the applications of Bayesian methods,* ed. A. Aykac and C. Brumet, 1-10. Amsterdam: North Holland.

de Kleer, J. 1986. An assumption-based truth maintenance system. *Artificial Intelligence* 29:241-88.

de Kleer, J., and Brown, J. S. 1986. Theories of causal ordering. *Artificial Intelligence* 29 (no. 1):33-62.

de Kleer, J., and Williams, B. C. 1986. Reasoning about multiple-faults. *Proc., 5th Natl. Conf. on AI* (AAAI-86), Philadelphia, 132-39.

de Kleer, J. and Williams, B. C. 1987. Diagnosing Multiple Faults. *Artificial Intelligence* 32 (no. 1): 97-130.

Dechter, R. 1987. Decomposing an N-ary relation into a tree of binary relations. *Proc., 6th Conf. on Principles of Database Systems,* San Diego, 185-89.

Dechter, R., and Pearl, J. 1985. The anatomy of easy problems: A constraint-satisfaction formulation. *Proc., 8th Intl. Joint Conf. on AI* (IJCAI-85), Los Angeles, 1066-72.

Dechter, R., and Pearl, J. 1987a. The cycle-cutset method for improving search performance in AI applications. *Proc., 3rd IEEE Conf. on AI Applications,* Orlando, Fla., 224-30.

Dechter, R., and Pearl, J. 1987b. Tree-clustering schemes for constraint-processing. *Proc., 7th Natl. Conf. on AI* (AAAI-88), Minneapolis:150-54. Also, *Artificial Intelligence* 38 (no. 3):353-66.

Dechter, R., and Pearl, J. 1987c. Network-based heuristics for constraint-satisfaction problems. *Artificial Intelligence* 34 (no. 1): 1-38.

Dell, G. S. 1985. Positive feedback in hierarchical connectionist models: Applications to language production. *Cognitive Science* 9 (no. 1):3-24.

Dempster, A. P. 1967. Upper and lower probabilities induced by a multivalued mapping. *Ann. Math. Statistics* 38:325-39.

Dempster, A. P. 1968. A generalization of Bayesian inference. *J. Royal Statist. Soc.,* ser. B 30:205-47.

Dempster, A. P. 1972. Covariance selection. *Biometrica* 28:157-75.

Diaconis, P., and Zabell, S. L. 1986. Some alternatives to Bayes's Rule. In *Information pooling and group decision making,* ed. B. Grofman and O. Guillermo, 25-38. Greenwich, Conn.: JAI Press.

Dijkstra, E. W. 1972. Hierarchical ordering of sequential processes. In *Operating Systems Techniques,* ed. C. A. R. Hoare and R. H. Perrott, 72-93. New York: Academic Press.

Domotor, Z. 1981. Higher order probabilities. *Philosophical Studies* 40:31-46.

Doyle, J. 1979. A truth maintenance system. *Artificial Intelligence* 12 (no. 3):231-72.

Doyle, J. 1988. Artificial intelligence and rational self-government. Technical Report CMU-CS-88-124, Carnegie-Mellon University.

Dubois, D., and Prade, H. 1988. Default reasoning and possibility theory. *Artificial Intelligence* 35 (no. 2):243-57.

Duda, R. O., and Hart, P. E. 1973. *Pattern recognition and scene analysis.* New York: Wiley.

Duda, R. O., Hart, P. E., and Nilsson, N. J. 1976. Subjective Bayesian methods for rule-based inference systems. *Proc., Natl. Comp. Conf.* (AFIPS) 45:1075-82.

Duda, R. O., Hart, P. E., Barnett, P., Gaschnig, J., Konolige, K., Reboh, R., and Slocum, J. 1978. Development of the PROSPECTOR consultant system for mineral exploration. Final report for SRI Projects 5821 and 6915, SRI International Artificial Intelligence Center.

Duncan, O. D. 1975. *Introduction to structural equation models*. New York: Academic Press.

Etherington, D. W. 1982. Finite default theories. M.S. thesis, Department of Computer Science, University of British Columbia (Vancouver, B.C.).

Etherington, D. W. 1987. More on inheritance hierarchies with exceptions: Default theories and inferential distance. *Proc., 6th Natl. Conf. on AI* (AAAI-87), Seattle, 352-57.

Etherington, D. W., and Reiter, R. 1983. On inheritance hierarchies with exceptions. *Proc., 6th Intl. Joint Conf. on AI* (IJCAI-83), Karlsruhe, W. Germany, 104-8.

Even, S. 1979. *Graph algorithms*. Potomac, Md.: Computer Science Press.

Fagin, R. 1977. Multivalued dependencies and a new form for relational databases. *ACM Trans. on Database Systems* 2 (no. 3):262-78.

Fagin, R., and Halpern, J. Y. 1988. Reasoning about knowledge and probability. In *Proceedings of the second conference on theoretical aspects of reasoning about knowledge*, Asilomar, Calif., ed. M. Vardi, 277-93. Los Altos, Calif: Morgan Kaufmann.

Fahlman, S. 1979. *NETL: A system for representing and using real-world knowledge*. Cambridge: MIT Press.

Falkenhainer, B. 1986. Towards a general purpose belief maintenance system. *Proc., 2nd Workshop on Uncertainty in AI*, Philadelphia, 71-76.

Feller, W. 1950. *An introduction to probability theory and applications*, vol. 1 (3rd ed. 1968). New York: Wiley.

Ferguson, T. S. 1967. *Mathematical statistics: A decision theoretic approach*. New York: Academic Press.

Field, H. 1978. A note on Jeffrey conditionalization. *Philosophy of Science* 45:361-67.

Fine, T. 1973. *Theories of Probability*. New York: Academic Press.

Fishburn, P. C. 1986. The axioms of subjective probability. *Statistical Science* 1 (no. 3):335-58.

Fisher, R. A. 1957. The underworld of probability. *Sankhya* 18:201-10.

Friedman, R. D. 1986. Diagramatic approach to evidence (with discussion by W. Edwards and G. Shafer). *Boston University Law Review* 66 (no. 3,4):571-633.

Frueder, E. C. 1982. A sufficient condition of backtrack-free search. *JACM* 29 (no. 1):24-32.

Gabbay, D. M. 1985. Theoretical foundations for non-monotonic reasoning in expert systems. In *Logics and models of concurrent systems*, ed. K. R. Apt. Berlin: Springer-Verlag.

Gafni, E. M., and Bertsekas, D. P. 1981. Distributed algorithms for generating loop-free routes in networks with frequently changing topology. *IEEE Trans. on Communications* COM-29 (no. 1):11-18.

Gaifman, C. 1986. A theory of higher order probabilities. In *Theoretical Aspects of Reasoning about Knowledge,* ed. J. Y. Halpern, 275-92. Los Altos, Calif.: Morgan Kaufmann.

Gallager, R. G. 1968. *Information theory and reliable communications,* 13-27. New York: Wiley.

Gardner, M. 1961. *Second Scientific American book of mathematical puzzles and diversions.* New York: Simon and Schuster.

Geffner, H. 1988. On the logic of defaults. *Proc., 7th Natl. Conf. on AI* (AAAI-88), St. Paul, Minn: 449-54.

Geffner, H., and Pearl, J. 1987a. A distributed approach to diagnosis. Technical Report R-66, Cognitive Systems Laboratory, University of California, Los Angeles. Short version in *Proc., 3rd IEEE Conf. on AI Applications,* Orlando, Fla., 156-62.

Geffner, H., and Pearl, J. 1987b. A framework for reasoning with defaults. Technical Report R-94, Cognitive Systems Laboratory, University of California, Los Angeles. Also in *Knowledge Representation and Defeasible Reasoning,* ed. H. Kyburg, et al., Kluer Academic Publishers, 1990, pp. 69-95.

Geffner, H., and Pearl, J. 1987c. An improved constraint propagation algorithm for diagnosis. *Proc., 10th Intl. Joint Conf. on AI* (IJCAI-87), Milan, 1105-11.

Geiger, D. 1987. Towards the formalization of informational dependencies (M.S. thesis). Technical Report R-102, Cognitive Systems Laboratory, University of California, Los Angeles.

Geiger, D., and Pearl, J. 1988a. Logical and algorithmic properties of conditional independence. Technical Report R-97, Cognitive Systems Laboratory, University of California, Los Angeles. Also, forthcoming, *Annals of Statistics.*

Geiger, D., and Pearl, J. 1988b. On the logic of causal models. *Proc., 4th Workshop on Uncertainty in AI, Minneapolis.*

Geman, S., and Geman, D. 1984. Stochastic relaxations, Gibbs distributions and the Bayesian restoration of images. *IEEE Trans. on Pattern Analysis and Machine Intelligence* PAMI-6 (no. 6):721-42.

Genesereth, M. R. 1984. The use of design descriptions in automated diagnosis. *Artificial Intelligence* 24 (no. 1):411-36.

Genesereth, M. R., and Nilsson, N. J. 1987. *Logical foundations of Artificial Intelligence.* Los Altos, Calif: Morgan Kaufmann.

Ginsberg, M. L. 1984. Non-monotonic reasoning using Dempster's rule. *Proc., 3rd Natl. Conf. on AI* (AAAI-84), Austin, 126-29.

Ginsberg, M. L., ed. 1987. *Readings in non-monotonic reasoning.* Los Altos, Calif: Morgan Kaufmann.

Glymour, C., Scheines, R., Spirtes, P., and Kelly, K. 1987. *Discovering causal structure*. New York: Academic Press.

Goldman, S. A., and Rivest, R. L. 1986. Making maximum entropy computations easier by adding extra constraints. *Proc. 6th Ann. Workshop on Max. Entropy and Bayesian Methods in App. Statistics*, Seattle. Also in *Uncertainty in artificial intelligence 2*, ed. J. F. Lemmer and L. N. Kanal, 133-48. Amsterdam: North Holland.

Golumbic, M. C. 1980. *Algorithmic graph theory and perfect graphs*. London: Academic Press.

Good, I. J. 1950. *Probability and the weighing of evidence*. London: Griffin.

Good, I. J. 1961. A causal calculus. *Philosophy of science* 11:305-18. Also in Good [1983].

Good, I. J. 1962. Subjective probability as the measure of a non-measurable set. In *Logic, methodology, and the philosophy of science*, ed. E. Nagel, P. Suppes, and A. Tarski, 319-29. Stanford: Stanford University Press.

Good, I. J. 1983. *Good thinking: The foundations of probability and its applications*. Minneapolis: University of Minnesota Press.

Goodman, L. A. 1970. The multivariate analysis of qualitative data: Interaction among multiple classifications. *J. Amer. Statist. Assoc.* 65:226-56.

Goodman, I. R. 1987. A measure-free approach to conditioning. *Proc. 3rd Workshop on Uncertainty in AI*, Seattle, 270-277.

Goodman, I. R., and Nguyen, H. T. 1985. *Uncertainty models for knowledge based systems*. Amsterdam: North Holland.

Gordon, J., and Shortliffe, E. H. 1985. A method of managing evidential reasoning in a hierarchical hypothesis space. *Artificial Intelligence* 26 (July):323-57.

Grnarov, A., Kleinrock, L., and Gerla, M. 1979. A new algorithm for network reliability computation. *Proc., Computer Networking Symposium*, Gaithersburg, Mass., 17-20.

Grosof, B. N. 1986. Non-monotonicity in probabilistic reasoning. *Proc., AAAI Workshop on Uncertainty in AI*, Philadelphia, 91-98.

Haberman, S. J. 1974. The general log-linear model. Ph.D. diss., Department of Statistics, University of Chicago.

Hacking, I. 1975. *The emergence of probability*. London: Cambridge University Press.

Hájek, P. 1985. Combining functions for certainty degrees in consulting systems. *Intl. Journal of Man-Machine Studies* 22:59-65.

Hájek, P. 1987. Logic and plausible inference in expert systems. *Proc. of AI Workshop on Inductive Reasoning*, Roskilde, Denmark.

Hájek, P., and Valdes, J. J. 1987. Algebraic foundations of uncertainty processing in rule-based expert systems. Technical report, Ceskoslovenka Akademie Ved, Matematicky Ustav.

Halpern, J. Y., and Rabin, M. 1987. A logic to reason about likelihood. *Artificial Intelligence* 32 (no. 3):379-406.

Hammersley, J. M., and Clifford, P. 1971. Markov fields on finite graphs and lattices. Unpublished manuscript cited in Isham [1981].

Hanks, S., and McDermott, D. V. 1986. Default reasoning, nonmonotonic logics, and the frame problem. *Proc., 5th Natl. Conf. on AI* (AAAI-86), Philadelphia, 328-33.

Hanks, S., and McDermott, D. V. 1987. Nonmonotonic logic and temporal projection. *Artificial Intelligence* 33:379-412.

Harper, W., Stalnaker, R., and Pearce, P., eds. 1981. *IFs, conditionals, belief, decision, chance, and time.* Dordrecht, Netherlands: D. Reidel.

Harman, G. 1986. *Change in view.* Cambridge: MIT Press.

Harsanyi, J. C. 1985. Acceptance of empirical statements: A Bayesian theory without cognitive utilities. *Theory and Decision* 18:1-30.

Hart, P. E., Nilsson, N. J., and Raphael, B. 1968. A formal basis for the heuristic determination of minimum cost paths. *IEEE Trans. on Systems, Man and Cybernetics* SSC-4 (no. 2):100-107.

Heckerman, D. 1986a. Probabilistic interpretations for MYCIN's certainty factors. In *Uncertainty in artificial intelligence,* ed. L. N. Kanal and J. F. Lemmer, 167-96. Amsterdam: North Holland.

Heckerman, D. 1986b. A rational measure of confirmation. Technical Report, Memo-KSL-86-25, Medical Computer Science Group, Stanford University; also in *Uncertainty in Artificial Intelligence* 2, ed. L. N. Kanal and J. F. Lemmer, 11-22. Amsterdam: North Holland.

Heckerman, D., and Jimison, H. 1987. A perspective on confidence and its use in focusing attention during knowledge acquisition. *Proc., 3rd Workshop on Uncertainty in AI,* Seattle, 123-31.

Henrion, M. 1986a. Propagating uncertainty by logic sampling in Bayes' networks. Technical Report, Department of Engineering and Public Policy, Carnegie-Mellon University.

Henrion, M. 1986b. Should we use probability in uncertain inference systems? *Proc., Cognitive Science Society Meeting, August 1986,* Amherst, Mass., 320-30.

Hinton, G. E., Sejnowski, T. J., and Ackley, D. H. 1984. Boltzmann machines: Constraint satisfaction networks that learn. Technical Report CMU-CS-84-119, Department of Computer Science, Carnegie-Mellon University.

Hoel, P. G., Port, S. C., and Stone, C. J. 1971. *Introduction to probability theory.* Boston: Houghton Mifflin.

Horty, J., Thomason, R., and Touretzky, D. 1987. A skeptical theory of inheritance in nonmonotonic semantic networks. *Proc., 6th Natl. Conf. on AI* (AAAI-87), Seattle, 358-63.

Horvitz, E. J., and Heckerman, D. 1986. The inconsistent use of measures of certainty in artificial intelligence research. In *Uncertainty in artificial intelligence,* ed. L. N. Kanal and J. F. Lemmer, 137-51. Amsterdam: North Holland.

Horvitz, E. J., Heckerman, D., and Langlotz, C. P. 1986. A framework for comparing alternative formalisms for plausible reasoning. *Proc., 5th Natl. Conf. on AI* (AAAI-86), Philadelphia, 210-14.

Howard, R. A. 1976a. The used car buyer. In *Readings in decision analysis,* ed. R. A. Howard, J. E. Matheson, and K. L. Miller, 491-520. Menlo Park, Calif.: Stanford Research Institute.

Howard, R. A. 1976b. Risk preference. In *Readings in decision analysis,* ed. R. A. Howard, J. E. Matheson, and K. L. Miller, 429-66. Menlo Park, Calif.: Stanford Research Institute.

Howard R. A., and Matheson, J. E. 1981. Influence diagrams. In *Principles and applications of decision analysis,* vol. 2 (1984). Menlo Park, Calif.: Strategic Decisions Group.

Howard, R. A., Matheson, J. E., and Miller, K. L. 1976. *Readings in decision analysis.* Menlo Park, Calif.: Stanford Research Institute.

Hummel, R., and Manevitz, L. M. 1987. Combining bodies of dependent information. *Proc., 10th Intl. Joint Conf. on AI* (IJCAI-87), Milan, 1015-17.

Hunter, D. 1989. Causality and maximum entropy updating. *Intl. Journal of Approximate Reasoning,* 3(1):87-114

Isham, V. 1981. An introduction to spatial point processes and Markov random fields. *Intl. Statist. Review* 49:21-43.

Iwasaki, Y., and Simon, H. A. 1986. Causality in device behavior. *Artificial Intelligence* 29 (no. 1):3-32.

Jaynes, E. T. 1979. Where do we stand on maximum entropy? In *The maximum entropy formalism,* ed. R. D. Levine and M. Tribus. Cambridge: MIT Press.

Jeffrey, R. 1965. *The logic of decisions.* New York: McGraw-Hill. (2nd Ed., 1983, Chicago:University of Chicago Press.)

Jeffrey, R. 1968. Probable knowledge. In *The problem of inductive logic,* ed. I. Lakatos. Amsterdam: North Holland.

Jeffreys, H. 1939. *Theory of probability.* Oxford: Clarenchou Press.

Joereskog, K. G. 1982. *Systems under indirect observation.* Amsterdam: North Holland.

Kahneman, D., Slovic, P., and Tversky, A., eds. 1982. *Judgment under uncertainty: Heuristics and biases.* Cambridge: Cambridge University Press.

Kanal, L. N. 1981. Markov mesh models. In *Image modeling,* ed. A. Rosenfeld, 239-43. New York: Academic Press.

Kanal, L. N., and Lemmer, J. F., eds. 1986. *Uncertainty in artificial intelligence.* Amsterdam: North Holland.

Kelly, C. W., III, and Barclay, S. 1973. A general Bayesian model for hierarchical inference. *Organizational Behavior and Human Performance* 10:388-403.

Kenley, R. C. 1986. Influence diagram models with continuous variables. Ph.D. diss., Engineering-Economic Systems Department, Stanford University.

Kenney, R. L., and Raiffa, H. 1976. *Decisions with multiple objectives: Preferences and value tradeoffs.* New York: Wiley.

Kenny, D. A. 1979. *Correlation and causality.* New York: Wiley.

Keynes, J. M. 1921. *A treatise on probability.* London: MacMillan.

Kiiveri, H., Speed, T. P., and Carlin, J. B. 1984. Recursive causal models *Journal of Australian Math Soc.* 36:30-52.

Kim, J. H. 1983. CONVINCE: A conversation inference consolidation engine. Ph.D. diss., Department of Computer Science, University of California, Los Angeles.

Kim, J. H., and Pearl, J. 1983. A computational model for combined causal and diagnostic reasoning in inference systems. *Proc., 8th Intl. Joint Conf. on AI* (IJCAI-83), Karlsruhe, West Germany.

Kim, J. H., and Pearl, J. 1987. CONVINCE: A conversational inference consolidation engine. *IEEE Trans. on Systems, Man and Cybernetics* 17 (no. 2):120-32.

Kirkpatrick, S., Gelatt, C. D., Jr., and Vecchi, M. P. 1983. Optimization by simulated annealing. *Science* 220:671-80.

Kolmogorov, A. N. 1950. *Foundations of the theory of probability.* New York: Chelsea Publishing.

Kong, A. 1986. Multivariate belief functions and graphical models. Ph.D diss., Department of Statistics, Harvard University.

Krantz, D. H., Duncan, L. R., Suppes, P., and Tversky, A. 1971. *Foundations of measurement.* New York: Academic Press.

Kulikowski, C., and Weiss, S. 1982. Representation of expert knowledge for consultation: The CASNET and EXPERT projects. In *Artificial intelligence in medicine,* ed. P. Szolovits, 21-55. Boulder, Colo.:Westview.

Kullback, S., and Leibler, R. A. 1951. Information and sufficiency. *Ann. Math. Statistics* 22:79-86.

Kyburg, H. E. 1961. *Probability and the logic of rational belief.* Middleton, Conn.: Wesleyan University Press.

Kyburg, H. E. 1983. The reference class. *Philosophy of Science* 50:374-97.

Kyburg, H. E. 1987a. Higher order probabilities. *Proc., 3rd Workshop on Uncertainty in AI,* Seattle, 30-38.

Kyburg, H. E. 1987b. Bayesian and non-Bayesian evidential updating. *Artificial Intelligence* 31: 271-94.

Kyburg, H. E., and Smokler, H. E., eds. 1980. *Studies in subjective probability.* New York: Krieger.

Laskey, K. B., and Lehner, P. E. 1988. Belief maintenance: An integrated approach to uncertainty management. *Proc., 7th Natl. Conf. on AI* (AAAI-88), St. Paul, Minn.: 210-14

Lauritzen, S. L. 1982. *Lectures on contingency tables.* 2nd ed. Aalborg, Denmark: University of Aalborg Press.

Lauritzen, S. L., and Spiegelhalter, D. J. 1988. Local computations with probabilities on graphical structures and their applications to expert systems. *J. Royal Statist. Soc.,* B, 50 (no. 2):154-227.

Lazarsfeld, P. F. 1966. Latent structure analysis. In *Measurement and prediction,* ed. S. A. Stouffer, L. Guttman, E. A. Suchman, P. F. Lazarfeld, S. A. Star, and J. A. Claussen. New York: Wiley.

Lemmer, J. F. 1983. Generalized Bayesian updating of incompletely specified distributions. *Large Scale Systems* 5:51-68.

Lemmer, J. F., and Barth, S. W. 1982. Efficient minimum information updating for Bayesian inferencing in expert systems. *Proc., Natl. Conf. on AI,* Pittsburgh, 924-27.

Lesser, V. R., and Erman, L. D. 1977. A retrospective view of HEARSAY II architecture. *Proc., 5th Intl. Joint Conf. on AI* (IJCAI-77), Cambridge, Mass., 790-800.

Levi, I. 1980. *The enterprise of knowledge.* Cambridge: MIT Press.

Lewis, D. 1976. Probabilities of conditionals and conditional probabilities. *Philosophical Review* 85 (no. 3):297-315.

Lindley, D. V. 1982. Scoring rules and the inevitability of probability. *International Statistical Review* 50:1-26.

Loui, R. P. 1986a. Defeat among arguments: A system of defeasible inference. Technical Report 190. Department of Computer Science, University of Rochester (Rochester, N.Y.).

Loui, R. P. 1986. Real rules of inference: Acceptance and non-monotonicity in AI. TR 191, Department of Computer Science, University of Rochester (Rochester, N.Y.).

Loui, R. P. 1987. Theory and computation of uncertain inference and decision. Ph.D diss., Department of Computer Science, University of Rochester (Rochester, N.Y.).

Lowrance, J. D. 1982. Dependency-graph models of evidential support. COINS Technical Report 82-26, University of Massachusetts at Amherst.

Lowrance, J. D., Garvey, T. D., and Strat, T. M. 1986. A framework for evidential-reasoning systems. *Proc., 5th Natl. Conf. on AI* (AAAI-86), Philadelphia, 896-901.

Maier, D. 1983. *The theory of relational databases.* Rockville, Md.: Computer Science Press.

Maler, O., and Ben-Bassat, M. 1986. Control strategies in uncertainty inference networks. Technical report, Faculty of Management, Tel Aviv University.

Malvestuto, F. M. 1986. Decomposing complex contingency tables to reduce storage requirements. *Proc., 3rd Intl. Workshop on Scientific and Statistical Database Management,* Luxembourg, 66-71.

McAllester, D. 1980. An outlook on truth maintenance. AI Memo No. 551, Artificial Intelligence Laboratory, Massachusetts Institute of Technology.

McCarthy, J. 1980. Circumscription: A form of non-monotonic reasoning. *Artificial Intelligence* 13:27-39.

McCarthy, J. 1986. Applications of circumscription to formalizing common-sense knowledge. *Artificial Intelligence* 28 (no. 1):89-116.

McCarthy, J., and Hayes, P. 1969. Some philosophical problems from the standpoint of artificial intelligence. In *Machine Intelligence,* ed. B. Meltzer and D. Michie, vol. 4, 463-502. Edinburgh, U. K.: Edinburgh University Press.

McDermott, D. V. 1987. Critique of pure reason (with discussion). *Computational Intelligence* 3 (Nov.):151-60.

McDermott, D. V., and Doyle, J. 1980. Non-monotonic logic 1. *Artificial Intelligence* 13 (no. 1,2):41-72.

Meditch, J. S. 1969. *Stochastic optimal linear estimation and control.* New York: McGraw-Hill.

Michalski, R. S., and Winston, P. H. 1986. Variable precision logic. *Artificial Intelligence* 29:121-96.

Miller, R. A., Poole, H. E., and Myers, J. P. 1982. INTERNIST-1: An experimental computer-based diagnostic consultant for general internal medicine. *New England Journal of Medicine* 307 (no. 8):468-70.

Montanari, U. 1974. Networks of constraints, fundamental properties and applications to picture processing. *Information Science* 7:95-132.

Morris, P. 1987. Curing anomalous extensions. *Proc., 6th Natl. Conf. on AI* (AAAI-87), Seattle, 437-42.

Niles, H. E. 1922. Correlation, causation, and Wright theory of "path coefficients." *Genetics* 7:258-73.

Nilsson, N. J. 1986. Probabilistic logic. *Artificial Intelligence* 28 (no. 1):71-87.

Pauker, S. P., and Kassirer, J. P. 1987. Decision analysis. *New England Journal of Medicine* 316 (no. 5):250-58.

Pearl, J. 1978. On the connection between the complexity and credibility of inferred models. *Intl. Journal of General Systems* 4:255-64.

Pearl, J. 1982. Reverend Bayes on inference engines: A distributed hierarchical approach. *Proc., Natl. Conf. on AI,* Pittsburgh, 133-36.

Pearl, J. 1984. *Heuristics: Intelligent search strategies for computer problem solving.* Reading, Mass.: Addison-Wesley.

Pearl, J. 1986a. On evidential reasoning in a hierarchy of hypotheses. *Artificial Intelligence* 28 (no.1):9-15.

Pearl, J. 1986b. A constraint-propagation approach to probabilistic reasoning. In *Uncertainty in Artificial Intelligence,* ed. L. N. Kanal and J. F. Lemmer, 357-70. Amsterdam: North Holland.

Pearl, J. 1986c. Fusion, propagation and structuring in belief networks. *Artificial Intelligence* 29 (no. 3):241-88.

Pearl, J. 1987a. Evidential reasoning using stochastic simulation of causal models. *Artificial Intelligence* 32 (no. 2):245-57.

Pearl, J. 1987b. Probabilistic semantics for inheritance hierarchies with exceptions. Technical Report 870052 (R-93), Cognitive Systems Laboratory, University of California, Los Angeles.

Pearl, J. 1987c. Deciding consistency in inheritance networks. Technical Report CSD 870053 (R-96), Cognitive Systems Laboratory, University of California, Los Angeles.

Pearl, J. 1987d. Distributed revision of composite beliefs. *Artificial Intelligence* 33 (no. 2):173-215.

Pearl, J. 1988a. On logic and probability. *Computational Intelligence* 4 (no. 1):99-103.

Pearl, J. 1988b. Embracing causality in formal reasoning. *Artificial Intelligence* 35 (no. 2):259-71.

Pearl, J., and Geffner, H. 1988. Probabilistic semantics for a subset of default reasoning. Technical Report R-93-III, Cognitive Systems Laboratory, University of California, Los Angeles.

Pearl, J., and Paz, A. 1985. GRAPHOIDS: A graph-based logic for reasoning about relevance relations. Technical Report 850038 (R-53-L), Cognitive Systems Laboratory, University of California, Los Angeles. Short version in *Advances in artificial intelligence 2,* ed. B. Du Boulay, D. Hogg., and L. Steels, 357-63, Amsterdam: North Holland.

Pearl, J., and Tarsi, M. 1986. Structuring causal trees. *Journal of Complexity* 2 (no. 1):60-77.

Pearl, J., and Verma, T. S. 1987. The logic of representing dependencies by directed graphs. *Proc., 6th Natl. Conf. on AI* (AAAI-87), Seattle, 374-79.

Pearl, J., and Verma T. S. 1991. A Theory of Inferred Causation, in Allen, J. A., Fikes, R., and Sandewall, E. (Eds.) *Principles of Knowledge Representation and Reasoning: Proceedings of the Second International Conference.* San Mateo, CA: Morgan Kaufmann.

Peirce, C. 1955. *Abduction and induction.* New York: Dover.

Peng, Y., and Reggia, J. A. 1986. Plausibility of diagnostic hypotheses. *Proc., 5th Natl. Conf. on AI* (AAAI-86), Philadelphia, 140-45.

Perez, A., and Jirousek, R. 1985. Constructing an intensional expert system (INES). In *Medical Decision Making,* 307-315. Amsterdam: Elsevier Sc. Pub.

Pinto, J. A. 1986. Relevance-based propagation in Bayesian networks (M.S. thesis). Technical Report 860098 (R-59), Computer Science Department, University of California, Los Angeles.

Pollock, J. 1974. *Knowledge and justifications.* Princeton: Princeton University Press.

Polya, G. 1954. *Mathematics and plausible reasoning.* Princeton: Princeton University Press.

Poole, D. L. 1987. Defaults and conjectures: Hypothetical reasoning for explanation and prediction. Research Report CS-87-54, University of Waterloo (Kitchener, Ontario).

Pople, H. 1982. Heuristic methods for imposing structures on ill-structured problems. In *Artificial intelligence in medicine,* ed. P. Szolovits. Boulder, Colo.: Westview.

Prade, H. 1983. A synthetic view of approximate reasoning techniques. *Proc., 6th Intl. Joint Conf. on AI* (IJCAI-83), Karlsruhe, W. Germany, 130-36.

Quillian, M. 1968. Semantic memory. In *Semantic information processing,* ed. M. Minsky, 216-70. Cambridge: MIT Press.

Quinlan, J. R. 1983. INFERNO: A cautious approach to uncertain inference. *The Computer Journal* 26:255-69.

Raiffa, H. A. 1968. *Decision analysis: Introductory lectures on choices under uncertainty.* Reading, Mass.: Addison-Wesley.

Raiffa, H. A., and Schlaifer, R. 1968. *Applied statistical decision theory.* Cambridge: MIT Press.

Ramsey, F. P. 1931. Truth and probability. In *The foundations of mathematics and other logical essays,* ed. R. B. Braithwaite. New York: Humanities Press. Reprinted in Kyburg and Smokler [1980], 23-52.

Rebane, G., and Pearl, J. 1987. The recovery of causal poly-trees from statistical data. *Proc., 3rd Workshop on Uncertainty in AI,* Seattle, 222-28.

Reggia, J. A., Nau, D. S., and Wang, Y. 1983. Diagnostic expert systems based on a set-covering model. *Intl. Journal of Man-Machine Studies* 19:437-60.

Reichenbach, H. 1949. *Theory of probability.* Berkeley: University of California Press.

Reiter, R. 1980. A logic for default reasoning. *Artificial Intelligence* 13:81-132.

Reiter, R. 1987a. A theory of diagnosis from first principles. *Artificial Intelligence* 32 (no. 1):57-95.

Reiter, R. 1987b. Nonmonotonic reasoning. In *Annual review of computer science,* vol. 2, 147-86. Palo Alto, Calif.: Annual Reviews.

Reiter, R., and Criscuolo, G. 1981. On interacting defaults. *Proc., 4th Intl. Joint Conf. on AI* (IJCAI-81), Vancouver, B.C., 270-76.

Reiter, R., and Criscuolo, G. 1983. Some representational issues in default reasoning. *Intl. J. Comput. Math.* 9:1-13.

Reiter, R., and de Kleer, J. 1987. Foundations of assumption-based truth maintenance systems. *Proc., 6th Natl. Conf. on AI* (AAAI-87), Seattle, 183-88.

Rich, E. 1983. Default reasoning as likelihood reasoning. *Proc., 6th Intl. Joint Conf. on AI* (IJCAI-83), Karlsruhe, W. Germany, 348-51.

Roberts, R. B., and Goldstein, I. 1978. The FRL manual. AI Memo No. 409, Massachusetts Institute of Technology.

Rosenfeld, A., Hummel, A., and Zucker, S. 1976. Scene labeling by relaxation operations. *IEEE Trans. SMC* 6:420-33.

Rosenthal, A. 1975. A computer scientist looks at reliability computations. In *Reliability and fault true analyses*, eds. Barlow et al., 133-52. Philadelphia: SIAM.

Ross, L., and Anderson, C. A. 1982. Shortcomings in the attribution process: On the origins and maintenance of erroneous social assessments. In *Judgement under uncertainty: Heuristics and biases,* ed. D. Kahneman, P. Slovic, A. Tversky, 129-52. Cambridge: Cambridge University Press.

Rumelhart, D. E., and McClelland, J. L. 1982. An interactive activation model of context effects in letter perception, part 2: The contextual enhancement effect and some tests and extensions of the model. *Psychological Review* 89:60-94.

Rumelhart, D. E., and McClelland, J. L. 1986. *Parallel distributed processing.* Cambridge, Mass.: MIT Press.

Ruspini, E. 1987. Epistemic logics, probability and the calculus of evidence. *Proc., 10th Intl. Joint Conf. on AI* (IJCAI-87), Milan, 924-31.

Russell, B. 1913. On the notion of cause. *Proceedings, The Aristotelian Society* 13:1-20.

Sandewall, E. 1986. Non-monotonic inference rules for multiple inheritance with exceptions. *Proceedings of the IEEE* 74 (no. 10):1345-53.

Savage, L. J. 1954. *The foundations of statistics.* New York: Wiley.

Savage, L. J., ed. 1962. *The foundations of statistical inference.* New York: Wiley.

Schank, R. 1972. Conceptual dependency: A theory of natural language understanding. *Cognitive Psychology* 3 (no. 4):552-631.

Schubert, L. K. 1976. Extending the expressive power of semantic networks. *Artificial Intelligence* 7 (no. 2):163-98.

Schubert, L. K. 1988. Cheeseman: A travesty of truth. *Computational Intelligence* 4 (no. 1):118-21.

Schum, D. A. 1987. *Evidence and inference for the intelligence analyst.* Lanham, Md.: University Press of America.

Schum, D. A., and Martin, A. W. 1982. Formal and empirical research on cascaded inference in jurisprudence. *Law and Society Review* 17:105-57.

Shachter, R. D. 1986. Evaluating influence diagrams. *Operations Research* 34 (no. 6):871-82.

Shachter, R. D., and Heckerman, D. 1987. Thinking backward for knowledge acquisition. *AI Magazine* 8:55-62.

Shachter, R. D., and Kenley, R. C. 1989. Gaussian influence diagrams. *Management Science* 35:527-50.

Shafer, G. 1976. *A mathematical theory of evidence.* Princeton: Princeton University Press.

Shafer, G. 1981. Constructive probability. *Synthese* 48:1-60.

Shafer, G. 1982. Bayes's two arguments for the rule of conditioning. *The Annals of Statistics* 10 (no. 4):1075-84.

Shafer, G. 1985. Conditional probability. *Intl. Statist. Review* 53:261-77.

Shafer, G. 1986a. Savage revisited. *Statistical Science* 1:463-501.

Shafer, G. 1986b. The combination of evidence. *Intl. Journal of Intelligent Systems* 1:155-79.

Shafer, G. 1987. Belief functions and possibility measures. In *Analysis of fuzzy information,* ed. J. Bezdek, vol. 1: Mathematics and logic, 51-84. Boca Raton, Fla.: CRC Press.

Shafer, G. 1988. Combining AI and OR. Working Paper No. 195, School of Business, University of Kansas (Lawrence).

Shafer, G., and Logan, R. 1987. Implementing Dempster's rule for hierarchical evidence. *Artificial Intelligence* 33 (no. 3):271-98.

Shafer, G., Shenoy, P. P., and Mellouli, K. 1987. Propagating belief functions in qualitative Markov trees. *Intl. Journal of Approximate Reasoning* 1 (no. 4): 349-400.

Shannon C. E., and Weaver, W. 1949. *The mathematical theory of communication.* Urbana: University of Illinois Press.

Shastri, L., and Feldman, J. A. 1984. Semantic networks and neural nets. Technical Report 131, Computer Science Department, University of Rochester (Rochester, N.Y.).

Shenoy, P. P., and Shafer, G. 1986. Propagating belief functions with local computations. *IEEE Expert* 1 (no. 3):43-52.

Shoham, Y. 1986. Chronological ignorance: Time, nonmonotonicity, necessity, and causal theories. *Proc., 5th Natl. Conf. on AI* (AAAI-86), Philadelphia, 389-93.

Shoham, Y. 1988. *Reasoning about change in time and causation from the standpoint of artificial intelligence.* Cambridge: MIT Press.

Shore, J. E. 1986. Relative entropy, probabilistic inference, and AI. In *Uncertainty in artificial intelligence,* ed. L. N. Kanal and J. F. Lemmer, 211-15. Amsterdam: North Holland.

Shortliffe, E. H. 1976. *Computer-based medical consultation: MYCIN.* New York: Elsevier.

Shortliffe, E. H., and Buchanan, B. G. 1975. A model of inexact reasoning in medicine. *Mathematical Biosciences* 23:351-379. Reprinted as Chapter 11 in Buchanan and Shortliffe [1984].

Shrobe, H., ed. 1988. *Exploring artificial intelligence: Survey talks from the national conferences on artificial intelligence.* San Mateo: Morgan Kaufmann.

Simon, H. A. 1954. Spurious correlations: A causal interpretation. *J. Amer. Statist. Assoc.* 49:469-92.

Simon, H. A. 1980. The meaning of causal ordering. In *Qualitative and quantitative social research,* ed. R. K. Merton, J. S. Coleman, and P. H. Rossi, 65-81. New York: Free Press.

Simpson, E. H. 1951. The interpretation of interaction in contingency tables. *J. Royal Statist. Soc.,* ser. B 13:238-41.

Smets, P. 1988. Belief functions (with discussion). In Smets et al. [1988], 253- 86.

Smets, P., Mamdani, A., Dubois, D., and Prade, H., eds. 1988. *Non-standard logics for automated reasoning.* London: Academic Press.

Smith, C. A. B. 1961. Consistency in statistical inference and decision. *J. Royal Statist. Soc.,* ser. B 23:218-58.

Smith, J. Q. 1989. Influence diagrams for statistical modeling. *The Annals of Statistics* 17(2):654-72.

Sowa, J. F. 1984. *Conceptual structures: Information processing in mind and machine.* Reading, Mass.: Addison-Wesley.

Spiegelhalter, D. J. 1986. Probabilistic reasoning in predictive expert systems. In *Uncertainty in artificial intelligence,* ed. L. N. Kanal and J. F. Lemmer, 47-68. Amsterdam: North Holland.

Spiegelhalter, D. J., and Knill-Jones, R. P. 1984. Statistical and knowledge-based approaches to clinical decision-support systems. *J. Royal Statist. Soc.,* ser. A 147:35-77.

Stephanou, H., and Sage, A. 1987. Perspectives on imperfect information processing. *IEEE Trans. on Systems, Man and Cybernetics* SMC-17 (no. 5):780-98.

Suppes, P. 1970. *A probabilistic theory of causation.* Amsterdam: North Holland.

Szolovits, P., and Pauker, S. G. 1978. Categorical and probabilistic reasoning in medical diagnosis. *Artificial Intelligence* 11:115-44.

Tarjan, R. E. 1976. Graph theory and Gaussian elimination. In *Sparse matrix computations,* ed. J. R. Bunch and D. J. Rose, 3-22. New York: Academic Press.

Tarjan, R. E., and Yannakakis, M. 1984. Simple linear-time algorithms to test chordality of graphs, test acyclicity of hypergraphs and selectively reduce acyclic hypergraphs. *SIAM J. Computing* 13:566-79.

Thompson, T. R. 1985. Parallel formulation of evidential reasoning theories. *Proc., 8th Intl. Joint Conf. on AI* (IJCAI-85), Los Angeles, 321-27.

Touretzky, D. 1984. Implicit ordering of defaults in inheritance systems. *Proc., 3rd Natl. Conf. on AI* (AAAI-84), Austin, 322-25.

Touretzky, D. 1986. *The mathematics of inheritance systems.* Los Altos, Calif.: Morgan Kaufmann.

Tribus, M. 1969. *Rational descriptions, decisions and designs.* Elmsford, N.Y.: Pergamon.

Tversky, A., and Kahneman, D. 1977. Causal schemata in judgments under uncertainty. In *Progress in social psychology,* ed. M. Fishbein. Hillsdale, N.J.: Lawrence Erlbaum.

Verma, T. S. 1986. Causal networks: Semantics and expressiveness. Technical Report R-65, Cognitive Systems Laboratory, University of California, Los Angeles. Also, 1988. In *Proc., 4th Workshop on Uncertainty in AI,* Minneapolis, Minn.: 352-59.

von Neumann, J., and Morgenstern, O. 1947. *Theory of games and economic behavior.* 2d ed. Princeton: Princeton University Press.

von Winterfeldt, D., and Edwards, W. 1986. *Decision analysis and behavioral research.* New York: Cambridge University Press.

Vorobev, N. N. 1962. Consistent families of measures and their extensions. *Theory of Probability and Appl.* 7:147-63.

Wald, A. 1950. *Statistical decision functions.* New York: Wiley.

Waltz, D. G. 1972. Generating semantic descriptions from drawings of scenes with shadows. AI Technical Report No. 271, Artificial Intelligence Laboratory, Massachusetts Institute of Technology.

Wermuth, N., and Lauritzen, S. L. 1983. Graphical and recursive models for contingency tables. *Biometrika* 70:537-52.

Wigmore, J. H. 1913. *The principles of judicial proof.* Boston: Little.

Wold, H. 1964. *Econometric model building.* Amsterdam: North Holland.

Woods, W. A. 1975. What's in a link? Foundations for semantic networks. In *Representation and understanding,* ed. D. Bobrow and A. Collins, 35-82. New York: Academic Press.

Wright, S. 1921. Correlation and causation. *Journal of Agricultural Research* 20:557-85.

Wright, S. 1934. The method of path coefficients. *Ann. Math. Statistics* 5:161-215.

Xu, L., and Pearl, J. 1987. Structuring causal tree models with continuous variables. *Proc., 3rd Workshop on Uncertainty in AI,* Seattle, 170-79.

Yager, R. 1987. Using approximate reasoning to represent default knowledge. *Artificial Intelligence* 31:99-112.

Yager, R. Ovchinnikov, S., Tong, R. M., and Nguyen, H. T., eds. 1987. *Fuzzy sets and applications: Selected papers by L. A. Zadeh.* New York: Wiley.

Zabell, S. L. 1987. The probabilistic analysis of testimony. Technical report, Department of Mathematics and Statistics, Northwestern University.

Zadeh, L. A. 1981. Possibility theory and soft data analysis. In *Mathematical frontier of the social and policy sciences,* ed. L. Cobb and R. M. Thrall, 69-129. Boulder, Colo.: Westview.

Zadeh, L. A. 1984. Review of *A mathematical theory of evidence,* by Glen Shafer. *AI Magazine* 5 (no. 3):81.

Zadeh, L. A. 1986. A simple view of the Dempster-Shafer theory of evidence and its implication for the rule of combination. *AI Magazine* 7 (no. 2):85-90.

Author Index

A

Abend, K. 120, 132
Ackley, D. H. 407
Adams, E. 25, 72, 481, 482, 484, 485,
 487, 488, 516
Aleliunas, R. A. 27
Andersen, S. K. 3, 27
Anderson, C. A. 280
Andreassen, S. 3, 27

B

Baldwin, J. F. 24, 445
Barbosa, V. C. 222, 233, 263
Barclay, S. 232, 39
Barth, S. W. 71
Bayes, T. 17, 70-71
Beeri, C. `89, 112, 132, 262
Ben-Bassat, M. 27, 240, 326, 327
Bentler, P. N. 347
Berman, P. 27
Bernouli, J. 70
Bertelé, U. 144
Bertsekas, D. P. 221
Blalock, H. M. 125
Bobrow, D. 345
Bonissone, P. P. 10, 27
Booker, L. 256
Brachman, R. J. 26, 516
Brioschi, F. 144
Brown, C. M. 373
Brown, F. M. 22
Brown, J. S. 408

Buchanan, B. G. 27, 342
Bundy, A. 11, 456, 463

C

Cardano, G. 16, 70
Carlin, J. B. 125
Carlson, R. W. 27, 240
Chandrasekaran, B. 3, 27
Chandy, K. M. 221
Charniak, E. 502
Cheeseman, P. 27, 372, 415, 463, 476
Chin, H. L. 223
Chou, P. B. 373
Chow, C. K. 386-389, 408
Clancey, W. J. 3
Clifford, P. 106
Cohen, P. R. 3, 11, 27
Cooper, G. F. 144, 196, 200, 223, 260,
 262, 272
Cox, R. 19, 27
Criscuolo, G. 469, 471, 473, 516

D

D'Ambrosio, B. 24, 455, 462, 463
David, F. N. 70
Davis, R. 27, 263
Dawid, A. P. 85, 88, 133, 495
Day, D. 27
de Finetti, B. 19, 27, 327, 357, 360, 363,
 366, 463
de Kleer, J. 240, 262, 263, 265, 272, 327,
 408, 452, 453, 454, 455, 463
Dechter, R. 233, 262, 384, 408, 431

Decker, K. S.   10, 27
Delisio, J.   27
Dell, G. S.   149
De Morgan, A.   1, 70
Dempster, A. P.   358, 413, 415, 462
Diaconis, P.   71, 462
Dijkstra, E. W.   221
Domotor, Z.   358
Doyle, J.   185, 240, 262, 327, 450, 451, 470, 499, 504
Dubois, D.   26, 465, 516
Duda, R. O.   3, 27, 81, 104, 382, 459
Duncan, L. R.   16, 19
Duncan, O. D.   125, 347

E

Edwards, W.   327
Erman, L. D.   147
Etherington, D. W.   450, 471, 489
Even, S.   388

F

Fagin, R.   16, 88, 112, 132, 133, 262
Fahlman, S.   489
Falck, B.   27
Falkenhainer, B.   24, 455, 463, 445
Feldman, J. A.   145, 148
Feller, W.   120, 216, 223
Ferguson, T. S.   327
Field, H.   66
Fine, T.   16, 19
Fishburn, P. C.   16
Fisher, R. A.   358, 457
Friedman, R. D.   232
Frueder, E. C.   384

G

Gabbay, D. M.   516
Gafni, E. M.   221, 233
Gaifman, C.   358
Gallager, R. G.   322, 394
Gans, S. S.   10, 27
Gardner, M.   423, 58
Garvey, T. D.   3, 13

Geffner, H.   26, 258, 287, 485, 493, 516-519
Geiger, D.   88, 89, 96, 107, 122, 131, 133, 136-137
Gelatt, C. D., Jr.   262
Geman, D.   132, 221
Geman, S.   132, 221
Genesereth, M. R.   263
Gerla, M.   456
Ginsberg, M. L.   3, 24, 438, 445, 450, 469, 516
Glymour, C.   408
Goldman, S. A.   115
Goldstein, I.   489
Goldstmidt, M.   519
Golumbic, M. C.   132
Good, I. J.   19, 232, 327, 358, 457, 463
Goodman, I. R.   425, 464
Goodman, L. A.   132
Gordon, J.   373
Greenberg,   27
Grnarov, A.   456
Grosof, B. N.   491

H

Haberman, S. J.   132
Hacking, I.   70
Hájek, P.   12, 446
Halpern, J. Y.   16
Hammersley, J. M.   106
Hanks, S.   466, 505
Har, P. E.   104
Harman, G.   280, 281, 287
Harper, W.   72
Harsanyi, J. C.   282, 286
Hart, P. E.   3, 27, 81, 260, 382
Hartley, T. J.   120, 132
Hayes, P.   15, 22
Heckerman, D.   6, 11, 27, 45, 46, 52, 126, 343, 360, 366
Henrion, M.   9, 212, 233
Hinton, G. E.   407
Horty, J.   493
Horvitz, E. J.   6, 27
Howard, R. A.   104, 125, 133, 232, 301, 304, 309, 327

Hummel, A. 148
Hummel, R. 425
Hunter, D. 464

I

Iwasaki, Y. 408
Isham, V. 105, 132, 96

J

Jaynes, E. T. 61, 415, 491
Jeffrey, R. 62, 64
Jeffreys, H. 70
Jimison, H. 360, 366
Jirousek, R. 3
Joereskog, K. G. 347

K

Kahneman, D. 151, 327
Kalme, C. 188
Kanal, L. N. 26, 120, 132
Kassirer, J. P. 27
Kelly, C. W., III 39, 232
Kelly, K. 408
Kenley, R. C. 348, 355
Kenney, R. L. 327
Kenny, D. A. 125, 347
Keynes, J. M. 70
Kiiveri, H. 125
Kim, J. 27, 232
Kirkpatrick, S. 262
Kjeldsen, R. 27
Kleinrock, L. 456
Kolmogorov, A. N. 70
Kong, A. 337, 432
Krantz, D. H. 16, 19
Kullback, S. 388
Kyburg, H. E. 71, 282, 366, 372, 373, 462

L

Langlotz, C. P. 27
Laskey, K. B. 462-463

Lauritzen, S. L. 83, 88, 96, 105, 115, 125, 132, 137, 204
Lazarsfeld, P. F. 399, 401, 408, 412
Lehner, P. E. 462-463
Leibler, R. A. 388
Lemmer, J. F. 26, 71, 132
Lesser, V. R. 147
Levi, I. 282
Lewis, D. 71
Lindley, D. V. 19, 27
Lipnick, E. 27, 240
Liu, C. N. 386, 387, 388, 408
Logan, R. 337, 373
Loui, R. P. 282, 287, 327, 493
Lowrance, J. D. 3, 13, 148, 149

M

Maier, D. 112, 132, 262
Maler, O. 326
Malvestuto, F. M. 390
Mamdani, A. 26, 465, 516
Manevitz, L. M. 425
Martin, A. W. 39, 232
Matheson, J. E. 104, 125, 133, 232, 304, 309, 327
McAllester, D. 148, 450
McCarthy, J. 15, 22, 25, 185, 477
McClelland, J. L. 149, 212
McDermott, D. V. 470, 502, 505, 509, 516
Meditch, J. S. 120, 348, 355, 382
Mellouli, K. 13, 88, 432
Michalski, R. S. 23
Miller, K. L. 327
Miller, R. A. 27
Misra, J. 221
Mittal, S. 3, 27
Montanari, U. 13, 81, 418
Morgenstern, O. 290, 327
Morris, P. 507
Myers, J. P. 27

N

Nau, D. S. 272
Nguyen, H. T. 464

Niles, H. E. 131
Nilsson, N. J. 3, 10, 27, 81, 104, 260,
         457, 460, 463, 516

P

Pauker, S. G. 27
Paz, A. 14, 88, 94, 97, 132, 139, 141
Pearce, P. 72
Pearl, J. 14, 26, 27, 88, 94, 96, 97, 104,
         107, 122, 133, 139, 141, 232, 233,
         258, 260, 262, 287, 301, 311, 384,
         392, 404, 406, 408, 431, 485, 488,
         493, 516, 517
Peng, Y. 200, 227, 233, 260, 262, 272
Perez, A. 3
Pinto, 327
Pollock, J. 27, 475
Polya, G. 7, 53, 161
Poole, D. L. 502
Poole, H. E. 27
Pople, H. 27, 240
Portigal, L. D. 27, 240
Prade, H. 26, 465, 516
Price, R. 29
Puri, V. K. 27, 240

Q

Quillian, M. 373
Quinlan, J. R. 10, 27, 148, 463

R

Rabin, M. 16
Raiffa, H. A. 327, 382
Ramsey, F. P. 19, 27
Raphael, B. 260
Rebane, G. 232, 392, 408
Reggia, J. A. 200, 227, 233, 260, 262,
         272
Reichenbach, H. 27
Reiter, R. 240, 454, 468, 469, 470, 471,
         472, 473, 477, 516
Rich, E. 24, 516
Riesbeck, C. K. 502

Rivest, R. L. 115
Roberts, R. B. 489
Rosenfeld, A. 148
Ross, L. 280
Rumelhart, D. E. 149, 212
Ruspini, 462
Russell, B. 18

S

Sage, A. 26
Sandewall, E. 516
Savage, L. J. 19, 327
Schank, R. 81
Scheines, R. 408
Schlaifer, R. 327, 382
Schubert, L. K. 373, 475, 476
Schum, D. A. 39, 232
Sejnowski, T. J. 407
Shachter, R. D. 52, 125, 126, 144, 233,
         310, 355
Shafer, G. 11, 13, 15, 19, 71, 88, 262,.
         334, 337, 357, 358, 373, 415, 425,
         432, 462
Shannon, C. E. 321
Shastri, L. 145, 148
Shenoy, P. P. 11, 13, 88, 262, 334, 337,
         373, 432
Shoham, Y. 14, 18, 408, 515
Shore, J. E. 388
Shortliffe, E. H. 3, 4, 27, 45, 337, 342,
         373
Shrobe, H. 462
Simon, H. A. 384, 396, 408
Simpson, E. H. 495
Slovic, P. 327
Smets, P. 26, 462, 465, 516
Smith, C. A. B. 457, 463
Smith, J. Q. 133
Smokler, H. E. 71
Sowa, J. F. 81
Speed, T. P. 125
Spiegelhalter, D. J. 115, 132, 196, 204,
         233, 360, 364, 373
Spirtes, P. 408
Stalnaker, R. 72
Stephanou, H. 26

Strat, T. M.   3, 13
Suppes, P.   16, 18, 19, 384, 408
Suthers, D.   27
Szolovits, P.   27

T

Tarjan, R. E.   112, 201, 262
Tarsi, M.   404
Thompson, T. R.   26
Touretzky, D. S.   26, 450, 471, 488-489,
   493, 516, 520
Tribus, M.   61, 373
Tversky, A.   16, 19, 151, 327

V

Valdes, J. J.   12
Vechi, M. P.   262
Verma, T. S.   119, 133
von Neumann, J.   290, 327
von Winterfeldt, D.   327
Vorobev, N. N.   132

W

Wagner, T. J.   389
Wald, A.   327
Waltz, D. G.   148

Wang, Y.   272
Weaver, W.   321
Weil, M. H.   240, 27
Wermuth, N.   125, 137
Wigmore, J. H.   232
Williams, B. C.   240, 262, 263, 265, 272,
   327, 453, 455, 463
Winston, P. H.   23, 516
Wold, H.   125
Woldbye, M.   3, 27
Woods, W. A.   81, 373
Wright, S.   125, 131, 347

X

Xu, L.   406, 408

Y

Yager, R.   464, 516
Yannakakis, M.   112, 132, 201, 262

Z

Zabell, S. L.   71, 462
Zadeh, L.   418, 425, 440
Zucker, S.   148

Subject Index

A

Abduction 7, 19, 381
Active paths 118
Adams'
 axioms 516
 logic 25, 480, 485, 516
Answering queries 223, 279
Antecedents 440
Anticipatory nodes 170, 181, 256
Arc reversal 310
Assumption-based reasoning 17, 205,
 261, 472
 see Conditioning
Assumptions, behind ruler 440, 450, 451
ATMS 452
 numerical uncertainties in 455
Attention, controlling 324
Axioms
 of "almost all" 480, 516
 of conditional independence 84
 of *d*-separation 128
 of graph separation 94
 of probability 16, 27, 30

B

Basic probability assignment 420
Bayes conditionalization 17, 64, 68, 71
Bayes' Rule 17, 34, 55
 history of 70
Bayesian belief networks 125
Bayesian networks 13, 50, 116-117, 119,
 125
 advantages of 116
 construction 119, 122

expressiveness 126
 test for 120
BEL* 247
BEL 152, 418, 422
Belief acceptance 240, 281-286
Belief commitments 468, 240
Belief functions 418-466
 applicability 427-428, 461
 computation 428-438, 440-446,
  455-457
 definition 418, 420
 history 462
 meaning 423, 427, 439, 447-450
Belief networks 12-13, 50
Belief revision 17, 240, 245, 450
 complexity 262
 conditioning 261
 propagation 250
 Stochastic simulation 262
Belief updating 37, 242
 approximate methods 195
 by clustering 197
 by conditioning 204
 by elimination 144
 by propagation 146
 by stochastic simulation 210
 complexity 144, 174
 under constraints 225
Bel 418
 see belief functions
 vs. BEL 422
Best explanation 246, 326
 multiple 257, 271
Bidirectional inferences 6, 149
Bidirectional propagation 157
Blocked paths 116, 118
Boltzmann machine 408

Boundary conditions   170, 181, 256
Boundary DAGs   119
Boundary strata   119
Broadcasting   321

C

Canonical models   184, 193, 346
Cascaded inferencing   39, 42, 161
Causal argument   255
Causal basin   393
Causal directionality   19, 51-52, 125-126,
     396, 408, 504, 513
   test for   396-397
Causal explanation   284
Causal models   128, 347, 383-386, 408
Causal nets   13
   see Bayesian networks
Causal reasoning   24, 383, 497
Causal rules   501
Causal schemata   122, 151, 383
Causal support   35, 164, 182, 499, 501
Causality   13-14, 50, 125, 128, 383
   and maximum entropy   463
   and temporal ordering   18, 126, 515
   in default reasoning   497-509
   probabilistic definition   18-19, 397
Causation   18-19, 51, 123, 408, 463
Causes
   direct   123
   interacting   7, 19, 49, 504
   multiple   7, 49, 176-176, 346
Certainty factors   3-4, 11, 24, 45
Chain rule   32, 109, 123
Chance nodes   300, 307
Chordal graphs   112, 127, 132, 201
Chordality
   axiom   128, 130
   test for   112
Chow tree   232
Chow's method   387-390
Chronological ignorance   14, 515
Circular reasoning   7, 149, 160
Circumscription   25, 497
Clique trees   111
   see Join trees
Cliques   105

Clustering   195, 197, 260, 356
Combination functions   10, 356
Compatibility constraints   418, 423, 427
Compatibility functions   105, 107
Completeness
   of Adams' axioms   481, 485, 516
   of dependency axioms   89, 95, 122
   of probability models   34, 124, 415, 457
Completeness conjecture   88, 122
Concurrency   219
Conditional dependency   79
Conditional independence   31, 36, 39, 44,
     80, 83, 385
   and graph separation   86, 92
   axioms of   84
Conditional probabilities   6, 12, 17, 24,
     30
Conditional sentences   71-72
   as constraints   71
Conditioning   17, 195, 204, 261, 355
Confidence   357
Confidence measures   363
Confirmation   342
Conjunctive queries   226
Connectionist paradigm   212, 408
Consequences   289
Consequent   440
Consistency   104, 457, 487-488
   of defaults   473
   of dependencies   89
   of probability models   124
Constraint networks   13, 430
Constraint
   propagation   145, 148
   satisfaction   145
Context   17, 59, 363, 452
Context-dependence   19, 24-25
Contingencies   360, 365, 426, 439, 450
Continuous variables   344-355, 405
Contraction axiom   84-85, 100, 103
Control   318
   centralized   325
   functions   314
   of attention   324
   of propagation   319
   of tests   319
   perception of   396
   subgoaling   325

CONVINCE   27, 232
Correlated evidence   6, 8
Correlation
  coefficients   137, 401, 413
  spurious   384
  vs. causation   396
Covariance matrix   137, 413
Credit assignment   190
Cutsets   93-94, 454
Cycle cutset   262, 287

D

DAG isomorph   128, 391
DAGs   116, 128
Decision analysis   289, 327
Decision nodes   300
Decision theory   327
Decision trees   299
Declarative
  statements   12
  systems   3
Decomposable distributions   113
Decomposable models   108, 113, 127
Decomposition   84-85, 87, 94, 103
Default assumptions   468
Default conventions   477
Default logic   468
  Reiter's   468
Default reasoning   25, 473
  semantics   481
Default rules   468
Defeaters   7
  see Suppressors
Dempster's rule   428-434
Dempster-Shafer   3-4, 12-13, 24, 61,
  415-416
Dempster-Shafer theory   359, 415-440,
  462
Dependence
  axioms for   82, 84, 88
  importance of   80
  in databases   13, 88, 133
  logic of   121
  probabilistic   82
  qualitative notion   79

representation of   79
  see Independence
Dependencies
  induced   11, 19, 93, 116
  nontransitive   11, 19, 51, 116
Dependency maps   91-92
Dependency models   91
Detachment   5, 8
Diagnosis   263, 334
  circuit   263
  medical   272
Diagnostic estimation   351
Diagnostic inference   6
Diagnostic support   34
Diagnostic tree   334
Dining philosophers   221
Direct causes   123
Distributed control   219
Distributions
  star decomposable   398, 401
  tree-decomposable   400
D-map   92
Dot products   153
d-separation   116, 118, 121, 133
  definition   117
D-S
  see Dempster-Shafer   415
Dummy nodes   170

E

Edge reversal policy   221
Edge-deletion method   97, 101-102
Elementary events   33
Elimination methods   144, 310
Embedded multivalued dependencies
  (EMVDs)   88, 133
EMVDs   88, 133
Entailment
  probabilistic   459
  probability of   423
Entropy   321, 323, 492
Environments   452
Epistemological adequacy   15
ε-semantics   482
Evidence nodes   170, 181
Evidential rules   501

Evidential support   35, 164, 182, 191, 499, 501
Exception independence   185
Exceptions   440
  reasoning with   1, 24
  in TMS   451-452
Expectations
  evoking   151, 497, 501-504
Expected monetary value   298
Expert systems   2-3, 27, 57, 151
  rule-based   4-11, 52, 147, 161, 440-446, 459
Explaining away   7, 19, 49, 351, 357
Explanation   246
  best   240, 278
  causal   285
  corpus   285
  evoking   151, 497, 501-504
  generating   279, 454
  most probable   240, 283, 286
  nature of   281
  second-best   271
exp-max procedure   301
Extensional systems   3-12, 445
Extensions   246, 418, 457

F

Focal element   420
Focusing attention   318
Frame of discernment   334, 363, 418
Frame problem   22
Fusion   163
Fuzzy
  logic   3, 464
  sets   464

G

Galleries   13
Game against nature   299
Generating explanations   279, 454
Graph separation   85, 92, 117
  axioms   94
  in DAGs   128

Graphical representations   69, 78, 81, 92, 127, 131
  directed graphs   116, 128
  undirected graphs   90, 96
Graph-isomorph dependencies   93
Graphoids   13, 87-88, 100
  axioms   84
  history of   132

H

Heuristic approaches to uncertainty   3
Hidden causes   383-386, 398-407
Hierarchical inferences   42, 232
Hierarchy of hypotheses
  causal   42, 116, 232, 383
  taxonomic   373
Higher-order probabilities   357
Hypothetical middle   17, 19
Hysteresis   280

I

Ignorance   357, 425, 439
I-map   96, 111
  definition   92, 119
  test for   98-99
Implicit suppressors   507
Incidence calculus   456, 463
Incrementality   2
Independence   2, 31, 79, 83
  induced by mediating variables   44, 386
Induced dependencies   19, 93, 116
Induction   7, 381
Inductive pattern   53
Inferential distance   472, 490, 493
INFERNO   10-11, 463
Influence, causal   123
Influence diagrams   13, 125, 306
  evaluating   307
Informational dependencies   93
Information
  sources of   313
  value of   313
Informativeness   319
Inheritance networks   472, 488-493
  consistency of   488

Instantiated variables 152
Intensional systems 3, 12, 27
Interpretations 246
  see Explanations
Intersection axiom 84-85, 87, 94, 97,
    103, 111, 117
Inversion formula 32
Irrelevance 6, 13 14
  axioms of 85
  inference rule 493
IS-A 335

J

Jeffrey's Rule 62, 71, 172
Join trees 111-113, 132, 200, 204, 261
Joint distribution functions 33, 51, 78

L

λ message 164, 169, 182, 248
λ* message 248, 253, 255
Label 453
Learning 381
Likelihood 16, 34-35, 37-38
  ratio 11, 34, 45, 152, 338, 343, 421
  vector 40, 46, 66, 153
Link
  matrices 124
  parameters 104, 124
Local computation 50, 147, 174, 286,
    344-345
Locality principle 5, 7
Locally Markov 98, 107
Logic
  conditional 25, 482
  default 25, 468-473
  nonmonotonic 24-26, 283, 287,
    467-481
  of proportions 493-496
  relevance-based 26, 493
  sampling 212
  vs. probability 21, 24-26, 54, 60, 283,
    287, 467, 513-516
Logicist school 2, 513
Log-likelihood 38
Loops 195, 260

Lotteries 291
  EMV of 298
  value of 292
Lottery paradox 282

M

Markov blanket 97, 120-121, 216
Markov boundary 97, 99-102
Markov chain 120
Markov fields 105-106, 132
Markov networks 96, 104
  construction 97-98, 100, 102, 105
  product forms 105, 109, 115, 388
Markov trees 108, 387
Material implications 24, 424, 459,
    449-450
Maximal cliques 105
Maximum cardinality search 112
Maximum-entropy 61, 321, 415, 463,
    491
Maximum-expected-utility 290, 295
Membership problem 89, 122
Message passing 240, 339
Meta-reasoning 425
Minimal I-map 96, 116, 119
Mixing rule 88
Model completion 61, 415, 425
Model-based systems 3
Modularity 5, 7, 35, 55, 383
Monotonicity 55, 468, 487
Most-probable-explanation (MPE) 250,
    283, 452
Multiple causes 7, 49, 175-176, 184, 346
Multiple explanations 175, 186, 257, 271
Multiple extensions 240, 471
Multi-valued variables 39, 150
Mutual information 321
MYCIN 3, 5, 7, 11, 27, 151, 501
Myopic policies 327, 314

N

Neighbor system 97
Network representations 12, 51, 81, 127
No-good set 454
Noisy OR-gates 184, 189, 227

Nontransitive dependencies   19, 51, 116
Normal defaults   470
Normalization
  constants   105, 153, 338
  Dempster's   429, 439

O

Object-oriented languages   147
Odds   34
Orthogonal sum   433

P

π message   164, 169, 182
π^* message   248, 253, 255
Parameter learning   382
Partitions   334
Path analysis   125, 131
Paths
  active   118
  blocked   118
  d-separated   118
Payoffs   286, 291
Perfect map   92, 96, 122, 341
Persistence   57, 505, 510, 513
Plan   299
Planning   300
Plausibility measure   421
Plausible inference   53
Polytrees   176, 232, 347
  recovery   390, 392
  skeleton   390
Possibilities   418, 427
Possibility theory   462
Posterior probability   32
Preconditions   451
Prediction   47
Predictive estimation   351
Predictive inference   6
Preference relation   294
Premises   441, 451
Prior probability   32
Probabilistic logic   457, 463
Probabilistic models   33
Probabilistic reasoning   14-27
  axiomatic basis   16, 19, 27, 30

Probabilistic semantics   482, 516
Probabilities of probabilities   357
Probabilities of provability   462
Probability   426
  and frequencies   15
  and human reasoning   20
  and logic   24, 54, 60, 467
  and nonmonotonic logic   23
  and nonmonotonic reasoning   17, 484
  and precision   20
  as a language   16
  autoepistemic interpretation   17
  axiomatic basis   16, 19, 27, 30
  history of   70
  infinitesimal   25, 482
  subjective   358
  uncertainty about   61, 357, 439
Probability intervals   61, 438, 462
Probability theory
  aim   14
  axioms   30
  Bayesian   17, 29-34, 70-71
  context dependencies   15
Procedure-based systems   3
Product forms   111, 123-124, 387
Production systems   3
Propagating uncertainties
  in chains   153
  in polytrees   175
  in taxonomic hierarchies   337
  in trees   162
Propagation rules   374
  for belief revision   255
  for continuous quantities   348
  in chains   161
  in polytrees   182
  in taxomonic hierarchies   339
  in trees   169
Protocol   71
  see Query
Provability   415, 423, 427
Pseudo-graphoids   97

Q

Qualitative Markov networks   13
Qualitative physics   345

Qualitative reasoning 16, 23
Query sensitivity 58-62, 71, 423

R

Ranges 346
Reasoning by cases 472, 494
Reasoning patterns
  for continuous quantities 357
Reasoning with exceptions 1
  in TMS 451
Recursive models 125, 137
Recursive updating 37
Reference classes 366
Relevance 13, 18, 491
Relevance-based control 318
Relevance-based logic 26, 491, 493
Reversibility 280
Risk aversion 298
Root nodes 170, 181
Rule networks 4, 441
Rule schemata 469
Rule-based computation 145-148, 161
Rule-based systems 3, 27, 52, 57, 151,
    440-446, 459
Rules
  as conditional probabilities 6, 25, 57,
    161, 343, 446, 480, 483, 510
  as constraints 440
  as conventions 447
  as material implication 24, 449-450,
    459
  certainty weights 5, 343, 440
  exceptions 440
  interpretation 4-6
  procedural interpretation 4-5, 24
  semantic interpretation 24
  transitivity of 24, 449, 486

S

Second-best interpretation 271
Semantic networks 372
Semantic
  interpretation of uncertainty 4, 6
Semi-graphoids 88, 101, 117, 119

Semi-normal defaults 471
Sensitivity matrices 320
Series-parallel networks 443, 456
Shannon's mutual information 322
Simpson's Paradox 495
Simulated-annealing 262
Singly connected networks 176
  see Polytrees
Skeletons 390
Spanning tree 389
  maximum weight 388, 392
Specific evidence 151
Specificity 24, 449-450, 484, 496
Spurious correlations 384, 396
Star-decomposability 401
Stationarity 216
Stochastic simulation 195, 210, 262, 456
Strong union axiom 94
Structure learning 382
Sub-explanation 247
Subgoals 325
  nested 326
Suppressors 7, 507
σ-weighted average 351, 357
Symmetry axiom 84-85, 94, 103

T

T norms 11
Target hypothesis 318
Taxonomic hierarchies 333
Thousand prisoner problem 60, 71, 423
Three prisoners paradox 58-62, 71, 417
TMS 451
Transitivity
  of connectedness 94
  of dependence 11, 19, 51, 116
  of rules 24, 449, 486
Tree-decomposable distribution 400
Tree-dependent distribution 387-388
Tree-reconstruction procedure 402
Triangularity axiom 480, 485-486
Triangulation 112, 115, 201
Truth-maintenance systems 24, 416, 450,
    463
Typicality information 468

U

Uncertain evidence (cascaded
     inference)   42, 148
 as likelihood ratio   45, 66, 151, 343
 as random switch   419
Uncertainty about probabilities   61, 357,
     439
Utility
 and explanations   282-285
 assessment of   294
 definition of   294
Utility functions   297
Utility theory   290, 327
 axioms   294

V

Value of information   426
Variables   30
 auxiliary   130, 385

compound   50, 82, 195, 197
continuous   344
domain   152
instantiated   152
multi-valued   39, 150
Virtual conditionalization   66, 71
Virtual evidence   44, 66, 71, 151

W

Weak transitivity   129, 137
Weak union   84-85, 87, 97, 103
Weight   423
 uncommitted   423

Y

Yale shooting problem   505, 509

Printed and bound by CPI Group (UK) Ltd, Croydon, CR0 4YY

03/10/2024

01040435-0004